PHP Bible

2nd Edition

Tim Converse and Joyce Park

WILEY

Wiley Publishing, Inc.

Best-Selling Books • Digital Downloads • e-Books • Answer Networks •
e-Newsletters • Branded Web Sites • e-Learning

PHP Bible, 2nd Edition

Published by
Wiley Publishing, Inc.
10475 Crosspoint Boulevard
Indianapolis, IN 46256
www.wiley.com

ISBN: 0-7645-4955-3

Manufactured in the United States of America

10 9 8 7 6 5 4 3 2 1

2B/RX/QZ/QS/IN

For general information on our other products and services or to obtain technical support, please contact our Customer Care Department within the U.S. at (800) 762-2974, outside the U.S. at (317) 572-3993 or fax (317) 572-4002.

Wiley also publishes its books in a variety of electronic formats. Some content that appears in print may not be available in electronic books.

Library of Congress Control Number: 2002110239

About the Authors

Tim Converse has written software to recommend neckties, answer questions about space stations, pick value stocks, and make a simulated breakfast. He has an M.S. in Computer Science from the University of Chicago, where he taught several programming classes. He is now a software engineer at Inktomi Corporation.

Joyce Park has an M.A. in history from the University of Chicago and has worked on several content-rich PHP Web sites, including the award-winning MysteryGuide.com. Her writing has garnered praise from the editors and readers of Slashdot, OSOpinion, Linux.com, and many others worldwide. Joyce is now a senior Web developer at KnowNow, Inc.

Credits

Acquisitions Editor
Debra Williams Cauley

Project Editor
Sharon Nash

Technical Editor
Richard Lynch

Editorial Manager
Mary Beth Wakefield

Vice President & Executive Group Publisher
Richard Swadley

Vice President and Executive Publisher
Bob Ipsen

Vice President and Publisher
Joseph B. Wikert

Executive Editorial Director
Mary Bednarek

Project Coordinator
Erin Smith

Proofreading
Mary Lagu

Indexing
Johnna VanHoose Dinse

Senior Permissions Editor
Carmen Krikorian

Media Development Specialist
Travis Silvers

Media Development Coordinator
Kate Rzepka

To our parents:

For their love, for their sacrifices,

and for letting us read a lot when we were kids

Preface

Welcome to the *PHP Bible, 2nd Edition*!

Although we're biased, we believe that the PHP Web-scripting language is the hands-down winner in its niche — by far the easiest and most flexible server-side tool for getting great Web sites up and running in a hurry. Although millions of Web programmers worldwide *could* be wrong, in this particular case, they're not.

As we write this book, PHP is in version 4.2 and has continued to grow in reach, adoption, and features since we wrote the first edition of this book two years ago.

What Is PHP?

PHP is an open-source, server-side, HTML-embedded Web scripting language that is compatible with all the major Web servers (most notably Apache). PHP enables you to embed code fragments in normal HTML pages — code that is interpreted as your pages are served up to users. PHP also serves as a "glue" language, making connecting your Web pages to server-side databases easy.

Why PHP?

We devote nearly all of Chapter 1 to this question. The short answer is that it's free, it's open-source, it's full-featured, it's cross-platform, it's stable, it's fast, it's clearly designed, it's easy to learn, and it plays well with others.

What's New in the Second Edition?

We've significantly expanded the size of this book in this new edition, both to cover new features and to improve coverage of features that we didn't have time to discuss the first time.

New features

A lot has changed and a lot has been added to the most recent versions of PHP. Among other changes, we cover the following:

- The new superglobal arrays, introduced in PHP version 4.1 and necessary as of PHP 4.2 because of changes in the default treatment of global variables. We've rewritten the code from the first edition to comply with post-4.2 PHP.

- The new DOM XML API, introduced in version 4.2.

- Web-services functionality, including coverage of XML-RPC and SOAP.

New chapters

The first edition had 32 chapters. After merging a couple of those and adding new material, we now have 39 chapters. Among the new chapters are those covering the following topics:

- PHP's Oracle functions.
- A chapter on generating graphics on-the-fly using the GD library.
- A chapter devoted to integrating other people's PHP with your own PHP.

More code

We received a lot of great feedback from readers on the first edition, most of it strongly positive. What complaints we got centered on the amount of code that we provided.

Many of the first edition's code examples were in the form of snippets designed to illustrate some particular point from the text. After talking to readers and after reading one particularly insightful review on Amazon, we realized that, although this approach works well for some people, others prefer having entire standalone examples that can be modified and reused.

We've listened, and as a result, we've substantially increased the number of standalone code samples. Among the many new pieces of code are the following:

- A running example through Chapters 9-13 (a fitness calculator) illustrating concepts from each chapter.
- Lengthy standalone mini-applications in the chapters on object-oriented programming and graphics.
- Two new case-study chapters at the end of the book (a user-authentication system and a trivia game) using techniques drawn from the entire book.

Who This Book Is For

This book is for anyone who wants to build Web sites that have more complex behavior than is possible with static HTML pages. Within that population, we had the following three particular audiences in mind:

- Web site designers who know HTML and want to move into creating dynamic Web sites
- Experienced programmers (C, Java, Perl, and so on) without Web experience who want to quickly get up to speed in server-side Web programming
- Web programmers who have used other server-side technologies (Active Server Pages, Java Server Pages, or Cold Fusion, for example) and want to upgrade or simply add another tool to their kit.

We assume that the reader is familiar with HTML and has a basic knowledge of the workings of the Web, but we do not assume any programming experience beyond that. To help save time for more experienced programmers, we include a number of notes and asides that compare PHP to other languages and help indicate which chapters and sections may be safely skipped. Finally, see our appendixes, which offer specific advice for C programmers, ASP coders, and pure-HTML designers.

This Book Is Not the Manual

The PHP Documentation Group has assembled a great online manual, located at www.php.net and served up (of course) by PHP. This book is not that manual or even a substitute for it. We see it as complementary to the manual and expect that you will want to go back and forth between them to some extent.

In general, you'll find the online manual to be very comprehensive, covering all aspects and functions of the language, but inevitably without a great amount of depth in any one topic. By contrast, we have the leisure of zeroing in on aspects that are most used or least understood and give background, explanations, and lengthy examples.

How the Book Is Organized

This book is divided into three parts, as the following sections describe.

Part I: The Basics

Chapters 1 through 4 give an introduction to PHP and tell you what you need to know to get started.

Chapters 5 through 13 are a guide to the most central facets of PHP (with the exception of database interaction): the syntax, the datatypes, and the most basic built-in functions. You may want to skim here and then use a reference.

Chapters 14 and 15 are a guide to PHP style and the most common pitfalls of PHP programming.

Part II: PHP and Databases

Chapters 16 and 17 give a general orientation to Web programming with SQL databases, including advice on how to choose the database system that is right for you.

Chapter 18 is devoted to PHP functions for MySQL, and Chapter 19 does the same for Oracle.

Chapters 20 through 23 are detailed, code-rich case studies of PHP/database interactions.

Chapters 24 and 25 give tips and gotchas specific to PHP/database work.

Part III: Advanced Techniques

In each of Chapters 26 through 39, we cover a more advanced, self-contained topic, including the new built-in session-handling functions, using cookies, generating JavaScript code, connecting PHP to mail programs, XML support, object-oriented programming in PHP, generating graphics, security, Web services, code integration, and configuration options.

Conventions Used in This Book

We use a monospace font to indicate literal PHP code. Pieces of code embedded in lines of text look like this, while full code listing lines look as follows:

```
print("this");
```

If the visual appearance of a PHP-created Web page is crucial, we include a screenshot figure. If it is not, we show textual output of PHP in monospace. If we want to distinguish the PHP output as seen in your browser from the actual output of PHP (which your browser renders), we call the former *browser output*.

If included in a code context, *italics* indicate portions that should be filled in appropriately, as opposed to being taken literally. In normal text, an italicized *term* means a possibly unfamiliar word or phrase with a definition in the glossary.

What the Icons Mean

Icons similar to the following example are sprinkled liberally throughout the book. Their purpose is to visually set off certain important kinds of information.

TIP: Tip icons indicate PHP tricks or techniques that may not be obvious and that enable you to accomplish something more easily or efficiently.

NOTE: Note icons usually give additional information or clarification but can be safely ignored if you are not already interested. Notes in this book are often audience-specific, targeted to people who already know a particular programming language or technology.

CAUTION: Caution icons indicate something that does not work as advertised, something that is easily misunderstood or misused, or anything else that can get programmers into trouble.

NEW FEATURE: New feature icons indicate functionality that is new and importantly different in PHP 4.

CROSS-REFERENCE: We use this icon whenever related information is in a different chapter or section.

The Web Site and Sample Code

All the sample code from the book, as well as supplementary material we develop after press time, can be found at our Web site at www.troutworks.com/phpbook. You can also find the sample code at www.wiley.com/compbooks/converse.

We want to hear from you! Please send us e-mail at phpbook@troutworks.com with comments, errata, kudos, flames, or any other communication that you care to send our way.

Acknowledgments

This project began out of a conversation with Debra Williams, our acquisitions editor at Wiley. She managed the project, found additional contributors, and maintained a sense of humor as she insulated naive first-time authors from the harsh realities of the publishing business. For the second edition, she insulated naive second-time authors. She also stepped up and made some important and difficult decisions along the way.

Barb Guerra was the project editor for the first edition. For the second edition, Sharon Nash took over, and (among many other things) dealt with some particularly hairy issues around templates and word-processing formats. Sharon took most of this hassle onto herself, urging us to focus on the content, and we are grateful for that.

Richard Lynch did double-duty by signing up as our technical reviewer for both editions. His deep PHP knowledge and common sense (evident to anyone who reads the PHP mailing list) improved the manuscript and saved us from making many stupid mistakes.

We didn't write this book by ourselves. Dustin Mitchell single-handedly wrote the chapter on security and cryptography, and Patrick McCuller and Ariel Garcia contributed early drafts of chapters that appeared in the first edition.

Thanks to the Webmasters of the PHP team for permission to reproduce a graph of PHP usage; the folks at Zend for permission to use screenshots of their Zend Studio product; Infopop Corporation for providing us with code used in UBBThreads for the chapter on integration; Amazon.com for data in the Web services chapter; KnowNow, Inc. for permission to excerpt code owned by them; Mimi Yin for her fabo design work; Alex Selkirk for permission to reproduce material from Opencortex.org; Tim Perdue for inspiration; and Jeff Barr of Syndic8.com for timely aid.

Our obvious thanks go to everyone who created PHP itself (Rasmus Lerdorf, Zeev Suraski, Andi Gutmans, Thies Arntzen, Stig Bakken, Sascha Schumann, Andrei Zmievski, Dan Libby, Sam Ruby, and a host of other contributors), the people who have documented PHP (Stig Bakken, Alexander Aulbach, Egon Schmid, Lars Torben Wilson, Jim Winstead, and others), and everyone on the PHP mailing list. Special thanks to Rasmus, Sascha, and Richard Lynch for mailing-list answers to our own questions. Finally, we would both like to thank our spouses for their support while this book was being written and revised. In a very literal sense, we couldn't have done it without them.

Contents

Part I

PHP: The Basics

Why PHP?

In This Chapter

- What is PHP?
- A history of PHP
- Reasons to love PHP
- PHP's competitive advantage

This first chapter is an introduction to PHP. In it, we'll try to address some of the most common questions about PHP, such as "What is it?" and "How does it compare to similar technologies?" Most of the chapter is taken up with an enumeration of the many, many reasons to love PHP. If you're a techie looking for some ammunition to lob at your PHB ("Pointy-Haired Boss" for those who don't know the Dilbert cartoons) or a manager asking yourself what is this P-whatever thing your geeks keep whining to get, this chapter will provide some preliminary answers.

What Is PHP?

PHP is the Web development language written by and for Web developers.

PHP stands for *PHP: Hypertext Preprocessor.* The product was originally named *Personal Home Page Tools,* and many people still think that is what the acronym stands for. But as it expanded in scope, a new and more appropriate (albeit GNUishly recursive) name was selected by community vote. You can use any extension you want to designate a PHP file, but the recommended ones have been `.php`, `.php3`, and `.phtml`. PHP is currently in its fourth major rewrite, called PHP4 or just plain PHP.

PHP is a server-side scripting language, which can be embedded in HTML or used as a standalone binary (although the former use is much, much, much more common). Proprietary products in this niche are Microsoft's Active Server Pages, Macromedia's ColdFusion, and Sun's Java Server Pages. Some journalists used to call PHP "the open source ASP" because its functionality is similar to that of the Microsoft product/concept/whatever-it-is — although this formulation was misleading, as PHP was developed before ASP. But over the past couple of years, PHP and server-side Java have gained so much momentum, while ASP has lost mindshare, that this comparison no longer seems so apposite.

We'll explore server-side scripting more thoroughly in Chapter 2, but for the moment you can think of it as a collection of super-HTML tags or small programs that run inside your Web pages — except on the server side, before they get sent to the browser. For example, you can use PHP to add common headers and footers to all the pages on a site, or to store form-submitted data in a database.

Strictly speaking, PHP has little to do with layout, events, the DOM, or really anything about what a Web page looks and sounds like. In fact, most of what PHP does is invisible to the end user. Someone looking at a PHP page will not necessarily be able to tell that it was not written in HTML, because the end result of PHP *is* HTML.

PHP is an official module of Apache HTTP Server, the market-leading free Web server that runs about 55 percent of the World Wide Web (according to the widely quoted Netcraft Web server survey). This means that the PHP scripting engine can be built into the Web server itself, leading to faster data manipulation. Like Apache Server, PHP is fully cross-platform, meaning it runs native on several flavors of Unix, as well as on Windows and now on Mac OS X. All projects under the aegis of the Apache Software Foundation — including PHP — are open source software.

The History of PHP

Rasmus Lerdorf — software engineer, Apache team member, and international man of mystery — is the creator and original driving force behind PHP. The first part of PHP was developed for his personal use in late 1994. This was a CGI wrapper that helped him keep track of people who looked at his personal site. The next year, he put together a package called the *Personal Home Page Tools* (a.k.a. the *PHP Construction Kit*) in response to demand from users who had stumbled into his work by chance or word of mouth. Version 2 was soon released under the title PHP/FI and included the *Form Interpreter*, a tool for parsing SQL queries.

By the middle of 1997, PHP was being used on approximately 50,000 sites worldwide. It was clearly becoming too big for any single person to handle, even someone as focused and energetic as Rasmus. A small core development team now runs the project on the open source "benevolent junta" model, with contributions from developers and users around the world. Zeev Suraski and Andi Gutmans, the two Israeli programmers who developed the PHP3 and PHP4 parsers, have also generalized and extended their work under the rubric of Zend.com (*Zee*v, A*nd*i, *Zend,* get it?).

The fourth quarter of 1998 initiated a period of explosive growth for PHP, as all open source technologies enjoyed massive publicity. In October 1998, according to the best guess, just over 100,000 unique domains used PHP in some way. Just over a year later, PHP broke the one-million domain mark. When we wrote the first edition of this book in the first half of 2000, the number had increased to about two million domains. As we write this, approximately 9 million public Web servers (in the software sense, not the hardware sense) have PHP installed on them.

Public PHP deployments run the gamut from mass-market sites such as Excite webmail and the Indianapolis 500 Web site, which serve up millions of pageviews per day, through "mass-niche" sites such as Sourceforge.net and Epinions.com, which tend to have higher functionality needs and hundreds of thousands of users, to e-commerce and brochureware sites such as Restoration Hardware and Sade.com (Web home of the British singer), which must be visually attractive and easy to update. There are also PHP-enabled parts of sites, such as the forums on the Internet Movie Database (imdb.com); and a large installed base of non-public PHP deployments, such as LDAP directories (MCI WorldCom built one with over 100,000 entries) and trouble-ticket tracking systems.

With the crashing of the dot-com bubble, PHP is poised to be used on more sites than ever. Demand for Web-delivered functionality has decreased very little and emerging technological standards continue to pop up all the time; but available funding for hardware, licenses, and especially headcount has drastically decreased. In the post-crash Web world, PHP's shallow learning curve, quick implementation of new functionality, and low cost of deployment are hard arguments to beat.

Reasons to Love PHP

There are ever so many reasons to love PHP. Let us count a few.

PHP is free

PHP costs you nothing. Zip, zilch, nada, not one red cent. Nothing up front, nothing over the lifetime of the application, nothing when it's over. Did we mention that the Apache/PHP/MySQL combo runs great on cheap, low-end hardware that you couldn't even *think* about for IIS/ASP/SQL Server?

For purposes of comparison, Table 1-1 shows some current retail figures for similar products in the United States. All prices quoted are for a single-processor public Web server with the most common matching database and development tool; *$0* means a no-cost alternative is a common real-world choice. One caveat: At press time, Microsoft had not yet released the .NET Server package which will include its next-generation Web server; but it's probably safe to assume that prices will rise rather than fall.

Table 1-1: Comparative Out-of-Pocket Costs

Item	ASP	ColdFusion 5	JSP	PHP
Development tool	$0 – 2499	$599	$0 - ~2000	$0 - 249
Server	$1,199	$1,295	$0 - ~35,000	$0
RDBMS	$4999	$4999	$15,000	$0

Open source software: don't fear the cheaper

But as the bard so pithily observed, we are living in a material world — where we've internalized maxims like, "You get what you pay for," "There's no such thing as a free lunch," and "Things that sound too good to be true usually are." You (or your boss) may, therefore, have some lingering doubts about the quality and viability of no-cost software. It probably doesn't help that until recently software that didn't cost money — formerly called *freeware*, *shareware*, or *free software* — was generally thought to fall into one of three categories:

♦ Programs filling small, uncommercial niches

♦ Programs performing grungy, low-level jobs

♦ Programs for people with bizarre socio-political "issues"

It's time to update some stereotypes once and for all. We are clearly in the middle of a sea change in the business of software. Much (if not most) major consumer software is distributed without cost today: E-mail clients, Web browsers, games, and even full-service office suites are all being given away as fast as their makers can whip up Web versions or set up FTP servers. Consumer software is increasingly seen as a loss-leader, the flower that attracts the pollinating honeybee — in other words, a way to sell more server hardware, operating systems, connectivity, advertising, optional widgets, or stock shares. Therefore, the full retail price of a piece of software is no longer a reliable gauge of its quality or the eccentricity-level of its user.

On the server side, open source products have come on even stronger; not only do they compete with the best commercial stuff, in many cases there's a feeling that they far exceed the competition. Don't take our word for it! Ask IBM, any hardware manufacturer, NASA, France Telecom, Siemens, Kinko's, the Queen of England, or the Mexican school system. If your boss still needs to be convinced, further ammunition is available at:

```
http://www.opensource.org
http://www.fsf.org
```

The PHP license

The freeness of open source and Free software is guaranteed by a gaggle of licensing schemes, most famously the *GPL* (*Gnu General Public License*) or *copyleft*. PHP used to be released under both the GPL and its own license, with each user free to choose between them. This has recently changed: The program as a whole is now released under its own extremely laissez-faire PHP4 license; whereas Zend as a standalone product is released under the *Q Public License* (this clause applies *only* if you unbundle Zend from PHP and try to sell it).

You can read the fine print about the relevant licenses at these Web sites:

```
http://www.php.net/license.html
http://www.troll.no/qpl/annotated.html
```

Most people get PHP via free download, but you may have paid for it as part of a Linux distribution, a technical book, or some other product. In that case, you may now be mentally disputing our assertion that PHP costs nothing. Here's the twist: Although you can't require a fee for most open source software, you *can* charge for delivering that software in a more convenient format — such as by putting it on a disk and shipping the disk to the customer. You can also charge anything the market will bear for being willing to perform certain services or accept certain risks that the development team may not wish to undertake. For instance, you are allowed to charge money for guaranteeing that every copy of the software you distribute will be virus-free or of reasonable quality, taking on the risk of being sued if a bunch of customers get bad CD-ROMs with hard-drive-erasing viruses on them.

Usually, open source software users can freely choose the precisely optimal cost-benefit equation for each particular situation: no cost and no warranties, or expensive but well supported, or something in between. However, no organized attempt has been made yet to sell service and support for PHP (although presumably that will be one of the value-adds of Zend). Other open source products, such as Linux, have companies like Red Hat standing by to answer your questions; but the commercialization process is still in the early stages for PHP.

PHP is easy

PHP is easy to learn, compared to the other ways to achieve similar functionality. Unlike Java Server Pages or C-based CGI, PHP doesn't require you to gain a deep understanding of a major programming language before you can make a trivial database or remote-server call. Unlike Perl, which has been semi-jokingly called a "write-only language," PHP has a syntax that is quite easy to parse and human-friendly. And unlike ASP.NET, PHP is stable and ready to solve your problems today.

Many of the most useful specific functions (such as those for opening a connection to an Oracle database, or fetching e-mail from an IMAP server) are predefined for you. A lot of complete scripts are waiting out there for you to look at as you're learning PHP. In fact, it's entirely possible to use PHP just by modifying freely available scripts rather than starting from scratch — you'll still need to understand the basic principles, but you can avoid many frustrating and time-consuming minor mistakes.

We must mention one caveat: "Easy" means different things to different people, and for some Web developers it has come to connote a graphical, drag-and-drop, What You See Is What You Get development environment. To become truly proficient at PHP, you need to be comfortable editing HTML by hand. You can use WYSIWYG editors to design sites, format pages, and insert client-side features before you add PHP functionality to the source code. There are even ways, which we'll detail in Chapter 3, to add PHP functions to your favorite editing environment. However, it's not realistic to think you can take full advantage of PHP's capabilities without ever looking at source code.

Most advanced PHP users (including most of the development team members) are diehard hand-coders. They tend to share certain gut-level, subcultural assumptions — for instance, that hand-written code is beautiful and clean and maximally browser-compatible, and therefore the only way to go — that they do not hesitate to express in vigorous terms. The PHP community offers help and trades tips mostly by e-mail; and if you want to participate, you have to be able to parse plain-text source code with facility. Some WYSIWYG users occasionally ask list members to diagnose their problems by looking at their Web pages instead of their source code, but this rarely ends well.

That said, let us reiterate that PHP really is easy to learn and write, especially for those with a little bit of experience in a C-syntaxed programming language. It's just a little more involved than HTML but probably simpler than JavaScript, and definitely less conceptually complex than JSP or ASP.NET.

PHP is embedded in HTML

PHP is embedded within HTML. In other words, PHP pages are ordinary HTML pages that "escape" into PHP mode only when necessary. Here is an example:

```
<HEAD>
<TITLE>Example.com greeting</TITLE>
</HEAD>
<BODY>
<P>Hello,
<?php
// We have now escaped into PHP mode.
// Instead of static variables, the next three lines
// could easily be database calls or even cookies;
// or they could have been passed from a form.
$firstname = 'Joyce';
$lastname = 'Park';
$title = 'Ms.';
echo "$title $lastname";
// OK, we are going back to HTML now.
?>
.  We know who you are!  Your first name is <?php echo $firstname;
?>.</P>

<P>You are visiting our site at <?php echo date('Y-m-d H:-i:s'); ?></P>

<P>Here is a link to your account management page:  <A
HREF="http://www.example.com/accounts/<?php echo "$firstname$lastname";
?>/"><?php echo $firstname; ?>'s account management page</A></P>
</BODY>
</HTML>
```

When a client requests this page, the Web server *preprocesses* it. This means it goes through the page from top to bottom, looking for sections of PHP, which it will try to resolve. For one thing, the parser will suck up all assigned variables (marked by dollar signs) and try to plug them into later PHP commands (in this case, the echo function). If everything goes smoothly, the preprocessor will eventually return a normal HTML page to the client's browser, as shown in Figure 1-1.

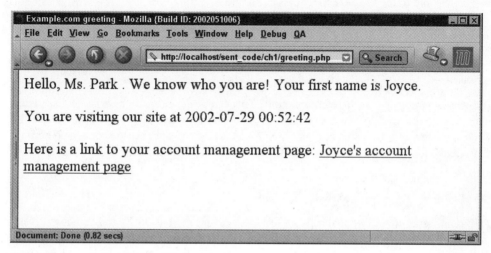

Figure 1-1: A result of preprocessed PHP

If you peek at the source code from the client browser (select Source or Page Source from the View menu, or right-click on AOL), it will look like this:

```
<HEAD>
<TITLE>Example.com greeting</TITLE>
</HEAD>
<BODY>
<P>Hello,
Ms. Park
. We know who you are!  Your first name is Joyce.</P>

<P>You are visiting our site at 2002-04-21 19-34-24</P>

<P>Here is a link to your account management page:  <A
HREF="http://www.example.com/accounts/JoycePark/">Joyce's account
management page</A></P>
</BODY>
</HTML>
```

This code is exactly the same as if you wrote the HTML by hand. So simple!

The HTML-embeddedness of PHP has many helpful consequences:

- ♦ PHP can quickly be added to code produced by WYSIWYG editors.
- ♦ PHP lends itself to a division of labor between designers and scripters.
- ♦ Every line of HTML does not need to be rewritten in a programming language.

♦ PHP can reduce labor costs and increase efficiency due to its shallow learning curve and ease of use.

Perhaps the sweetest thing of all about embedded scripting languages is that they don't need to be compiled into binary code before they can be tested or used — just write and run. PHP is interpreted (as are many newish computer languages), although the Zend Engine does some behind-the-scenes precompiling into an intermediate form for greater speed with complex scripts.

But what if you happen to *want* compilation? This can be desirable if you wish to distribute nonreversible binaries so others can use the code without being able to look at the source. The Zend team now offers an precompiler, *Zend Encoder*, that will deliver the code in an non-reversible intermediate representation, as well as substantially speeding up large complex PHP scripts.

PHP is cross-platform

PHP runs native on every popular flavor of Unix (including Mac OS X) and Windows. A huge percentage of the world's HTTP servers run on one of these two classes of operating systems.

PHP is compatible with the three leading Web servers: Apache HTTP Server for Unix and Windows, Microsoft Internet Information Server, and Netscape Enterprise Server (a.k.a. iPlanet Server). It also works with several lesser-known servers, including Alex Belits' fhttpd, Microsoft's Personal Web Server, AOLServer, and Omnicentrix's Omniserver application server.

Table 1-2 shows a brief matrix of the possible OS/Web-server combinations.

Table 1-2: Operating Systems and Web Servers for PHP

Variables	*UNIX*	*Windows*
Flavors	AIX, A/UX, BSDI, Digital UNIX/Tru64, FreeBSD, HP-UX, IRIX, Linux, Mac OS X, NetBSD, OpenBSD, SCO UnixWare, Solaris, SunOS, Ultrix, Xenix, and more	Windows 95/98/ME Windows NT/2000/XP
Web servers	Apache, fhttpd, Netscape	IIS, PWS, Netscape, Apache, Omni

Now that PHP runs on Macintosh, PHP is almost totally cross-platform. You can develop on almost any client OS using your favorite tools and then upload your PHP scripts to a server on almost any OS. We'll discuss the development process in more detail in Chapter 3.

PHP isn't tag-based

PHP is a real programming language. ColdFusion, by contrast, is a bunch of predefined tags, like HTML. In PHP, you can define functions to your heart's content just by typing a name and a definition. In ColdFusion, you have to use tags developed by other people, or go through the Custom Tag Extension development process.

As a witty PHP community member once said, "ColdFusion makes easy things easy, and medium-hard things impossible." And as every programmer will agree: Once you experience the power of curly brackets and loops, you never go back to tags.

PHP is stable

The word *stable* means two different things in this context:

   ♦ That the server doesn't need to be rebooted often.

   ♦ That the software doesn't change radically and incompatibly from release to release.

Happily, both of these connotations apply to PHP.

Apache Server is generally considered to be the most stable of major Web servers, with a reputation for enviable uptime percentages. Although it is not the fastest nor the easiest to administer, once you get it set up, Apache HTTP Server seemingly never crashes. It also doesn't require server reboots every time a setting is changed (at least on the Unix side). PHP inherits this reliability; plus, its own implementation is solid yet lightweight. In a two-and-a-half-month head-to-head test conducted by the Network Computing labs in October 1999, Apache Server with PHP handily beat both IIS/Visual Studio and Netscape Enterprise Server/Java for stability of environment.

PHP is also stable in the sense of feature stability. The development team has thus far enjoyed a clear vision of their project and refused to be distracted by every new fad and ill-thought-out user demand that comes along. Much of its effort goes into incremental improvements, such as getting the parser to run faster, communicating with more major databases, or adding better session support. Historically, very few functions or constructions have had to be dropped between versions of PHP.

PHP is fast

PHP is pleasingly zippy in its execution, especially when compiled as an Apache module on the Unix side.

PHP 4 is now much faster for almost every use than CGI scripts. There is an unfortunate grain of truth to the joke that CGI stands for "Can't Go Instantly." Although many CGI scripts are written in C, one of the lowest-level and therefore speediest of the major programming languages, they are hindered by the fact that each request must spawn an entirely new process after being handed off from the http daemon. The time and resources necessary for this handoff and spawning are considerable, and there can be limits to the number of concurrent processes that can be running at any one time. Other CGI scripting languages such as Perl and Tcl can be quite slow. Most Web sites have moved away from use of CGI for performance and security reasons.

Although it takes a slight performance hit by being interpreted rather than compiled, this is far outweighed by the benefits PHP derives from its status as a Web server module. When compiled this way, PHP becomes part of the http daemon itself. Because there is no transfer to and from a separate application server (as there is with ColdFusion, for instance) requests can be filled with maximum efficiency.

Although no extensive formal benchmarks have compared the two, much anecdotal evidence and many small benchmarks suggest that PHP is at least as fast as ASP or JSP in most applications.

PHP is open

We've already dealt with the cost advantages of open source software in the "PHP is free" section of this chapter. The other major consequence of these licenses is that the complete source code for the software must be included in any distribution.

In fact, the Unix version of PHP is *only* released as source code; so far, the development team has staunchly resisted countless pleas to distribute official binaries for any of the Unixes. At first, new users (particularly those who are also new to Unix) tend to feel that source code is about as useful as a third leg, and most would vastly prefer a nice convenient rpm. But there are both pragmatic and idealistic reasons for including folders full of pesky .c and .h files.

The most immediate pragmatic advantage is that you can compile your PHP installation with only the stuff you really need for any given situation. This approach has performance and security advantages. For instance, you can put in hooks to the database(s) of your choice. You can recompile as often as you want: maybe when an Apache security release comes out, or when you come to the conclusion you need XML support.

What sets open source software apart from its competitors is not just price but control. Plenty of consumer software is now given away under various conditions. However, careful scrutiny of the relevant licenses will generally reveal limits as to how the software can be used. Maybe you can run it at home, but not at the office. Perhaps you can load it on your laptop, but you're in violation if you use it for business purposes. Or, most commonly, you can use it for anything you want, but forget about looking at the code — much less changing it. There are even "community licenses" that force you to donate your improvements to the codebase but charge you for use of the product at the end!

> **CAUTION:** Don't even *think* about coming back with a riposte that involves violating a software license — we're covering our ears; we're *not* listening! Especially with the explosion in no-cost software, there's just no good reason to break the law. Besides, it's bad karma for software developers: What goes around, comes around, don't ya know?

Table 1-3 shows examples of the various source and fee positions in today's software marketplace:

Table 1-3: Source/Fee Spectrum

Fee Structure	Closed Source	Controlled Source	Open Source
Fee for all uses	Macromedia ColdFusion	—	—
Fee for some uses	Corel WordPerfect	Sun Java	MySQL
No fee for any use	Microsoft IE	Sun StarOffice	GPLed software

Genuinely open source software like PHP cannot seek to limit the purposes for which it is used, the people who are allowed to use it, or a host of other factors. The most critical of these rights is the one allowing users to make and distribute any modifications along with the original software. In the most extreme case, where one or more developers decide to release a separate, complete version of a piece of software, this practice is referred to as "*code forking*."

If somewhere down the road you develop irreconcilable differences with the PHP development team, you can take every bit of code they've labored over for all these years and use it as the basis of your own product. You couldn't call it PHP, and you'd have to include stuff in your documentation that gave due credit to the authors. In most circumstances it's just a stupid idea — but you always have the right to fork, and it has been exercised many times with other software projects for reasons good, bad, and ugly. The rationale is that source code distributions make it next to impossible for any single person or group to hijack a program to the detriment of the community as a whole, because every user always has the power to take all the source and walk.

Users new to the open source model should be aware that this right is also enjoyed by the developers. At any time, Rasmus, Zend, and company can choose to defect from the community and put all their future efforts into a commercial or competing product based on PHP. Of course, the codebase up to this point would still be available to anyone who wanted to pick up the baton, and for a product as large as PHP that could be a considerable number of volunteer developers.

This leads to one other oft-forgotten advantage of open source software: You can be pretty sure the software will be around in a few years, no matter what. In these days of products with the life spans of morning glories, it's hard to pick a tool with staying power. Fans of OS/2, Amiga, NeXT, Newton, Firefly, Netscape, BeOS, Napster, and a host of other once-hot technologies know the pain of abandonment when a company goes belly-up, decides to stop supporting a technology, or is sold to a buyer with a new agenda. We were ourselves seduced and tossed aside by another (now-defunct) server-side scripting tool before we discovered

PHP; and although we've gotten past the denial and anger, there's still a hollow feeling when we think of the years we gave to our ex-scripting language. The open source model reduces the chances of an ugly emergency port in a couple of years and thus makes long-term planning more realistic.

PHP plays well with others

PHP makes it easy to communicate with other programs and protocols. The PHP development team seems committed to providing maximum flexibility to the largest number of users.

Database connectivity is especially strong, with native-driver support for about 15 of the most popular databases plus ODBC. In addition, PHP supports a large number of major protocols such as POP3, IMAP, and LDAP. PHP4 also has new support for Java and distributed object architectures (COM and CORBA), making n-tier development a possibility for the first time.

Most things that PHP does not support are ultimately attributable to closed-source shops on the other end. For instance, Microsoft has not thus far been eager to cooperate with open source projects like PHP. Potential users who complain about lack of native Mac OS 9 or .NET support on the PHP mailing list are simply misinformed about where the fault lies.

PHP adds new features quickly

Users of proprietary Web development technologies can sometimes be frustrated by the glacial speed at which new features are added to the official product standard to support emerging technologies. With PHP, this is not a problem. All it takes is one developer, a C compiler, and a dream to add important new functionality. This is not to say that the PHP team will accept every random contribution into the official distribution without community buy-in; but independent developers can and do distribute their own extensions which may be later folded into the main PHP package in more or less unitary form. For instance, Dan Libby's elegant xmlrpc-epi extension was adopted as part of the PHP distribution in version 4.1, a few months after it was first released as an independent package.

PHP development is also constant and ongoing. Although there are clearly major inflection points, such as the transition between PHP 3 and PHP 4, these tend to be most important deep in the guts of the parser — people were actually working on major extensions throughout the transition period without critical problems. Furthermore, the PHP group subscribes to the open source philosophy of "release early, release often," which gives developers many opportunities to follow along with changes and report bugs. Compare this release scheme to the .NET transition, which has left developers with almost a year in which Microsoft is not really improving IIS but has not yet released a prime-time version of .NET server.

PHP is popular and growing

PHP is fast becoming one of the most popular choices for so-called two-tier development (Web plus data). Figure 1-2 charts growth since 1999.

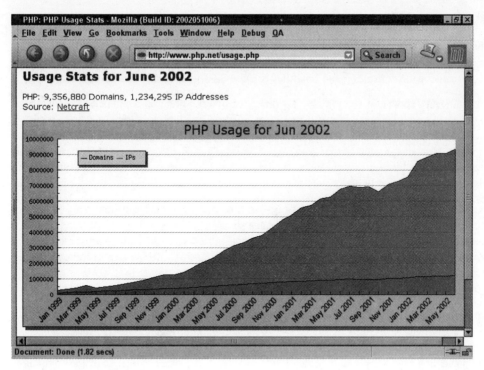

Figure 1-2: Netcraft survey of PHP use

Although it's not clear from this graphic, the period October 1998 through October 1999 showed 800 percent growth in the number of domains. As Web sites become even more ubiquitous, and as more of them go beyond simple static HTML pages, PHP is expected to gain ground quickly in absolute numbers of users.

Although it's somewhat more difficult to get firm figures, it seems that PHP is also in a strong position relative to similar products. Microsoft Active Server Pages technology appears to be utilized on about 24 percent of Web servers, whereas ColdFusion is implemented on approximately 4 percent of surveyed domains. PHP is used on over 24 percent of all Web servers, as measured by a larger and more accurate sample, and is now said to be the most popular server-side scripting language on the Web

Active Server Pages and ColdFusion used to be highly visible because they tended to be disproportionately selected by large e-commerce sites. However, the realities of the Web finally caught up with us — and it is the flashy e-commerce sites which were disproportionately thinned by the dot-bomb crash. It is now becoming clearer that the vast majority of Web sites are informational rather than direct revenue centers and, therefore, do not repay high development expenses in an immediate way. PHP enjoys substantial advantages over its competitors in this development category, which has turned out to be the majority of the Internet.

PHP is not proprietary

The history of the personal computer industry to date has largely been a chronicle of proprietary standards: attempts to establish them, clashes between them, their benefits and drawbacks for the consumer, and how they are eventually replaced with new standards.

But in the past few years the Internet has demonstrated the great convenience of voluntary, standards-based, platform-independent compatibility. For example, e-mail works so well because it enjoys a clear, firm standard to which every program on every platform must conform. New developments that break with the standard (for example, HTML-based e-mail "stationery") are generally regarded as deviations, and their users find themselves having to bear the burdens of early adoption.

Furthermore, customers (especially the big-fish businesses with large systems) are fed up with spending vast sums to conform to a proprietary standard — only to have the market uptake not turn out as promised. Much of the current momentum towards XML and Web services is driven by years of customer disappointment with Java RMI, CORBA, COM, and even older proprietary methods and data formats.

Right now, software developers are in a period of experimentation and flux concerning proprietary versus open standards. Companies want to be sure they can maintain profitability while adopting open standards. There have been some major legal conflicts related to proprietary standards, which are still being resolved. These could eventually result in mandated changes to the codebase itself, or even affect the future existence of the companies involved. In the face of all this uncertainty, a growing number of businesses are attracted to solutions that they know will not have these problems in the foreseeable future.

PHP is in a position of maximum flexibility because it is, so to speak, *antiproprietary*. It is not tied to any one server operating system, unlike Active Server Pages. It is not tied to any proprietary cross-platform standard or middleware, as Java Server Pages or ColdFusion are. It is not tied to any one browser or implementation of a programming language or database. PHP isn't even doctrinaire about working only with other open source software. This independent but cooperative pragmatism should help PHP ride out the stormy seas that seem to lie ahead.

The PHP community

PHP is developed and supported in a collaborative fashion by a worldwide community of users. Some animals (such as the core developers) are more equal than others — but that's hard to argue with, because they put in the most work, had the best ideas, and have managed to maintain civil relationships with the greatest number of other users.

The main advantage for most new users is technical support without charge, without boundaries, and without the runaround. People on the mailing list are available 24/7/365 to answer your questions, help debug your code, and listen to your gripes. The support is human and real. PHP community members might tell you to read the manual, take your question over to the appropriate database mailing list, or just stop your whining — but they'll never tell you to wipe your C drive and then charge you for the privilege. Often they'll look at your code and tell you what you're doing wrong, or even help you design an application from the ground up.

As you become more comfortable with PHP, you may wish to contribute. Bug tracking, offering advice to others on the mailing lists, posting scripts to public repositories, editing documentation, and, of course, writing C code are all ways you can give back to the community.

Summary

PHP isn't the panacea for every Web development problem, but it has a lot of advantages. It's built by Web developers for Web developers and supported by a large and enthusiastic community. It sits on a sweet-spot of lightness, power, reliability, and ease of use. It offers best-of-breed connectivity to backend servers of all types. And did we mention it's free? To know PHP is to love it for many of the most common Web development tasks.

Chapter 2
Server-Side Web Scripting

In This Chapter

♦ Understanding static and dynamic Web pages

♦ Client-side versus server-side scripting

♦ An introduction to server-side scripting

This chapter is about server-side scripting and its relationship to both static HTML and common client-side technologies. By the end, you can expect to gain a clear understanding of what kinds of things PHP can and cannot do for you, along with a general understanding of how it can interact with client-side code.

Static HTML

The most basic type of Web page is a completely static, text-based one, written entirely in HTML. Take the simple HTML-only page that Figure 2-1 shows as an example.

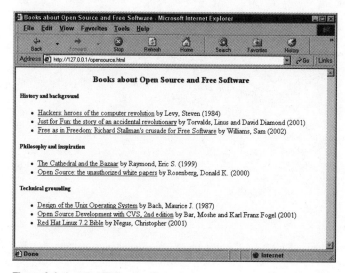

Figure 2-1: A static HTML example

The following example displays the source code for the Web page shown in Figure 2-1:

```
<HTML>
<HEAD>
<TITLE>Books about Open Source and Free Software</TITLE>
<META NAME=KEYWORDS CONTENT="Open Source, Free Software, software
development, books">
</HEAD>

<BODY>
<CENTER><H3>Books about Open Source and Free Software</H3></CENTER>

<H5>History and background</H5>
<UL>
<LI><A HREF="bkLevyHackers.html">Hackers:  heroes of the computer
revolution</A> by Levy, Steven (1984)</LI>
<LI><A HREF="bkTorvaldsFun.html">Just for Fun:  the story of an
accidental revolutionary</A> by Torvalds, Linus and David Diamond
(2001)</LI>
<LI><A HREF="bkWilliamsFreedom.html">Free as in Freedom:  Richard
Stallman's crusade for Free Software</A> by Williams, Sam (2002)</LI>
</UL>

<H5>Philosophy and inspiration</H5>
<UL>
<LI><A HREF="bkRaymondBazaar.html">The Cathedral and the Bazaar</A> by
Raymond, Eric S. (1999)</LI>
<LI><A HREF="bkRosenbergSource.html">Open Source:  the unauthorized
white papers</A> by Rosenberg, Donald K. (2000)</LI>
</UL>


<H5>Technical grounding</H5>
<UL>
<LI><A HREF="bkBachSystem.html">Design of the Unix Operating System</A>
by Bach, Maurice J. (1987)</LI>
<LI><A HREF="bkBarCVS.html">Open Source Development with CVS, 2nd
edition</A> by Bar, Moshe and Karl Franz Fogel (2001)</LI>
<LI><A HREF="bkNegusBible.html">Red Hat Linux 7.2 Bible</A> by Negus,
Christopher (2001)</LI>
</UL>

</BODY>
</HTML>
```

After a client computer makes an HTTP request for this page from the server machine across the Web or an intranet, as shown in Figure 2-2, the server simply passes along whatever text it finds in the file.

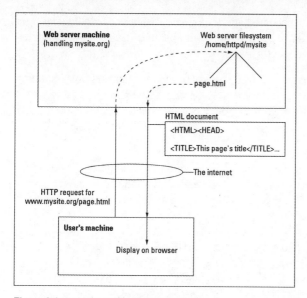

Figure 2-2: A simple HTTP request and response

After this data gets back to the client machine, the browser does its best to render the page according to its understanding of precisely what kind of code it is, user preferences, monitor size, and other factors. The contents of the HTML file on the server are exactly the same as the source code of the page on the client.

Very plain, static HTML, such as the code in this example, offers certain advantages, such as the following:

♦ Any browser can display it adequately.

♦ Many kinds of devices can display it adequately.

♦ Each request is fulfilled quickly and uses minimal resources.

♦ HTML is easy to learn or produce automatically.

♦ Web developers can make small changes to individual pages quickly.

Of course, static HTML has its downsides, including the following limitations:

♦ It makes control of design and layout difficult.

♦ It doesn't scale up to a large number of pages.

♦ It's not very interactive.

♦ It makes including meaningful metadata about the page difficult.

♦ It can't cope with rapidly changing content or personalization.

♦ It's not very attractive.

For all these reasons, static HTML has become a mark of amateurishness or ideological rigor (as in the home pages of computer science professionals who believe all Web pages should conform to HTML 3.1 and be readable on all devices).

Numerous additional technologies were developed in response to these limitations, including JavaScript, Cascading Style Sheets, and Java applets on the client side and server-side scripting with database connectivity on the server side. Upcoming technologies include XML and XSL, both of which appear as part of various other specifications (XHTML, XSLT, XPath, ICE, and so on).

You can save yourself a lot of headaches if you take the time to understand exactly what functionality each of these technologies can and can't be expected to add to your Web site. The basic question to ask yourself about any given Web site task: Where is the computation happening — on the client or on the server?

> **NOTE:** What does *dynamic* mean? A basic and often-repeated distinction exists between "static" and "dynamic" Web pages — but *dynamic* can mean almost anything beyond plain-vanilla HTML. Web developers use the term to describe both client- and server-side functions. On the client, it can mean multimedia presentations, scrolling headlines, pages that update themselves automatically, or elements that appear and disappear. On the server, the term generally denotes content that is assembled on-the-fly.

Client-Side Technologies

The most common additions to plain HTML are on the client side. These add-ons include formatting extensions such as Cascading Style Sheets and Dynamic HTML; client-side scripting languages such as JavaScript; Java applets; and Flash. Support for all these technologies is (or is not, as the case may be) built into the Web browser. They perform the tasks described in Table 2-1 with some overlap.

Table 2-1: Client-Side HTML Extensions

Client-Side Technology	Main Use	Example Effects
Cascading Style Sheets, Dynamic HTML	Formatting pages: controlling size, color, placement, layout, timing of elements	Overlapping, different colored/sized fonts Layers, exact positioning
Client-side scripting (JavaScript, VBScript)	Event handling: controlling consequences of defined events	Link that changes color on mouseover Mortgage calculator
Java applets	Delivering small standalone applications	Moving logo Crossword puzzle
Flash animations	Animation	Short cartoon film

The page shown in Figure 2-3 is based on the same content as that in Figure 2-1.

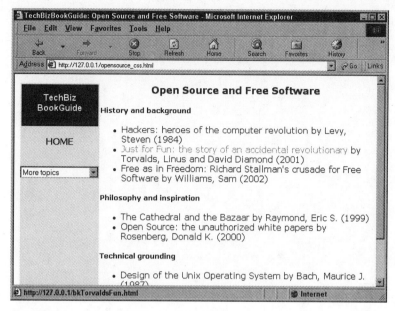

Figure 2-3: An example of HTML plus client-side scripting

As you can see from the following source code for Figure 2-3, however, this example adds style sheets and client-side scripting as well as somewhat more sophisticated HTML:

```
<HTML>
<HEAD>
<TITLE>TechBizBookGuide: Open Source and Free Software</TITLE>
<META NAME=KEYWORDS CONTENT="Open Source, Free Software, software
development, books">
<STYLE TYPE="text/css">
<!--
BODY, P      {color: black; font-family: verdana; font-size: 10 pt}
H1         {margin-top: 10; color: white; font-family: arial; font-size:
12 pt}
H2         {margin-bottom: -10; color: black; font-family: verdana; font-
size: 18 pt}
A:link, A:visited    {color: #000080; text-decoration: none}
.roll    {  }
A.roll:hover  {color: #8FBc8F}
-->
</STYLE>

<SCRIPT LANGUAGE="JavaScript">
<!--
```

```
     function ListVisit(form, i) {
        // get the URL from options
        var site = form.elements[i].selectedIndex;
        // if it's not the first (null) option, go there
        if( site >= 1 ) {
            top.location = form.elements[i].options[ site].value;
        }
        // and then reselect the null (it functions as a label)
        form.elements[i].selectedIndex = 0;
     }

//-->
</SCRIPT>
</HEAD>

<BODY>
<TABLE BORDER=0 CELLPADDING=0 WIDTH=100%>
<TR>
<TD BGCOLOR="#F0F8FF" ALIGN=CENTER VALIGN=TOP WIDTH=17%>
   <TABLE CELLPADDING=5 WIDTH=100%>
   <TR ALIGN=CENTER>
   <TD BGCOLOR="#000080">
   <H1>TechBiz<BR>BookGuide</H1>
   </TD></TR></TABLE>
   <BR>
   <A HREF="index.php"><B>HOME</B></A><BR><BR>
   <BR>
   <FORM action="">
   <SELECT NAME="topics" onChange="ListVisit(this.form, 0)">
   <OPTION>More topics
   <OPTION VALUE="commercial.html">Commercial software
   <OPTION VALUE="hardware.html">Hardware
   <OPTION VALUE="telephony.html">Telephony
   </SELECT></FORM><BR>
</TD>
<TD BGCOLOR="#FFFFFF" ALIGN=LEFT VALIGN=TOP WIDTH=83%>
<CENTER><H3>Open Source and Free Software</H3></CENTER>

<H5>History and background</H5>
<UL>
<LI><A HREF="bkLevyHackers.html" class="roll">Hackers:  heroes of the
computer revolution</A> by Levy, Steven (1984)</LI>
<LI><A HREF="bkTorvaldsFun.html" class="roll">Just for Fun:  the story
of an accidental revolutionary</A> by Torvalds, Linus and David Diamond
(2001)</LI>
<LI><A HREF="bkWilliamsFreedom.html" class="roll">Free as in Freedom:
Richard Stallman's crusade for Free Software</A> by Williams, Sam
(2002)</LI>
</UL>
```

```
<H5>Philosophy and inspiration</H5>
<UL>
<LI><A HREF="bkRaymondBazaar.html" class="roll">The Cathedral and the
Bazaar</A> by Raymond, Eric S. (1999)</LI>
<LI><A HREF="bkRosenbergSource.html" class="roll">Open Source:  the
unauthorized white papers</A> by Rosenberg, Donald K. (2000)</LI>
</UL>


<H5>Technical grounding</H5>
<UL>
<LI><A HREF="bkBachSystem.html" class="roll">Design of the Unix
Operating System</A> by Bach, Maurice J. (1987)</LI>
<LI><A HREF="bkBarCVS.html" class="roll">Open Source Development with
CVS, 2nd edition</A> by Bar, Moshe and Karl Franz Fogel (2001)</LI>
<LI><A HREF="bkNegusBible.html" class="roll">Red Hat Linux 7.2 Bible</A>
by Negus, Christopher (2001)</LI>
</UL>

</TD>
</TR></TABLE>
</BODY>
</HTML>
```

Unfortunately, the best thing about client-side technologies is also the worst thing about them: They depend entirely on the browser. Wide variations exist in the capabilities of each browser and even between versions of the same brand of browser. Individuals can also choose to configure their own browsers in awkward ways: Some people disable JavaScript for security reasons, for example, which makes it impossible for them to view sites that overuse JavaScript for navigation (as we deliberately did in the preceding code sample).

Furthermore, many consumers are very slow to upgrade their browsers for reasons of cost or technical anxiety or both. The savvy Web developer should also consider the implications of device-based browsing, universal accessibility, and a global audience. The fact that the huge mass-market sites that are trying to reach the widest audiences, such as Yahoo! and Amazon, continue to resist using style sheets and JavaScript more than five years after these standards were adopted is no accident. Against the urging of the World Wide Web Consortium, many sites continue to stubbornly cling to their FONT tags and BGCOLOR attributes as the only way to survive in the face of customers who insist on using AOL 3.0 on five-year-old Macintoshes with 13-inch monitors. The stubborn unwillingness of the public to upgrade is the bane of client-side developers, causing them to frequently suffer screaming nightmares and/or existential meltdowns in the dark, vulnerable hours before dawn. The bottom-line irony is that, even after five years of explosive Web progress, the only thing that a developer can absolutely, positively know that the client is going to see is plain text-based HTML (or, rather, the subset of HTML that's widely supported and has stood the tests of time and usefulness).

Finally, client-side technologies cannot do anything that requires connecting to a backend server. JavaScript cannot assemble a customized drop-down list on-the-fly from user preferences stored in a database — if a change is needed in the list, the Web developer must go in and edit the page by hand. (Server-side JavaScript does exist, but no one much uses it.) This gap is filled by server-side scripting.

In summation, anything to do with layout or browser events happens on the client. Generally speaking, anything that looks cool or depends on the movements of the mouse is client-side. The faster you see some event happening, the more likely that the client is handling it, because high speed indicates that no request to and download from the server is necessary.

> **NOTE:** *Java applets*, also known as *client-side Java*, are considerably less dependent on the browser than are other client-side technologies. As the name suggests, applets are complete little Java applications that are delivered across the Internet. But instead of interacting directly with the client's operating system as do applications that written in other programming languages, Java applets run on a piece of middleware known as a *Java Virtual Machine*. You can think of the JVM as an operating system living on top of your real operating system, like the aliens taking over human bodies in a gazillion cheesy sci-fi movies. Most recent browsers incorporate a JVM, and you can also download one separately. This division of labor enables applets to use the rendering capabilities of a browser without being limited to the browser's relatively puny functionality.
>
> Applets have suffered under an early reputation for picayune pointlessness because they were initially used for a category of thing that we might term "dancing Chihuahuas" — logos that look as if they're made out of gelatin, scrolling headlines, bouncing links, and other headache-inducing frivolities. Luckily, applets have since been redeemed by useful, humanistic purposes such as crossword puzzles, Tower of Hanoi simulations, and virtual ways to "try on" ensembles of clothing and accessories.

Server-Side Scripting

Figure 2-4 shows a schematic representation of a server-side scripting data flow.

Client-side scripting is the glamorous, eye-catching part of Web development. In contrast, server-side scripting is invisible to the user. Pity the poor server-side scripters, toiling away in utter obscurity, trapped in the no-man's land between the Web server and the database while their arty brethren brazenly flash their wares before the public gaze.

Server-side Web scripting is mostly about connecting Web sites to backend servers, such as databases. This enables the following types of two-way communication:

♦ **Server to client:** Web pages can be assembled from backend-server output.

♦ **Client to server:** Customer-entered information can be acted upon.

Common examples of client-to-server interaction are online forms and some drop-down lists (usually the ones that require you to click a button) that the script assembles dynamically on the server.

Server-side scripting products consist of two main parts: the scripting language and the scripting engine (which may or may not be built into the Web server). The engine parses and interprets pages written in the language.

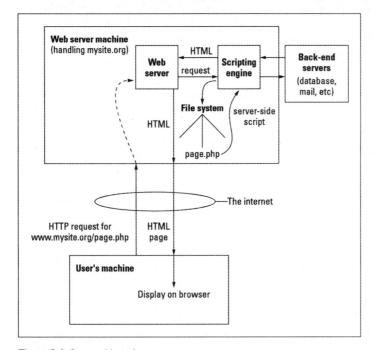

Figure 2-4: Server-side tasks

Often, the same company or team develops both parts for use only with each other — PHP 3 and ColdFusion are both examples of this practice. However, exceptions to this rule do exist. Java Server Pages, for example, are written in a standard programming language rather than in a special-purpose scripting language; but third parties (for example, Macromedia JRun, Apache Tomcat) have developed several interchangeable scripting engines.

In theory, Active Server Pages enables you to use almost any scripting language and one of several matching ActiveX scripting engines (although, in practice, using anything but the Windows/IIS/VBScript/JScript combination is highly problematic). PHP 4 is also a "bikini" scripting technology now, because the scripting engine (Zend) is theoretically separable from the PHP programming language.

Figure 2-5 shows a simple example of server-side scripting — a page assembled on-the-fly from a database, followed by the server-side source and the client-side source. We include database calls (which we don't get around to explaining until Part II of this book) and leave out some of the included files, because we intend this example to show the final product of PHP rather than serve as a piece of working code.

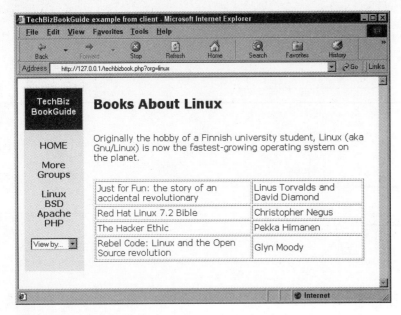

Figure 2-5: Server-side scripting example

The following PHP code shows the source on the server:

```
<HTML>
<HEAD>
<TITLE>TechBizBookGuide example from server</TITLE>
<?php include_once("tbbg-style.css"); ?>
<?php include_once("javascript.inc"); ?>
</HEAD>
<BODY>
<?php
include_once("tbbg-navbar.txt");
$org = $_GET['org'];
?>
<TD BGCOLOR="#FFFFFF" ALIGN=LEFT VALIGN=TOP WIDTH=83%>
   <TABLE CELLPADDING=5 WIDTH=100%><TR><TD ALIGN=LEFT VALIGN=MIDDLE>
   <H2>Books about <?php print("$org"); //passed in from URL
?></H2><BR></TD></TR>
   <TR><TD WIDTH=50% ALIGN=LEFT>
   <?php
   $dbh = mysql_connect('localhost', 'mysqluser') or die("Unable to open
database");
   mysql_select_db("techbizbookguide") or die("Unable to access
database");
   $query = "SELECT Blurb FROM Org WHERE OrgName = '$org'";
   $qresult = mysql_query($query) or die(mysql_error());
```

```
   $blurb = mysql_fetch_array($qresult) or die(mysql_error());
   print("$blurb[0]");
   ?>
   </TD></TR>
   <TR><TD ALIGN=LEFT>
      <TABLE BORDER=1 CELLPADDING=3>
      <?php
      $query2 = "SELECT ID, Title, AuthorFirst, AuthorLast FROM bookinfo
WHERE OrgName='$org' ORDER BY AuthorLast";
      $qresult2 = mysql_query($query2) or die(mysql_error());
      while ($titlelist = mysql_fetch_array($qresult2)) {
         $bookID = $titlelist[0];
         $title = $titlelist[1];
         $authorfirst = $titlelist[2];
         $authorlast = $titlelist[3];
         print("<TR><TD><A HREF=\"book.php?bn=$bookID\" class=\"roll\">
$title</A></TD><TD>$authorfirst $authorlast</TD>");
      }
      ?>
      </TR></TABLE>
   </TD></TR></TABLE>
</TD></TR></TABLE>
</BODY></HTML>
```

After the preceding PHP source code is parsed by the PHP scripting engine, the following client-side code will be produced by the Web server and sent to the browser.

```
<HTML>
<HEAD>
<TITLE>TechBizBookGuide example from client</TITLE>
<STYLE TYPE="text/css">
<!--
BODY      {color: black; font-family: verdana; font-size: 10 pt}
H1        {margin-top: 10; color: white; font-family: arial; font-size:
12 pt}
H2        {margin-bottom: -10; color: black; font-family: verdana; font-
size: 18 pt}
A:link, A:visited    {color: #000080; text-decoration: none}
.roll     { }
A.roll:hover   {color: #008080}
-->
</STYLE>
<SCRIPT LANGUAGE="JavaScript">
<!--
   function ListVisit(form, i) {
      // get the URL from options
      var site = form.elements[i].selectedIndex;
      // if it's not the first (null) option, go there
      if( site >= 1 ) {
```

```
            top.location = form.elements[i].options[site].value;
            }
        // and then reselect the null (it functions as a label)
        form.elements[i].selectedIndex = 0;
    }
    //-->
</SCRIPT>
</HEAD>

<BODY>
<TABLE BORDER=0 CELLPADDING=0 WIDTH=100%>
<TR>
<TD BGCOLOR="#F0F8FF" ALIGN=CENTER VALIGN=TOP WIDTH=17%>
    <TABLE CELLPADDING=5 WIDTH=100%>
    <TR ALIGN=CENTER>
    <TD BGCOLOR="#000080">
    <H1>TechBiz<BR>BookGuide</H1>
    </TD></TR></TABLE>
    <BR>
    <A HREF="index.php"><B>HOME</B></A><BR><BR>
    <B>More</B><BR>
    <B>Groups</B><BR><BR>
    <A HREF="techbizbook.php?org=linux" class="roll"><B>Linux</B></A>
    <BR>
    <A HREF="techbizbook.php?org=bsd" class="roll"><B>BSD</B></A>
    <BR>
    <A HREF="techbizbook.php?org=apache" class="roll"><B>Apache</B></A>
    <BR>
    <A HREF="techbizbook.php?org=php" class="roll"><B>PHP</B></A>
    <BR><BR>
    <FORM action="">
    <Select onChange="ListVisit(this.form, 0)">
    <OPTION>View by...
    <OPTION VALUE="author.php">Author
    <OPTION VALUE="people.php">People
    <OPTION VALUE="themes.php">Themes
    <OPTION VALUE="role.php">Roles
    <OPTION VALUE="size.php">Group size
    </SELECT></FORM><BR>
</TD>
<TD BGCOLOR="#FFFFFF" ALIGN=LEFT VALIGN=TOP WIDTH=83%>
    <TABLE WIDTH=100% CELLPADDING=15><TR><TD ALIGN=LEFT VALIGN=MIDDLE>
    <H2>Books About Linux</H2><BR></TD></TR>
    <TR><TD WIDTH=50% ALIGN=LEFT>Originally the hobby of a Finnish
university student, Linux (aka Gnu/Linux) is now the fastest-growing
operating system on the planet.</TD></TR>
    <TR><TD ALIGN=LEFT>
        <TABLE BORDER=1 CELLPADDING=3>
```

```
      <TR><TD><A HREF="book.php?book=1" class="roll">Just for Fun:  the
story of an accidental revolutionary</A></TD><TD>Linus Torvalds and
David Diamond</TD>
      <TR><TD><A HREF="book.php?book=2" class="roll">Red Hat Linux 7.2
Bible</A></TD><TD>Christopher Negus</TD>
      <TR><TD><A HREF="book.php?book=3" class="roll">The Hacker
Ethic</A></TD><TD>Pekka Himanen</TD>
      <TR><TD><A HREF="book.php?book=4" class="roll">Rebel Code: Linux
and the Open Source revolution</A></TD><TD>Glyn Moody</TD>
      </TR></TABLE>
   </TD></TR></TABLE>
</TD></TR></TABLE>
</BODY></HTML>
```

This particular page isn't significantly more impressive to look at than the plain HTML version at the beginning of the chapter. Passing one different variable, however, results in the automatic generation of any number of unique pages — in this case, pages listing the books by criteria other than the author's last name — without any further work. If we add some new books about another company to the database, these lists automatically get updated to reflect the new data on each subsequent page load.

As you can see from these two different source-code listings, you cannot view server-side scripts from the client. All the heavy lifting happens before the code gets shoved down the pipe to the client. After emerging from the Web server, the code appears on the other end as normal HTML and JavaScript, which also means that you can't tell which server-side scripting language was used unless something in the header or URL gives it away. These scripts, incidentally, were written in PHP and the MySQL database; you can learn all about these techniques in Part II of this book.

TIP: There are client-side methods and server-side methods to accomplish many tasks. Sending e-mail, for example, the client-side way is to open up the mail client software with a preaddressed blank e-mail message after the user clicks a MAILTO link; the server-side method is to make the user fill out a form, the contents of which are formatted as e-mail and sent via an SMTP server. You can also choose between client methods and server methods of browser-sniffing, form-validation, drop-down lists, and arithmetic calculation. Sometimes you see subtle but meaningful differences in functionality (server-side drop-downs can be assembled dynamically; client-side cannot) but not always.

How to choose? Know your audience. Server-side methods are generally a bit slower at runtime because of the extra transits they must make, but they don't assume anything about your visitor's browser capabilities and take less developer time to maintain. These qualities make them good for mass-market and educational sites. If you're one of the lucky few developers who's absolutely positive that your visitors all have up-to-date browsers and good throughput, you can feel free to go wild with the scripting and graphics. Finally, remember that you can use PHP to generate both static HTML and JavaScript — thus enjoying the best of both worlds, as we explain in Chapter 28.

> **NOTE:** Recent developments in programming languages are increasingly blurring the difference between *programming* and *scripting*. PHP, for example, definitely uses most of the same control structures as other programming languages do. Fully interpreted HTML-embedded languages such as ASP, however, are still considered to be on the scripting side of the line, whereas separately compiled binaries are a definite mark of programming. But because PHP 4 is now dynamically compiled, it's officially a "real" programming language — and don't let anyone tell you otherwise. This change accounts for much of the screaming speed of PHP4, which moves into the same class as Perl.

What Is Server-Side Scripting Good for?

The client looks good, but the server cooks good. What server-side scripting lacks in eye-candy sex appeal, it more than makes up for in sheer usefulness. Most Web users probably interact with the products of server-side scripting on a daily, if not an hourly, basis.

One category of thing that the server just absolutely can't help you with is real-time, 3-D shoot-'em-ups. The more immediately responsive and graphics-intensive a project needs to be, the less suitable PHP is for it. At the moment, the Web is simply too slow a channel for these purposes (although broadband pioneers are eager to change that).

On the other hand, server-side scripting languages such as PHP perfectly serve most of the truly useful aspects of the Web, as such as the items in this list:

- Content sites (both production and display)
- Community features (forums, bulletin boards, and so on)
- E-mail (Web mail, mail forwarding, sending mail from a Web application)
- Customer-support and technical-support systems
- Advertising networks
- Web-delivered business applications
- Directories and membership rolls
- Surveys, polls, and tests
- Filling out and submitting forms online
- Personalization technologies
- Groupware
- Catalog, brochure, and informational sites
- Any other application that needs to connect a backend server (database, LDAP, and so on) to a Web server

PHP can handle all these essential tasks — and then some.

But enough rhetoric! Now that you have a firm grasp of the differences between client-side and server-side technologies, you can get on to the practical stuff. In the next chapter, we show you how to get, install, and configure PHP for yourself (or find someone to do it for you).

Summary

To understand what PHP (or any server-side scripting technology) can do for you, having a firm grasp on the division of labor between client and server is crucial. In this chapter, we work through examples of plain, static HTML; HTML with client-side additions such as JavaScript and Cascading Style Sheets; and PHP-generated Web pages as viewed from both the server and the client.

Client-side scripting can be visually attractive and quickly responsive to user inputs, but anything beyond the most basic HTML is subject to browser variation. Static client-side scripts also require more developer time to maintain and update, because pages cannot be dynamically generated from a constantly changing datastore. Server-side programming and scripting languages, such as PHP, can connect databases and other servers to Web pages.

PHP4 differs architecturally from some other server-side tools and even from PHP3. PHP 4 is dynamically compiled, which makes it faster at runtime. PHP4 also separates the scripting engine, Zend, from the scripting language (PHP).

Chapter 3

Getting Started with PHP

In This Chapter

- ◆ Deciding to outsource or self-host
- ◆ Finding the right ISP
- ◆ Avoiding common hosting pitfalls
- ◆ Installing PHP
- ◆ Choosing a PHP development tool

In this chapter, we'll discuss the pros and cons of the various Web hosting options: outsourcing, self-hosting, and various compromises. Then we'll give detailed directions for installing PHP and finish with a few tips on finding the right development tool. By the end of the chapter, you should be ready to write your first script.

Hosting versus DIY

The first major decision you need to make is: Who will host your PHP-enabled Web site, you or a Web hosting service? Also, will you need a separate development setup; and if so, who will host it? If you've already made these decisions, feel free to skip right to the installation section of this chapter, "Installing PHP."

The ISP option

Remote hosting is becoming a more popular option as a range of companies begins to offer PHP-enabled Web sites. These are some basic pros and cons to keep in mind.

The good

Outsourced hosting has a lot of advantages. The ISP will (in theory) handle many of the crucial technical and administrative details necessary to keep a site running, such as:

- ◆ Hardware
- ◆ Software upgrades
- ◆ InterNIC registration, IP addressing, DNS
- ◆ Mail servers (POP/IMAP and SMTP)

- Bandwidth
- Power supply
- Backups
- Security

There's no cozier feeling than the one you get just before you fall asleep, knowing that some poor schmo at your ISP will be getting the pager message in the middle of the night if something goes wrong with your site. Lurking crackers, downed power lines, munged backup tapes — all that is your host's headache now. Especially for developers who have little experience with system administration issues, outsourcing can be a major time saver.

Web hosting is also extremely cost effective in most situations. PHP on Linux or one of the BSDs is almost ridiculously inexpensive and widely available. Currently, only a few companies offer PHP on an NT server platform, and some of them can be pricey. As the Miracles so eloquently urge: You better shop around (shop, shop ooh).

The bad

Of course, there can be some serious disadvantages to Web hosting too.

Most of these have to do with control. When you go ISP, you're basically a guest in someone else's house and have to play by his rules. Maybe you're a welcome paying guest, a veritable parlor boarder — but the fact remains that when you live in someone else's establishment, you can't just strip down to your undies and lipsync your way through a high-volume version of "Proud Mary" on the dining room table whenever you feel like it. People are trying to eat, pal.

A few years ago, the most central issue for PHP was module versus CGI. PHP runs best and fastest as a module, in other words built into the Web server itself rather than running as a separate process. Almost everyone prefers to use the module version if he can. However, some ISPs prefer to run the CGI version of PHP because it's much simpler to administer safely on a shared Web server. Thankfully, as more Web hosting services set up shop, it's much easier to find one which will give you the module.

Currently, the biggest problem with outsourced PHP hosting is the non-availability of other programs. Obviously ISPs have a strong incentive to control the programs you are allowed to run on their servers. However, a lot of a PHP's value is as a glue between various services and protocols. It can be extremely frustrating to be prevented from running a common and useful utility, such as ImageMagick or HTML Tidy, because your Web host won't allow you to run unauthorized binaries or link to libraries outside your home directory.

A good rule of thumb is: The more common your needs are, the more possible and appropriate it is to outsource your hosting. The more oddball and/or bleeding edge your needs are, the more you're going to be pushed to host your own whether you want to or not. Of course the unspoken realpolitik addendum to this is: The bigger you are and the more money you have to spend, the more weight you have available to throw around.

A few factors will make it considerably more difficult for you to find a hosting service:

♦ Generally objectionable content (hate, porn)

♦ Unsolicited mailings (a.k.a spam)

♦ Content that attracts crackers (security info)

♦ Potentially legally actionable content

♦ Need for unusual server-side hardware, OS, or software

♦ Need for super-high bandwidth, especially if unpredictable

If you're in one of these situations, you need to mention it up front — you'll just get the boot anyway once they find out. Chances are good that you won't get to do much shopping around — if you can find any hosting situation, grab it before they change their minds, and look for a better deal later.

Finally, we must mention the most important negative factor of all: the frustration and anxiety caused by a bad hosting experience. Words cannot describe the tooth-grinding, stomach-churning, scream-suppressing state of existence caused by your site crashing just when you've been featured on Slashdot, thereby making you look like a total technoposer as well as losing all the good pub you so richly deserve.

That's not even mentioning more common problems like lost e-mail, disappearing DNS, unexplained site outages, deleted databases (this actually happened to us once), lack of backups, suffering through an hour-long telephone wait just to talk to some tech supportie who's never been within ten feet of a server, never getting a response to your polite e-mails, and being overbilled for the privilege (not that we're bitter, and anyway our lawyer says we can't name any names).

Bottom line: If you choose hosting, you do so at your own peril. Always be ready to make a quick getaway, which might entail eschewing the cheapest or most fully featured deal in favor of one without long-term contracts and/or prepayments. Conversely, don't be an utter jerk when you deal with the employees of your hosting company. If you've never outsourced hosting before, take the time to understand the difference between things you can legitimately blame on the Web host (bad tech support), and things that are basically Acts of Fate (Internet traffic in your entire metro area goes out).

The details

If you've decided on the hosting option, you will enjoy a plethora of choices in today's marketplace. However, novice shoppers should be aware that the term *ISP* (or even *Web host*) can mean almost anything these days.

Table 3-1 provides a guide to the specializations and their most appropriate uses (the companies mentioned are intended as examples only; this does not constitute an endorsement or recommendation of their services).

Table 3-1: Varieties of ISPs

Type of ISP	Keywords	PHP Users
Consumer ISP (Earthlink, RoadRunner)	Home DSL, cable modem	Home self-hosting of small sites
Free Web host	Free Web hosting under certain circumstances	Small sites, often in exchange for showing ads
Commercial Web hosting	Web hosting, virtual hosting, colocation, dedicated server	Most outsourced sites
Site development	Design, promotion, custom development, consulting	Sites that want to outsource Web development as well as hosting
Access provider (UUNet)	T-1, DS-3, commercial DSL	Self-hosters

Although finding a good Web hosting service sometimes seems as difficult as finding a lifelong mate, there are now listing resources to make it easier:

```
http://hosts.php.net
http://www.od-site.com/php
http://www.ispcheck.com
```

Pay special attention to the user comments, good and bad. Ask your friends and colleagues about their experiences. Search the PHP user list archives — people occasionally make recommendations and comment on bad experiences they've had.

Probably the single most contentious post-signup issue is throughput. Be wary of the phrase *unlimited traffic/bandwidth/hits*. Recall the query of the wise middle-aged baseball manager when the elderly team owner offered him the job for life: "Whose life are we talking about?" Analogously, a level of bandwidth that would never be tested by Joe's Epic Poetry Appreciation Site is probably not going to feel quite so roomy to a Web site featuring free streaming video of scantily clad supermodels. Before you sign up for any deal, you need to assess where you're going to fall on this continuum.

> **CAUTION:** Be extra careful of the amount of disk space that comes with your service plan, especially if you have a large or graphics-heavy site. If you exceed the limit, you will generally be charged exorbitant rates for every fraction of a megabyte of extra space per month. One thing that contributes to this problem is log files; delete them or download them to some cheaper form of storage on a regular basis.

> **TIP:** How to guesstimate your bandwidth needs: 1GB of traffic per month is equal to 100,000 views of files averaging 10K (including graphics, text, ads unless they're third-party served, everything — measuring from a client, not the server).

The self-hosting option: pros and cons

Self-hosting is becoming a realistic option for more sites as the price of connectivity goes down. It's the ultimate in command and control, and it offers substantial security advantages — if you have the expertise to take advantage of them. Running your own setup means problems get solved faster because you don't have to waste time hanging on a tech support line, and many just feel it's more fun: There's just no substitute for being able to put your hands on the actual server machine whenever you want. Remember that if you have unusual, objectionable, or cutting-edge needs, you may be forced to serve your own site whether you want to or not.

On the flip side, self-hosting requires tons more work and can be quite a bit more expensive, especially for the smallish-to-midsize site. Plus, a self-hosted site is only going to be as good as your available skill set. So if no one on your team knows much about security, you can expect to have security problems (although, at least, you'll be aware of your weaknesses, unlike the false comfort that comes when your hosting service fails to inform you that their security expert quit three months ago).

More existentially, you have no one to blame but yourself if things go wrong. If you can look yourself in the mirror every morning and think "It's all on me and I feel great," you have the necessary self-confidence for self-hosting.

Compromise solutions

Of course, outsourcing and self-hosting are actually poles on a continuum. Several "compromise" solutions exist that attempt to offer the best of both worlds.

Colocation

Colocation means you crate up your server machine and ship it to the hosting company, who will hook up your machine to its network and monitor it for you. You are responsible for purchasing, licensing, insuring, installing, configuring, and maintaining all software and hardware, except the uninterruptible power supply. The host does not mess with your box at all, beyond the occasional reboot — for which it generally charges you extra. If you want any technical support whatsoever, you must either go to the location yourself or pay hundreds of dollars an hour for the staff's gentle ministrations — and if you're in a colocation situation, chances are good you're using products for which they have no training.

Dedicated server

A *dedicated server* is just what it sounds like: The hosting service will buy a server, fit it out to your tastes (on your dime, of course), and hook it up to its network; then all the processor cycles belong to you. Generally, you get technical support with your service. This is much more secure than a shared server environment and relatively cost-effective for a midsize site.

Outsource production, self-host development

This option involves two complete setups: an *outsourced production site* and an identical in-house *development server* or servers. Dividing things up this way can offer the best of both worlds, letting someone else take the emergency pager messages in the middle of the night while still enjoying the intimacy of playing on your very own server. If you're located in an area with limited connectivity choices, this option can be a lifesaver. It is also one of the best choices for larger sites with more developers.

Installing PHP

If you've decided to completely outsource PHP hosting and have a competent sysadmin to perform all workstation installs, feel free to skip the rest of this chapter. However, we are bound to recommend that you install your own software at first, even if it's only on your personal development machine, so you have more exposure to and understanding of the development environment.

Before you can begin

Before you can install PHP on any platform, you need:

- ◆ A server or workstation with enough RAM for your OS

- ◆ A Unix, Mac OS X, or Windows operating system installed

- ◆ A working, dedicated Internet connection if you are running a production site; and/or installation on an intranet for a development site; or neither if you are running a totally standalone PHP setup (although without an Internet connection, you must find another source for the necessary software packages).

Help for these prerequisites is beyond the scope of this book. You might want to look at the following sources for networking information:

```
World of Windows Networking (http://www.wown.com)

Linux Documentation Project (http://www.linuxdoc.org/HOWTO/HOWTO-
INDEX/howtos.html)
```

If you plan to install PHP on Windows, you'll also need:

- ◆ A working PHP-supported Web server. Under previous versions of PHP, IIS/PWS was the easiest choice because a module version of PHP was available for it; but PHP 4 offers a much wider selection of modules for Windows.

- ◆ A correctly installed PHP-supported database (if you plan to use one)

♦ For Windows 95 only, the DCOM update, which you can download without cost from `http://download.microsoft.com/msdownload/dcom/95/x86/en/dcom95.exe`

♦ The PHP Windows binary distribution (download it at `http://www.php.net/downloads.php`)

♦ A utility to unzip files (search `http://download.cnet.com` for PC file compression utilities)

If you plan to install PHP on Unix, you'll also need:

♦ The PHP source distribution (`http://www.php.net/downloads.php`).

♦ The latest Apache source distribution (`http://www.apache.org/dist/` — look for the highest odd number that ends with the `.tar.gz` suffix)

♦ A working PHP-supported database if you plan to use one

♦ Any other supported software to which PHP must connect (mail server, BCMath package, JDK, and so forth)

♦ An ANSI C compiler

♦ Gnu make (starting with PHP 4, it can't be any other make version, which is particularly relevant for non-GPLed Unices like Solaris and BSD — you can freely download it at `http://www.gnu.org/software/make`)

♦ Bison and flex (Enter `find . -name bison -print` and `find . -name flex -print` from the `/usr` directory to check if you have them already, or just let gcc check for them during the make process. If not, you can download Bison from `http://www.gnu.org/software/bison` and flex from `ftp://ftp.ee.lbl.gov`.)

> **TIP:** Remember that any extra servers or software libraries to which PHP will connect need to be installed *before* you build. A database is the most common type of external server. Other examples are the BCMath package, an IMAP server, the mcrypt library, and the expat XML parser (unless you use Apache, with which it is bundled).

Now you're ready to actually install PHP. The difference between building as an Apache module and building as a CGI executable is very small. In fact, it comes down to leaving off the `--with-apache` or `--with-apxs` flags when configuring. Many users compile both the module and the CGI versions at the same time for convenience.

> **TIP:** In the past, various parties have offered programs (such as PHPTriad, Nusphere MySQL, and Zend Launchpad) which install Apache, PHP, and sometimes MySQL for you in one fell swoop. Unfortunately, at press time all these products seem to be in problematic situations. Nusphere is in serious legal difficulty after being accused of violating the MySQL license, the maintainer of PHPTriad announced he was no longer maintaining the product, and Zend Launchpad has simply disappeared from the site.

Installation procedures

Due to PHP's strong commitment to cross-platform operability, there are far too many specific installation methods to fully list here. We have tried to cover what we believe to be the most popular platforms for PHP, but trying to write out the installation instructions for every possible operating system and Web server would have resulted in a prohibitively long chapter.

Furthermore, while PHP installation procedures under Unix have been stable for years, Windows installs have gone through quite a bit of flux since PHP4.0 was released. Part of this is due to actions on the part of the PHP team, part of this is due to changes in the Windows product line such as the introduction of Windows XP and planned changes in IIS. PHP now also runs on Macintosh OS X, and that installation process is quite unstable as of this writing.

Due to such rapid change, we can only caution you that for the freshest information on installation you should visit the PHP Website (`http://www.php.net/docs.php`) on each download. Even if you've installed PHP a gazillion times before, there might be something new and different on the gazillion-and-first occasion.

Unix and Apache

The first time you build your own HTTP daemon from source, you might be a little apprehensive. But the process is fairly straightforward, and it's worth the effort to compile your Web server yourself instead of being dependent on other people's RPMs, which are often weeks or months out of date. And hey, it's a genuine rush when it works! Once you do it a couple of times, it's a breeze — one of us once had a job where we recompiled the Apache server at least weekly if not daily, and after that it was totally routine.

For those who have already successfully built an earlier version of PHP, the procedure is exactly the same — only it takes a lot longer than before.

> **CAUTION:** Your Red Hat or Mandrake Linux installation may have come with RPM versions of Apache and PHP. You *must* remove these packages before compiling your new PHP! In addition, you may have RPM versions of third-party servers, such as MySQL or PostgreSQL, which are installed differently than their source counterparts. If you encounter problems, look in the documentation for installation locations.

In the following directions, the code fragments are what you will type into each shell prompt.

> **TIP:** Remember to log in as the root user first if you are installing in a root-owned directory.

To start your build, just follow these steps:

1. If you haven't already done so, unzip and untar your Apache source distribution. Unless you have a reason to do otherwise, `/usr/local` is the standard place.

```
gunzip -c apache_1.3.x.tar.gz
tar -xvf apache_1.3.x.tar
```

2. Initial configuration of Apache server. If you are installing somewhere other than /usr/local, this is the time to say so with the --prefix flag as shown below. If you are installing in /usr/local, don't worry that the apache directory mentioned below doesn't exist — it will by the end of the build process.

```
cd apache_1.3.x
./configure --prefix=/usr/local/apache
```

3. Unzip and untar your PHP source distribution. Unless you have a reason to do otherwise, /usr/local is the standard place. If Apache and PHP are not under the same directory, you must replace every .. below with the full pathname to the relevant package.

```
cd ..
gunzip -c php-4.x.tar.gz
tar -xvf php-4.x.tar
cd php-4.x
```

4. Configure your PHP build. (Configuring PHP is a topic so large and important that it would not fit into this chapter, so please flip over to Chapter 37 for more information.) The most common are the options to build as an Apache module, which you almost certainly want, and with specific database support. Java and XML support are also increasingly popular. The example build here is an Apache module with MySQL and XML support, but your flags may be completely different.

```
./configure --with-apache=../apache_1.3.x --with-mysql --with-xml --
enable-track-vars
```

5. Make and install the PHP module.

```
make
make install
```

6. Configure and make the Apache daemon. Do not worry that libphp4.a doesn't exist in that location yet! Apache will make it for you.

```
cd ../apache_1.3.x
./configure --activate-module=src/modules/php4/libphp4.a
make
```

7. If you already have an httpd executable, you should stop it and get rid of it now. In current versions of Apache, this step will create a new directory /usr/local/apache (without the version number) which will contain the binaries and configuration files you should use.

```
make install
```

8. Install the php.ini file. Edit this file to get configuration directives; see the options listed in Chapter 37. At this point, we highly recommend new users set error reporting to E_ALL (15) on their development machines.

```
cd ../../php-4.x
cp php.ini-dist /usr/local/lib/php.ini
```

9. Tell your Apache server where you want to serve files from, and what extension(s) you want to identify PHP files (`.php` is the standard, but you can use `.html`, `.phtml`, or whatever you want). Go to your HTTP configuration files (`/usr/local/apache/conf` or whatever your path is), and open `httpd.conf` with a text editor. Search for the word `DocumentRoot` (which should appear twice), and change both paths to the directory you want to serve files out of (in our case, `/home/httpd`). We recommend a home directory rather than the default `/usr/local/apache/htdocs` because it is less insecure. Add at least one PHP extension directive, as shown in the first line below; in the second line, we've also added a second handler to have all HTML files parsed as PHP (which does impose a small performance hit and should not be done if your architecture uses the `.html` file extension strictly for HTML-only files). This would also be a good time for you to ensure that Apache knows what domain alias or IP address to listen for. (If you have no idea what this means, search `httpd.conf` for the word `ServerName`, add the word `localhost` right after it, and use that as your domain name until you get a better one.)

```
AddType application/x-httpd-php .php
AddType application/x-httpd-php .html
```

10. Restart your server. Every time you change your HTTP configuration or `php.ini` files, you must stop and start your server again. An HUP signal will not suffice.

```
cd ../bin
./apachectl start
```

11. Set the document root directory permissions to world-executable. PHP files need only be world-readable (`644`). If necessary, replace `/home/httpd` with your document root below.

```
chmod 755 /home/httpd/html/php
```

12. Open a text editor. Type: `<?php phpinfo(); ?>`. Save this file in your Web server's document root as `info.php`. Start any Web browser and browse the file — you must always use an HTTP request (`http://www.testdomain.com/info.php` or `http://localhost/info.php` or `http://127.0.0.1/info.php`) rather than a filename (`/home/httpd/info.php`) for the file to be parsed correctly. You should see a long table of information about your new PHP4 installation. Congratulations!

CROSS-REFERENCE: Many Apache production servers do not use a `php.ini` file because it can be undesirable to have two different configuration files in two different locations. You can replicate many of the configuration directives of `php.ini` in your Apache `httpd.conf` file. At a minimum, you probably want to set the include path and error reporting levels, because the default settings for these are often unsatisfactory. See Chapter 37 for more details.

Mac OS X and Apache

One of the most exciting developments in open source recently has been the partial opening of the Macintosh platform. Most observers view OS X as a super-stylish GUI on top of a full BSD implementation — possibly the combination that will put a Unix machine in every home.

In keeping with this dual nature, Mac users have the choice of either a binary or a source installation. In fact, your OS X probably came with Apache and PHP preinstalled. This is likely to be quite an old build, and it probably lacks many of the less common extensions. However, if all you want is a quick and dirty Apache + PHP + MySQL/PostgreSQL setup on your laptop, this is certainly the easiest way to fly. All you need to do is edit your Apache configuration file and turn on the Web server. So just follow these steps (and again, the code following each step is what you enter to actually perform the step):

1. Open the Apache config file in a text editor as root.

```
sudo open -a TextEdit /etc/httpd/httpd.conf
```

2. Edit the file. Uncomment the following lines:

```
Load Module php4_module
AddModule mod_php4.c
AddType application/x-httpd-php .php
```

3. You may also want to uncomment the `<Directory /home/*/Sites>` block or otherwise tell Apache which directory to serve out of.

4. Restart the Web server.

```
sudo apachectl graceful
```

5. Now open a text editor. Type `<?php phpinfo(); ?>`. Save this file in your Sites folder as `info.php`. Start any Web browser and browse the file — you must always use an HTTP request (`http://www.testdomain.com/~username/info.php` or `http://localhost/~username/info.php` or `http://127.0.0.1/~username/info.php`) rather than a filename (`/home/username/info.php`) for the file to be parsed correctly. You should see a long table of information about your new PHP4 installation. Congratulations!

If you find you don't have the PHP module, or if you'd like to upgrade your module to a newer version, you can download it from several locations on the Internet. One such source is Marc Liyanage in Switzerland, whose URL we are using below. If you have another preferred binary, substitute the URL to that location in this command:

```
curl -O http://www2.entropy.ch/download/libphp4.so.gz
gunzip libphp4.so.gz
sudo apxs -i -a -n php4 libphp4.so
sudo apachectl graceful
```

Source builds on OS X can be tricky. The directory structure and some of the necessary tools are different, and Apple's own included binaries have been nonstandard. At the moment, compilation from source is not recommended for new PHP users without significant Unix experience. If you want to try it anyway, a good article is available at Stepwise.com:

```
http://www.stepwise.com/Articles/Workbench/2001-10-11.01.html
```

The installation situation on OS X is likely to be in flux for the foreseeable future. Always check the OS X installation page at `http://www.php.net/manual/en/install.macosx.php` before installation of a fresh version of PHP.

Windows NT/2000/XP and IIS

The Windows server installation of PHP4 running IIS 4 or 5 is much simpler than on Unix, since it involves a precompiled binary rather than a source build.

There are currently two choices of binary for Windows: the Installshield self-installer version, and the manual zipfile. The self-installer may seem easier, but it has several limitations: It only works with IIS 4 or 5 and Xitami Web servers; it only provides the CGI version rather than the module; it lacks automatic setup of extensions; and it is notably insecure. Any serious PHP installation on Windows will choose the manual installation instead.

To start your installation, follow these steps:

1. Extract the binary archive using your unzip utility; `C:\PHP` is a common location.

2. Copy some `.dll` files from your PHP directory to your systems directory (usually `C:\Winnt\System32`). You need `php4ts.dll` for every case. You will also probably need to copy the file corresponding to your Web server module — `C:\PHP\Sapi\php4isapi.dll`. It's possible you will also need others from the `dlls` subfolder — but start with the two mentioned above and add more if you need them.

3. Copy either `php.ini-dist` or `php.ini-optimized` (preferably the latter) to your Windows directory (`C:\Winnt` or `C:\Winnt40`), and rename it `php.ini`. Open this file in a text editor (for example, Notepad). Edit this file to get configuration directives; see the options listed in Chapter 37. We highly recommend new users set error reporting to `E_ALL` (15) on their development machines at this point. For now, the most important thing is the `doc_root` directive under the `Paths and Directories` section — make sure this matches your `IIS Inetpub` folder (or wherever you plan to serve out of).

4. Stop and restart the WWW service. Go to the Start menu, Settings, Control Panel, Services. Scroll down the list to IIS Admin Service. Select it and click Stop. After it stops (the status message will inform you), select World Wide Web Publishing Service and click Start. Stopping and restarting the service from within Internet Service Manager (by right-clicking the globe icon) will not suffice. Since this is Windows, you may also wish to reboot.

5. Open a text editor (for example, Notepad). Type: **`<?php phpinfo(); ?>`**. Save this file in your Web server's document root as `info.php`. Start any Web browser and browse the file — you must always use an HTTP request

(http://www.testdomain.com/info.php or http://localhost/info.php or http://127.0.0.1/info.php) rather than a filename (C:\inetpub\wwwroot\info.php) for the file to be parsed correctly. You should see a long table of information about your new PHP4 installation. Congratulations!

> **TIP:** Some Windows users have reported they must put their php.ini files in the same directory as their php.exe executables for the CGI version of PHP. This is not ideal for security reasons because it would be better to keep this file out of the Web tree entirely. Now that PHP offers good modules for many common Windows Web servers, use one of these if you can.

Windows 95/98/Me and PWS

As of this writing, Microsoft appears to have discontinued free distribution of its Personal Web Server (PWS) product, a crippled version of Internet Information Server (IIS) for desktop development.

On balance, this is probably a net positive. PWS was a way for IIS users who wanted to check out PHP at the lowest cost and risk (or so they thought) by installing it on a Windows 95/98/Me box. But these operating systems weren't intended to be used as server platforms, and they did not want to go along quietly. Therefore, to install a Web server and third-party scripting engine, it was necessary to perform fairly major surgery by delving into the Registry by hand. This introduced the possibility of serious damage to the system, and there was no really good way to uninstall cleanly.

It may be some time until Microsoft's new Web server platform is stabilized, especially for desktop use. Until then, we recommend Windows users get to know the friendly and humble workhorse called Apache HTTP server. PHP scripts you develop on Apache on your desktop will eventually run fine on IIS (or .NET Web Server or whatever it's finally called) if the PHP development team's previous record is any guide.

> **TIP:** Even though it's possible to use folder names with spaces in them under Windows, we recommend you do not do so for PHP-enabled directories because it can cause installer problems. Your code will also be less portable.

Windows 95/98/Me and Apache

PHP 4.0 introduced the long-awaited Windows Apache module. Until then, Apache users on Windows could only run the CGI version of PHP, which was slow and less secure. PHP 4.1 brought significant improvements in performance and stability for this module. The Apache developers are also putting a special effort into rapidly improving their Windows HTTP server. For all these reasons, there is really no better time to try Apache — plus it works great even on those aging Win95/98/Me machines.

To install Apache with PHP on Windows 95/98/ME:

1. Download Apache server from
   `http://www.apache.org/dist/httpd/binaries/win32`. You want the current
   stable release version with the `no_src.msi` extension (You can try the `.exe` version if
   there is one, but it doesn't work on all systems and isn't any easier). Double click the
   installer file to install; `C:\Program Files` is a common location. The installer will
   also ask you whether you want to run Apache as a service (takes more cycles, but it's
   available from the taskbar) or from the command line or DOS prompt or whatever they
   call it now. We recommend you do not install as a service, as this may cause problems
   with startup and shutdown on some computers.

2. Extract the PHP binary archive using your unzip utility; `C:\PHP` is a common location.

3. Copy some `.dll` files from your PHP directory to your system directory (usually
   `C:\Windows`). You need `php4ts.dll` for every case. You will also probably need to
   copy the file corresponding to your Web server module —
   `C:\PHP\Sapi\php4apache.dll` — to your Apache modules directory. It's possible
   that you will also need others from the `dlls` subfolder — but start with the two
   mentioned above and add more if you need them.

4. Copy either `php.ini-dist` or `php.ini-optimized` (preferably the latter) to your
   Windows directory, and rename it `php.ini`. Open this file in a text editor (for example,
   Notepad). Edit this file to get configuration directives; see the options listed in Chapter
   37. At this point, we highly recommend new users set error reporting to `E_ALL` (15) on
   their development machines.

5. Tell your Apache server where you want to serve files from and what extension(s) you
   want to identify PHP files (`.php` is the standard, but you can use `.html`, `.phtml`, or
   whatever you want). Go to your HTTP configuration files (`C:\Program
   Files\Apache Group\Apache\conf` or whatever your path is), and open
   `httpd.conf` with a text editor. Search for the word `DocumentRoot` (which should
   appear twice) and change both paths to the directory you want to serve files out of. (The
   default is `C:\Program Files\Apache Group\Apache\htdocs`.) Add at least
   one PHP extension directive as shown in the first line of the following code:.

```
LoadModule php4_module modules/php4apache.dll
AddType application/x-httpd-php .php .phtml
```

6. You may also need to add the following line:

```
AddModule mod_php4.c
```

7. This would also be a good time for you to ensure that Apache knows what domain alias
   or IP address to listen for. (If you have no idea what this means, search `httpd.conf` for
   the word `ServerName`, add the word `localhost` right after it, and use that as your
   domain name until you get a better one).

8. Stop and restart the WWW service. Go to the Start menu, Programs, Apache HTTP
   Server, Control Apache HTTP Server, Stop/Start; or run Apache from the MS-DOS
   prompt.

9. Open a text editor (for example, Notepad). Type: `<?php phpinfo(); ?>`. Save this file in your Web server's document root as `info.php`. Start any Web browser and browse the file — you must always use an HTTP request (`http://www.testdomain.com/info.php` or `http://localhost/info.php` or `http://127.0.0.1/info.php`) rather than a filename (`C:\Program Files\Apache Group\Apache\htdocs\info.php`) for the file to be parsed correctly. You should see a long table of information about your new PHP4 installation. Congratulations!

> **CROSS-REFERENCE:** If you follow these directions and don't get the results you expected, don't panic! Check out Chapter 15 for common gotchas and quirks. If that doesn't help, check out the comments on the relevant pages in the PHP online manual — users leave specific tips for specific setups they've had problems with.

Other Web servers

PHP 4 has been successfully built and run with many other Web servers, such as Netscape Enterprise Server, Xitami, Zeus, and thttpd. Module support for AOLServer, NSAPI, and fhttpd is available. See the relevant pages on the PHP online manual's installation section.

Development tools

When it comes to development tools, PHP unfortunately can fall between the cracks — between tools originally designed for other programming languages and those mainly used to create pretty HTML. It's certainly possible to write a complex 2000-line program that touches several other services and filesystems, then outputs the string 1 to the browser on completion. On the other hand, there are many people whose main use of PHP is to slap common headers and footers on what amounts to a bunch of static HTML pages. With such a diversity of usages, it's perhaps not so amazing that the perfect PHP development environment — user-friendly enough for the designers, but light and powerful enough for the geeks — has been elusive.

Those coming to PHP from a strictly client-side perspective probably have the hardest adjustment to make. There's no such thing as a plush development environment with wizards and drag-and-drop icons and built-in graphics manipulation. If that sort of thing is important to you, you can use a WYSIWYG editor to format the page and then add PHP functionality later using a text editor. The downside of this strategy is, of course, that machine-written code is often not very human-readable — but one must suffer to be pretty.

> **CAUTION:** Be particularly careful with using Microsoft FrontPage as a PHP editor, as it seems to cause problems for many users. At a minimum, you will need to enable (by choosing the option in your `php.ini` file) and use ASP-style tags; or use JavaScript-style `<SCRIPT>` tags consistently, which can be a pain.

Old-school programmers will have less of a learning curve, since they can treat PHP like any other server-side programming language that may or may not happen to output HTML to a browser. Most PHP users in this category seem to prefer simple text editors. Generally, these products will afford you a modest amount of help, such as syntax highlighting, brace matching, or tag closing — most of which is about helping you avoid stupid mistakes rather than actually writing the script for you.

The most exciting development in PHP tools to date has been the release of Zend Studio, which is in 2.0 release as of this writing. This product combines a powerful debugger with an attractive (although still non-WYSIWYG) editing environment. The intelligent product design will clearly help you save time on repetitive tasks such as looking up the exact syntax of PHP functions and zeroing in on bugs faster — and since developer time is money, the modest cost of the product should be quickly recouped in increased productivity. You can really tell that the makers of this IDE know PHP inside and out — Zend Studio is the first development tool for PHP that isn't obviously repurposed from some other use. Figure 3-1 is a screenshot of the main Zend Studio console:

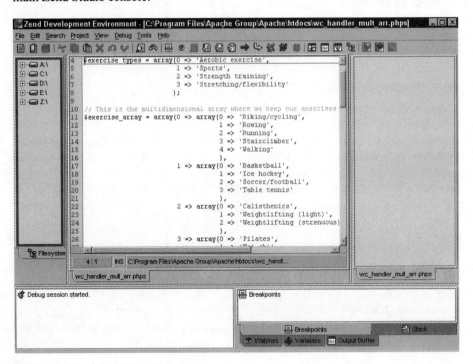

Figure 3-1: Screenshot of Zend Studio IDE

As you can see from Figure 3-1, Zend Studio gives you the ability to "run" a PHP script and view the HTML output in the window on the right — instead of having to View Source on a browser, which can be frustrating due to nonstandard results and funky viewers. The debugging functions give you plenty of power — you can step through a script line by line or step into and out of functions, set breakpoints, perform a stacktrace, track all the global and local variables used by a page or watch a particular variable — in an easy-to-use GUI, as well as alerting you to problematic issues such as undeclared variables. Syntax highlighting and code indentation are lovely and easily customizable — these are notoriously difficult for new users to handle in `emacs` or `vi` — and code completion can save you many, many lookups in the PHP online manual ("Is it `strreplace` or `str_replace`, and what order do the arguments come in?"). You can also get autocomplete help with your HTML, especially handy for remembering the allowable attributes of each tag. You can even register your own user-defined functions on the code completion list, making them easy to use without having to constantly refer to the definition — a godsend if you love to pass tons of variables into your functions. The bigger and more complex and more heavily functionalized your codebase is, the more an IDE like this can help you.

Remember that your development client doesn't necessarily have to be on the same operating system as the server — this is the beauty of truly cross-platform development. This is particularly valuable if you're using a Unix server, where (to paraphrase *The Blues Brothers*) "We have both kinds of editor: `emacs` and `vi`." It must be admitted that Macintosh and Windows have a wider selection of slicker, more user-friendly text editors. Unix, on the other hand, makes it easy to support multiple client OSes. Many development shops take advantage of this "best of all worlds" situation. `emacs`, `vi`, and Zend Studio are editors that come in all the major client platforms — so if your team standardizes on one of those, you will be able to accommodate all client OS preferences.

Table 3-2 shows a matrix of the most popular programmer's editors, with information on the different operating systems they run on.

> **CAUTION:** If you're going to have developers using multiple OSes, remember that linebreaks and some other characters are incompatible between Windows and Unix. Unix-style linebreaks show up as black boxes in Notepad; while Windows linebreaks look like ^M in Unix text editors. Your PHP scripts will probably still work fine, but you'll drive each other crazy if you have to edit each other's code. The best way to deal with the incompatible linebreaks issue, and a heck of a good idea for a lot of other reasons, is to use a version control system such as CVS.

In addition to these popular choices, Keith Edmunds maintains a longer running list of PHP-suitable text editors, many available at no or low cost:

`http://www.itworks.demon.co.uk/phpeditors.htm`

Take a deep breath — after all that installing and configuring, you should now be ready to write your first PHP script.

Table 3-2: Popular PHP Editors by Platform

Platform	Product	Description
Macintosh	BBEdit (`www.barebones.com`)	Many Mac developers can't imagine life without it. Integrated in the Mac version of WYSIWYG package Macromedia Dreamweaver. A no-cost version, BBEdit Lite, is also available.
Unix Windows Macintosh	emacs (`www.gnu.org/software/emacs`) xemacs (`www.xemacs.org`)	Not for the faint of heart. Good PHP syntax highlighting is finally available at `http://sourceforge.net/projects/php-mode/`. Available on every OS imaginable.
Unix Windows Macintosh	vim (`www.vim.org`)	An improved variant of `vi`, now standard on many Unices. This is the kinder, gentler Unix hacker's editor, with a notably friendly community. It was the first major editor to have PHP syntax highlighting. Available on almost every OS.
Linux Windows Macintosh	Zend Studio (`www.zend.com`)	The first development tool specifically designed for PHP. debugger, code completion, and HTML output viewer.
Windows	HomeSite (`http://www.macromedia.com/software/homesite/`)	Perennially popular Windows commercial text editor. Integrated with the Windows version of WYSIWYG package Macromedia Dreamweaver.
Windows	Notepad (included with all Windows systems)	Believe it or not, many people build fine sites using this crudest of tools.

Summary

Before you can use PHP, you need to decide whether you will self-host, outsource, or adopt a compromise solution, such as colocation. Some important factors in the decision are cost, size and traffic of site, unusual hardware or software needs, type of content, and desire for control. The best candidates for external Web hosting are small sites without unusual requirements; or sites large enough to require at least one entire server to themselves.

If you decide to self-host or maintain a development environment, detailed installation instructions are provided above for the most common platforms. PHP4 supports many other Web servers, but installation directions for all of them would have made this chapter unreasonably lengthy.

Finally, before you can start developing, you will want to give some thought to which development tools are best adapted to PHP. Although the long-awaited PHP-specific IDE is now available from Zend, most PHP developers still simply use their favorite text editor. It is possible to add PHP to the product of a WYSIWYG editor, but it can be messy.

Chapter 4
Adding PHP to HTML

In This Chapter

♦ Escaping into PHP mode

♦ Choosing PHP tag styles

♦ Writing a Hello World program in PHP

♦ Including files

After all those preliminary exertions, we finally get to the point of writing our first PHP scripts. Here you'll learn about PHP mode, PHP tags, and how to include other files in your PHP scripts. You'll also write your very first PHP program.

Your HTML Is Already PHP-Compliant!

PHP is already perfectly at home with HTML — in fact, it is generally embedded within HTML. As you'll see in later chapters, PHP rides piggyback on some of the cleverer parts of the HTML standard, such as forms and cookies, to do all kinds of useful things.

Anything that is compatible with HTML on the client side is also compatible with PHP. PHP could not care less about chunks of JavaScript, calls to music and animation, applets, or anything else on the client side. PHP will simply ignore those parts, and the Web server will happily pass them on to the client.

It should thus be clear that you can use any method of developing Web pages, and simply add PHP to that. If you're comfortable having teams work on each page using huge multimedia graphics suites, you can keep on doing that. The general point is, you don't need to change tools or workflow order — just do what you've been doing and add the server-side functionality at the end.

Escaping from HTML

By now you're probably wondering: How does the PHP parser recognize PHP code inside your HTML document? The answer is that you tell the program when to spring into action by using special PHP tags at the beginning and end of each PHP section. This process is called *escaping from HTML* or, alternatively, *escaping into PHP*.

> **CAUTION:** Not to confuse you, but *escape* in this sense should not be confused with another common use of the term *escape* in PHP: putting a backslash in front of certain special characters (such as tab and newline) within double-quoted strings.

Everything within these tags is understood by the PHP parser to be PHP code. Everything outside of these tags does not concern the server and will simply be passed along and left for the client to sort out whether it's HTML or JavaScript or something else.

There are four styles of PHP tags, and different rationales for using them. However, part of the decision is simply individual preference: what the individual programmer is comfortable with, or what a team has decided upon for reasons of their own.

Canonical PHP tags

The PHP tag style that is most universally effective is:

```
<?php   ?>
```

If you use this style, you can be positive that your tags will always be correctly interpreted. Unless you have a very, very strong reason to prefer one of the other styles, use this one. Some or all of the other styles of PHP tag may be phased out in the future — this is the only one that is certain to be safe.

Short-open (SGML-style) tags

Short or short-open tags look like this:

```
<?   ?>
```

Short tags are, as one might expect, the shortest option. Those who escape into and out of HTML frequently in each script will be attracted by the prospect of fewer keystrokes. However, the price of shorter tags is pretty high. You must do one of two things to enable PHP to recognize the tags:

- ♦ Choose the `--enable-short-tags` configuration option when you're building PHP.

- ♦ Set the `short_open_tag` setting in your `php.ini` file to on. This option must be disabled to parse XML with PHP because the same syntax is used for XML tags.

> **CAUTION:** There used to be a third way to enable short-open tags: the `short_open()` function. This is no longer supported in PHP 4.

There are several reasons to resist the temptation of the short-open tag. The main downside is that this syntax is not compatible with XML — and since XHTML is a type of XML, this implies that none of your code will be able to validate as XHTML. PHP code written with short-open tags is less portable because you can't be sure another machine will have enabled them. Short-open tags are also harder to pick out visually on the page, and many syntax-highlighting schemes don't support them. Beginners should be encouraged to start off with the canonical style tag if at all possible.

The short-open tag was one of many hacky ease-of-use ideas that ended up biting the PHP community years later. The PHP development team must now struggle to balance desires for a more standard and consistent syntax with a large installed userbase, which has written a huge pile of code in the old style. As XML becomes more and more central to Web development, the short-open tag faces a shaky future. Do yourself a favor and start moving towards the canonical PHP tags now.

> **TIP:** If you've made the virtuous decision to eschew the short-open tag, remember to disable it in your `php.ini` file. You want to see an error when you inadvertently forget to complete your tag correctly.

ASP-style tags

ASP-style tags are tags that mimic the tags used by Microsoft Active Server Pages to delineate code blocks. ASP-style tags look like this:

```
<%    %>
```

People who use FrontPage as a development tool often choose this style. To use ASP-style tags, you will need to set the configuration option in your `php.ini` file. Obviously, if you use ASP-style tags and the `.asp` suffix (which you may wish to do if you're converting from an ASP site or spoofing ASP for some reason), you will need to disable ASP on your IIS server. Otherwise, two different scripting engines will be trying to parse the same blocks of code with unpredictable results.

HTML script tags

HTML script tags look like this:

```
<SCRIPT LANGUAGE="PHP">  </SCRIPT>
```

Although this is effective and also gets around the FrontPage problems, it can be cumbersome in certain situations, such as quick pop-in variable replacement. In particular, be careful if you use lots of JavaScript on your site since the close-script tags are fatally ambiguous. The HTML script tag is best used for fairly sizable blocks of PHP code.

Hello World

Now we're ready to write our first PHP program. Open up a new file in your preferred editor. Type:

```
<HTML>
<HEAD>
<TITLE>My first PHP program</TITLE>
</HEAD>

<BODY>
```

```
<?php
print("Hello, cruel world<BR><BR>\n");
phpinfo();
?>
</BODY>
</HTML>
```

In most browsers, nothing but the PHP section is strictly necessary. However, it's a good idea to get in the habit of always using a well-formed HTML structure in which to embed your PHP.

If you don't see something pretty close to the output shown in Figure 4-1, we have a problem — most likely some kind of installation or configuration glitch.

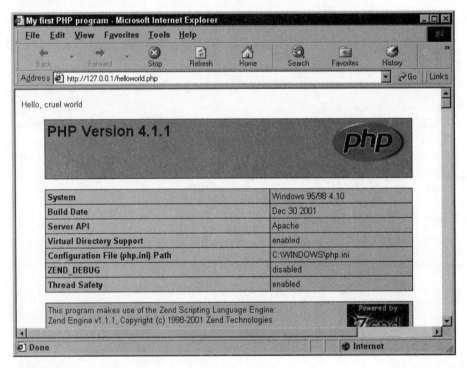

Figure 4-1: Your first PHP script

Refer back to Chapter 3 for installation instructions and forward to Chapter 37 for configuration options. Chapter 15 diagnoses some common early problems and gives debugging hints.

Jumping in and out of PHP mode

At any given moment in a PHP script, you are either in PHP mode or you're out of it in HTML. There's no middle ground. Anything within the PHP tags is PHP; everything outside is plain HTML as far as the server is concerned.

You can escape into PHP mode with giddy abandon, as often and as briefly or lengthily as necessary. For example:

```
<?php $id = 1; ?>
<FORM METHOD="POST" ACTION="registration.php">
<P>First name:
<INPUT TYPE="TEXT" NAME="firstname" SIZE=20>
<P>Last name:
<INPUT TYPE="TEXT" NAME="lastname" SIZE=20>
<P>Rank:
<INPUT TYPE="TEXT" NAME="rank" SIZE=10>
<INPUT TYPE="HIDDEN" NAME="serial number" VALUE="<?php print("$id");
?>">
<INPUT TYPE="SUBMIT" VALUE="INPUT">
</FORM>
```

Notice that things that happened in the first PHP mode instance — in this case, a variable being assigned — are still valid in the second. In the next chapter, you'll learn more about what happens to variables when you skip in and out of PHP mode. In Chapter 14, you'll also learn about different styles of using PHP mode.

Including files

Another way you can add PHP to your HTML is by putting it in a separate file and calling it by using PHP's include functions. There are four include functions:

♦ include('/filepath/filename')

♦ require('/filepath/filename')

♦ include_once('/filepath/filename')

♦ require_once('/filepath/filename')

In previous versions of PHP, there were significant differences in functionality and speed between the include functions and the require functions. This is no longer true; the two sets of functions differ only in the kind of error they throw on failure. Include() and include_once() will merely generate a warning on failure, while require() and require_once() will cause a fatal error and termination of the script.

As suggested by the names of the functions, include_once() and require_once() differ from simple include() and require() in that they will only allow a file to be included once per PHP script. This is extremely helpful when you are including files that contain PHP functions, because redeclaring functions results in an automatic fatal error. In larger PHP systems, it's quite common to include files which include other files which include other files — it can be difficult to remember whether you've included a particular function before, but with `include_once()` or `require_once()` you don't have to.

How do you decide on a preferred `include` function? Basically you must decide whether you want to force yourself to write good code on pain of fatal error, or whether you want it to run regardless of certain common errors on your part. The strictest alternative is `require()`, which will bring everything grinding to a halt if your code isn't perfect; the least strict is `include_once()`, which will good-naturedly hide the consequences of some of your bad coding habits.

The most common use of PHP's `include` capability is to add common headers and footers to all the Web pages on a site.

For example, a simple header file (cleverly named `header.inc`) might look like this:

```
<HTML>
<HEAD>
<TITLE>A site title</TITLE>
</HEAD>

<BODY>
```

Similarly, a footer file called `footer.inc` might consist of:

```
<P>Copyright 1995 - 2002</P>
</BODY>
</HTML>
```

They are called from a PHP page this way:

```
<?php require_once($DOCUMENT_ROOT . '/header.inc'); ?>
<P>This is some body text for this particular page.</P>
<?php require_once($DOCUMENT_ROOT . '/footer.inc'); ?>
```

Obviously, this single move greatly enhances the maintainability and scalability of an entire site. Now, if you want a different look and feel or if you need to update the copyright notice, you can alter one file instead of identical lines in dozens of HTML pages.

> **TIP:** When including files, remember to set the `include_path` directive correctly in your `php.ini` file. Remember that you can include files from above or entirely outside your Web tree by proper use of this directive. See Chapter 37 for more information.

As you can see from the example above, PHP's `include` functions simply pass along the contents of the included file *as text*. Many people think that because an `include` function occurs inside PHP mode, the included file will also be in PHP mode. This is not true! Actually, the server escapes back into HTML mode at the beginning of each included file and silently returns to PHP mode at the end, just in time to catch the semicolon.

As always, you need to say when you intend something to be PHP by using PHP opening and closing tags. Any part of an included file that needs to be executed as PHP should be enclosed in valid PHP tags. If the entire file is PHP (very common in files of functions), the entire file must be enclosed within PHP tags.

Take the following file, `database.inc`:

```
$db = mysql_connect('localhost', 'db_user', 'db_password');
mysql_select_db('my_database');
```

> **CAUTION:** We can't emphasize this enough: If you're having problems including PHP files, particularly if you're seeing output you don't expect or not seeing output you do expect, be *ABSOLUTELY POSITIVE* that you've put PHP tags at the beginning and end of the included file.

If you were to foolishly include this file from a PHP script, your database variables would be visible to the world in plain text — because you neglected to use PHP tags, the parser assumes this block of code is HTML. A correct version of the `database.inc` file would look like this:

```
<?php
$db = mysql_connect('localhost', 'db_user', 'db_password');
mysql_select_db('my_database');
?>
```

> **CAUTION:** For all PHP files which are included from other files, you must ensure that there are no empty new lines at the end of the file. Remember, anything outside a PHP block is considered HTML, even a blank line. Blank lines, or even blank spaces outside a closing PHP tag, will be interpreted as output. If you include the file in a situation where you cannot have output — say before using HTTP headers — your script will fail with a big error message about the output stream having already been started in your included file. See Chapter 15 for an example.

Summary

PHP is easy to embed in HTML. You can use whatever HTML-production method you're already comfortable with, and simply add the PHP sections later. PHP additions can range from simply echoing a single-digit integer to writing long chunks of code.

Every PHP block, short or long, is set off by PHP tags. There are several styles of PHP tag, but everyone should be encouraged to use the canonical style. You can also include PHP in files by using the `include` functions — but remember that the contents of the included files will not be recognized as PHP unless surrounded by PHP tags.

## Chapter 5

Syntax, Variables, and Printing

In this chapter, we cover the basic syntax of PHP — the rules that all well-formed PHP code must follow. We also explain how to use variables to store and retrieve information as your PHP code executes. Finally, we look at the simplest ways to display text that will show up in your user's browser window.

PHP Is Forgiving

The first and most important thing to say about the PHP language is that it tries to be as forgiving as possible. Programming languages vary quite a bit in terms of how stringent a syntax they enforce. Pickiness can be a *good* thing because it helps make sure that the code you're writing is really what you mean. If you are writing a program to control a nuclear reactor and you forget to assign a variable, it is far better to have the program be rejected than to create behavior different from what you intended. PHP's design philosophy, however, is at the other end of the spectrum. Because PHP started life as a handy utility for making quick-and-dirty Web pages, it emphasizes convenience for the programmer over correctness; rather than have a programmer do the extra work of redundantly specifying what is meant by a piece of code, PHP requires the minimum and then tries its best to figure out what was meant. Among other things, this means that certain syntactical features that show up in other languages, such as variable declarations and function prototypes, are simply not necessary.

With that said, though, PHP can't read your mind; it has a minimum set of syntactical rules that your code must follow. Whenever you see the words `parse error` in your browser window instead of the cool Web page you thought you had just written, it means that you've broken these rules to the point that PHP has given up on your page.

HTML Is Not PHP

The second most important thing to understand about PHP syntax is that it applies only within PHP. Because PHP is embedded in HTML documents, every part of such a document is interpreted as either PHP or HTML, depending on whether that section of the document is enclosed in PHP tags.

PHP syntax is relevant only within PHP, so we assume for the rest of this chapter that PHP mode is in force — that is, most code fragments will be assumed to be embedded in an HTML page and surrounded with the appropriate tags.

PHP's Syntax Is C-Like

The third most important thing to know about PHP syntax is that, broadly speaking, it is like the C programming language. If you happen to be one of the lucky people who already know C, tthis is very helpful; if you are uncertain about how a statement should be written, try it first the way you would do it in C, and if that doesn't work . . . look it up in the manual. The rest of this section is for the other people, the ones who don't already know C. (C programmers might want to skim the headers of this section and also see Appendix A, which is specifically for C programmers.)

PHP is whitespace insensitive

Whitespace is the stuff you type that is typically invisible on the screen, including spaces, tabs, and carriage returns (end-of-line characters). PHP's whitespace insensitivity does not mean that spaces and such never matter. (In fact, they are crucial for separating the "words" in the PHP language.) Instead, it means that it never matters how many whitespace characters you have in a row — one whitespace character is the same as many such characters.

For example, each of the following PHP statements that assigns the sum of 2 + 2 to the variable $four is equivalent:

```
$four = 2 + 2;      // single spaces
$four <tab>=<tab>2<tab>+<tab>2  ;     // spaces and tabs
$four            =
2
+
2;  // multiple lines
```

The fact that end-of-line characters count as whitespace is handy, because it means you never have to strain to make sure that a statement fits on a single line.

PHP is sometimes case sensitive

Having read that PHP isn't picky, you may be surprised to learn that it is sometimes case sensitive (that is, it cares about the distinction between lowercase and capital letters). In particular, all variables are case sensitive. If you embed the following code in an HTML page:

```
<?php
  $capital = 67;
  print("Variable capital is $capital<BR>");
  print("Variable CaPiTaL is $CaPiTaL<BR>");
?>
```

The output you will see is:

```
Variable capital is 67
Variable CaPiTaL is
```

because the different capitalization schemes make for different variables. (Surprisingly, under the default settings for error reporting, code like this fragment will not produce a PHP error — see the section "Unassigned variables" later in the chapter.)

On the other hand, unlike in C, function names are *not* case sensitive, and neither are the basic language constructs (`if`, `then`, `else`, `while`, and the like).

Statements are expressions terminated by semicolons

Here is a typical statement in PHP, which in this case assigns a string of characters to a variable called `$greeting`:

```
    $greeting = "Welcome to PHP!";
```

The rest of this subsection is about how such statements are built from smaller components and how the PHP interpreter handles the evaluation of statements. (If you already feel comfortable with statements and expressions, feel free to skip ahead.)

The smallest building blocks of PHP are the *indivisible tokens*, such as numbers (`3.14159`), strings (`"two"`), variables (`$two`), constants (`TRUE`), and the special words that make up the syntax of PHP itself (`if`, `else`, and so forth). These are separated from each other by whitespace and by other special characters such as parentheses and braces.

The next most complex building block in PHP is the *expression*, which is any combination of tokens that has a value. A single number is an expression, as is a single variable. Simple expressions can also be combined to make more complicated expressions, usually either by putting an *operator* in between (for example, `2 + (2 + 2)`), or by using them as input to a function call (for example, `pow(2 * 3, 3 * 2)`). Operators that take two inputs go in between their inputs, whereas functions take their inputs in parentheses immediately after their names, with the inputs (known as *arguments*) separated by commas.

Expressions are evaluated

Whenever the PHP interpreter encounters an expression in code, that expression is immediately *evaluated*. This means that PHP calculates values for the smallest elements of the expression, and then successively combines those values that are connected by operators or functions, until it has produced an entire value for the expression. For example, successive steps in an imaginary evaluation process might look like:

```
$result = 2 * 2 + 3 * 3 + 5;
        (= 4 + 3 * 3 + 5)   //imaginary evaluation steps
        (= 4 + 9 + 5)
        (= 13 + 5)
        (= 18)
```

with the result that the number 18 is stored in the variable $result.

Precedence, associativity, and evaluation order

There are two kinds of freedom PHP has in expression evaluation: how it groups or associates subexpressions and the order in which it evaluates them. For example, in the evaluation process just shown, multiplications were associated more tightly than additions, which affects the end result.

The particular ways that operators group expressions are called *precedence* rules — operators that have higher precedence win in "grabbing" the expressions around them. If you want, you can memorize the rules, such as the fact that *always has higher precedence than +. Or, you can just use the following cardinal rule: When in doubt, use parentheses to group expressions.

For example:

```
$result1 = 2 + 3 * 4 + 5 // is equal to 19
$result2 = (2 + 3) * (4 + 5) // is equal to 45
```

Operator precedence rules remove much of the ambiguity about how subexpressions are associated. But what about when two operators have the same precedence? Consider this expression:

```
$how_much = 3.0 / 4.0 / 5.0;
```

Whether this is equal to 0.15 or 3.75 depends on which division operator gets to "grab" the number 4.0 first. There is an exhaustive list of rules of associativity in the online manual, but the rule to remember is that associativity is usually left-before-right — that is, the preceding expression would evaluate to 0.15, because the leftmost of the two division operators wins the dispute over precedence.

The final wrinkle is order of evaluation, which is not quite the same thing as associativity. For example, look at the arithmetic expression:

```
3 * 4 + 5 * 6
```

We know that the multiplications will happen before the additions, but that is not the same as knowing which multiplication PHP will perform first. In general, you need not worry about evaluation order, because in almost all cases it will not affect the result. You can construct weird examples where the result does depend on order of evaluation, usually by making assignments in subexpressions that are used in other parts of the expression. For example:

```
$huh = ($this = $that + 5) + ($that = $this + 3);  // BAD
```

But don't do this, okay? PHP may or may not have a predictable order of evaluation of expressions, but you shouldn't depend on it — so we're not going to tell you! (The one legitimate use of relying on left-to-right evaluation order is in "short-circuiting" Boolean expressions, which we will cover in Chapter 7.

Expressions and types

Usually, the programmer is careful to match the types of expressions with the operators and functions that combine them. Common expressions are *mathematical* (with mathematical operators combining numbers), or *Boolean* (combining true-or-false statements with *and*s and *or*s), or *string expressions* (with operators and functions constructing strings of characters). As with the rest of PHP, however, the treatment of types is surprisingly forgiving. For example, consider the following expression, which deliberately mixes the types of subexpressions in an inappropriate way:

```
2 + 2 * "nonsense" + TRUE
```

Rather than produce an error, this evaluates to the number 3. (You can take this as a puzzle for now, but we will explain how such a thing can happen in the next chapter.)

Assignment expressions

A very common kind of expression is the *assignment*, where a variable is set to equal the result of evaluating some expression. These have the form of a variable name (which always starts with a $), followed by a single equal sign, followed by the expression to be evaluated. For example:

```
$eight = 2 * (2 * 2)
```

assigns the variable $eight the value you would expect.

An important thing to remember is that even assignment expressions are expressions and so have values themselves! The value of an expression that assigns a variable is the same as the value that is assigned. This means that you can use assignment expressions in the middle of more complicated expressions. If you evaluate the statement:

```
$ten = ($two = 2) + ($eight = 2 * (2 * 2))
```

each variable would be assigned a numerical value equal to its name.

Finally, a *statement* in PHP is any expression that is followed by a semicolon (;). If expressions correspond to phrases, statements correspond to entire sentences, and the semicolon is the full stop at the end. Any sequence of valid PHP statements that is enclosed by the PHP tags is a valid PHP program.

Reasons for expressions and statements

There are usually only two reasons to write an expression in PHP: for its *value* or for a *side effect*. The value of an expression is what is passed on to any more complicated expression that includes it; side effects are anything else that happens as a result of the evaluation. The most typical side effects involve assigning or changing a variable, printing something to the user's screen, or making some other persistent change to the program's environment (such as interacting with a database).

Although statements are expressions, they are not themselves included in more complicated expressions. This means that the only good reason for a statement is a side effect! It also means that it is possible to write legal (yet totally useless statements) such as the second of these:

```
print("Hello");  // side effect is printing to screen

2 * 3 + 4;  // useless - no side effect

$value_num = 3 * 4 + 5;  // side effect is assignment

store_in_database(49.5);  // side effect to DB
```

Braces make blocks

Although statements cannot be combined like expressions, you can always put a sequence of statements anywhere a statement can go by enclosing them in a set of curly braces.

For example, The `if` construct in PHP has a test (in parentheses) followed by the statement that should be executed if the test is true. If you want more than one statement to be executed when the test is true, you can use a brace-enclosed sequence instead. The following pieces of code (which simply print a reassuring statement that it is still true that $1 + 2$ is equal to 3) are equivalent:

```
if (3 == 2 + 1)
  print("Good - I haven't totally lost my mind.<BR>");

if (3 == 2 + 1)
  {
    print("Good - I haven't totally ");
    print("lost my mind.<BR>");
  }
```

You can put any kind of statement in a brace-enclosed block, including, say, an `if` statement that itself has a brace-enclosed block. This means that `if` statements can have other `if` statements inside them. In fact, this kind of nesting can be done to an arbitrary number of levels.

Comments

A *comment* is the portion of a program that only exists for the human reader. The very first thing that a program executor does with program code is to strip out the comments, so they cannot have any effect on what the program does. Comments are invaluable in helping the next person who reads your code figure out what you were thinking when you wrote it, even when that person is yourself a week from now.

PHP drew its inspiration from several different programming languages, most notably C, Perl, and Unix shell scripts. As a result, PHP supports styles of comments from all those languages, and those styles can be intermixed freely in PHP code.

C-style multiline comments

The *multiline* style of commenting is the same as in C: A comment starts with the character pair /* and terminates with the character pair */. For example:

```
/*  This is
    a comment in
    PHP */
```

The most important thing to remember about multiline comments is that they cannot be nested. You cannot put one comment inside another. If you try, the comment will be closed off by the first instance of the */ character pair, and the rest of what was intended to be an enclosing comment will instead be interpreted as code, probably failing horribly. For example:

```
/* This comment will /* fail horribly on the
    last word of this */ sentence
*/
```

This is an easy thing to do unintentionally, usually when you try to deactivate a block of commented code by "commenting it out."

Single-line comments: # and //

In addition to the /* . . . */ multiple-line comments, PHP supports two different ways of commenting to the end of a given line, one inherited from C++ and Java and the other from Perl and shell scripts. The shell-script-style comment starts with a pound sign, whereas the C++ style comment starts with two forward slashes. Both of them cause the rest of the current line to be treated as a comment, as in the following:

```
#  This is a comment, and
 #  this is the second line of the comment
 // This is a comment too.  Each style comments only
 // one line so the last word of this sentence will fail
horribly.
```

The very alert reader might argue that single-line comments are incompatible with what we said earlier about whitespace insensitivity. That would be correct — you will get a very different result if you take a single-line comment and replace one of the spaces with an end-of-line character. A more accurate way of putting it is that, after the comments have been stripped out of the code, PHP code is whitespace insensitive.

Variables

The main way to store information in the middle of a PHP program is by using a variable — a way to name and hang on to any value that you want to use later.

Here are the most important things to know about variables in PHP (more detailed explanations will follow):

◆ All variables in PHP are denoted with a leading dollar sign ($).

◆ The value of a variable is the value of its most recent assignment.

◆ Variables are assigned with the = operator, with the variable on the left-hand side and the expression to be evaluated on the right.

◆ Variables do not need to be declared before assignment.

◆ Variables have no intrinsic type other than the type of their current value.

◆ Variables that are used before they are assigned have default values.

PHP variables are Perl-like

All variables in PHP start with a leading $ sign just like scalar variables in the Perl scripting language, and in other ways they have similar behavior (need no type declarations, may be referred to before they are assigned, and so on). Perl hackers may need to do no more than skim the headings of this section, which is really for the rest of us.

After the initial $, variable names must be composed of letters (uppercase or lowercase), digits (0-9), and underscore characters (_). Furthermore, the first character after the $ may not be a number.

Declaring variables

This subheading is here simply because programmers from some other languages might be looking for it — in languages such as C, C++, and Java, the programmer must declare the name and type of any variable before making use of it. However in PHP, because types are associated with values rather than variables, no such declaration is necessary — the first step in using a variable is to assign it a value.

Assigning variables

Variable assignment is simple — just write the variable name and then add a single equal sign (=), and then the expression that you want to assign to that variable.

```
$pi = 3 + 0.14159; // approximately
```

Note that what is assigned is the result of evaluating the expression, not the expression itself. After the preceding statement is evaluated, there is no way to tell that the value of $pi was created by adding two numbers together.

Reassigning variables

There is no interesting distinction in PHP between assigning a variable for the first time and changing its value later. This is true even if the assigned values are of different types. For example, the following is perfectly legal:

```
$my_num_var = "This should be a number - hope it's reassigned";
$my_num_var = 5;
```

If the second statement immediately follows the first one, the first statement has essentially no effect.

Unassigned variables

Many programming languages will object if you try to use a variable before it is assigned; others will let you use it, but if you do you may find yourself reading the random contents of some area of memory. In PHP, the default error-reporting setting allows you to use unassigned variables without errors, and PHP ensures that they have reasonable default values.

> **CROSS-REFERENCE:** If you would like to be warned about variables that have not been assigned, you should change the error-reporting level to E_ALL (the highest level possible) from the default level of error reporting. You can do this either by including the statement error_reporting(E_ALL); at the top of a script, or by changing your php.ini file to set the default level (see Chapter 37).

Default values

Variables in PHP do not have intrinsic types — a variable does not know in advance whether it will be used to store a number or a string of characters. So how does it know what type of default value to have when it hasn't yet been assigned?

The answer is that, just as with assigned variables, the type of a variable is interpreted depending on the context in which it is used. In a situation where a number is expected, a number will be produced, and this works similarly with character strings. In any context that treats a variable as a number, an unassigned variable will be evaluated as 0; in any context that expects a string value, an unassigned variable will be the empty string (the string that is zero characters long).

Checking assignment with IsSet

Because variables do not have to be assigned before use, in some situations you can actually convey information by selectively setting or not setting a variable! PHP provides a function, called IsSet, which tests a variable to see whether it has been assigned a value.

As the following code illustrates, an unassigned variable is distinguishable even from a variable that has been given the default value:

```
$set_var = 0; //set_var has a value
              //never_set does not
```

```
print("set_var print value: $set_var<BR>");
print("never_set print value: $never_set<BR>");
if ($set_var == $never_set)
  print("set_var is equal to never_set!<BR>");
if (IsSet($set_var))
  print("set_var is set.<BR>");
else
  print("set_var is not set.<BR>");
if (IsSet($never_set))
  print("never_set is set.<BR>");
else
  print("never_set is not set.");
```

Oddly enough, this code will produce the following output:

```
set_var print value: 0
never_set print value:
set_var is equal to never_set!
set_var is set.
never_set is not set.
```

The variable $never_set has never been assigned, so it produces an empty string when a string is expected (as in the print statement) and a zero value when a number is expected (as in the comparison test that concludes that the two variables are the same). Still, IsSet can tell the difference between $set_var and $never_set.

The act of assigning a variable is not irrevocable — the function unset() will restore a variable to an unassigned state (for example, unset($set_var); will make $set_var into an unbound variable, regardless of its previous assignments).

Variable scope

Scope is the technical term for the rules about when a name (for, say, a variable or function) has the same meaning in two different places, and in what situations two names that are spelled exactly the same way can actually refer to different things.

Any PHP variable that is not inside a function has *global* scope and extends throughout a given "thread" of execution. In other words, if you assign a variable near the top of a PHP file, the variable name has the same meaning for the rest of the file; and if it is not reassigned, it will have the same value as the rest of your code executes (except inside the body of functions).

The assignment of a variable will not affect the value of variables with the same name in other PHP files or even in repeated uses of the same file. For example, let's say that you have two files: startup.php, and next_thing.php, which are typically visited in that order by a user. Let's also say that near the top of startup.php, you have the line:

```
$username = "Jane Q. User";
```

which is only executed in certain situations. Now, you might hope that, after setting that variable in `startup.php`, it would also be preset automatically when the user visited `next_thing.php`, but no such luck. Each time a PHP page executes, it assigns and reassigns variables as it goes, and those variables "disappear" at the end of a page's production. Assignments of variables in one file do not affect variables of the same name in a different file or even in other requests for the same file.

Obviously, there are many situations in which you would like to hold onto information for longer than it takes to generate a particular Web page. There are a variety of ways you can accomplish this, and the different techniques are a lot of what the rest of this book is about. For example, You can pass information from page to page using GET and POST variables (Chapter 9), store information persistently in a database (all of Part II of this book), associate it with a user's session using PHP's new session mechanism (Chapter 27), or store it on a user's hard disk via a cookie (Chapter 27).

Functions and variable scope

Except inside the body of a function, variable scope in PHP is quite simple: Within any given execution of a PHP file, just assign a variable, and its value will be there for you later. We haven't yet covered how to define your own functions, but it's worth a look-ahead note: Variables assigned within a function are *local* to that function, and unless you make a special declaration in a function, that function won't have access to the global variables that are defined outside the function, even when they are defined in the same file. (We will discuss the scope of variables in functions in depth when we cover function definitions in Chapter 8.)

You can switch modes if you want

One scoping question that we had the first time we saw PHP code was: Does variable scope persist across tags? For example, we have a single file that looks like:

```
<HTML>
<HEAD>
<?php
  $username = "Jane Q. User";
?>
</HEAD>
<BODY>
<?php
  print("$username<BR>");
?>
</BODY>
</HTML>
```

Should we expect our assignment to `$username` to survive through the second of the two PHP-tagged areas? The answer is yes — variables persist throughout a thread of PHP execution (in other words, through the whole process of producing a Web page in response to a user's request). This is a single manifestation of a general PHP rule, which is that the *only* effect of the tags is to let the PHP engine know whether you want your code to be interpreted as PHP or passed through untouched as HTML. You should feel free to use the tags to switch back and forth between modes whenever it is convenient.

Constants

In addition to variables, which may be reassigned, PHP offers constants, which have a single value throughout their lifetime. Constants do not have a $ before their names, and by convention the names of constants usually are in uppercase letters. Constants can only contain scalar values (numbers and string). Constants have global scope, so they are accessible everywhere in your scripts after they have been defined — even inside functions.

For example, the built-in PHP constant E_ALL represents a number that indicates to the error_reporting() function that all errors and warnings should be reported. A call to error_reporting() might look like this:

```
error_reporting(E_ALL);
```

This is identical to calling error_reporting() on the integer value of E_ALL, but is better because the actual value of E_ALL may change from one version of PHP to the next.

It's also possible to create your own constants using the define() form, although this is more unusual than referring to built-in constants. The code:

```
define(MY_ANSWER, 42);
```

would cause MY_ANSWER to evaluate to 42 everywhere it appears in your code. There is no way to change this assignment after it has been made.

Output

Most of the constructs in the PHP language execute *silently* — they don't print anything to output. The only way that your embedded PHP code will display anything in a user's browser program is either by means of statements that print something to output or by calling functions that, in turn, call print statements.

Echo and print

The two most basic constructs for printing to output are echo and print. Their language status is somewhat confusing, because they are basic constructs of the PHP language, rather than being functions. As a result, they can be used either with parentheses or without them. (Function calls always have the name of the function first, followed by a parenthesized list of the arguments to the function.)

Echo

The simplest use of echo is to print out a string as argument, for example:

```
echo "This will print in the user's browser window.";
```

Or, equivalently:

```
echo("This will print in the user's browser window.");
```

Both of these statements will cause the given sentence to be displayed, without displaying the quote signs. (*Note for C programmers:* Think of the HTTP connection to the user as the "standard output stream" for these functions.)

You can also give multiple arguments to the unparenthesized version of echo, separated by commas, as in:

```
echo "This will print in the ", "user's browser window.";
```

The parenthesized version, however, will not accept multiple arguments:

```
echo ("This will produce a ", "PARSE ERROR!");
```

Print

The command print is very similar to echo, with two important differences:

- ◆ Unlike echo, print can accept only one argument.
- ◆ Unlike echo, print returns a value, which represents whether the print statement succeeded.

The value returned by print will be 1 if the printing was successful, and 0 if unsuccessful. (It is rare that a syntactically correct print statement will fail, but in theory this return value provides a means to test, for example, if the user's browser has closed the connection.)

Both echo and print are usually used with string arguments, but PHP's type flexibility means that you can throw pretty much any type of argument at them without causing an error. For example, the following two lines will print exactly the same thing:

```
print("3.14159");  // print a string
print(3.14159);    // print a number
```

Technically, what is happening in the second line is that, because print expects a string argument, the floating-point version of the number is converted to a string value before print gets hold of it. However, the effect is that both print and echo will reliably print out numbers as well as string arguments.

For the sake of simplicity and uniformity, we will typically use the parenthesized version of print in our examples, rather than using echo.

> **CROSS-REFERENCE:** In addition to the printing functions discussed here, there are two printing functions that are used mostly for debugging: print_r() and var_dump(). The point of these functions is to help you visualize what's going on with compound data structures like arrays, so we cover them along with the details of arrays in Chapter 11.

Variables and strings

C programmers are accustomed to using a function called `printf`, which allows you to splice values and expressions into a specially formatted printing string. PHP has analogous functions (which we will cover in Chapter 9), but as it turns out we can get much of the same functionality just by using `print` (or `echo`) with quoted strings. For example, the fragment:

```
$animal = "antelope";
$animal_heads = 1;
$animal_legs = 4;
print("The $animal has $animal_heads head(s).<BR>");
print("The $animal has $animal_legs leg(s).<BR>");
```

will produce the following output in the browser:

```
The antelope has 1 head(s).
The antelope has 4 leg(s).
```

The values for the variables we included in the string have been neatly spliced into the printed output. This makes it very easy to quickly produce Web pages with content that varies depending on how variables have been set. It is not due to any magical properties of `print`, however — the magic is really happening in the interpretation of the quoted string itself.

Single versus double quotation marks

PHP does some preprocessing of doubly quoted strings (strings with quotes like "this") before constructing the string value itself. For one thing, variables are replaced by their values (as in the preceding example). To see that this replacement is really about the quoted string rather than the `print` construct, consider the following code:

```
$animal = "antelope"; // first assignment
$saved_string = "The animal is $animal<BR>";
$animal = "zebra"; // reassignment
print("The animal is $animal<BR>"); //first display line
print($saved_string); //second display line
```

What output would you expect here? As it turns out, your browser would display:

```
The animal is zebra
The animal is antelope
```

And the browser displays the preceding output in exactly that order. This is because "`antelope`" is spliced into the string `$saved_string`, before the `$animal` variable is reassigned. In addition to splicing variable values into doubly quoted strings, PHP also replaces some special multiple-character *escape sequences* with their single-character values. The most commonly used is the end-of-line sequence ("\n") — in reading a string like:

```
"The first line \n\n\nThe fourth line"
```

PHP would first replace each "\n" with the single end-of-line character. If you viewed the HTML source produced by this line, you would see a couple of blank lines in the middle of the output. (In a browser window, however, everything would probably be on the same line — see "HTML and line breaks" later in this chapter.)

Singly quoted strings (like `'this'`) behave differently — PHP does not perform any variable interpolation on them, and it pays attention to only two escape sequences. (You can include a literal `'` in the middle of your string by escaping it as `\'`, and a literal `\` by escaping it as `\\`.) With these two exceptions, PHP interprets singly quoted strings as the literal string of characters that were typed. If you type a '$' character into such a string and send it to output with `print`, you will see a '$' in your browser window.

> **CROSS-REFERENCE:** In addition to single-quoting and double-quoting, there's another very useful way to construct strings for output, called the *heredoc* syntax. This syntax allows for variable interpolation, just as the double-quote syntax does, but removes the need for escaping quote signs. We cover this syntax in detail in Chapter 10.

HTML and linebreaks

One mistake often made by new PHP programmers (especially those from a C background) is to try to break lines of text in their browsers by putting end-of-line characters (`"\n"`) in the strings they print. To understand why this doesn't work, you have to distinguish the *output* of PHP (which is usually HTML code, ready to be sent over the Internet to a browser program) from the way that output is rendered by the user's browser. Most browser programs will make their own choices about how to split up lines in HTML text, unless you force a line break with the `<BR>` tag. End-of-line characters in strings will put line breaks in the HTML source that PHP sends to your user's browser, but they will usually have no effect on the way that text looks in a Web page.

Summary

PHP code follows a basic set of syntactical rules, mostly borrowed from programming languages such as C and Perl. The syntactical requirements of PHP are minimal, and in general PHP tries to display results when it can rather than generating an error.

PHP code is whitespace insensitive, and although variable names are case sensitive, basic language constructs and function names are not. Simple PHP expressions are combined into larger expressions by operators and function calls, and statements are expressions with a terminating semicolon. Variables are denoted by a leading $ character and are assigned using the = operator. They need no type declarations and have reasonable default values if used before they are assigned. Variable scope is global except inside the body of functions, where it is local to the function unless explicitly declared otherwise.

The simplest way to send output to the user is by using either `echo` or `print`, which output their string arguments. They are particularly useful in combination with doubly quoted strings, which automatically replace embedded variables with their values.

Chapter 6
Types in PHP

In This Chapter

♦ Understanding the eight PHP types: integer, double, Boolean, NULL, string, array, object, and resource

♦ Creating, reading, printing, and manipulating objects of different types

♦ Converting from one type to another

All programming languages have some kind of type system, which specifies the different kinds of values that can appear in programs. These different types often correspond to different bit-level representations in computer memory, although in many cases programmers are insulated from having to think about (or being able to mess with) representations in terms of bits. PHP's type system is simple, streamlined, and flexible, and it insulates the programmer from low-level details.

In this chapter we cover the fundamental types of PHP (integers, doubles, Booleans, NULL, strings, arrays, objects, and resources) and show how they are read in, printed out, assigned to variables, converted, and combined. The chapter is both as overview and a reference — those familiar with programming can skim it those less familiar can read only the early parts of sections, and both can check back later for those details that didn't seem to matter the first time around.

The First Rule: Don't Worry, Be Happy

PHP makes it easy not to worry too much about typing of variables and values, both because it does not require variables to be typed and also because it handles a lot of type conversions for you.

No variable type declarations

As we saw in the last chapter, the type of a variable does not need to be declared in advance. Instead, the programmer can jump right ahead to assignment and let PHP take care of figuring out the type of the expression that is assigned:

```
$first_number = 55.5;
$second_number = "Not a number at all";
```

Automatic type conversion

PHP does a good job of automatically converting types when necessary. Like most other modern programming languages, PHP will "do the right thing" when, for example, doing math with mixed numerical types. The result of the expression

```
$pi = 3 + 0.14159
```

is a floating-point (double) number, with the integer 3 implicitly converted into floating point before the addition is performed.

Types assigned by context

PHP goes further than most languages in performing automatic type conversions. Consider:

```
$sub = substr(12345, 2, 2);
print("sub is $sub<BR>");
```

The `substr` function is designed to take a string of characters as its first input and return a substring of that string, with the start point and length determined by the next two inputs to the function. Instead of handing the function a character string, however, we gave it the integer `12345`. What happens? As it turns out, there is no error, and we get the browser output:

```
sub is 34
```

Because `substr` expects a character string rather than an integer, PHP converts the number `12345` to the character string `'12345'`, which `substr` then slices and dices.

Because of this automatic type conversion, it is very difficult to persuade PHP to give a type error — in fact, PHP programmers need to exercise a little care sometimes to make sure that type confusions do not lead to error-free but unintended results.

Type Summary

PHP has a total of eight types: integers, doubles, Booleans, strings, arrays, objects, NULL, and resources.

- *Integers* are whole numbers, without a decimal point, like 495.
- *Doubles* are floating-point numbers, like 3.14159, or 49.0.
- *Booleans* have only two possible values: TRUE and FALSE.
- *NULL* is a special type that only has one value: NULL.
- *Strings* are sequences of characters, like `'PHP 4.0 supports string operations.'`
- *Arrays* are named and indexed collections of other values.
- *Objects* are instances of programmer-defined classes, which can package up both other kinds of values and functions that are specific to the class.

♦ *Resources* are special variables that hold references to resources external to PHP (such as database connections).

NEW FEATURE: Note that the Boolean, NULL, and resource types are new as of PHP 4 and did not exist in PHP 3.

Of these, the first five are *simple types*, and the next two (arrays and objects) are *compound* — the compound types can package up other arbitrary values of arbitrary type, whereas the simple types cannot. We will treat the compound types (arrays and objects) lightly in this chapter because they really deserve chapters of their own. Finally, the resource type is a somewhat special type that PHP programmers do not manipulate directly, other than requesting resources via special functions and passing them on to other functions that need them.

The Simple Types

The simple types in PHP (integers, doubles, Booleans, NULL, and strings) should mostly be familiar to those with programming experience (although we will not assume that experience and will explain them in detail). The only thing likely to surprise C programmers is how few types there are.

Many programming languages have several different sizes of numerical types, with the larger ones allowing a greater range of values, but also taking up more room in memory. For example, the C language has a `short` type (for relatively small integers), a `long` type (for possibly larger integers), and an `int` type (which might be intermediate, but in practice is sometimes identical either to the `short` or `long` type). It also has floating-point types, which vary in their precision. This kind of typing choice made sense in an era when tradeoffs between memory use and functionality were often agonizing. The PHP designers made what we think is a good decision to simplify this by having only two numerical types, corresponding to the largest of the integral and floating-point types in C.

Integers

Integers are the simplest type — they correspond to simple whole numbers, both positive and negative. Integers can be assigned to variables, or they can be used in expressions, like so:

```
$int_var = 12345;
$another_int = -12345 + 12345; // will equal zero
```

Read formats

Integers can actually be read in three formats, which correspond to bases: *decimal* (base 10), *octal* (base 8), and *hexadecimal* (base 16). Decimal format is the default, octal integers are specified with a leading `0`, and hexadecimals have a leading `0x`. Any of the formats can be preceded by a `-` sign to make the integer negative. For example:

```
$integer_10 = 1000;
$integer_8 = -01000;
$integer_16 = 0x1000;
print("integer_10: $integer_10<BR>");
print("integer_8: $integer_8<BR>");
print("integer_16: $integer_16<BR>");
```

yields the browser output:

```
integer_10: 1000
integer_8: -512
integer_16: 4096
```

Note that the read format only affects how the integer is converted as it is read — the value stored in $integer_8 does not remember that it was originally written in base 8. Internally, of course, these numbers are represented in binary format; and we see them in their base 10 conversion in the preceding output because that is the default for printing and incorporating int variables into strings.

Range

How big (or small) can integers get? Because PHP integers correspond to the C long type, which in turn depends on the word-size of your machine, this is difficult to answer definitively. For most common platforms, however, the largest integer is $2^{31} - 1$ (or 2,147,483,647), and the smallest (most negative) integer is $-(2^{31} - 1)$ (or –2,147,483,647).

As far as we know, there is no PHP constant (like MAXINT in C) that will tell you the largest integer on your implementation — if in doubt, see the Addendum at the very end of this chapter. If you really need integers even larger or smaller than the above, PHP does have some arbitrary-precision functions — see the BC section of the Math chapter (Chapter 12).

Doubles

Doubles are floating-point numbers, such as:

```
$first_double = 123.456;
$second_double = 0.456
$even_double = 2.0;
```

Note that the fact that $even_double is a "round" number does not make it an integer. Integers and doubles are stored in different underlying formats, and the result of:

```
$five = $even_double + 3;
```

is a double, not an integer, even if it prints as 5. In almost all situations, however, you should feel free to mix doubles and integers in mathematical expressions, and let PHP sort out the typing.

By default, doubles print with the minimum number of decimal places needed — for example, the code:

```
$many = 2.2888800;
$many_2 = 2.2111200;
$few = $many + $many_2;
print("$many + $many_2 = $few<BR>");
```

produces the browser output:

```
2.28888 + 2.21112 = 4.5
```

CROSS-REFERENCE: If you need finer control of printing, see the `printf` function in Chapter 10.

Read formats

The typical *read format* for doubles is `-X.Y` where the `-` optionally specifies a negative number, and both `X` and `Y` are sequences of digits between 0 and 9. The `X` part may be omitted (if the number is between –1.0 and 1.0), and the `Y` part can also be omitted. Leading or trailing zeros have no effect. All the following are legal doubles:

```
$small_positive = 0.12345;
$small_negative = -.12345
$even_double = 2.00000;
$still_double = 2.;
```

In addition, doubles can be specified in scientific notation, by adding the letter e and a desired integral power of 10 to the end of the previous format — for example, `2.2e-3` would correspond to 2.2×10^{-3}. The floating-point part of the number need not be restricted to a range between 1.0 and 10.0. All the following are legal:

```
$small_positive = 5.5e-3;
print("small_positive is $small_positive<BR>");
$large_positive = 2.8e+16;
print("large_positive is $large_positive<BR>");
$small_negative = -2222e-10;
print("small_negative is $small_negative<BR>");
$large_negative = -0.00189e6;
print("large_negative is $large_negative<BR>");
```

The preceding code produces the following browser output:

```
small_positive is 0.0055
large_positive is 2.8E+16
small_negative is -2.222E-07
large_negative is -1890
```

Notice that, just as with octal and hexadecimal integers, the read format is irrelevant once PHP has finished reading in the numbers — the preceding variables retain no memory of whether they were originally specified in scientific notation. In printing out the values, PHP is making its own decisions to print the more extreme values in scientific notation, but this has nothing to do with the original read format.

Booleans

Booleans are true-or-false values, which are used in control constructs like the "testing" portion of an `if` statement. As we will see in the next chapter, Boolean truth values can be combined using logical operators to make more complicated Boolean expressions.

A genuine Boolean type is a new addition to PHP 4 — PHP 3 had no distinct Boolean type but instead simply treated certain values of other types as being true and false. (This approach should be familiar to Perl hackers.) This difference doesn't make as much difference as you might think, because you can still use other types in a Boolean context — PHP 4 will just do an automatic type conversion first. (See "PHP3 Booleans versus PHP4 Booleans" at the very end of this section for a couple of cases in which the PHP 3 and PHP 4 behaviors are different.)

Boolean constants

PHP provides a couple of constants especially for use as Booleans: ~~TRUE~~ and ~~FALSE~~, which can be used like so:

```
if (TRUE)
  print("This will always print<BR>");
else
  print("This will never print<BR>");
```

Interpreting other types as Booleans

Here are the rules for determine the "truth" of any value that is not already of the Boolean type:

- ◆ If the value is a number, it is false if exactly equal to zero and true otherwise.
- ◆ If the value is a string, it is false if the string is empty (has zero characters) *or* is the string `"0"`, and is true otherwise.
- ◆ Values of type NULL are always false.
- ◆ If the value is a compound type (an array or an object), it is false if it contains no other values, and it is true otherwise. For an object, *containing a value* means having a member variable that has been assigned a value.
- ◆ Valid resources are true (although some functions that return resources when they are successful will return FALSE when unsuccessful).

> **CROSS-REFERENCE:** For a more complete account of converting values across types, see "Assignment and Coercion" later in this chapter.

Examples

Each of the following variables has the truth value that is embedded in its name when it is used in a Boolean context.

```
$true_num = 3 + 0.14159;
$true_str = "Tried and true"
$true_array[49] = "An array element"; // see next section
$false_array = array();
$false_null = NULL;
$false_num = 999 - 999;
$false_str = ""; // a string zero characters long
```

Don't use doubles as Booleans

Note that, although Rule 1 implies that the double 0.0 converts to a false Boolean value, it is dangerous to use floating-point expressions as Boolean expressions, due to possible rounding errors. For example:

```
$floatbool = sqrt(2.0) * sqrt(2.0) - 2.0;
if ($floatbool)
  print("Floating-point Booleans are dangerous!<BR>");
else
  print("It worked ... this time.<BR>");
print("The actual value is $floatbool<BR>");
```

The variable $floatbool is set to the result of subtracting two from the square of the square root of two — the result of this calculation should be equal to zero, which means that $floatbool is false. Instead, the browser output we get is:

```
Floating-point Booleans are dangerous!
The actual value is 4.4408920985006E-16
```

The value of $floatbool is very close to 0.0, but it is nonzero and, therefore, unexpectedly true. Integers are much safer in a Boolean role — as long as their arithmetic happens only with other integers and stays within integral sizes, they should not be subject to rounding errors.

PHP3 Booleans versus PHP4 Booleans

Because PHP 3 has no independent Boolean type, the real values of the constants TRUE and FALSE are of other types, and some experimentation can reveal what those values are. Remember, though, that using these constants in a non-Boolean context is in the poorest possible taste and also likely to lead to PHP 4 incompatibilities. The general rule to follow is: Do not make explicit equality comparisons with Booleans — just incorporate them into tests directly.

For example, imagine that as a result of some cool function you wrote, you now have a value assigned to the variable $truth_value. This variable might be a number or a string, but it should have the right truth value when interpreted according to the conversion rules stated earlier. What is the right way to use this variable? The right way, which will work in either PHP 3 or PHP 4, is the following:

```
if ($truth_value) // good PHP! Safe in PHP3 or PHP4
  print("truth_value is true!<BR>");
```

The wrong way looks like:

```
if ($truth_value == TRUE) // bad PHP! Compares to Boolean
   print("truth_value is true!<BR>");
```

The behavior of PHP 3 and PHP 4 might be different in the bad example, in the case where $truth_value is, say, the number 3. PHP 4 may convert 3 to the Boolean value TRUE before doing the equality comparison; whereas PHP 3 will test the number 3 to see if it is equal to whatever the actual value of TRUE is, and the test will probably fail.

NULL

The world of Booleans may seem like a small one, since the Boolean type has only two possible values. The *NULL type*, however, takes this to the logical extreme: The type NULL has only one possible value, which is the value NULL. To give a variable the NULL value, simply assign it like this:

```
$my_var = NULL;
```

The special constant NULL is capitalized by convention, but actually it is case insensitive; you could just as well have typed:

```
$my_var = null;
```

So what is special about NULL? NULL represents the *lack* of a value (You can think of it as the *non-value*, or the *unvalue*). A variable that has been assigned the value NULL is nearly indistinguishable from a variable that has not been set at all. In particular, a variable that has been assigned the NULL has the following properties:

♦ It evaluates to FALSE in a Boolean context.

♦ It returns FALSE when tested with IsSet() (No other type has this property.)

♦ PHP will not print warnings if you pass the variable to functions and back again, whereas passing a variable that has never been set will sometimes produce warnings.

The NULL value is best used for situations where you want a variable not to have a value, intentionally, and you want to make it clear to both a reader of your code and to PHP that this is what you want. The latter point is particularly relevant when passing variables to functions.

For example, the following pseudo-code may print a warning (depending on your error-reporting settings) if the variable $authorization has never been assigned before you pass it to your test_authorization() function.

```
if (test_authorization($authorization)) {
  // code that grants a privilege of some sort
}
```

On the other hand, code like this:

```
$authorization = NULL;
// code that might or might not set $authorization
if (test_authorization($authorization)) {
  // code that grants a privilege of some sort
}
```

does not cause an unbound-variable warning, assuming that you have written
`test_authorization()` to handle arguments that might be NULL. It also makes clear to a
reader of the code that you intend for the variable to lack a value unless there's a case where it
is assigned.

Strings

Strings are character sequences, as in the following:

```
$string_1 = "This is a string in double quotes.";
$string_2 = 'This is a somewhat longer, singly quoted string';
$string_39 = "This string has thirty-nine characters.";
$string_0 = ""; // a string with zero characters
```

Strings can be enclosed in either single or double quotation marks, with different behavior at
read time. Singly quoted strings are treated almost literally, whereas doubly quoted strings
replace variables with their values as well as specially interpreting certain character sequences.

Singly quoted strings

Except for a couple of specially interpreted character sequences, singly quoted strings read in
and store their characters literally. The following code:

```
$literally = 'My $variable will not print!\\n';
print($literally);
```

produces the browser output:

```
My $variable will not print!\n
```

Singly quoted strings also respect the general rule that quotes of a different type will not break
a quoted string. This is legal:

```
$singly_quoted = 'This quote mark: " is no big deal';
```

To embed a single quote (such as an apostrophe) in a singly quoted string, escape it with a
backslash, as in the following:

```
$singly_quoted = 'This quote mark\'s no big deal either';
```

Although in most contexts backslashes are interpreted literally in singly quoted strings, you
may also use two backslashes (\\) as an escape sequence for a single (nonescaping)
backslash. This is useful when you want a backslash as the final character in a string, as in:

```
$win_path = 'C:\\InetPub\\PHP\\';
```

```
print("A Windows-style pathname: $win_path<BR>");
```

which displays as

```
A Windows-style pathname: C:\InetPub\PHP\
```

> **NOTE:** We could have used single backslashes to produce the first two backslashes in the output, but the escaping is necessary at the end of the string so that the closing quote will *not* be escaped.

These two escape sequences (\\ and \') are the *only* exceptions to the literal-mindedness of singly quoted strings.

Doubly quoted strings

Strings that are delimited by double quotes (as in "this") are preprocessed in both the following two ways by PHP:

♦ Certain character sequences beginning with backslash (\) are replaced with special characters.

♦ Variable names (starting with $) are replaced with string representations of their values.

The escape-sequence replacements are:

♦ \n is replaced by the newline character

♦ \r is replaced by the carriage-return character

♦ \t is replaced by the tab character

♦ \$ is replaced by the dollar sign itself ($)

♦ \" is replaced by a single double-quote (")

♦ \\ is replaced by a single backslash (\)

The first three of these replacements make it easy to visibly include certain whitespace characters in your strings. The \$ sequence lets you include the $symbol when you want it, without it being interpreted as the start of a variable. The \" sequence is there so that you can include a double-quote symbol without terminating your doubly quoted string. Finally, because the \ character starts all these sequences, you need a way to include that character literally, without it starting an escape sequence — to do this, you preface it with itself.

Just as with singly quoted strings, quotes of the opposite type can be freely included without an escape character:

```
$has_apostrophe = "There's no problem here";
```

Variable interpolation

Whenever an unescaped $ symbol appears in a doubly quoted string, PHP tries to interpret what follows as a variable name and splices the current value of that variable into the string. Exactly what kind of substitution occurs depends on how the variable is set:

♦ If the variable is currently set to a string value, that string is interpolated (or spliced) into the doubly quoted string.

♦ If the variable is currently set to a nonstring value, the value is converted to a string, and then that string value is interpolated.

♦ If the variable is not currently set, PHP interpolates nothing (or, equivalently, PHP splices in the empty string).

An example:

```
$this = "this";
$that = "that";
$the_other = 2.2000000000;
print("$this,$not_set,$that+$the_other<BR>");
```

produces the PHP output

```
this,,that+2.2<BR>
```

which in turn, when seen in a browser, looks like:

```
this,,that+2.2
```

If you find any part of this example puzzling, it is worth working through exactly what PHP does to parse the string in the `print` statement. First, notice that the string has four $ signs, each of which is interpreted as starting a variable name. These variable names terminate at the first occurrence of a character that is not legal in a variable name. Legal characters are letters, numbers, and underscores; the *illegal* terminating characters in the preceding `print` string are (in order) a comma, another comma, the plus symbol (+), and a left angle bracket (<). The first two variables are bound to strings (`'this'` and `'that'`), so those strings are spliced in literally. The next variable (`$not_set`) has never been assigned, so it is omitted entirely from the string under construction. Finally, the last variable (`$the_other`) is discovered to be bound to a double — that value is converted to a string (`"2.2"`), which is then spliced into our constructed string.

> **CROSS-REFERENCE:** For more about converting numbers to strings, see the "Assignment and Coercion" section that follows in this chapter.

As we said in Chapter 5, all this interpretation of doubly quoted strings happens when the string is *read,* not when it is printed. If we saved the example string in a variable and printed it out later, it would reflect the variable values in the preceding code even if the variables had been changed in the meantime.

> **CROSS-REFERENCE:** In addition to single-quotes and double-quotes, there is another way to create strings (called the *heredoc* syntax), that in some ways makes it even easier to splice in the values of variables. We cover it in in Chapter 10.

Newlines in strings

Although PHP offers an escape sequence (\n) for newline characters, it is good to know that you can literally include new lines in the middle of strings, which PHP also treats as a newline characters. This capability turns out to be convenient when creating HTML strings, because browsers will ignore the line breaks anyway, and so we can format our strings with line breaks to make our PHP code lines short:

```
print("<HTML><HEAD></HEAD><BODY>My HTML page is too big
to fit on a single line, but that doesn't mean that I
need multiple print statements!</BODY></HTML>");
```

We produced this statement in our text editor by literally hitting the Enter key at the end of the first two lines — these newlines are preserved in the string, so the single `print` statement will produce three distinct lines of PHP output. (Your mileage may vary depending on your text editor — if your editor automatically wraps lines in displaying them, you may see three lines of code that are actually one long line.) Of course, the browser program will ignore these newlines and will make its own decisions about whether and where to break the lines in display, but you will see the linebreaks if you use View Source in your browser to see the HTML itself.

Limits

There are no artificial limits on string length — within the bounds of available memory, you ought to be able to make strings that are arbitrarily long.

Arrays

The PHP *array* type gives the programmer a way to group a bunch of different values together and index them by number (and also, as we'll see later, by name). If you ever find yourself using variables with names like $thing1, $thing2, $thing3..., it might be time to use an array instead ($things[1], $things[2], $things[3],...), where the array as a whole is stored in a variable called $things. Array elements are referred to via indices in brackets (the [1], [2], [3]... in this example), and elements of different type can be assigned into the same array.

The best way to learn about PHP arrays is by example. Here is some simple code that inspects an array variable both before and after the very first value is assigned into it:

```
print("my_array is $my_array<BR>");
print("my_array[0] is $my_array[0]<BR>");
print("my_array[5] is $my_array[5]<BR>");
$my_array[5] = "Slot #6";
```

```
print("my_array is $my_array<BR>");
print("my_array[0] is $my_array[0]<BR>");
print("my_array[5] is $my_array[5]<BR>");
```

The browser output this yields is:

```
my_array is
my_array[0] is
my_array[5] is
my_array is Array
my_array[0] is
my_array[5] is Slot #6
```

Let's explain this in terms of what is true before and after that first assignment is made. Before the assignment, despite the name, PHP doesn't know that the variable $my_array is destined to become an array — it is simply an unassigned variable like any other. This means that it is interpreted as the empty string when included in a doubly quoted string. As it turns out, an array index reference ([5]) into an unassigned variable is treated as an unassigned variable also. The result is that the first three print statements end inconclusively in is.

After the assignment, $my_array is now officially an array, and as a result it prints with the generic "Array" string when it is included in a doubly quoted string. The array slot indexed by the number 5 has been filled with the string "Slot #6" (in recognition of the fact that, in most languages, array elements are numbered beginning with zero) and can be recovered with the index 5. This is really the only thing that has changed — the zero[th] slot of $my_array is still unbound, just as it was before the assignment was made.

Array implementation

Arrays are one of the coolest and most useful features of PHP, and although they look deceptively like arrays in other languages, they are really implemented quite differently.

In most programming languages, you would declare an array with a statement like:

```
int int_array[10]; // NOT PHP!
```

which amounts to setting up a block of 10 contiguous integer variables in memory, which can be accessed by indexes of int_array ranging from 0 to 9.

By contrast, PHP arrays are *associative* — when you make an array assignment, you are really adding a new array slot, associated with a new index that can be used to recover the value. (This behavior may make sense to programmers who are familiar with hash tables — PHP arrays are more like hash tables than like arrays in other languages.)

One implication of the associative nature of arrays is that you don't need to be afraid to assign a very high array slot, like:

```
my_array[100000000] = "not scary" // this is OK
```

because it won't result in a sudden allocation of 100 million array slots. The slots indexed by lower numbers probably do not yet exist, and so they do not use up any memory.

Strings as array indices

Our array examples so far have used only integers as indices, but string values may also be used, such as:

```
$tasty['Spanish'] = "paella";
$tasty['Japanese'] = "sashimi";
$tasty['Scottish'] = "haggis?";
```

These indices are used in the same way as numerical indices, and numerical and string indices may be used in the same array without conflicting with each other.

Where is the structure type?

Some programming languages (C, Pascal) offer a "structure" or "record" type that allows variables of different types to be packaged together. The rule of thumb in such languages for choosing a compound type is: If all of the contained values will be of the same type, use an array, and otherwise use a structure.

Now, PHP does have an *object* type that, in addition to its more exotic properties, can act much like a record or structure type. Even before this was introduced, however, PHP did not really need a structure type, because its arrays are not restricted to only one type of value. If you are porting code to PHP from a language with a structure type, for example, one possibility is to use an associative array with string indices corresponding to the original field names.

Other array features

We have only scratched the surface of arrays in this chapter — in addition, arrays can be multidimensional; can have their values assigned using a variety of methods; and have a wealth of associated functions that make them easy to inspect, iterate over, and manipulate. We will return to arrays in Chapter 11.

Objects

Another basic PHP datatype is the *object* — PHP's entry into the glamorous world of object-oriented programming (OOP). Like an array, an object is a compound type that lets you package other data values together in a single unit. Objects have additional, more complex properties, including the capability to package up functions as well as data, and the capability to define new object types in terms of other object types (inheritance).

We treat objects and object-oriented programming fully and exhaustively in Chapter 26, and encourage you to jump to that chapter to learn more.

Resources

Resources are special values that refer to memory or resources that are external to the PHP language itself. You don't have to know too much about resources for casual PHP programming — we'll briefly explain what resources are all about, but feel free to skip to "How to handle resources" that follows.

What are resources?

The resource type is needed when PHP communicates with some external program (which may be a database or a graphics program) that allocates memory in response to requests from PHP. In general, PHP programmers do not have to worry about freeing memory within PHP — if you create a string in a PHP script (which will take up some space in memory), you can forget all about it and let your script run until the end. PHP (or the Web server it is attached to) will reclaim all memory associated with your script when your script is done, if not earlier.

External programs (databases, and so on.) might not be smart enough to do this deallocation. You might conceivably have space reserved in your database's memory for your script long after your script has gone to script heaven. The way this problem gets handled in PHP is that all special functions that request memory from such external programs return "resources" which PHP tracks to see if your script can still get to them. If nobody can reach the resource, PHP makes sure that the external program does the right kind of cleanup. PHP does this by counting references to the resource — if the reference count goes to zero, then the resource can be freed.

How to handle resources

In general, PHP programmers do not create resources by themselves — they call special functions that return values of the resource type, and then pass them on to other functions that require resources. For example, (as we'll see in the second part of this book), you might call the function `mysql_connect()` (which returns a resource value that refers to a connection to a MySQL database), save the result in a variable, and then pass it on to `mysql_query()` (which uses the connection to query the database).

Essentially all you have to do with this connection resource is store it in a variable and pass that variable to functions that require it. You can depend on PHP to clean up the resource after your script is done. If, for whatever reason, you feel that the resource is tying up enough memory during script execution that you want the memory freed before the script is done, you should be able to do something like this:

```
$my_resource = mysql_connect();  // stores  variable
// .. code that uses the connection resource ..
$my_resource = NULL; // variable no longer refers to resource
```

The reassignment of `$my_resource` should cause PHP to check that no other piece of code is using the `MySQL` resource and then free it.

Type Testing

Especially because variables can change types due to reassignment, it is sometimes necessary to find out the type of a value at program execution time. PHP offers both a general type-testing function (gettype()) and individual Boolean functions for each of the five types. These functions, some of which have alternate names, are summarized in Table 6-1.

Table 6-1: Functions for Type Testing

Function	Behavior
gettype(arg)	Returns a string representing the type of arg: either integer, double, string, array, object, or unknown type
is_int(arg) is_integer(arg) is_long(arg)	Returns a true value if arg is an integer, and a false one if not
is_double(arg) is_float(arg) is_real(arg)	Returns a true value if arg is a double, and a false one if not
is_bool(arg)	Returns a true value if arg is a Boolean value (TRUE or FALSE), and a false one if not
is_null(arg)	Returns a true value if arg is of the NULL type, and a false one if not.
is_string(arg)	Returns a true value if arg is a string, and a false one if not
is_array(arg)	Returns a true value if arg is an array, and a false one if not
is_object(arg)	Returns a true value if arg is an object, and a false one if not
is_resource(arg)	Returns a true value if arg is a a resource, and a false one if not.

Assignment and Coercion

As we have said, PHP often automatically converts from one type to another when the context demands it, and as it turns out the PHP programmer can also force some of these conversions to happen. In either situation, the programmer should know what to expect.

Type conversion behavior

Here are some general rules for PHP's conversion from one type to another:

- **Integer to double:** The exact corresponding double is created (for example, the int 4 becomes the double 4.0).

- **Double to integer:** The fractional part is dropped, truncating the number toward zero.

- **Number to Boolean:** FALSE if exactly equal to 0, TRUE otherwise.

- **Number to string:** A string is created that looks exactly the way the number would print. Integers are printed as a sequence of digits, and doubles are printed with the minimum precision needed. Extreme double values will be converted to scientific notation.

- **Boolean to number:** 1 if TRUE, 0 if FALSE.

- **Boolean to string:** '1' if TRUE, the empty string if FALSE.

- **Null to number:** 0

- **Null to boolean:** FALSE

- **String to number:** Equivalent to "reading" a number from the string, then making a conversion to the given type. If a number cannot be read, the value is zero. Not all of the string needs to be read for the reading to be considered a success.

- **String to Boolean:** FALSE if it is an empty string or the string is '0', TRUE otherwise.

- **Simple type (number or string) to array:** Equivalent to creating a new array with the simple value assigned to index zero.

- **Array to number:** Undefined (see note below).

- **Array to Boolean:** FALSE if the array has no elements, TRUE otherwise.

- **Array to string:** 'Array'.

- **Object to number:** Undefined (see note below).

- **Object to boolean:** TRUE if the object contains any member variables that have a value, and FALSE otherwise

- **Object to string:** 'Object'.

- **Resource to Boolean:** FALSE

- **Resource to number:** Undefined (see note below).

- **Resource to string:** Something like 'Resource id #1' (but this should not be relied upon).

In the preceding list, we noted that some types have an undefined result when converted to numerical values. In this context, "undefined" simply means that the PHP developers are not making a commitment as to what kind of behavior you'll get in future versions of PHP, so it would be a bad idea to depend on a particular behavior in your code. You may find that these types can be converted to numbers in expressions in your particular version of PHP, but that may not work in the next version.

Explicit conversions

PHP offers three different ways for the programmer to manipulate types: conversion functions, type casts (as in the C language), and calling `settype()` on variables:

♦ The functions `intval()`, `doubleval()`, and `strval()` will convert their respective arguments to an integer, a double, or a string, respectively. (At this writing, there does not seem to be a `boolval()` function.)

♦ Any expression can be preceded by a type cast (the name of the type in parentheses), which converts the expression result to the desired type.

♦ any variable can be given as a first argument to `settype()`, which will change the type of that variable to the type named in the second string argument.

For example, Each of the following approaches will put the correct count of canines (101) into the integer variable `$dog_count`:

```
$dog_count = intval (strval (doubleval("101 Dalmatians")));

$dog_count = (int) (string) (double) "101 Dalmatians";

$dog_count = "101 Dalmatians"
settype($dog_count, "double");
settype($dog_count, "string");
settype($dog_count, "int");
```

> **TIP:** Of course, each approach in the example takes an indirect route, converting needlessly to string and double types — it would suffice to convert immediately to the integer type.

Six of the basic type names (integer, double, Boolean, string, array, and object) are valid in casts and are valid string arguments to `settype()`. In addition, certain alternate names are valid in casts (but not in `settype()`): `(int)` instead of `(integer)`, `(float)` or `(real)` instead of `(double)`, and `(bool)` instead of `(boolean)`. It is not valid to cast to type resource, and casting to type NULL is pointless. (Because the result can only be the value NULL, you might as well simply assign instead.)

Conversion examples

Just for fun, Listing 6-1 shows some PHP code that displays various type conversions in an HTML table, with the resulting table shown in Figure 6-1. (This code is not intended as a style example, and it uses several constructs that have not yet been covered — feel free to just look at the output).

Listing 6-1: Type conversions

```
$type_examples[0] = 123; // an integer
$type_examples[1] = 3.14159; // a double
$type_examples[2] = "a non-numeric string";
$type_examples[3] = "49.990 (begins with number)";
```

```
$type_examples[4] = array(90,80,70);

print("<TABLE BORDER=1><TR>");
print("<TH>Original</<TH>");
print("<TH>(int)</<TH>");
print("<TH>(double)</<TH>");
print("<TH>(string)</<TH>");
print("<TH>(array)</<TH></TR>");

for ($index = 0; $index < 5; $index++)
  {
    print("<TR><TD>$type_examples[$index]</TD>");
    $converted_var =
       (int) $type_examples[$index];
    print("<TD>$converted_var</TD>");
    $converted_var =
       (double) $type_examples[$index];
    print("<TD>$converted_var</TD>");
    $converted_var =
       (string) $type_examples[$index];
    print("<TD>$converted_var</TD>");
    $converted_var =
       (array) $type_examples[$index];
    print("<TD>$converted_var</TD></TR>");
  }
print("</TABLE>");
```

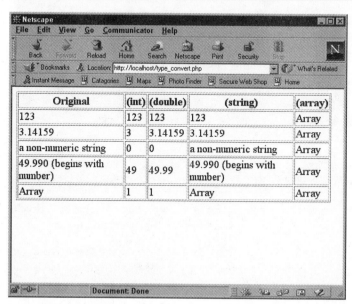

Figure 6-1: Type conversion examples

Other useful type conversions

The functions listed in Table 6-2 do not exactly convert types, but they return a different type than their main argument in a useful way.

Table 6-2: Other Type-Conversion Functions

From\To	Integer	String	Array
Integer		ord()	
Double	ceil(), floor(), round()		
String	chr()		explode()
Array		implode()	

The function `ceil()` takes a double and returns the integer greater than or equal to that double. For example:

```
$my_double = 4.7;
$my_int = ceil($my_double); // $my_int is equal to 5
$my_double = -4.7;
$my_int = floor($my_double) // $my_int is equal to -4
```

The `floor()` function is the opposite of `ceil()`. (We'll drop the intermediate assignment to $my_double now.)

```
$my_int = floor(4.7); // $my_int is equal to 4
$my_int = floor(-4.7); // $my_int is equal to -5
```

The `round()` function takes a double and returns the nearest integer. If the fractional part of the double is exactly one half, the rounding is to the nearest even number.

```
$my_int = round(4.7); // $my_int is equal to 5
$my_int = round(-4.7); // $my_int is equal to -5
$my_int = round(-4.5); // $my_int is equal to -4
```

> **TIP:** If you're looking for a truncate function (simply dropping the fractional part and, therefore, rounding toward zero), notice that this is the behavior you get simply from typecasting from `double` to `int`.

The function `chr()` takes an integer and returns a one-character string with that ASCII value, whereas `ord()` reverses this, returning the ASCII value of the first character in a string.

Finally, `implode()` and `explode()` allow a certain kind of conversion between strings and arrays. `implode()` creates a string out of the array it is given as second argument, separating the elements with the string that is its first argument. For example:

```
$words[0] = "My";
```

```
$words[1] = "short";
$words[2] = "sentence.";
$sentence = implode(" ", $words);
print("$sentence<BR>");
```

produces the browser output:

```
My short sentence.
```

`explode()` reverses the process, creating an array from a string:

```
$words = explode(" ", "My short sentence.");
```

Integer overflow

One clever automatic type conversion built into PHP relatively recently is that when integer values *overflow* (that is, they are assigned a value larger than they can hold), they become doubles — this makes some sense, because doubles can accommodate larger magnitudes than integers can. For example:

```
$too_big = 111;
for ($count = 0; $count < 5; $count++)
  {
    $too_big = 1000 * $too_big;
    print("Is $too_big still an integer?<BR>");
  }
```

produces the following browser output:

```
Is 111000 still an integer?
Is 111000000 still an integer?
Is 111000000000 still an integer?
Is 1.11E+14 still an integer?
Is 1.11E+17 still an integer?
```

The shift you see in this example from literal integers to scientific notation reflects a change of `$too_big`'s type from integer to double. Of course, this may lose some information, because the precision of doubles is limited, but it is in keeping with the PHP philosophy of doing the best it can in preference to causing an error.

Finding the largest integer

If you need to know the largest integer your PHP will support and, for some reason, you believe that it is not the usual $2^{31} - 1$, here's a handy function (which uses concepts not yet covered):

```
function maxint()
{ /* quick-and-dirty function for PHP int size --
    assumes largest integer is of form 2^n - 1 */
  $to_test = 2;
  while(1)
```

```
    {
        $last = $to_test;
        $to_test = 2 * $to_test;
        if (($to_test < $last) || (!is_int($to_test)))
            return($last + ($last - 1));
    }
}
/* sample use */
$maxint = maxint();
print("Maxint is $maxint<BR>");
```

Summary

PHP 4 has eight types: integer, double, Boolean, NULL, string, array, object, and resource. Five of these are simple types: Integers are whole numbers, doubles are floating-point numbers, Booleans are true-or-false values, NULL has just one value (NULL), and strings are sequences of characters. *Arrays* are a compound type that holds other PHP values, indexed either by integers or by strings. *Objects* are instances of programmer-defined classes, which can contain both member variables and member functions, and which can inherit functions and data types from other classes. (We address objects in Chapter 26.) Finally, *resources* are special references to memory allocated from external programs, which memory PHP frees automatically when they are no longer needed.

Only values are typed in PHP — variables have no inherent type other than the value of their most recent assignment. PHP automatically converts value types as demanded by the context in which the value is used. The programmer can also explicitly control types by means of both conversion functions and type casts.

## Chapter 7

Control

In This Chapter

♦ Creating and combining logical tests

♦ Branching with `if` and `switch`

♦ Looping with `while` and `for`

♦ Aborting page execution with `exit` and `die`

It's difficult to write interesting programs if you can't make the course of program execution depend on anything. In a weak sense, the behavior of code that prints out variables depends on the variable values, but that is as exciting as filling out a template — as programmers, we want programs that react to something (the world, the time of day, user input, or the contents of a database) by doing something different.

This kind of program reaction requires a *control structure,* which indicates how different situations should lead to the execution of different code. In the last chapter, we informally used the `if` control structure without really explaining it; in this chapter, we lay out every kind of control structure offered by PHP and study their workings in detail.

> **NOTE:** Experienced C programmers: Of all the features in PHP, control is probably the most reliably C-like — all the structures you are used to are here, and they work the same way. You might want to jump to the Summary section at the end of the chapter.

The two broad types of control structures we will talk about are *branches* and *loops.* A branch is a fork in the road for a program's execution — depending on some test or other, the program goes either left or right, possibly following a different path for the rest of the program's execution. A loop is a special kind of branch where one of the execution paths jumps back to the beginning of the branch, repeating the test and possibly the body of the loop.

Before we can make interesting use of control structures, however, we have to be able to construct interesting tests. We'll start from the very simplest of tests, working our way up from the constants TRUE and FALSE, and then move on to using these tests in more complicated code.

Boolean Expressions

Every control structure in this chapter has two distinct parts: the *test* (which determines which part of the rest of the structure executes), and the *dependent code* itself (whether separate branches or the body of a loop). Tests work by evaluating a *Boolean expression*, an expression with a result that is treated as either true or false.

Boolean constants

The simplest kind of expression is a simple value, and the simplest Boolean values are the constants TRUE and FALSE. We can use these constants anywhere we would use a more complicated Boolean expression, and vice versa. For example, we can embed them in the test part of an if-else statement:

```
if (TRUE)
 print("This will always print<BR>");
else
 print("This will never print<BR>");
```

Or, equivalently:

```
if (FALSE)
 print("This will never print<BR>");
else
 print("This will always print<BR>");
```

Logical operators

Logical operators combine other logical (a.k.a. Boolean) values to produce new Boolean values. The standard logical operations (and, or, not, and exclusive-or) are supported by PHP, which has alternate versions of the first two, as shown in Table 7-1.

Table 7-1: Logical Operators

Operator	Behavior
and	Is true if and only if both of its arguments are true.
or	Is true if either (or both) of its arguments are true.
!	Is true if its single argument (to the right) is false and false if its argument is true.
xor	Is true if either (but not both) of its arguments are true.
&&	Same as and, but binds to its arguments more tightly. (See the discussion of precedence later in the chapter.)
||	Same as or but binds to its arguments more tightly.

The && and || operators will be familiar to C programmers. The ! operator is usually called *not*, since it negates the argument it operates on.

As an example of using logical operators, consider the following expression:

```
(($statement_1 && $statement_2) ||
($statement_1 && !$statement_2) ||
(!$statement_1 && $statement_2) ||
(!$statement_1 && !$statement_2))
```

This is a *tautology*, meaning that it is always true regardless of the values of the statement variables. There are four possible combinations of truth values for the two variables, each of which is represented by one of the && expressions. One of these four must be true; and because they are linked by the || operator, the entire expression must be true.

Here's another, slightly trickier tautology, using xor:

```
(($statement_1 and $statement_2 and
  $statement_3) xor
 ((!($statement_1 and $statement_2)) or
  (!($statement_1 and $statement_3)) or
  (!($statement_2 and $statement_3))))
```

In English, this expression says, "Given three statements, one and only one of the following two things hold — either 1) all three statements are true, or 2) there are two statements that are not both true."

Precedence of logical operators

Just as with any operators, some logical operators have higher precedence than others, although precedence can always be overridden by grouping subexpressions together using parentheses. The logical operators listed in declining order of precedence are: !, &&, ||, and, xor, or. Actually, and, xor, and or have much lower precedence than the others, so that the assignment operator (=) binds more tightly than and, but less tightly than &&.

> **CROSS-REFERENCE:** A complete table of operator precedence and associativity can be found in the online manual at www.php.net.

Logical operators short-circuit

One very handy feature of Boolean operators is that they associate left-to-right, and they *short-circuit*, meaning that they do not even evaluate their second argument if their truth value is unambiguous from their first argument. For example, imagine that you wanted to determine a very approximate ratio of two numbers, but also wanted to avoid a possible division-by-zero error. You can first test to make sure that the denominator is not zero, by using the != (not-equal-to) operator:

```
if ($denom != 0 && $numer / $denom > 2)
   print("More than twice as much!");
```

In the case where $denom is zero, the && operator should return false regardless of whether the second expression is true or false. Because of short-circuiting, the second expression is not evaluated, and so an error is avoided. In the case where $denom is not zero, the && operator does not have enough information to reach a conclusion about its truth value, and so the second expression is evaluated.

So far, all we've formally covered are the TRUE and FALSE constants, and how to combine them to make other true-or-false values. Now we'll move on to operators that actually let you make meaningful Boolean tests.

Comparison operators

Table 7-2 shows the comparison operators, which can be used for either numbers or strings (although you should see the cautionary sidebar entitled "Comparing Things That Are Not Integers").

Table 7-2: Comparison Operators

Operator	Name	Behavior
==	Equal	True if its arguments are equal to each other, false otherwise
! =	Not equal	False if its arguments are equal to each other, true otherwise
<	Less than	True if the left-hand argument is less than its right-hand argument, false otherwise
>	Greater than	True if the left-hand argument is greater than its right-hand argument, false otherwise
<=	Less than or equal to	True if the left-hand argument is less than its right-hand argument *or* equal to it, and false otherwise
>=	Greater than or equal to	True if the left-hand argument is greater than its right-hand argument *or* equal to it, and false otherwise
===	Identical	True if its arguments are equal to each other and of the same type, and false otherwise (This operator is a new addition in PHP 4.)

As an example, here are some variable assignments, followed by a compound test that is always true:

```
$three = 3;
$four = 4;
```

```
$my_pi = 3.14159;
if (($three == $three) and
    ($four === $four) and
    ($three != $four) and
    ($three < $four) and
    ($three <= $four) and
    ($four >= $three) and
    ($three <= $three) and
    ($my_pi > $three) and
    ($my_pi <= $four))
 print("My faith in mathematics is restored!<BR>");
else
 print("Sure you typed that right?<BR>");
```

> **CAUTION:** Watch out for a very common mistake: confusing the assignment operator (=) with the comparison operator (==). The statement if ($three = $four). will (probably unexpectedly) set the variable $three to be the same as $four; and what's more the test will be true if $four is a true value!

Operator precedence

Although over-reliance on precedence rules can be confusing for the person who reads your code next, it's useful to note that comparison operators have higher precedence than Boolean operators. This means that a test like the following:

```
    if ($small_num > 2 && $small_num < 5) ...
```

doesn't need any parentheses other than those shown.

String comparison

The comparison operators may be used to compare strings as well as numbers (see the cautionary sidebar). We would expect the following code to print its associated sentence (with apologies to Billy Bragg):

```
if (("Marx" < "Mary") and
    ("Mary" < "Marzipan"))
{
  print("Between Marx and Marzipan in the ");
  print("dictionary, there was Mary.<BR>");
}
```

The comparisons are case sensitive, and the only reason that this example will print anything is that we have inappropriately capitalized Marzipan. Due to the capitalization of Dennis, the following will not print anything:

```
if (("deep blue sea" < "Dennis") and
    ("Dennis" < "devil"))
{
  print("Between the deep blue sea and ");
```

```
print("the devil, that was me.<BR>");
}
```

COMPARING THINGS THAT ARE NOT INTEGERS

Although comparison operators work with numbers or strings, a couple of gotchas lurk here.

First of all, although it is always safe to do less-than or greater-than comparisons on doubles (or even between doubles and integers), it can be dangerous to rely on equality comparisons on doubles, especially if they are the result of a numerical computation. The problem is that a rounding error may make two values that are theoretically equal differ slightly.

Second, although comparison operators work for strings as well as numbers, PHP's automatic type conversions can lead to counterintuitive results when the strings are interpretable as numbers. For example, the code:

```
$string_1 = "00008";

$string_2 = "007";

$string_3 = "00008-OK";

if ($string_2 < $string_1)

  print("$string_2 is less than $string_1<BR>");

if ($string_3 < $string_2)

  print("$string_3 is less than $string_2<BR>");

if ($string_1 < $string_3)

  print("$string_1 is less than $string_3<BR>");
```

gives this output (with comments added):

```
007 is less than 00008   // numerical comparison
00008-OK is less than 007 // string comparison
00008 is less than 00008-OK // string comp. - contradiction!
```

When it can, PHP will convert string arguments to numbers, and when both sides can be treated that way, the comparison ends up being numerical, not alphabetic. The PHP 4 designers view this as a feature, not a bug. Our view is that, if you are comparing strings that have any chance of being interpreted as numbers, you're better off using the `strcmp()` function (see Chapter 10).

The ternary operator

One especially useful construct is the *ternary conditional operator*, which plays a role somewhere between a Boolean operator and a true branching construct. Its job is to take three expressions and use the truth value of the first expression to decide which of the other two expressions to evaluate and return. The syntax looks like:

```
test-expression ? yes-expression : no-expression
```

The value of this expression is the result of `yes-expression` if `test-expression` is true; otherwise, it is the same as `no-expression`.

For example, The following expression assigns to `$max_num` either `$first_num` or `$second_num`, whichever is larger:

```
$max_num = $first_num > $second_num ? $first_num : $second_num;
```

As we will see, this is equivalent to:

```
if ($first_num > $second_num)
   $max_num = $first_num;
else
   $max_num = $second_num;
```

but is somewhat more concise.

Branching

The two main structures for branching are `if` and `switch`. If is a workhorse and is usually the first conditional structure anyone learns. `Switch` is a useful alternative for certain situations where you want multiple possible branches based on a single value, and where a series of `if` statements would be cumbersome.

If-else

The syntax for `if` is:

```
if (test)
   statement-1
```

Or, with an optional `else` branch:

```
if (test)
   statement-1
else
   statement-2
```

When an `if` statement is processed, the `test` expression is evaluated, and the result is interpreted as a Boolean value. If `test` is true, *statement-1* is executed. If `test` is not true, and there is an `else` clause, then *statement-2* is executed. If `test` is false, and there is no `else` clause, then execution simply proceeds with the next statement after the `if` construct.

Note that a *statement* in this syntax can either be a single statement that ends with a semicolon, a brace-enclosed block of statements, or another conditional construct (which itself counts as a single statement). Conditionals can be nested inside each other to arbitrary depth. Also, the Boolean expression can be a genuine Boolean (TRUE, FALSE, or the result of a Boolean operator or function), or it can be a value of another type that is interpreted as a Boolean.

> **CROSS-REFERENCE:** For the full story on how values of non-Boolean types are treated as Booleans, see Chapter 6. The short version is that the number 0, the string "0", and the empty string, "", are false, and almost every other value is true.

The following example, which prints a statement about the absolute difference between two numbers, shows both the nesting of conditionals and the interpretation of the test as a Boolean:

```
if ($first - $second)
  if ($first > $second)
    {
      $difference = $first - $second;
      print("The difference is $difference<BR>");
    }
  else
    {
      $difference = $second - $first;
      print("The difference is $difference<BR>");
    }
else
  print("There is no difference<BR>");
```

This code relies on the fact that the number 0 is interpreted as a false value — if the difference is zero, then the test fails, and the no differencemessage is printed. If there is a difference, a further test is performed. (This example is artificial, because a test like $first != $second would accomplish the same thing more comprehensibly.)

Else attachment

At this point, former Pascal programmers may be warily wondering about else attachment — that is, how does an else clause know which if it belongs to? The rules are simple and are the same as in most languages other than Pascal. Each else is matched with the nearest unmatched if that can be found, while respecting the boundaries of braces. If you want to make sure that an if statement stays solo and does not get matched to an else, wrap it up in braces like so:

```
if ($num % 2 == 0) // $num is even?
  {
    if ($num > 2)
      print("num is not prime<BR>");
  }
else
  print("num is odd<BR>");
```

This code will print num is not prime if $num happens to be an even number greater than 2, num is odd if $num is odd, and nothing if $num happens to be 2. If we had omitted the curly braces, the else would attach to the inner if, and so the code would buggily print num is odd if $num were equal to 2 and would print nothing if $num were actually odd.

> **NOTE:** In this chapter's examples, we often use the modulus operator (%), which is explained in Chapter 12. For the purposes of these examples, all you need to know is that if $x % $y is zero, then $x is evenly divisible by $y.

Elseif

It's very common to want to do a cascading sequence of tests, as in the following nested if statements:

```
if ($day == 5)
  print("Five golden rings<BR>");
else
  if ($day == 4)
    print("Four calling birds<BR>");
  else
    if ($day == 3)
      print("Three French hens<BR>");
    else
      if ($day == 2)
        print("Two turtledoves<BR>");
      else
        if ($day == 1)
          print("A partridge in a pear tree<BR>");
```

> **NOTE:** We have indented this code in to show the real syntactic structure of inclusions — although this is always a good idea, you will often see code that does not bother with this, and where each else line starts in the first column.

This pattern is common enough that there is a special elseif construct to handle it. We can rewrite the preceding example as:

```
if ($day == 5)
  print("Five golden rings<BR>");
elseif ($day == 4)
  print("Four calling birds<BR>");
elseif ($day == 3)
  print("Three French hens<BR>");
elseif ($day == 2)
  print("Two turtledoves<BR>");
elseif ($day == 1)
  print("A partridge in a pear tree<BR>");
```

BRANCHING AND HTML MODE

As you may have learned from earlier chapters, you should feel free to use the PHP tags to switch back and forth between HTML mode and PHP mode, whenever it seems convenient. If you need to include a large chunk of HTML in your page that has no dynamic code or interpolated variables, it can be simpler and more efficient to escape back into HTML mode and include it literally than it is to send it using print or echo.

What may not be as obvious is that this strategy works even inside conditional structures. That is, you can use PHP to decide what HTML to send and then "send" that HTML by temporarily escaping back to HTML mode.

For example, the following cumbersome code uses print statements to construct a complete HTML page based on the supposed gender of the viewer. (We're assuming a nonexistent Boolean function called female() that tests for this.)

```
<HTML><HEAD>
<?php
if (female())
  {
    print("<TITLE>The women-only site</TITLE><BR>");
    print("</HEAD><BODY>");
    print("This site has been specially constructed ");
    print("for women only.<BR> No men allowed here!");
  }
else
  {
    print("<TITLE>The men-only site</TITLE><BR>");
    print("</HEAD><BODY>");
    print("This site has been specially constructed ");
    print("for men only.<BR> No women allowed here!");
  }
?>
</BODY></HTML>
```

Instead of all these print statements, we can duck back into HTML mode within each of the two branches:

```
<HTML><HEAD>

<?php

if (female())

  {

?>

<TITLE>The women-only site</TITLE>
```

```
</HEAD><BODY>
This site has been specially constructed
for women only.<BR> No men allowed here!
<?php
  }
else
  {
?>
<TITLE>The men-only site</TITLE><BR>
</HEAD><BODY>
This site has been specially constructed
for men only.<BR> No women allowed here!
<?php
  }
?>
</BODY></HTML>
```

This version is somewhat more difficult to read, but the only difference is that it replaces each set of `print` statements with a block of literal HTML that starts with a closing PHP tag (`?>`) and ends with a starting PHP tag (`<?php`).

In this book's examples, we mostly avoid this kind of conditional inclusion, simply because we feel that it may be harder for the novice PHP programmer to decipher. But that shouldn't stop you — literal inclusion has advantages, including fast execution. (In HTML mode, all the PHP engine must do is pass on characters and watch for the next PHP start tag, which is inevitably faster than parsing and executing `print` statements, especially if they include doubly quoted strings.)

The `if, elseif` construct allows for a sequence of tests that executes only the first branch that has a successful test. In theory, this is syntactically different from the previous example (we have a single construct with five branches, rather than a nesting of five two-branch constructs), but the behavior is identical. Use whichever syntax you find more appealing.

Switch

For a specific kind of multiway branching, the `switch` construct can be useful. Rather than branch on arbitrary logical expressions, `switch` takes different paths according to the value of a single expression. The syntax is as follows, with the optional parts enclosed in square brackets ([]):

```
switch(expression)
{
   case value-1:
      statement-1
      statement-2
      ...
      [break;]
   case value-2:
      statement-3
      statement-4
      ...
      [break;]
   ...
   [default:
      default-statement]
}
```

The expression can be a variable or any other kind of expression, as long as it evaluates to a simple value (that is, an integer, a double, or a string). The construct executes by evaluating the expression and then testing the result for equality against each case value. As soon as a matching value is found, subsequent statements are executed in sequence until the special statement (break;) or until the end of the switch construct. (As we'll see in the "Looping" section, break can also be used to break out of looping constructs.) A special default tag can be used at the end, which will match the expression if no other case has matched it so far.

For example, we can rewrite our if-else example as follows:

```
switch($day)
{
  case 5:
    print("Five golden rings<BR>");
    break;
  case 4:
    print("Four calling birds<BR>");
    break;
  case 3:
    print("Three French hens<BR>");
    break;
  case 2:
    print("Two turtledoves<BR>");
    break;
  default:
    print("A partridge in a pear tree<BR>");
}
```

This will print a single appropriate line for days 2–5; for any day other than those, it will print `A partridge in a pear tree`.

> **CAUTION:** The single most confusing aspect of `switch` is that all cases after a matching case will execute, unless there are `break` statements to stop the execution. In the "partridge" example, the `break` statements ensure that we see only one line from the song at a time. If we remove the `break` statements, we will see a sequence of lines counting down to the final line, just as in the song.

Looping

Congratulations! You just passed the boundary from scripting into "real programming." The branching structures we have looked at so far are useful, but there are limits to what can be computed with them alone. On the other hand, it's well established in theoretical computer science that any language with tests plus unbounded looping can do pretty much anything that any other language can do. You may not actually want to write a C compiler in PHP, for example, but it's nice to know that no inherent language limits are going to stop you.

Bounded loops versus unbounded loops

A *bounded loop* is a loop that will execute a fixed number of times — you can tell by looking at the code how many times the loop will iterate, and the language guarantees that it won't loop more times than that. An *unbounded loop* is one that repeats until some condition becomes true (or false), and that condition is dependent on the action of the code within the loop. Bounded loops are predictable, whereas unbounded loops can be as tricky as you like.

Unlike some languages, PHP doesn't actually have any constructs specifically for bounded loops — `while`, `do-while`, and `for` are all unbounded constructs — but as we will see in this section, an unbounded loop can do anything a bounded loop can do.

> **CROSS-REFERENCE:** In addition to the looping constructs in this chapter, PHP provides functions for iterating over the contents of arrays, which will be covered in Chapter 11.

While

The simplest PHP looping construct is `while`, which has the following syntax:

```
while (condition)
  statement
```

The `while` loop evaluates the *condition* expression as a Boolean — if it is true, it executes *statement* and then starts again by evaluating *condition*. If the condition is false, the `while` loop terminates. Of course, just as with `if`, *statement* may be a single statement or it may be a brace-enclosed block. The body of a `while` loop may not execute even once, as in:

```
while (FALSE)
  print("This will never print.<BR>");
```

Or it may execute "forever," as in this code snippet:

```
while (TRUE)
  print("All work and no play makes
         Jack a dull boy.<BR>");
```

or it may execute a predictable number of times, as in:

```
$count = 1;
while ($count <= 10)
  {
    print("count is $count<BR>");
    $count = $count + 1;
  }
```

which will print exactly ten lines. (For more interesting examples, see the "Looping examples" section later in this chapter.)

Do-while

The do-while construct is similar to while, except that the test happens at the end of the loop. The syntax is:

```
do statement
  while (expression);
```

The statement is executed once, and then the expression is evaluated. If the expression is true, the statement is repeated until the expression becomes false. The only practical difference between while and do-while is that the latter will always execute its statement at least once. For example:

```
$count = 45;
do
  {
    print("count is $count<BR>");
    $count = $count + 1;
  }
  while ($count <= 10)
```

prints the single line:

```
count is 45
```

For

The most complicated looping construct is for, which has the following syntax:

```
for (initial-expression;
     termination-check;
     loop-end-expression)
  statement
```

In executing a `for` statement, first the *initial-expression* is evaluated just once, usually to initialize variables. Then *termination-check* is evaluated — if it is false, the `for` statement concludes, and if it is true, the statement executes. Finally, the *loop-end-expression* is executed and the cycle begins again with *termination-check*. As always, by *statement* we mean either a single (semicolon-terminated) statement, a brace-enclosed block, or a conditional construct.

If we rewrote the preceding `for` loop as a `while` loop, it would look like this:

```
initial-expression;
while (termination-check)
   {
     statement
     loop-end-expression;
   }
```

Actually, although the typical use of `for` has exactly one initial-expression, one termination-check, and one loop-end-expression, it is legal to omit any of them. The termination-check is taken to be always true if omitted, so:

```
for (;;)
   statement
```

is equivalent to:

```
while (TRUE)
   statement
```

It is also legal to include more than one of each kind of `for` clause, separated by commas. The termination-check will be considered to be true if any of its subclauses are true; it is like an `'or'` test. For example, the following statement:

```
for ($x = 1, $y = 1, $z = 1;    //initial expressions
     $y < 10, $z < 10;          // termination checks
     $x = $x + 1, $y = $y + 2,  // loop-end expressions
     $z = $z + 3)
  print("$x, $y, $z<BR>");
```

would give the browser output:

```
1, 1, 1
2, 3, 4
3, 5, 7
```

Although the `for` syntax is the most complex of the looping constructs, it is often used for simple bounded loops, using the following idiom:

```
for ($count = 0; $count < $limit; $count = $count + 1)
   statement
```

Looping examples

Now let's look at some examples.

A bounded for loop

Listing 7-1 shows a typical use of bounded `for` loops. The page produced by Listing 7-1 is shown in Figure 7-1.

Listing 7-1: A division table

```php
<?php
  $start_num = 1;
  $end_num = 10;
?>
<HTML>
<HEAD>
<TITLE>A division table</TITLE>
</HEAD>
<BODY>
<H2>A division table</H2>
<TABLE BORDER=1>
<?php
  print("<TR>");
  print("<TH> </TH>");
  for ($count_1 = $start_num;
       $count_1 <= $end_num;
       $count_1++)
    print("<TH>$count_1</TH>");
  print("</TR>");

  for ($count_1 = $start_num;
       $count_1 <= $end_num;
       $count_1++)
  {
    print("<TR><TH>$count_1</TH>");
    for ($count_2 = $start_num;
         $count_2 <= $end_num;
         $count_2++)
    {
      $result = $count_1 / $count_2;
      printf("<TD>%.3f</TD>",
             $result);  // see Chapter 10
    }
    print("</TR>\n");
  }
?>
</TABLE>
</BODY>
</HTML>
```

Figure 7-1: A division table

The main body of this code simply has one `for` loop nested inside another, with each loop executing ten times, resulting in a 10 × 10 table. Each iteration of the outer loop prints a row, whereas each inner iteration prints a cell. The only novel feature is the way we chose to print out the numbers — we used `printf` (covered in Chapter 10), which allows us to control the number of decimal places that are printed.

An unbounded while loop

Now let's look at a loop that is not so obviously bounded. The sole purpose of the code in Listing 7-2 is to approximate the square root of 81 (using Newton's method). The approximation starts with a guess of 1 and then "zeros in" on the actual square root of 9 by improving the guesses. A trace of this approximation is shown in Figure 7-2.

Listing 7-2: Approximating a square root

```
<HTML>
<HEAD>
<TITLE>Approximating a square root</TITLE>
</HEAD>
<BODY>
<H3>Approximating a square root</H3>

<?php
$target = 81;
$guess = 1.0;
```

```
$precision = 0.0000001;

$guess_squared = $guess * $guess;
while (($guess_squared - $target > $precision) or
       ($guess_squared - $target < - $precision))
{
  print("Current guess: $guess is the square
        root of $target<BR>");
  $guess = ($guess + ($target / $guess)) / 2;
  $guess_squared = $guess * $guess;
}
print("$guess squared = $guess_squared<BR>");
?>
</BODY>
</HTML>
```

Now, although it nicely illustrates a potentially unbounded loop, this approximation example is very artificial — first, because PHP already has a perfectly good square-root function (sqrt) and second, because the number 81 is hardcoded into the page. We can't use this page to find the square root of any other number.

> **CROSS-REFERENCE:** In the next chapter, we'll show how to wrap code like this into a function that can take the number as a parameter; and in Chapter 9, we'll look at how you can pass that parameter from one page to another.

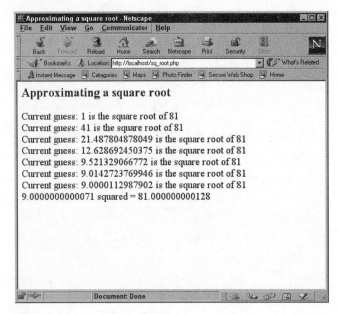

Figure 7-2: Approximating a square root

Break and continue

The standard way to get out of a looping structure is for the main test condition to become false. The special commands `break` and `continue` offer an optional side exit from all the looping constructs, including `while`, `do-while`, and `for`:

♦ The `break` command exits the innermost loop construct that contains it.

♦ The `continue` command skips to the end of the current iteration of the innermost loop that contains it.

For example, the following code:

```
for ($x = 1; $x < 10; $x++)
{
  // if $x is odd, break out
  if ($x % 2 != 0)
    break;
  print("$x ");
}
```

prints nothing because 1 is odd, which terminates the `for` loop immediately. On the other hand, the code:

```
for ($x = 1; $x < 10; $x++)
{
  // if $x is odd, skip this loop
  if ($x % 2 != 0)
    continue;
  print("$x ");
}
```

prints:

```
2 4 6 8
```

because the effect of the `continue` statement is to skip the printing of any odd numbers.

Using the `break` command, the programmer can choose to dispense with the main termination test altogether. Consider the following code, which prints out a list of prime numbers (that is, numbers that are not divisible by something other than one or the number itself):

```
$limit = 500;
$to_test = 2;
while(TRUE)
{
  $testdiv = 2;
  if ($to_test > $limit)
    break;
  while (TRUE)
  {
```

```
    if ($testdiv > sqrt($to_test))
      {
        print "$to_test ";
        break;
      }
    // test if $to_test is divisible by $testdiv
    if ($to_test % $testdiv == 0)
      break;
    $testdiv = $testdiv + 1;
  }
  $to_test = $to_test + 1;
}
```

In the preceding code, we have two while loops — the outer loop works through all the numbers between 1 and 500, and the inner loop actually does the testing with each possible divisor. If the inner loop finds a divisor, the number is not prime, so it breaks out without printing anything. If, on the other hand, the testing gets as high as the square root of the number, we can safely assume that the number must be prime, and the inner loop is broken without printing. Finally, the outer loop is broken when we have reached the limit of numbers to test. The result in this case is a list of primes less than 500:

```
2 3 5 7 11 13 17 19 23 29 31 37 41 43 47 53 59 61 67 71 73 79 83 89 97
101 103 107 109 113 127 131 137 139 149 151 157 163 167 173 179 181 191
193 197 199 211 223 227 229 233 239 241 251 257 263 269 271 277 281 283
293 307 311 313 317 331 337 347 349 353 359 367 373 379 383 389 397 401
409 419 421 431 433 439 443 449 457 461 463 467 479 487 491 499
```

Notice that it is crucial to this code that break only interrupts the inner while loop.

> **CROSS-REFERENCE:** There is another iteration construct, called foreach, that is only used for iterating over arrays. We cover it later in the chapter on arrays. (Chapter 11).

A note on infinite loops

If you've ever programmed in another language, you've probably had the experience of accidentally creating an infinite loop (a looping construct whose exit test never becomes true and so never returns). The first thing to do when you realize this has happened is to interrupt the program, which will otherwise continue "forever" and use up a lot of CPU time. But what does it mean to interrupt a PHP script? Is it sufficient to click the Stop button on your browser?

As it turns out, The answer is dependent on some PHP configuration settings — you can set the PHP engine to ignore interruptions from the browser (like the result of clicking Stop) and also to impose a time limit on script execution (so that "forever" will only be a short time). The default configuration for PHP 4 is to ignore interruptions, but with a script time limit of 30 seconds — the time limitation means that you can afford to forget about infinite loops that you may have started.

CROSS-REFERENCE: For more on the configuration of PHP, see Chapter 37.

Alternate Control Syntaxes

PHP offers another way to start and end the bodies of the `if`, `switch`, `for`, and `while` constructs. It amounts to replacing the initial brace of the enclosed block with a colon, and the closing brace with a special ending statement for that construct (`endif`, `endswitch`, `endfor`, and `endwhile`). For example, the `if` syntax becomes:

```
if (expression):
  statement1
  statement2
  ..
endif;
```

Or:

```
if (expression):
  statement1
  statement2
  ..
elseif (expression2):
  statement3
  ..
else:
  statement4
  ..
endif;
```

Note that the `else` and `elseif` bodies also begin with colons. The corresponding `while` syntax is:

```
while (expression):
  statement
endwhile;
```

Which syntax you use is a matter of taste. The non-standard syntax is in PHP largely used for historical reasons and for the comfort of people who are familiar with it from the early versions of PHP. We will consistently use the standard syntax in the rest of this book.

Terminating Execution

Sometimes you just have to give up, and PHP offers a construct that helps you do just that. The `exit()` construct takes either a string or a number as argument, prints out the argument, and then terminates execution of the script. Everything that PHP produces up to the point of invoking `exit()` is sent to the client browser as usual, and nothing in your script after that point will even be parsed — execution of the script stops immediately. If the argument given to exit is a number rather than a string, the number will be the return value for the script's execution. Because exit is a construct, not a function, it's also legal to give no argument, and omit the parentheses.

The die() construct is an alias for exit() and so behaves exactly the same way. (We'll usually use the die() version because we find the name more evocative.) So what's the point of exit() and die()? One possible use is to cut off production of a Web page when your script has determined that there is no more interesting information to send, without bothering to wrap up the different branches in a conditional construct. This usage can make long scripts somewhat difficult to read and debug, however.

A better use for die() is to make your crashes informative. It's good to get into the habit of testing for unexpected conditions that would crash your script if they were true, and throw in a die() statement with an informative message. If you're correct in your expectations, the die() will never be invoked; if you're wrong, you will have an error message of your own, rather than a possibly obscure PHP error. For example, consider the following pseudocode, which assumes that we have functions to make a database connection, and we then use that database connection:

```
$connection = make_database_connection();
if (!$connection)
   die("No database connection!");
use_database_connection($connection);
```

This example assumes that our imaginary function make_database_connection(), like many PHP functions, returns a useful value if it succeeds, and a false value if it fails. An even more compact version of the preceding code takes advantage of the fact that or has lower precedence than the = assignment operator.

```
$connection = make_database_connection()
   or die("No database connection!");
use_database_connection($connection);
```

This works because the or operator short-circuits, and therefore the die() construct will only be evaluated if the expression $connection = make_database_connection() has a false value. Because the value of an assignment expression is the value assigned, this code ends up being equivalent to the earlier version. (Note that this would not work the same way if we used || instead of or, because || has higher precedence than assignment, and so $connection would end up being assigned to the true-or-false result of the || expression.)

Summary

PHP has a C-like set of control structures, which branch or loop depending on the value of Boolean expressions, which in turn can be combined using Boolean operators (and, or, xor, !, &&, ||). The structures if and switch are used for simple branching; while, do-while, and for are used for looping; and exit() (or die()) terminates script execution.

Table 7-3 summarizes all the control structures from this chapter, with the exception of the alternative: .. endif syntax.

Table 7-3: PHP Control Structures

Name	Syntax	Behavior
If (or if-else)	```if (test) statement-1 -or- if (test) statement-1 else statement-2 -or- if (test) statement-1 elseif (test2) statement-2 else statement-3```	Evaluate *test* and if it is true, execute *statement-1*. If *test* is false and there is an else clause, execute *statement-2*. The elseif construct is a syntactic shortcut for else clauses where the included statement is itself an if construct. Statements may be single statements terminated with a semicolon or brace-enclosed blocks.
Ternary operator	```expression-1 ? expression-2 : expression-3```	Evaluate *expression-1* and interpret it as a Boolean. If it is true, evaluate *expression-2* and return it as the value of the entire expression. Otherwise, evaluate and return *expression-3*.
Switch	```switch(expression) { case value-1: statement-1 statement-2 … [break;] case value-2: statement-3 statement-4 … [break;] … [default: default-statement] }```	Evaluate *expression,* and compare its value to the value in each case clause. When a matching case is found, begin executing statements in sequence (including those from later cases), until the end of the switch statement or until a break statement is encountered. The optional default case will execute if no other case has matched the expression.

While	`while (condition)` `statement`	Evaluate *condition* and interpret it as Boolean. If *condition* is false, the `while` construct terminates. If it is true, execute *statement,* and keep executing it until *condition* becomes false. Terminate the `while` loop if the special `break` command is encountered, and skip the rest of the current iteration if `continue` is encountered.
Do-while	`do statement` `while (condition);`	Perform *statement* once unconditionally, then keep repeating statement until *condition* becomes false. (The `break` and `continue` commands are handled as in `while`.)

For	`for (initial-expression;`
	   `termination-check;`
	   `loop-end-expression)`
	   `statement`
		Evaluate *initial-expression* once unconditionally. Then if *termination-check* is true, evaluate *statement,* and then *loop-end-expression,* and repeat that loop until *termination-check* becomes false. Clauses may be omitted, or multiple clauses of the same kind can be separated with commas — a missing termination-check is treated as true. (The `break` and `continue` commands are handled as in `while`.)

Exit (or die)	`exit(message-string or`
	`return-value), or`
	`equivalently`
	`die(message-string or`
	`return-value)`
		Terminate script immediately, without further parsing. The die() construct is an alias for exit().

Chapter 8

Using and Defining Functions

Any real programming language has some kind of capability for *procedural abstraction* — a way to name pieces of code so that you can use them as building blocks in writing other pieces of code. Some scripting languages lack this capability, and we can tell you from our own sorrowful experience that complex server-side code can quickly become unmanageable without it.

PHP's mechanism for this kind of abstraction is the *function.* There are really two kinds of functions in PHP — those that have been built into the language by the PHP developers and those that are defined by individual PHP programmers.

In this chapter, we look at how to use the large body of functions already provided in PHP and then, a bit later, how to define your own functions. Luckily, there is no real difference between using a built-in function and using your own functions.

Using Functions

The basic syntax for using (or *calling*) a function is:

```
function_name(expression_1, expression_2, ..., expression_n)
```

This includes the name of the function followed by a parenthesized and comma-separated list of input expressions (which are called the *arguments* to the function). Functions can be called with zero or more arguments, depending on their definitions.

When PHP encounters a function call, it first evaluates each argument expression and then uses these values as inputs to the function. After the function executes, the returned value (if any) is the result of the entire function expression.

All the following are valid calls to built-in PHP functions:

```
sqrt(9) // square root function, evaluates to 3
rand(10, 10 + 10) // random number between 10 and 20
strlen("This has 22 characters") // returns the number 22
pi() // returns the approximate value of pi
```

These functions are called with 1, 2, 1, and 0 arguments, respectively.

Return values versus side effects

Every function call is a PHP expression, and (just as with other expressions) there are only two reasons why you might want to include one in your code: for the *return value* or for the *side effects*.

The *return value* of a function is the value of the function expression itself. You can do exactly the same things with this value as with the results of evaluating any other expression. For example, You can assign it to a variable, as in:

```
$my_pi = pi();
```

Or you can embed it in more complicated expressions, as in:

```
$approx = sqrt($approx) * sqrt($approx)
```

Functions are also used for a wide variety of *side effects*, including writing to files, manipulating databases, and printing things to the browser window. It's okay to make use of both return values and side effects at the same time — for example, it is very common to have a side-effecting function return a value that indicates whether or not the function succeeded.

The result of a function may be of any type, and it is common to use the array type as a way for functions to return multiple values.

Function Documentation

The architecture of PHP has been cleverly designed to make it easy for other developers to extend. The basic PHP language itself is very clean and flexible, but there is not a lot there — most of PHP's power resides in the large number of built-in functions. This means that developers can contribute simply by adding new built-in functions, which is nice especially because it does not change anything that PHP users may be relying on.

Although this book covers many of these built-in functions, explaining some of them in greater detail than the online manual can, the manual at www.php.net is the authoritative source for function information. In this book, we get to choose our topics to some extent, whereas the PHP documentation group has the awesome responsibility of covering every aspect of PHP in the manual. Also, although we hope to keep updating this book in future editions, the manual will have the freshest information on new additions to the ever-growing PHP functionality. It's worth looking at some of the different resources that the PHP site and manual offer.

> **NOTE:** Although the following information is correct at this writing (the 2nd Edition, written in 2002), some details may date or become inapplicable if the online manual is reorganized.

To find the manual, head to www.php.net and look for the Documentation tab at the top of the page. The Documentation page that this tab leads to has links to manual information in a wide variety of formats. Our favorite version is the default (currently in the View Online row of the Formats table on the Documentation page), which allows users to post their own clarifying comments to each page. (*Please note:* The manual annotation system is not the right place to post questions! For that, see the section on mailing lists under the Support tab on www.php.net, or see Appendix D. But it *is* the right place to explain something in your own words once you understand it. If you offer a better explanation, it might well show up in a later version of the documentation, which is a cool way to contribute. It's also definitely the right place to point out confusing aspects and potential gotchas.)

The largest section of the manual is the function reference, where each built-in function gets its own page of documentation. Typically each group of functions has a page of general explanation, leading to pages for individual functions. Each function page starts off with the name of the function and a one-line description. This is followed by a C-style header declaration of the function (explained in the next section), followed by a slightly longer description and possibly an example or two, and then (in the annotated manual) clarifications and gotcha reports from users.

Headers in documentation

For those unfamiliar with C function headers, the very beginning of a function documentation page might be confusing. The format is:

```
return-type function-name(type1 arg1, type2 arg2, . . .);
```

This specifies the type of value the function is expected to return, the name of the function, and the number and expected types of its arguments.

Here is a typical header description:

```
string substr(string string, int start[, int length]);
```

This says that the function substr() will return a string and expects to be given a string and two integers as its arguments. Actually, the square brackets around length indicate that this argument is optional — so substr() should be called either with a string and an int, or a string and two ints.

Unlike in C, the argument types in these documentary headers are not absolute requirements. If you call substr() with a number as its first argument, you will not get an error. Instead, PHP will convert the first argument to a string as it begins to execute the function. However, The argument types do document the intent of the function's author, and it is a good idea either to use the function as documented or to understand the type conversion issues well enough that you are sure the result will be what you expect.

In general, the type names used in function documentation will be those of the basic types or of their aliases: integer (or int), double (or float, real), Boolean, string, array, object, resource, and NULL. In addition, you may see the types void and mixed. The void return type means that the function does not return a value at all; whereas the "mixed" argument type means that the argument might be of any type.

Finding function documentation

What's the best way to find information about a function in the manual? That is likely to depend on what kind of curiosity you have. The most common questions about functions are:

♦ I want to use function X. Now, how does X work again?

♦ I'd really like to do task Y. Is there a function that handles that for me?

For the first type of curiosity, the full version of the online manual offers an automatic lookup by function name. The "Search For" box in the upper-right-hand corner of the manual pages defaults to a mode where it searches for specific function names and displays the corresponding function page if found. (You can also make other choices, including searching the mailing list or the entire online documentation — the latter is a good choice when you don't know the name of the function you want, but can guess at words that appear on its manual page.)

For the second type of curiosity, your best bet is probably to use the hierarchical organization of the function reference, which is split (at press time) into about 108 chapters. For example, the substr function shown in the "Headers in Documentation" section is found in the "String Functions" section. You can browse the chapter list of the function reference for the best fit to the task you want to do. Alternatively, if you happen to know the name of a function that seems to be in the same general area as your task, you can use the Quick Ref button to jump to that chapter.

Defining Your Own Functions

User-defined functions are not a requirement in PHP. You can produce interesting and useful Web sites simply with the basic language constructs and the large body of built-in functions. However, if you find that your code files are getting longer, harder to understand, and more difficult to manage, it may be an indication that you should start wrapping some of your code up into functions.

What is a function?

A *function* is a way of wrapping up a chunk of code and giving that chunk a name, so that you can use that chunk later in just one line of code. Functions are most useful when you will be using the code in more than one place, but they can be helpful even in one-use situations, because they can make your code much more readable.

Function definition syntax

Function definitions have the following form:

```
function function-name ($argument1, $argument2, ..)
{
  statement1;
  statement2;
  ...
}
```

That is, function definitions have four parts:

- ◆ The special word `function`
- ◆ The name that you want to give your function.
- ◆ The function's parameter list — dollar-sign variables separated by commas
- ◆ The function body — a brace-enclosed set of statements

Just as with variable names, the name of the function must be made up of letters, numbers, and underscores, and it must not start with a number. Unlike variable names, function names are converted to lowercase before they are stored internally by PHP, so a function is the same regardless of capitalization.

The short version of what happens when a user-defined function is called is:

1. PHP looks up the function by its name (you will get an error if the function has not yet been defined).

2. PHP substitutes the values of the calling arguments (or the *actual parameters*) into the variables in the definition's parameter list (or the *formal parameters*).

3. The statements in the body of the function are executed. If any of the executed statements are `return` statements, the function stops and returns the given value. Otherwise, the function completes after the last statement is executed, without returning a value.

> **NOTE:** The alert and experienced programmer will have noticed that the preceding description implies call-by-value, rather than call-by-reference. In the last section of this chapter, we explain the difference and show how to get call-by-reference behavior.

Function definition example

As an example, imagine that we have the following code that helps decide which size of bottled soft drink to buy. (This is sometime next year, when supermarket shoppers routinely use their wearable wireless Web browsers to get to our handy price-comparison site.)

```
$liters_1 = 1.0;
$price_1 = 1.59;
$liters_2 = 1.5;
$price_2 = 2.09;

$per_liter_1 = $price_1 / $liters_1;
$per_liter_2 = $price_2 / $liters_2;
if ($per_liter1 < $per_liter2)
  print("The first deal is better!<BR>");
else
  print("The second deal is better!<BR>");
```

Because this kind of comparison happens in our Web site code all the time, we would like to make part of this a reusable function. One way to do this would be the following rewrite:

```
function better_deal ($amount_1, $price_1,
                      $amount_2, $price_2)
{
  $per_amount_1 = $price_1 / $amount_1;
  $per_amount_2 = $price_2 / $amount_2;
  return($per_amount_1 < $per_amount_2);
}

$liters_1 = 1.0;
$price_1 = 1.59;
$liters_2 = 1.5;
$price_2 = 2.09;

if (better_deal($liters_1, $price_1,
                $liters_2, $price_2))
  print("The first deal is better!<BR>");
else
  print("The second deal is better!<BR>");
```

Our `better_deal` function abstracts out the three lines in the previous code that did the arithmetic and comparison. It takes four numbers as arguments and returns the value of a Boolean expression. As with any Boolean value, we can embed it in the test portion of an `if` statement. Although this function is longer than the original code, there are two benefits to this rewrite: We can use the function in multiple places (saving lines overall), and if we decide to change the calculation, we only have to make the change in one place.

Alternatively, if the only way we ever use these price comparisons is to print out which deal is preferred, we can include the printing in the function, like this:

```
function print_better_deal ($amount_1, $price_1,
                            $amount_2, $price_2)
{
  $per_amount_1 = $price_1 / $amount_1;
  $per_amount_2 = $price_2 / $amount_2;
```

```
  if ($per_amount_1 < $per_amount_2)
    print("The first deal is better!<BR>");
  else
    print("The second deal is better!<BR>");
}

$liters_1 = 1.0;
$price_1 = 1.59;
$liters_2 = 1.5;
$price_2 = 2.09;

print_better_deal($liters_1, $price_1,
                  $liters_2, $price_2);
```

Our first function used the `return` statement to send back a Boolean result, which was used in an `if` test. The second function has no `return` statement, because it is used for the side effect of printing text to the user's browser. When the last statement of this function is executed, PHP simply moves on to executing the next statement after a function call.

Formal parameters versus actual parameters

In the preceding examples, the arguments we passed to our functions happened to be variables, but this is not a requirement. The actual parameters (that is, the arguments that are in the function call) may be any expression that evaluates to a value. In our examples, we could have passed numbers to our function calls rather than variables, as in:

```
print_better_deal(1.0, 1.59, 1.5, 2.09);
```

Also, notice that in the examples we had a couple of cases where the actual parameter variable had the same name as the formal parameter (for example, `$price_1`), and we also had cases where the actual and formal names were different. (`$liters_1` is not the same as `$amount_1`.) As we will see in the next section, this name agreement doesn't matter either way — the names of a function's formal parameters are completely independent of the world outside the function, including the function call itself.

Argument number mismatches

What happens if you call a function with fewer arguments than appear in the definition, or with more? As you might have come to expect by now, PHP handles this without anything crashing, but it may print a warning depending on your settings for error reporting.

Too few arguments

If you supply fewer actual parameters than formal parameters, PHP will treat the unfilled formal parameters as if they were unbound variables. However, under the usual settings for error reporting in PHP 4, you will also see a warning printed to the browser.

The default error-reporting setting in PHP 4 reports on every kind of error except runtime notices, which are the least serious condition that is detected. The reason you see warnings about too few arguments to a function is that this is treated as a runtime-warning situation (the next most serious category). If you really need function calls that sometimes provide too few arguments and seeing warnings is unacceptable, you have two options for suppressing the warnings:

- You can temporarily change the value of error reporting in your script, with a statement like `error_reporting(E_ALL - (E_NOTICE + E_WARNING));`. This will turn off both runtime notices and runtime warnings from the point where it appears in your script up to the next `error_reporting()` statement (if any). (Note that this is dangerous, as lots of other problems might produce warnings besides the one you're interested in.)

- You can suppress errors for any single expression by using the error-control operator `@`, which you can put in front of any expression to suppress errors from that expression only. For example, if the function call `my_function()` is producing a warning, `@my_function()` will not. Note that this is dangerous as well because all types of errors except for parse errors will be suppressed.

We don't advise using either of these band-aids, but provide them because we are such non-judgmental people by nature. PHP actually provides ways to write functions that expect variable numbers of arguments (see "Variable numbers of arguments" in the "Advanced Function Tricks" section later in the chapter), and using them is a much better idea than shooting the messenger.

> **TIP:** Rather than decreasing PHP's reportage of errors, we advise increasing it to the maximum level possible when you are developing new code. You can do this globally by changing the `php.ini` file (see Chapter 37), or simply by including the statement `error_reporting(E_ALL);` at the top of your scripts. Among other things, this increase in reportage will mean that you will be warned about variables you have forgotten to assign, which is one of the most frequent causes of time-wasting bugs.

Too many arguments

If you hand too many arguments to a function, the excess arguments will simply be ignored, even when error reporting is set to `E_ALL`. As we will see in the "Advanced Function Tricks" section, this tolerance turns out to be helpful in defining functions that can take a variable number of arguments.

Functions and Variable Scope

As we said in Chapter 5, outside of functions, the rules about variable scope are simple: Assign a variable anywhere in the execution of a PHP code file, and the value will be there for you later in that file's execution. The rules become somewhat more complicated in the bodies of function definitions, but not much.

The basic principle governing variables in function bodies is: Each function is its own little world. That is, barring some special declarations, the meaning of a variable name inside a function has nothing to do with the meaning of that name elsewhere. (This is a feature, not a bug — you want functions to be reusable in different contexts, and so having the behavior be independent of the context is a good thing. If not for this kind of scoping, you would waste a lot of time chasing down bugs caused by using the same variable name in different parts of your code.)

> **NEW FEATURE:** As of PHP 4.1, there is a small set of global variables which *are* automatically visible from within function definitions, in contradiction to the previous paragraph and the following one. These are the *superglobal arrays* ($_POST, $_GET, $_SESSION, and so on) which contain keys and values corresponding to variable bindings from different sources. For more on these variables and their uses, see the next chapter.

The only variable values that a function has access to are the formal parameter variables (which have the values copied from the actual parameters), plus any variables that are assigned inside the function. This means that you can use local variables inside a function without worrying about their effects on the outside world. For example, consider this function and its subsequent use:

```
function SayMyABCs ()
{
  $count = 0;
  while ($count < 10)
    {
      print(chr(ord('A') + $count));
      $count = $count + 1;
    }
  print("<BR>Now I know $count letters<BR>");
}
$count = 0;
SayMyABCs();
$count = $count + 1;
print("Now I've made $count function call(s).<BR>");
SayMyABCs();
$count = $count + 1;
print("Now I've made $count function call(s).<BR>");
```

The intent of `SayMyABCs()` is to print out a sequence of letters. (The functions `chr()` and `ord()` translate between letters and their numeric ASCII codes — we use them here just as a trick to generate letters in sequence.) The output of this code is:

```
ABCDEFGHIJ
Now I know 10 letters
Now I've made 1 function call(s).
ABCDEFGHIJ
```

```
Now I know 10 letters
Now I've made 2 function call(s).
```

Both the function definition and the code outside the function make use of variables called $count, but they refer to different variables and do not clash.

The default behavior of variables assigned inside functions is that they do not interact with the outside world, and they act as though they are newly created each time the function is called. Both of these behaviors, however, can be overridden with special declarations.

Global versus local

The scope of a variable defined inside a function is *local* by default, meaning that (as we explained in the previous section) it has no connection with the meaning of any variables outside the function. Using the global declaration, you can inform PHP that you want a variable name to mean the same thing as it does in the context outside the function. The syntax of this declaration is simply the word global, followed by a comma-delimited list of the variables that should be treated that way, with a terminating semicolon. To see the effect, consider a new version of the previous example. The only difference is that we have declared $count to be global, and we have removed its initial assignment to zero inside the function:

```
function SayMyABCs2 ()
{
  global $count;
  while ($count < 10)
    {
      print(chr(ord('A') + $count));
      $count = $count + 1;
    }
  print("<BR>Now I know $count letters<BR>");
}
$count = 0;
SayMyABCs2();
$count = $count + 1;
print("Now I've made $count function call(s).<BR>");
SayMyABCs2();
$count = $count + 1;
print("Now I've made $count function call(s).<BR>");
```

Our revised version prints the following browser output:

```
ABCDEFGHIJ
Now I know 10 letters
Now I've made 11 function call(s).

Now I know 11 letters
Now I've made 12 function call(s).
```

This is buggy behavior, and the global declaration is to blame. There is now only one $count variable, and it is being increased both inside and outside the function. When the second call to SayMyABCs() happens, $count is already 11, and so the loop that prints letters is never entered.

Although this example shows global to bad advantage, it can be quite useful, especially because (as we'll see in Chapter 9) PHP provides some variable bindings to every page even before any of your own code is executed. It can be helpful to have a way for functions to see these variables without the bother of passing them in as arguments with each call.

Static variables

By default, functions retain no memory of their own execution, and with each function call local variables act as though they have been newly created. The static declaration overrides this behavior for particular variables, causing them to retain their values in between calls to the same function. Using this, we can modify our earlier function SayMyABCs2() to give it some memory:

```
function SayMyABCs3 ()
{
  static $count = 0; //assignment only if first time called
  $limit = $count + 10;
  while ($count < $limit)
    {
      print(chr(ord('A') + $count));
      $count = $count + 1;
    }
  print("<BR>Now I know $count letters<BR>");
}
$count = 0;
SayMyABCs3();
$count = $count + 1;
print("Now I've made $count function call(s).<BR>");
SayMyABCs3();
$count = $count + 1;
print("Now I've made $count function call(s).<BR>");
```

This memory-enhanced version gives us the following output:

```
ABCDEFGHIJ
Now I know 10 letters
Now I've made 1 function call(s).
KLMNOPQRST
Now I know 20 letters
Now I've made 2 function call(s).
```

The static keyword allows for an initial assignment, which has an effect only if the function has not been called before. The first time SayMyABCs3() executes, the local version of

$count is set to zero. The second time the function is called, it has the value it had at the end of the last execution, so we are able to pick up our studies where we left off. Notice that changes to $count outside the function still have no effect on the local value.

Function Scope

Although the rules about the scope of variable names are fairly simple, the scoping rules for function names are even simpler. There is just one rule in PHP 4: Functions must be defined once (and only once) somewhere in the script that uses them. (See the "New Feature" note about differences between this behavior and PHP 3.) The scope of function names is implicitly global, and so a function that is defined in a script is available everywhere in that script. For clarity's sake, however, it is often a good idea to define all your functions first before any code that calls those functions.

> **NEW FEATURE:** In PHP 3, functions could be used only after they were defined. This meant that the safest practice was to define (or include the definitions of) all functions early in a given script, before actually using any of them. PHP 4 actually precompiles scripts before running them, and one effect of this pre-compilation is that it discovers all function definitions before actually running the code. This means that functions and code can appear in any order in a script, as long as all functions are defined once (and only once).

Include and require

It's very common to want to use the same set of functions across a set of Web site pages, and the usual way to handle this is with either include or require, both of which import the contents of some other file into the file being executed. Using either one of these forms is vastly preferable to *cloning* your function definitions (that is, repeating them at the beginning of each page that uses them) because when you want to modify your functions, you will only have to do it once.

For example, at the top of a PHP code file we might have lines like:

```
include "basic-functions.inc"
include "advanced-function.inc";
(.. code that uses basic and advanced functions ..)
```

which import two different files of function definitions. (Note that parentheses are optional with both include() and require().) As long as the only things in these files are function definitions, the order of their inclusion does not matter.

Both include and require have the effect of splicing in the contents of their file into the PHP code at the point that they are called. The only difference between them is how they fail if the file cannot be found. The include construct will cause a warning to be printed, but processing of the script will continue; require, on the other hand, will cause a fatal error if the file cannot be found.

> **NEW FEATURE:** Note that `include` and `require` are now more similar in their behavior than they used to be. Prior to PHP 4.0.2, `require` had its file contents spliced in statically, before the actual execution of the page; whereas the contents from `include` were spliced in dynamically as the page executed. Among other things, this led to subtle differences in behavior when the `include`/`require` form was in conditional code. Now, however, both `include` and `require` have the same dynamic behavior. This means, for example, that if an `include`/`require` form is in a loop that is executed ten times, ten inclusions will be made.

Including only once

Sometimes you really want a file to be included once, but not more than once. This is true most often in the case of function definitions. For example, two different function definition files might, in turn, include the same file of utility functions — if a top level page includes both of these files, the utility functions might be included twice, leading to complaints from PHP that functions are being defined twice.

To the rescue come `include_once` and `require_once`, which act just like their counterparts except that they will not include a file named by a given string if that file has already been included. It's usually better to use the `_once` version, in general, for including function and class definition files.

> **NEW FEATURE:** The `include_once` and `require_once` constructs are new as of PHP 4.0.1pl2.

The include path

When you `include` a filename, PHP searches for a file by that name in the directories specified in the `include_path` (which is settable in your `php.ini` file). The default path includes the same directory as the one the top-level code page is in. See Chapter 37 for details about how to add locations to your `include` path.

> **WARNING:** Remember that `included` (and `required`) files are parsed by default in HTML mode rather than in PHP mode. This means that any `included` file that is meant to be interpreted as PHP needs to have the usual PHP tags at the beginning and end.

Recursion

Some compiled languages, like C and C++, impose somewhat complex ordering constraints on how functions are defined. To know how to compile a function, the compiler must know about all the functions that the function calls, which means the called functions must be defined first. So what do you do if two functions each call the other, or one function calls itself? Issues like this led the designers of C to a separation of function declarations (or prototypes) from function definitions (or implementations). The idea is that you use declarations to inform the compiler in advance about the types of arguments and return types of the functions you plan to use, which is enough information for the compiler to handle the actual definitions in any order.

In PHP, this problem goes away, and so there is no need for separate function prototypes. In PHP 3, functions need to be defined before they are used, but defining one function to call another does not yet count as use of either function. When PHP 3 encounters the definition of function A, it does not object if the body of A includes calls to function B, which has not yet been defined. Function B just needs to be defined by the time function A is actually called. In PHP 4, even the ordering issue is not an issue.

This means that *recursive functions* (functions that call themselves) are no problem in PHP4. For example, we can define a recursive function and then immediately call it:

```
function countdown ($num_arg)
  {
    if ($num_arg > 0)
      {
        print("Counting down from $num_arg<BR>");
        countdown($num_arg - 1);
      }
  }
countdown(10);
```

This produces the browser output:

```
Counting down from 10
Counting down from 9
Counting down from 8
Counting down from 7
Counting down from 6
Counting down from 5
Counting down from 4
Counting down from 3
Counting down from 2
Counting down from 1
```

As with all recursive functions, it's important to be sure that the function has a *base case* (a nonrecursive branch) in addition to the recursive case, and that the base case is certain to eventually occur. If the base case is never invoked, the situation is much like a `while` loop where the test is always true — we will have an infinite loop of function calling. In the case of the preceding function, we know that the base case will happen, because every invocation of the recursive case reduces the countdown number, which must eventually become zero. Of course, this assumes that the input is a positive integer, rather than a negative number or a double. Notice that our "greater than zero" test guards against infinite recursion even in these cases, whereas a "not equal to zero" test would not.

Similarly, *mutually recursive functions* (functions that each call each other) work without a hitch. For example, the following definitions plus function call:

```
function countdown_first ($num_arg)
  {
```

```
   if ($num_arg > 0)
     {
       print("Counting down (first) from $num_arg<BR>");
       countdown_second($num_arg - 1);
     }
  }
function countdown_second ($num_arg)
  {
    if ($num_arg > 0)
      {
        print("Counting down (second) from $num_arg<BR>");
        countdown_first($num_arg - 1);
      }
  }

countdown_first(5);
```

produces the browser output:

```
Counting down (first) from 5
Counting down (second) from 4
Counting down (first) from 3
Counting down (second) from 2
Counting down (first) from 1
```

Advanced Function Tricks

Now we move on to some more exotic properties of functions, including ways to use variable numbers of arguments, ways to have functions actually modify the variables they are passed, and (cooler still) using functions as data.

> **NOTE:** This final section is more challenging than the rest of the chapter, and it may be of interest only to the adventurous, the curious, or more experienced programmers.

Variable numbers of arguments

It's often useful to have the number of actual arguments that are passed to a function depend on the situation in which it is called. There are three possible ways to handle this in PHP, one of which is only available in PHP 4:

♦ Define the function with default arguments — any that are missing in the function call will have the default value, and no warning will be printed.

♦ Use an array argument to hold the values — it is the responsibility of the calling code to package up the array, and the function body must appropriately take it apart.

♦ Use the variable-argument functions (func_num_args(), func_get_arg(), and func_get_args()) introduced in PHP 4.

Default arguments

To define a function with default arguments, simply turn the formal parameter name into an assignment expression. If the actual call has fewer parameters than the definition has formal parameters, PHP will match actual with formal until the actual parameters are exhausted, and then will use the default assignments to fill in the rest.

For example, the following function has all its variables defined with defaults:

```
function tour_guide($city = "Gotham City",
                    $desc = "vast metropolis",
                    $how_many = "dozens",
                    $of_what = "costumed villains")
{
  print("$city is a $desc filled with
        $how_many of $of_what.<BR>");
}
tour_guide();
tour_guide("Chicago");
tour_guide("Chicago", "wonderful city");
tour_guide("Chicago", "wonderful city",
           "teeming millions");
tour_guide("Chicago", "wonderful city",
           "teeming millions",
           "gruff people with hearts of
            gold and hard-luck stories to tell");
```

The browser output is something like this, with the intra-sentence line breaks, of course, determined by your browser:

```
Gotham City is a great metropolis filled with dozens of costumed
villains.
Chicago is a great metropolis filled with dozens of costumed villains.
Chicago is a wonderful city filled with dozens of costumed villains.
Chicago is a wonderful city filled with teeming millions of costumed
villains.
Chicago is a wonderful city filled with teeming millions of gruff people
with hearts of gold and hard-luck stories to tell.
```

The main limitation of default arguments is that the matching of actual to formal parameters is determined by the ordering of both — it's first-come, first-served. This means that there is absolutely no way to use the default-argument mechanism to tell someone about hard-luck stories in Gotham City.

Arrays as multiple-argument substitutes

If you are dissatisfied with the flexibility of multiple arguments, you can bypass the whole argument-counting issue by using an array as your communication channel.

The following example uses this strategy and, in addition, uses a few tricks like the ternary operator (introduced in Chapter 7) and the associative array (touched on in Chapter 6 and covered completely in Chapter 11):

```
function tour_brochure($info_array)
{
$city =
 IsSet($info_array['city']) ?
  $info_array['city'] : "Gotham City";
$desc =
 IsSet($info_array['desc']) ?
  $info_array['desc'] : "great metropolis";
$how_many =
 IsSet($info_array['how_many']) ?
  $info_array['how_many'] : "dozens";
$of_what =
 IsSet($info_array['of_what']) ?
  $info_array['of_what'] : "costumed villains";

print("$city is a $desc filled with
      $how_many of $of_what.<BR>");
}
```

This function checks the single incoming array argument for four different values associated with particular strings. Using the ternary conditional operator ?, local variables are assigned to either the incoming value (if it has been stored in the array) or to our comic-book defaults. Now, let's try calling this function with a couple of different arrays:

```
tour_brochure(array()); // empty array
$tour_info =
 array('city' => 'Cozumel',
      'desc' => 'destination getaway',
      'of_what' => 'sandy beaches');
tour_brochure($tour_info);
```

In this example, we call `tour_brochure` first with an empty array (corresponding to no arguments) and then with an array that has three of the four possible associative values stored in it. The browser output we get is:

```
Gotham City is a great metropolis filled with dozens of costumed
villains.
Cozumel is a destination getaway filled with dozens of sandy beaches.
```

In both cases, the `dozens` amount is defaulted, because neither array had anything stored under the `how_many` association.

Multiple arguments in PHP4

Finally, PHP 4 offers some functions that can be used inside function bodies to recover the number and values of arguments. They are:

♦ func_num_args():Takes no arguments and returns the number of arguments that passed to the function it is called from.

♦ func_get_arg():Takes an integer argument *n* and returns the *n*th argument to the function it is called from. Arguments are numbered starting from zero.

♦ func_get_args():Takes no arguments and returns an array containing all the arguments in the function it is called from, with array indices starting from zero.

All three of these functions will produce a warning if called outside a function body, and func_get_arg() will give a warning if it is called with an index higher than the index of the final argument that was passed.

If your function is going to handle the decoding of arguments using these functions, you can take advantage of the fact that PHP doesn't complain about function calls that have more arguments than formal parameters in the definition. Simply define your function to take no arguments and then use the functions to catch any that are actually passed.

As an example, consider the following two functions, both of which return an array of the arguments they are given:

```
function args_as_array_1 ()
{
$arg_count = func_num_args();
$counter = 0;
$local_array = array();
while ($counter < $arg_count)
  {
   $local_array[$counter] =
     func_get_arg($counter);
   $counter = $counter + 1;
  }
return($local_array);
}

function args_as_array_2 ()
{
   return(func_get_args());
}
```

The first cumbersome function uses func_get_arg() to retrieve the individual arguments and bounds the loop using the result of func_num_args(), so that no attempt is made to retrieve more arguments than were actually passed. Each argument is individually stored in an array, which is then returned. Packaging up the arguments like this is already done for free by func_get_args(), so the second version of the function is extremely short.

As another example, let's rewrite our earlier tour_guide() function to use the multiple-argument functions instead of default arguments:

```
function tour_guide_2()
{
$num_args = func_num_args();
$city = $num_args > 0 ?
  func_get_arg(0) : "Gotham City";
$desc = $num_args > 1 ?
  func_get_arg(1) : "great metropolis";
$how_many = $num_args > 2 ?
  func_get_arg(2) : "dozens";
$of_what = $num_args > 3 ?
  func_get_arg(3) : "costumed villains";

print("$city is a $desc filled with
      $how_many of $of_what.<BR>");
}
tour_guide2();
```

This has exactly the same behavior as the default-argument version and is subject to the same limitation. The arguments are passed in by position, and so there is no way to replace "costumed villains" with something else while leaving "Gotham City" as the default.

Call-by-value versus call-by-reference

The default behavior for user-defined functions in PHP is *call-by-value*. This means that when you pass variables to a function call, PHP makes copies of the variable values to pass on to the function. So, whatever the function does, it is not able to change the actual variables that appear in the function call. This behavior can be good or bad. It's a nice reassurance if you only want to use a function for its returned value, but it can also be a source of confusion and frustration if changing the passed variable is actually your goal.

Let's demonstrate call-by-value with a fragile and extremely inefficient implementation of subtraction:

```
function my_subtract ($num1, $num2)
{
  if ($num1 < $num2)
    die("Negative numbers are imaginary");
  $return_result = 0;
  while($num1 > $num2)
    {
      $num1 = $num1 - 1;
      $return_result = $return_result + 1;
    }
  return($return_result);
}
$first_op = 493;
$second_op = 355;
```

```
$result1 = my_subtract($first_op, $second_op);
print("result1 is $result1<BR>");
$result2 = my_subtract($first_op, $second_op);
print("result2 is $result2<BR>");
```

Reassuringly, we find that our result is the same both times we perform the same subtraction:

```
result1 is 138
result2 is 138
```

This is true even though my_subtract changes the value of its formal parameter $num1 — that variable only holds a copy of the value that was in the actual parameter $first_op, and so $first_op cannot be affected.

Call-by-reference

PHP offers two different ways to have functions actually modify their arguments: in the function definition and in the function call.

If you want to define a function to operate directly on a passed variable, simply put an ampersand in front of the formal parameter in the definition, like so:

```
function my_subtract_ref (&$num1, &$num2)
{
  if ($num1 < $num2)
    die("Negative numbers are imaginary");
  $return_result = 0;
  while($num1 > $num2)
    {
      $num1 = $num1 - 1;
      $return_result = $return_result + 1;
    }
  return($return_result);
}
$first_op = 493;
$second_op = 355;
$result1 = my_subtract_ref($first_op, $second_op);
print("result1 is $result1<BR>");
$result2 = my_subtract_ref($first_op, $second_op);
print("result2 is $result2<BR>");
```

Now, if we perform exactly the same subtraction calls as we did the first time, we get the output:

```
result1 is 138
result1 is 0
```

This is because the formal parameter $num1 refers to the same thing as the actual parameter $first_op — changing one means changing the other.

You can also force a function to take arguments by reference by prepending the actual parameters with ampersands (although this is a deprecated capability, and so may disappear in future PHP versions). That is, we can use our original call-by-value function and get the by-reference behavior, like so:

```
$first_op = 493;
$second_op = 355;
$result1 = my_subtract(&$first_op, &$second_op);
print("result1 is $result1<BR>");
$result2 = my_subtract(&$first_op, &$second_op);
print("result2 is $result2<BR>");
```

producing, once again:

```
result1 is 138
result1 is 0
```

As of PHP 4, variable references can now be used outside of function calls as well. In general, assigning a variable reference (`&$varname`) to a variable will make the two variables aliases of each other rather than distinct variables with the same value. For example:

```
$name_1 = "Manfred von Richtofen";
$name_2 = "Percy Blakeney";
$alias_1 = $name_1; // vars have same value
$alias_2 = &$name_2; // vars are the same

$alias_1 = "The Red Baron"; // doesn't change real name
$alias_2 = "The Scarlet Pimpernel"; // anonymous forever

print("$alias_1 is $name_1<BR>");
print("$alias_2 is $name_2<BR>");
```

gives the browser output:

```
The Red Baron is Manfred von Richtofen
The Scarlet Pimpernel is The Scarlet Pimpernel
```

Variable function names

One of the neater tricks you can do in PHP is to use variables in place of the names of user-defined functions. That is, rather than typing a literal function name into your code, you type a dollar-sign variable — the function that is actually called at runtime will depend on the string that that variable has been assigned to. In some sense, this allows us to use functions as data. This kind of trick will be familiar to advanced C programmers and to even beginning users of any kind of Lisp language (for example, Scheme or Common Lisp).

For example, the following two function calls are exactly equivalent:

```
function customized_greeting ()
{
```

```
   print("You are being greeted in a customized way!<BR>");
}
customized_greeting();
$my_greeting = 'customized_greeting';
$my_greeting();
```

and produce the same output:

```
You are being greeted in a customized way!
You are being greeted in a customized way!
```

Because function names are just strings, they can also be used as arguments to functions or be returned as a function's result.

An extended example

Just for fun, let's see what kinds of trouble we can get into by using some of the more advanced features of functions, including using function names as function arguments.

Listing 8-1 shows an extended example of functions that implement a substitution cipher — a rudimentary kind of cryptography that scrambles messages by substituting one letter of the alphabet for another.

NOTE: This code is both longer and more advanced than anything in the book so far. It is both skippable and skimmable for those who don't want to work through the details.

Listing 8-1: A substitution cipher

```
/* Part 1 - cipher algorithm and utility functions */
function add_1 ($num)
{
  return(($num + 1) % 26);
}

function sub_1 ($num)
{
  return(($num + 25) % 26);
}

function swap_2 ($num)
{
  if ($num % 2 == 0)
    return($num + 1);
  else
    return($num - 1);
}

function swap_26 ($num)
{
```

```
   return(25 - $num);
}

function lower_letter($char_string)
{
 return ((ord($char_string) >= ord('a')) &&
         (ord($char_string) <= ord('z')));
}

function upper_letter($char_string)
{
 return ((ord($char_string) >= ord('A')) &&
         (ord($char_string) <= ord('Z')));
}

/* Part 2 - the letter_cipher function */
function letter_cipher ($char_string, $code_func)
{
  if (!(upper_letter($char_string) ||
       lower_letter($char_string)))
    return($char_string);
  if (upper_letter($char_string))
    $base_num = ord('A');
  else
    $base_num = ord('a');
  $char_num = ord($char_string) -
                 $base_num;
  return(chr($base_num +
             ($code_func($char_num)
              % 26)));
}

/* Part 3 - the main string_cipher function */
function string_cipher($message, $cipher_func)
{
  $coded_message = "";
  $message_length = strlen($message);
  for ($index = 0;
       $index < $message_length;
       $index++)
    $coded_message .=
      letter_cipher($message[$index], $cipher_func);
  return($coded_message);
}
```

Listing 8-1 is in three parts. In the first part, we define a few functions that do simple math on the numbers from 0 through 25, which will represent the letters A–Z in our cipher codes. Function add_1 simply adds 1 to the number it is given, modulo 26 (which just means that numbers that are 26 and larger "wrap around" to start from zero again). 0 becomes 1, 1 becomes 2, . . . and 25 becomes 0. Sub_1 shifts numbers in the other direction, by adding 25 (which in this modular arithmetic is equivalent to subtracting 1) — 25 becomes 24, 24 becomes 23, . . . and 0 becomes 25. Swap_2 trades the places of pairs of numbers (0 to 1, 1 to 0, 2 to 3, 3 to 2, . . .). Swap_26 trades high numbers for low numbers (25 to 0, 0 to 25, 24 to 1, 1 to 24, . . .). Each one of these functions will be the basis of a simple cipher code. Finally, we have a couple of utility functions that test whether a character is an uppercase or lowercase letter.

Part 2 is a single function called letter_cipher(), whose job it is to take a math function, like the ones in Part 1, and apply it to encode a single letter. First, it tests whether the string it is handed (which should be a single character) is an alphabetic letter; if not, it returns it as is. If the character is a letter, it is transformed into a number using ord(), and the appropriate letter (a or A) is subtracted to bring the number into the 0–25 range. When it is in that range, we apply the cipher function whose name was passed in as a string, and then we convert the number back into a letter and return it.

Finally, Part 3 is the single string_cipher() function, which takes a string message and a cipher function and returns a new string that is the message encoded via the function. This code uses a couple of features we haven't seen before (including the string concatenation operator =, which we will cover in Chapter 10). For now, however, it's enough to know that this function builds a new string, letter by letter, from the message string, and that each new letter is the result of applying $cipher_func to the numerical representation of the old letter.

Now let's write some code to try out string_cipher():

```
$original = "My secret message is ABCDEFG";
print("Original message is: $original<BR>");

$coding_array = array('add_1',
                      'sub_1',
                      'swap_2',
                      'swap_26');
for ($count = 0;
     $count < sizeof($coding_array);
     $count++)
{
  $code = $coding_array[$count];
  $coded_message =
    string_cipher($original, $code);
  print("$code encoding is: $coded_message<BR>");
}
```

This testing code takes our four predefined letter-encoding functions, stashes them in an array, and then loops through the array, encoding the $original message and printing out the encoded version. The browser output looks like the following:

```
Original message is: My secret message is ABCDEFG
add_1 encoding is: Nz tfdsfu nfttbhf jt BCDEFGH
sub_1 encoding is: Lx rdbqds ldrrzfd hr ZABCDEF
swap_2 encoding is: Nz tfdqfs nfttbhf jt BADCFEH
swap_26 encoding is: Nb hvxivg nvhhztv rh ZYXWVUT
```

We can take this function-as-data approach one step further and write a function that applies more than one cipher to a message in sequence. This function also uses the variable-argument functions of PHP 4:

```php
function chained_code ($message)
{
  /* takes a message, then an arbitrary number of
     cipher-code function names. Returns
     result of applying each code to the previous
     result. */
  $argc = func_num_args();
  $coded = $message;
  for ($count = 1; $count < $argc; $count++)
    {
      $function_name = func_get_arg($count);
      $coded =
         string_cipher($coded,
                       $function_name);
    }
  return($coded);
}
```

The first argument to `chained_code()` should be a message string, followed by any number of names corresponding to cipher functions. The coded message is the result of applying the first coding function to the message, then applying the second coding function to the result, and so on. We can test it with various combinations of our predefined letter-coding functions, as follows:

```php
$tricky =
  chained_code($original,
              'add_1', 'swap_26',
              'add_1', 'swap_2');
print("Tricky encoded version is $tricky<BR>");

$easy =
  chained_code($original,
              'add_1', 'swap_26',
              'swap_2', 'sub_1',
              'add_1', 'swap_2',
              'swap_26', 'sub_1');
print("Easy encoded version is $easy<BR>");
```

with these results:

```
Tricky encoded version is Ma guwjuh muggysu qg YZWXUVS
Easy encoded version is My secret message is ABCDEFG
```

As you can see, the "tricky" encoding of our message is a combination of our previous codes that doesn't correspond exactly to any of those single coding functions. And the "easy" coding is an even more complicated combination of those functions that produces . . . our original message unchanged! (No, it's not that our cipher code doesn't work — we'll leave it to you to figure out why that particular sequence of coding functions brings us around to our starting message again.)

The moral of our little cryptographic scripting story is that, although the cipher code was mildly complicated, it was made considerably simpler by PHP's support for using function names as function arguments.

Summary

Most of the power of PHP resides in the large number of built-in functions provided by PHP's benevolent army of open-source developers. Each of these functions should be documented (albeit briefly) in the online manual at `http://www.php.net`.

You can also write your own functions, which are then used in exactly the same way as the built-in functions. Functions are written in a simple C-style syntax, as in the following:

```
function my_function ($arg1, $arg2, ..)
{
statement1;
statement2;
..
return($value);
}
```

User-defined functions can use arguments of any PHP type and can also return values of any type. The types of arguments and return value do not need to be declared.

In PHP 4, the ordering of function definitions and function calls makes no difference, as long as every function that is called is defined exactly once. There is no need for separate function declarations or prototypes. Variables assigned inside a function are local to that function, unless specified otherwise with the `global` declaration. Local variables may be declared to be *static,* which means that they hold onto their values in between function calls.

The default behavior for user-defined functions is *call-by-value*, meaning that functions work on copies of their arguments and so cannot modify the original variables in the function call. You can force *call-by-reference* behavior by preceding parameters with &, on either the definition side or the calling side. PHP offers more than one way to let functions take a variable number of arguments. Finally, the functions to be called can be determined at runtime, by substituting a string variable for the literal name of the user-defined function — this allows functions to be treated as data and passed back and forth between other functions.

## Chapter 9

Passing Information Between Pages

In This Chapter

♦ Why HTTP is like a rolling stone

♦ GET arguments

♦ A better use for GET-style URLs

♦ POST arguments

♦ Formatting form variables

♦ PHP superarrays

♦ Extended example: an exercise calculator

In this chapter, we'll briefly discuss some things you need to know about passing data between Web pages. Some of this information is not specific to PHP but is a consequence of the PHP/HTML interaction or of the HTTP protocol itself.

HTTP Is Stateless

The most important thing to recall about the way the Web works is that the HTTP protocol itself is stateless. If you were a poetic soul, you might say that each HTTP request is on its own with no direction home, like a complete unknown . . . you know how the rest goes.

For the less lyrical among us, this means that each HTTP request — in most cases, this translates to each HTML screen being asked for and delivered — is independent of all the others, knows nothing substantive about the identity of the client, and has no memory. Each request spawns a discrete process, which goes about its humble but worthy task of serving up one single solitary file and then is automatically killed off (although that sounds so harsh; maybe we can say "flits back to the pool of available processes" instead?).

Even if you design your site with very strict one-way navigation (Page 1 leads only to Page 2, which leads only to Page 3, and so on), the HTTP protocol will never know or care that someone browsing Page 2 must have come from Page 1. You cannot set the value of a variable on Page 1 and expect it to be imported to Page 2 by the exigencies of HTML itself. You can use HTML to display a form, and someone can enter some information using it — but unless you employ some extra means to pass the information to another page or program, the variable will simply vanish into the ether as soon as you move to another page.

This is where a form handling technology like PHP comes in. PHP will catch the variable tossed from one page to the next and make it available for further use. PHP happens to be unusually good at this type of data-passing function, which makes it fast and easy to employ for a wide variety of Web site tasks.

HTML forms are mostly useful for passing a few values from a given page to one single other page of a Web site. There are more persistent ways to maintain state over many pageviews, such as cookies and sessions, which we cover in Chapter 27. This chapter will focus on the most basic techniques of information-passing between Web pages, which utilize the GET and POST methods in HTTP to create dynamically-generated pages and to handle form data.

> **NOTE:** This is where old-school ASP developers invariably say, "PHP sucks!" because they think ASP session variables are magic. Not to burst anyone's bubble, but Microsoft is just using cookies to store session variables — thereby opening the door to all kinds of potential problems.

GET Arguments

The GET method passes arguments from one page to the next as part of the *Uniform Resource Indicator* (you may be more familiar with the term *Uniform Resource Locator* or *URL*) query string. When used for form handling, GET appends the indicated variable name(s) and value(s) to the URL designated in the ACTION attribute with a question-mark separator and submits the whole thing to the processing agent (in this case a Web server).

This is an example HTML form using the GET method (save the file under the name team_select.html):

```
<HTML>
<HEAD>
<TITLE>A GET method example, part 1</TITLE>
</HEAD>

<BODY>
<FORM ACTION="http://localhost/baseball.php" METHOD="GET">
<P>Root, root, root for the:<BR>
<SELECT NAME="Team" SIZE=2>
<!--It's a good idea to use the VALUE attribute even though it is not
mandatory with the SELECT element. In this example, it's extremely
necessary. -->
<OPTION VALUE="Cubbies">Chicago Cubs (National League)</OPTION>
<OPTION VALUE="Pale Hose">Chicago White Sox (American League)</OPTION>
</SELECT>
<P><INPUT TYPE=submit" NAME=""Submit" VALUE="Select"></P>
</FORM>
```

```
</BODY>

</HTML>
```

When the user makes a selection and clicks the Submit button, the browser agglutinates these elements in this order, with no spaces between the elements:

♦ The URL in quotes after the word ACTION (http://localhost/baseball.php)

♦ A question mark (?) denoting that the following characters constitute a GET string.

♦ A variable NAME, an equal sign, and the matching VALUE (Team=Cubbies)

♦ An ampersand (&) and the next NAME-VALUE pair (Submit=Select); further name-value pairs separated by ampersands can be added as many times as the server query-string-length limit allows.

The browser thus constructs the URL string:

```
http://localhost/baseball.php?Team=Cubbies&Submit=Select
```

It then forwards this URL into its own address space as a new request. The PHP script to which the preceding form is submitted (baseball.php) will grab the GET variables from the end of the request string, and do something useful with them — in this case, plug one of two values into a text string.

The following code sample shows the PHP form handler for the preceding HTML form:

```
<HTML>
<HEAD>
<TITLE>A GET method example, part 2</TITLE>
<STYLE TYPE="text/css">
<!--
BODY  {font-size: 24pt;}
-->
</STYLE>
</HEAD>

<BODY>
<P>Go,
<?php echo $_GET['Team']; ?>
!</P>
</BODY>
</HTML>
```

Finally, you should see a page that says Go, Cubbies! in big type.

The GET method of form handling offers one big advantage over the POST method: It constructs an actual new and differentiable URL query string. Users can now bookmark this page (and thus find the oh-so-necessary encouraging word when their team starts to fade in the doldrums of August). The result of forms using the POST method are not bookmarkable.

However, just because you *can* achieve the desired functionality with GET arguments doesn't mean you should. The disadvantages of GET for most types of form handling are so substantial that the original HTML 4.0 specification deprecated its use. These flaws include:

♦ The GET method is not suitable for logins because the username and password are fully visible onscreen as well as potentially stored in the client browser's memory as a visited page.

♦ Every GET submission is recorded in the Web server log, data set included.

♦ Because the GET method assigns data to a server environment variable, the length of the URL is limited. You may have seen what seem like very long URLs using GET — but you really wouldn't want to try passing a 300-word chunk of HTML-formatted prose using this method.

> **CAUTION:** The original HTML spec called for query strings to be limited to 255 characters. Although this stricture was later loosened to mere "encouragement" of a 255-character limit, using a longer string is asking for trouble.

The GET method of form handling had to be reinstated by the W3C after much outcry, largely because of the bookmarkability factor. However, despite the fact that it's still implemented as the default choice for form handling in all browsers, GET now comes with a strong recommendation to deploy it only in *idempotent* usages — in other words, those that have no permanent side-effects. Putting two and two together, the single most appropriate form-handling use of GET is the search box. Unless you have a compelling reason to use GET for non-search-box form handling, use POST instead.

A Better Use for GET-Style URLs

Although the actual GET method of form handling is deprecated, the style of URL associated with it turns out to be very useful for site navigation. This is especially true for dynamically generated sites such as those often constructed with PHP, because the appended-variable style of URL works particularly smoothly with a template-based content-development system.

As an illustration, imagine you are the proud proprietor of an information-rich Web site about solar cars. You've toiled long and hard over informative and attractive pages such as these:

```
suspension_design.html
windtunnel_testing.html
friction_braking.html
```

But as your site grows, a flat-file site structure like this can take a lot of time to administer, as even the most trivial changes must be repeated on every page. If the structure of these pages is very similar, you might want to move to a template-based system with PHP.

You might decide to utilize a single template with separate text files for each topic (containing information, photos, comments, and so on):

```
topic.php
  suspension_design.inc
  windtunnel_testing.inc
  friction_braking.inc
```

Or you might decide you needed a larger, more specialized choice of template files:

```
vehicle_structure.php
  tubular_frames.inc
mechanical_systems.php
  friction_braking.inc
electrical_systems.php
  solar_array.inc
racing.php
  race_strategy.inc
```

A simple template file might look something like this (because we haven't included the necessary .inc text files, this example will not actually work):

```
<HTML>
<HEAD>
<TITLE>Solar-car topics</TITLE>
<STYLE TYPE="text/css"">
<!--
BODY  {font: verdana; font-size: 12pt}
-->
</STYLE>
</HEAD>

<BODY>
<TABLE BORDER=0 CELLPADDING=0 WIDTH=100%>
<TR>
<!-- Navbar, with Get-style URLs. -->
<TD BGCOLOR="#4282B4" ALIGN=CENTER VALIGN=TOP WIDTH=25%>
  <P>
  <A HREF="mechanical_systems.php?Name=friction_braking"><B>Friction
braking</B></A>
  <BR>
  <A HREF="mechanical_systems.php?Name=steering"><B>Steering</B></A>
  <BR>
  <A HREF="mechanical_systems.php?Name=suspension"><B>Suspension</B></A>
  <BR>
  <A HREF="mechanical_systems.php?Name=tires"><B>Tires and
wheels</B></A>
  <BR>
  </P>
</TD>
```

```
<!-- Main body of content -->
<TD BGCOLOR="#FFFFFF" ALIGN=LEFT VALIGN=TOP WIDTH=75%>
<?php include("$_GET['Name'].inc"); ?>
</TD></TR></TABLE>
</BODY>
</HTML>
```

Notice that the links on the navbar, when clicked, will be handled by the browser as if they were the product of a GET submission.

But even with this solution, you still have to tend part of your garden by hand: making sure each include file is properly formatted in HTML, adding a new link to the navbar each time you add a new page to the site, and other such chores. Following the general rule to separate form and content as much as is feasible, you might choose to go to another level of abstraction with a database. In that case, a URL such as:

```
http://localhost/topic.php?topicID=2
```

would point to a PHP template that makes database calls. (Using a number variable rather than a word makes for faster database interaction.) This system could also automatically add a link to the navbar whenever you added new topics to the database, and so it could produce Web pages entirely without ongoing human intervention (all right, maybe "entirely" is an exaggeration – but with many fewer person-hours of grunt labor).

POST Arguments

POST is the preferred method of form submission today, particularly in *non-idempotent* usages (those which will result in permanent changes), such as adding information to a database. The form data set is included in the body of the form when it is forwarded to the processing agent (in this case PHP). No visible change to the URL will result according to the different data submitted.

The POST method has these advantages:

♦ It is more secure than GET because user-entered information is never visible in the URL query string, in the server logs, or (if precautions, such as always using the password HTML input type for passwords, are taken) onscreen.

♦ There is a much larger limit on the amount of data that can be passed (a couple of kilobytes rather than a couple of hundred characters).

However, POST has these disadvantages:

♦ The results at a given moment cannot be bookmarked.

♦ This method can be incompatible with certain firewall setups, which strip the form data as a security measure.

We use the POST method consistently in this book for form handling — especially when putting data into a system via a file write or SQL INSERT. We use GET only for site navigation and Search boxes — in other words, for pulling data back out of a data store and displaying it. All the rest of the forms in this chapter use the POST method.

GET AND POST BOTH

Did you know that with PHP you can use both GET and POST variables on the same page? You might want to do this for a dynamically generated form, for example.

But what if you (deliberately or otherwise) use the same variable name in both the GET and the POST variable sets? PHP keeps all ENVIRONMENT, GET, POST, COOKIE, and SERVER variables in the $GLOBALS array if you have set the register_globals configuration directive to "on" in your php.ini file. If there is a conflict, it is resolved by overwriting the variable values in the order you set, using the variables_order option in php.ini. Later trumps earlier, so if you use the default "EGPCS" value, cookies will triumph over posts that will themselves obliterate GETs. You can control the order of overwriting by simply changing the order of the letters on the appropriate line of this file, or even better turning register_globals off and using the new PHP superglobal arrays instead. See the section on Superglobals below.

Formatting Form Variables

PHP is so efficient at passing data around because the developers made a very handy but (in theory) slightly sketchy design decision. PHP automatically, but invisibly, assigns the variables for you on the new page when you submit a data set using GET or POST. Most of PHP's competitors make you explicitly do this assignment yourself on each page; if you forget to do so or make a mistake, the information will not be available to the processing agent. PHP is faster, simpler, and mostly more goof-proof.

But because of this automatic variable assignment, you need to always use a good NAME attribute for each INPUT. NAME attributes are not strictly necessary in HTML proper – your form will render fine without them – but the data will be of little use because the HTML form-field NAME attribute will be the variable name in the form handler.

In other words, in this form:

```
<FORM ACTION="<?php echo $_SERVER['PHP_SELF']; ?>" METHOD="POST">
<INPUT TYPE="text" NAME="email">
<INPUT TYPE="submit" NAME="submit" VALUE="Send">
</FORM>
```

the text field named email will cause the creation of a PHP variable called $_POST['email'] (or $HTTP_POST_VARS['email'] if you use the older style of variable arrays; or just $email if you have register_globals turned on) when the form is submitted. Similarly, the Submit button will lead to the creation of a variable called $_POST['submit'] on the next page. The name you use in the HTML form will be the name of your variable in the PHP form handler.

Remember that you cannot use a variable name beginning with a number — so you should not name your form field something like 5 (you laugh, but we've seen people try to do it) — and PHP variable names are case sensitive. Also, *please* try to use informative variable names rather than a succession of form fields named myvar and e.

Another thing to keep in mind when creating your HTML forms is that, if you ever want this form to be displayed with prefilled inputs, you need to set the VALUE attribute. This is particularly relevant to two kinds of forms: those that are used to edit data from a database; and those that are intended to possibly be submitted more than once. The latter case is very common in situations where a form should redisplay on error with values already prefilled — for instance, a registration form that will not work until the user provides a valid email address or other required data.

For example, the following form (which represents a retirement savings calculator) is designed to be submitted multiple times while the user fiddles around with the values. Every time you submit the form, the values from the previous go-round will be filled in for you automatically. Note the use of the VALUE attribute in the form fields in this code sample:

```
<HTML>
<HEAD>
<TITLE>A POST example: retirement savings worksheet</TITLE>
<STYLE TYPE="text/css">
<!--
BODY      {font-size: 14pt}
.heading    {font-size: 18pt; color: red}
-->
</STYLE>
</HEAD>

<?php
// This test, along with the Submit button value in the form below,
// will check to see if the form is being rendered for the first time
// (in which case it will display with only the default annual gain
// filled in)

if (!IsSet($_POST['Submit']) || $_POST['Submit'] != 'Calculate') {
  $_POST['CurrentAge'] = "";
  $_POST['RetireAge'] = "";
  $_POST['Contrib'] = "";
  $Total = 0;
  $AnnGain = 7;
} else {
  $AnnGain = $_POST['AnnGain'];
  $Years = $_POST['RetireAge'] - $_POST['CurrentAge'];
  $YearCount = 0;
  $Total = $_POST['Contrib'];

  while ($YearCount <= $Years) {
```

```
    $Total = round($Total * (1.0 + $AnnGain/100) + $_POST['Contrib']);
    $YearCount = $YearCount + 1;
  }
}
?>
<BODY>

<DIV ALIGN=CENTER ID=Div1 class=heading>A retirement-savings
calculator</DIV>

<P class=blurb>Fill in all the values (except "Nest Egg") and see how
much money you'll have for your retirement under different scenarios.
You can change the values and resubmit the form as many times as you
like. You must fill in the two "Age" variables. The "Annual return"
variable has a default inflation-adjusted value (7% = 8% growth minus 1%
inflation) which you can change to reflect your greater optimism or
pessimism.</P>

<FORM ACTION="<?php echo $_SERVER['PHP_SELF']; ?>" METHOD="POST">
<P>Your age now:  <INPUT TYPE="text" SIZE=5 NAME="CurrentAge"
VALUE="<?php echo $_POST['CurrentAge']; ?>">
<P>The age at which you plan to retire:  <INPUT TYPE="text" SIZE=6
NAME="RetireAge" VALUE="<?php echo $_POST['RetireAge']; ?>">
<P>Annual contribution:  <INPUT TYPE="text" SIZE=15 NAME="Contrib"
VALUE="<?php echo $_POST['Contrib']; ?>">
<P>Annual return:  <INPUT TYPE="text" SIZE=5 NAME="AnnGain" VALUE="<?php
echo $AnnGain; ?>"> %
<BR><BR>
<P><B>NEST EGG</B>:  <?php echo $Total; ?>
<P><INPUT TYPE="submit" NAME="Submit" VALUE="Calculate">
</FORM>
</BODY>
</HTML>
```

Figure 9-1 shows the result of the preceding code.

Consolidating forms and form handlers

As you can see in the example above, often it is handy to make the HTML form and the form handler into one script. This practice has many advantages, such as making it easier to change the name of the file without harming functionality; making it easier to display error messages and prefilled form fields; and achieving better control over your variable namespace. For example, you are making a login form that redisplays with an error message if the login is unsuccessful. If you have separate forms and form handlers, you'll probably have to do something yucky with GET vars and redirection. If you consolidate, it's very simple to control the display without these machinations. See Chapter 38 for an example of this very usage in a login form.

Figure 9-1: A form using the `POST` method with `VALUE` attributes

When you consolidate, generally the form-handling code should come before the form display. This order may be something of a shift in thinking for those who are used to writing the form before the handler, but if you think it through, you will see the logic of the practice. You have to give yourself an opportunity to set variables and make choices before you can decide what to show the user. This is especially relevant if you will be redirecting the user to a different page under certain circumstances, via the `header()` function, because this decision point must come before any HTML output has been displayed to the browser.

Generally there are two ways you can check to see whether you're displaying a form for the first time or whether it's already been submitted at least once. Either you can use the `Submit` button, as we do in the example above; or you can set a hidden variable if you tend to have all your `Submit` buttons say the same thing (like "Submit"). The latter method is safer, because some browsers don't actually submit the `Submit` value if a user hits `Enter` instead of clicking the button.

Using array variables with forms

In all the examples so far, each form field created a variable of the string or integer types. This implies that there is a one-to-one relationship between a form field and a form-handler variable. But PHP also allows you to post an array-type variable. (If you don't yet have a good grip on arrays, come back to this section after you read Chapter 11).

This is an example of a script that creates an array from the names of the form fields in an HTML form:

```php
<?php

/**********************************************************
 * "How geeky are you?" script, showing with screens. *
 * Screen 1: : quiz form.   Screen 2: results page.    *
 **********************************************************/

// The header which appears in both cases
// -------------------------------------------
$header_str = <<< EOHEADER
<HTML>
<HEAD>
<STYLE TYPE="text/css">
<!--
BODY, P, TD      {color: black; font-family: verdana; font-size: 9 pt}
H1          {color: black; font-family: arial; font-size: 12 pt}
-->
</STYLE>
</HEAD>

<BODY>
<TABLE BORDER=0 CELLPADDING=10 WIDTH=100%>
<TR>
<TD BGCOLOR="#F0F8FF" ALIGN=CENTER VALIGN=TOP WIDTH=150>
</TD>

<TD BGCOLOR="#FFFFFF" ALIGN=LEFT VALIGN=TOP WIDTH=83%>
  <table cellspacing=0 cellpadding=20 border=0 width="530"><tr><td
valign=top>
EOHEADER;


// The footer which appears in both cases
// -------------------------------------------
$footer_str = <<< EOFOOTER
  </td></tr></table>
</TD></TR></TABLE>

</BODY>
</HTML>
EOFOOTER;


// Screen 1: quiz form
// --------------------
$quiz_str = <<< EOQUIZ
```

```
<h2>How geeky are you?</h2>
<form action="geek_quiz.php" method="POST">
<br /><br />
0.  Have you ever had a dream in which you were debugging?<br />
Yes <input type="checkbox" name="affirm[0]" value="1"/>
<br /><br />
1.  Do you know the name of the company founded by Danny Hillis?<br />
Yes <input type="checkbox" name="affirm[1]" value="1"/>
<br /><br />
2.  Can you edit a file in both emacs and vi without recourse to any
documentation?<br />
Yes <input type="checkbox" name="affirm[2]" value="1"/>
<br /><br />
3.  Is the computer you're using at this moment hooked up to a KVM
switch?<br />
Yes <input type="checkbox" name="affirm[3]" value="1"/>
<br /><br />
4.  Are you wearing a logowear T-shirt?<br />
Yes <input type="checkbox" name="affirm[4]" value="1"/>
<br /><br />
5.  Have you ever written a chess program?<br />
Yes <input type="checkbox" name="affirm[5]" value="1"/>
<br /><br />
6.  Have you ever set up an SMTP server?<br />
Yes <input type="checkbox" name="affirm[6]" value="1"/>
<br /><br />
7.  Have you ever discussed the merits of a commercial LISP
implementation?<br />
Yes <input type="checkbox" name="affirm[7]" value="1"/>
<br /><br />
8.  Have you ever used the phrase "I can do that in two lines of code"
in public?<br />
Yes <input type="checkbox" name="affirm[8]" value="1"/>
<br /><br />
9.  Have you ever refused an otherwise welcome sexual advance because
you were debugging?<br />
Yes <input type="checkbox" name="affirm[9]" value="1"/>
<br /><br />
<input type="submit" name="submit" value="Evaluate"></form>
EOQUIZ;


// ------------------
// Now for some logic
// ------------------
echo $header_str;
if (!isSet($_POST['submit'])) {
  // First time, show the quiz form
  echo $quiz_str;
```

```
} elseif ($_POST['submit'] == 'Evaluate') {

  // Count up the yes answers
  $num_affirm = count($_POST['affirm']);

  // Come up with a 4 different blurbs
  if ($num_affirm >= 0 && $num_affirm <= 3) {
    $result_str = "<P>Why even pretend to be something you're so clearly
not?</P>\n";
  } elseif ($num_affirm >= 4 && $num_affirm <= 6) {
    $result_str = "<P>Come back when you've learned more craft,
Grasshopper.</P>\n";
  } elseif ($num_affirm >= 7 && $num_affirm <= 8) {
    $result_str = "<P>Pretty geeky, but not yet a Code God.</P>\n";
  } elseif ($num_affirm >= 9 && $num_affirm <= 10) {
    $result_str = "<P>We're not worthy to be in the presence of your bad
geeky self!</P>\n";
  }

  echo $result_str;
}
echo $footer_str;
?>
```

Figure 9-2 illustrates the output of the preceding code.

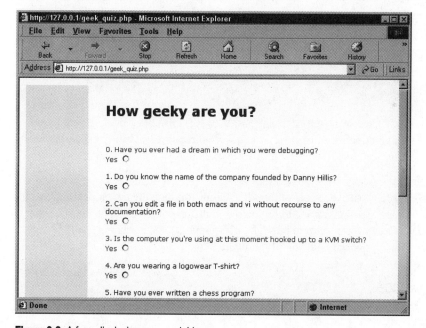

Figure 9-2: A form displaying array variables

Because, ultimately, we just want to count how many Yes answers there are, it would be cumbersome to set each check box as a separate variable and then count them. As you can see in the preceding code(line 93), with an array it is a simple matter of calling the count() function. In many other situations, it takes much less code to loop through an array than to separately test a bunch of strings.

As you can see in the form HTML, the way you create an array variable with an HTML form is by using a name with a bracket after it. This can be an empty bracket, a bracket with an integer inside like the one we used above, or a bracket with a string inside. When you understand arrays better and have an idea of what you want an array to do for you, it will be clearer which of these alternatives you need in any given instance.

PHP Superglobal Arrays

A change that has been coming for a long time in PHP 4 is the gradual phasing out of automatic global variables in favor of the new *superglobal* arrays. Understanding superglobal arrays before you understand arrays may present difficulties; if so, we recommend you read Chapter 11 and come back to this section later.

In the good old days before PHP 4.1, you could write a piece of code like this and expect it to work:

```php
<?php
if (isSet($submit)) {
  echo $email;
} else {
?>
<FORM ACTION="<?php echo $PHP_SELF; ?>" METHOD="POST">
<INPUT TYPE="text" NAME="email">
<INPUT TYPE="submit" NAME="submit" VALUE="Send">
</FORM>
```

All GET, POST, COOKIE, ENVIRONMENT, and SERVER variables were made global by the register_globals directive in php.ini, and were directly accessible by their names by default.

This was bad for several reasons. For one thing, every so often a COOKIE variable would accidentally overwrite a POST variable of the same name although the developer didn't want that to happen. For another thing, it led to big messy undifferentiated global namespaces. And most importantly, allowing variables to be set by user input is very insecure. The PHP world had far too many inexperienced coders writing things like:

```php
<?php
if ($secretpassword == 'opensesame') {
  $allaccesspass = 1;
}
```

```
if ($allaccesspass == 1) {
  include('/admin_index.html');
} else {
  include('/doweknowyou.html');
}
?>
```

without giving too much thought to the idea that a cracker could easily just call this page with a GET variable named allaccesspass set to 1 – and negate the advantages of any password check.

The PHP team, in its infinite wisdom, decided to phase out the practice of registering globals, and force everyone to call his variables as indices in an array (for example, $_POST['secretpassword']). This had already been possible in PHP 4, via arrays named $HTTP_GET_VARS, $HTTP_POST_VARS, $HTTP_POST_VARS, and so on; but few developers had used this syntax because frankly it was a lot of extra keystrokes for a small increase in security. So the PHP team is also taking this opportunity to rename these arrays with shorter names: $_GET, $_POST, $_COOKIE, $_ENV, and $_SERVER.

These superglobal arrays also have one cool feature which may ameliorate some pain: They are automatically global everywhere. This means, for instance, you no longer have to pass cookie values into a function or declare the $HTTP_COOKIE_VARS array global before you can access those values in a function. This will help those who functionalize to the max, and will be a small amelioration for everyone else.

As of PHP 4.2, register_globals is officially turned off by default, and the old-style variable array names are deprecated. It will take quite a while to move the entire PHP community over to the new superglobal arrays, but we feel obligated to try to use them as much as possible in this book to set a good example.

Extended example: an exercise calculator

Chapters 9 through 13 of this book feature an extended example that will build on itself from chapter to chapter. Starting with a simple HTML form and form handler, you will add concepts as you move through string, array, math, and filesystem functions. At the end, you will have built a simple exercise calculator system that allows you to figure out how many calories were burned by your daily workouts and to store this information in a file.

In this first episode, we are simply going to move a string POST variable from a form to a form handler using PHP. This HTML form is called workout_calc_var.html:

```
<HTML>
<HEAD>
<STYLE TYPE="text/css">
<!--
BODY, P     {color: black; font-family: verdana; font-size: 10 pt}
H1          {color: black; font-family: arial; font-size: 12 pt}
```

```
-->
</STYLE>
</HEAD>

<BODY>
<TABLE BORDER=0 CELLPADDING=10 WIDTH=100%>
<TR>
<TD BGCOLOR="#F0F8FF" ALIGN=CENTER VALIGN=TOP WIDTH=150>
</TD>
<TD BGCOLOR="#FFFFFF" ALIGN=LEFT VALIGN=TOP WIDTH=83%>
<H1>Workout calculator (passing a variable)</H1>
<P>Enter an exercise, and we'll tell you how long you'd have to do
it<BR>to burn one pound of fat.</P>
<FORM METHOD="post" ACTION="wc_handler_var.php">
<INPUT TYPE="text" SIZE=50 NAME="exercise">
<BR><BR>
<INPUT TYPE="submit" NAME="submit" VALUE="Burn, baby, burn!">
</FORM>
</TD>
</TR>
</TABLE>

</BODY>
</HTML>
```

Figure 9-3 represents the output of the preceding HTML.

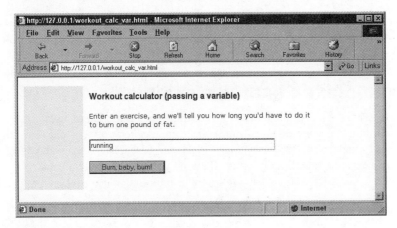

Figure 9-3: A simple form passing a string variable

The matching form handler is called wc_handler_var.php:

```
<?php
$exercise = $_POST['exercise'];
?>
```

```
<HTML>
<HEAD>
<STYLE TYPE="text/css">
<!--
BODY, P      {color: black; font-family: verdana; font-size: 10 pt}
H1           {color: black; font-family: arial; font-size: 12 pt}
-->
</STYLE>
</HEAD>

<BODY>
<TABLE BORDER=0 CELLPADDING=10 WIDTH=100%>
<TR>
<TD BGCOLOR="#F0F8FF" ALIGN=CENTER VALIGN=TOP WIDTH=150>
</TD>
<TD BGCOLOR="#FFFFFF" ALIGN=LEFT VALIGN=TOP WIDTH=83%>
<H1>Workout calculator handler, part 1</H1>
<P>We've successfully passed the contents of the text input field,<BR>
as a variable called "exercise" with a value of <B><?php echo $exercise;
?></B>.<BR>
But before we can do anything interesting with it, we need to learn
about strings.</P>
</TD>
</TR>
</TABLE>

</BODY>
</HTML>
```

Figure 9-4 represents the output of `wc_handler_var.php` on success.

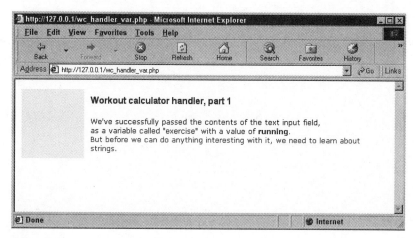

Figure 9-4: Data successfully passed from one page to another

In the next chapter (Chapter 10), we will learn to take this string input and do interesting things with it.

Summary

The HTTP protocol is stateless. This means a plain HTML page is incapable of receiving information from any other page. It can be used to pass values via a URL or an HTML form, but a separate program called a *form handler* must step in to recognize and perform actions on the passed values. In first-generation Web development, these form handlers were Perl or C CGI scripts; but nowadays Web developers are more likely to use an HTML-embedded programming language like PHP. PHP makes it particularly easy to write form handlers and even to combine them with HTML display on a single Web page.

Information is passed between Web pages using one of four main methods: GET, POST, a cookie, or sessions. GET is mainly used to construct complex URL strings for use with dynamically generated pages. It is deprecated for use with most HTML forms. POST is the method recommended for most forms. Forms are the main way to pass information from one Web page to a single other Web page. We deal with the persistent state methods, cookies and sessions, in Chapter 27.

Chapter 10

Strings and String Functions

In This Chapter

♦ Creating and manipulating strings

♦ Inspecting, comparing, and searching strings

♦ Advanced string functions

Although images, sound files, videos, animations, and applets make up an important portion of the World Wide Web, much of the Web is still text — one character's worth after another, like this sentence. The basic PHP datatype for representing text is the *string*.

In this chapter, we cover almost all PHP's capabilities for manipulating strings (although we leave the pattern-matching power of regular expressions for separate treatment in Chapter 30). We start with the basics of strings, move to the most commonly used operators and functions, and move towards increasingly specialized and rarely used capabilities (which you may want to skip or skim until you encounter a situation that calls for one of them). Finally, at the end, we return to basics by continuing the "exercise calculator" example from Chapter 9.

Strings in PHP

Strings are sequences of characters that can be treated as a unit — assigned to variables, given as input to functions, returned from functions, or sent as output to appear on your user's Web page. The simplest way to specify a string in PHP code is to enclose it in quotes, whether single quotes (') or double quotes ("), like this:

```
$my_string = 'A literal string';
$another_string = "Another string";
```

The difference between single and double quotes lies in how much interpretation PHP does of the characters between the quote signs before creating the string itself. If you enclose a string in single quotes, almost no interpretation will be performed; if you enclose it in double quotes, PHP will splice in the values of any variables you include, as well as make substitutions for certain special character sequences that begin with the backslash (\) character. For example, if you evaluate the following code in the middle of a Web page:

```
$statement = 'everything I say';
$question_1 =
```

```
  "Do you have to take $statement so literally?\n<BR>";
$question_2 =
  'Do you have to take $statement so literally?\n<BR>';
echo $question_1;
echo $question_2;
```

you should expect to see the browser output:

```
Do you have to take everything I say so literally?
Do you have to take $statement so literally?\n
```

> **CROSS-REFERENCE:** For the details on exactly how PHP interprets both singly and doubly quoted strings, see the "Strings" section of Chapter 6.

Interpolation with curly braces

In most situations, you can simply include a variable in a doubly quoted string, and the variable's value will be spliced into the string when it is interpreted. There are two situations where the string parser might very reasonably get confused and need more guidance from you. The first situation is when your notion of where the variable name should stop is not the same as the parser's, and the other occurs when the expression you want to have interpolated is not a simple variable. In these cases, you can clear things up by enclosing the value you want interpolated in curly braces: { }.

For example, PHP has no difficulty with the following code:

```
$sport = 'volleyball';
$plan = "I will play $sport in the summertime";
```

The parser in this case encounters the $ symbol, and then begins collecting characters for a variable name until it runs into the space after $sport. Spaces cannot be part of a variable name, so it is clear that the variable in question is $sport, and PHP successfully finds a value for that variable ('volleyball'), and splices the value in.

Sometimes, though, it is not convenient to stop a variable name with a space. Take this example.

```
$sport1 = 'volley';
$sport2 = 'foot';
$sport3 = 'basket';
$plan1 = "I will play $sport1ball in the summertime";  //wrong
$plan2 = "I will play $sport2ball in the fall";  //wrong
$plan3 = "I will play $sport3ball in the winter";  //wrong
```

You will not get the desired effect here, because PHP interprets $sport1 as being part of the variable name $sport1ball, which is probably unbound. Instead, you need something like:

```
$plan1 = "I will play {$sport1}ball in the summertime"; //right
```

which asks PHP to evaluate only the variable expression within the braces before interpolating.

For similar reasons, PHP has difficulty interpolating complex variable expressions, like multidimensional arrays and object variables, unless curly braces are used. The general rule is that if you have a { which is immediately followed by a $, then PHP will evaluate the variable expression up until the closing }, and interpolate the resulting value into the string. (If for some reason you need a literal {$ to appear in your string, you can accomplish it by escaping either character with a backslash (\).)

Characters and string indexes

Unlike some programming languages, PHP has no distinct character type that is different from the string type. In general, functions that would take character arguments in other languages expect strings of length 1 in PHP.

You can retrieve the individual characters of a string by including the number of the character, starting at 0, enclosed in curly braces immediately following a string variable. These characters will actually be one-character strings. For example, the following code:

```
$my_string = "Doubled";
for ($index = 0; $index < 7; $index++) {
  $string_to_print = $my_string{$index};
  print("$string_to_print$string_to_print");
}
```

gives the browser output:

```
DDoouubbolleedd
```

with each character of the string being printed twice per loop. (The number 7 is hard-coded in this example only because we haven't yet covered how to find out the length of a string — see the function `strlen()` in the later section "Inspecting strings.")

> **NEW FEATURE:** In the first edition of this book, our examples for retrieving individual characters used square brackets rather than curly braces (for example, `$my_string[3]` rather than `$my_string{3}`). While you can still use the square (array-like) brackets to do this, this usage is is now deprecated, and the curly brace syntax is preferred.

String operators

PHP offers only one real operator on strings: the dot (.) or concatenation operator. This operator, when placed between two string arguments, produces a new string that is the result of putting the two strings together in sequence. For example:

```
$my_two_cents = "I want to give you a piece of my mind";
$third_cent = "And another thing ...";
print($my_two_cents . "..." . $third_cent);
```

gives the browser output:

```
I want to give you a piece of my mind ... And another thing
```

Note that we are not passing multiple string arguments to the print statement — we are handing it one string argument, which was created by concatenating three strings together. The first and third strings are variables, but the middle one is a literal string enclosed in double quotes.

> **NOTE:** Note that the concatenation operator is not + as in Java, and it does not overload anything else. If you forget this and add strings using +, they will be interpreted as numbers, with the result that 'one' + 'two' equals 0 (because no successful string-to-number conversion can be made).

Concatenation and assignment

Just as with arithmetic operators, PHP has a shorthand operator (. =) that combines concatenation with assignment. The following statement:

```
$my_string_var .= $new_addition;
```

is exactly equivalent to:

```
$my_string_var = $my_string_var . $new_addition;
```

Note that, unlike commutative addition and multiplication, with this shorthand operator it matters that the new string is added to the right. If you want the new string tacked on to the left, there's no alternative shorter than:

```
$my_string_var = $new_addition . $my_string_var;
```

The heredoc syntax

In addition to the single-quote and double-quote syntaxes, PHP offers another way to specify a string, called the *heredoc syntax*. This syntax turns out to be extremely useful for specifying large chunks of variable-interpolated text, because it spares you from the need to escape internal quotes. It is especially useful in creating pages that contain HTML forms.

The operator in the heredoc syntax is <<<. What is expected immediately after this is a label (unquoted) that indicates the beginning of a multiline string. PHP will continue including subsequent lines into this string until it sees the same label again, beginning a line. The ending label may optionally be followed by a semicolon, but by nothing else.

An example:

```
$my_string_var = <<<EOT
Everything in this rather unnecessarily wordy
ramble of prose will be incorporated into the
string that we are building up inevitably, inexorably,
character by character, line by line, until we reach that
```

```
blessed final line which is this one.
EOT;
```

It is important to note that the final EOT above must *not* be indented at all — otherwise it will be taken to be just more text to be included. The label need not be literally `EOT` — it can be whatever you like within the normal rules for variable names in PHP.

Interpolation of variables happens exactly the same way as with double-quoted strings. The nice thing about heredoc, though, is that quote signs can be included without any escaping and without prematurely terminating the string. Another example:

```
echo <<<ENDOFFORM
<FORM METHOD=POST ACTION="{$_ENV['PHP_SELF']}">
<INPUT TYPE=TEXT NAME=FIRSTNAME VALUE=$firstname>
<INPUT TYPE=SUBMIT NAME=SUBMIT VALUE=SUBMIT>
</FORM>
ENDOFFORM;
```

This has the effect of echoing a very simple form to the browser.

String Functions

PHP gives you a huge variety of functions for the munching and crunching of strings. If you're ever tempted to roll your own function that reads strings character-by-character to produce a new string, pause for a moment to think whether the task might be common. If so, there is probably a built-in function that handles it.

In this section, we present the basic functions for inspecting, comparing, modifying, and printing strings. If you want to be really comfortable with string manipulation in PHP, you should probably have at least a passing acquaintance with everything in this section.

> **NOTE:** A note for C programmers. Many of the PHP string function names should be familiar to you. Just keep in mind that, because PHP takes care of memory management for you, the functions that return strings are allocating the string storage on their own and do not need to be given a preallocated string to write into.

Inspecting strings

What kinds of questions can you ask strings? First on the list is how long the string is, using the `strlen()` function (the name is short for *string length*).

```
$short_string = "This string has 29 characters";
print("It does have " . strlen($short_string) .
        " characters");
```

This code gives the following output:

```
It does have 29 characters
```

Knowing the string's length is particularly useful for situations in which we'd like to loop through a string character by character. A useless but illustrative example, using the preceding example string, is:

```
for ($index = 0; $index < strlen($short_string); $index++)
  print($short_string{$index});
```

This simply prints:

```
This string has 29 characters
```

which is the string we started with.

Finding characters and substrings

The next category of question you can ask your strings is what they contain. For example, the `strpos()` function finds the numerical position of a particular character in a string, if it exists.

```
$twister = "Peter Piper picked a peck of pickled peppers";
print("Location of 'p' is " . strpos($twister, 'p') .'<BR>');
print("Location of 'q' is " . strpos($twister, 'q') .'<BR>');
```

gives us the browser output:

```
Location of 'p' is 8
Location of 'q' is
```

The reason that the `'q'` location is apparently blank is that `strpos()` returns false if the character in question cannot be found, and a false value prints as the empty string.

> **CAUTION:** The `strpos()` function is one of those cases where PHP's type-looseness can be problematic. If no match can be found, the function returns a false value; if the very first character is a match, the function returns 0 (because the indexing count starts with 0 rather than 1). Both of these values look false if used in a Boolean test. One way to distinguish them is to use the identity comparison operator (`===`, introduced as of PHP 4), which is only true if its arguments are the same and of the same type — you can use it to test if the returned value is 0 (or is FALSE) without risk of confusion with other values that might be the same after type coercion. If you are using PHP 3, you need to do explicit type testing with, for example, `is_integer()`.

The `strpos()` function can also be used to search for a substring rather than a single character, simply by giving it a multicharacter string rather than a single-character string. You can also supply an extra integer argument specifying the position to begin searching forward from.

Searching in reverse is also possible, using the `strrpos()` function (Note the extra r, which you can think of as standing for *reverse*). This function takes a string to search and a single-character string to locate, and it returns the last position of occurrence of the second argument in the first argument. (Unlike with strpos(), the string that is searched for must only have one character.) If we use this function on our example sentence, we find a different position:

```
$twister = "Peter Piper picked a peck of pickled peppers";
printf("Location of 'p' is " . strrpos($twister, 'p') .'<BR>');
```

Specifically, we find the third p in peppers:

```
Location of 'p' is 40
```

ARE STRINGS IMMUTABLE?

In some programming languages (like C), it is common to manipulate strings by directly changing them — that is, storing new characters into the middle of an existing string, replacing old characters. Other languages (like Java) try to keep the programmer out of certain kinds of trouble by making string classes that are *immutable* (or unchangeable) — you can make new strings by creating modified copies of old ones, but once you have made a string, you are not allowed to change it by directly changing the characters that make it up.

Where does PHP fit in? As it turns out, PHP strings can be changed, but the most common practice seems to be to treat strings as immutable.

Strings can be changed by treating them as character arrays and assigning directly into them, like this:

```
$my_string = "abcdefg";
```

```
$my_string[5] = "X";
```

```
print($my_string . "<BR>");
```

which will give the browser output:

```
abcdeXg
```

However, this modification method seems to be undocumented and shows up nowhere in the online manual, even though the corresponding extraction method (now updated to use curly braces) is highlighted. Also, almost all PHP string-manipulation functions return modified copies of their string arguments rather than making direct changes, which seems to indicate that this is the style that the PHP designers prefer. Our advice is not to use this direct-modification method to change strings, unless you know what you are doing and there is some large benefit in terms of memory savings.

Comparison and searching

Is this string the same as that string? It's a question that your code is likely to have to answer frequently, especially when dealing with input typed by the end user.

> **NOTE:** For the == operator, two strings are the same if they contain exactly the same sequence of characters. It does not test any stricter notion of being the same, such as being stored at the same memory address, but it does pay attention to case (or capitalization).

The simplest method to find an answer is to use the basic comparison operator (==), which does equality testing on strings as well as numbers.

CAUTION: Comparing two strings using == (or the corresponding < and > operators) is trustworthy if both the arguments are in fact strings, and you know that no type conversion is being performed. (See Chapter 6 for more on this.) Using strcmp() (described next) is always trustworthy.

The most basic workhorse string-comparison function is strcmp(). It takes two strings as arguments and compares them byte by byte until it finds a difference. It returns a negative number if the first string is less than the second and a positive number if the second string is less. It returns 0 if they are identical.

The strcasecmp() function works the same way, except that the equality comparison is case insensitive. The function call strcasecmp("hey!", "HEY!") should return 0.

Searching

The comparison functions just described tell you whether one string is equal to another. To find out if one string is contained within another, use the strpos() function (covered earlier) or the strstr() function (or one of its relatives).

The strstr() function takes a string to search in and a string to look for (in that order). If it succeeds, it returns the portion of the string that starts with (and includes) the first instance of the string it is looking for. If the string is not found, a false value is returned. For example, here is a successful search followed by an unsuccessful search:

```
$string_to_search = "showsuponceshowsuptwice";
$string_to_find = "up";
print("Result of looking for $string_to_find" .
      strstr($string_to_search, $string_to_find));
$string_to_find = "down";
print("Result of looking for $string_to_find" .
      strstr($string_to_search, $string_to_find));
```

which gives us:

```
Result of looking for up: uponceshowsuptwice
Result of looking for down:
```

The blank space after the colon in the second line is the result of trying to print a false value, which prints as the empty string. The strstr() function also has an alias by the name of strchr(). Other than the name, the two functions are identical. Just as with strcmp(), strstr() has a case-insensitive version, by the name of stristr(). (That i in the middle stands for "insensitive"). It is identical to strstr() in every way, except that the comparison treats lowercase letters as indistinguishable from their uppercase counterparts. The string functions we have covered so far are summarized in Table 10-1.

Table 10-1: Simple Inspection, Comparison, and Searching Functions

Function	Behavior
strlen()	Takes a single string argument and returns its length as an integer.
strpos()	Takes two string arguments: a string to search, and the string being searched for. Returns the (0-based) position of the beginning of the first instance of the string if found, and a false value otherwise. It also takes a third optional integer argument, specifying the position at which the search should begin.
strrpos()	Like strpos(), except that it searches backward from the end of the string, rather than forward from the beginning. The search string must only be one character long, and there is no optional position argument.
strcmp()	Takes two strings as arguments and returns 0 if the strings are exactly equivalent. If strcmp() encounters a difference, it returns a negative number if the first different byte is a smaller ASCII value in the first string, and a positive number if the smaller byte is found in the second string.
strcasecmp()	Identical to strcmp(), except that lowercase and uppercase versions of the same letter compare as equal.
strstr()	Searches its first string argument to see if its second string argument is contained in it. Returns the substring of the first string that starts with the first instance of the second argument, if any is found — otherwise, it returns false.
strchr()	Identical to strstr().
stristr()	Identical to strstr() except that the comparison is case independent.

Substring selection

Many of PHP's string functions have to do with slicing and dicing your strings. By *slicing,* we mean choosing a portion of a string; and by *dicing,* we mean selectively modifying a string. Keep in mind that (most of the time) even dicing functions do not change the string you started out with. Usually such functions return a modified copy, leaving the original argument intact.

The most basic way to choose a portion of a string is the substr() function, which returns a new string that is a subsequence of the old one. As arguments, it takes a string (that the substring will be selected from), an integer (the position at which the desired substring starts), and an optional third integer argument that is the length of the desired substring. If no third argument is given, the substring is assumed to continue until the end. (Remember that, as with all PHP arguments that deal with numerical string positions, the numbering starts with 0 rather than 1.)

For example, the statement:

```
echo(substr("Take what you need, and leave the rest behind",
     23));
```

prints out the string `leave the rest behind`; whereas the statement:

```
echo(substr("Take what you need, and leave the rest behind",
     5, 13));
```

prints out `what you need` — a 13-character string starting at (0-based) position 5.

Both the start-position argument and the length argument can be negative, and in each case the negativity has a different meaning. If the start-position is negative, it means that the starting character is determined by counting backward from the end of the string, rather than forward from the beginning. (A start position of –1 means start with the last character, –2 means second-to-last, and so on.)

Now, you might expect that a negative length would similarly imply that the substring should be determined by counting backward from the start character, rather than forward. This is not the case — it is always true that the character at the start-position is the first character in the returned string (not the last). Instead, a negative-length argument means that the final character is determined by counting backward from the end, rather than forward from the start position.

Some examples, with positive and negative arguments:

```
$alphabet_test = "abcdefghijklmnop";
print("3: " . substr($alphabet_test, 3) . "<BR>");
print("-3: " . substr($alphabet_test, -3) . "<BR>");
print("3, 5: " . substr($alphabet_test, 3, 5) . "<BR>");
print("3, -5: " . substr($alphabet_test, 3, -5) . "<BR>");
print("-3, -5: " . substr($alphabet_test, -3, -5) . "<BR>");
print("-3, 5: " . substr($alphabet_test, -3, 5) . "<BR>");
```

This gives us the output:

```
3: defghijklmnop
-3: nop
3, 5: defgh
3, -5: defghijk
-3, -5:
-3, 5: nop
```

> **CAUTION:** In the `substr()` example with a start position of –3 and a length of –5, the ending position is before the starting position, which in a sense specifies a string with *negative length*. The manual at www.php.net/manual currently says that such negative length calls to `substr()` will result in returning a string containing the single character at the start position. Instead, as in the preceding example, PHP 4.0.0 seems to return empty strings in such cases. Caveat coder.

Notice that there is an intimate relationship between the functions substr(), strstr(), and strpos(). The substr() function selects a substring by numerical position, strstr() selects a substring by its content, and strpos() finds the numerical position of a given substring. In the case where we're sure in advance that the string $containing has the string $contained as a substring, then the expression:

```
strstr($containing, $contained)
```

should be equivalent to the code:

```
substr($containing, strpos($containing, $contained))
```

String cleanup functions

Although they are technically substring functions, just like the others in this chapter, the functions chop(), ltrim(), and trim() are really used for cleaning up untidy strings. They trim whitespace off of the end, beginning, and beginning-and-end, respectively, of their single string argument. Some examples:

```
$original = "  More than meets the eye   ";
$chopped = chop($original);
$ltrimmed = ltrim($original);
$trimmed = trim($original);
print("The original is '$original'<BR>");
print("Its length is " . strlen($original) . "<BR>");
print("The chopped version is '$chopped'<BR>");
print("Its length is " . strlen($chopped) . "<BR>");
print("The ltrimmed version is '$ltrimmed'<BR>");
print("Its length is " . strlen($ltrimmed) . "<BR>");
print("The trimmed version is '$ltrimmed'<BR>");
print("Its length is " . strlen($trimmed) . "<BR>");
```

The result as viewed by a browser is:

```
The original is ' More than meets the eye '
Its length is 28
The chopped version is ' More than meets the eye'
Its length is 25
The ltrimmed version is 'More than meets the eye '
Its length is 26
The trimmed version is 'More than meets the eye'
Its length is 23
```

The original string had three spaces at the end (subject to removal by chop() or trim()), and two at the beginning (removed by ltrim() and trim()). We were careful to describe our result "as viewed by a browser" because the multiple spaces have apparently been collapsed to one in the output, as browsers will do. If we viewed the HTML source produced by PHP originally, we would still see sequences of two and three spaces.

In addition to spaces, these functions remove whitespace like that denoted by the escape sequences \n, \r, \t, and \0 (end-of-line characters, tabs, and the null character used to terminate strings in C programs).

You will hear the name chop() more frequently, but the identical function can also be called with the more logical name of rtrim(). Finally, notice that although chop() sounds extremely destructive, it does not harm the $original argument, which retains the same value.

String replacement

The substring functions we've seen so far are all about choosing a portion of the argument, rather than building a genuinely new string. Enter the functions str_replace() and substr_replace().

The str_replace() function enables you to replace all instances of a particular substring with an alternate string. It takes three arguments: the string to be searched for, the string to replace it with when it is found, and the string to perform the replacement on. For example:

```
$first_edition =
    "Burma is similar to Rhodesia in at least one way.";
$second_edition = str_replace("Rhodesia", "Zimbabwe",
                              $first_edition);
$third_edition = str_replace("Burma", "Myanmar",
                              $second_edition);
print($third_edition);
```

gives us:

```
Myanmar is similar to Zimbabwe in at least one way.
```

This replacement will happen for all instances of the search string that are found. If our outdated encyclopedia could be snarfed into a single PHP string, we could update it in one pass.

One subtlety to be aware of: What happens when multiple instances of the search string overlap? For example, with code like:

```
$tricky_string = "ABA is part of ABABA";
$maybe_tricked = str_replace("ABA", "DEF", $tricky_string);
print("Substitution result is '$maybe_tricked'<BR>");
```

The behavior we see is:

```
Substitution result is 'DEF is part of DEFBA'
```

which is probably as reasonable as any other alternative.

As we've seen, str_replace() picks out portions to replace by matching to a target string; by contrast, substr_replace() chooses a portion to replace by its absolute position. The function takes up to four arguments: the string to perform the replacement on, the string to replace with, the starting position for the replacement, and (optionally) the length of the section to be replaced. For example:

```
print(substr_replace("ABCDEFG", "-", 2, 3));
```

gives us:

```
AB-FG
```

The CDE portion of the string has been replaced with the single -. Notice that we are allowed to replace a substring with a string of a different length. If the length argument is omitted, it is assumed that you want to replace the entire portion of the string after the start position.

The substr_replace() function also takes negative arguments for starting position and length, which are treated exactly the same way as in the substr() function (described in the earlier section "Substring selection").

Finally, we have a couple more whimsical functions that produce new strings from old. The strrev() function simply returns a new string with the characters of its input in reverse order. The str_repeat() function takes a string argument and an integer argument and returns a string that is the appropriate number of copies of the string argument tacked together. For example:

```
print(str_repeat("cheers ", 3));
```

gives us:

```
cheers cheers cheers
```

for the end of this section at long last.

The substring search and replacement functions are summarized in Table 10-2.

Tokenizing and parsing functions

Sometimes you need to take strings apart at the seams, and you have your own notions of what should count as a seam. The process of breaking up a long string into "words" is called *tokenizing,* and among other things it is part of the internals of interpreting or compiling any computer program, including PHP. PHP offers a special function for this purpose, called strtok().

The strtok() function takes two arguments: the string to be broken up into tokens, and a string containing all the *delimiters* (characters that count as boundaries between tokens). On the first call, both arguments are used, and the string value returned is the first token. To retrieve subsequent tokens, make the same call, but omit the source string argument. It will be remembered as the current string, and the function will remember where it left off. For example:

Table 10-2: Substring and String Replacement Functions

Function	Behavior
substr()	Returns a subsequence of its initial string argument, as specified by the second (position) argument and optional third (length) argument. The substring starts at the indicated position and continues for as many characters as specified by the length argument or until the end of the string, if there is no length argument. A negative position argument means that the start character is located by counting backward from the end, whereas a negative length argument means that the end of the substring is found by counting back from the end, rather than forward from the start position.
chop()-, or-rtrim()	Returns its string argument with trailing (right-hand side) whitespace removed. Whitespace is , \n, \r, \t, and \0.
ltrim()	Returns its string argument with leading (left-hand side) whitespace removed.
Trim()	Returns its string argument with both leading and trailing whitespace removed.
Str_replace()	Used to replace target substrings with another string. Takes three string arguments: a substring to search for, a string to replace it with, and the containing string. Returns a copy of the containing string with *all* instances of the first argument replaced by the second argument.
Substr_replace()	Puts a string argument in place of a position-specified substring. Takes up to four arguments: the string to operate on, the string to replace with, the start position of the substring to replace, and the length of the string segment to be replaced. Returns a copy of the first argument with the replacement string put in place of the specified substring. If the length argument is omitted, the entire tail of the first string argument is replaced. Negative position and length arguments are treated as in substr().

```
$token = strtok(
    "open-source HTML-embedded server-side Web scripting",
    " ");
while($token){
  print($token . "<BR>");
  $token = strtok(" ");
}
```

gives the browser output:

```
open-source
HTML-embedded
server-side
Web
scripting
```

The original string would be "broken" at each space. At our discretion, we could change the delimiter set, like so:

```
$token = strtok(
    "open-source HTML-embedded server-side Web scripting",
    "-");
while($token){
  print($token . "<BR>");
  $token = strtok("-");
}
```

This gives us (less sensibly):

```
open
source HTML
embedded server
side Web scripting
```

Finally, we can break the string at all these places at once, by giving it a delimiter string like " - ", containing both a space and a dash. The code:

```
$token = strtok(
    "open-source HTML-embedded server-side Web scripting",
    " -");
while($token){
  print($token . "<BR>");
  $token = strtok(" -");
}
```

prints:

```
open
source
HTML
embedded
server
side
Web
scripting
```

Notice that in every case the delimiter characters do not show up anywhere in the retrieved tokens.

The strtok() function doles out its tokens one by one. You can also use the explode() function to do something similar, except it stores the tokens all at once into an array. After the tokens are in the array, you can do anything you like with them, including sort them.

The explode() function takes two arguments: a separator string and the string to be separated. It returns an array where each element is a substring between instances of the separator in the string to be separated. For example:

```
$explode_result = explode("AND", "one AND a two AND a three");
```

results in the array $explode_result having three elements, each of which is a string: "one ", " a two ", and " a three". In this particular example, there would be no capital letters anywhere in the strings contained in the array, because the AND separator does not show up in the result.

The separator string in explode() is significantly different from the delimiter string used in strtok(). The separator is a full-fledged string, and all its characters must be found in the right order for an instance of the separator to be detected. The delimiter string of strtok() specifies a set of single characters, any one of which will count as a delimiter. This makes explode() both more precise and more brittle — if you leave out a space or a newline character from a long string, the entire function will be broken.

Because the entire separator string disappears into the ether when explode() is used, this function can be the basis for many useful effects. The examples given in most PHP documentation use short strings for convenience, but remember that a string can be almost any length — and explode() is especially useful with longer strings that might be tedious to parse some other way. For instance, you can use it to count how many times a particular string appears within a text file by turning the file into a string and using explode() on it, as in this example (which uses some functions we haven't explained yet, but we hope make sense in context).

```php
<?php
//First, turn a text file into a string called $filestring.
$filename = "complex_layout.html";
$fd = fopen($filename, "r");
$filestring = fread($fd, filesize($filename));
fclose ($fd);

//Explode on the beginning of the <TABLE> HTML tag
$tables = explode("<TABLE", $filestring); // assumes uppercase
//Count the number of pieces
$num_tables = count($tables);

//Subtract one to get the number of <TABLE> tags, and echo
echo ($num_tables - 1);
?>
```

The explode() function has an inverse function, implode(), which takes two arguments: a "glue" string (analogous to the separator string in explode()), and an array of strings like that returned by explode(). It returns a string created by inserting the glue string between each string element in the array.

You can use the two functions together to replace every instance of a particular string within a text file. Remember that the separator string will vanish into the ether when you perform an explode() — if you want it to appear in the final file, you have to replace it by hand. In this example, we're changing the font tags on a Web page.

```php
<?php
//Turn text file into string
$filename = "someoldpage.html";
$fd = fopen($filename, "r");
$filestring = fread($fd, filesize($filename));
fclose ($fd); $parts = explode("arial, sans-serif", $filestring); $whole
= implode("arial, verdana, sans-serif", $parts);

//Overwrite the original file
$fd = fopen($filename, "w");
fwrite($fd, $whole);
fclose ($fd);
?>
```

Case functions

These functions change lowercase to upper and vice versa. The first two (de)capitalize entire strings, whereas the second two operate only on first letters of words.

strtolower()

The strtolower() function returns an all-lowercase string. It doesn't matter if the original is all uppercase or mixed. This fragment:

```php
<?php
$original = "They DON'T KnoW they're SHOUTING";
$lower = strtolower($original);
echo $lower;
?>
```

returns the string "they don't know they're shouting".

strtoupper()

The strtoupper() function returns an all-uppercase string, regardless of whether the original was all lowercase or mixed.

```php
<?php
$original = "make this link stand out";
echo("<B>strtoupper($original)</B>");
?>
```

ucfirst()

The `ucfirst()` function capitalizes only the first letter of a string.

```php
<?php
$original = "polish is a word for which pronunciation depends on
capitalization";
echo(ucfirst($original));
?>
```

ucwords()

The `ucwords()` function capitalizes the first letter of each word in a string.

```php
<?php
$original = "truth or consequences";
$capitalized = ucwords($original);
echo "While $original is a parlor game, $capitalized is a town in New
Mexico.";
?>
```

> **NOTE:** Neither `ucwords()` nor `ucfirst()` convert anything into lowercase. They only make the appropriate leading letters into uppercase. If there are inappropriate capital letters in the middle of words, they will not be corrected.

Escaping functions

One of the virtues of PHP is that it is willing to talk to almost anybody. In its role as a "glue" language, PHP talks to database servers, to LDAP servers, over sockets, and over the HTTP connection itself. Frequently it accomplishes this communication by first constructing a message string (like a database query) and then shipping it off to the receiving program. Often, however, the program attaches special meanings to certain characters, which therefore have to be *escaped,* meaning that the receiving program is told to take them as a literal part of the string rather than treating them specially.

Many users deal with this issue by enabling magic-quotes, which ensures that quotes are escaped before strings are inserted into databases. However, if that's not feasible or desirable, there are good old-fashioned strip-slashing and add-slashing by hand. The `addslashes()` function escapes quotes, double quotes, backslashes, and NULLs with backslashes, because these are the characters that typically need to be escaped for database queries.

```php
<?php
$escapedstring = addslashes("He said, 'I'm a dog.'");
$query = "INSERT INTO test (quote) values ('$escapedstring')";
$result = mysql_query($query) or die(mysql_error());
?>
```

This will prevent the SQL statement from thinking it's finished right before the letter `I`. When you pull the data back out, you'll need to use `stripslashes()` to get rid of the slashes.

```php
<?php
$query = "SELECT quote FROM test WHERE ID=1";
$result = mysql_query($query) or die(mysql_error());
$new_row = mysql_fetch_array($result);
$quote = stripslashes($new_row[0]);

echo $quote;
```

The `quotemeta()` function escapes a wider variety of characters, all of which usually have a special meaning in the Unix command-line:'.', '\' '+', '*', '?', '[', '^', ']', '(', '$', and ')'. For example, the code:

```php
$literal_string =
  'These characters ($, *) are very special to me\n<BR>';
$qm_string = quotemeta($literal_string);
echo $qm_string;
```

will print:

```
These characters \(\$, \*\) are very special to me\\n
```

> **CROSS-REFERENCE:** For escaping functions that are specific to HTML, see the "Advanced String Functions" section later in this chapter.

Printing and output

The workhorse constructs for printing and output are `print` and `echo`, which we covered in detail in Chapter 5. The standard way to print the value of variables to output is to include them in a doubly quoted string (which will interpolate their values), and then give that string to `print` or `echo`.

If you need even more tightly formatted output, PHP also offers `printf()` and `sprintf()`, which are modeled on C functions of the same name. The two functions take identical arguments: a special format string (described later in this section), and then any number of other arguments which will be spliced into the right places in the format string to make the result.

The only difference between `printf()` and `sprintf()` is that `printf()` sends the resulting string directly to output, whereas `sprintf()` returns the result string as its value.

> **NOTE:** To C programmers: This `sprintf()` function is slightly different from C's version in that you need not supply an allocated string for `sprintf()` to write into — PHP allocates the result string for you.

The complicated bit about these functions is the format string. Every character that you put in the string will show up literally in the result, except the % character and characters that immediately follow it. The % character signals the beginning of a *conversion specification*, which indicates how to print one of the arguments that follow the format string.

After the %, there are five elements that make up the conversion specification, some of which are optional: padding, alignment, minimum width, precision, and type.

♦ The single (optional) *padding* character is either a 0 or a space ( ). This character is used to fill any space that would otherwise be unused, but that you have insisted (with the minimum width argument) be filled with something. If this padding character is not given, the default is to pad with spaces.

♦ The optional *alignment* character (-) indicates whether the printed value should be left- or right-justified. If present, the value will be left-justified; if absent, it will be right-justified.

♦ An optional *minimum width* number that indicates how many spaces this value should take up, at a minimum. (If more spaces are needed to print the value, it will overflow beyond its bounds.)

♦ An optional precision specifier, which is a dot (.) followed by a number. It indicates how many decimal points of *precision* a double should print with. (This has no effect on printing things other than doubles.

♦ A single character indicating how the *type* of the value should be interpreted. The f character indicates printing as a double, the s character indicates printing as a string, and then the rest of the possible characters (b, c, d, o, x, X) mean that the value should be interpreted as an integer and printed in various formats. Those formats are b for binary, c for printing the character with the correponding ASCII values, o for octal, x for hexadecimal (with lowercase letters) and X for hexadecimal with uppercase letters.

An example of printing the same double in several different ways:

```
<pre>
<?php
$value = 3.14159;
printf("%f,%10f,%-010f,%2.2f\n",
        $value, $value, $value, $value);
?>
</pre>
```

gives us:

```
3.141590, 3.141590,3.141590000000000, 3.14
```

The <pre></pre> construct is HTML that tells the browser to format the enclosed block literally, without collapsing many spaces into one, and so on.

Advanced String Functions

We have now covered the most basic things to do with strings: making them, breaking them, comparing them, finding substrings, and printing them out. Now, we'll delve into some more exotic string functions, which we've categorized by type and/or purpose. These are the sort of functions that might only be relevant to you if you're working on a particular kind of project. Some of these sections might make you want to say "Why would anyone want to do that?" — if so, please ignore them until you the day that you suddenly realize that you need to do that thing exactly.

HTML functions

PHP offers a number of Web-specific functions for string manipulation, which are summarized in Table 10-3.

Table 10-3: HTML-Specific String Functions

Function	Behavior
htmlspecialchars()	Takes a string as argument and returns the string with replacements for four characters that have special meaning in HTML. Each of these characters is replaced with the corresponding HTML entity, so that it will look like the original when rendered by a browser. The & character is replaced by & " " (the double-quote character) is replaced by " < is replaced by < > is replaced by &gt.
htmlentities()	Goes further than htmlspecialchars(), in that it replaces all characters that have a corresponding HTML entity with that HTML entity.
get_html_translation_table()	Takes one of two special constants (HTML_SPECIAL_CHARS and HTML_ENTITIES), and returns the translation table used by htmlspecialchars() and htmlentities(), respectively. The translation table is an array where keys are the character strings and the corresponding values are their replacements.
nl2br()	Takes a string as argument and returns that string with \<BR\> inserted before all newlines (\n). This is helpful, for example, in maintaining the apparent line length of text paragraphs when they are displayed in a browser.
strip_tags()	Takes a string as argument and does its best to return that string stripped of all HTML tags and all PHP tags.

Hashing using MD5

MD5 is a string-processing algorithm that is used to produce a digest or signature of whatever string it is given. The algorithm boils its input string down into a fixed-length string of 32 hexadecimal values (0,1,2, ... 9,a,b, ... f). MD5 has some very useful properties:

♦ MD5 always produces the same output string for any given input string.

♦ The fixed-length results of applying MD5 are very evenly spread over the range of possible values.

♦ There is no known way to efficiently produce an input string corresponding to a given MD5 output string, or to produce two inputs that yield the same output.

PHP's implementation of MD5 is available in the function md5(), which takes a string as input, and produces the 32-character digest as output. For example, evaluating this:

```
print("md5 of 'Tim' is " . md5('Tim') . "<BR>");
print("md5 of 'tim' is " . md5('tim') . "<BR>");
print("md5 of 'time' is " . md5('time') . "<BR>");
```

gives us the browser output:

```
md5 of Tim is dc2054afd537ddc98afd9347136494ac
md5 of tim is b15d47e99831ee63e3f47cf3d4478e9a
md5 of time is 07cc694b9b3fc636710fa08b6922c42b
```

Although the input strings seem close to each other in some sense, there is no apparent similarity in the output strings. And since the range of possible output values is so huge (16 to the 32nd power), the chances that any two distinct strings will *collide* by producing the same MD5 value is vanishingly small.

The characteristics of MD5 make it useful for a wide variety of tasks, including:

♦ **Checksumming a message or file.** If you are worried about errors that might happen in transfer, you can transmit an MD5 digest, along with the message, and run the message through MD5 again after transfer. If the two versions of the digest do not match, then something is amiss.

♦ **Detecting if a file's contents have changed.** Similar to checksumming, MD5 is often used in this way by search engines as a check on whether a Web page has changed, making re-indexing necessary. It is cheaper to store the MD5 digest than the entire original file.

♦ **Encrypting passwords.** You might store an MD5'ed password in your database, and compare the result of MD5'ing an entered password against that entry.

♦ **Splitting strings or files into buckets.** If you want to divide a set of strings into N randomly dispersed sets, you can MD5 the strings, take the first few hex characters, translate them into a number, and take that number modulo the number of bins you want.

In addition to the md5() function, PHP offers md5_file(), which takes a filename as argument and returns an MD5 hash of the file's contents.

Strings as character collections

PHP offers some pretty specialized functions that treat strings more as collections of characters than as sequences.

The first is strspn(), which you can use to see what portion of a string is composed only of a given set of characters. For example:

```
$twister = "Peter Piper picked a peck of pickled peppers";
$charset = "Peter picked a";
print("The segment matching '$charset' is " .
     strspn($twister, $charset) . " characters long");
```

gives us:

```
The segment matching 'Peter picked a' is 26 characters long
```

because the first character not found in $charset is the o in of, and there are 26 characters that precede it.

The strcspn() function (where that internal c stands for *complement*) does the same thing, except that it accepts characters that are *not* in the character set argument. For example, the statement:

```
echo(strcspn($twister, "abcd"));
```

prints the number 14, because it accepts a 14-character sequence with the last character being the c in picked.

Finally, although it uses some properties of arrays that we have not yet studied, check out the following for an acute analysis of alliteration:

```
$twister = "Peter Piper picked a peck of pickled peppers";
print("$twister<BR>");
$letter_array = count_chars($twister, 1);
while ($cell = each($letter_array)){
  $letter = chr($cell['key']);
  $frequency = $cell['value'];
  print("Character: '$letter'; frequency:  $frequency<BR>");
}
```

This gives the browser output:

```
Peter Piper picked a peck of pickled peppers
Character: ' '; frequency: 7
Character: 'P'; frequency: 2
Character: 'a'; frequency: 1
Character: 'c'; frequency: 3
```

```
Character: 'd'; frequency: 2
Character: 'e'; frequency: 8
Character: 'f'; frequency: 1
Character: 'i'; frequency: 3
Character: 'k'; frequency: 3
Character: 'l'; frequency: 1
Character: 'o'; frequency: 1
Character: 'p'; frequency: 7
Character: 'r'; frequency: 3
Character: 's'; frequency: 1
Character: 't'; frequency: 1
```

The `count_chars()` function returns a report on the occurrences of characters in its string argument, packaged up as an array where the keys are the ASCII values of characters, and the values are the frequencies of those characters in the string. The second argument to `count_chars()` is an integer that determines which of several modes the results should be returned in. In mode 0, an array of key/value pairs is returned, where the keys are every ASCII value from 0 to 255, and the corresponding values are the frequencies of each character in the string. Modes 1 and 2 are variants that include only ASCII values that occurred in the string (mode 1) or that did not occur (mode 2). Finally, modes 3 and 4 return a string instead of an array, where the string contains all characters that occur (mode 3) or do not occur (mode 4).

These functions are summarized in Table 10-4.

> **CROSS-REFERENCE:** For an explanation of how to take apart array formats like that returned by `count_chars()`, see Chapter 11. The `chr()` function used in the preceding example, which maps from ASCII numbers to the corresponding characters, is covered in Chapter 6.

Table 10-4: Functions for Examining Character Contents

Function	Behavior
`count_chars()`	Takes a single string argument and an integer mode argument from 0 to 4. Returns a report about frequencies of characters in the string argument, as either an array or a string. (See the preceding text for more detail.)
`strspn()`	Takes two string arguments and returns the length of the initial substring of the first argument that is composed entirely of characters found in its second argument.
`strcspn()`	Takes two string arguments and returns the length of the initial substring of the first argument that is composed entirely of characters that are *not* found in its second argument.

String similarity functions

How similar is this string to that string? Well, it depends what you mean by *similar*, right?

If the kind of similarity you want is similarity of spelling, consider the Levenshtein metric. The `levenshtein()` function takes two strings and returns the minimum number of additions, deletions, and replacements of letters needed to transform one into the other. For example:

◆ `levenshtein('Tim', 'Time')` returns 1

◆ `levenshtein('boy', 'chefboyardee')` returns 9

◆ `levenshtein('never', 'clever')` returns 1 (incorrectly, in PHP 4.1.2. It should return 2. The bug should be fixed in PHP 4.2)

If the similarity you are interested in is phonetic, consider the functions `soundex()` and `metaphone()`. Both of them take an input string and return a key string representing the pronunciation category of the word (in English). If two input word strings map to exactly the same output key, they most likely have a similar pronunciation.

Extended Example: An Exercise Calculator

In this section we continue the "exercise calculator" example from the previous chapter, by using a variety of string functions to process strings posted from a user form. In the previous example, we had just managed to pass off a string variable from an HTML form to the PHP page designed to receive it. In this version, we actually do some analysis of the string we receive. (See "Analysis," at the end of this section, to see why this example will still need to be improved in later chapters.)

Listing 10-1 shows the HTML form used to prompt the user for an exercise to analyze. This is largely the same as the corresponding form in Chapter 9, with a different form-handling target.

Listing 10-1: The entry form

```
<HTML>
<HEAD>
<STYLE TYPE="text/css">
<!--
BODY, P {color: black; font-family: verdana; font-size: 10 pt}
H1      {color: black; font-family: arial; font-size: 12 pt}
-->
</STYLE>
</HEAD>
<BODY>
<TABLE BORDER=0 CELLPADDING=10 WIDTH=100%>
<TR>
<TD BGCOLOR="#F0F8FF" ALIGN=CENTER VALIGN=TOP WIDTH=150>
</TD>
```

```
<TD BGCOLOR="#FFFFFF" ALIGN=LEFT VALIGN=TOP WIDTH=83%>
<H1>Workout calculator (passing a string)</H1>
<P>Enter an exercise, and we'll tell you how long you'd have to do
it<BR>to burn one pound of fat.</P>
<FORM METHOD="post" ACTION="wc_handler_str.php">
<INPUT TYPE="text" SIZE=50 NAME="exercise">
<BR><BR>
<INPUT TYPE="submit" NAME="submit" VALUE="Burn, baby, burn!">
</FORM>
</TD>
</TR>
</TABLE>
</BODY>
</HTML>
```

Listing 10-2 shows a revised form-handling page that displays different exercise stats depending on the particular exercise entered by the user.

> **CAUTION:** We very intentionally used the modern $_POST superglobal to catch the value of the string posted by the form. This means, however, that the code in Listing 10-2 will not run in any version of PHP earlier than PHP 4.1. To adapt it to an earlier version, replace $_POST with '$HTTP_POST_VARS'.

Listing 10-2: Form handler using string functions

```
<?php$exercise = $_POST['exercise']; // NOTE: only works in PHP 4.1+
// Make sure they aren't trying to do naughty things
if (strlen($exercise) > 50) {
  echo "You aren't playing by the rules.  Bad dog!";
  exit;
}
// Try to parse the input string
// ----------------------------
// Make sure there aren't any spaces before or after
$exercise = trim($exercise);

// Convert to all lowercase for better string matching
$exercise = strtolower($exercise);

// Try to standardize on gerund form, if possible
if (strpos($exercise, 'ing') > 0) {
  // Already good
  $exercise_str = $exercise;
} elseif ($exercise == 'bike' || $exercise == 'cycle') {
  $exercise_str = 'cycling';
} elseif ($exercise == 'run' || $exercise == 'jog') {
  $exercise_str = 'running';
} elseif ($exercise == 'soccer' || $exercise == 'football') {
```

```php
    $exercise_str = 'soccer';
} elseif (strstr($exercise, 'weight') || strstr($exercise, 'strength'))
{
    $exercise_str = 'weight lifting';
}


// Now assign a number of hours to burn one pound of fat to each sport
if ($exercise_str == 'cycling' || $exercise_str == 'biking') {
    $hours = '5 hours and 40 minutes';
} elseif ($exercise_str == 'running' || $exercise_str == 'jogging') {
    $hours = '4 hours and 30 minutes';
} elseif ($exercise_str == 'soccer' || $exercise_str == 'football') {
    $hours = '4 hours and 30 minutes';
} elseif ($exercise_str == 'weight lifting') {
    $hours = '7 hours and 30 minutes';
} else {
    // Nullify all other exercises
    $exercise_str = '';
    $hours = '';
}

// Construct a sentence
// --------------------

if ($exercise_str != "" && $hours != "") {
    $message = 'It would take '.$hours.' of '.$exercise_str.' to burn one
pound of fat.';
} elseif ($exercise_str == "" && $hours == "") {
    // If the exercise isn't in the list above, give a
    // default message.
    $message = 'Sorry, we do not have data for that exercise.';
} else {

    // There are two other logical possibilities
    // 1.  We recognize the exercise but don't have a duration
    // for it
    // 2.  We don't recognize the exercise but somehow have a
    // duration
    // neither should happen, but just in case...
    $message = 'Something has gone horribly wrong!';
}
// Now lay out the page
// --------------------
$page_str = <<< EOPAGE
<HTML>
<HEAD>
<STYLE TYPE="text/css">
<!--
```

```
BODY, P        {color: black; font-family: verdana; font-size: 10 pt}
H1             {color: black; font-family: arial; font-size: 12 pt}
-->
</STYLE>
</HEAD>

<BODY>
<TABLE BORDER=0 CELLPADDING=10 WIDTH=100%>
<TR>
<TD BGCOLOR="#F0F8FF" ALIGN=CENTER VALIGN=TOP WIDTH=150>
</TD>
<TD BGCOLOR="#FFFFFF" ALIGN=LEFT VALIGN=TOP WIDTH=83%>
<H1>Workout calculator handler, part 2</H1>
<P>The workout calculator says, "$message"</P>
</TD>
</TR>
</TABLE>
</BODY>
</HTML>
EOPAGE;

echo $page_str;

?>
```

In order, the code in Listing 10-2:

♦ Receives the posted string from the HTML form.

♦ Tries to put the received string into a standard form by trimming off whitespace, converting to lowercase, and translating some known variations.

♦ Uses the cleaned-up and translated string to look up data on a given exercise.

♦ Uses the heredoc syntax to construct a response page.

Figures 10-1 and 10-2 show what would be displayed as the user enters the word *bike*.

So, do we like our exercise calculator yet? The main problem is that it is highly likely that the form will not know how to handle what the user types (other than by printing a generic message). Also, if you raise error reporting up to E_ALL, you will see some warnings due to uninitialized variables. The user is also not given any clue as to what kinds of input the form will be able to handle.

In general, unless you are building a system (like a search engine) where the whole point is dealing with free text, it is a bad idea to have the results of your code depend on analysis of user-entered strings. If you want the user to make choices, you should constrain those choices so that you know what is coming. User-entered text is fine as long as its ultimate fate is to be viewed by another human being (after, say, being stored in a database or forwarded by an e-mail program).

Figure 10-1: The entry form

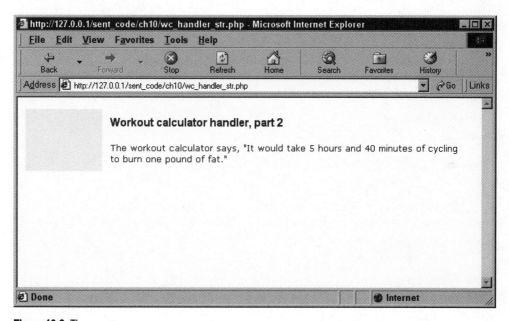

Figure 10-2: The answer

To gracefully constrain the user's choices, you need HTML user-interface elements other than the text box, such as check boxes, radio buttons and pull-down lists. And to make use of those UI elements on the receiving side, we really need to exploit the power of arrays more fully. We will extend this example in the next chapter by doing just that.

Summary

Strings are sequences of characters, and the string is one of the eight basic datatypes in PHP. Unlike in some other languages, there is no distinct character type, since single characters behave as strings of length 1. Literal strings are specified in code by either single (') or double (") quotes. Singly quoted strings are interpreted nearly literally, while doubly-quoted strings interpret a number of escape sequences and automatically interpolate variable values.

The main string operator is ' . ', which concatenates two strings together. In addition, there is a dizzying array of string functions, which help you inspect, compare, search, extract, chop, replace, slice, and dice strings to your heart's content. For the most sophisticated string manipulation needs, PHP supports both POSIX and Perl-compatible regular expressions (covered in Chapter 30).

Chapter 11

Arrays and Array Functions

In This Chapter

♦ How arrays work in PHP

♦ Using multidimensional arrays

♦ Imitating other data structures with arrays

♦ Sorting and other transformations

Arrays are definitely one of the coolest and most flexible features of PHP. Unlike vector arrays from other languages (C, C++, Pascal), PHP arrays can store data of varied types and automatically organize it for you in a large variety of ways.

> **CROSS-REFERENCE:** This chapter treats arrays and array functions in some depth. For a very quick introduction to the syntax and use of arrays, see Chapter 6.

The Uses of Arrays

Throughout much of this chapter, we will be looking at the inner workings of arrays and exploring all the built-in PHP functions that manipulate them. Before we get too deep into that, however, it's worth listing the common ways that arrays are used in real PHP code:

♦ Many built-in PHP environment variables are in the form of arrays (for example, $_SESSION, which contains all the variable names and values that are being propagated from page to page via PHP's session mechanism). If you want access to them, you need to understand, at a minimum, how to reference arrays.

♦ Most database functions transport their info via arrays, making a compact package of an arbitrary chunk of data.

♦ It's easy to pass entire sets of HTML form arguments from one page to another in a single array (see Chapter 9).

♦ Arrays make a nice container for doing manipulations (sorting, counting, and so on) of any data you develop while executing a single page's script.

Almost any situation that calls for a number of pieces of data to be packaged and handled as one is appropriate for a PHP array.

What Are PHP Arrays?

PHP arrays are *associative* arrays with a little extra machinery thrown in. The *associative* part means that arrays store element values in association with key values, rather than in a strict linear index order. (If you have seen arrays in other programming languages, they are likely to have been *vector* arrays rather than associative arrays — see the sidebar for an explanation of the difference.) If you store an element in an array, in association with a key, all you need to retrieve it later from that array is the key value. For example, storage is as simple as this:

```
$state_location['San Mateo'] = 'California';
```

which stores the element `'California'` in the array variable `$state_location`, in association with the lookup key `'San Mateo'`. After this has been stored, you can look up the stored value by using the key, like so:

```
$state = $state_location['San Mateo'];   // equals 'California'
```

Simple, no?

If all you want arrays for is to store key/value pairs, the preceding information is all you need to know. Similarly, if you want to associate a numerical ordering with a bunch of values, all you have to do is use integers as your key values, as in:

```
$my_array[1] = "The first thing";
$my_array[2] = "The second thing"; // and so on ...
```

> **NOTE:** For Perl programmers. Arrays in PHP are much like hashes in Perl, with some syntactic differences. For one thing, all variables in PHP are denoted with a leading $, not just scalar variables. Secondly, even though the array is associative, the indices are grouped by square brackets ([ ]) rather than curly braces ({ }). Finally, there is no array or list type that is indexed only by integers. The convention is to use integers as associative indices, and the array itself maintains an internal ordering for iteration purposes.

In addition to the machinery that makes this kind of key/value association possible, arrays track some other things behind the scenes. Because of this, we sometimes treat them as other kinds of data structures. As we will see, arrays can be multidimensional. They can store values in association with a sequence of key values rather than a single key. Also, arrays automatically maintain an ordered list of the elements that have been inserted in them, independent of what the key values happen to be. This makes it possible to treat arrays as linked lists. In general, we will reveal the workings of this extra machinery as we explore the functions that use it.

> **NOTE:** A note for C++ programmers. You should be aware that arrays can handle some of the same tasks that require the use of template libraries in C++. Much of the reason for having templates in the first place is to get around restrictions having to do with strict typing of data. PHP's looser typing system makes it possible, for example, to write general algorithms that iterate over the contents of arrays without committing as to the type of the array elements themselves.

ASSOCIATIVE ARRAYS VERSUS VECTOR ARRAYS

If you have programmed in languages like C, C++, and Pascal, you are probably used to a particular usage of the word *array*, one that doesn't match the PHP usage very well at all. A more specific term for a C-style array is a *vector array*, whereas a PHP-style array is an *associative array*.

In a vector array, the contained elements all need to be of the same type, and usually the language compiler needs to know in advance how many such elements there are likely to be. For example, In C you might declare an array of 100 double-precision floating-point numbers with a statement like:

```
double my_array[100]; // This is C, not PHP!
```

The restriction on types and the advance declaration of size have an associated benefit: Vector arrays are very fast, both for storage and lookup. The reason is that the compiler will usually lay out the array in a contiguous block of computer memory, as large as the size of the element type multiplied by the number of elements. This makes it very easy for the programming language to locate a particular array slot — all it needs to know is the starting memory address of the array, the size of the element type, and the index of the element it wants to look up, and it can directly compute the memory address of that slot.

By contrast, PHP arrays are associative (and so some would call them *hashes,* rather than arrays). Rather than having a fixed number of slots, PHP creates array slots as new elements are added to the array. Rather than requiring elements to be of the same type, PHP arrays have the same type-looseness that PHP variables have — you can assign arbitrary PHP values to be array elements. Finally, because vector arrays are all about laying out their elements in numerical order; the "keys" that are used for lookup and storage must be integer numbers. PHP arrays can have keys of arbitrary type, instead, including string keys. So, you could have successive array assignments like:

```
$my_array[1] = 1;

$my_array['orange'] = 2;

$my_array[3] = 3;
```

without any paradox. The result is that your array has three values (1, 2, 3), each of which is stored in association with a key (1, 'orange', and 3, respectively).

The extra flexibility of associative arrays comes at a price, because there is a little bit more going on between your code and the actual computation of a memory address than is true with vector arrays. For most Web programming purposes, however, this extra access time is not a significant cost.

The fact that integers are legal keys for PHP arrays means that you can easily imitate the behavior of a vector array, simply by restricting your code to use only integers as keys.

> **NOTE:** A general note for programmers familiar with other languages. PHP does not need very many different kinds of data structures, in part because of the great flexibility offered by PHP arrays. By careful choice of a subset of array functions, you can make arrays "pretend" to act like vector arrays, structure/record types, linked lists, hash tables, or stacks and queues — data structures that in other languages either require their own data types or more abstruse language features such as pointers and explicit memory management.

Creating Arrays

There are three main ways to create an array in a PHP script: by assigning a value into one (and thereby implicitly creating it), by using the `array()` construct, and by calling a function that happens to return an array as its value.

Direct assignment

The simplest way to create an array is to act as though a variable is already an array and assign a value into it, like this:

```
$my_array[1] = "The first thing in my array that I just made";
```

If `$my_array` was an unbound variable (or bound to a nonarray variable) before this statement, it will now be a variable bound to an array with one element. If instead `$my_array` was already an array, the string will be stored in association with the integer key 1. If no value was associated with that number before, a new array slot will be created to hold it; if a value was associated with 1, the previous value will be overwritten. (You can also assign into an array by omitting the index entirely as in `$my_array[]`, described later in this chapter.)

The array() construct

The other way to create an array is via the `array()` construct, which creates a new array from the specification of its elements and associated keys. In its simplest version, `array()` is called with no arguments, which creates a new empty array. In its next simplest version, array() takes a comma-separated list of elements to be stored, without any specification of keys. The result is that the elements are stored in the array in the order specified and are assigned integer keys beginning with zero. For example, the statement:

```
$fruit_basket = array('apple', 'orange', 'banana', 'pear');
```

causes the variable `$fruit_basket` to be assigned to an array with four string elements (`'apple'`, `'banana'`, `'orange'`, `'pear'`), with the indices 0, 1, 2, and 3 respectively. In addition (as we'll see in the "Iteration" section later in this chapter), the array will remember the order in which the elements were stored.

The assignment to `$fruit_basket`, then, has exactly the same effect as the following:

```
$fruit_basket[0] = 'apple';
$fruit_basket[1] = 'orange';
```

```
$fruit_basket[2] = 'banana';
$fruit_basket[3] = 'pear';
```

assuming that the $fruit_basket variable was unbound at the first assignment. The same effect could also have been accomplished by omitting the indices in the assignment, like so:

```
$fruit_basket[] = 'apple';
$fruit_basket[] = 'orange';
$fruit_basket[] = 'banana';
$fruit_basket[] = 'pear';
```

In this case, PHP again assumes that you are adding sequential elements that should have numerical indices counting upward from zero.

> **NOTE:** Yes, the default numbering for array indices starts at zero, not one. This is the convention for arrays in most programming languages. We're not sure why computer scientists start counting at zero (mathematicians, like everyone else in the world, start with one), but it probably has its origin in the kind of pointer arithmetic that calculates memory addresses for vector arrays. Addresses for successive elements of such arrays are found by adding successively larger offsets to the array's address, but the offset for the first element is zero (because the first element's address is the same as the array's address).

Specifying indices using array()

The simple example of array() in the preceding section assigns indices to our elements, but those indices will be the integers, counting upward from zero — we're not getting a lot of choice in the matter. As it turns out, array() offers us a special syntax for specifying what the indices should be. Instead of element values separated by commas, you supply key-value pairs separated by commas, where the key and value are separated by the special symbol =>.

Consider the following statement:

```
$fruit_basket = array(0 => 'apple', 1 => 'orange',
                      2 => 'banana', 3 => 'pear');
```

Evaluating it will have exactly the same effect as our earlier version — each string will be stored in the array in succession, with the indices 0, 1, 2, 3 in order. Instead, however, we can use exactly the same syntax to store these elements with different indices:

```
$fruit_basket = array('red' => 'apple', 'orange' => 'orange',
                      'yellow' => 'banana', 'green' => 'pear');
```

This gives us the same four elements, added to our new array in the same order, but indexed by color names rather than numbers. To recover the name of the yellow fruit, for example, we just evaluate the expression:

```
$fruit_basket['yellow'] // will be equal to 'banana'
```

Finally, as we said earlier, you can create an empty array by calling the array function with no arguments. For example:

```
$my_empty_array = array();
```

creates an array with no elements. This can be handy for passing to a function that expects an array as argument.

Functions returning arrays

The final way to create an array in a script is to call a function that returns an array. This may be a user-defined function, or it may be a built-in function that makes an array via methods internal to PHP.

Many database-interaction functions, for example, return their results in arrays that the functions create on-the-fly. Other functions exist simply to create arrays that are handy to have as grist for later array-manipulating functions. One such is range(), which takes two integers as arguments and returns an array filled with all the integers (inclusive) that are between the arguments. In other words:

```
$my_array = range(1,5);
```

is equivalent to:

```
$my_array = array(1, 2, 3, 4, 5);
```

Retrieving Values

After we have stored some values in an array, how do we get them out again?

Retrieving by index

The most direct way to retrieve a value is to use its index. If we have stored a value in $my_array at index 5, then $my_array[5] should evaluate to the stored value. If $my_array has never been assigned, or if nothing has been stored in it with an index of 5, then $my_array[5] will behave like an unbound variable.

The list() construct

There are a number of other ways to recover values from arrays without using keys, most of which exploit the fact that arrays are silently recording the order in which elements are stored. We cover this in more detail in the "Iteration" section, but one such example is list(), which is used to assign several array elements to variables in succession. Suppose, for example, the following two statements are executed:

```
$fruit_basket = array('apple', 'orange', 'banana');
list($red_fruit, $orange_fruit) = $fruit_basket;
```

This will have the result of assigning the string 'apple' to the variable $red_fruit, and the string 'orange' to the variable $orange_fruit (with no assignment of 'banana', because we didn't supply enough variables). The variables in list() will be assigned to elements of the array in the order they were originally stored in the array. Notice the unusual behavior here — the list() construct is on the left-hand side of the assignment operator (=), where we normally only find variables.

In some sense, list() is the opposite or inverse of array() because array() packages its arguments into an array, and list() takes the array apart again into individual variable assignments. If we evaluate:

```
list($first, $second) = array($first, second);
```

the original values of $first and $second will be assigned to those variables again, after having been briefly stored in an array.

> **NOTE:** We have been careful to refer to both array() and list() as constructs, rather than functions. This is because they are not in fact functions — like certain other specialized PHP language features (if, while, function, and so on) they are interpreted specially by the language itself and are not run through the usual routine of function-call interpretation. Remember that the arguments to a function call are evaluated before the function is really invoked on those arguments, so constructs that need to do other kinds of interpretation on what they are given cannot be implemented as function calls. It's a useful exercise to look hard at the example uses of both array() and list() to figure out why treating them as function calls could not result in the behavior advertised.

Multidimensional Arrays

So far the array examples we have looked at have all been one-dimensional, with only one level of bracketed keys. However, PHP can easily support multiple-dimensional arrays, with arbitrary numbers of keys. And just as with one-dimensional arrays, there is no need to declare our intentions in advance — the first reference to an array variable can be an assignment like:

```
$multi_array[1][2][3][4][5] = "deeply buried treasure";
```

That is a five-dimensional array with successive keys that happen, in this case, to be five successive integers.

Actually, in our opinion, thinking of arrays as multidimensional makes matters more confusing than they need to be. Instead, just remember that the values that are stored in arrays can themselves be arrays, just as legitimately as they can be strings or numbers. The multiple-index syntax in the preceding example is simply a concise way to refer to a (four-dimensional) array that is stored with a key of 1 in $multi_array, which in turn has a (three-dimensional) array stored in it, and so on. Note also that you can have different "depths" of reference in different parts of the array, like so:

```
$multi_level_array[0] = "a simple string";
$multi_level_array[1]['contains'] = "a string stored deeper";
```

The integer key of 0 stores a string, and the key of 1 stores an array that, in turn, has a string in it. However, you cannot continue on with this assignment:

```
$multi_level_array[0]['contains'] = "another deep string";
```

without the result of losing the first assignment to 'a simple string'. The key of 0 can be used to store a string or another array, but not both at once.

If we remember that multidimensional arrays are simply arrays that have other arrays stored in them, it's easier to see how the array() creation construct generalizes. In fact, even this seemingly complicated assignment is not that complicated:

```
$cornucopia = array('fruit' =>
                 array('red' => 'apple',
                       'orange' => 'orange',
                       'yellow' => 'banana',
                       'green' => 'pear'),
                 'flower' =>
                 array('red' => 'rose',
                       'yellow' => 'sunflower',
                       'purple' => 'iris'));
```

It is simply an array with two values stored in association with keys. Each of these values is an array itself. After we have made the array, we can reference it like this:

```
$kind_wanted = 'flower';
$color_wanted = 'purple';
print("The $color_wanted $kind_wanted is " .
    $cornucopia[$kind_wanted][$color_wanted]);
```

See the browser output:

```
The purple flower is iris
```

> **NOTE:** There's a reason that we used the string concatenation operator . in the preceding print statement, rather than simply embedding the $cornucopia[$kind_wanted][$color_wanted] in our print string as we do with other variables. PHP3 string parsing can be confused by multiple array indices within a double-quoted string, so it needs to be concatenated separately. PHP4 handles this in a better way — you are safe embedding array references in a string as long as you enclose the reference in curly braces, like this:
>
> ```
> print( "The thing we want is
> {$cornucopia[$kind_wanted][$color_wanted]}");
> ```

Finally, notice that there is no great penalty for misindexing into a multidimensional array when we are trying to retrieve something; if no such key is found, the expression is treated like an unbound variable. So, if we tried the following instead:

```
$kind_wanted = 'fruit';
$color_wanted = 'purple'; //uh-oh, we didn't store any plums
print("The $color_wanted $kind_wanted is " .
    $cornucopia[$kind_wanted][$color_wanted]);
```

The worst that happens is the unsatisfying:

```
The purple fruit is
```

This is the worst thing that happens, of course, unless you have raised your error_reporting level to E_ALL, as we advise you to do some points in this book. In that case, you will get a warning message about an undefined index ('purple') just as you would if you had an unbound variable.

Inspecting Arrays

Now we can make arrays, store values in arrays, and then pull the values out again when we want them. Table 11-1 summarizes a few other functions we can use to ask questions of our arrays.

Table 11-1: Simple Functions for Inspecting Arrays

Function	Behavior
is_array()	Takes a single argument of any type and returns a true value if the argument is an array, and false otherwise.
count()	Takes an array as argument and returns the number of nonempty elements in the array. (This will be 1 for strings and numbers.)
sizeof()	Identical to count().
in_array()	Takes two arguments: an element (that might be a value in an array), and an array (that might contain the element). Returns true if the element is contained as a value in the array, false otherwise. (Note that this does not test for the presence of keys in the array.)
IsSet($array[$key])	Takes an array[key] form and returns true if the key portion is a valid key for the array. (This is a specific use of the more general function IsSet(), which tests whether a variable is bound.)

Deleting from Arrays

Deleting an element from an array is simple, exactly analogous to getting rid of an assigned variable. Just call unset(), as in the following:

```
$my_array[0] = 'wanted';
$my_array[1] = 'unwanted';
```

```
$my_array[2] = 'wanted again';
unset($my_array[1]);
```

Assuming that $my_array was unbound when we started, at the end it has two values ('wanted', 'wanted again'), in association with two keys (0 and 2, respectively). It is as though we had skipped the original 'unwanted' assignment (except that the keys are numbered differently)

Note that this is *not* the same as setting the contents to an empty value. If, instead of calling unset(), we had the following statement:

```
$my_array[1] = '';
```

at the end we would have three stored values ('wanted', '', 'wanted again') in association with three keys (0, 1, and 2, respectively).

Iteration

We've seen how to put things into arrays, how to find them once we have put them there, and how to delete them when we don't want them anymore. What we need next is techniques for dealing with array elements in bulk. Iteration constructs help us do this by letting us step or loop through arrays, element by element or key by key.

We'll first delve briefly into the internal representation of arrays to understand how PHP supports iteration. (Although important, this subsection is skippable — if you want to use it but don't want to know how it works, you can jump down to "Using Iteration Functions.")

Support for iteration

In addition to storing values in association with their keys, PHP arrays silently build an ordered list of the key/value pairs that are stored, in the order that they are stored. The reason for this is to support operations that iterate over the entire contents of an array. (Notice that this is difficult to do simply by building a loop that increments an index, because array indices are not necessarily numerical.)

There is, in fact, sort of a hidden pointer system built into arrays. Each stored key/value pair points to the next one, and one side effect of adding the first element to an array is that a current pointer points to the very first element, where it will stay unless disturbed by one of the iteration functions.

> **NOTE:** Each array remembers a particular stored key/value pair as being the current one, and array iteration functions work in part by shifting that current marker through the internal list of keys and values. Although we will call this marker the *current pointer*, PHP does not support full pointers in the sense that C and C++ programmers may be used to, and this usage of the word will only turn up in the context of iterating through arrays.

This linked-list pointer system is an alternative way to inspect and manipulate arrays, which exists alongside the system that allows key-based lookup and storage. Figure 11-1 shows an abstract view (not necessarily reflecting the real implementation) of how these systems locate elements in an array.

Internal structure of an array

Figure 11-1: Internal structure of an array

Using iteration functions

To explore the iteration functions, let's construct a sample array that we can iterate over.

```
$major_city_info = array();
$major_city_info[0] = 'Caracas';
$major_city_info['Caracas'] = 'Venezuela';
$major_city_info[1] = 'Paris';
$major_city_info['Paris'] = 'France';
$major_city_info[2] = 'Tokyo';
$major_city_info['Tokyo'] = 'Japan';
```

In this example, we created an array and stored some names of cities in it, in association with numerical indices. We also stored the names of the relevant countries into the array, indexed by the city names. (We could have accomplished all this with one big call to array(), but the separate statements make the structure of the array somewhat clearer.)

Now, we can use the array key system to pull out the data we have stored. If we want to rely on the convention in the preceding example (cities stored with numerical indices, countries stored with city-name indices), we can write a function that prints out the city and the associated country, like so:

```
function city_by_number ($number_index, $city_array)
{
  if (IsSet($city_array[$number_index]))
    {
      $the_city = $city_array[$number_index];
      $the_country = $city_array[$the_city];
      print("$the_city is in $the_country<BR>");
    }
}
city_by_number(0, $major_city_info);
city_by_number(1, $major_city_info);
city_by_number(2, $major_city_info);
```

If we have set $major_city, as in the previous block of code, the browser output we should expect is:

```
Caracas is in Venezuela
Paris is in France
Tokyo is in Japan
```

Now, this method of retrieval is fine when we know how the array is structured and we know what all the keys are. But what if you would simply like to print everything that an array contains?

Our favorite iteration method: foreach

Our favorite construct for looping through an array is foreach. Although it is probably inherited from Perl's foreach, it has a somewhat odd syntax (which is not the same as Perl's odd syntax). It comes in two flavors — which one you decide to use will depend on whether you care about the array's keys or just the values.

```
foreach ($array_variable as $value_variable) {
  // .. do something with the value in $value_variable
}  // Note that this is an example template, not real PHP code

foreach ($array_variable as $key_var => $value_var) {
// .. do something with $key_var and/or $value_var
}
```

Although in the above pseudo-code we assume that the array of interest is in the variable $array_variable, you can have any expression that evaluates to an array in that position, for example:

```
foreach (function_returning_array() as $value_variable) {
```

```
    // .. do something with the value in $value_variable
}
```

> **NOTE:** Like `array()` and `list()`, and unlike the genuine iteration functions in the rest of this section, `foreach` is a language construct, not a function. (See the earlier note about `list()` for an explanation of the difference.)

As an example, let's write a function to print out all the names from our sample array:

```
function print_all_foreach ($city_array)
{
  foreach ($city_array as $name_value) {
    print("$name_value<BR>");
  }
}
print_all_foreach($major_city_info);
print_all_foreach($major_city_info);// again, as an experiment
```

As output, we get all the names, in the order we stored them, twice over:

```
Caracas
Venezuela
Paris
France
Tokyo
Japan
Caracas
Venezuela
Paris
France
Tokyo
Japan
```

The reason we printed the contents twice was to show that calling the function is repeatable.

Iterating with current() and next()

We like `foreach`, but it is really only good for situations where you want to simply loop through an array's values. For more control, let's look at `current()` and `next()`.

The `current()` function returns the stored value that the current pointer points to. (See Figure 11-1 earlier in the chapter for a diagram of the array internals.) When an array is newly created with elements, the element pointed to will always be the first element. The `next()` function first advances that pointer and then returns the current value pointed to. If the `next()` function is called when the current pointer is already pointing to the last stored value and, therefore, "runs off the end" of the array, the function returns a false value.

As an example, we can print out an array's contents with the iteration functions `current()` and `next()`. (Notice that the final function call is repeated again.)

```
function print_all_next($city_array)
{   // warning — doesn't quite work. See the function each()
  $current_item = current($city_array);
  if ($current_item)
    print("$current_item<BR>");
  else
    print("There's nothing to print");
  while($current_item = next($city_array))
    print("$current_item<BR>");
}
print_all_next($major_city_info);
print_all_next($major_city_info);// again, to see what happens
```

> **CAUTION:** There is a gotcha lurking in the preceding code example, which doesn't bite us in this particular example but makes this function untrustworthy as a general method for finding everything in an array. That is that we may have stored a false value in the array, which our `while` loop won't be able to distinguish from the false value that `next()` returns when it has run out of array elements. See the discussion of the `each()` function later in this chapter under "Empty values and the `each()` function" for a solution.

When we execute this array-printing code, we get the following again:

```
Caracas
Venezuela
Paris
France
Tokyo
Japan
Caracas
Venezuela
Paris
France
Tokyo
Japan
```

Now, how is it that we are seeing the same thing from the second call to `print_all_next()`? How did the current pointer get back to the beginning to start all over again the second time? The answer lies in the fact that PHP function calls are "call-by-value," meaning that they copy their arguments rather than operating directly on them. Both of the function calls, then, are getting a fresh copy of their array argument, which has never itself been disturbed by a call to `next()`.

> **CROSS-REFERENCE:** For more on what circumstances functions copy their arguments rather than operating on them directly, see Chapter 8.

We can test this explanation by passing the arrays by reference rather than by value. If we define the same function but call it with ampersands (&) like this:

```
print_all_next(&$major_city_info);
print_all_next(&$major_city_info);// again
```

We get the following printing behavior:

```
Caracas
Venezuela
Paris
France
Tokyo
Japan
There's nothing to print
```

> **NOTE**: The trick we used to test the array behavior (passing a variable reference to a function) has recently been deprecated, so you may get a warning when running this code, in addition to seeing the results printed above.

The reason is that this time the current pointer of the global version of the array was moved by the first function call.

> **NOTE:** Most of the iteration functions have both a returned value and a side effect. In the case of the functions next(), prev(), reset(), and end(), the side effect is to change the position of the internal pointer, and what is returned is the value from the key/value pair pointed to *after* the pointer's position is changed.

Starting over with reset()

In the preceding section, we wrote a function intended to print out all the values in an array, and we saw how it could fail if the array's internal pointer did not start off at the beginning of the list of key/value pairs. The reset() function gives us a way to "rewind" that pointer to the beginning — it sets the pointer to the first key/value pair and then returns the stored value. We can use it to make our printing function more robust by replacing the call to current() with a call to reset().

```
function print_all_array_reset($city_array)
{  // warning — still not reliable. See the function each()
  $current_item = reset($city_array); //rewind, return value
  if ($current_item)
    print("$current_item<BR>");
  else
    print("There's nothing to print");
  while($current_item = next($city_array))
    print("$current_item<BR>");
}
```

This function is somewhat more predictable in that it will always start with the first element, regardless of the pointer's location in the array it is handed. (Whether this is a good idea depends, of course, on what the function is used for and whether its arguments are passed by value or by reference.)

Perhaps confusingly, we use our call to `reset()` in the preceding example both for its side effect (rewinding the pointer) and for its return value (the first value stored). Alternatively, we could replace the first real line of the function body with these two lines:

```
reset($city_array);  // rewind to the first element
$current_item = current($city_array); // the first value
```

Reverse order with end() and prev()

We have seen the functions `next()`, which moves the current pointer ahead by one, and `reset()`, which rewinds the pointer to the beginning. Analogously, there are also the functions `prev()`, which moves the pointer back by one, and `end()`, which jumps the pointer to the last entry in the list. We can use these, for example, to print our array entries in reverse order.

```
function print_all_array_backwards($city_array)
{  // warning — still not reliable. See the function each()
  $current_item = end($city_array); //fast-forward to last
  if ($current_item)
    print("$current_item<BR>");
  else
    print("There's nothing to print");
  while($current_item = prev($city_array))
    print("$current_item<BR>");
}
print_all_array_backwards($major_city_info);
```

If we call this on the same `$major_city_info` data as in previous examples, we get the same printout in reverse order:

```
Japan
Tokyo
France
Paris
Venezuela
Caracas
```

Extracting keys with key()

So far we have only printed out the values stored in arrays, even though we are storing keys as well. The keys are also retrievable from the internal linked list of an array by using the `key()` function — this acts just like `current()` except that it returns the key of a key/value pair, rather than the value. (See Figure 11-1 from a few pages back.) Using the `key()` function, we can modify one of our earlier printing functions to print out keys as well as values.

```
function print_keys_and_values($city_array)
```

```
{  // warning - See the discussion of each() below
  reset($city_array);
  $current_value = current($city_array);
  $current_key = key($city_array);
  if ($current_value)
    print("Key: $current_key; Value: $current_value<BR>");
  else
    print("There's nothing to print");
  while($current_value = next($city_array))
  {
      $current_key = key($city_array);
      print("Key: $current_key; Value: $current_value<BR>");
  }
}
print_keys_and_values($major_city_info);
```

With the same data as before, this gives us the browser output:

```
Key: 0; Value: Caracas
Key: Caracas; Value: Venezuela
Key: 1; Value: Paris
Key: Paris; Value: France
Key: 2; Value: Tokyo
Key: Tokyo; Value: Japan
```

Empty values and the each() function

We have written several functions that print out the contents of arrays by iterating through them and, as we have pointed out, all but the `foreach` version have the same weakness. Each one of them tests for completion by seeing whether `next()` returns a false value. This will reliably happen when the array runs out of values, but it will also happen if and when we encounter a false value that we have actually stored. False values include the empty string (`""`), the number 0, and the Boolean value FALSE, any or all of which we might reasonably store as a data value for some task or other.

To the rescue comes `each()`, which is somewhat similar to `next()` but has the virtue of returning false only after it has run out of array to traverse. Oddly enough, if it has not run out, `each()` returns an array itself, which holds both keys and values for the key/value pair it is pointing at. This characteristic makes `each()` confusing to talk about because you need to keep two arrays straight: the array that you are traversing and the array that `each()` returns every time that it is called. The array that `each()` *returns* has the following four key/value pairs:

- Key: 0; Value: *current-key*
- Key: 1; Value: *current-value*
- Key: `'key'`; Value: *current-key*

♦ Key: `'value'`; Value: *current-value*

The *current-key* and *current-value* are the key and value from the array being traversed. In other words, the returned array packages up the current key/value pair from the traversed array and offers both numerical and string indices to specify whether you are interested in the key or the value.

NOTE: In addition to having a different type of return value, `each()` differs from `next()` in that `each()` returns the value that was pointed to *before* moving the current pointer ahead, whereas `next()` returns the value *after* the pointer is moved. This means if you start with a current pointer pointing to the first element of an array, successive calls to `each()` will cover each array cell, whereas successive calls to `next()` will skip the first value.

We can use `each()` to write a more robust version of a function to print out all keys and values in an array:

```
function print_keys_and_values_each($city_array)
{  // reliably prints everything in array
  reset($city_array);
  while ($array_cell = each($city_array))
  {
    $current_value = $array_cell['value'];
    $current_key = $array_cell['key'];
    print("Key: $current_key; Value: $current_value<BR>");
  }
}
print_keys_and_values_each($major_city_info);
```

Applying this function to our standard sample array gives the following browser output:

```
Key: 0; Value: Caracas
Key: Caracas; Value: Venezuela
Key: 1; Value: Paris
Key: Paris; Value: France
Key: 2; Value: Tokyo
Key: Tokyo; Value: Japan
```

This is exactly the same as was produced by our earlier function `print_keys_and_values()`. The difference is that our new function will not stop prematurely if one of the values is false or empty.

Walking with array_walk()

Our last iteration function lets you pass an arbitrary function of your own design over an array, doing whatever your function pleases with each key/value pair. The `array_walk()` function takes two arguments: an array to be traversed and the name of a function to apply to each key/value pair. (It also takes an optional third argument, discussed later in this section.)

The function that is passed in to `array_walk()` should take two (or three) arguments. The first argument will be the value of the array cell that is visited, and the second argument will be the key of that cell. For example, here is a function that prints out a descriptive statement about the string length of an array value:

```
function print_value_length($array_value, $array_key_ignored)
{
  $the_length = strlen($array_value);
  print("The length of $array_value is $the_length<BR>");
}
```

(Notice that this function intentionally does nothing with the second argument.) Now let's pass this function over our standard sample array using `array_walk()`:

```
array_walk($major_city_info, 'print_value_length');
```

which gives the browser output:

```
The length of Caracas is 7
The length of Venezuela is 9
The length of Paris is 5
The length of France is 6
The length of Tokyo is 5
The length of Japan is 5
```

The final flexibility that `array_walk()` offers is accepting an optional third argument that, if present, will be passed on, in turn, as a third argument to the function that is applied. This argument will be the same throughout the array's traversal, but it offers an extra source of runtime control for the passed function's behavior.

> **CAUTION**: You should not alter an array while you are iterating through the array using `array_walk()`. There is no guarantee how `array_walk()` will behave if you do this.

Table 11-2 shows a summary of the behavior of the array iteration functions that we covered in this section. Notice that `foreach` and `list` are not included because they are not functions.

Stacks and Queues

Stacks and *queues* are abstract data structures, frequently used in computer science, that enforce a certain kind of access discipline on the objects they contain, without necessarily committing to what those objects are. PHP arrays are well suited to imitating other kinds of data structures, and the loose typing of PHP array elements makes it easy for them to imitate stacks and queues. PHP provides some array functions specifically for this purpose — if you use them exclusively, you can forget that arrays are involved at all.

Table 11-2: Functions for Iterating over Arrays

Function	Arguments	Side Effect	Return Value
current()	One array argument	None.	The value from the key/value pair currently pointed to by the internal "current" pointer (or false if no such value).
next()	One array argument	Advances the pointer by one. If already at the last element, it will move the pointer "past the end," and subsequent calls to current() will return false.	The value pointed to after the pointer has been advanced (or false if no such value).
prev()	One array argument	Moves the pointer back by one. If already at the first element, will move the pointer "before the beginning."	The value pointed to after the pointer has been moved back (or false if no such value).
reset()	One array argument	Moves the pointer back to point to the first key/value pair, or "before the beginning" if the array is empty.	The first value stored in the array, or false for an empty array
end()	One array argument	Moves the pointer ahead to the last key/value pair.	The last value that is currently in the list of key/value pairs.
pos()	One array argument	None. (This function is an alias for current().)	The value of the key/value pair that is currently pointed to.

`each()`	One array argument	Moves the pointer ahead to the next key/value pair.	An array that packages the keys and values of the key/value pair that was current before the pointer was moved (or false if no such pair). The returned array stores the key and value under its own keys 0 and 1, respectively, and also under its own keys 'key' and 'value.'
`array_walk()`	1) An array argument, 2) the name of a two- (or three-) argument function to call on each key/value, and 3) an optional third argument.	This function invokes the function named by its second argument on each key/value pair. Side effects depend on the side effects of the passed function.	(Returns 1.)

A *stack* is a container that stores values and supports last-in-first-out (LIFO) behavior. This means that the stack maintains an order on the values you store, and the only way you can get a value back is by retrieving (and removing) the most recently stored value. The usual analogy is a stack of cafeteria trays in one of those dispensers that keeps the top tray at a constant level. You can push new trays down on top of the old ones, and you can take trays off the top, but you can't grab an older tray without taking the newer ones first. The act of adding into the stack is called *pushing* a value onto the stack, whereas the act of taking off the top is called *popping* the stack. Another analogy is the way some Web browsers store the pages you have visited for use by the Back button; visiting a new page pushes a new URL onto that stack, and using the Back button pops the stack.

A *queue* is similar to a stack, but its behavior is first-in-first-out (FIFO). The usual analogy here is what the British call a *queue* and what Americans call a *line*, where people line up in order to wait for something. The rule is that whoever has been in the queue the longest is the next to be served.

The stack functions are `array_push()` and `array_pop()`. The `array_push()` function takes an initial array argument and then any number of elements to push onto the stack. The elements will be inserted at the end of the array, in order from left to right. The array_pop() function takes such an array and removes the element at the end, returning it. Take the following fragment:

```
$my_stack = array();  // needed — array_push() will not create
array_push($my_stack, "the first", "the middle");
array_push($my_stack, "the last");
while ($popped = array_pop($my_stack))
  print("Popped the stack and got: $popped<BR>");
```

This will produce the browser output:

```
Popped the stack and got: the last
Popped the stack and got: the middle
Popped the stack and got: the first
```

PHP4 also offers functions that behave exactly the same way as array_push() and array_pop(), except that they work at the other end, adding to and removing from the beginning of the array. The array_unshift() function is analogous to array_push(), and array_shift() is like array_pop(). If you choose one function from column A and one from column B, you can get the behavior of a queue. For example, we can rewrite our previous example to push into the beginning of the array (using array_unshift()) and pop from the end (using array_pop(), as before):

```
$my_queue = array();// needed — array_unshift() will not create
array_unshift($my_queue, "the first");
array_unshift($my_queue,"the middle");
array_unshift($my_queue, "the last");
while ($popped = array_pop($my_queue))
  print("Popped the queue and got: $popped<BR>");
```

It produces the output:

```
Popped the queue and got: the first
Popped the queue and got: the middle
Popped the queue and got: the last
```

CAUTION: The array_unshift() and array_shift() functions are somewhat different from array_push() and array_pop() in that the former do some renumbering of the array indices if the indices are integers. The idea is that some people may be relying on the numerical indices to order the array contents, so using array_unshift() to insert a new element at the beginning should assign an index of 0 to the new element, and renumber those above. Similarly, popping an element from the beginning with array_shift() causes integral indices of other elements to be reduced. (This is not an issue with array_push and array_pop because changes are at the end, and no renumbering is needed.) If you are using string indices exclusively, this renumbering has no effect. This is a general pattern with PHP array functions: Some of them treat integer indices like any other associative indexes, whereas others assume that integers imply order, and redo them if the order has changed.

The stack and queue functions are summarized in Table 11-3.

Table 11-3: Stack and Queue Functions

Function	Arguments	Side Effect	Returns
Array_push()	An initial array argument, then any number of values to be pushed onto the stack	Modifies the array by adding the elements in order to the end of the array.	The number of elements in the array after the push.
array_pop()	A single array argument	Removes the element at the end of the array.	Returns the last (removed) value, or a false value if the array is empty.
array_unshift()	An initial array argument, then any number of values to be pushed onto the front of the array	Modifies the array by adding the successive elements to the beginning. (The last argument will be at the beginning of the array.)	The number of elements in the array after the new elements are added.
array_shift()	A single array argument	Removes the element at the beginning of the array.	Returns the first (removed) value, or a false value if the array is empty.

Transformations of Arrays

PHP4 offers a host of functions for manipulating your data once you have it nicely stored in an array. What the functions in this section have in common is that they take your array, do something with it, and return the results in another array. (We will defer the array-sorting functions until the next section.)

Earlier in the chapter, we incrementally developed a function to print out the entire contents of an array, and in this section will use the last of these (print_keys_and_values_each()) to show the arrays that are being returned in examples.

Retrieving keys and values

The array_keys() function returns the keys of its input array in the form of a new array where the keys are the stored values. The keys of the new array are the usual automatically incremented integers, starting from 0. The array_values() function does exactly the same thing, except the stored values are the values from the original array. If we start with an array like the following:

```
$pizza_requests = array('Alice' => 'pepperoni',
                        'Bob' => 'mushrooms',
                        'Carl' => 'sausage',
```

```
                          'Dennis' => 'mushrooms');
```

and then we print the arrays resulting from calls to the these two functions:

```
print("Array keys:<BR>");
print_keys_and_values_each(array_keys($pizza_requests));
print("Array values:<BR>");
print_keys_and_values_each(array_values($pizza_requests));
```

we get output like this:

```
Array keys:
Key: 0; Value: Alice
Key: 1; Value: Bob
Key: 2; Value: Carl
Key: 3; Value: Dennis
Array values:
Key: 0; Value: pepperoni
Key: 1; Value: mushrooms
Key: 2; Value: sausage
Key: 3; Value: mushrooms
```

The second of these (array_values()) may seem uninteresting because we have essentially taken our old array and produced a new one with the keys renamed to successive numbers.

We can do something slightly more useful (and more helpful for ordering) with the function array_count_values(). This takes an array and returns a new array where the old values are now the new keys and the new values are the number of times each old value occurs in the original array.

```
print_keys_and_values_each(
    array_count_values($pizza_requests));
```

gives us:

```
Key: pepperoni; Value: 1
Key: mushrooms; Value: 2
Key: sausage; Value: 1
```

Flipping, reversing, shuffling

A even odder function is array_flip(), which changes the keys of an array into the values, and vice versa. For example:

```
print_keys_and_values_each(array_flip($pizza_requests));
```

gives us:

```
Key: pepperoni; Value: Alice
Key: mushrooms; Value: Dennis // what happened to Bob?
Key: sausage; Value Carl
```

Notice that, although array keys are guaranteed to be unique, array values are not — because of this, any duplicate values in the original array become the same key in the new array. Only one of the original keys will survive to become the corresponding new value.

Reversing an array is simpler: `array_reverse()` returns a new array with the key/value pairs in reverse order. So, with the usual printing test:

```
print_keys_and_values_each(array_reverse($pizza_requests));
```

we get the result:

```
Key: Dennis; Value: mushrooms
Key: Carl; Value: sausage
Key: Bob; Value: mushrooms
Key: Alice; Value: pepperoni
```

In this case, although the internal order has been reversed, all the key/value pairs end up being the same. However, this function (like several other PHP array functions) treats integer keys somewhat specially. It assumes that the ordering of integer keys on those key/value pairs should also be reversed for the later use of code that pays attention to the ordering of keys, rather than using the internal linked-list ordering. So, `array_reverse()` swaps integer keys to make the new key ordering match the internal list.

If you need some extra randomness in your life, the `shuffle()` function can give it to you — `shuffle()` takes an array argument and randomizes the order of the elements in the array. It uses `rand()`, a function that generates successive random numbers. Before you use `shuffle()`, you need to have seeded the random-number generator with a call to `srand()`. (See the discussion of `random-number generation` in Chapter 12.) A reasonable calling sequence looks like this:

```
srand((double)microtime() * 1000000);  // for random # gen
shuffle($pizza_requests);
print_keys_and_values_each(array_flip($pizza_requests));
```

which *might* give us output like:

```
Key: Carl; Value: sausage
Key: Bob; Value: mushrooms
Key: Dennis; Value: mushrooms
Key: Alice; Value: pepperoni
```

(Of course, we emphasize *might* because the point is that the order is not predictable. See "How random is `shuffle()`?" later in this chapter for more on how unpredictable it is.)

> **CROSS-REFERENCE:** For more on random-number generation, see Chapter 12. If you want to use the `shuffle()` function without having to consult Chapter 12, simply make sure that any page that uses `shuffle()` has the call to `srand()` once (and only once) in the script, before any calls to `shuffle()`, as in the preceding example.

> **CAUTION:** Unlike many of the array functions in this chapter, `shuffle()` is *destructive*, meaning that it operates directly on its array argument and changes it, rather than returning a newly created array. (Functions that return a new thing without disturbing their arguments might be called *constructive*, or just *nondestructive*.) Among other things, this means that the correct way to call the shuffle function is not
>
> ```
> $my_new_array = shuffle($my_old_array); //WRONG!
> ```
>
> especially because the `shuffle()` function does not return a value. Instead, the right call is
>
> ```
> shuffle($my_array);    // change the array itself
> ```

These array-manipulating functions, and a few extra besides, are summarized in Table 11-4.

Table 11-4: Array Transformation Functions

Function	Behavior
`array_keys()`	Takes a single array argument and returns a new array where the new values are the keys of the input array, and the new keys are the integers incremented from zero.
`array_values()`	Takes a single array argument and returns a new array where the new values are the original values of the input array, and the new keys are the integers incremented from zero.
`array_count_values()`	Takes a single array argument and returns a new array where the new keys are the old array's values, and the new values are a count of how many times that original value occurred in the input array.
`array_flip()`	Takes a single array argument and changes that array so that the keys are now the values and vice versa.
`array_reverse()`	Takes a single array argument and changes the internal ordering of the key/value pairs to reverse order. Numerical keys will also be renumbered.
`shuffle()`	Takes a single array argument and randomizes the internal ordering of key/value pairs. Also renumbers integer keys to match the new ordering. This function itself uses the random-number generator `rand()`, so `srand()` must be called to seed the generator before the call to `shuffle()`.
`Array_merge()`	Takes two array arguments, merges them, and returns the new array, which has (in order) the first array's elements and then the second array's elements. (*Note:* This is most useful for arrays that are being used for simple linked lists rather than for their associative keys, because keys that appear in both arrays will have one of the values overwritten. Also, numerical keys will be renumbered from 0 to reflect the new ordering.)

`Array_pad()`	Takes three arguments: an input array, a pad size, and a value to pad with. Returns a new array that is "padded" by the following rules: If the pad size is greater than the length of the input array, the array is lengthened with the pad value to the pad size, as though by successive assignments like `$my_array[] = $pad_value`. A negative pad size will act the same way with the absolute value of that pad size, except that the padding will occur at the beginning of the array rather than the end. If the array is already longer than the (absolute value of) the pad size, the function has no effect.
`array_slice()`	Takes three arguments: an input array, an integer offset, and an (optional) integer length. Returns a new array that is a "slice" of the old one — a subsequence of its list of key/value pairs. The starting and stopping point of the slice are determined by the offset and length. A positive offset means that the starting point is that number of elements after the beginning; a negative offset means that it is that many elements before the end. The optional length argument specifies how long the resulting slice is (if positive) or how many elements before the end it should stop (if negative). If the length argument is not present, the slice continues to the end of the array.
`array_splice()`	Removes a chunk (or a slice) of an array and replaces it with the contents of another array. Takes four arguments: an input array, an offset, an optional integer length, and an optional replacement array. Returns a new array containing the slice that was removed from the input array. The rules for using the offset and length arguments to determine the slice that is removed are the same as in the previous `array_slice()` function. If no replacement array is supplied, this function simply (destructively) removes a slice of the input array and returns it. If there is a replacement array, the elements of that array are inserted in place of the removed slice.

Translating between Variables and Arrays

PHP4 offers a couple of unusual functions for mapping between the name/value pairs of regular variable bindings and the key/value pairs of an array. The `compact()` function translates from variable bindings to an array, and the `extract()` function goes in the opposite direction. These are summarized briefly in Table 11-5.

Table 11-5: Array/Variable-Binding Functions

Function	Behavior
`compact()`	Takes a specified set of strings, looks up bound variables (if any) in the current environment that are named by those strings, and returns an array where the keys are the variable names, and the values are the corresponding values of those variables.
	This function takes any number of arguments, each of which is either a string or an array that contains strings at some level of index depth. The entire set of strings that are included in the argument(s) is used as the candidate set of variable names. Strings that do not correspond to bound variables are ignored.
`extract()`	Takes an array (plus two optional arguments explained in the next paragraph) and imports the key/value pairs into the current variable-binding context. The array keys become the variable names, and the corresponding array values become the values of the variables. Any keys that do not correspond to a legal variable name will not produce an assignment.
	The optional arguments are an integer (intended to receive one of a small set of constants) and a prefix string. The point of these arguments is to specify what should happen in the case of a collision between the name of an existing variable and one that would be created from an array key.
	The intended possible constants for the optional integer arguments are 1) `EXTR_OVERWRITE`, 2) `EXTR_SKIP`, 3) `EXTR_PREFIX_SAME`, and 4) `EXTR_PREFIX_ALL`. The corresponding behaviors are 1) go ahead and overwrite existing variables, 2) skip any new assignments that would require overwriting, 3) use the optional prefix string to distinguish the new variable from the old one, or 4) prefix all the new variables with the string. For example, `extract(array('my_var' => 4), EXTR_PREFIX_SAME, 'diff_');` would cause `$my_var` to be 4 if `$my_var` were not already bound; otherwise, it would assign the value 4 to `$diff_my_var`.

Sorting

Finally, PHP4 offers a host of functions for sorting arrays. As we saw earlier, a tension sometimes arises between respecting the key/value associations in an array and treating numerical keys as ordering info that should be changed when the order changes. Luckily, PHP offers variants of the sorting functions for each of these behaviors and also allows sorting in ascending or descending order and by user-supplied ordering functions. The function names are terse, but each letter (other than the `'sort'` part) has its meaning. The decoder ring is something like:

♦ An initial a means that the function sorts by value but maintains the association between key/value pairs the way it was.

♦ *An initial k means that it sorts by key but maintains the key/value associations.

♦ A lack of that initial a or k means that it sorts by value but doesn't maintain the key/value association. In particular, numerical keys will be renumbered to reflect the new ordering.

♦ An r before the sort means that the sorting order will be reversed.

♦ An initial u means that a second argument is expected: the name of a user-defined function that specifies the ordering of any two elements that are being sorted. (See the description in Table 11-6.)

Table 11-6: Array Sorting Functions

Function	*Behavior*
asort()	Takes a single array argument. Sorts the key/value pairs by value but keeps the key/value mapping the same. Good for associative arrays.
arsort()	Same as asort(), but sorts in descending order.
ksort()	Takes a single array argument. Sorts the key/value pairs by key but maintain the key/value associations the same.
krsort()	Same as ksort(), but sorts in descending order.
sort()	Takes a single array argument. Sorts the key/value pairs of an array by their values. Keys may be renumbered to reflect the new ordering of the values.
rsort()	Same as sort(), but sorts in descending order.
uasort()	Sorts key/value pairs by value using a comparison function. Similar to asort(), except the actual ordering of the values is determined by the second argument, which is the name of a user-defined ordering function. That function should return a negative number if its first argument is before the second (according to the comparison function), a positive number if the first argument comes after the second, and zero if the elements are the same.
uksort()	Sorts key/value pairs by key, using a comparison function. Similar to uasort(), except that the ordering is by key, rather than by value.
usort()	Sorts an array by value using a supplied comparison function. Similar to uasort(), except that (as in sort()), the key/value associations are not maintained.

Example: How Random Is Shuffle()?

This subsection has several purposes: to demonstrate a nontrivial use of array functions, to investigate the randomness claims of the shuffle() function, and to show you a function that you might want to use instead of shuffle(). We got into this because we kept hearing complaints that shuffle() seemed to give insufficiently random results. It's always hard to know what to make of anecdotal reports of isolated instances of nonrandomness, so we thought some testing was called for.

Listing 11-1 shows some code to display a text matrix for `shuffle()`. This test repeatedly takes a an ordered array with ten elements, runs it through `shuffle()`, and constructs a 10x10 matrix from the repeated results. Each count in the matrix represents the number of times an element started at position x and ended at position y. Take, for example, the number at position 0.0 represents the number of times that an element started off at the beginning of the list and was still at the beginning after the list was shuffled.

Listing 11-1: Testing `shuffle()`

```php
<?php
srand((double) microtime() * 1000000);

function run_tests() {
   global $shuffle_counts;
   $shuffle_array = array(0,1,2,3,4,5,6,7,8,9);
   shuffle($shuffle_array);

   $element_counter = 0;
   foreach ($shuffle_array as $element) {
      if (isSet($shuffle_counts[$element_counter][$element])) {
         $shuffle_counts[$element_counter][$element] += 1;
      }
      else {
         $shuffle_counts[$element_counter][$element] = 1;
      }
      $element_counter++;
   }
}

for ($i = 0; $i < 1000; $i++) {
   run_tests();
}

print("<H3>Counts from shuffled arrays</H3>");
print("<TABLE BORDER=1><TR>");
print("<TH>Positions:</TH>");
for ($pos = 0; $pos < 10; $pos++) {
   print("<TH>$pos</TH>");
}
print("</TR>");
for ($val = 0; $val < 10; $val++) {
   print("<TR><TH>Value $val</TH>");
   for ($pos = 0; $pos < 10; $pos++) {
      print("<TD>" . $shuffle_counts[$pos][$val]. "</TD>");
   }
   print("</TR>");
```

```
}
print("</TABLE>");
?>
```

Figure 11-2 shows a representative run from this test. The code repeats the shuffle test 1000 times, so each row (and each column) has 1000 counts to spread around — the question is how randomly the results are spread. If shuffle() had never been called at all, we would expect to see the diagonal cells (top-left to bottom-right) with values of exactly 1000, and zeroes elsewhere. Clearly, shuffle() is doing better than that. However, if the results of the shuffle were perfectly random, the expected value for each cell would be the same (100). Of course, we would expect to see random variation from cell to cell, but no persistent pattern. Instead, counts along the diagonal seem to be disproportionately high, especially the top-left and bottom-right corners, indicating that elements in the first or last position often ended up staying there. (We understand that a single run is yet another anecdotal report, so feel free to run the code yourself until you are convinced.)

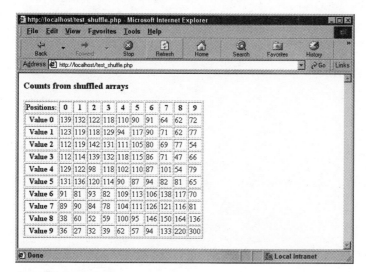

Figure 11-2: Randomness of shuffle

Listing 11-2 shows a similar test, along with a hand-rolled shuffling function (create_randomized_array). Now, note that this function is not doing exactly the same task as PHP's shuffle(). Shuffle() randomizes an array in place, without using extra storage. Our function, instead, produces a new array from an old one. Also, ours pays no attention to keys and returns a simple array produced from the values of the input array. With that said, however, it seemingly does a better job if your goal is simply to produce a shuffled version of a list of elements. Figure 11-3 shows the corresponding results of the 10x10 matrix test. (We use the create_randomized_array function for the trivia game example in Chapter 39, in preference to shuffle().)

Listing 11-2: Testing a replacement for shuffle

```php
<?php
srand((double) microtime() * 1000000);

function create_randomized_array ($in_array) {
   // Assumes input is simple list, with keys
   //   equal to 0,...,n
   // Returns similar list, with keys as in input
   //   but values in randomized order
   // Assumes prior call to srand()
   $in_array_length = count($in_array);
   $working_array = array();
   for ($i = 0; $i < $in_array_length; $i++) {
      $rand_value = rand();
      $working_array[$i] = $rand_value;
   }
   asort($working_array);  // orders by random value
   $return_array = array();
   $working_keys = array_keys($working_array);
   foreach ($working_keys as $int_key) {
      array_push($return_array,
         $in_array[$int_key]);
   }
   return($return_array);
}
function run_tests() {
   global $random_counts;
   $random_array = array(0,1,2,3,4,5,6,7,8,9);
   $random_array = create_randomized_array($random_array);

   $element_counter = 0;
   foreach ($random_array as $element) {
      if (IsSet($random_counts[$element_counter][$element])) {
 $random_counts[$element_counter][$element] += 1;
      }
      else {
 $random_counts[$element_counter][$element] = 1;
      }
      $element_counter++;
   }
}

for ($i = 0; $i < 1000; $i++) {
  run_tests();
}

print("<H3>Counts from randomized arrays</H3>");
print("<TABLE BORDER=1><TR>");
```

```
print("<TH>Positions:</TH>");
for ($pos = 0; $pos < 10; $pos++) {
  print("<TH>$pos</TH>");
}
print("</TR>");
for ($val = 0; $val < 10; $val++) {
  print("<TR><TH>Value $val</TH>");
  for ($pos = 0; $pos < 10; $pos++) {
    print("<TD>" . $random_counts[$pos][$val]. "</TD>");
  }
  print("</TR>");
}
print("</TABLE>");

?>
```

Figure 11-3: Randomness of the `shuffle()` replacement

Printing Functions for Visualizing Arrays

Before we continue with the exercise-calculator example we began in Chapters 9 and 10, we should mention a couple of printing functions that are very useful for visualizing and debugging arrays, especially multidimensional arrays.

The first function is `print_r()`, which is short for *print recursive*. This takes an argument of any type and prints it out, which includes printing all its parts recursively. For a simple value (a number or string), this means simply that the value is printed; for compound types like arrays and objects it means that all elements (and all parts of those elements) are printed. The layout that makes the compound structure clear involves spaces, so it's best to wrap its output in an HTML <pre></pre> construct so that the spaces are printed literally.

The var_dump() function is similar, except that it prints additional information about the size and type of the values it discovers. An example is worth a thousand words here, so we will create a simple multidimensional array and print it using both functions:

```php
<?php

$my_array = array("key1" => "value1",
                  "key2" => array("subkey1" => "value2"));

print("The result of print_r:<BR><pre>");
print_r($my_array);
print("</pre><BR>");
print("The result of var_dump:<BR><pre>");
var_dump($my_array);
print("</pre><BR>");
?>The resulting output from this sample looks like this:The result of
print_r:
Array
(
    [key1] => value1
    [key2] => Array
        (
            [subkey1] => value2
        )

)

The result of var_dump:
array(2) {
  ["key1"]=>
  string(6) "value1"
  ["key2"]=>
  array(1) {
    ["subkey1"]=>
    string(6) "value2"
  }
}
```

Extended Example: An Exercise Calculator

Now we'll continue our exercise-calculator example that we started in Chapters 9 and 10, and make further improvements using PHP arrays.

When we left this example in Chapter 10, we were allowing the user to type in the name of an exercise into a Web form, and we were hoping to match the submitted string with an exercise known to the receiving script. Instead, let's take our advice from late in Chapter 10, and constrain inputs from the user to a set we know we can recognize on the receiving end.

Listing 11-3 shows an HTML form that presents a set of exercises that the user can choose from. This uses a radio-button input, so that the user can choose only one exercise to submit.

Listing 11-3: Entry form with radio buttons

```
<HTML>
<HEAD>
<STYLE TYPE="text/css">
<!--
BODY, P, TD
{color: black; font-family: verdana; font-size: 10 pt}
H1
{color: black; font-family: arial; font-size: 12 pt}
-->
</STYLE>
</HEAD>

<BODY>
<TABLE BORDER=0 CELLPADDING=10 WIDTH=100%>
<TR>
<TD BGCOLOR="#F0F8FF" ALIGN=CENTER VALIGN=TOP WIDTH=150>
</TD>
<TD BGCOLOR="#FFFFFF" ALIGN=LEFT VALIGN=TOP WIDTH=83%>
<H1>Workout calculator (radio buttons with arrays)</H1>
<P>Select one of the following exercises, and we'll tell
   you how long <BR>
   you'd have to do it to burn one pound of fat.</P>

<FORM METHOD="post" ACTION="wc_handler_ckbx.php">
<table>
<tr>
  <td><input type="radio"
      name="exercise" value="0"> Biking/cycling</td>
</tr><tr>
  <td><input type="radio"
      name="exercise" value="1"> Running</td>
</tr><tr>
  <td><input type="radio"
      name="exercise" value="2"> Soccer/football</td>
</tr><tr>
  <td><input type="radio"
      name="exercise" value="3"> Stairclimber</td>
</tr><tr>
  <td><input type="radio"
      name="exercise" value="4"> Weightlifting</td>
</tr><tr>
```

```
  <td> </td>
</tr><tr>
  <td><input type="submit"
      name="submit" value="Burn, baby, burn!"></td>
</tr>
</table>
</FORM>

</TD>
</TR>
</TABLE>

</BODY>
</HTML>
```

Figure 11-4 shows how the entry form looks in a browser.

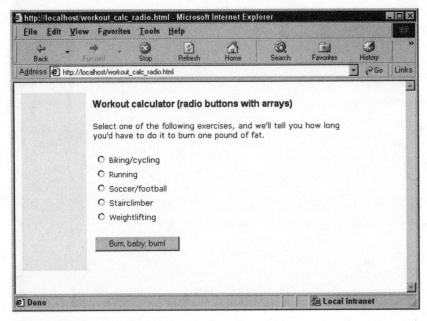

Figure 11-4: Entry form with radio buttons

The radio-button entry form passes a particular POST variable named `'exercise'`, which can have several different numerical values depending on which button the user clicks on. Listing 11-4 shows some handler code which can catch such a submission; the job of this code is to figure out which button was clicked and to print some appropriate info, which has been stored in advance in arrays in the receiving code file. Figure 11-5 shows the result of catching the user submission and displaying appropriately.

Listing 11-4: Handler for radio-button selection

```php
<?php

// This is the array where we keep our exercise names
$name_array = array(
                    0 => 'Biking/cycling',
                    1 => 'Running',
                    2 => 'Soccer/football',
                    3 => 'Stairclimber',
                    4 => 'Weightlifting'
                );

// This is the array where we keep our duration data
$duration_array = array(
                    0 => '5 hours and 40 minutes',
                    1 => '4 hours and 30 minutes',
                    2 => '4 hours and 30 minutes',
                    3 => '5 hours',
                    4 => '7 hours and 30 minutes'
                );

// Now pull out the chosen exercise from the submission
if (is_array($_POST) && count($_POST) > 1) {
  $exercise_value = $_POST['exercise'];
  $exercise_name = $name_array[$exercise_value];
  $hours = $duration_array[$exercise_value];
}   //Usually you'd test an array for a count of 0, but here
  //there is 1 automatic POST element -- $_POST['submit'].

// Construct a sentence
// --------------------
if (isSet($hours)) {
  $message = 'It would take '.$hours.' of '.$exercise_name.
    ' to burn one pound of fat.';
} else {
  // Hmmm, they didn't pick one or something odd happened
  $message = 'Ummm, did you pick an exercise?';
}

// Now lay out the page
// --------------------
$page_str = <<< EOPAGE
<HTML>
<HEAD>
<STYLE TYPE="text/css">
<!--
BODY, P      {color: black; font-family: verdana; font-size: 10 pt}
```

```
H1           {color: black; font-family: arial; font-size: 12 pt}
-->
</STYLE>
</HEAD>

<BODY>
<TABLE BORDER=0 CELLPADDING=10 WIDTH=100%>
<TR>
<TD BGCOLOR="#F0F8FF" ALIGN=CENTER VALIGN=TOP WIDTH=150>
</TD>
<TD BGCOLOR="#FFFFFF" ALIGN=LEFT VALIGN=TOP WIDTH=83%>
<H1>Workout calculator handler (radio buttons with arrays)</H1>
<P>The workout calculator says, "$message"</P>
</TD>
</TR>
</TABLE>

</BODY>
</HTML>
EOPAGE;

echo $page_str;

?>
```

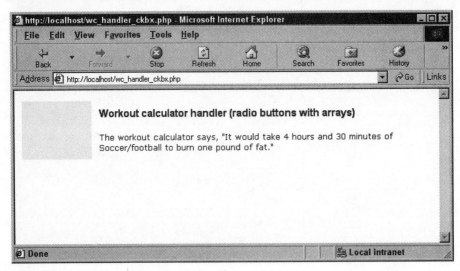

Figure 11-5: Displaying the result of radio-button entry

As usual, this is fine as far as it goes, but what if we want to submit more than one choice? For one thing, the point of the radio-button HTML construct is to allow only one choice, so we will have to abandon it; for another, the receiving code is only set up to extract one exercise.

To relax this constraint, let's use HTML check boxes instead of radio buttons for the form itself. And while we're doing that, let's use a nice feature of PHP form processing and give the choices variable names that look like indexes into a single array variable (`exercise[0]`, `exercise[1]`, and so on). On the receiving end, we can simply treat `exercise` as a single array that has arrived in the `$_POST`. Listing 11-5 shows the modified HTML form, and Listing 11-6 shows the receiving code.

Listing 11-5: Entry form with check boxes

```
    <HTML>
<HEAD>
<STYLE TYPE="text/css">
<!--
BODY, P, TD      {color: black; font-family: verdana; font-size: 10 pt}
H1          {color: black; font-family: arial; font-size: 12 pt}
-->
</STYLE>
</HEAD>


<BODY>
<TABLE BORDER=0 CELLPADDING=10 WIDTH=100%>
<TR>
<TD BGCOLOR="#F0F8FF" ALIGN=CENTER VALIGN=TOP WIDTH=150>
</TD>
<TD BGCOLOR="#FFFFFF" ALIGN=LEFT VALIGN=TOP WIDTH=83%>
<H1>Workout calculator (multiple checkboxes with arrays)</H1>
<P>Select one or more of the following exercises, and we'll tell you<BR>
how long you'd have to do each one to burn one pound of fat.</P>

<FORM METHOD="post" ACTION="wc_handler_array.php">
<table>
<tr>
  <td><input type="checkbox" name="exercise[0]"
value="1"> Biking/cycling</td>
</tr>
<tr>
  <td><input type="checkbox" name="exercise[1]"
value="1"> Running</td>
</tr>
<tr><td><input type="checkbox" name="exercise[2]"
value="1"> Soccer/football</td>
</tr>
<tr>
  <td><input type="checkbox" name="exercise[3]"
value="1"> Stairclimber</td>
</tr>
<tr>
```

```
  <td><input type="checkbox" name="exercise[4]"
value="1"> Weightlifting</td>
</tr>
<tr>
  <td> </td>
</tr>
<tr>
  <td><input type="submit" name="submit" value="Burn, baby, burn!"></td>
</TR>
</TABLE>
</FORM>

</TR></TABLE>

</BODY>
</HTML>
```

To save space, we'll skip the screenshots for this example; the submitting form looks similar to the radio-button example except for the prompting language, and the receiving page simply prints out multiple choices rather than a single choice.

Listing 11-6: Handler for check boxes

```php
<?php

// This is the array where we keep our exercise names
$name_array = array(
                0 => 'Biking/cycling',
                1 => 'Running',
                2 => 'Soccer/football',
                3 => 'Stairclimber',
                4 => 'Weightlifting'
              );

// This is the array where we keep our duration data
$duration_array = array(
                0 => '5 hours and 40 minutes',
                1 => '4 hours and 30 minutes',
                2 => '4 hours and 30 minutes',
                3 => '5 hours',
                4 => '7 hours and 30 minutes'
              );

// Now step through the exercises and see which ones they chose
if (is_array($_POST) && count($_POST) > 1) {
  $message = '';
  foreach ($_POST['exercise'] as $key => $val) {
    if ($val == 1) {
      $exercise_name = $name_array[$key];
```

```
        $hours = $duration_array[$key];
        $message .=
          "</P>\n<P>It would take $hours of $exercise_name " .
        "to burn one pound of fat.";
      }
    }
}
else {
   // Hmmm, they didn't pick one or something strange happened
   $message = 'Ummm, did you pick an exercise?';
} //If you don't have this test, an empty form will cause an error.
   //Usually you'd test an array for a count of 0, but here
   //there is 1 automatic POST array element -- $_POST['submit'].


// Now lay out the page
// --------------------
$page_str = <<< EOPAGE
<HTML>
<HEAD>
<STYLE TYPE="text/css">
<!--
BODY, P     {color: black; font-family: verdana; font-size: 10 pt}
H1          {color: black; font-family: arial; font-size: 12 pt}
-->
</STYLE>
</HEAD>

<BODY>
<TABLE BORDER=0 CELLPADDING=10 WIDTH=100%>
<TR>
<TD BGCOLOR="#F0F8FF" ALIGN=CENTER VALIGN=TOP WIDTH=150>
</TD>
<TD BGCOLOR="#FFFFFF" ALIGN=LEFT VALIGN=TOP WIDTH=83%>
<H1>Workout calculator handler (multiple checkboxes with arrays)</H1>
<P>The workout calculator says:
$message</P>
</TD>
</TR>
</TABLE>

</BODY>
</HTML>
EOPAGE;

echo $page_str;

?>
```

Taking this one step further, we can also submit multidimensional arrays via HTML form. All we need to do is name our FORM variables with multiple levels of brackets (like exercise[1][2]), and we'll have a multidimensional array on the receiving end.

Listing 11-7 shows our slightly modified entry form, and Listing 11-8 shows receiving code that iterates through the submitted multidimensional array, doing the appropriate unpacking.

Listing 11-7: Entry form for multidimensional arrays

```
<HTML>
<HEAD>
<STYLE TYPE="text/css">
<!--
BODY, P, TD      {color: black; font-family: verdana; font-size: 10 pt}
H1         {color: black; font-family: arial; font-size: 12 pt}
-->
</STYLE>
</HEAD>


<BODY>
<TABLE BORDER=0 CELLPADDING=10 WIDTH=100%>
<TR>
<TD BGCOLOR="#F0F8FF" ALIGN=CENTER VALIGN=TOP WIDTH=150>
</TD>
<TD BGCOLOR="#FFFFFF" ALIGN=LEFT VALIGN=TOP WIDTH=83%>
<H1>Workout calculator (multidimensional arrays)</H1>
<P>Select one or more of the following exercises, and we'll tell you<BR>
how long you'd have to do each one to burn one pound of fat.</P>

<FORM METHOD="post" ACTION="wc_handler_mult_arr.php">
<table>
<tr>
  <td><B>Aerobic exercise</B></td>
</tr>
<tr>
  <td><input type="checkbox" name="exercise[0][0]"
      value="1"> Biking/cycling</td>
</tr>
<tr>
  <td><input type="checkbox" name="exercise[0][1]"
      value="1"> Rowing</td>
</tr>
<tr>
  <td><input type="checkbox" name="exercise[0][2]"
      value="1"> Running</td>
</tr>
<tr>
  <td><input type="checkbox" name="exercise[0][3]"
      value="1"> Stairclimber</td>
</tr>
```

```
</tr>
<tr>
  <td><input type="checkbox" name="exercise[0][4]"
      value="1"> Walking</td>
</tr>
<tr>
  <td><B>Sports</B></td>
</tr>
<tr>
  <td><input type="checkbox" name="exercise[1][0]"
      value="1"> Basketball</td>
</tr>
<tr>
  <td><input type="checkbox" name="exercise[1][1]"
      value="1"> Ice hockey</td>
</tr>
<tr>
  <td><input type="checkbox" name="exercise[1][2]"
      value="1"> Soccer/football</td>
</tr>
<tr>
  <td><input type="checkbox" name="exercise[1][3]"
      value="1"> Table tennis</td>
</tr>
<tr>
  <td><B>Strength training</B></td>
</tr>
<tr>
  <td><input type="checkbox" name="exercise[2][0]"
      value="1"> Calisthenics</td>
</tr>
<tr>
  <td><input type="checkbox" name="exercise[2][1]"
      value="1"> Weightlifting (light)</td>
</tr>
<tr>
  <td><input type="checkbox" name="exercise[2][2]"
      value="1"> Weightlifting (strenuous)</td>
</tr>
<tr>
  <td><B>Stretching/flexibility</B></td>
</tr>
<tr>
  <td><input type="checkbox" name="exercise[3][0]"
      value="1"> Pilates</td>
</tr>
<tr>
  <td><input type="checkbox" name="exercise[3][1]"
      value="1"> Tai chi</td>
```

```
</tr>
<tr>
  <td><input type="checkbox" name="exercise[3][2]"
      value="1"> Yoga</td>
</tr>
<tr>
  <td> </td>
</tr>
<tr>
  <td><input type="submit" name="submit"
      value="Burn, baby, burn!"></td>
</td></tr>
</table>
</TR>
</TABLE>
</FORM>

</BODY>
</HTML>
```

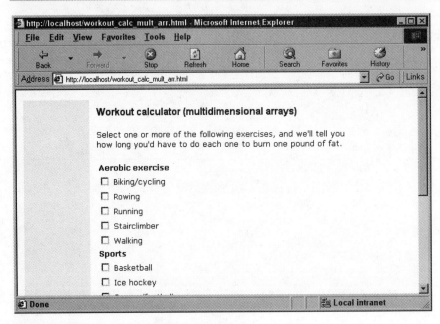

Figure 11-6: Entry form using a multidimensional array

Listing 11-8: Handler for multidimensional array form

```
<?php

// Exercise types
```

```
$exercise_types = array(0 => 'Aerobic exercise',
                        1 => 'Sports',
                        2 => 'Strength training',
                        3 => 'Stretching/flexibility'
                       );

// This is the multidimensional array where we keep our exercises
$exercise_array =
  array(0 => array(0 => 'Biking/cycling',
                   1 => 'Rowing',
                   2 => 'Running',
                   3 => 'Stairclimber',
                   4 => 'Walking'
                  ),
        1 => array(0 => 'Basketball',
                   1 => 'Ice hockey',
                   2 => 'Soccer/football',
                   3 => 'Table tennis'
                  ),
        2 => array(0 => 'Calisthenics',
                   1 => 'Weightlifting (light)',
                   2 => 'Weightlifting (strenuous)',
                  ),
        3 => array(0 => 'Pilates',
                   1 => 'Tai chi',
                   2 => 'Yoga',
                  )
       );

// This is the array where we keep our duration data
$duration_array =
  array(0 => array(0 => '5 hours and 40 minutes',
                   1 => '4 hours and 10 minutes',
                   2 => '4 hours and 30 minutes',
                   3 => '5 hours',
                   4 => '10 hours and 10 minutes'
                  ),
        1 => array(0 => '5 hours',
                   1 => '5 hours',
                   2 => '4 hours and 30 minutes',
                   3 => '10 hours and 10 minutes'
                  ),
        2 => array(0 => '6 hours and 30 minutes',
                   1 => '13 hours and 30 minutes',
                   2 => '7 hours and 30 minutes',
                  ),
        3 => array(0 => '8 hours and 45 minutes',
                   1 => '10 hours and 10 minutes',
                   2 => '16 hours',
```

```
                )
        );

// Now step through the exercises and see which one they chose
if (is_array($_POST) && count($_POST) > 1
    && is_array($_POST['exercise'])) {
  $message = '';
  foreach ($_POST['exercise'] as $key_1 => $val) {
    // $val should be an array
    if (!is_array($val)) {
      $message .= "Something's wrong -- value not array<BR>";
    }
    else {
      // Add heading
      $heading = $exercise_types[$key_1];
      $message .= "</P>\n<P><B>$heading</B>";
      foreach ($val as $key_2 => $val_2) {
        if ($val_2 == 1) {
          $exercise_name = $exercise_array[$key_1][$key_2];
          $hours = $duration_array[$key_1][$key_2];
          $message .= "</P>\n<P>It would take $hours of ".
            "$exercise_name to burn one pound of fat.";
        }
      }
    }
  }
} else {
  // Hmmm, they didn't pick one or something wack happened
  $message = 'Ummm, did you pick an exercise?';
}

// Now lay out the page
// --------------------
$page_str = <<< EOPAGE
<HTML>
<HEAD>
<STYLE TYPE="text/css">
<!--
BODY, P
{color: black; font-family: verdana; font-size: 10 pt}
H1
{color: black; font-family: arial; font-size: 12 pt}
-->
</STYLE>
</HEAD>

<BODY>
<TABLE BORDER=0 CELLPADDING=10 WIDTH=100%>
<TR>
```

```
<TD BGCOLOR="#F0F8FF" ALIGN=CENTER VALIGN=TOP WIDTH=150>
</TD>
<TD BGCOLOR="#FFFFFF" ALIGN=LEFT VALIGN=TOP WIDTH=83%>
<H1>Workout calculator handler (multidimensional arrays)</H1>
<P>The workout calculator says:
$message</P>
</TD>
</TR>
</TABLE>

</BODY>
</HTML>
EOPAGE;

echo $page_str;

?>
```

There are several layers of array packaging that the receiving code in Listing 11-8 pulls apart: First, it uses the 'exercise' key to find the right value in the $_POST array. The value it finds is itself an array. It then uses two nested foreach loops to delve down through the two layers of indexing to the actual exercises submitted. Figure 11-7 shows the result.

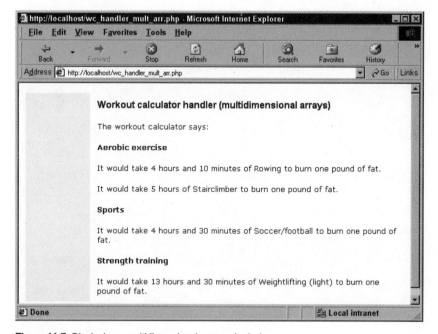

Figure 11-7: Displaying a multidimensional array submission

Summary

The array is a basic PHP datatype and plays the role of both record types and vector array types in other languages. PHP arrays are associative, meaning that they store their values in association with unique *keys* or *indices*. Indices can be either strings or numbers, and are denoted as indices by square brackets. (The expression `$my_array[4]` refers to the value stored in `$my_array` in association with the integer index 4, and not necessarily to the 4th element of `$my_array`.)

The loose typing of PHP means that any PHP value can be stored as an array. In turn, this means that arrays can be stored as array elements. *Multidimensional arrays* are simply arrays that contain other arrays as elements, with a reference syntax of successive brackets. (The expression `$my_array[3][4]` refers to the element (indexed by 4) of an array which is an element (indexed by 3) of `$my_array`.)

The array is the standard vehicle for PHP functions that return structured data, and so PHP programmers should learn to unpack arrays, even if they are not interested in constructing them. PHP also offers a huge variety of functions for manipulating data after you have it stored in an array, including functions for counting, summarizing, and sorting.

Chapter 12
Math

In This Chapter

- ♦ Understanding the basic numerical types and arithmetic operations
- ♦ Exponential, trigonometric, and base-conversion functions
- ♦ Generating random numbers
- ♦ Arbitrary-precision arithmetic

If you need to do serious numerical, scientific, or statistical computation, a Web-scripting language is probably not where you want to be doing it. With that said, however, PHP does offer a generous array of functions that nicely cover most of the mathematical tasks that arise in Web scripting. It also offers some more advanced capabilities such as arbitrary-precision arithmetic and access to hashing and cryptographic libraries.

The PHP designers have, quite sensibly, not tried to reinvent any wheels in this department. Instead, they found about eighteen perfectly good wheels by the side of the road and built a lightweight fiberglass chassis to connect them all together. Many of the more basic math functions in PHP are simple wrappers around their C counterparts (for more on this, see the sidebar "A Glimpse behind the Curtain" in the "Simple Mathematical Functions" section).

Numerical Types

PHP has only two numerical types: *integer* (also known as *long*), and *double* (a.k.a. *float*), which correspond to the largest numerical types in C. PHP does automatic conversion of numerical types, so they can be freely intermixed in numerical expressions and the "right thing" will typically happen. PHP also converts strings to numbers where necessary.

In situations where you want a value to be interpreted as a particular numerical type, you can force a typecast by prepending the type in parentheses, such as:

```
(double) $my_var
(integer) $my_var
```

Or you can use the functions `intval()` and `doubleval()`, which convert their arguments to integers and doubles, respectively.

> **CROSS-REFERENCE:** For more details on the integer and double types, see Chapter 6.

Mathematical Constants

When we wrote the first edition of this book (around the release of PHP version 4.0), there was only one documented math constant: M_PI (the value of pi as a double). However, many new constants were introduced at that time or with PHP v4.0.2. Most of these new constants have to do with pi (or multiples thereof), e (or multiples thereof), or square roots, with a few oddballs thrown in. The general naming scheme is M_<constant-name>. In cases where the constant is a ratio (x/y), the name is M_X_Y, and in cases where there is an operation on a number, the name is M_OPERNUM (e.g. M_SQRT2). The current set of constants (drawn directly from the online manual) is shown in Table 12-1 (two constants per row).

Table 12-1: Mathematical Constants

Constant	Description	Constant	Description
M_PI	Pi	M_SQRT2	sqrt(2)
M_PI_2	pi/2	M_SQRT3	sqrt(3)
M_PI_4	pi/4	M_SQRT_1_2	1/sqrt(2)
M_1_PI	1/pi	M_LOG2E	$\log_2(e)$
M_2_PI	2/pi	M_LOG10E	$\log_{10}(e)$
M_SQRTPI	sqrt(pi) (the square root of pi)	M_LN2	$\log_e(2)$
M_2_SQRTPI	2/sqrt(pi)	M_LN_10	$\log_e(10)$
M_E	the constant e	M_LN_PI	loge(pi)
M_EULER	the Euler constant		

Mathematical Operators

Most of the mathematical action in PHP is in the form of built-in functions, rather than in operators. In addition to the comparison operators covered in Chapter 7, PHP offers five operators for simple arithmetic, as well as some *shorthand* operators that make incrementing and assigning statements more concise.

Arithmetic operators

The five basic arithmetic operators are those you would find on a four-function calculator, plus the modulus operator (%). (If you are unfamiliar with modulus, see the discussion following.) They are summarized in Table 12-2.

Table 12-2: Arithmetic Operators

Operator	Behavior	Examples
+	Sum of its two arguments.	`4 + 9.5` evaluates to `13.5`

-	If there are two arguments, the right-hand argument is subtracted from the left-hand argument. If there is just a right-hand argument, then the negative of that argument is returned.	`50 - 75` evaluates to `-25`
		
		`- 3.9` evaluates to `-3.9`

*	Product of its two arguments.	`3.14 * 2` evaluates to `6.28`
/	Floating-point division of the left-hand argument by the right-hand argument.	`5 / 2` evaluates to `2.5`

%	Integer remainder from division of left-hand argument by the absolute value of the right-hand argument. (See discussion in the following section.)	`101 % 50` evaluates to `1`
		
		`999 % 3` evaluates to `0`
		
		`43 % 94` evaluates to `43`
		
		`-12 % 10` evaluates to `-2`
		
		`-12 % -10` evaluates to `-2`

Arithmetic operators and types

With the first three arithmetic operators (+, -, *), you should expect *type contagion* from doubles to integers; that is, if both arguments are integers, the result will be an integer, but if either argument is a double, then the result will be a double. With the division operator, there is the same sort of contagion, and in addition the result will be a double if the division is not even.

> **TIP:** If you want integer division rather than floating-point division, simply coerce or convert the division result to an integer. For example, `intval(5 / 2)` evaluates to the integer 2.

Modular arithmetic is sometimes taught in school as *clock arithmetic*. The process of taking one number modulo to another amounts to "wrapping" the first number around the second, or (equivalently) taking the remainder of the first number after dividing by the second. The result of such an operation is always less than the second number.

Roughly speaking, a conventional civilian analog clock displays hours elapsed modulo 12, while military time is modulo 24. (The *roughly* in the previous sentence is because the real modulus function converts numbers to the range 0 to n-1, rather than the range 1 to n. If bell-tower clocks respected this, noontime would be marked by silence, rather than by twelve chimes.)

The modulus operator in PHP (%) expects integer arguments — if it is given doubles, they will simply be converted to integers (by truncation) first. The result is always an integer.

Most programming languages have some form of the modulus operator, but they differ in how they handle negative arguments. In some languages, the result of the operator is always positive, and -2 % 26 equals 24. In PHP, though, -2 % 26 is -2, and, in general, the statement $mod = $first_num % $second_num is exactly equivalent to the expression:

```
if ($first_num >= 0)
   $mod = $first_num % abs($second_num);
else
   $mod = - (abs($first_num) % abs($second_num));
```

where abs() is the absolute value function.

Incrementing operators

PHP inherits a lot of its syntax from C, and C programmers are famously proud of their own conciseness. The incrementing/decrementing operators taken from C make it possible to more concisely represent statements like $count = $count + 1, which tend to be typed frequently.

The increment operator (++) adds one to the variable it is attached to, and the decrement operator (--) subtracts one from the variable. Each one comes in two flavors, *postincrement* (which is placed immediately after the affected variable), and *preincrement* (which comes immediately before). Both flavors have the same side effect of changing the variable's value, but they have different values as expressions. The postincrement operator acts as if it changes the variable's value after the expression's value is returned, whereas the preincrement operator acts as though it makes the change first and then returns the variable's new value. You can see the difference by using the operators in assignment statements, like this:

```
$count = 0;
$result = $count++;
print("Post ++: count is $count, result is $result<BR>");
$count = 0;
$result = ++$count;
print("Pre ++: count is $count, result is $result<BR>");
$count = 0;
$result = $count--;
print("Post --: count is $count, result is $result<BR>");
$count = 0;
$result = --$count;
print("Pre --: count is $count, result is $result<BR>");
```

which gives the browser output:

```
Post ++: count is 1, result is 0
Pre ++: count is 1, result is 1
Post --: count is -1, result is 0
Pre --: count is -1, result is -1
```

In this example, the statement $result = $count++; is exactly equivalent to

```
$result = $count;
$count = $count + 1;
```

while `$result = ++$count;` is equivalent to

```
$count = $count + 1;
$result = $count;
```

Assignment operators

Incrementing operators like ++ save keystrokes when adding one to a variable, but they don't help when adding another number or performing another kind of arithmetic. Luckily, all five arithmetic operators have corresponding assignment operators (+= , -= , *= , /= , and %=) that assign to a variable the result of an arithmetic operation on that variable, in one fell swoop. The statement:

```
$count = $count * 3;
```

can be shortened to:

```
$count *= 3;
```

and the statement:

```
$count = $count + 17;
```

becomes:

```
$count += 17;
```

Comparison operators

PHP includes the standard arithmetic comparison operators, which take simple values (numbers or strings) as arguments and evaluate to either TRUE or FALSE:

> **CROSS-REFERENCE:** For examples of using the comparison operators and also some gotcha issues with comparing doubles and strings, see Chapter 7.

- The < (less than) operator is true if its left-hand argument is strictly less than its right-hand argument, and false otherwise.

- The > (greater than) operator is true if its left-hand argument is strictly greater than its right-hand argument, and false otherwise.

- The <= (less than or equal) operator is true if its left-hand argument is less than or equal to its right-hand argument, and false otherwise.

- The >= (greater than or equal) operator is true if its left-hand argument is greater than or equal to its right-hand argument, and false otherwise.

- The == (equal to) operator is true if its arguments are exactly equal, and false otherwise.

♦ The ! = (not equal) operator is false if its arguments are exactly equal, and true otherwise.

♦ The === operator (identical to) is true if its two arguments are exactly equal, and of the same type.

NEW FEATURE: The *identical to* operator (===) is new to PHP4 and at times can be a necessary antidote to PHP's automatic type conversions. None of the following expressions will have a true value:

```
2 === 2.0

2 === "2"

"2.0" === 2.0

0 === FALSE
```

This behavior can be invaluable, for example, if you have a function that returns a string when it succeeds (which might be the empty string), and a FALSE value when it fails. Testing the truth of the return value would confuse FALSE with the empty string, whereas the identical operator can distinguish them.

Precedence and parentheses

Operator *precedence* rules govern the relative "stickiness" of operators, deciding which operators in an expression get first claim on the arguments that surround them. You can find a complete table of all operator precedences in the manual at http://www.php.net, but the important precedence rules for arithmetic are:

♦ Arithmetic operators have higher precedence (that is, bind more tightly) than comparison operators.

♦ Comparison operators have higher precedence than assignment operators.

♦ The *, /, and % arithmetic operators have the same precedence.

♦ The + and – arithmetic operators have the same precedence.

♦ The *, /, and % operators have higher precedence than + and –.

♦ When arithmetic operators are of the same precedence, associativity is left-to-right (that is, a number will associate with an operator to its left in preference to the operator on its right).

If you find the precedence rules difficult to remember, the next person who reads your code may have the same problem, so feel free to parenthesize when in doubt. For example, can you easily figure out the value of this expression?

```
1 + 2 * 3 - 4 - 5 / 4 % 3
```

As it turns out, the value is 2, as we can see more easily when we add parentheses that are not, strictly speaking, necessary:

```
((1 + (2 * 3)) - 4) - ((5 / 4) % 3)
```

Simple Mathematical Functions

The next step up in sophistication from the arithmetic operators consists of miscellaneous functions that perform tasks like converting between the two numerical types (which we discussed in Chapter 6) and finding the minimum and maximum of a set of numbers (see Table 12-3).

Table 12-3: Simple Math Functions

Function	Behavior
floor()	Takes a single argument (typically a double) and returns the largest integer that is less than or equal to that argument.
ceil()	Short for ceiling — takes a single argument (typically a double) and returns the smallest integer that is greater than or equal to that argument.
round()	Takes a single argument (typically a double) and returns the nearest integer. If the fractional part is exactly 0.5, it returns the nearest even number.
abs()	Short for absolute value — if the single numerical argument is negative, the corresponding positive number is returned; if the argument is positive, the argument itself is returned.
min()	Takes any number of numerical arguments (but at least one) and returns the smallest of the arguments.
max()	Takes any number of numerical arguments (but at least one) and returns the largest of the arguments.

For example, the result of the following expression:

```
min(3, abs(-3), max(round(2.7), ceil(2.3), floor(3.9)))
```

is 3, because the value of every function call is also 3.

Base Conversion

The default base in PHP for reading in or printing out numbers is 10. In addition, you can instruct PHP to read octal numbers in base 8 (by starting the number with a leading 0) or hexadecimal numbers in base 16 (by starting the number with a 0x).

> **CROSS-REFERENCE:** For more on read formats of numbers, including octal and hexadecimal notation, see Chapter 6.

A GLIMPSE BEHIND THE CURTAIN

How are built-in PHP functions really implemented? This is likely to be of interest only to C programmers and/or those who care about the inner workings of PHP, but we thought that it might be revealing to see why so many PHP functions work just like their C counterparts.

What follows is the actual implementation for the PHP function ceil, which is intended to convert a double to the smallest integer that is greater than or equal to it.

```
PHP_FUNCTION(ceil)
{
  zval **value;

  if (ARG_COUNT(ht)!=1||getParametersEx(1,&value)==FAILURE) {
            WRONG_PARAM_COUNT;
  }
    convert_scalar_to_number_ex(value);

    if ((*value)->type == IS_DOUBLE) {
      RETURN_LONG((long)ceil((*value)->value.dval));
        } else if ((*value)->type == IS_LONG) {
          RETURN_LONG((*value)->value.lval);
        }
    RETURN_FALSE;
}
```

Although the capitalized portions (including the PHP_FUNCTION declaration) are macros specific to the PHP framework, much of the body of this code is straight C. The code might look dense and confusing at first, but most of the action has to do with PHP's special treatment of types. Here is roughly what is happening, in order:

1.   The arguments that ceil() was called with are retrieved and counted — if the count is anything other than 1, the function call returns with an error.

2.   The single argument is converted to a number if it is a scalar type other than a number — this handles the possibility of string arguments, as in ceil("5.4").

3.   Now the numerical argument is tested to see whether it is a PHP long (a.k.a. integer) or a PHP double. If it turns out to be a long, the value as a long is returned.

4.   The interesting case is if the value is a PHP double. If so, the C double value is extracted, it is run through the C function ceil, the result is converted to a C long, and then that value is wrapped up and returned as a PHP long.

In other words, the PHP implementation of ceil is simply the C function ceil, wrapped up in a lot of type conversion and argument checking. This is the case with many of PHP's functions that have exact analogues in C.

Once numbers are read in, of course, they are represented in binary format in memory, and all the basic arithmetic and mathematical calculations are carried out internally in base 2. PHP also has a number of functions for translating between different bases, which are summarized in Table 12-4.

Table 12-4: Base Conversion Functions

Function	Behavior
BinDec()	Takes a single string argument representing a binary (base 2) integer, and returns a string representation of that number in base 10.
DecBin()	Like BinDec(), but converts from base 10 to base 2.
OctDec()	Like BinDec(), but converts from base 8 to base 10.
DecOct()	Like BinDec(), but converts from base 10 to base 8.
HexDec()	Like BinDec(), but converts from base 16 to base 10.
DecHex()	Like BinDec(), but converts from base 10 to base 16.
baseconvert()	Takes a string argument (the integer to be converted) and two integer arguments (the original base, and the desired base). Returns a string representing the converted number — digits higher than 9 (from 10 to 35) are represented by the letters a–z. Both the original and desired bases must be in the range 2–36.

All the base conversion functions are special-purpose, converting from one particular base to another, except for base_convert(), which accepts an arbitrary start base and destination base. Here's an example of base_convert() in action:

```
function display_bases($start_string, $start_base)
{
  for ($new_base = 2; $new_base <= 36; $new_base++)
    {
      $converted =
        base_convert($start_string, $start_base, $new_base);
        print("$start_string in base $start_base
            is $converted in base $new_base<BR>");
    }
}

display_bases("1jj", 20);
```

which yields the browser output:

```
1jj in base 20 is 1100011111 in base 2
1jj in base 20 is 1002121 in base 3
1jj in base 20 is 30133 in base 4
```

```
1jj in base 20 is 11144 in base 5
1jj in base 20 is 3411 in base 6
1jj in base 20 is 2221 in base 7
1jj in base 20 is 1437 in base 8
1jj in base 20 is 1077 in base 9
1jj in base 20 is 799 in base 10
1jj in base 20 is 667 in base 11
1jj in base 20 is 567 in base 12
1jj in base 20 is 496 in base 13
1jj in base 20 is 411 in base 14
1jj in base 20 is 384 in base 15
1jj in base 20 is 31f in base 16
1jj in base 20 is 2d0 in base 17
1jj in base 20 is 287 in base 18
1jj in base 20 is 241 in base 19
1jj in base 20 is 1jj in base 20
1jj in base 20 is 1h1 in base 21
1jj in base 20 is 1e7 in base 22
1jj in base 20 is 1bh in base 23
1jj in base 20 is 197 in base 24
1jj in base 20 is 16o in base 25
1jj in base 20 is 14j in base 26
1jj in base 20 is 12g in base 27
1jj in base 20 is 10f in base 28
1jj in base 20 is rg in base 29
1jj in base 20 is qj in base 30
1jj in base 20 is po in base 31
1jj in base 20 is ov in base 32
1jj in base 20 is o7 in base 33
1jj in base 20 is nh in base 34
1jj in base 20 is mt in base 35
1jj in base 20 is m7 in base 36
```

Notice that although all the base-conversion functions take string arguments and return string values, you can use decimal numerical arguments and rely on PHP's type conversion (but see the cautionary note that follows). In other words, both DecBin("1234") and DecBin(1234) will yield the same result.

> **CAUTION:** Don't confuse the read formats of numbers with their representations as strings for the purposes of base conversion. For example, although 10 in base 16 is the number 16 in base 10, the expression HexDec(0x10) evaluates to the string "22". Why? There are really three conversions happening: when 0x10 is read (converts from hex to internal binary), when the argument is auto-converted (from internal binary number to the decimal string "16"), and in the operation of the function (from assumed base 16 to decimal "22"). If you want just one conversion, then the desired expression is HexDec("10").

> **NOTE:** The base conversion functions expect their string arguments to be integers, not floating-point numbers. That means you can't use these functions to convert a binary 10.1 to a decimal 2.5.

Exponents and Logarithms

PHP includes the standard exponential and logarithmic functions, in both base 10 and base e varieties (shown in Table 12-5).

Table 12-5: Exponential Functions

Function	Behavior
pow()	Takes two numerical arguments and returns the first argument raised to the power of the second. The value of pow($x, $y) is x^y.
exp()	Takes a single argument and raises e to that power. The value of exp($x) is e^x.
log()	The "natural log" function. Takes a single argument and returns its base e logarithm. If e^y = x, then the value of log($x) is y.
log10()	Takes a single argument and returns its base-10 logarithm. If 10^y = x, then the value of log10($x) is y.

Unlike with exp() and the base e, there is no single-argument function to raise 10 to a given power, but in its place you can use the two-argument function pow() with 10 as the first argument.

You can verify for yourself that exponential and power functions of the same base are inverses of each other, by testing an "identity" like this:

```
$test_449 = 449.0;
$test_449 = pow(10, exp(log(log10($test_449))));
print("test_449 is $test_449<BR>");
```

which gives the browser output:

```
test_449 is 449
```

Trigonometry

Although explaining the math behind the PHP functions in this chapter is beyond the scope of this book, we've made an exception just this once. (See the sidebar "Trigonometry in One Paragraph." Anyone who doesn't already know trigonometry will, of course, find the sidebar completely impenetrable, but we hope that those who know trig will at least be amused by how short it is.)

PHP offers the standard set of basic trigonometric functions as well as the constant M_PI, an approximation of pi as a double that prints as 3.1415926535898. This constant can be used anywhere you would use the literal number itself, and it is also interchangeable with the pi() function. (For other constants derived from pi, see the "Mathematical Constants" section at the beginning of this chapter.) Both of the following statements have the same result:

```
$my_pi = M_PI;
$my_pi = pi();
```

The basic trig functions are summarized in Table 12-6.

Table 12-6: Trigonometric Functions

Function	Behavior
pi()	Takes no arguments and returns an approximation of pi (3.1415926535898). Can be used interchangeably with the constant M_PI.
Sin()	Takes a numerical argument in radians and returns the sine of the argument as a double.
Cos()	Takes a numerical argument in radians and returns the cosine of the argument as a double.
Tan()	Takes a numerical argument in radians and returns the tangent of the argument as a double.
Asin()	Takes a numerical argument and returns the arcsine of the argument in radians. Inputs must be between −1.0 and 1.0 [inputs outside that range will return a result of NaN (for "not a number")]. Results are in the range −pi / 2 to pi / 2.
Acos()	Takes a numerical argument and returns the arccosine of the argument in radians. Inputs must be between −1.0 and 1.0 [inputs outside that range will return a result of NaN (for "not a number")]. Results are in the range 0 to pi.
Atan()	Takes a numerical argument and returns the arctangent of the argument in radians. Results are in the range −pi / 2 to pi / 2.
Atan2()	A variant of atan() that takes 2 arguments. Atan($y, $x) is identical to atan($y/$x) when $x is positive, but the quadrant of atan2's result depends on the signs of both $y and $x. Range of the result is from −pi to pi.

Rather than writing down a table of sample function results, let's resort to our usual trick of writing code that automatically displays examples as an HTML table. Listing 12-1 shows both a generalized function for displaying a set of one-argument functions applied to a set of numerical arguments and then the result of using this display function to make trigonometric example tables. The results are displayed in Figure 12-1.

TRIGONOMETRY IN ONE PARAGRAPH

Imagine a circle with a radius of 1, centered at 0,0 in the coordinate plane. Start at the right-hand edge (at position (1,0)), and trace a certain distance along the circle counter-clockwise. For example, a distance of 2 pi would take you once around the circle and back to your starting point. Clockwise travel counts as a negative distance. For any such distance, the sine function tells you the y-value of the coordinate you arrive at, the cosine function tells you the x-value of that coordinate, and the tangent function is a ratio of the two, from which you can infer the slope of the line tangent to the circle at that point. The functions arccosine, arcsine, and arctangent are in some sense inverses of their corresponding functions — they map back from an x, y, or y/x ratio to the distance of a circular trip that would arrive at that x-coordinate, y-coordinate, or ratio thereof. Because adding a multiple of 2 pi to any distance brings you around to the same point again, these inverse functions might have an infinite number of answers per input, making them ill-defined — instead, they are restricted to a range corresponding to one particular trip around half of the circle and so have well-defined results.

Listing 12-1: Displaying trigonometric function results

```php
<?php

function display_func_results($func_array, $input_array)
{
/* print a function header */
print("<TABLE BORDER=1><TR><TH>INPUT\\FUNCTION</TH>");
for($y = 0;
        $y < count($func_array);
        $y++)
    print("<TH>$func_array[$y]</TH>");
print("</TR><TR>");
/* print the rest of the table */
for($x = 0;
    $x < count($input_array);
    $x++)
  {
    /* print column entries for inputs */
    print("<TH>".
          sprintf("%.4f", $input_array[$x])
          ."</TH>");
    for($y = 0;
        $y < count($func_array);
        $y++)
    {
      $func_name = $func_array[$y];
      $input = $input_array[$x];
```

```
      print("<TD>");
      printf("%4.4f", $func_name($input));
      print("</TD>");
    }
    print("</TR><TR>");
  }
print("</TR></TABLE>");
}
?>

<HTML>
<HEAD>
<TITLE>Trigonometric Function Examples</TITLE>
</HEAD>
<BODY>

<?php
/* using the function displayer */
print("<H3>Trigonometric function examples</H3>");
display_func_results(array("sin", "cos", "tan"),
                     array(-1.25 * pi(),
                           -1.0 * pi(),
                           -0.75 * pi(),
                           -0.5 * pi(),
                           -0.25 * pi(),
                           0,
                           0.25 * pi(),
                           0.5 * pi(),
                           0.75 * pi(),
                           pi(),
                           1.25 * pi()));

?>
</BODY>
</HTML>
```

> **CROSS-REFERENCE:** The `display_func_results()` function of Listing 12-1 uses several tricks we've seen in previous chapters: using a string variable as the name of a function to call (covered near the end of Chapter 8), and using the string concatenation operator (`.`) to pull together a print string in the middle of a print statement (covered in Chapter 9).

Figure 12-1 shows the basic trigonometric functions over an input range of `-5/4 pi` to `5/4 pi` and the basic inverse trigonometric function over inputs from `-1.0` to `1.0`. The very large tangent values are due to denominators that should theoretically be zero but instead differ slightly from zero due to rounding error.

Figure 12-1: Trigonometric function examples

> **NEW FEATURE:** In Listing 12-1 we take advantage of the *variable function feature* in PHP, which enables us to retrieve and call trigonometric functions by their stored names. Although previous versions of PHP permitted user-defined functions to be called this way, the capability to do the same with built-in functions is new in PHP 4.

Randomness

PHP's functions for generating pseudo-random numbers are summarized in Table 12-7. (If you are new to random number generation and are wondering what the *pseudo* is all about, please see the accompanying sidebar.)

There are two random number generators (invoked with rand() and mt_rand(), respectively), each with the same three associated functions: a seeding function, the random-number function itself, and a function that retrieves the largest integer that might be returned by the generator.

The particular pseudo-random function that is used by rand() may depend on the particular libraries that PHP was compiled with. By contrast, the mt_rand() generator always uses the same random function (the Mersenne Twister) and the author of mt_rand()'s online documentation argues that it is also faster and "more random" (in a cryptographic sense) than `rand()`. We have no reason to believe that this is not correct, and so we prefer `mt_rand()` to `rand()`.

Table 12-7: Random Number Functions

Function	Behavior
srand()	Takes a single positive integer argument and seeds the random number generator with it.
rand()	If called with no arguments, returns a "random" number between 0 and RAND_MAX (which can be retrieved with the function getrandmax()). The function can also be called with two integer arguments to restrict the range of the number returned — the first argument is the minimum and the second is the maximum (inclusive).
getrandmax()	Returns the largest number that may be returned by rand().
mt_srand()	Like srand(), except that it seeds the "better" random number generator.
mt_rand()	Like rand(), except that it uses the "better" random number generator.
mt_getrandmax()	Returns the largest number that may be returned by mt_rand().

NOTE: On some PHP versions and some platforms, you can apparently get seemingly random numbers from `rand()` and `mt_rand()` without seeding first — this should not be relied upon, however, both for reasons of portability and because the unseeded behavior is not guaranteed.

Seeding the generator

The typical way to seed either of the PHP random-number generators (using `mt_srand()` or `srand()`) looks like this:

```
mt_srand((double)microtime()*1000000);
```

This sets the seed of the generator to be the number of microseconds that have elapsed since the last "whole" second. (Yes, the typecast to "double" is necessary here, because `microtime()` returns a string, which would treated as an integer in the multiplication but for the cast.) Please use this seeding statement even if you don't understand it — just place it in any PHP page, once only, before you use the corresponding `mt_rand()` or `rand()` functions, and it will ensure that you have a varying starting point, and therefore random sequences that are different every time. This particular seeding technique has been thought through by people who understand the ins and outs of pseudo-random number generation, and so is probably better than any attempt an individual programmer might make to try something trickier.

PSEUDO-RANDOM NUMBER GENERATORS

As with all programming languages, the "random" number functions offered by PHP are really implemented by pseudo-random number generators. This is because conventional computer architectures are deterministic machines that will always produce the same results given the same starting conditions and inputs and have no good source of randomness. (Here we're talking about the ideal computer as it is supposed to work, not the actual physically embodied, power-interruptible, cosmic-ray flippable, seemingly very random machines we all struggle with daily!) You could imagine connecting a conventional computer to a source of random bits such as a mechanical coin-flip reader, or a device that observed quantum-level events, but such peripherals don't seem to be widely available at this time.

So we must make do with pseudo-random generators, which produce a deterministic sequence of numbers that looks random enough for most purposes. They typically work by running their initial input number (the *seed*) through a particular mathematical function to produce the first number in the sequence; each subsequent number in the sequence is the result of applying that same function to the previous number in the sequence. The sequence will repeat at some point (once it generates a particular number for the second time, it is doomed to follow the same sequence as it did the first time around), but a good iteration function will generate a very long sequence of numbers that have little apparent pattern before the loop occurs.

How do you choose a seed to start off with? Because of the generator's determinism, if you hard-code a PHP page to have a particular seed, that page will always see the same sequence from the generator. (Although this is not usually what you want, it can be an invaluable trick when you are trying to debug behavior that depends on the particular numbers that are generated.) The typical seeding technique is to use a fast-changing digit from the system clock as the initial seed — although those numbers are not exactly random, they are likely to vary quickly enough that subsequent page executions will start with a different seed every time.

Here is some representative code that uses the pseudo-random functions:

```
print("Seeding the generator<BR>");
mt_srand((double)microtime() * 1000000);
print("With no arguments: " . mt_rand() . "<BR>");
print("With no arguments: " . mt_rand() . "<BR>");
print("With no arguments: " . mt_rand() . "<BR>");
print("With two arguments: " .
      mt_rand(27, 31) . "<BR>");
print("With two arguments: " .
      mt_rand(27, 31) . "<BR>");
print("With two arguments: " .
      mt_rand(27, 31) . "<BR>");
```

with the browser output:

```
Seeding the generator
With no arguments: 992873415
With no arguments: 656237128
With no arguments: 1239053221
With two arguments: 28
With two arguments: 31
With two arguments: 29
```

> **TIP:** Although the random-number functions only return integers, it is easy to convert a random integer in a given range to a corresponding floating-point number (say, one between 0.0 and 1.0 inclusive) with an expression like `rand() / getrandmax()`. You can then scale and shift the range as desired (to, say, a number between 100.0 and 120.0) with an expression like `100.0 + 20.0 * (rand() / getrandmax())`.

Obviously, if you run exactly this code, you will get numbers that differ from those above, because the point of seeding the generator this way is to ensure that different executions produce different sequences of numbers.

> **CAUTION:** In some old versions of PHP3, the `rand()` function buggily ignored its arguments, returning numbers between 0 and `getrandmax()` regardless of restrictions. We have also heard some reports of that behavior under more recent Windows implementations. If you suspect that you are suffering from such a bug, you can define your own restricted version of `rand()` like so:
>
> ```
> function my_rand ($min, $max)
> {
>   return(rand() % (($max - $min) + 1)
>          + $min);
> }
> ```
>
> Unlike `rand()`, this version requires the `min` and `max` arguments.

Example: Making a random selection

Now let's use the random functions for something useful (or, at least, something that could be used for something useful). The following two functions let you construct a random string of letters, which could, in turn, be used as a random login or password string:

```
function random_char($string)
{
  $length = strlen($string);
  $position = mt_rand(0, $length - 1);
  return($string[$position]);
}
function random_string ($charset_string, $length)
{
```

```
    $return_string = ""; // the empty string
  for ($x = 0; $x < $length; $x++)
    $return_string .= random_char($charset_string);
  return($return_string);
}
```

The random_char() function chooses a character (or, actually, a substring of length 1) from its input string. It does this by restricting the mt_rand() function to positions within the length of the string (with chars numbered starting at zero), and then returning the character that is at that random position. The random_string() function calls random_char() a number of times on a string representing the universe of characters to be chosen from and concatenates a string of the desired length.

Now, to demonstrate this code, we first seed the generator, define our universe of allowable characters, and then call random_string() a few times in a row:

```
mt_srand((double)microtime() * 1000000);
$charset = "abcdefghijklmnopqrstuvwxyz";

$random_string = random_string($charset, 8);
print("random_string: $random_string<BR>");
$random_string = random_string($charset, 8);
print("random_string: $random_string<BR>");
$random_string = random_string($charset, 8);
print("random_string: $random_string<BR>");
```

with the result:

```
random_string: eisexkio
random_string: mkvflwfy
random_string: gpulbwth
```

In this example, we only seed the generator once, and we draw that seed value from the system clock. Notice what happens if we make the mistake of repeatedly seeding the generator with the same value:

```
mt_srand(43);
$random_string = random_string($charset, 8);
print("random_string: $random_string<BR>");

mt_srand(43);
$random_string = random_string($charset, 8);
print("random_string: $random_string<BR>");

mt_srand(43);
$random_string = random_string($charset, 8);
print("random_string: $random_string<BR>");
```

Because the sequence that is generated depends deterministically on the seed, we get the same behavior each time:

```
random_string: qgkxvurw
random_string: qgkxvurw
random_string: qgkxvurw
```

In these examples, we chose to draw random characters from strings, but this kind of selection process is generalizable to draw items from arrays or to be used in any situation that requires choosing random members from a set. All you need is the universe of items, a way to put them in numerical order, and a way to retrieve them by order number, and you can then use the rand() or mt_rand() function to choose a random order number for the retrieval.

Arbitrary Precision (BC)

The integer and double types are fine for most of the mathematical tasks that arise in Web scripting, but each instance of these types is stored in a fixed amount of computer memory, and so the size and precision of the numbers these types can represent is inherently limited. Although the exact range of these types may depend on the architecture of your server machine, integers typically range from $-2^{31} - 1$ to $2^{31} - 1$, and doubles can represent about 13 to 14 decimal digits of precision. For tasks that require greater range or precision, PHP offers the *arbitrary-precision* math functions (also known as *BC functions*, from the name of the Unix-based, arbitrary-precision calculating utility).

> **NOTE:** Especially if you compiled PHP yourself, the arbitrary-precision functions may not have been included in the compilation — you need to have included the flag --enable-bcmath at configuration time. To check whether the functions are present, try evaluating bcadd("1", "1") — if you get an unbound function error, you will have to reconfigure and recompile PHP.

Instead of using the fixed-length numerical types, the BC functions have strings as arguments and return values. Because strings in PHP are limited only by available memory, numbers can be as long as you like. The underlying computations are performed in decimal and are done much as you would do them with pen and paper (if you were very fast and very patient). When operating with integers, the BC functions are exact and use as many digits as needed; when operating with floating-point numbers, computations are done to as many decimal places as you specify. The BC functions are summarized in Table 12-8.

Most of the functions take an optional scale factor (an integer) as a final argument, which determines how many decimal places will be in the result. If such an argument is not supplied, the scale is the default scale, which, in turn, can be set by calling bcscale(). The default for the default value (that is, if bcscale() has never been called) can also be set in the initialization file php.ini.

Table 12-8: Arbitrary-Precision (BC) Math Functions

Function	Behavior
bcadd()	Takes two string arguments representing numbers, and an optional integer scale parameter. Returns the sum of the first two arguments as a string, with the number of decimal places in the result determined by the scale parameter. If no scale parameter is supplied, the default scale is used (which is settable by bcscale()).
bcsub()	Similar to bcadd(), except that it returns the subtraction of the second argument from the first.
bcmul()	Similar to bcadd() but returns the product of its arguments.
bcdiv()	Similar to bcadd() but returns the result of dividing the first argument by the second.
bcmod()	Returns the modulus (remainder) of the first argument as divided by the second. Because the return type is "integral," no scale argument is taken.
bcpow()	Raises the first argument to the power of the second argument. The number of decimal places in the result is set by the scale factor if supplied.
bcsqrt()	Returns the square root of its argument, with number of decimal places set by the optional scale factor.
bcscale()	Sets the default scale factor for subsequent BC function calls.

An arbitrary-precision example

Here's an example of using the arbitrary-precision functions for exact integer arithmetic. The following code:

```
for ($x = 1; $x < 25; $x++) {
  print("$x to the $x power is " . bcpow($x, $x) . "<BR>");
}
```

will print like this:

```
1 raised to the power of 1 is 1
2 raised to the power of 2 is 4
3 raised to the power of 3 is 27
4 raised to the power of 4 is 256
5 raised to the power of 5 is 3125
6 raised to the power of 6 is 46656
7 raised to the power of 7 is 823543
8 raised to the power of 8 is 16777216
```

```
9 raised to the power of 9 is 387420489
10 raised to the power of 10 is 10000000000
11 raised to the power of 11 is 285311670611
12 raised to the power of 12 is 8916100448256
13 raised to the power of 13 is 302875106592253
14 raised to the power of 14 is 11112006825558016
15 raised to the power of 15 is 437893890380859375
16 raised to the power of 16 is 18446744073709551616
17 raised to the power of 17 is 827240261886336764177
18 raised to the power of 18 is 39346408075296537575424
19 raised to the power of 19 is 1978419655660313589123979
20 raised to the power of 20 is 104857600000000000000000000
21 raised to the power of 21 is 5842587018385982521381124421
22 raised to the power of 22 is 341427877364219557396646723584
23 raised to the power of 23 is 20880467999847912034355032910567
24 raised to the power of 24 is 1333735776850284124449081472843776
25 raised to the power of 25 is 88817841970012523233890533447265625
```

If we had used the regular PHP integer type for this computation, the integers would have "overflowed" well before the end, and the rest of the loop would have been calculated in approximate floating point.

Converting code to arbitrary-precision

Let's see what it's like to take an existing piece of mathematical code and retrofit it to use the arbitrary-precision functions.

The following function approximates pi, using the series approximation:

```
sqrt ( 12 - (12/2²) + (12/3²) - (12/4²) + (12/5²) - ...)
```

(As we'll see, this series does not converge fast enough for our purposes, but it has the virtue of being a simple formula.)

```php
function pi_approx($iterations, $print_frequency)
{
  $squared_approx = 12;
  $next_sign = -1;
  $denom = 2;

  for ($iter = 0; $iter < $iterations; $iter++)
    {
      $squared_approx += $next_sign * 12/(pow($denom,2));
      $denom++;
      $next_sign = - $next_sign;
      if ($denom % $print_frequency == 0)
        {
          $estimate = sqrt($squared_approx);
          print("$denom iterations: $estimate<BR>");
        }
```

```
    }
}
```

In addition to performing the calculation itself, this code periodically prints out its current estimate of pi, so we can see how we are doing. We can call it as follows, and then print out PHP's value for comparison:

```
pi_approx(10000, 1000);
print("PHP value: " . pi() . "<BR>");
```

The result looks like:

```
1000 iterations: 3.1415936094742
2000 iterations: 3.1415928924416
3000 iterations: 3.1415927597285
4000 iterations: 3.1415927132878
5000 iterations: 3.1415926917946
6000 iterations: 3.14159268012
7000 iterations: 3.141592673081
8000 iterations: 3.1415926685124
9000 iterations: 3.1415926653804
10000 iterations: 3.1415926631401
PHP value: 3.1415926535898
```

Now, not only are we not that close, but we can't hope to be more accurate than PHP's value for pi, because that already uses all the precision available in the double type.

To convert this to an arbitrary-precision version, we must replace all the math functions and operators that need precision with their BC counterparts, like so:

```
function pi_approx_bc($iterations, $print_frequency, $scale)
{
  $squared_approx = "12";
  $next_sign = -1;
  $denom = 2;
  for ($iter = 0; $iter < $iterations; $iter++)
    {
      $squared_approx
        = bcadd(
            $squared_approx,
            bcmul($next_sign,
                  bcdiv(12,
                        bcpow($denom,
                              2,
                              $scale),
                        $scale),
                  $scale),
            $scale);
      $denom++;
      $next_sign = - $next_sign;
```

```
    if ($denom % $print_frequency == 0)
      {
        $estimate = bcsqrt($squared_approx,$scale);
        print("$denom iterations: $estimate<BR>");
      }
    }
}
```

Notice that although the BC functions want string arguments, we can as always use regular numbers in their places and rely on PHP to convert the arguments to strings for us. Also notice that we did not bother making the numerical computations that do not require great precision into BC computations (for instance, we still have $denom++ rather than bcadd($denom, 1). Finally, we added a scale argument to the entire function, which turns the decimal precision of each BC function it calls.

Unfortunately, both your authors and our browsers ran out of patience with this series before it got even got to the level of precision of PHP's value. Here are some late results of calling (pi_approx_bc(1250000, 50000, 50):

```
50000 iterations: 3.141592653971772741297235510683477263712976869266596
100000 iterations: 3.141592653685287159245987692543905949271462053371113
150000 iterations: 3.141592653632234839562316495039222042729332175382022
[..]
1150000 iterations: 3.141592653590515303104552554096025800032655499955003
1200000 iterations: 3.141592653590456384611480874034589189444055471472111
1250000 iterations: 3.141592653590404393933040187100721577035010223888304
```

The correct digits in the preceding output are about one digit shy of the PHP value. This is the fault of the series we chose, rather than the arbitrary-precision libraries — with a more sophisticated and speedier approximation series, you too can serve up millions of digits of pi to your eager audience.

Somewhat more satisfyingly, evaluating:

```
print("The square root of two is " . bcsqrt(2, 40));
```

gives us many more digits of precision than we could get using doubles:

```
The square root of two is 1.4142135623730950488016887242096980785696
```

Extended Example: An Exercise Calculator

Now let us return to the exercise-calculator example that we've been developing since Chapter 9. In addition to mixing in a little bit of arithmetic calculation, we'll also reorganize the code a bit.

One problem with the code as we left it was that we had our data in two different code files, and in more than one array. Changes to the data require updating more than one file, and take some care to make sure that everything stays in sync.

We could always keep this data in a text file or in a database. For this chapter, however, let's just make a single PHP code file where we define a single array with everything we need: types of exercises, names of exercises, and the calories per minute that each exercise consumes, assuming a person of average weight. Such an array is shown in Listing 12-2; we'll call this file exercise_include.php.

Listing 12-2: `exercise_include.php`

```php
<?php
// categories of exercise with associated calories per minute
// (not medically trustworthy because we made them up)
$exercise_info =
  array('Aerobic exercise' =>
   array('biking/cycling' => 9,
            'rowing' => 8,
            'running' => 14,
            'stairclimber' => 6,
        'walking' => 5),
 'Sports' =>
          array('basketball' => 12,
               'ice hockey' => 9,
               'soccer/football' => 11,
               'table tennis' => 7),
  'Strength training' =>
          array('calisthenics' => 11,
               'weightlifting (light)' => 9,
               'weightlifting (strenuous)' => 13),
 'Stretching/flexibility' =>
          array('pilates' => 5,
               'tai chi' => 6,
               'yoga' => 5)
     );
?>
```

Although we'll stick to having separate form submission and form handler pages, let's make the form submission page a PHP file too, rather than using straight HTML. This will let us generate the form elements from the data we defined in exercise_include.php.

Listing 12-3: Form submission code for fitness calculator

```php
<?php include_once("exercise_include.php");
?>
<html>
<head>
<style TYPE="text/css">
<!—
BODY, P, TD       {color: black; font-family: verdana; font-size: 10 pt}
H1         {color: black; font-family: arial; font-size: 12 pt}
-->
```

```
</STYLE>
</head>

<xbody>
<table BORDER=0 CELLPADDING=10 WIDTH=100%>
<tr>
<td BGCOLOR="#F0F8FF" ALIGN=CENTER VALIGN=TOP WIDTH=150>
</td>
<td BGCOLOR="#FFFFFF" ALIGN=LEFT VALIGN=TOP WIDTH=83%>
<h1>Workout calculator (math)</h1>
<p>For one or more of the following exercises, enter<br>
the duration in minutes and your current weight<br>
and we'll tell you how many calories you burned.</p>

<form METHOD="post" ACTION="wc_handler_math.php">
<table>
<tr>
  <td><input type="text" size=5 name="weight"><b>Weight (kilos)</b></td>
</tr>
<tr>
  <td> </td>
</tr>

<?php
$type_counter = 0;
foreach ($exercise_info
          as $exercise_type => $per_exercise_info) {
  print("<tr><td><b>$exercise_type</b></td></tr>");
  $exercise_counter = 0;
  foreach ($per_exercise_info
            as $exercise_name => $exercise_intensity) {
    print("<tr><td>
          <input type = \"text\" size = 5
            name=\"exercise[$type_counter][$exercise_counter]\"
          > $exercise_name</td></tr>");
    $exercise_counter++;
  }
  $type_counter++;
}
?>
<tr>
  <td> </td>
</tr>
<tr>
  <td><input type="submit" name="submit"
      value="Burn, baby, burn!"></td>
</td></tr>
</table>
</tr>
```

```
</table>

</form>

</body>
</html>
```

Although mostly a static HTML page, the hierarchy of exercises specified in `exercise_include.php` can be used to print out the data-entry portion of the form. Notice that we print the names and types of exercises, but do not propagate them as form variables; we plan to use the very same array from `exercise_include.php` on the other end to distinguish the meaning of the submitted variables.

The submission form itself is shown in Figure 12-2.

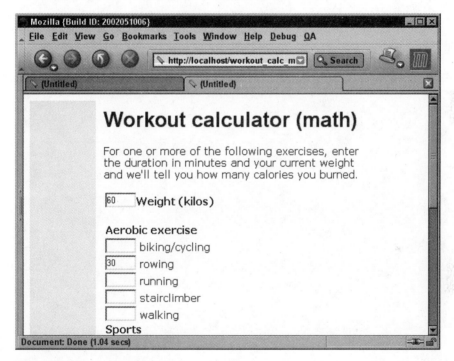

Figure 12-2: The calculator entry form

Now the job of the receiving page is more complex than in previous chapters. We will be receiving an array in `$_POST['exercise']` that has a hierarchical structure similar to the one defined in `exercise_include.php`.

The difference is that the former includes the minutes spent at each exercise, while the latter includes the rate at which that exercise burns calories. The receiving page's job is to use both arrays to produce a report for the user about calories actually burned.

The handler code is shown in Listing 12-4. First of all, we receive the submitted weight. Then we move on to iterating through the data array defined in `exercise_include.php` and querying the `$_POST['exercise']` array for nonzero minutes submitted for each exercise.

We're relying on the fact that the iteration uses the same data array and does the same counting in both the sending and receiving pages; this means that if we find nonzero minutes in a given position, we can correlate that with the name, type, and calories/minute drawn from the data file.

Whenever we find a "hit" (some positive minutes entered for an exercise we know about), we simply calculate the calories burned (calories/minute x minutes), and then adjust that value for the user's weight. We round each value before adding it into a total, largely so that the individual entries will agree with the rounded sum.

Listing 12-4: Handler code for the fitness calculator (wc_handler_math.php)

```php
<?php
include_once("exercise_include.php");
$weight = $_POST["weight"];

// scale linearly assuming 65-kilo norm
$weight_factor = $weight / 65.0;

$exercise_accumulator = array();
$type_counter = 0;
if (is_array($_POST) && count($_POST) > 1
    && is_array($_POST['exercise'])) {
  foreach ($exercise_info
            as $exercise_type => $per_exercise_info) {
    $exercise_counter = 0;
    foreach ($per_exercise_info
      as $exercise_name => $exercise_intensity) {
      $minutes =
        $_POST['exercise'][$type_counter][$exercise_counter];
      if ($minutes > 0) {
        $exercise_accumulator[$exercise_type][$exercise_name]
          = round($minutes * $exercise_intensity *
                  $weight_factor);
      }
    $exercise_counter++;
  }
  $type_counter++;
  }
}
```

```
// now we use $exercise_accumulator to build a display string
$total_calories = 0;
$message = "";
foreach ($exercise_accumulator
           as $exercise_type => $per_exercise_info) {
  $message .= "<P><B>$exercise_type</B></P>";
  foreach ($per_exercise_info
    as $exercise_name => $calories_burned) {
      $message .= "<P>".
          ucfirst("$exercise_name: $calories_burned calories</P>");
      $total_calories += $calories_burned;
  }
}
if ($message == "" || $weight == 0) {
   $message =
     "<P>Did you enter your weight and at least one exercise?";
}
else {
   $message .=
     "<P><B>Total calories burned: $total_calories</B></P>";
}


// Now lay out the page
// --------------------
$page_str = <<< EOPAGE
<HTML>
<HEAD>
<STYLE TYPE="text/css">
<!--
BODY, P
{color: black; font-family: verdana; font-size: 10 pt}
H1
{color: black; font-family: arial; font-size: 12 pt}
-->
</STYLE>
</HEAD>

<BODY>
<TABLE BORDER=0 CELLPADDING=10 WIDTH=100%>
<TR>
<TD BGCOLOR="#F0F8FF" ALIGN=CENTER VALIGN=TOP WIDTH=150>
</TD>
<TD BGCOLOR="#FFFFFF" ALIGN=LEFT VALIGN=TOP WIDTH=83%>
<H1>Workout calculator handler (Math)</H1>
<P>The workout calculator says:
$message</P>
</TD>
```

```
</TR>
</TABLE>

</BODY>
</HTML>
EOPAGE;

echo $page_str;
?>
```

The resulting handler page is shown in Figure 12-3.

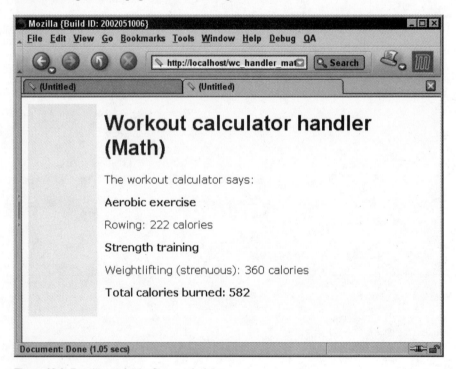

Figure 12-3: Result page for the fitness calculator

In addition to doing more numeric calculation that our calculator from previous chapters, this version does a better job of splitting up data and code, at the cost of some extra complexity.

Summary

The highlights of PHP math are summarized in Table 12-9.

Table 12-9: Summary of PHP Math Operators and Functions

Category	Description
Arithmetic operators	Operators +, -, *, /, % perform basic arithmetic on integers and doubles.
Incrementing operators	The ++ and -- operators change the values of numerical variables, increasing them by one or decreasing them by one (respectively). The value of the postincrement form ($var++) is the same as the variable's value before the change; the value of the preincrement form (++$var) is the variable's value after the change.
Assignment operators	Each arithmetic operator (like +) has a corresponding assignment operator (+=). The expression $count += 5 is equivalent to $count = $count + 5.
Comparison operators	These operators (<, <=, >, >=, ==, !=) compare two numbers and return either true or false. The === operator is true if and only if its arguments are equal and of the same type.
Basic math functions	floor(), ceil(), and round() convert doubles to integers, min() and max() take the minimum and maximum of their numerical arguments, and abs() is the absolute value function.
Base conversion functions	Special-purpose functions (OctDec(), DecOct(), BinDec(), DecBin(), HexDec(), DecHex()) convert between particular pairs of bases, whereas base_convert() translates between arbitrary bases.
Exponential functions	Functions having to with raising numbers to powers or the inverse: log() (natural log), log10() (base-10 log), exp() (e raised to the power of the argument), and pow() (first argument to the power of the second).
Trigonometric functions	Functions having to do with angular measures: pi() (and the equivalent constant M_PI), sin(), cos(), tan(), acos(), asin(), atan(), and atan2() (a two-argument version of atan()).
Arbitrary-precision (BC) functions	Functions that do arithmetic on arbitrary-length strings representing decimal integers and floating-point numbers: bdadd(), bcsub(), bcmult(), bcdiv(), bcmod(), bcpow(), bcsqrt(). Most of these functions take an optional scale parameter specifying the number of decimal points of precision desired — the default for that parameter is settable using bcscale().

Chapter 13

Filesystem and System Functions

In This Chapter

♦ Understanding PHP file permissions

♦ Filesystem functions

♦ Directory functions

♦ Network functions

♦ Date and time functions

♦ Calendar conversion functions

♦ Extended example: an exercise calculator

> **CAUTION:** Many of the functions in this chapter have serious security implications. You are inviting bad news if you use them without thinking pretty hard about the consequences! We'll try to point out the most scary ones as we go, but nothing that allows the system to be altered via HTTP should be undertaken lightly.

This chapter contains information on the multiplicity of system functions built into PHP. Many of these functions duplicate system functions via HTTP. Among the most useful are file reading and writing functions and those that return dates or times.

> **CAUTION:** Some of these functions are Unix-only. The Windows system is deliberately made less available to users, especially to non-Administrator users, and lacks many utilities that Unix-heads take for granted. If you're having problems and you run on Windows, make sure the function is enabled on your platform.

Understanding PHP File Permissions

Many PHP users, who have a developer orientation rather than any sysadmin experience, unfortunately do not take the time to understand Unix filesystem permissions. You really need to have a firm grasp of the basics to make good decisions about using many of the functions in this section. If you already do, feel free to skip the rest of this section.

Unfortunately, most explanations of the subject are quite general and user's eyes can easily glaze over in a hail of `rwxes` and three-digit numbers. So we're going to break it down for you into two simple default rules specifically for PHP users.

♦ Unless you have a good reason to do otherwise, your PHP files should all be set to `644` (`rw-r--r--`).

♦ Unless you have a good reason to do otherwise, your PHP-enabled directories should all be set to `751` (`rwxr-x--x`).

For some reason, many users seem to believe that PHP files need to be executable. This is only true for files that you write with the intention of their being called on the command line (for example, `./myscript.php`). Files that will be run through a Web server only need to be readable by the Web server user (usually Nobody, or some other user with very limited permissions). It's rather inconvenient to make the files not writable by you, which is why our default recommendation is `644` (`rwxr--r--`) rather than `444` (`r--r--r--`), but this is a matter of convenience only — on a production system, where you shouldn't be altering code anyway, you might very well want to set them to `444`. Your PHP scripts will run perfectly fine at `444` (read-only).

Directory permissions are also very often misunderstood. Many users seem to believe that directories need to be readable for files to run. Actually the *read* directory permission means a user can list the contents of that directory (via the `ls` command, for instance). The *execute* directory permission is closer to what we think of as readable. For your PHP scripts to run, the directory only needs to be world-executable (`751` or `rwxr-x--x`). Do not make the directory writable by others unless you know what you're doing.

This Web page gives a good short explanation of Unix file permissions:

`www.freeos.com/articles/3127/`

File Reading and Writing Functions

This is a supremely useful set of functions, particularly for data sets too small or scattered to merit the use of a database. File reading is pretty safe unless you keep unencrypted passwords lying around; but file writing can be quite unsafe.

> **TIP:** Remember that although the Web server (and client-side languages such as JavaScript) can only act on files located under the document root, PHP can access files at any location in the file system — including those above or entirely outside the Web server document root — as long as the file permissions and `include_path` are set correctly. For instance, if your Web server document root is located at `/usr/local/apache/htdocs`, Apache will only be able to serve files from this directory and its subdirectories; but PHP can open, read, and write to files in `/usr/local`, `/home/php`, `/export/home/httpd`, or any other directory that you make readable and includable by the PHP and/or Web server user.

A file manipulation session might involve the following steps:

1. Open the file for read/write.
2. Read in the file.
3. Close the file (may happen later).
4. Perform operations on the file contents.
5. Write results out.

Each step has a corresponding PHP filesystem function.

This archetypal example illustrates some subtleties of the syntax for manipulating file contents:

```
$fd = fopen($filename, "r+") or die("Can't open file $filename");
$fstring = fread($fd, filesize($filename));
$fout = fwrite($fd, $fstring);
fclose($fd);
```

The effect of this particular example will be to *double* the file — in other words, the end result will be a file with the original contents of the file written out twice. This function will not overwrite the file, as you might expect. In the following sections, we walk you through this archetypal file manipulation session, step by step.

File open

It's essentially mandatory to assign the result of fopen() to a variable (traditionally $fd for *file descriptor*, or $fp for *file pointer*).

> **CAUTION:** The PHP manual claims that fopen() returns an integer on success. This is not exactly true; for all practical purposes, it returns a string that says Resource id #1. Do not attempt to test the success of your file open by using is_int() or is_numeric(). Use die() instead.

If it's successful in opening the file, PHP will return a resource ID, which it requires for further operations such as fread or fwrite. Otherwise, the value will be false.

> **CAUTION:** The system only makes a certain number of file descriptors available, which is a good argument for closing files as soon as you can. If you anticipate a large demand and have access to system settings, you may increase the number. However, if you fail to close a file descriptor, PHP will do it for you when the script ends.

Files may be opened in any of six modes (similar to permissions levels). If you try to do mode-inappropriate things, you will be denied. The modes are:

♦ Read-only ("r").

♦ Read and write if the file exists already ("r+"): will write to the beginning of the file, "doubling" original contents of the file if you read the file in as a string, edit it, and then write the string out to the file.

♦ Write-only ("w"): will create a file of this name, if one doesn't already exist; and will erase the contents of any file of this name before writing! You cannot use this mode to read a file, only to write.

♦ Write and read even if the file doesn't exist already ("w+"): will create a file of this name, if one doesn't already exist, and will erase the contents of any file of this name before writing!

♦ Write-only to the end of a file whether it exists or not ("a").

♦ Read and write to the end of a file whether it exists or not ("a+"), "doubling" original contents of the file if you read the file in as a string, edit it, and then write the string out to the file.

You need to be very sure you have read in the contents of any pre-existing file before using "w" or "w+" on it. Your chance of losing data with the other modes is much less.

> **TIP:** Any of these modes may also have the letter "b" appended if you want to read or write a binary file on Windows.

There are four main types of file connections that can be opened: *HTTP, FTP, standard I/O,* and *filesystem.*

> **TIP:** Some users have reported problems with the "+" modes. Many of these problems actually appear to be caused by slightly faulty understanding of the six modes. When in doubt, try opening in separate read and write modes. See the section on File-writing below.

HTTP fopen

An HTTP `fopen()` tries to open an HTTP 1.0 connection to a file of a type which would normally be served by a Web server (such as HTML, PHP, ASP, and so on). PHP actually "fakes out" the Web server into thinking the request is coming from a normal Web browser surfin' the Net rather than a file-open operation.

You should be able to use forward slashes like this on either Unix or Windows:

```
$fd = fopen("http://www.example.com/openfile.html/", "r");
```

Remember that technically a URL without a trailing slash is malformed, but through incorrect usage most Web servers will automatically rewrite the URL with the slash and try redirecting it. Versions of PHP before 4.0.5 did not support redirects, so all HTTP `fopen()` requests would fail without the trailing slash. After 4.0.5, the trailing slash became optional.

Remember that you need not necessarily use an HTTP connection just because you're looking at an HTML file. If you have filesystem access, you can open from the filesystem instead and treat the file as a text file. The HTTP `fopen()` alternative is mostly useful for getting HTML pages from remote Web servers — as when you try to "scrape" data from an HTML page. The effect will be much like viewing an HTML page and saving the source code.

Beginning with PHP 4.3.0, you will be able to make HTTPS `fopen`s by using `"https://"` rather than `"http://"`.

HTTP `fopen()`s are read-only. You will not be able to write to a remote HTML file using this type of file manipulation.

FTP fopen

An FTP `fopen()` attempts to establish an FTP connection to a remote server by pretending to be an FTP client. This is the trickiest of the four options because you need to use an FTP username and password in addition to the hostname and path.

```
$fd = fopen("ftp://username:password@example.com/openfile.txt/", "r");
```

The FTP server must support passive mode for this method to work correctly. Also, FTP file opens can only be read *or* write, not both at once; and writes can only be to new files, not to existing ones.

PHP has many specific FTP functions, sufficient to implement a complete FTP client in PHP. If you want to do anything except a simple FTP file download, you should probably use them instead. See the PHP manual at:

```
www.php.net/manual/en/ref.ftp.php
```

Standard I/O fopen

Standard I/O read/writes are indicated by `php://stdin`, `php://stdout`, or `php://stderr` (depending on the desired stream). The standard I/O `fopen()` comes into play mostly when PHP is used on the command line or as a system scripting language, à la Perl, because standard I/O is usually associated with terminal windows. This usage is so rare in PHP that we have only seen one real-life example of any length.

A command-line script using a standard I/O `fopen` looks like this:

```
#! /usr/local/bin/php
<?php
$fp = fopen("php://stdin", "r");
while (!feof($fp)) {
  echo fgets($fp, 4096);
}
echo "\n";
?>
```

You would run it like this from the command line:

```
echo "goo goo ga ga" | ./stdin_test.php
```

Filesystem fopen

The most common and useful way to use `fopen()` is from the filesystem. Unless specifically directed otherwise, PHP will attempt to open from the filesystem.

On Windows systems, you can choose to use the Windows format with backslashes if desired — but remember to escape them:

```
$fp = fopen("c:\\php\\phpdocs\\navbar.inc", "r");
```

You can use forward slashes from both Windows and Unix. You should not use a trailing slash for filesystem `fopen()` calls.

> **TIP:** Remember that your files and potentially your directories need to be readable or writable by the PHP (or Web server, if module) process UID rather than by you as a system user. If you share a server, this means any of the other legitimate PHP users may be able to read and/or write to your files.

File read

The `fread()` function takes a file-pointer identifier and a file size in bytes as its arguments. If the file size given is not sufficient to read in the whole file, you will have mysterious problems (unless you're passing in a smaller file size on purpose, which is useful when reading huge files in chunks). Unless you have a reason to do otherwise (such as a huge, unwieldy file), it's best just to let PHP fill in the file size itself, by using the `filesize()` function with the name of the file (or a variable) as the argument:

```
$fstring = fread($fd, filesize($filename));
```

A common error is to type `filesize($fd)` rather than `filesize($filename)`.

This is an extremely useful function because it allows you to turn any file into a string, which can then be manipulated with PHP's large variety of useful string functions. Any string can also be broken up into an array through use of a function like `file()` or `explode()`, which gives you access to the large arsenal of PHP array-manipulation functions. PHP gives you more slicing and dicing functions than a whole set of Ginsu knives!

If you wish to send the entire contents of a file to standard output (meaning, for most PHP installations, echoing it to the Web browser window), use `readfile()` instead. This function has file opening built in, so you need not use a separate function to open the file first. The `readfile()` function is equivalent to the combination of `fopen()` and `fpassthru()`.

Beginning with PHP 4.3.0, a new function called `file_get_contents()` is available. This function returns the entire contents of a file as a string, including the `fopen()`. It is equivalent to `fopen()` and `fread()`, or to `readfile()` except returning the contents as a string rather than straight to standard output.

If you wish to read in and perform operations on a file line by line, you can use fgets() instead of fread(). Beginning in PHP 4.2.0, if you do not specify a line length as the second argument to fgets(), the function will default to 1024 bytes per line.

```
$fd = fopen("samplefile.inc", "r") or die('Cannot find file');
while (!feof($fd)) {
  $line = fgets($fd, 4096);
  if ($line === $targetline)
    {echo "A match was found!";}
}
fclose($fd);
```

If you would rather read the file in as an array, you can use the function file() instead. You might want to do this if you're reading one of the many types of data files that use newlines to indicate rows — such as a spreadsheet saved to tab-delimited text format. This creates an array, each element of which is a line from the original file including an ending newline character. The function file() does not require a separate file open or file close step. A single operation using file(), such as:

```
$line_array = file($filename);
```

is the equivalent of this:

```
$fd = fopen($filename, "r") or die("Can't open file $filename");
$fstring = fread($fd, filesize($filename));
$line_array = explode("\n", $fstring);
```

> **CAUTION:** The file() function will only work correctly when PHP recognizes newlines. Hopefully PHP will handle newlines from other operating systems correctly — current Windows and Unix versions of PHP seem to identify newline characters from the other operating system — but we cannot guarantee that this will be true of every case.

Finally, if you'd like to read in a file character by character, you can use the fgetc() function. This will return a character from the file pointer, until the end-of-file. In practice, this function is not used very much because it's so inefficient to read in a file one character at a time. You'd probably only use fgetc() in situations where you wanted to test the first or second character in the file.

Constructing file downloads by using fpassthru()

Besides reading in a file for manipulation by PHP, you can use fpassthru() in combination with the PHP header() construct to assemble and send file downloads. For instance, let's say you keep lots of tab-delimited data lying around in files, and occasionally you need to let someone download some data from them. Your users are typical businesspeople, not techies, so you know they use IE and would prefer the data as an Excel spreadsheet. So you give the user an HTML form which they can use to ask for the data from a particular day, and when it submits you assemble a download and send it like so:

```php
<?php

// This example assumes there is one data file per day,
// and your form lets the user specify the date they want to see.

$file = $_POST['date'].'.'.'txt';
$fp = $fopen($file, "r");
header("Content-Type:application/xls");
header("Content-Disposition:attachment; filename=$_POST['date'].xls");
// Notice we changed the file name and type
header("Content-Transfer-Encoding:binary");
fpassthru($fp);
?>
```

CAUTION: File downloads in PHP are surprisingly tricky because every browser implements the file download behavior differently — even different versions of the same browser can have different behaviors. The method above works fine in IE 6.0, but in Mozilla 1.0 the file will claim to be of type "application.xls" but will download as "20020526.xls.php". Most of the methods necessary to get a perfect file download are hacks and involve tricking the browser into thinking it's downloading the file directly — for instance by tacking /$_POST['data'].xls onto the end of the URL (e.g. http://example.com/sample.php/20020526.xls). Also, if you saved the script above as "data.xls", and jiggered your Web server into parsing ".xls" files as PHP, you could get a great download in just about every browser. No single perfect method exists for every browser, but this is one situation where you can't just go by what you read in the PHP online manual.

File write

TIP: For file writing via PHP, directory permissions must be set to at least 703.

File writing is pretty straightforward if you've successfully opened in the correct mode for your intended purpose. The function fwrite() takes arguments of a file pointer and a string, with an optional length in bytes, which should not be used unless you have a specific reason to do so. It returns the number of characters written.

```php
$fout = fwrite($fp, $fstring);
if ($fout != strlen($fstring)){
  echo "file write failed!";
}
```

The function fputs() is identical to fwrite() in every way. They are simply aliases for one another, but fputs() is the C-style function name.

Keep in mind that opening a file in "w" or "w+" modes will result in the complete and utter obliteration of any file contents. These modes are meant for clean overwrites only. If you want to write to the beginning or end of a file, use "r+" or "a+" respectively.

Probably the most common error with PHP file-writing modes involves using a Web interface (in other words, an HTML form) to edit a text file. If you want to open a file, read in and view the contents, then write an edited version to the same filename, you cannot depend on "w+" mode. The "w" modes erase the contents of the file *immediately upon opening it* — thus although you can fread() from a "w+" file, there will be no text to read until after you write to it. To get around this issue, you need to open once in read mode and once in write mode, as in the example below:

```php
<?php
if (IsSet($submitted)) {
  $fd = fopen($filename, "w+") or die("Can't open file $filename");
  $fout = fwrite($fd, $newstring);
  fclose($fd);
}
$fd = fopen($filename, "r") or die("Can't open file $filename");
$initstring = fread($fd, filesize($filename));
fclose($fd);
echo "<HTML>";
echo "<FORM METHOD='POST' ACTION=\"$_SERVER['PHP_SELF']\">";
echo "<INPUT TYPE='text' SIZE=50 NAME='newstring'
VALUE=\"$initstring\">";
echo "<INPUT TYPE='HIDDEN' NAME='submitted' VALUE=1>";
echo "<INPUT TYPE='SUBMIT'>";
echo "</FORM>";
echo "</HTML>";
?>
```

Let us reiterate that file writing is not at all a good idea unless you can control your environment very tightly! In other words, a well-hardened intranet server might be appropriate, but file writing on a production Web site can be a security risk. For more information, see Chapter 36.

As we explain in Chapter 37, in PHP4 there is a very easy mechanism to disable the capability to file-write. This is a great idea especially if your site is entirely database-driven, in which case you don't have any legitimate need to write to the filesystem with PHP anyway. To disable file writing, simply add fwrite to the list of disabled functions in php.ini:

```
disabled_functions = "fwrite"
```

If you don't use php.ini and need to set this value in Apache httpd.conf, remember that it requires a php_admin_value flag (rather than php_value):

```
php_admin_value disabled_functions="fwrite";
```

File close

File closing is straightforward:

```
fclose($fd);
```

Unlike `fopen()`, the result of `fclose()` does not need to be assigned to a variable. File closing may seem like a waste of time; but your system has only so many file descriptors available, and you may run out if you do not close your files. On the other hand, PHP will close all open files when your script ends; and at least one version of PHP 3 had a buggy `fclose()` function which would crash the server. You know your own setup best, and you can make the call.

Filesystem and Directory Functions

Most of these functions will be quite familiar to Unix users, as they closely replicate common system commands.

Many of the functions in this section are dangerous. Because they duplicate functions that can and should be performed from the local system, they can be a cracker's bonanza without providing much value to legitimate users. Strongly consider disabling them using PHP4's new `disable_functions` directive (as discussed in the preceding section on file writing)!

The one piece of good news is that some of these functions will only work if the PHP process is running as the superuser. Because this is not the default case in the Web browser, presumably these functions are intended to be used by the scripting version of PHP, and only trusted users who know what they're doing are even in a position to shoot themselves in the foot this way. Of course, if you are foolish enough to run your Web server as root, you are doubly screwed.

The most common and safest functions are listed first in the following sections; the less common and less safe are in Table 13-1.

feof

The `feof` function tests for end-of-file on a file pointer and takes a filename as argument. It's used mostly in a `while` loop to perform the same function on each line in a file:

```
while (!feof($fd)) {
  $line = fgets($fd, 4096);
  echo $line;
}
```

file_exists

The `file_exists` function is a simple function you will use again and again if you use filesystem functions at all. It simply checks the local filesystem for a file of the specified name.

```
if (!file_exists("testfile.php")) {
  $fd = fopen("testfile.php", "w+");
}
```

The function returns true if the file exists, false if not found. The results of this test are stored in a cache, which may be cleared by use of the function clearstatcache().

filesize

Another simple but useful function is filesize, which returns and caches the size of a file in bytes. We use it in all the fread() examples earlier in this chapter. Never pass in a filesize as an integer if you can possibly do it by using filesize() instead.

Table 13-1: Filesystem Functions

Function	Description
basename (*filepath*, [*suffix*])	Returns the filename portion of a stated path.
chgrp(*file*, *group*)	Changes file to any group to which the PHP process belongs. Inoperative on Windows systems.
chmod(*file*, *mode*)	Changes to the stated octal mode. Inoperative on Windows systems.
chown(*file*, *user*)	If executed by the superuser, changes file owner to stated owner. Inoperative but returns true on Windows systems.
clearstatcache	Clears cache of file status info.
copy(*file*, *destination*)	Copies file to stated destination.
delete(*file*)	See "unlink."
dirname(*path*)	Returns the directory portion of a stated path.
diskfreespace("/dir")	Returns the number of free bytes in a given directory.
fgetcsv(fp, *length*, *delimiter*)	Reads in a line and parses for CSV format.
fgetss(fp, *length* [, allowable_tags])	Gets a file line (delimited by a newline character) and strips all HTML and PHP tags except those specifically allowed.
fileatime(*file*)	Returns (and caches) last time of access.
filectime(*file*)	Returns (and caches) last time of inode change.
filegroup(*file*)	Returns (and caches) file group ID number. Names can be determined by using posix_getgrid().

`fileinode(file)`	Returns (and caches) file inode.
`filemtime(file)`	Returns (and caches) last time of modification.
`fileowner(file)`	Returns (and caches) owner ID number. Names can be determined by using `posix_getpwuid()`.
`fileperms(file)`	Returns (and caches) file permissions level.
`filetype(file)`	Returns (and caches) one of: `fifo`, `char`, `dir`, `block`, `link`, `file`, `unknown`.
`flock(file, operation)`	Advisory file locking. Operation value must be 1 (shared), 2 (exclusive), 3 (release), or +4 (don't block while locking).
`fpassthru(fp)`	Standard output of all data from file pointer to EOF.
`fseek(fp, offset, whence)`	Moves file pointer offset number of bytes into file stream from the position indicated by `whence`.
`ftell(fp)`	Returns offset position into file stream.
`set_file_buffer(fp [, buffersize])`	Sets a buffer for file writing; 8K is the default.
`Is_dir(directory)`	Returns (and caches) `true` if named directory exists.
`Is_executable(file)`	Returns (and caches) `true` if named file is executable.
`Is_file(file)`	Returns (and caches) `true` if named file is a regular file.
`Is_link(file)`	Returns (and caches) `true` if named file is a symlink.
`Is_readable(file)`	Returns (and caches) `true` if named file is readable by PHP.
`is_writable (file/directory)`	Returns (and caches) `true` if named file or directory is writable by PHP.
`link(target, link)`	Creates hard link. Inoperative on Windows systems.
`linkinfo(path)`	Confirms existence of link. Inoperative on Windows systems.
`mkdir(path, mode)`	Makes directory at location *path* with the given permissions in octal mode.
`pclose(fp)`	Closes process file pointer opened by `popen()`.
`popen(command, mode)`	Opens process file pointer.
`readlink(link)`	Returns target of a symlink. Inoperative on Windows systems.
`rename(oldname, newname)`	Renames file.

`rewind(fp)`	Resets file pointer to beginning of file stream.
`rmdir(directory)`	Removes an empty directory.
`stat(file)`	Returns a selection of info about file.
`lstat(file)`	Returns a selection of info about file or symlink.
`symlink(target, link)`	Creates a symlink from target to link. Inoperative on Windows systems.
`touch(file, [time])`	Sets modification time; creates file if it does not exist.
`umask(mask)`	Returns `umask`, and sets to `mask & 0777`. With no argument passed, it simply returns the `umask`.
`unlink(file)`	Deletes file.

Network Functions

The network functions are a bunch of relatively little-used functions that provide network information or connections. Many of these may be more useful from the command line than the Web page, unless you're writing some kind of monitoring tool.

Syslog functions

The `syslog` functions allow you to open the system log for a program, generate a message, and close it again.

♦ `openlog([ident], option, facility)` is entirely optional when used with `syslog()`. The ident value is generated automatically.

♦ `syslog(priority, message) generates a system log entry`

♦ `closelog()` is entirely optional when used with `syslog()`. It takes no arguments.

DNS functions

PHP offers some very slick DNS-querying functions, outlined in the Table 13-2 below. These functions allow PHP scripts to do some jiggering between IP address (which is available via the Apache REMOTE_ADDR variable, for instance) and host name, or vice versa.

Table 13-2: DNS Functions

Function	*Description*
`checkdnsrr($host, [$type])`	Checks for existence of DNS records. Default is MX; other types are A, ANY, CNAME, NS, SOA.
`gethostbyaddr($Ipaddress)`	Gets host name corresponding to address.

`gethostbyname($hostna me)`	Gets address corresponding to hostname.
`gethostbynamel($hostn ame)`	Gets list of addresses corresponding to hostname.
`getmxrr($hostname, [mxhosts array], [weight])`	Checks for existence of `MX` records corresponding to hostname, places in `mxhosts` array, fills in weight info.

Socket functions

A *socket* is a kind of dedicated connection that allows different programs (which may be on different machines) to communicate by sending text back and forth. PHP socket functions allow scripts to establish such connections to socket-based servers. For instance, Web and database servers communicate via `fsockopen()` — so you could theoretically write your own Web server in PHP using this function, if you had lost all contact with reality. The connection can then be read from or written to with the standard file-writing functions (`fputs()`, `fgets()`, and so on).

The standard socket-opening function is `fsockopen()`. The `pfsockopen()` function is identical except that sockets are not destroyed when your script exits; instead, the connection is pooled for later use. The blocking behavior of socket connections can be toggled with `set_socket_blocking()`. When blocking is enabled, functions that read from sockets will hang until there is some input to return; when it is disabled, such functions will return immediately if there is no input. These functions are summarized in Table 13-3.

Table 13-3: Socket Functions

Function	*Description*
`fsockopen($hostname, $port, [error number], [error string], [timeout in seconds])`	Opens the socket connection to specified port on the host, and returns a file pointer suitable for use by functions like `fgets()`.
`getservbyname($service, $protocol)`	Returns the port number of the specified service.
`getservbyport($port, $protocol)`	Returns service name on port.
`pfsockopen($hostname, $port, [error number], [error string], [timeout in seconds])`	Opens the specified persistent socket connection.
`set_socket_blocking($socket descriptor, $mode)`	`TRUE` for blocking mode, `FALSE` for nonblocking. Default is nonblocking.

Date and Time Functions

These functions are basic tools used in many self-defined functions. You may use them simply to output the date or time, to keep track of microtime for a PHP performance-tracking utility, or to initiate a function over a particular date range (such as putting a "Happy Holidays" message on your site during holiday seasons).

These are pretty straightforward to use if you understand the Unix timestamp. They fall into three main categories: functions that return date or time, functions that format date or time, and functions that validate date.

> **TIP:** The Unix timestamp measures time as a number of seconds since the beginning of the Unix epoch (midnight Greenwich Mean Time on January 1, 1970). Despite the name, these functions mostly work on Windows also.

If you don't know either date or time

The fastest way to get a time is to use the function `time()`. This will return the Unix timestamp for your locale, which will look something like "961906652." If you plan to pass this timestamp to another function or program, this is the best format. Alternatively, you can then use one of the functions in the next section to format the timestamp into something a bit more human-readable.

You could also use `microtime()` to return the current time in seconds and microseconds since the Unix epoch. This can be supremely helpful for utilities that are designed to measure performance. The format is "0.74321900 961906846," where the first part is microseconds and the second is the Unix timestamp. If you're trying to (for instance) measure the performance of different parts of your Web page, you really just want the microseconds part, which can be cut out like so:

```php
<?php
$stampmebaby = microtime();
$chunks = explode(" ", $stampmebaby);
$microseconds = $chunks[0];
echo $microseconds;
?>
```

A function used to return date information is `getdate($timestamp)`. When used with the argument `time()`, as in `getdate(time())`, it returns an associative array with the following numeric elements derived from the Unix timestamp:

- Seconds
- Minutes
- Hours
- Mday (day of the month — for example, `1-31`)

- ♦ Wday (day of the week — for example, 1-7)

- ♦ Mon (month — for example, 1-12)

- ♦ Year (numeric, for example, 1984)

- ♦ Yday (day of the year — for example, 1-356)

- ♦ Weekday (day of the week — for example, Sunday-Saturday)

- ♦ Month (for example, January-December)

You can also use the getdate() function with a Unix timestamp other than that representing the current time.

If you want to get the time and format it in one step, you can use date() instead of getdate(). In the absence of a Unix timestamp argument, date() will default to the current local date. This has the advantage of allowing nicer formatting, as we will explain in the next subsection. The function strftime() will also format the current Unix timestamp for you (as we explain in the next subsection) unless another is specified.

If you've already determined the date/time/timestamp

The functions in this section come into play if you already have a timestamp and merely wish to format the information more finely. For instance, You may like to express your dates European style (2000.20.04) rather than American (4/20/2000).

The main method to format a timestamp is using date($format...$formatn[, $timestamp]). You pass a series of codes indicating your formatting preferences, plus an optional timestamp. For instance:

```
date('Y-m-d');
```

returns a string like "2002-05-27". You can choose a date with two-zero day identifiers or strictly numeric date identifiers, 12- or 24-hour format, or abbreviated month name. (See the PHP manual for all the options.) An analogous function is gmdate($format...$formatn [, $timestamp]), which will return a Greenwich Mean Date.

The function strftime($format...$formatn[, $timestamp]) is similar but specializes in formatting the time rather than the date; gmstrftime($format...$formatn [, $timestamp]) returns the time in formatted Greenwich Mean Time

The function mktime() allows you to convert any date into a timestamp. It's subtly different in the order of arguments from the Unix command of the same name, so pay attention. The function gmmktime() gives the Greenwich alternative to your own time zone.

Finally, checkdate($month, $day, $year) allows you to quickly ensure that a particular date is a valid one. This is great for leap-year questions.

Calendar Conversion Functions

Finally, we have some optional calendar conversion routines, which are now available as an extension.

> **TIP:** Many new users have made the mistake of thinking "calendar functions" mean date functions. Not so. These functions strictly convert between different (largely historical) calendar systems. See "Date and time functions" earlier in this chapter if you feel you have entered this section in error.

If you happen to be a French historian, you'll be happy to know PHP can automatically convert between the French Revolutionary calendar and the Gregorian calendar with but a couple of commands. What can we say to that but: *Bon Thermidor, Citoyens et Citoyennes*!

Seriously, these functions have real uses — particularly on the global Internet. (And not to be ungrateful or anti-Judeo-Christian-centric . . . but Joyce is patiently and lazily waiting for someone to add the Chinese lunar calendar to PHP, so she can always know when Chinese New Year celebrations will occur.)

To use calendar functions, you need to compile your own PHP from source with the `enable-calendar` flag. Until PHP 4.1 or so, the process of building in calendar functions was shakier, but it seems to have stabilized recently

Conversion between systems is made possible because all the calendar functions share a universal referent, the so-called "Julian Day Number" (a.k.a. "Julian Day Count"). This is an integer that represents the days since noon on the first of January, 4713 BC by the Julian calendar (which wasn't in use at the time, but why niggle?). This date would be the 14th of January in the Gregorian calendar, which is commonly used in secular societies today. The so-called "Julian Date" is a double that represents the days and hours since Julian Day Zero — but PHP does not allow this level of specificity; we're just mentioning it here in case anyone is looking for this information.

> **TIP:** Remember that the Julian day changes at noon rather than midnight, which is the convention today.

PHP's calendar conversion functions translate a date in some calendar into or out of Julian Day Count. To convert between two calendars, you will need to use two separate functions: one to give the date from one calendar as a Julian Day Number, and the other to convert JD into another calendar's date. In this example, we are converting a Gregorian date into its equivalent in the Jewish calendar.

```
$jd_no = gregoriantojd(8, 11, 1945);
$hebrew = jdtojewish($jd_no);
echo $hebrew;
```

This will return a date of `2, 6 [Elul], 5705`. Conversion to the Jewish calendar is somewhat complicated by the fact that it uses lunar months and its days begin at sunset rather than midnight.

The calendars offered at the moment are:

◆ French Republican

◆ Gregorian

◆ Jewish

◆ Julian

◆ Unixian

Each of these calendars has associated "JDTo*X*" and an "*X*ToJD" functions.

Finally, there are two other pairs of miscellaneous calendar functions. JDMonthName() and JDDayofWeek() return the month and day of week of any Julian Day Number in any of the supported calendars; whereas easter_date() and easter_days() will tell you when (Western or Catholic, as opposed to Eastern or Orthodox) Easter falls/fell/will fall in any given year. easter_date() is the more straightforward method but can only be used within a Unix date range (1970–2037). It returns the Unix timestamp of Easter midnight in the specified year.

Extended Example: An Exercise Calculator

At the end of the previous chapter, Chapter 12, the exercise calculator produced a display of calories burned per day's exercise. Now we will store this output in a file and also write a Web-based tool which will allow us to view our exercise diary in a handy monthly format.

Writing data to a file

When you enter your weight and the activities you performed on a given day into the exercise calculator in the previous chapter, it will calculate and display the number of calories you burned that day. But at the same time, you can also capture this data for permanent storage by writing it out to a file.

In this example, we're going to write one file per month. Then you'll be able to look back over your activities on a month-by-month basis, which seems about right for exercise unless you're a total gym rat who analyzes each day's exercise with obsessive glee.

You want to add this code to the end of wc_handler_math.php from the previous chapter:

```php
<?php

// Construct the string
$year_month = date('Y-m');
$day = date('d');
$weight_today = $_POST['weight'];
$cals_today = $total_calories;

$today_str = "$day\t$weight_today\t$cals_today\n";
```

```
// Write out the string
$filename = $year_month.'.txt';
$fd = fopen($filename, "a") or die("Can't open file $filename");
$fout = fwrite($fd, $today_str);
fclose($fd);
echo "Wrote to $filename";
?>
```

This is the simplest form in which you might want to keep the data. If you wanted to, you could record exactly the exercises and durations that you enjoyed that day. You'd do that by replacing the section above commented "`Construct the string`" with this:

```
for ($i = 0; $i <= 3; $i++) {
  foreach ($_POST['exercise'][$i] as $key => $val) {
    if ($val != "") {
      $exer_str .= "$key|$val\t";
    }
  }
}

$today_str = "$day\t$weight_today\t$cals_today\t$exer_str\n";
```

Now let's imagine that you want to both write out the data to a file, and FTP it to some remote location — perhaps to your personal trainer's server. In that case, you'd want to add these lines to the end of the file. Remember that with an FTP file open, you cannot write to the end of an existing file — you can only write to new files. Therefore, you need to write to a differently named file every day.

```
// FTP the file to trainer's server
$ftp_file = "$year-month-$day.txt";
$fd = fopen("ftp://username:password@example.com/$ftp_file/", "w") or
die("Can't open file $ftp_file");
$fout = fwrite($fd, $today_str);
fclose($fd);
echo "FTPed $ftp_file";
```

Displaying data from a file

Now let's say you want to review your sports and fitness activities each month. You can easily read the monthly file you've been writing data to and display the contents in an attractive table. Many of the steps you need to take to accomplish this task amount to reversing the steps you took to write the data to the file in the first place.

Name this script `display_exercise_data.php`. You will pass the specific month you want to look at in the URL as a GET variable, like this:
`display_exercise_data.php?month=2002-05`.

This is the code for `display_exercise_data.php`. When running it in the browser, be sure to pass in a month as shown in the previous paragraph:

```php
<?php

/******************************************************
 * Script to display a month's worth of exercise data *
 ******************************************************/

$month = $_GET['month'];
$filename = $month.'.txt';
if (!file_exists($filename)) {
  echo "There's no file for that month.  Please check the URL and try
again.";
  exit;
}
$day_array = file($filename);

// Deconstruct each day's string
foreach ($day_array as $val) {
  if ($val != "") {
    $data = explode("\t", $val);
    $day = $data[0];
    $weight = $data[1];
    $cals = $data[2];
    $table_str .= "\n<TR
COLSPAN=3><TD>$day</TD><TD>$weight</TD><TD>$cals</TD></TR>";
  }
}

// Print out the nice page
$page_str = <<< EOPAGE
<html>
<head>
<style TYPE="text/css">
<!--
BODY, P, TD      {color: black; font-family: verdana; font-size: 10 pt}
H1        {color: black; font-family: arial; font-size: 12 pt}
-->
</STYLE>
</head>

<table BORDER=0 CELLPADDING=10 WIDTH=100%>
<tr>
<td BGCOLOR="#F0F8FF" ALIGN=CENTER VALIGN=TOP WIDTH=17%>
</td>
<td BGCOLOR="#FFFFFF" ALIGN=LEFT VALIGN=TOP WIDTH=83%>
<h1>Workout calculator (filesystem)</h1>
<p>This is a record of your fitness during the month $month</p>
```

```
<table border=1>
<tr COLSPAN=3><th>Day</th><th>Weight (kilos)</th><th>Calories</th></tr>
$table_str
</table>

</body>
</html>
EOPAGE;
echo $page_str;

?>
```

The results for a partial month look like Figure 13-1:

Figure 13-1: Displaying the contents of a data file

Obviously if you keep more detailed data (for example, the exact exercises and durations), you can display that. You could also choose to graph this data on-the-fly with PHP's graphics functions, discussed in detail in Chapter 33. This example is merely an illustration of how to store and access data from a text file.

Summary

PHP has numerous filesystem and system functions built in, which can be extremely handy if sometimes potentially insecure. A large number of PHP functions duplicate Unix systems utilities, such as chmod() and copy(). PHP can also boast some extra-clever functions such as those for DNS-querying. Although we recommend turning off some of these functions, others can be useful in trusted hands and a well-planned environment.

PHP's file opening, reading, and writing functions are extremely powerful tools. Most problems with these functions result from a slightly incorrect understanding of the file-opening modes. In addition to filesystem `fopen()`, PHP also supports very slick HTTP, HTTPS, FTP, and standard I/O file-opening.

Finally, PHP offers a plethora of time, date, and calendar functions so you always know what time it is.

Chapter 14
PHP Style

This chapter is about the major points of PHP style and how it can enhance the functionality, maintainability, and attractiveness of your code. This discussion is intended to help new PHP developers make the main stylistic decisions, most of which are common to all programming languages.

We also hope this chapter may help new PHPers decipher other people's code. It can be very alarming to someone just learning scripting to read three different tutorials, which appear totally incongruent but lack any explanation of the discrepancies. The information in this chapter will help you tease out the functionally important bits of code from the mere stylistic quirks and thus gain a better understanding of what you're seeing.

The Uses of Style

The primary goal of a program is, of course, functionality. After all, if your PHP script chokes, who's even going to care how good it looks? Error messages are never all that stylin'. But there is a vast difference between simply whipping up something that will work and writing well-formed code that can be clearly understood by others.

PHP programmers confront all the same style issues that other programmers do, including:

- **Readability:** Sure, you understood it when you wrote it, but what about the next person who reads it? What about if the next person is you?

- **Maintainability:** What happens when your health-advice site finally makes that conversion from Fahrenheit to Celsius? (A wrong answer: Replacing 790 occurrences of the string 98.6 in your source code.)

- **Robustness:** Your Web site works fine when it's getting the inputs you expect. What about when it gets the inputs you don't expect?

- **Conciseness and efficiency:** Fast code is better than slow code, and (others things equal) code using fewer keystrokes is better than code with more keystrokes (but other things are almost never equal).

This chapter will give a quick overview of some strategies for achieving these goals in PHP, before moving on to some code organization issues that are unique to PHP.

Readability

Before a PHP script can aspire to be maintainable or elegant, it has to be human-readable. The human eye likes clear patterns, logical organization, and meaningful repetition. It also helps to have the most significant word or character at the beginning of a line, instead of buried in the middle.

If you develop HTML mostly through use of a WYSIWYG tool, your notions of legibility may be very odd indeed. These programs are notorious for writing badly structured graphics-oriented HTML, filled with invisible GIFs and absolute sizing and other little horrors.

Trying to add PHP directly to HTML files like this is an exercise in frustration, like trying to dance with someone who has no rhythm. If you insist on doing so, remember: It's not PHP's fault, so please direct your abuse to the other vendor. However, in lieu of yet another moralistic Unix-centric anti-WYSIWYG lecture, we'll now try to make a concrete suggestion or two for those who can't totally avoid such tools.

Probably the single most effective step you can take to increase legibility is to run all machine-produced HTML through a utility that will make it more human-readable. It doesn't take very long at all and will improve matters substantially. A good one for Unix is HTML Tidy, freely available from:

```
www.w3.org/People/Raggett/tidy/
```

This utility will also clean up common errors in your HTML source, such as missing end tags. Furthermore, it has some (admittedly limited at this point) capability to cope with PHP, if you've used the standard `<?php ... ?>` tags — so you can also try cleaning up those "I'm in such a hurry, so just this once I'll save a Microsoft Office document in HTML format and then stick in a couple of PHP tags" situations. It will read Microsoft Office documents saved as HTML, although HTML Tidy is not available on the Windows platform (at press time).

A somewhat more labor-intensive approach that gives you finer control is to run the code through an HTML validator. This is a utility (many are Web-delivered) that lists all the specific points at which a page is not in compliance with HTML standards. However, unlike HTML Tidy, it does not actually rewrite the source code; you can choose to make changes on a point-by-point basis.

The next most effective way to increase code legibility involves lobbying your boss to move the whole shop over to a development environment that supports both a good WYSIWYG editor and a good text editor. Although this is not an endorsement, a well-known product of this description is Macromedia Dreamweaver, which is available in both Mac and Windows versions, has some PHP support, and can interoperate with a variety of image manipulation packages.

Even PHP developers who code entirely by hand can help themselves in the long run by selecting a congenial text editor (as discussed in Chapter 3). Why waste time closing HTML tags or chasing down a missing parenthesis if you don't have to? Most text editors today have the capability to automatically close tags and brackets appropriately, and otherwise help you avoid trivial but time-consuming mistakes.

You want something that is available on your preferred development platform and can be configured to closely match your personal style. Some people love syntax highlighting in many colors on black, others think it's too much like programming a Lite-Brite; some people use tab indentations, others prefer spaces; some people like the program to do everything but make coffee for them, others want a dumb but obedient terminal. It's all good, and you can find almost any combination of features you want — if you're willing to put the time into customizing your editor. Because a programmer's text editor is like a desperado's horse — you have to ride that nag until one of you drops — this is definitely time well spent. All text editors today have Web sites with lots and lots of screenshots; look around until you see the configuration of your dreams.

> **CAUTION:** Make sure your chosen editor is compatible with whatever your coworkers are using. Some editors strip out tab-indenting, cause documents to be formatted oddly, use strange quote marks, and so forth. Your codevelopers won't elect you Employee of the Month if they have to reformat every page after you look at it.

One of our pet peeves is about programmers who haven't yet accepted that computer memory is no longer worth any kind of premium, and thus it's counterproductive to spend time trying to squeeze a program into the smallest space possible. This practice is unfortunately recapitulated by some misguided technical book and magazine publishers, who still ask their authors to use various dodges to reduce the length of printed code samples, like so:

```
<?php if($UserID && strlen($Horse)>0) {
 if($Horse=="Man O'War") print("Chestnut, white snip");
 elseif($Horse=="Native Dancer") print("Light grey");
 elseif($Horse=="Seattle Slew") print("Black");
} else {
print("Please try again."); }?>
```

This example features indentations consisting of a single space per level, absence of repetitive but meaningful file elements such as HTML headers, and an overall lack of breathing room. None of this is at all incorrect, but neither does it particularly aid readability. Compare that format to this (and try to imagine both being embedded in a much longer, more complex script that you've been assigned to change ASAP):

```
<HTML><BODY>
<?php
if($UserID && strlen($Horse)>0)
{
    if($Horse == "Man O'War")
        print("Chestnut, white snip");
    elseif($Horse == "Native Dancer")
        print("Light grey");
    elseif($Horse == "Seattle Slew")
        print("Black");
}
else
{
    print("Please try again.");
}
?>
</BODY></HTML>
```

New programmers might do well to keep in mind that the code in books or even on the Internet (where space literally costs *nothing*) does not necessarily represent the pinnacle of human legibility.

And finally, not to belabor the obvious, neatness does count. This becomes more true as the number of developers rises and issues of maintainability come to the fore.

Comments

Putting comments in code is just like flossing your teeth: important for health and hygiene, the object of many good intentions, all too often skipped "just this once," and long regretted later if undone.

The problem is that there's no immediate glory to be had from commenting — all the benefits are longer term and diffuse. Let's face it: You rarely hear hackers oohing and aahing over the beautiful commenting of the guy in the next cubicle, and few Web sites' go-live dates are allowed to slip so that the programmers can put the finishing touches on their comments. Commenting comes into its own later, when your team leader quits (in the middle of a major site redesign) to join a neo-Luddite community; and the rest of you are sitting around scratching your heads and thinking "Huh?" in unison, as you desperately try to write up some documentation in time for the scheduled release. So what kinds of things should you comment? We feel you *must* explain:

♦ Anything with future "what the heck was I thinking?" potential (usually due to extreme cleverness or extreme ugliness)

♦ Anything you suspect might be a temporary expedient

- Anything that will lead to dire consequences if tampered with by ignorant people

Things that ideally should be noted include:

- The date the file was originally created, and the name of the creator
- The date the file was most recently altered, and the name of the alterer, and possibly an explanation of the rationale behind the alteration
- Any other files or programs that depend on the existence of this file
- The intended purpose of the file and of its constituent parts
- Things you might want to mention in documentation you're planning to write later
- The reason why you want to save something that isn't being used (alternate versions, archive copies, and so on), conditions under which it might become okay to throw it away, or your plans for what to do with it

Obviously, you're in a better position than we to decide whether these items are strictly necessary. If you're using PHP for a very small, purely personal site, maybe commenting would be superfluous; but the bigger and more complex the site, the more you need to annotate your own work. In theory, it's possible to overcomment; but, in practice, few programmers are guilty of this offense.

> **TIP:** As we detailed in Chapter 5, there are several styles of PHP comments. Remember that none of these will be visible from the client machine, even when HTML source is viewed. If you want client-readable hidden text, you must use HTML comments.

PHPDoc

For very large and complex programs, code-embedded comments are not sufficient. You want separate documentation that someone can read without delving into the code itself. The problem with documentation like this, however, is not just how anyone gets the time to write it (since that is often low priority), but how it stays in sync with the code (which is even lower priority). When starting a new day job, we have more than once confronted a very common choice: Should we get to know the code by reading the current code itself or by consulting some very nicely-written documentation of the code as it was two years ago?

One approach, used with some languages, is to employ a tool that produces documentation by extracting specially-formatted, embedded comments from the code. For example, If you have followed a certain commenting convention, you can point the `javadoc` tool at your Java code and it will extract class and method comments into a set of HTML pages documenting the API. This is not a magic solution for the problem of keeping docs in sync with code. (It will break down, for example, if people begin writing new methods by copying old methods, and leaving the original comments in place.) But at least developers have to write only one description of a given method rather than two.

There is an analogous `phpdoc` tool under development, which uses PHP (naturally) to scan PHP code for special comments, producing HTML output. The current version imposes some mild restrictions on the code it processes (for example, you can't mix class definitions and normal function definitions in the same file), and there is inherent overhead involved in maintaining the comment blocks. If you are doing a large-team project, though, especially one making heavy use of object-oriented PHP, you might find `phpdoc` to be helpful. For more on phpdoc, see www.phpdoc.de/.

File and variable names

Some people act like thinking up variable names is equivalent to being forced to write an epic poem — they go into a kind of writer's block and become creatively incapacitated. For instance, we once had an intern who was apparently unable to think up a single name, or even a halfway decent scheme for doing so. This person's habit was to name every new file according to simple sequential order: `file16.html`, `file17.html`, `file18.html`, and so forth. Each variable on a Web page was called `var1`, `var2`, and so on. This story would be a lot funnier if it had happened to someone else.

Because PHP generally requires a lot more variables than HTML, you need a robust naming scheme for all occasions. The following sections include a few tips.

Long versus short

Longer is generally better because it's more informative. You can break up long names with underscores or capitalization if necessary.

Even though most filesystems technically allow for long filenames, the results are not pretty when viewed as icons — so GUI users may be consciously or unconsciously averse to using long filenames. Icon labels are usually quite short and, thus, naturally lend themselves to very concise filenames. Try giving a file a long, complex name (like `PoachedPeachesRecipe.php`) and putting it on your desktop — the result is just viscerally displeasing.

> **CAUTION:** Most GUI-oriented filesystems allow and even encourage filenames with spaces in them (for example, `My Document.doc`). Unix systems do in theory, but in practice it's not such a good idea. However, PHP will try to cope gracefully with such filenames, but it may not be able to do so in all situations.

One benefit of using PHP for dynamic content generation is that you can use shorter filenames that will be expanded and differentiated by GET-style query strings. For example, a static site might use this style of filename to uniquely identify each page:

```
FeatureHitchcockBirds.html
MiniseriesIrvinSpy.html
```

A dynamic site, on the other hand might identify the same pages like this:

```
feature.php?ID=1
```

```
miniseries.php?ID=2
```

In this situation, you can have the best of both worlds: short filename plus unique identifier. (The only downside of this is that some search engines still discriminate against pages with dynamic arguments, under the theory that the contents are likely to change with every pageview and, therefore, won't be worth indexing.)

PHP sets no particular limit on the length of variable names. So feel free to invent lengthy but informative variables like `$AddressOfClientCompanyInSasketchewan`. Hey, it's your script — we're just living in it. You only need to be careful if you plan to use a lot of long-name variables as part of a GET-method form.

Underscores versus camelcaps

There are two typical ways to break up long variable and file names in Unix. Underscores look like this:

```
$name_of_favorite_beer
```

whereas *camelcaps* look like this, with the internal capital letters giving the name a humped profile:

```
$NameOfFavoriteBeer
```

It's a purely personal preference, which style you use (unless you have agreed on a particular style -- see the "PEAR coding style" section later in this chapter). PHP itself uses underscores (`$PHP_SELF`), but this usage by PHP could be construed as an argument in favor of either scheme for PHP programmers. Just remember you can't use dashes and should be careful with dots.

CAUTION: Unix filenames are case sensitive all the time. Filenames in other OSs, such as Windows, are not case sensitive. If you might be in a position to move PHP files between OSes, be careful.

The main thing to strive for here is consistency. It's frustrating to spend a lot of time trying to figure out why `$My_Number` was never assigned, only to find out that it's because you called it `$MyNumber` when you assigned it.

Reassigning variables

Situations arise in which you deliberately want to keep using the same variable name over and over rather than coming up with new names. This happens when you need to be certain only one variable of a particular type will be valid at any given time. For instance, you might want to be sure there can be no confusion about which of two database queries will be used for an operation, which you can ensure by using the same name for both (for example, `$query`). PHP will overwrite the former with the latter, and your variable will always be minty fresh.

The PEAR coding standards

Although we have talked in a very free and easy way about how all these stylistic choices are up to you, there are situations where it is actually good to have a consensus on what code should look like, and then enforce that. This is particularly true when many programmers will contribute code to a project. The reasons that are usually advanced for a uniform style are:

♦ It makes it easier to read code from multiple programmers, because you don't have to get used to a new indenting or layout style every time you see new code.

♦ It makes life easier for version control software (like CVS). If I change a code file that you created and my editor changes the indentation, there will be a lot of apparent but spurious differences.

Believe it or not, fierce battles have raged over the pros and cons of putting a space between a function name and its parenthesized arguments, or the question of whether to put a curly brace at the end of a line or at the beginning of the next. But the benefits of a uniform style is that these questions can be settled after a smart person, or a set of smart people, has considered all the arguments in all directions and then settled the question once and for all (possibly arbitrarily).

The *PEAR project* is a repository for high-quality, reusable PHP code and PHP extensions (see `http://pear.php.net`). As part of the "high-quality" part of this, the PEAR team decided to agree on a particular coding style and then to enforce it (in other words, until your code follows the style, it will not be accepted into PEAR). If you are interested in using a consistent style for your project, you might consider using PEAR's, even if you have no plans to submit your code to them.

Much more detail on the coding standard can be found at the PEAR site, but we will briefly list some of the highlights here (while noting with regret that the code in this book is non-compliant):

♦ Use `<?php .. ?>` tags rather than `<? .. ?>`.

♦ Indent code by four spaces per level (no tabs).

♦ Put a space between control structures (`if`, `while`) and the parenthesis that starts the test clause.

♦ Do not put a space between function name and the parenthesis that starts the argument list (in both function calls and definitions).

♦ Put the initial curly brace of a function definition on its own line, rather than immediately following the argument list.

♦ Use the `//` and `/* .. */` commenting styles, rather than `#`.

♦ Use `phpdoc` commenting (see the "PHPDoc" section earlier in this chapter) for documentation of object-oriented classes and methods.

Maintainability

Many seasoned programming veterans, especially those who are also managers, tout the importance of maintainability above that of any other virtue.

The problem is, of course, that maintainability is in direct conflict with all the other goals — especially speed. When Internet Time gets into the ring with Hypothetical Future Code Maintenance By Someone Probably Not Myself, everyone knows how the story is going to end. Still, the main mental mantras of maintainability are worth keeping in mind:

♦ The things that are most likely to be changed should be the easiest to find.

♦ Changing those things should not have unpredictable effects.

♦ Each change should have to be made in only one place.

Avoid magic numbers

A *magic number* is a numerical value that might someday have to be changed but is buried deep in code, often in multiple places. Imagine, for example, these lines of code found in your bank's hypothetical PHP-based Web site:

```
print("The interest rate on your CD can be as high as
      5.5%!<BR>");
$sample_gains = 5000 * 1.055;
print("After a year, a \$5000 investment could grow to
      \$$sample_gains!<BR>");
```

Now, when times get tighter and the rate goes down to 5.0%, someone has to find and change every instance of the rate. So, someone does a text search for 5.5, which misses the 1.055 in the second line here, and now your bank is engaging in false advertising.

For simple sites, a better alternative can be as easy using an $interest_rate variable, which is assigned very visibly at the top of a script — a change in rate means a change only to that assignment statement. More complex sites might produce their pages as function calls, with variables like $interest_rate being passed in as an actual parameter. Finally, some sites will go so far as to have all their content imported from a database, so that no piece of information has to ever be changed directly in code.

Functions

Having tried to maintain a complex site using a Web-scripting language that did not support functions, we can say from our own experience that functions are crucial to maintenance. The art of procedural abstraction via functions needs a book in itself, but here's some brief advice:

♦ Always look for opportunities to bundle naked PHP code into a function, especially in cases where it might be reused.

♦ Try to keep function definitions short — if a definition gets too long, break it up into multiple functions.

♦ Always load all your function definitions before any code that calls any functions.

Include files

One of the great benefits of dynamic Web page generation over static HTML is the opportunity to fight redundancy. Anyone who has ever managed a static site of any size knows how much of each file is boilerplate — and even editing a single character on each page isn't a picnic if your site has 200 pages.

PHP makes it very easy to drop in anything, from one character to a whole separate program, into your scripts by using the built-in `include` or `require` functions. The syntax is simply:

```php
<?php include("filename.ext"); ?>
```

You can also use a variable filename, like this:

```php
<?php
$LastName = "Park";
include("$LastName.inc");
?>
```

which will result in the contents of the file `Park.inc` being spliced in at the location of the include statement.

You can use any extension you want for the included file. Popular choices include `.txt`, `.inc`, and even `.html` to remind yourself that the file will show up in HTML mode.

A few things to remember:

♦ PHP will drop the entire text of the file into your PHP script *in HTML mode* (as explained in Chapter 4). If the included file is itself meant to be parsed as PHP, you must use valid PHP tags at the beginning and end. If any part of the file is meant to be parsed as PHP, you must use valid PHP tags around that section.

♦ Recall the difference (explained in detail in Chapter 5) between `include/require` and `include_once/require_once`. In general, if what you are including or requiring is a set of function or class definitions, you should use the `once` variant. If it is straight PHP or HTML, then which variant you load depends on whether you would ever want that literal block to repeat in your output; if not, then the `once` version is probably still what you want.

♦ `include` can also be used to assemble complex Web pages from text files instead of from a database. In some cases, this can even be faster — usually when the included data is just a sizable text file(s). However, after you go to the trouble to make a database connection for any reason, it's probably just as fast to store your big chunks of text there, too.

Object wrappers

Although we haven't covered PHP's object system in detail yet, it's worth noting that consistent use of objects can make code more maintainable, much as functions do. For example, some developers of database-enabled PHP sites are disciplined enough to wrap up all of their database-specific functionality in the methods of an object, so that the rest of their code doesn't even know what kind of database is supporting the site. In theory, then, if they decide to move from a mySQL database to an Oracle database, only the object-level code will have to be changed.

> **CROSS-REFERENCE:** For detail on PHP's support for object-oriented programming, see Chapter 26.

Consider using version control

For large multiprogrammer projects in industrial settings, version control isn't something to "consider" — it's a must. Similarly, large decentralized open-source projects could not survive without *CVS* (Concurrent Versions System). Even if you are working by yourself or with one other person on a hobby project, using version control can free you to do more experimentation, secure in the knowledge that you can get to the older versions of your code if something goes awry.

See www.cvshome.org for more information on CVS. SourceForge also offers free Web-based CVS project hosting for open-source projects (www.sourceforge.net/).

Robustness

The two commandments of robustness are:

♦ Code should detect unexpected situations and respond gracefully rather than dying.

♦ If code must die, better that it die informatively.

Fancy languages like Java have elaborate exception-handling systems that require code to specify in advance the ways that it might die, and what significance should be attached to such deaths. Unfortunately PHP has nothing like this — the humble PHP programmer must make do with conditional tests and branches, and (like a spy's cyanide tooth) the die() function.

Writing robust code is at first a difficult task of imagination, where the programmer tries to think ahead to all the things that might go wrong and to cover those cases. The ideal situation is for that habit of mind to become a habit of code, so that the coder has a standard set of tests that wrap around the standard potential problems. Although most of the robustness issues in PHP are the same as in any language, there are two kinds of situations to cover that are more specific to PHP: problems with an external service, and problems having to do with variable type.

> **NEW FEATURE**: It is no longer true that the only alternative for error-handling is `die()`. The `set_error_handler()` function (introduced in version 4.0.1 and improved in 4.0.2) allows the programmer to intercept arbitrary errors and specify a function that decides how to handle them.

Unavailability of service

PHP is in part a "glue" language, offering a single environment where a variety of different code libraries and external services can be invoked. Any given PHP page might open a file, connect to a database, query an LDAP server, send an HTTP header, or send mail via an SMTP server. The important habit to develop is covering cases where for some external reason a service is unavailable, or times out, or behaves oddly, or gets interrupted in the middle.

Often such services have error states that can be retrieved and printed if the only option left is to informatively die. For example, a reasonable construct for making a connection to a mySQL database is:

```
$connection = mysql_connect([arguments]) or
              die("Connection failed:  $php_errormsg<BR>");
```

This is preferable to the weird and unexpected errors you would see if your code went happily ahead assuming that it had a live database connection. An alternative that is better from a security point of view is:

```
$connection = mysql_connect(...) or error_log($php_errormsg);
if (!$connection){
 die("Connection Failed");
}
```

because this will avoid displaying interesting facts about your PHP and database configuration to the user's browser.

Unexpected variable types

Although the type-looseness of PHP is for the most part a good thing, it leaves a little bit of uncertainty for the programmer about exactly what type a variable or value will turn out to be. Unless you come to know all the type-conversion rules very well, it can be surprising to have code that is accustomed to strings suddenly run across a value that is a number, all because some PHP construct decided that any string composed only of numerical digits must really be a number at heart. One interesting robustness check is to use a text editor to search your code for $ (thereby finding every variable) and ask yourself for each one what would happen if the type turned out to be surprisingly different.

Conciseness and Efficiency

Conciseness and efficiency are not the same thing. Concise code accomplishes a given task in a small number of lines or keystrokes, and efficient code runs using a small amount of execution time or computer memory. In this section, we give some quick tips toward writing concise and efficient PHP code, along with our extremely opinionated commentary about in what senses these goals are worth striving for.

Efficiency: Only the algorithm matters

There was a time when computer memory and computer cycles were so precious that it was worth a lot of effort to boil down your code to the smallest number of resulting machine instructions possible. This is still true in certain areas of software development (kernel programming, graphics libraries), but for most development tasks saving a few instructions or a few K is not worth backing off on any other goal. This is especially true for Web scripting, where there is always going to be some overhead of purely Internet-related execution delay. If it takes half a second for a user to fetch your page, regardless of how your page is produced, then an extra five milliseconds on the server side will be lost in the noise.

With that said, there's one variety of efficiency that matters and will probably always matter: the broad algorithm or approach that your code uses for a task. For example, if your code locates a name in a database by querying the database for all names and then doing a string comparison for each name to see if it's the one you want, you'll soon find out how much efficiency can matter.

Efficiency optimization tips

Here are some quick mantras to repeat to yourself as you code.

Don't reinvent the wheel

It's usually a bad idea to write code that duplicates a language-level facility, unless it's for purposes of fun or education. For example, any programmer worth his or her salt should write sorting routines at some point in their education, but no programmer should have to keep writing them (unless it is actually in their job description). Most high-level programming languages offer some kind of sorting capability (either as part of the language or in a library), and it's very likely that the programmer who wrote them did a better job than you will. PHP is no exception here — the array type supports several types of sorting, and most of the databases supported by PHP have sorting options built into the query language. Either of these options will be faster and more reliable than what you get by rolling your own.

Discover the bottleneck

Although it's good to try to use efficient algorithms from the beginning, it's often not worth doing other kinds of optimization until you find out that too much of some resource is being used. At that point, you want to tighten things up, and you'll get the most reward for your effort if you focus on the piggiest parts of your code. Most code follows the 90/10 rule: 90 percent of the time is spent in 10 percent of the code, and you want to locate that 10 percent.

One technique that programmers often use to locate that 10 percent is called *profiling*. A profiler is a utility that tracks code as it runs, noting the time spent in every function call, and producing a neat summary of the results. Unfortunately, at this writing, there is no good general profiling utility for PHP (although one may be on the way for later versions of PHP4). So the best bet for now is the poor man's profiling technique: printing the value of the function call `microtime()` in various places in your script to see where the time is going. If the 90/10 rule is in effect, the time sink will usually be glaringly obvious.

Focus on database queries

Although it involves a bit of look-ahead to the next part of the book, you should be aware that database queries are usually the biggest time sink for PHP sites that have database back ends. Especially if your database-enabled site doesn't do a lot of other computationally intensive work, your first suspicious glance should be at the queries, and your next task should be to try to identify a query that is particularly time-consuming. After you've identified a guilty query, there are a host of techniques available to speed that query up, many of which don't have anything to do with PHP.

> **CROSS-REFERENCE:** For details on optimizing database-enabled PHP sites, see Chapter 24.

Focus on the innermost loop

Let's say that you have a page with embedded looping constructs, like the following:

```
for ($x = 0; $x < 100; $x++)
{
  do_X();
  for ($y = 0; $y < 100; $y++)
    {
      do_XY();
      for ($z = 0; $z < 100; $z++)
        {
          do_XYZ();
        }
    }
}
```

Unless you have a really good reason to think otherwise, your optimization focus should be on the function `do_XYZ()` (which will execute 1,000,000 times) rather than on the other two functions (10,000 times and 100 times).

Conciseness: the downside

Before we get into how to write more concise code, let us say that we think conciseness is an overrated virtue, for the following reasons.

Conciseness rarely implies efficiency

Although it's true that somewhere in the guts of the PHP engine, the characters of the code you write are being consumed one by one (and so, in theory, more code takes more time), in practice, the Zend-based parsing engine of PHP4 is so zippy that the number of characters just doesn't matter. Ditto for the time or space consumed in extra variable assignments or the overhead of extra function calls.

Conciseness trades off with readability

Remember that every keystroke you omit might be the keystroke that would have let someone figure out what the heck you were thinking when you wrote the code. For example, take a look at the following admirably concise function:

```
function sieve($n) {
  for ($i = 2; $i <= sqrt($n); $i++)
    for ($j = $i, $ind = $i * $j; $ind <= $n;
         $j++, $ind = $i * $j)
    $carray[$ind] = 1;
  for ($i = $n, $plist = array(); $i > 1; $i--)
    if (!$carray[$i]) array_push($plist,$i);
  return($plist);
}
```

Obviously, this implements the Sieve of Erasthones, and $plist is a list of all the prime numbers less than $n. Obviously.

So why do programmers strive for conciseness? The first reason is that it saves them time (but only at the time of actual code writing). The second reason (and we're only half-joking) is that they're afraid some other programmer (probably one trained in C) will come along later, laugh at them, and point out that their code could have been written in only half the space.

Conciseness tips

If you must write code that fits in less space, try some of the following techniques.

Use return values and side effects at the same time

It's a very common trick to exploit the fact that the value of an assignment is the value assigned, as in the following pseudocode:

```
while ($next = GetNextOne())
   DoSomethingWith($next);
```

where GetNextOne() is some function that returns useful values in sequence and then returns a false value when it runs out of them. When a false value is returned, $next is false, and the while loop terminates.

Use incrementing and assignment operators

The incrementing operators (++ and --) shorten statements that involve adding or subtracting one from a variable, and the combined assignment operators (+=, *=, .=, and so on) make certain kinds of assignments more concise.

> **CROSS-REFERENCE:** The incrementing operators and the arithmetic assignment operators are covered in Chapter 10, and the combined string assignment operator (. =) is covered in Chapter 9.

Often these operators are used in combination with the previous trick, as in:

```
while ($count--)
   DoSomethingWith($count);
```

which (assuming that $count starts as a positive integer) would call its function for the very last time on the value 1.

Reuse functions

This is one case where conciseness is good, because functions are good. If you can identify any stretches of code that get duplicated in your pages, try to replace each one with a call to a single function that packages up that code. Your code will be shorter by the amount of the duplication and also easier to maintain.

There's nothing wrong with Boolean

Beginning programmers often have an odd distrust of Boolean values, not realizing that they can be passed around as freely as any other kind of value. This leads to code that wastes a lot of space, like the following:

```
function DivisibleByBad($num1, $num2)
{
   if ($num1 % $num2 == 0)
      return(TRUE);
   else
      return(FALSE);
}
/* using the function */
if (DivisibleByBad(9, 3))
  $divisible_result = TRUE;
else
  $divisible_result = FALSE;
if ($divisible_result == TRUE)
  print("It's divisible!<BR>");
else
  if ($divisible_result == FALSE)
     print("It's not divisible!<BR>");
```

A more concise version would look like:

```
function DivisibleByBetter($num1, $num2)
{
   return ($num1 % $num2 == 0);
}
/* using the function */
if (DivisibleByBetter(9,3))
```

```
  print("It's divisible!<BR>");
else
  print("It's not divisible!<BR>");
```

You could obviously take this one step further and get rid of the function itself, like so:

```
if (9 % 3 == 0)
  print("It's divisible!<BR>");
else
  print("It's not divisible!<BR>");
```

But (once again) *Functions Are Good* — an explanatory function name is a little piece of documentation in itself, and any function you write gives you a chance to reuse it later, which, in turn, makes your code more maintainable.

Use short-circuiting Boolean expressions

Certain kinds of Boolean tests aren't safe to apply until you've done other tests. It's tempting to deal with this by insulating the problematic tests with `if` constructs. For example, imagine that you want to print the ratio of two variables that are bound to integers, but only if they are bound to integers, and only if the ratio is greater than two. Also, you want to avoid a division-by-zero warning. You might overcautiously write:

```
if (IsSet($x))
  {
    if (IsSet($y))
    {
      if (Is_Integer($x))
      {
        if (Is_Integer($y))
        {
          if ($y != 0)
            {
              if ($x / $y > 2)
                print("Ratio is " . ($x / $y));
            }
        }
      }
    }
  }
```

You can be equally overcautious and still type a little less, as in:

```
if (IsSet($x) && IsSet($y) && Is_Integer($x) &&
    Is_Integer($y) && $y != 0 && $x / $y > 2)
  print("Ratio is " . ($x / $y));
```

The tests will be applied in left-to-right order, and if any test fails, the tests to the right of it will not be evaluated.

HTML Mode or PHP Mode?

There's a spectrum of ways to combine PHP and HTML, functionally all pretty much the same. Your choice will depend on extrinsic factors such as your particular team's workflow.

The easiest way to demonstrate all this is to simply write the same script in minimal PHP, maximal PHP, and medium PHP styles. We will also include a version using the *heredoc* construct (discussed in Chapter 10), which is our favorite of the four. Remember, these are equally correct and return much the same result. The stylistic decision is just a matter of preference and consistency, and (sometimes) slight differences in functionality.

Minimal PHP

The code in Listing 14-1 shows a simple self-submitting form, which returns some simple information about days of the week. First, it tells you what day it is today, and then gives you a chance to ask it what day it will be in a few days (using a form with a pull-down list). The typical text output looks like this:

```
4 days from this moment it will be Thursday
Today is Sunday
Please choose a number of days, and we'll tell you what day it will be
that many days from now
```

It is written using a *minimal PHP* style, meaning simply that, as much as possible, the code is pure HTML, dropping into PHP mode only when dynamic data must be displayed (such as the current day of the week, or an answer that depends on submitted data).

Listing 14-1: Minimal PHP

```
<HTML><HEAD TITLE="Calendar Server"></HEAD><BODY>
<H2>Welcome to the Calendar Server</H2>

<?php if (IsSet($_POST['DAYS'])) { ?>
  <P> <?php echo $_POST['DAYS'];?>
  days from this moment it will be
  <?php $date = getdate(time() +
                       ($_POST['DAYS'] * 86400));
       echo($date['weekday']);
}?>

<P>Today is <?php $date = getdate();
               echo($date['weekday']); ?>
<P>Please choose a number of days, and we'll
tell you what day it will be that many days from now:

<FORM METHOD=POST ACTION="<?php echo $_SERVER['PHP_SELF'];?>" >
<SELECT NAME=DAYS>
 <OPTION VALUE=1>1<OPTION VALUE=2>2<OPTION VALUE=3>3
 <OPTION VALUE=4>4<OPTION VALUE=5>5<OPTION VALUE=6>6
```

```
</SELECT>
<INPUT TYPE=SUBMIT NAME=SUBMIT VALUE=SUBMIT>
</FORM>
</BODY></HTML>
```

This code takes the minimal style to an extreme — note the funny business with the `'if'` statement near the top, where some straight HTML text ("days from this moment") is included conditionally, based on the results of the PHP statement that precedes it.

As we have said, this is a matter of taste, but we don't like this version very much. It's a bit hard to see exactly what is being produced by the PHP snippets that are spliced into the page.

Maximal PHP

At the opposite extreme, consider the code in Listing 14-2. This version is in PHP mode all the time, and simply prints out all the HTML it needs to as it goes.

Listing 14-2: Maximal PHP

```
<?php
print("<HTML><HEAD TITLE=\"Calendar Server\"></HEAD><BODY>");
print("<H2>Welcome to the Calendar Server</H2>");

if (IsSet($_POST['DAYS'])) {
  print("<P>" .$_POST['DAYS'] .
        " days from this moment it will be ");
  $date = getdate(time() +
          ($_POST['DAYS'] * 86400));
  print($date['weekday']);
}

$date = getdate();
$day_of_week = $date['weekday'];
print("<P>Today is $day_of_week");
print("<P>Please choose a number of days, and we'll
tell you what day it will be that many days from now:");

$self = $_SERVER['PHP_SELF'];
print("<FORM METHOD=POST ACTION=\"$self\" >");
print("<SELECT NAME=DAYS>");
for ($i = 1; $i < 7; $i++) {
 print("<OPTION VALUE=$i>$i");
}
print("</SELECT>");
print("<INPUT TYPE=SUBMIT NAME=SUBMIT VALUE=SUBMIT>");
print("</FORM></BODY></HTML>");
?>
```

Another term for *maximal PHP* might be *CGI-style*, because we are not taking advantage of the HTML-embeddedness of PHP at all, and might as well be writing a CGI script in C or Perl (and who wants to do that?). Again, a matter of taste, but it's a little bit hard to visualize the structure of the HTML page that will result from running this.

Medium PHP

An intermediate version, that better exploits functions, is shown in Listing 14-3. It spends about half its text in PHP mode, defining functions, before dropping back to a minimal style for the rest of the script.

Listing 14-3: Medium PHP

```
<?php
function maybe_print_answer_date () {
  $seconds_in_day = 60 * 60 * 24;
  if (IsSet($_POST['DAYS'])) {
    print("<P>" .$_POST['DAYS'] .
          " days from this moment it will be ");
    $date = getdate(time() +
            ($_POST['DAYS'] * $seconds_in_day));
    print($date['weekday']);
  }
}

function print_day_options () {
 for ($i = 1; $i < 7; $i++) {
   print("<OPTION VALUE=$i>$i");
 }
}

function get_day_of_week($time) {
  $date = getdate($time);
  return($date['weekday']);
}

?>
<HTML><HEAD TITLE="Calendar Server"></HEAD><BODY>
<H2>Welcome to the Calendar Server</H2>
<?php maybe_print_answer_date(); ?>
<P>Today is <?php echo get_day_of_week(time());?>
<P>Please choose a number of days, and we'll
tell you what day it will be that many days from now:

<FORM METHOD=POST ACTION="<?php echo $_SERVER['PHP_SELF'];?>" >
<SELECT NAME=DAYS>
  <?php print_day_options(); ?>
</SELECT>
<INPUT TYPE=SUBMIT NAME=SUBMIT VALUE=SUBMIT>
```

```
</FORM>
</BODY></HTML>
```

Maybe the medium style is a little bit more verbose, but to our eyes, it's also a little easier to read and modify than the minimal and maximal styles.

The heredoc style

Listing 14-4 shows a rewrite of the medium style, using the heredoc syntax for constructing strings.

Listing 14-4: Heredoc style

```
<?php
function answer_string ($days) {
  $seconds_in_day = 60 * 60 * 24;
  $return_string = "";
  $day_string =
    day_of_week_string(time() + $days *
                       $seconds_in_day);

  $return_string .=
    $_POST['DAYS'] .
    " days from this moment it will be " .
    $day_string;
  return($return_string);

}

function day_of_week_string($time) {
  $date = getdate($time);
  return($date['weekday']);
}

function calendar_form_string () {
  $option_string = "";
  for ($i = 1; $i < 7; $i++) {
    $option_string .= "<OPTION VALUE=$i>$i";
  }
  $self_string = $_SERVER['PHP_SELF'];
  $return_string=<<<EOT
<FORM METHOD=POST ACTION="$self_string" >
<SELECT NAME=DAYS>$option_string</SELECT>
<INPUT TYPE=SUBMIT NAME=SUBMIT VALUE=SUBMIT>
</FORM>
EOT;
  return($return_string);
}
```

```
// set up string variables
$answer_string = IsSet($_POST['DAYS']) ?
                answer_string($_POST['DAYS']) :
                "";
$day_of_week = day_of_week_string(time());
$form_string = calendar_form_string();

// set up page string
$page_string=<<<EOT
<HTML><HEAD TITLE="Calendar Server"></HEAD><BODY>
<H2>Welcome to the Calendar Server</H2>
<P>$answer_string
<P>Today is $day_of_week
<P>Please choose a number of days, and we'll
tell you what day it will be that many days from now:
$form_string
</BODY></HTML>
EOT;

echo($page_string);
?>
```

Tim Perdue of SourceForge has made the stylistic argument that it's a bad idea for functions to print output to the browser. The heredoc example follows this advice, and only uses functions for calculations and for building strings that are returned. The heredoc construct is used twice, first to build a string corresponding to the form that will be displayed, and then (using the form string) to build the string corresponding to the entire page. The last act of the script is to echo out the string it has constructed.

This is the most verbose of the four, but the heredoc syntax has the advantage (over the maximal style) that we never have to do any escaping of quotes. Another advantage (over the minimal style) is that we can simply include variables in our page template without dropping out of HTML mode to do so. It probably the best version of the four at separating logic from page structure.

Separating Code from Design

Many of the topics in this chapter have obvious implications for the separation of code and design. Here are a few additional techniques we should mention.

Functions

As you can see from our Medium PHP example in Listing 14-3, using self-defined functions can be a very flexible and powerful formatting tool, as well as one of the things that makes PHP better than a tag-based scripting language.

Cascading style sheets in PHP

As you doubtless already know, there are four generally accepted ways to apply styles to your Web pages:

- ◆ By applying CSS formatting to individual tags.
- ◆ By using <STYLE> tags (optionally inside a pair of HTML comment tags).
- ◆ By using <LINK> tags.
- ◆ By using @import.

> **CAUTION:** In this book, we've typically used the <STYLE> tag in each code sample rather than an external style sheet. This is solely so you, Dear Reader, can see the style declarations we used to get the results we display in the figures. There is absolutely no PHP-intrinsic reason for this usage.

In PHP, you could also use the include function to apply styles in a nonstandard way, although it's not clear how much of a gain this would be. For instance, You could include a text file containing everything between the <STYLE> tags, instead of linking to an external style sheet.

We should also mention the anti-style sheet, a practice almost as long-deprecated as it is common: using outdated HTML tags such as FONT, BGCOLOR, and ALINK. Although you shouldn't do it at all, PHP can help you do it more efficiently if for some reason you must. This usage, for instance:

```
<FONT FACE="<?php include("fontlist.txt"); ?>" SIZE=+2>
```

would at least allow the poor, overworked Web developer to change the fonts throughout the whole site with a single edit of the text file. Not that we can condone this kind of thing! Only slightly less kludgy would be this alternative:

```
<P STYLE="font-family: <?php include("fontlist.txt"); ?>">Text here</P>
```

Templates and page consistency

As you can now imagine, PHP allows a wide variety of approaches to site design, which you can fit to your particular style and the organization of the people who work on the site. If your techies can't talk to your artists, you may want to set things up so that they never touch the same files; if you're a tech artist, you may express yourself by the very intermingling of code and graphics. If your site has a large number of pages or is very content-rich, you may find (as we have) that it's helpful to choose a particular kind of file organization or template, and stick to it across the site. One simplified example follows, which is similar to templates we have used on www.mysteryguide.com and www.sciencebookguide.com.

```
<?
/* load general functions */
include("general-functions.inc");
```

```
/* load functions specific to this page */
include("renaissance-functions.inc");
/* page-wide variables */
$PageTitle = "Painters of the Renaissance";
$db_connection = make_database_connection();
?>

<HTML>
<HEAD>
<TITLE>
    <?php print("$PageTitle"); ?>
</TITLE>
</HEAD>
<BODY>
<H3>
    <?php print("$PageTitle"); ?>
</H3>
<TABLE>
<TR><TD>
    <?php print-left-side($db_connection); ?>
</TD><TD>
    <?php print-right-side($db_connection); ?>
</TD></TR>
</TABLE>
    <?php print-footer($db_connection); ?>
</BODY><HTML>
```

In this example, every page loads the same file of site-wide utility functions, then loads a file of functions specific to that page, then defines variables that will be global for the page, and finally intersperses PHP commands in some boilerplate HTML. The content is in columns, and the actual content displayed depends on the particular page's functions, which always have the same names, but with definitions varying for each page. Changing what's displayed in the columns means either changing the per-page functions or (more likely) modifying the database contents. It would be possible for a nonprogrammer to do some limited design on this page by operating directly on the HTML and being careful to leave the PHP alone.

The preceding example is just one simplified possibility from a range of ways to divide up the labor of displaying a PHP page. Another that we like even better is the heredoc technique that we discuss in the section, "The heredoc style," earlier in the chapter. Your particular strategy will depend on the type of site, the size of the site, and the styles of the people contributing.

Finally, note that all these strategies really just adopt a convention about separating logic and display in PHP. If you need an even stronger distinction, there are PHP-based templating systems available that further insulate the display people from the innards of program logic. One example is YATS (Yet Another Template System), available at http://yats.sourceforge.net.

Summary

Most of the elements of PHP style are desirable in any programming language. You want to write readable code, with appropriately abstracted functions, consistent indentation, and explanatory comments. You want to stay away from magic numbers, "cloned" code repetition, overuse of global variables, and cryptically clever tricks. Your program should work on the inputs you expect, do something reasonable with inputs you didn't expect, and have the grace to die informatively in situations you *really* didn't expect.

Some of the PHP-specific style issues have to do with organizing file inclusions, how intimately you mix your PHP with your HTML, and more generally the separation of code from design. A wide range of styles are okay here, but you should strive for page-level and site-wide consistency.

In the Chapter 15, we move from such stylistic questions to a much more basic one: What do you do if your PHP code isn't working?

Chapter 15
Basic PHP Gotchas

In This Chapter

♦ Installation-related problems

♦ Blank and incomplete pages

♦ Parse errors

♦ Permissions problems

♦ Unbound variables

♦ Function problems

♦ Math problems

Even though we've tried to give clear instructions, and you've no doubt followed them to the letter, there are still many potential glitches that can arise. This chapter will lay out some of the most common ones by symptom and suggest some frequent causes.

> **CROSS-REFERENCE:** There is a whole other universe of gotchas involving database connectivity. This chapter deals with PHP-only problems. You may want to skip ahead to Chapter 25 if you're having problems with PHP and a database. Also, problems specific to certain more advanced features (including sessions, cookies, building graphics, e-mail, and XML) are dealt with in their individual chapters in Part III.

Installation-Related Problems

Instead of getting moralistic about people who rush through their installs without understanding the documentation, we'll point out a few common symptoms that characteristically appear when you've just installed PHP for the first time.

> **TIP:** If you are seeing similar errors but are confident that your installation is stable, follow the cross-references to later parts of this chapter.

Symptom: Text of file displayed in browser window

If you are seeing the text of the your PHP script instead of the resulting HTML, the PHP engine is clearly not being invoked. Check that you are accessing the site by invoking the `httpd`, not via the filesystem. Do this:

```
http://localhost/mysite/mypage.php
```

rather than this:

```
file:/home/httpd/html/mysite/mypage.php
```

Symptom: PHP blocks showing up as text under HTTP or browser prompts you to save file

The PHP engine is not being invoked properly. If you're properly requesting the file via HTTP as explained previously, the most common reason for this error is that you haven't specified all the filename extensions you want PHP to recognize, at least not for this directory. The second most common reason is that your php.ini file is in the wrong place or has a bad configuration directive.

> **CROSS-REFERENCE:** If you see PHP code in your Web browser and you have a stable installation, your problem is probably due to missing PHP tags. See the "Rendering Problems" section later in this chapter.

Symptom: Server or host not found/Page cannot be displayed

If your browser can't find your server, you may have a DNS (Domain Name Service) or Web-server configuration issue.

If you can get to the site via IP address rather than domain name, your problem is probably DNS-related. Maybe your DNS alias hasn't propagated throughout the Internet yet. This problem does occur occasionally, even after the site has been up for awhile, either because your DNS server goes down without a valid secondary server or because of local Internet conditions.

If you cannot get to the site via IP address, it's likely you haven't successfully bound the IP address to your network interface or configured httpd to handle requests for a particular domain (see Chapter 3).

Rendering Problems

This section covers problems where PHP does not report an error per se, but what you see is not what you thought you would get.

Symptom: Totally blank page

A blank page is very frequently an HTML problem rather than PHP per se (except insofar as you use PHP to produce HTML). If you *do not* use the maximal style of PHP (in other words, if there is any part of your script that should be renderable without first being preprocessed), the problem is almost sure to be in the HTML. So you should first try doing whatever you usually do to debug HTML.

> **NOTE:** In general, one of your best debugging tools when faced with puzzling browser output is simply to view the HTML source that the browser is trying to render. All browsers have some command for viewing such a source. For example, in Internet Explorer, it is Source selection under the View menu.

If you wrote the file using a plain text editor, quickly check to make sure you haven't left out something crucial, such as a closing </TABLE> or </FORM> tag. If you used a WYSIWYG editor at some stage, the problem is more likely to be an extra element of some kind.

You may get edifying results by viewing the HTML source from a client (especially if you use a maximal PHP style) or from a different browser. Internet Explorer is supposedly the most forgiving of mistakes, whereas Opera and Amaya are the strictest at enforcing HTML style.

Sometimes a page that appears blank in your browser is blank because there is simply no HTML to display. See the next symptom for possible causes of this.

Symptom: Document contains no data

In some situations your Web server may return no HTML whatsoever in response to a request. The exact symptom that presents when this happens varies by browser. In some versions of Netscape, for example, you will see a pop-up dialog that informs you that This document contained no data, and urges you to get professional help. IE5, on the other hand, will cheerfully display an empty page. If you view the HTML source, you may see nothing or you may see an autogenerated minimal set of HTML headers (an empty head or an empty body). But any way you slice it, if PHP isn't sending back any HTML, you're not going to see anything interesting in your browser.

One possible answer, in this case, is that the PHP module is not working at all. Test by browsing a different page in the same directory that you've previously verified is being correctly handled by PHP. If you are a developer who does not maintain your own site, you may need to talk to your sysadmin. If other pages work, and this one doesn't, the problem is likely to be with your code.

Another possible answer is that your code really is not generating any output. For example, loading a PHP code file that contains nothing but function definitions in PHP mode would give you this kind of problem.

A third possibility is that your code is actually making the PHP invocation crash before it can deliver any output. For example, if you define a recursive function that doesn't have a base case, like so:

```
function recurse_forever() {  // don't do this!
  recurse_forever();
}
recurse_forever();
```

PHP will try to execute the function until it runs out of memory, will crash in short order, and will return nothing. A diagnostic for this kind of problem is to put some kind of print statement at the beginning of your PHP code (at least, if you do not have access to the Zend debugger). If the print statement executes, and PHP is not blowing up, you should be able to see your printed string, regardless of what happens later — if not in the browser, then in the HTML source. If the string does not appear at all, it probably means that PHP died after encountering the `print` statement, but before actually shipping off any output. (In addition to infinitely recursing functions, we've seen this kind of behavior when using early versions of object serialization.)

Also see the "Time-Outs" section near the end of this chapter for more information on what happens when you write code that runs "forever."

Symptom: Incomplete or unintended page

These problems are usually in the HTML parts of the script. Figure 15-1 shows an interesting example, which is highly browser dependent; this is the IE5 product.

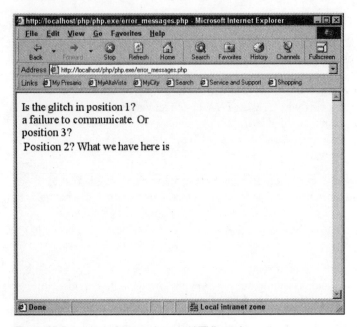

Figure 15-1: An incomplete or unintended HTML result

View the HTML source from a client. Sometimes the source will break off at the problematic point. If the source doesn't conveniently break off, try putting temporary error messages (in HTML mode) in different parts of the script to narrow down the location of the breakdown point, like this:

```
<HTML>
<HEAD></HEAD>
<BODY>Is the glitch in position 1?
<TABLE><TR><TD>Position 2? What we have here is </TD></TR>
<?php
$Problem = "a failure to communicate";
print("$Problem"); ?>. Or position 3?
</BODY>
</HTML>
```

This test would show the result seen in Figure 15-2, indicating that the temporary error messages in positions one and three are showing up in the right places relative to the other elements. It's position two that's out of place, indicating a likely problem (lack of a </TABLE> tag) with this line.

Figure 15-2: Using temporary HTML error messages

Your page may be incomplete due to a complete lack of PHP preprocessing, as in a script like this:

```
<HTML>
<HEAD></HEAD>
<BODY>
<P>What we have here is
<?php
$Problem = "a failure to communicate";
print("$Problem"); ?>.
```

```
</BODY>
</HTML>
```

This script will show up as seen in Figure 15-3.

Figure 15-3: Failure to be preprocessed

In other words, all HTML-mode stuff will show up, but no PHP-mode stuff or error messages will appear. This is indicative of the PHP module not working at all or of the page residing on a computer without a PHP-enabled Web server. (Don't laugh. It happens a lot when you forget that you've been working on a particular version of a page on your client.)

Symptom: PHP code showing up in Web browser

If you are seeing literal PHP code in your browser, rather than a rendering of the HTML it should be producing, probably you have omitted a PHP start tag somewhere. (This assumes that you have had PHP running successfully, and that you are using the correct tags for your installation. If not, see the "Installation-Related Problems" section near the beginning of this chapter.)

It's easy to forget that PHP treats included files as HTML, not PHP, unless you tell it otherwise with a start tag at the beginning of the file. For example, assume that we load the following PHP file:

```
<HTML><HEAD></HEAD><BODY>
<?php include("secret.php");
secret_function(); ?>
</BODY></HTML>
```

which includes the file secret.php, which in turn looks like this:

```
function secret_function ()
{
```

```
    print("Open sesame!");
}
```

The result is shown in Figure 15-4.

Figure 15-4: A PHP include appearing as HTML

This can be fixed by adding PHP tags to the included file like so:

```php
<?php
function secret_function ()
{
  print("Open sesame!");
}
?>
```

Failures to Load Page

A couple of different kinds of errors are seen when PHP is unable to find a file that you have asked it to load.

Symptom: Page cannot be found

If your browser can't find a PHP page you've created, and you have recently installed PHP, please see the section "Installation-Related Problems" earlier in this chapter. If you get this message when you have been loading other PHP files without incident, it's quite likely you are just misspelling the filename or path.

Symptom: Failed opening [file] for inclusion

Under the Windows NT/IIS version of PHP, we sometimes see errors like this:

```
Warning Failed opening 'C:\InetPub\wwwroot\asdf.php' for inclusion
(include_path='') in [no active file] on line 0
```

It turns out that this is the NT version of Page cannot be found — that is, PHP hasn't even gotten to loading the first line of the active file. There is no active file because no file by that name could be found.

It's also possible that you will see this message under NT as a result of incorrect permissions on the file you are trying to load.

Parse Errors

The most common category of error arises from mistyped or syntactically incorrect PHP code, which confuses the PHP parsing engine.

Symptom: Parse error message

Although the causes of parsing problems are many, the symptom is almost always the same: a parse error message like that in Figure 15-5.

Figure 15-5: A parse error message

These errors occur in PHP mode by definition. This is actually good, because PHP returns more informative error messages than HTML — notably the line number of the problematic parsable.

The most common causes of parse errors, detailed in the subsections that follow, are all quite minor and easy to fix, especially with PHP lighting the way for you. However, every parse error returns the identical message (except for filenames and line numbers) regardless of cause. Any HTML that may be in the file, even if it appears before the error-causing PHP fragment, will not be displayed or appear in the source code.

The missing semicolon

If each PHP instruction is not duly finished off with a semicolon, a parse error will result. In this sample fragment, the first line lacks a semicolon and, therefore, the variable assignment is never completed.

```
What we have here is
<?php
$Problem = "a silly misunderstanding"
print("$Problem"); ?>.
```

No dollar signs

Another very common problem is that a dollar sign prepending a variable name is missing. If the dollar sign is missing during the initial variable assignment, like so:

```
What we have here is
<?php
Problem = "a big ball of earwax";
print("$Problem"); ?>.
```

a parse error message will result. However, If instead the dollar sign is missing from a later output of the variable, like this:

```
What we have here is
<?php
$Problem = "a big ball of earwax";
print("Problem"); ?>.
```

PHP will not indicate a parse error. Instead, you will get the screen shown in Figure 15-6.

Figure 15-6: A missing dollar sign on variable output

> **TIP:** If you spend any significant portion of your time debugging PHP code, an editor that can jump to specific line numbers can be invaluable. Note that the actual mistake that caused the error may be on the line that PHP complains about, or before it, but never after it. For example, because there's nothing wrong with commands that span several lines, a missed semicolon won't cause a parse error until PHP tries to interpret subsequent lines as being part of the same statement.

Mode issues

Another family of glitches arises from faulty transitions in and out of PHP mode.

A parse error will result if you fail to close off a PHP block properly, as in:

```
What we have here is
<?php
$Problem = "an awful kerfuffle";
print("$Problem"); .
```

This particular mode issue is very common with short PHP blocks. Conversely, if you fail to begin the PHP block properly, the rest of the intended block will simply appear as HTML.

A slightly more tricky issue is engendered by the use of the minimal PHP style, which entails weaving in and out of HTML mode frequently. (See the discussion of minimal vs. maximal style in Chapter 14.) For instance, this fragment (which omits the ?> after the first curly brace, when we intend to return to HTML mode) will return a parse error:

```
<?php if(!IsSet($stage))
{
What we have here is
<?php
$Problem = "an awful kerfuffle ";
print("$Problem"); ?>.
<?php
} else {
print("$Stage"); }
?>
```

Another instance of a very common problem is this one, which combines the short block and weaving-in-and-out-of-HTML issues neatly:

```
<FORM>
<INPUT TYPE="TEXT" SIZE=15 NAME="FirstName" VALUE="<?php
print("$FirstName"); ?>">
<INPUT TYPE="TEXT" SIZE=15 NAME="LastName" VALUE="<?php
print("$LastName"); ?>">
<INPUT TYPE="TEXT" SIZE=10 NAME="PhoneNumber" VALUE="<?php
print($PhoneNumber); ?>"
<INPUT TYPE="SUBMIT" NAME="Submit">
</FORM>
```

A PHP double-quote and the HTML closing bracket have been forgotten on the PhoneNumber input line here. This will both cause a parse error and prevent the Submit button from displaying on a client browser.

The sample code is meant to demonstrate how easy it can be to forget an element on a crowded page with lots of small but important symbols. You can reduce this type of error by either using a good programmer's text editor or by completing and testing the HTML first and adding the PHP later (or both).

Unescaped quotes

Another type of parse error is characteristic of maximal PHP: the unescaped quote.

```php
<?php
print("She said, /"What we have here is ");
$Problem = "a difference of opinion\"";
print("$Problem"); ?>.
```

In this case, the double-quote just before the word What is falsely escaped by a forward slash rather than a backslash. If you simply forgot the backslash, the effect would be the same.

Unterminated strings

Failing to close off a quoted string can cause parse errors that refer to line numbers far away from the source of the problem. For example, a code file like this:

```php
print("I am a guilty print statement!);  // line 5
// 47 lines of PHP code omitted ...
print("I am an innocent print statement!"); // line 53
```

might well produce a parse error that complains about line 53. This is because PHP is happy to include any text you might want in a quoted string, including many lines of your own code. This inclusion finishes happily with the first double-quote in line 53, and then the parser finds the symbol I, which it can't figure out how to interpret as PHP code.

If the quote symbol that begins the unterminated string happens to be the last one in the file, the line number in the complaint will be the last line in the file — again, probably far away from the scene of the crime.

Other parse error causes

The problems we have named are not an exhaustive list of the sources of parse errors. Anything that makes a PHP statement malformed will confuse the parser, including unclosed parentheses, unclosed brackets, operators without arguments, control structure tests without parentheses, and so on. Sometimes the parse error will include a statement about what PHP was expecting and didn't find, which can be a helpful clue. If the line of the parse error is the very last line of the file, it usually means that some kind of enclosure (quotes, parentheses, braces) was opened and never closed, and PHP kept on hoping until the very end.

File Permissions

Most operating systems have some scheme of file and directory permissions that specifies which users have what kind of access to which files. The Web server runs as some user under this system, and so must have read permission for any files it looks at, including HTML and PHP source files.

Symptom: HTTP error 403

When a browser page presents you with error 403, it means that your file permissions are incorrect. Some browsers will not mention the error number but will complain that you do not have access to the given Web page.

The most common reason for this is that you haven't made this directory world-executable (Unix) or enabled script execution (Windows). Remember that PHP scripts may run under a user ID different than your own. Under Unix, PHP usually inherits the "nobody" UID, which (we hope) is pretty much restricted to the HTTP service. Under some Windows installations, each HTTP request is logged as the anonymous guest user.

Missing Includes

In addition to loading top-level source files, PHP also needs to be able to load in any files you bring in via include() or require().

Symptom: Include warning

This kind of error is shown in Figure 15-7.

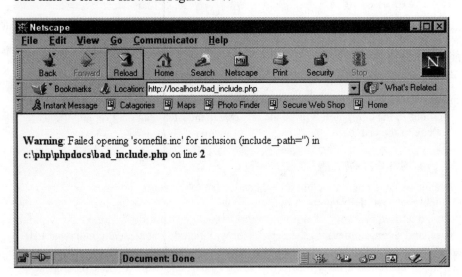

Figure 15-7: Include warning

The problem is that you call somewhere in the script for a file to be included, but PHP can't find it. Check to see that the path is correct. You might also have a case sensitivity or other typographic issue.

You will also get this message if your script tries to include a file that is in another directory with incorrect permissions for the PHP user. Generally, the directory must be specifically readable and executable by the Web-server user (often 'nobody' under Unix), or generally world-read/ executable (for example, 755under Unix systems) for this usage, and of course the file must be world-readable (often 744).

Unbound Variables

PHP is different from many programming languages in that variables do not have to be declared before being assigned, and (under its default settings) PHP will not complain if they are used before being assigned (or *bound*) either. As a result, forgetting to assign a variable will not result in direct errors — either you will see puzzling, but error-free output, or you will see a downstream error that is a result of variables not having the values you expected. (If you would rather be warned, you can set the error-reporting level by evaluating `error_reporting(E_ALL)`). Some symptoms of this kind of problem follow.

Symptom: Variable not showing up in print string

If you embed a variable in a double-quoted string (`"like $this"`) and then print out the string using `print` or `echo`, the variable's value should show up in the string. If it seems to not be there at all in the output (`"like "`), the variable has probably never been assigned.

Symptom: Numerical variable unexpectedly zero

Although it's possible to have a math error or misunderstanding result in this symptom, it's much more likely that you believe that the variable has been assigned when it actually hasn't been.

Causes of unbound variables

PHP automatically converts the types of variables depending on the context in which they are used, and this is also true of unbound variables. In general, unbound variables are interpreted as 0 in a numerical context, `""` in a string context, `FALSE` in a Boolean context, and as an empty array in an array context. The following code shows the effect of forgetting to bind two variables (`$two_string` and `$three`); the resulting display appears in Figure 15-8:

```php
<?php
$one_string = "one";
$three_string = "three";
$one = 1;
$two = 2;
```

```
print("This math is as easy as $one_string, $two_string,
$three_string!<BR>");
print("$one_string is equal to $one<BR>");
print("$two_string is equal to $two<BR>");
print("$three_string is equal to $three<BR>");
print("$one_string divided by $two_string is " .
        ($one / $two) . "<BR>");
print("$one_string divided by $three_string is " .
        ($one / $three) . "<BR>");
?>
```

Figure 15-8: The effect of unbound variables

Case problems

Variables in PHP are case sensitive, and so the same name with different capitalization results in a different variable. Even after a value is assigned to the variable $Mississippi$, the variable $mississippi$ will still be unbound. (Capitalization aside, variables that are this difficult to spell are probably to be avoided for the same reason.)

Scoping problems

As long as no function definitions are involved, PHP variable scoping is simple: Assign a variable, and its value will be there for you from that point on in that script's execution (until the variable is reassigned). However, the only variables that are available inside a function body are the function's formal parameters and variables that have been declared to be global — if you have a puzzling, unbound variable inside a function, this is probably something you've forgotten. In the following code, for example, the variable $serial\_no$ is neither passed in to the function nor declared to be global:

```
$name = "Bond, James Bond";
$rank = "Spy";
$serial_no = "007";

function Answer($name)
{
global $rank;
print("Name: $name; Rank: $rank;
      serial no: $serial_no<BR>");
}
Answer($name);
```

The resulting browser output looks like:

```
Name: Bond, James Bond, Rank: Spy, serial no:
```

because the variable is unbound inside the function.

> **TIP:** Under its default setting for error reporting, PHP will not warn about use of unbound variables. However, This setting can be changed, and doing so temporarily is often the fastest way to get to the bottom of unbound-variable problems. Simply put the line
>
> ```
> error-reporting(E_ALL);
> ```
>
> early in your script, and PHP will warn you about all such uses. You can delete the statement when done debugging, or return it to the default value explicitly with
>
> ```
> error-reporting(E_ALL - E_NOTICE);
> ```
>
> Alternatively, if you always want to be warned, you change the default error-reporting level in the php.ini file. The error-reporting levels and configuration issues are explained in more detail in Chapter 37.

Function Problems

Many problems having to do with function calls result in *fatal errors*, which means that PHP gives up on processing the rest of the script.

Symptom: Call to undefined function my_function()

PHP is trying to call the function my_function(), which has not been defined. This could be because you misspelled the name of a function (built-in or user-defined), or because you have simply omitted the function definition. If you use include/require files to load user-defined functions, make sure that you are loading the appropriate files.

If the problem involves a fairly specialized, built-in function (for instance, it is related to XML or arbitrary-precision math), it may be that you did not enable the relevant function family when you included PHP. If, for example, all the BC functions seem to be undefined, they probably were not included at compile time — to fix it (under Unix systems), you would need to reconfigure PHP and recompile.

Symptom: Call to undefined function ()

In this case, PHP is trying to call a function and doesn't even know the function's name. This is invariably because you have code of the form $my_function(), where the name of the function is itself a variable. Unless you are intentionally trying to exploit the variable-function-name feature of PHP, you probably accidentally put a $ in front of a sensible call to my_function(). Because $my_function is an unbound variable, PHP interprets it as the empty string — which is not the name of a defined function — and so gives this uninformative error message.

Symptom: Call to undefined function array()

This problem has a cause that is similar to the previous problem, although it still baffled us completely the first time we ran into it. It can arise when you have code like the following:

```
$my_amendments = array();
$my_amendments(5) = "the fifth";
```

Unless you look closely, this looks like an innocent pair of statements to create an array, and then store something in that array, with the number 5 as a key. And yet PHP is telling us that array() is an unbound function, even though we know that it is a very standard built-in function. What's going on?

The fault is actually with Line 2 above, rather than with Line 1. If we want to access an element of $my_amendments, the correct syntax is $my_amendments[5], with square brackets. Instead, we used parentheses, which the parser interprets as an attempted function call. It takes what is immediately before the left parenthesis to be a function. Instead what comes before the parenthesis is an array, which is not a function; and PHP gives up on us, with this obscure complaint.

Symptom: Cannot redeclare my_function()

This is a simple one — somewhere in your code you have two definitions of my_function(), which PHP will not stand for. Make sure that you are not using include to pull in the same file of function definitions more than once.

Symptom: Wrong parameter count

The function named in the error message is being called with either fewer or more arguments than it is supposed to handle.

Math Problems

The problems that follow are specific to math and the numerical data types.

Symptom: Division-by-zero warning

Somewhere in your code you have a division operator where the denominator is zero. The most common cause of this is an unbound variable, as in:

```
$numerator = 5;
$ratio = $numerator / $denominator;
```

where `$denominator` is unbound. It's also possible, of course, that the legitimate result of a computation is producing a zero denominator. In this case, the only thing to do is catch it with a test, and do something reasonable if the test applies. See the following:

```
$numerator = 5;
if ($denominator != 0)
    $ratio = $numerator / $denominator;
else
    print("I'm sorry, Dave, I cannot do that<BR>");
```

Symptom: Unexpected arithmetic result

Sometimes things just don't add up (or multiply up, or subtract up). If you are having this experience, check any complex arithmetic expressions for unbound variables (which would act as zeros) and for precedence confusions. If you have any doubt about the precedence of operators, add (possibly redundant) parentheses to make sure the grouping is as you intend.

Symptom: NaN (or NAN)

If you ever see this dreaded acronym, it means that some mathematical function you used has gone out of range or given up on its inputs. The value NAN stands for "Not a Number," and it has some special properties. Here's what happens if we try to take the arccosine of 45, even though arccosine is only defined when applied to numbers between −1.0 and 1.0:

```
$value = acos(45);
print("acos result is $value<BR>");
print("The type is " . gettype($value) . "<BR>");
$value_2 = $value + 5;
print("Derived result is $value<BR>");
print("The type is " . gettype($value_2) . "<BR>");
if ($value == $value)
  print("At least that much makes sense<BR>");
else
  print("Hey, value isn't even equal to itself!<BR>");
```

The browser output looks like:

```
acos result is NAN
The type is double
Derived result is NAN
The type is double
Hey, value isn't even equal to itself!
```

Oddly enough, NAN *is* a number, at least in the sense that its PHP type in this example turns out to be double rather than string. It also "infects" other values with not-a-numberness when used in math expressions. (This behavior is a feature, not a bug, when used in very complex calculations that must be correct. It's better to have the whole value be tagged as untrustworthy than have one subexpression be silently bogus.) Finally, any equality comparison that involves NAN will be false — NAN is neither less than, nor greater than, nor equal to any other number, including itself. It is always unequal (! =) to all numbers, including itself. (The NAN value is not a PHP-specific feature — it is part of the IEEE standard for floating-point arithmetic, which is implemented by the C functions that underlie PHP.)

Because of the contagion of NAN values, this kind of problem can be difficult to debug. The best way to try to find the original offending NAN is with diagnostic `print` statements, especially because comparison tests will give counterintuitive results. If you need to explicitly test for NANs, one hack is this function:

```
function is_nan($value)
{
  return($value != $value);
}
```

It uses the weird comparison properties of NAN as a type checker.

Time-Outs

Of course any download can occasionally time out before a complete page can be delivered. However, this shouldn't be happening frequently on your local development server! If it does, you may have an issue that has nothing to do with slow Internet channels or server overload.

The most interesting reason for a time-out is an infinite loop. These can be difficult to track down quickly, as in this example:

```
//compute the factorial of 10
$Fact = 1;
for ($Index = 1; $Index <= 10; $index++)
  $Fact *= $Index;
```

This code shows a nasty little collaboration between a loop and a case confusion — the lowercase $index that is incremented has nothing to do with the $Index that is being tested, and so the test will never become false.

Also see the discussion of infinite recursion in the "Document contains no data" section earlier in this chapter. Whether due to loop or a recursive loop, any PHP code that runs "forever" is not going to give you a happy result. The exact symptom you see is likely to depend on whether PHP runs out of memory first (and crashes, returning no HTML), or runs out of time first (and your browser informs you of a time-out).

Summary

In Table 15-1, we summarize the gotchas in this chapter by mapping symptoms to possible causes. We also offer some suggestions on how to fix the most common problems.

Table 15-1: From Symptoms to Causes

Symptom	Possible Causes	Advice
(New installation) Text of file displayed in browser window	The PHP engine is not being invoked, possibly because you are opening it via the local filesystem rather than as a request to your server.	Make sure that your request is to the Web server, either via localhost (`http://localhost/[path]`) if testing on the server machine, or by the full URL (`www.site.com/[path]`).
(New installation) PHP blocks showing up as text under HTTP, or browser prompts you to save file or visit an external file repository	PHP is not being invoked properly. Your Web server may not be set up to map the right suffixes (for example, `.php`) to the PHP engine, or there may be a problem with the location or contents of `php.ini`.	Check your Web server configuration, and the PHP init file (`php.ini`).
(New installation) Server or host not found/page cannot be displayed	Often due to Internet/DNS/Web-server configuration problems, rather than PHP.	Try loading a pure HTML file with a suffix you have not set up for PHP (for example, `.html`) to rule out PHP problems. Try getting to the same file using an IP address rather than a domain name — if that works, the problem is DNS-related.
Totally blank page	Usually due to malformed HTML (whether produced by PHP or not).	View the HTML source from a browser. Look especially for unclosed `<TABLE>`, `<FORM>`, or `<SELECT>` forms.
Document contains no data (or blank page with no HTML to look at)	PHP engine may not be working at all, or your code simply does not output anything. Also You may actually be crashing PHP	If other PHP pages work fine from the same server, then the problem is your code. Force your code to output something at the beginning, and try to find it in HTML source. If no joy, you probably have crashed PHP, possibly by calling a recursive function forever.

Incomplete or unintended page	Usually due to malformed HTML (whether produced by PHP or not).	View the HTML source from a browser. Try to narrow down the source of the problem with diagnostic printing statements (in either HTML or PHP).
PHP code showing up in browser window	If the PHP engine is installed and functioning properly, this is usually due to a missing PHP start tag.	Check start and end tags and make sure that any `include` files of PHP code have correct tags at beginning and end.
Page cannot be found	Usually means that the filename or path of the PHP file is incorrect.	Double-check the name and directory path.
Failed opening [file] for inclusion	Same as the preceding error, as reported under some NT configurations.	Double-check the name and directory path.
Parse error message	A variety of causes, including missing semicolons, variables without a $, unescaped quotes, unclosed quotes, brackets, or parentheses, and HTML being interpreted as PHP.	Locate the line of the parse error in the PHP file and look for one of the causes in that line or the lines immediately preceding. If the "error" is on the final line of the file, look for an unclosed quote, paren, or bracket, possibly much earlier in the file.
HTTP error 403	The file permissions are incorrect.	Check the permissions of the file itself and the directories (or folders) in the path to that file.
`Include` warning	For one reason or another, PHP was not able to load a file named in an `include` statement.	Check that the file actually exists, the spelling of the filename, the pathname, and (on Unix systems) the case of the name. Also make sure that the file permissions allow the file to be read.
Variable value not showing up in `print` string	The variable has not been assigned, and so its value in a printed string is the empty string.	Check that you are assigning the variable before the `print` statement and compare spelling and case (capitalization). Make sure that you are not embedding any objects or multidimensional arrays in quoted strings. You can also use the statement `error-reporting(15)` to tell PHP to warn about any unbound variables.

Numerical variable unexpectedly zero	Often due to the variable never having been assigned.	(See preceding.)
Call to undefined function `my_function()`	Function `my_function()` is being called without having been defined first.	If you are trying to call a function of your own, check that the definition (or inclusion of the file containing the definition) is before the use. If you are trying to call a built-in function, check the spelling. If it is correct, investigate whether that "family" of functions was included when you configured PHP (for example, either all the XML functions will work, or none will).
Call to undefined function `()`	An expression of the form `$my_function()` is being evaluated, and `$my_function` is not bound to the name of a defined function.	If you intend to be using the variable-function feature, then add (or correct) the assignment of `$my_function`. If you are just trying to call `my_function()`, remove the `$`.
Call to undefined function `array()`	You probably have an expression of the form `$array_var_name(3)`, when what you want is `$array_var_name[3]`	Decide whether you want an array expression or a function call — if the former, then change parens to square brackets.
Cannot redeclare `my_function()`	The function `my_function()` is being defined twice in a page's execution.	Look for double definitions of `my_function` in the PHP file, or double-inclusions of the file that defines it.
Wrong parameter count	The named function (usually a built-in function) is being called with an incorrect number of arguments.	Compare the function call to the definition in the online PHP manual (`www.php.net`)
Division-by-zero warning	A / operator has a right-hand argument of zero. Can be due to an unbound variable in the denominator.	Assign the unbound variable if that's the cause. If the desired logic could actually result in zero denominators, install a test to catch that case.

Unexpected arithmetic result	Frequently due to an unbound variable in an arithmetic expression.	Check for unbound variables (see preceding), and make sure that arithmetic expressions are parenthesized appropriately.
NAN value	A built-in math function is being given inputs outside its acceptable range. If that function's results are used in arithmetic, the results are also NAN.	Trace backward from the NAN value to function calls that contribute to its computation. Test with print statements, or test for values that fail to be self-equal (a diagnostic for NAN).
Page takes forever to load, or browser times out	Internet congestion, heavy load on your server machine, computationally intensive PHP code, or an infinite loop.	Check if Web sites other than your own are giving you the same trouble. Check all looping constructs in your code for errors that could cause them to never terminate.

Part II

PHP and Databases

## Chapter 16

Choosing a Database for PHP

In This Chapter

♦ What is a database?

♦ Why a database?

♦ Choosing a database

♦ Advanced features

♦ PHP-supported databases

♦ Database abstraction (or not)

♦ Our focus: MySQL and Oracle

Databases and PHP go together like cake and ice cream, Trinidad and Tobago, green eggs and ham — you get the picture.

After all, what's the Web about? Making vast stores of information available to a more or less wide public, that's what. Not that there aren't small "brochureware" sites galore; but the bigger and more frequently updated the data source, the more comparative value is provided by the Web over other media.

Perhaps the single greatest advantage of PHP over similar products is the unsurpassed choice and ease of database connectivity it offers. As detailed in the "Choosing a Database" section of this chapter, PHP supports native connections to a number of the most popular databases, open source and commercial alike. Almost any database that will open its API to the public seems to be included eventually. For any unsupported databases, there's generic ODBC support.

What Is a Database?

A *database* is a separate application that stores a collection of data. Each database has one or more distinct APIs for creating, accessing, managing, searching, and replicating the data it holds. Other kinds of data stores can be used, such as files on the filesystem or large hash tables in memory, but when people talk about databases they mean a standalone application such as Oracle or SQL Server or Sleepycat.

Why a Database?

If you're going to the trouble to use PHP at all, you're likely to need a database sooner or later — probably sooner. Even for something small, like a personal Weblog, you want to think hard about the advantages of using a database instead of static pages or included text files.

Maintainability and scalability

Having PHP assemble your pages on-the-fly from a template and a database is an addictive experience. Once you enjoy it, you'll never go back to managing a static HTML site of any size. For the effort of programming one page, you can produce an infinite number of uniform pages. Change one, and you've changed them all.

There are now Web sites with hundreds of thousands of separate pages – you can rest assured that no one is maintaining them all by hand. If you have a Web concept that may eventually grow to more than a few dozen pages, you should think about moving to a database sooner rather than later.

Portability

Because a database is an application rather than a part of the operating system, you can easily transfer its structure and contents from one machine to another or (in certain cases) even from one platform to another. This is especially valuable for contractors, who may develop a project without being able to control the environment in which it will eventually be deployed — they can deliver a package of PHP plus a MySQL database schema dump in one tarball or zipfile. There are even well-known PHP programs, such as vBulletin, which keep most of their code in a database to make it easier to distribute.

Avoiding awkward programming

Certain things can be done with PHP but probably shouldn't because they entail ugly or risky programming moves.

Say you happen to be the commander of the starship *Enterprise* and are keeping a Captain's log. Each episode is contained in a text file identified by its unique stardate, which is plugged into a template by PHP — but hey, you're a busy spaceman with whole galaxies to explore; you don't always have time to write in your log every day. You want to put automatically generated Next and Previous links on each page for those who wish to read in straight chronological order. It's pretty easy to use PHP to find the previous stardated entry; but any attempt to locate the next entry can quickly become an infinite loop — because it's easier to prove something does exist than that it doesn't. On the other hand, if you put your log data in a database, the whole job becomes trivial. The database will tell you which is the latest entry at any given moment.

There are other types of programming tasks that a database is highly optimized to do, and given the option, you should take advantage of these chores. For instance, you should never sort data sets on the PHP side — you should learn to write your queries so they come back pre-sorted. We discuss these efficiency issues in greater detail in Chapter 24.

Searching

Although it's possible to search multiple text files for strings (especially on Unix platforms) it's not something most Web developers will want to do all the time. After you search a few hundred files, the task becomes slow and hard to manage. Databases exist to make searching easy. With a single command, you can find anything from one ID number to a large text block to a JPEG-format image.

In some cases, information attains value only when put into a searchable database. For instance, relatively few people would want to read a long text list of movie directors and their films; but many might occasionally want to search a database of that information. You could argue that it's the searchability that creates the value here, as much as the information itself.

Security

A database adds another layer of security if used with its own password or passwords.

Say you use PHP to maintain a company's customer files, filled with information about the prices each customer paid for your product and complaints that customers made. This information would be gold for your competitors, and embarrassing if it leaked to anyone – but you need to put it on the Internet so it can be accessed by your worldwide army of salespeople. If you have PHP write each new customer record to a text file, you must give the HTTP daemon user (usually Nobody or Everybody) write access to your most sensitive directory. This is not a good idea. By having PHP write to a database instead, you can maintain read-only directory permissions and also ask for a second password before the database can be altered.

Or take the case of a content site with a large number of visitors, a smaller number of writers, and a handful of editors. You can easily set database permission levels for each group so that visitors can just look at the database content (as formatted in Web pages), writers can browse and change only their own entries, and editors can browse/change/delete anything in the site.

N-tier architecture

So far, we've only been considering so-called two-tier sites: PHP takes raw data from some kind of storage system and turns it into HTML. However, one of the intentions of PHP is to become the "glue" in three-tier or n-tier development. If you have anything more complex than the simplest two-tier architecture, you *really* need a database.

An n-tier architecture is an arbitrary number of software subsystems linked by a Web site on the front end and one or more databases on the back end. One fairly common n-tier architecture is that of a big e-commerce site, which has shopping carts linking up to order-taking systems linking up to supply-chain management routines — plus product databases, customer databases, credit-card debiting, FAQ-o-matics, recommendation engines, Web-log analysis tools, caching proxies, phone-center knowledge bases, and who knows what else lurking behind the scenes. Under these conditions, you need the advanced database capabilities that we'll describe in the "Advanced features" section of this chapter.

Potential downside: performance

You may be concerned about performance. It's true that a database-driven site on the same hardware and software will always be slower on than a static site. It's true that some databases are faster than others. However, the real question is whether the performance hit will even be detectable by you. If we're talking about adding milliseconds to your latency, who cares? Some of the concerns about performance you read on the Internet are so overblown that they verge on the absurd.

One thing to realize is that once you need to go into the database for even *one piece* of information per page, it's almost always cost-effective to put all your data in the database. Most of the overhead of a database query is front-loaded in establishing a connection. If you have to do that to get a name or title, downloading a couple thousand words of text is almost free.

In the end, only performance testing will establish whether a database is too slow for your particular setup and task – everything else is just talk. Many totally database-driven Web sites easily achieve subseconds of latency, which should be good enough for most purposes.

Choosing a Database

Although databases (even relational ones) have been around for a long time, they were quite expensive or limited in functionality until very recently. Therefore, even a lot of experienced programmers never had to learn much about choosing a database for a particular need. For that reason, we feel it's worthwhile to review the basic factors that go into making such a decision.

You may not have a choice

Realistically, you may not have much of a choice. Many people are specifically looking for the fastest way to put their legacy database online, rather than enjoying the luxury of deciding on a scripting language first and choosing a database later.

Furthermore, decisions about OS, Web server, and programming languages can make some of your decision for you. A custom Java application on a "Big Iron" Unix platform is just not going to mesh very smoothly with Microsoft SQL Server (In theory it's possible, but in practice you'd have to be a glutton for punishment — although the other way around isn't so bad). The bigger the system gets, the more constrained one's choices are likely to be by previous decisions.

The good news is that PHP is committed to supporting many databases and other back-end servers. It can help you knit up the loose ends of an architecture that has grown organically over time, as so many have. Some functions in PHP exist solely to aid in porting your data over to a more modern database.

Flat-file, relational, object-relational

Databases are kind of like kitchen equipment: The simpler the tool, the more skilled the operator needs to be to achieve a great result. Expert chefs can produce gourmet fare using nothing but a very sharp knife and a few old pots and pans; whereas amateurs must whip out the Cuisinart and the Calphalon to produce similar results.

So it is with databases. It can get almost laughable to read people's arguments about the purported failings of this or that database, knowing that the skill of the individual user is reflected by this piece of software more than by almost any other. Suffice it to say that many technical masterpieces live in the simplest hash tables, while untold botched messes are simmering along on the latest and greatest object-oriented Java-enabled DBMS.

You can use three main types of databases with PHP: *flat-file*, *relational*, and *object-relational*.

Flat-file or *hashing* databases, such as Gnu DBM and Berkeley DB (a.k.a. Sleepycat DB2), are mostly used by or within other programs such as e-mail servers. They provide the lightest-weight and fastest means of storing and searching for data such as username/password pairs or dated e-mail messages. Old-school C programmers usually have the most experience with this type of database.

These databases do not themselves create a representation of more complex relationships between data points. Instead, this is done by the accessing client program. Although the results can be extremely impressive, it all depends on your skill as a programmer.

The relational variety is now the most common type of database. People have different ideas of what constitutes a relational database, and we don't want to get pulled down into that particular definitional tar pit. Therefore, we're going to arbitrarily say that databases that speak fluent SQL are relational. Most of the popular databases commonly used with PHP are relational. See Chapter 17 for a longer discussion of relational databases.

But there's relational and relational. Certain very popular commercial databases, such as Filemaker Pro and Microsoft Access, were not designed to be used on the back end of a production Web site. Although they have a certain level of ODBC support, and therefore PHP can get data from them, they were mostly designed for ease of use rather than speed. Even worse, most users of these products refuse to avail themselves of what relational features there are, preferring to repeat text information in each entry rather than creating a separate table representing a relationship. Finally, these databases generally lack threading, locking, and other advanced features. People out there must be trying to use Microsoft Access with PHP, because they post to PHP mailing lists and forums, but evidently not for public sites with significant traffic. (We do, however, know developers who use Access or Filemaker Pro as development tools on their laptops so they can program on the airplane; and there are always porting and other projects using legacy data from these semi-relational databases.)

Finally there are object-oriented and object-relational databases, new and still developing models of data access. The object-oriented database is intended to work more smoothly with object-oriented programming languages; whereas the object-relational is a hybrid used for data types (such as astronomical and genetic data) that are not well served by ordinary relational databases. However, PHP is not itself wholly object-oriented and probably never will be, so it's hard to see why you'd select PHP as your scripting language of choice with one of these DBMSs.

ODBC/JDBC versus native API

There are two generic standard APIs for database access: Open Database Connectivity (ODBC), and Java Database Connectivity (JDBC). ODBC is closely associated with Microsoft, and JDBC is even more closely associated with Sun Microsystems. Nevertheless, other companies have implemented these standards in their own products, with the addition of specific drivers for each client program.

ODBC and JDBC are more or less mutually exclusive. Something called the *ODBC-JDBC bridge* is used to allow Java programs to access ODBC databases, but it is very slow. There are also proprietary drivers that do the same job more quickly.

There are also databases that clients can access through their own APIs rather than ODBC or JDBC. This is invariably faster because there are fewer layers in the stack. Most open source databases fall into this category. Some of these also have ODBC or JDBC drivers. So for instance, PHP can access MySQL with a native API, whereas a Java subsystem can use the same database via JDBC. Before you commit to any multiple-access scheme, be very sure the drivers you need are available, affordable, and maintainable.

Swappable databases

Although ODBC is slower than native APIs, it has the advantage of being an open standard. Therefore, PHP code written with the ODBC commands will mostly work with any ODBC-compliant database. This feature is very handy if you must start a project with a database that you know will not scale, such as Microsoft Access, and later switch to a more industrial-strength database. Although both are good products in their niches, it can be a lot of work to switch from a lightweight database like Mini SQL (a.k.a. mSQL) to an enterprise-ready server suite like IBM's DB2. (Again, a good programmer who is given the time and resources can make any application relatively easy to port, while an inexperienced or rushed developer may not be able to do so.)

Advanced Features to Look For

This section mentions specific SQL database features, with which you may not yet be familiar. We're hoping you will instantly have a gut feeling, even from so brief a description, if you truly need one or more of these features.

A GUI

Databases vary enormously in their user interface tools. Choices range from the starkest command-line interactions to massive Java-powered development toolkits. You pay for what you get, both in cash and in performance. Look for the lightest interface that meets your needs, because a GUI can add substantially to overhead costs.

One lower-cost alternative to the built-in GUI is a Web interface. These are often custom developed, but there are also third-party products which may meet your needs. For instance, MySQL has several freely available Web-based interfaces, which can be found by searching at Freshmeat (`www.freshmeat.net`) or SourceForge (`http://sf.net`). The most popular of these is probably PHPMyAdmin, which is available at the PHPMyAdmin Web site (`www.phpmyadmin.org`).

Subquery

A *subquery* or *subselect* is an embedded `select` statement, like this:

```
SELECT * FROM table1 WHERE id IN (SELECT id FROM table2);
```

There are ways to work around a lack of subselects, and not everyone needs them. However, they can save some time if you consistently need to make large selects, inserts, and deletes.

SELECT INTO

`SELECT INTO` is a handy feature if you need to move data from one table to another frequently. The syntax can vary a little. One method is:

```
SELECT INTO table2(col2, col3, col7) lastname, firstname, state FROM
table1 WHERE col5 = NULL;
```

Another way to get the same result is:

```
INSERT INTO table2(col2, col3, col7) SELECT lastname, firstname, state
FROM table1 WHERE col5 = NULL;
```

Complex joins

A *join* is a way of searching for something across tables, by using shared values to match up the tables. The simplest form is:

```
SELECT * FROM table1,table2 WHERE table1.id=table2.id;
```

This yields the complete contents of whichever rows in the two tables share ID numbers. More specific and extensive types of joins, including left or right, straight or cross, inner and outer, and self, exist but you may not need them.

Joins are very handy and timesaving, sometimes well nigh essential; but in practice few need the more esoteric forms, so don't reject a database out of hand for lacking a right outer join.

Threading and locking

Threading and *locking* are very important for multiple-tier sites and two-tier sites that have many contributors. They prevent two database calls from bumping into each other, so to speak, by giving editorial control to only a single transaction at a time.

An example that clearly illustrates the value of threading and locking is a Web site that sells tickets to popular rock concerts (assigned rather than "festival" seating). Obviously you would not want two people to be able to purchase the same seat at the same event due to a database error. The database needs some way to recognize unique requests and let only one user (or thread) make changes at any given moment.

Unless you're sure your project (a Web log, for instance) will have only one user at a time, be careful of committing to a nonthreaded database.

Transactional databases

This term refers to a database design that seeks to maximize data integrity. The *transactional* paradigm relies on commits and rollbacks. Transactions that are concluded successfully will be committed to the database. Those that are not successfully concluded will not be saved, or the database will be rolled back to its previous condition.

Generally transactions become more useful in situation where you want an all-or-nothing commit on a group of inserts. An e-commerce system might use rollbacks in situations where a customer's credit card is declined, choosing not to record the customer information, the purchase order, the inventory change, and so on. Rollbacks are also useful in the case of data corruption, as when a database server experiences a hardware failure incident.

An alternative data integrity design is called *atomic*. Proponents of the atomic paradigm claim it is much faster and just as safe, but transactions can be easier for a large number of programmers to work with because it puts more of the logic in the database layer.

Procedures and triggers

Procedures are stored, precompiled queries or routines on the database server. A common procedure would be one that selects out all the e-mail addresses of customers who made purchases on a particular day. If you use the same select statements over and over, procedures can package them in a handy and fast way for you.

Triggers are procedures that occur when some tripwire event is registered by the database. Depending on the database, you could write a trigger to send an account-statement e-mail to customers or associates of your site, and set it to go off at midnight every Sunday. Another handy use would be to send an e-mail to the database administrator every time an error is registered. Relatively few databases use triggers because they take a good deal of programmatic power and lots of extra cycles to track potential events.

Indexes

Indexes are a way to speed up searches of large data sets. You can think of it like this: Say you need to find a particular customer's file in a large stack of files tossed haphazardly on your desk (not that you would ever do this in real life, of course). Or you could look for the file in a set of filing cabinets sorted by some alphabetical scheme. Obviously the filing-cabinet system would be faster, because it would presort the documents into smaller buckets. In a nutshell, that is what indexes do.

If you have a million users, it will be very slow for a database to find one by last name because the program will have to look at each entry in the `Lastname` field and compare it to the string you're searching for. An index placed on that column will make it possible for the database to search only part of the data set, and this will result in a faster search.

However, indexes should not be used by everyone. For one thing, they typically slow down writes while speeding up reads. They don't necessarily speed up every type of query, and your data set may not be big enough to show an appreciable speed difference. Indexes are a scalability feature – they'll help you a lot if you have half a billion entries, but they very well may not help you at all if you have 500.

Foreign keys and integrity constraints

The relational structure of a database is often implicit in the ways fields of one table refer to row IDs of another, but your database won't necessarily do anything helpful to make sure that structure is respected as changes are made. One way your database can help is via *cascading deletes* — automatically deleting rows that depend on other rows being deleted (this is sometimes implemented as a trigger). For example, if you delete a hospital patient record, you might want all the "orphaned" rows in the corresponding table of patient visits to automatically be deleted too. Alternatively, a database system can simply not permit the deletion of parent rows unless potential orphans are deleted first. Whether this kind of a constraint is a lifesaver or just an annoying restriction depends on how crucial it is that the relational structure be completely reliable and consistent, and how frequently you need to do these kinds of dangerous operations.

Database replication

As your data store expands, you will need to think about scaling up. For a certain amount of time, one can just move the database server to faster machines with more processors and bigger disks — but sooner or later a growing database will need to be replicated on more than one server.

To do this, there must be some means of automatically keeping the different servers synched up. This usually involves a journaling system, and often a *master-slave* relationship between database servers. One database is designated the *master*, and all new data is inserted into it. A journal keeps track of these changes in chronological order. All the other servers are *slaves*, which serve up data rather than taking it in. They periodically read the master journal and make the same changes in themselves.

The next step up is some kind of failover mechanism, by which a slave can become the master database server if the master goes down. Think carefully about how bombproof your data needs to be, as this type of safety is expensive.

PHP-Supported Databases

If you've never chosen a database before, the large choice of PHP-supported products can be dizzying at first. Table 16-1 below will give you a first-glance introduction to the various databases most easily available to PHP users, with notes on drivers and licensing.

Table 16-1: PHP-Supported Databases

Database	Type	Support	Platform	License	Notes
Adabas D	R	ODBC (deprecated)	U, W	C	German, distributed with SuSE Linux
DBA/DBM	FF	Abstraction layer	U	OS, C	Sleepycat, Gnu DBM, cdb
dBase	P	Import only	W	C	No SQL
Empress	R	ODBC	U, W	C	Enterprise, JDBC driver avail.
filepro	P	Import only	U, W	C	Not for production
IBM DB2	R	ODBC	U, W	C	Enterprise, JDBC driver avail.
Informix	R	Native	U, W	C	Enterprise

Interbase	R	Native	U, W	C	Enterprise, JDBC driver avail.
MS Access	R	ODBC	W	C	Not for production
MS SQL Server	R	Native	W	C	Enterprise?
mSQL	R	Native	U	Sh	Very small
MySQL	R	Native	U, W	C, OS	Several licenses
Oracle	R	Native	U, W	C	Enterprise
Oracle8	R	Native	U, W	C	Enterprise, Java integration
PostgreSQL	O-R	Native	U	OS	Commercial support available
Solid	R	ODBC (deprecated)	U, W	C	Embedded db, Finnish company
Sybase	R	Native	U, W	C	Enterprise

Database abstraction (or not)

Database abstraction — writing wrapper functions or classes instead of using the bare PHP commands — is one of those quasi-religious topics in programming. Some excellent programmers swear by it and make good arguments for it. Others, just as experienced and articulate, think it sounds better than it usually works out to be. We know of top PHP teams that have members in both camps.

The truth of the matter is that it's more of an issue with PHP than with almost any other programming language because PHP is so strong in multiple database connectivity. Enterprise Java installations are often all about choosing between two or three very similar database products with JDBC connectivity; so Java developers don't argue nearly as much about the merits of database portability. Similarly, ODBC is the standard option for ASP developers. The issue of database abstraction basically arises just because PHP hooks up to so many database products with fast native APIs.

The arguments for database abstraction basically boil down to: You can swap databases without changing a lot of code, and sometimes it saves you some keystrokes. The arguments against database abstraction basically boil down to: If you have to swap databases, you've probably already screwed up big-time; and the practice limits you to the most basic, common

SQL functions used in a fixed pattern instead of letting you code in the way which takes maximal advantage of your particular database's feature set.

For instance, one of Oracle's coolest features is the capability to take an entire result set and dump it into a single-dimensional numerical PHP array. None of the other major databases used with PHP have this feature —they can only fetch a single row at once. To implement it yourself in a portable way could add considerable overhead to your query, because you'd have to fetch each row and rewrite it to a value in some second array. Of course, you can do this kind of thing — the question is, should you?

Not to say that database switching doesn't happen – we've personally had to do it more than once. However, the experienced mind quailsat the contention that you should be able to "plug in" different databases whenever the spirit moves you. Not to belabor the obvious, but it's a non-trivial task to change databases! It's not something most developers will want to contemplate unless the situation is absolutely dire. In every case in which we were personally involved, the database change was part of a complete site rewrite and involved a tremendous amount of pain for everyone involved — all-nighters, frantic attempts to flip through 1200-page database manuals, endless data transfer attempts which choked countless numbers of times. All of which is to suggest that database portability might be a good idea in theory, but in practice it usually means a bad, bad architectural mistake was made at some prior point. In the early days of the Web, bad architectural decisions were a matter of course because no one could predict which technologies and products would last. — As the rate of change has slowed somewhat, and clear leaders in various product categories have emerged, however, this type of rescue operation should become less necessary.

As always, our advice is to put your own needs first and be skeptical of unsolicited advice. Remember that many commercial and open source PHP packages that incorporate database abstraction may have a mission different from yours – often they are focused on getting the largest installed userbase and are willing to accept some non-optimal database code to achieve it. You might just need to focus on how to keep one particular site running most smoothly. Heavily discount any advice from those who have not actually had to switch databases. When people talk about their experiences swapping databases, find out how big the change was in programming terms – migrating from MS SQL Server to MySQL is less of a stretch than switching from MySQL to Oracle. Then make a decision about what's right for you in your particular situation.

> **TIP:** There's one particular situation in which you may have to accept database abstraction even if it's not the right technical decision. Our experience has been that many inexperienced clients or bosses want "the option" of switching from some perfectly functional database to Oracle or DB2 in the undefined future. This is a delicate social-engineering concern, because they have an investment in the idea that their online business will grow massively and become a real "enterprise." It is pointless to tell them that by the time they need Oracle or DB2, the sun will have consumed all its fuel and the Himalayas will be eroded into a flat plain. Smile and implement database wrapper functions.

Our Focus: MySQL and Oracle

We, like most every other team who has ever written a book about PHP, love MySQL and will use it in all the upcoming examples in Part II (except for Chapter 19, which covers Oracle). MySQL is quite likely the fastest, cheapest, simplest, most reliable database that also has most of the features you'd want and — this is the real differentiator — comes in more or less equally good Unix and Windows implementations. There's just an ineffable synergy between PHP and MySQL (especially on the Linux/Apache platform), recently recognized by the development teams, who have announced plans to move the products even closer together.

However, there are certain situations in which you need the power of an enterprise-ready transactional system like Oracle. MySQL and Oracle pretty much represent the low and high ends of the Web database server market; if you can work with those two, you can work with any database. Therefore, we will also discuss Oracle and give examples of its use in a larger production system.

Summary

The great advantage of the Web is its capability to make large quantities of information publicly available quickly and cheaply. This functionality has been tremendously enhanced by the recent increase in availability of inexpensive, reliable databases.

Since many experienced programmers may never have had to choose a database before, we describe some of the basic points that should be taken into account in the decision-making process. These include the basic database design (flat-file, relational, or object-relational), the API or driver, and ease of future porting. Optional features, such as transactions or a graphical interface, may also figure into the choice of database. PHP supports many databases of a variety of types, so you have an excellent chance of finding exactly the feature set you need.

Chapter 17
SQL Tutorial

In This Chapter

♦ Relational databases and SQL

♦ SQL standards

♦ Basic SQL statements

♦ Designing SQL databases

♦ Privileges and security

This chapter is a basic introduction to SQL databases in which we discuss standards, database design, data manipulation language, data definition language, and database security procedures common to all SQL databases.

This chapter is in no way a comprehensive guide to SQL or to any particular SQL database. To go beyond the simplest common features, you will need to consult your particular manufacturer's documentation and/or specific books. A couple of popular guides to SQL in general are:

♦ *SQL for Dummies, 4th edition* by Allen G. Taylor (Wiley 2001)

♦ *The Practical SQL Handbook* by Judith S. Bowman, Sandra L. Emerson, and Marcy Darnovsky (Addison-Wesley 1996)

You will also want to look at documentation and books relating to your specific SQL database.

Relational Databases and SQL

SQL is the language of relational databases. It is the *lingua franca*, the Medieval Latin, the Chinese characters of the relational database world — a common idiom that makes it possible for everyone to make himself understood across a wide range of differences. A simple query like a one-table `SELECT` will be more or less the same whether you're using a tiny database like mSQL or an expensive behemoth like Oracle 9i Enterprise.

The big advantage for you, the Web developer, is that, after you learn SQL, you will be able to interact with numerous databases across all platforms without a steep retraining curve. Just imagine how horrible life would be if Oracle, MySQL, and SQL Server all had entirely different sets of commands for putting data in and getting data out of their stores — as if Oracle used `SELECT` to ask for data sets, MySQL used `VALJ` (the developers are Swedish, you know), and SQL Server used `FIND IT IN THIS TABLE` (to better match the vocabulary of Windows). SQL is the common vocabulary and syntax that will save you from this nightmare. There will be some differences between products, but it's better to have 80% in common and 20% different than the other way around.

SQL Standards

According to Andrew Taylor, original inventor of SQL, *SQL* does *not* stand for "*S*tructured *Q*uery *L*anguage" (or anything else for that matter). But for the rest of the world, it does now. As you would expect from the (non-)title, SQL represents a stricter and more general method of data storage than the previous standard of flat-file DBM-style databases.

SQL is a standard under both ANSI and ECMA (international standards-maintenance organizations). You can read the standards on payment of a fee to these organizations:

```
www.ansi.org
www.ecma.org
```

However, within the general guidelines of the standard there is very considerable difference between the products of individual companies and open source database development organizations. The past few years, for instance, have seen the rapid growth of so-called *object-relational* databases, as well as of SQL products specifically slanted toward the Web market.

The key to choosing a database is to be selfish, or at least supremely self-centered. You will see plenty of unusually virulent postings out there opining that a certain advanced database feature (like triggers or cross joins) is a "must," and any SQL installation without this feature hardly deserves the name. Take this stuff with a grain of salt. It's far better to make a blind shopping list of functions you need in order of importance and then go out looking for the product that best meets your requirements.

That said, a good deal of SQL really is pretty standardized. You will be using a few SQL statements over and over and over, no matter which specific product you choose to deploy.

The Workhorses of SQL

The basic logical structure of a SQL database is very simple. A given SQL installation can usually contain multiple *databases* — for instance, one for customer data and one for product data. (It's problematic that both the SQL server itself and the collections of tables within it are commonly referred to by the term *database* — but what can you do?) Each database contains a number of *tables*. Each table is made up of carefully defined *columns*, and every entry can be thought of as an added *record* or row. (It's not really a row, but this is a concept so stuck in our visualization that we may as well go with it.)

Four so-called *data manipulation statements* are supported by every SQL server and will constitute an extremely high percentage of all the things you'll want to do with a relational database. These four horsemen of the database are SELECT, INSERT, UPDATE, and DELETE. These commands are your friends and helpmates; get comfy with them, and they will serve you well.

The thing to remember about these four SQL statements is that they only manipulate database *values,* not the structure of the database itself. In other words, you can use these commands to add data but not to make a database; and you can get rid of every piece of data in a database, but the shell will still be there — so, for instance, you wouldn't be able to name another database on the same server with the same name. If you want to add or get rid of columns, blow away entire databases as if they never existed, or make up new databases, you need to use other commands such as DROP, ALTER, and CREATE. We discuss these in the "Database Design" section later in this chapter.

> **TIP:** A note on SQL style. Many SQL queries that you see are written in one long line of code — which becomes totally illegible once you're dealing with more than four or five fields. A very accomplished PL/SQL programmer of our acquaintance recommends that you break up every SQL statement into as many lines as you need for maximum legibility. He also does not shy away from using indentation in a SQL query with many variables. (SQL queries are usually quite whitespace insensitive.). He has years of experience working on big Oracle installations, and his recommendations actually are very helpful — so that is the style we try to use in this book.

SELECT

SELECT is the main command you need to get information out of a SQL database. The basic syntax is extremely simple:

```
SELECT field1, field2, field3
FROM table
WHERE condition;
```

That's no harder than asking your coworker to get you last month's sales records from the file cabinet in the hallway.

In some cases, you'll want to ask for entire records instead of picking out individual pieces of information. This practice is deprecated for very good reasons (it may be slower than requesting just the data you need, and it can lead to problems if you redesign the table); but it is still widely used and, therefore, we need to mention it. A whole record is called for by using the wildcard (asterisk) symbol:

```
SELECT *
FROM my_table
WHERE ID <= 100;
```

Joins

Only one thing about SELECT statements is even slightly taxing: *joins*. Because joins are one of the main useful features of SQL, we should explain them in some detail here.

A SELECT statement on a single table without joins is easily imagined as being something like a row in a spreadsheet. This is not really how the data is stored or arranged in a SQL database, but for this purpose it's a handy visualization device.

But a SQL database is by definition relational. To understand the philosophy behind the relational database concept, you have to think back to some occasion on which you were forced to fill out a whole bunch of forms — such as applying for a loan, visiting a doctor's office for the first time, or dealing with some kind of governmental formality. (If you've never had this experience, it's because you're young enough to have lived entirely in a world of relational databases.) As you were writing down your name, address, phone, and social security number for the fifteenth time, you probably thought, "Why can't I just write my address down once, and then they could just look it up on a need-to-know basis." That's exactly the concept behind a relational database.

The way a relational database differs from paper forms is the main identifier. Humans do well with text and prefer to categorize by textual identifiers such as names. If a dentist's office or auto body shop stored its paper files in numerical order, it would be difficult for anyone to lay his hands on John Johnson's forms when John next required service. Frankly, most paper file users these days ask for your social security number as a backup — it works solely to differentiate you from other people in their files with exactly the same first, last, and middle names.

Databases, on the other hand, work fastest with integers. Because integers are unique by nature, a database only needs one to identify a person, place, or thing uniquely — no matter how many tables refer to that piece of information.

So instead of needing to repeat information several times, like this:

```
Name:  John Johnson
SS#:   123-45-6789

Name:  John Johnson
Fears:  Cats, Friday the 13th, Flying

Name:  Jane Jones
SS#:   987-65-4321

Name:  Jane Jones
Fears:  Heights, Flying
```

with a relational database you can write down each piece of information just once and then relate it to each other piece using integers, as shown in Tables 17-1 to 17-3.

Table 17-1: People

PersonID	Name	SS#
1	John Johnson	123-45-6789
2	Jane Jones	987-65-4321
3	Aloysius Snuffleupagus	564-73-8291

Table 17-2: Fears

FearID	Fear
1	Black cats
2	Friday the 13th
3	Peanut butter sticking to the roof of your mouth
4	Heights
5	Flying

Table 17-3: Person_Fear

ID	PersonID	FearID
1	1	1
2	1	2
3	1	5
4	2	4
5	2	5

This is clearly a neater and faster (for a database) way to store this information. But when you need to pull out the data into a human-readable form, there's a problem: You have to get and correlate information from more than one database. That's the job of a join.

To find out what phobias were suffered by Ms. Jones, you could first look up her personal unique ID:

```
SELECT PersonID
FROM People
WHERE Name = 'Jane Jones';
```

that returns the unique integer 2. Then you can define another SELECT statement using that information:

```
SELECT FearID
FROM Person_Fear
WHERE PersonID = 2;
```

You get the values 4 and 5 back, which you can use in a third query:

```
SELECT Fear
FROM Fears
WHERE FearID = 4 OR FearID = 5;
```

This returns the values Heights and Flying. We should make it clear that there is nothing inherently incorrect about doing it this way, as long as any performance loss is within parameters acceptable to you.

Alternatively, you can perform a join, which returns the same information in a single SELECT statement:

```
SELECT Fears.Fear
FROM Fears, Person_Fear, People
WHERE Fears.FearID = Person_Fear.FearID
AND Person_Fear.PersonID = People.PersonID
AND People.Name = 'Jane Jones';
```

An alternate syntax for this join is:

```
SELECT Fears.Fear
FROM (Fears INNER JOIN Person_Fear ON FearID INNER JOIN People on
PersonID)
WHERE People.Name = 'Jane Jones';
```

As you can see, you need only know one single piece of information to be able to get all the data in the database about that subject using joins. In effect, a join makes two or more tables into one for purposes of searching for a particular piece of information.

Joins come in several different flavors. The one in the preceding example is called an *inner join*, which is the most common and restrictive type. Another common type is the *outer join*. This is used to return a list of all fears even if they do not have people attached to them. In this example, we are using a *left outer join* (also known as a *natural join*):

```
SELECT Fear
FROM Fears LEFT JOIN People ON PersonID;
```

Fears that have people attached to them would appear in the data set multiple times, but also fears without people would each appear once.

You can also get a list of all people even if they do not have fears attached to them, using a *right outer join*:

```
SELECT Name
FROM Fears RIGHT JOIN People on PersonID;
```

Again, the fears that are actually attached to people appear multiple times, whereas the fears which are not suffered by any people still show up once in the data set. As you can see, left and right outer joins differ in which of the two tables you want the actual data set from: the first (left) or the second (right). Because you can switch them around at will, many people consistently use the left outer join for all outer joins.

> **CAUTION:** Ask yourself whether you really need to be using outer joins. Because outer joins require less precision to format, inexperienced SQL users often perform an outer join and then filter the results in the code layer. This is wasteful and slow. Outer joins are all about the NULL values, which are not easily returned by inner joins. An example of a good use for an outer join is a report where you want to see which of your registered users had and had not downloaded your latest software product, and how many times they had downloaded. If you are not in this situation, learn to use inner joins instead.

Finally, there is something known as the *self-join*, which is a more advanced technique and won't really make a lot of sense with the example data set. It's often used with *denormalized data*, which means data that deliberately bends the rules of good SQL design (for example, never repeating any data point) for performance reasons (for example, to reduce the number of complex multitable joins).

If you need to make complex and frequent joins, this may constrain the brand of SQL database you can use, because not all of them support every type of join.

Subselects

Before we leave the realm of SELECT statements, we should mention the *subselect*. This is a statement such as:

```
SELECT phone_number
FROM table
WHERE name = 'SELECT name FROM table2 WHERE ID = 1';
```

Subselects are more of a convenience than a necessity. They can be very handy if you're working with enormous batches of data; but you can get the same result with two simpler SELECTs. The subselect is faster if the subselect clause returns a large data set, but there are cases where two selects will not appreciably affect performance.

INSERT

The command you need to put new data into a database is INSERT. The basic syntax here is:

```
INSERT INTO table (col1, col2, col3) VALUES(val1, val2, val3);
```

Obviously the columns and their values need to match up; if you mix up your array items, nothing good will happen. If some of the rows will not have values for some of the fields, you will need to use an empty, null, or auto-incremented value — and, at a deeper level, you may need to have ensured beforehand that fields can be nullable or auto-incrementable. If this is not possible, you should simply leave out any columns you wish to default to an empty value in an INSERT statement.

A twist on the basic INSERT is the INSERT INTO...SELECT. This just means you can INSERT the results of a SELECT statement:

```
INSERT INTO customer(birthmonth, birthflower, birthstone) SELECT * FROM
birthday_info WHERE birthmonth = $birthmonth;
```

Not every SQL database has this capability. Also, you need to be careful with this command because you can cause problems for yourself quite easily — for instance you can overwrite data or experience locking issues. In general, it's not a good idea to select from the same database you're inserting into.

UPDATE

UPDATE is used to edit information already in the database, without deleting any rows. In other words, you can selectively change some information without having to delete an entire old record and insert a new one. The syntax is:

```
UPDATE table
SET field1='val1', field2='val2', field3='val3'
WHERE condition;
```

The conditional statement is just like a SELECT condition, such as WHERE ID>15 AND ID<21 or WHERE gender='F'.

DELETE

DELETE is pretty self-explanatory: You use it to delete the contents of one or more fields permanently from the database. The syntax is:

```
DELETE datapoint
FROM table
WHERE condition;
```

The most important thing to remember is the condition — if you don't set one, you will delete every entry in the specified columns from the database, without a confirmation or a second chance in many cases.

> **CAUTION:** Let us re-emphasize: you *must* remember to use a condition *every single time* you UPDATE or DELETE! If you do not, every single row in the table will experience the same alteration or deletion. Even very experienced programmers have forgotten to include the condition, to their vast professional embarrassment. You should also give a good deal of thought to restricting database permissions so the minimum number of people can perform these potentially dangerous operations.

Database Design

As should be obvious from the previous section, learning to use a SQL database isn't exactly rocket science — you can get a lot done with just a few simple commands. The hard part is designing the database in the first place and, of course, operating it in the real world over time. Not every Web developer will be asked to design a schema in a professional context, but it never hurts to know how.

At the most fundamental level, database design can be broken down into the following mantra *cum* children's jingle:

```
One to one,
One to many,
Many to many,
Many to one;
And always use a unique ID.
```

An example of *one-to-one data* for Americans is the social security number (other nations probably have similar identification cards with unique numbers). Each U.S. citizen has only one unique identifier; and it is, in fact, a crime to use the social security number of another individual or apply for more than one number. Database designers seize upon truly unique identifiers such as this because almost every other piece of personal information is subject to change — which accounts for the large number of businesses who inappropriately use the social security number for identification purposes.

Many-to-one and *one-to-many data* are the same, differing only in how the columns are placed in a database. An example of one-to-many data comes from the medical realm: patients to visits. Each patient will always be a discrete individual but may have any number of visits to the doctor. If you designed the table to represent visits to patients, it would instantly become many-to-one data.

Finally, *many-to-many data* is well represented by the relationship of authors to books. Not only can a given book have multiple authors; but each author may have written or co-authored many books. This is not a matrix of relationships that would be easy to represent efficiently in a spreadsheet, but it is precisely this category of data at which relational databases most excel.

Every data relationship falls into one of these categories. As a database designer, it's your job to decide which one of these represents what you need to know in the way you need to know it.

This is not as trivial as it sounds. Imagine you want to develop a database of movie information. One decision you might have to make is whether *movie* and *title* are in a one-to-one relationship with each other, or whether enough films have alternate titles to merit an *alternate title* field or even a one-to-many representation. There's no right answer here — the decision depends on exactly how the information will be used, how large the database will be, if the extra resources required to maintain a more precise data structure are worth the cost, and whether there's a better-than-even chance that today's tangential trivia will become tomorrow's crucial discovery. Some people may be surprised to learn that archiving information can be as much about ruthless excluding as about careful hoarding. As historians say, history is about forgetting as much as it is about remembering.

The simplest relationship is the one-to-one because you can group all these fields into a single table that can be searched more quickly. For instance, a table holding customer information might contain the following fields:

```
Customer ID
Customer name
Administrative contact
Technical contact
```

The hardest thing about the one-to-one relationship is definitively deciding that you will never need to make it into a one-to-many relationship. For instance, what if your biggest customer decides it wants to designate two technical contacts?

As soon as you have a one-to-many, many-to-one, or many-to-many relationship, you're looking at going from a single table to multiple tables: one each for the main variables, and one stating the relationship. Tables 17-4 through 17-6 show a common example of a many-to-many relationship:

Table 17-4: Customer

Customer_id	Name
1	Acme Bread
2	Baker Construction
3	Coolee Dam

Table 17-5: Interactions

Interaction_id	Type
1	Phone-support incident
2	On-site incident
3	Written complaint
4	Phone complaint
5	Kudo

Table 17-6: Customer-Interaction

Customer-interaction_id	Customer_id	Interaction_id
1	1	1
2	3	5
3	2	4
4	2	3
5	1	2

After you've decided on a database design, the mechanical details of constructing the database are minimal. The main data structure statements of SQL are CREATE, ALTER, and DROP.

CREATE is used to make a completely new table. All the work is in defining the columns of each table. First you declare the name of the table, and then you must detail the specific data types of that table's columns in what is called a *create definition*. A CREATE statement will take this form:

```
CREATE TABLE tablename (
  id_col INT NOT NULL AUTO_INCREMENT PRIMARY KEY,
  col1 TEXT NULL INDEX,
  col2 DATE NOT NULL
);
```

Different SQL servers have slightly different data types and definition options, so the syntax of one may not transfer exactly to another.

DROP can be used to completely delete a table and all its associated data. It's not the most subtle command:

```
DROP TABLE tablename;
```

Obviously you need to be very careful with this statement.

ALTER is the way to change a table's structure. You simply indicate which table you're changing and redefine its specs. Again, SQL products differ in functionality here. The ALTER statement usually takes this form:

```
ALTER TABLE table RENAME AS new_table;
ALTER TABLE new_table ADD COLUMN col3 VARCHAR(50);
ALTER TABLE new_table DROP COLUMN col2;
```

Privileges and Security

As we state in Chapter 36, security online is analogous to security in the real world. Any cop will tell you that you cannot make your home absolutely crime-proof. A more realistic goal is to increase the difficulty and risk to a level where a large percentage of intruders will choose to go to an easier target down the block.

Using a database with PHP can be similar to using two locks on your front door, substantially enhancing the safety of your site by reducing super-risky operations like system file writes — but only if you follow a few elementary rules of database hygiene. PHP makes many of these techniques a little easier to implement, which means you have fewer reasons to skimp on security.

Setting database permissions

The most fundamental rule of database use is to give each user or group only the minimum permissions necessary to do what needs to be done. You wouldn't let strangers walk into your house and kick back in your bedroom and read your diary — so why should you give them the option to do analogous things on your site? It's a little more work to manage multiple users and make sure all the permissions are set to the right levels at all times; but if that tiny pinprick of pain can prevent a massive infection later, you'd be extremely foolish to refuse this simple but effective prophylaxis.

Besides the threat of malicious/experimental outsiders, setting the correct permissions can protect you from your coworkers and yourself. Insiders have been known to cause massive problems through disgruntlement, ignorance, momentary brain freeze, or a combination of motives. You do not want to have to cope with the consequences of a fired employee's parting shot, or a new intern "trying out" the DROP database command just to see what happens.

A typical database permissions package might be something like:

♦ **Web visitor:** SELECT only

♦ **Contributor:** SELECT, INSERT, and maybe UPDATE

♦ **Editor:** SELECT, INSERT, UPDATE, and maybe DELETE and maybe GRANT

♦ **Root:** SELECT, INSERT, UPDATE, DELETE, GRANT, and DROP

DROP in particular is the nuclear bomb of SQL because it allows you to blow away an entire table or database with a single command. Someone's got to have the ability, but heavy lies the tiara of responsibility on the head of the root database user. Use the power wisely, grasshopper.

In many databases, including MySQL, passwords are encrypted using a different algorithm from system passwords (and, of course, they are typically stored in entirely different locations). Even if one is cracked, the other is not necessarily vulnerable. This assumes you take the time to set permissions correctly, pick good passwords, and usually employ a special command to insert usernames and passwords correctly into the grant table (as opposed to inserting them like other data).

> **TIP:** Database usernames and passwords should not be identical to system usernames and passwords. Never, ever, *ever* set any database password to the root system-user's password! If crackers should happen to get into your database via Web scripts, you don't want to offer them the key to the whole system.

Keep database passwords outside the Web tree

It's a good idea to separate passwords from the Web page that use them. With PHP's include()/include_once() and require()/require_once() functions, it's very easy to drop in text (such as database passwords) from another file at runtime. Remember that these included files do not have to be in a PHP or Web server-enabled directory! Whenever possible, keep them somewhere outside your Web tree, such as in the directory above your Web document root or in a home directory.

Taking the database variables out of PHP files is also good for other reasons. If you have many PHP scripts using the same database, they can all use the same password file. When you suspect the password has been compromised, or when you change the password on a regular schedule, you need only alter one script for all the files to be updated.

The unavoidable downside of this technique is that the file must be *readable* by the Apache user. Because the Apache user and the database user are seldom the same, that means in practice the file must be world-readable. This should still be safer than keeping the database variables inside a public Web root directory.

If you have a set of database variables you use infrequently — a configuration script or the like — you can keep it in a non-Apache-readable directory and change the permissions only on the rare occasions necessary. We infrequently have to go to the trouble to delete postings from our sites' forums. So it's not that much more work (and much more secure) to keep this file in a non-Apache-user-owned directory, once in awhile change the permissions just long enough to delete the offending post, and then immediately change everything back.

If for whatever reason, you decide to put your database username, password, hostname, and database name into a PHP script in plaintext, this is what you can expect. If the `httpd` is functioning normally, the database passwords should be as safe as any file on that server — which is to say, not extremely. But if the daemon goes down, there is some chance your raw PHP (including plaintext database variables) will be delivered in a human-readable form. You can reduce this risk by avoiding the use of the `.html` suffix for PHP files.

In PHP3, if database connectivity goes down and you haven't specified silent mode, you would see something like the following:

```
Warning: MySQL Connection Failed: Access denied for user:
'someuser@localhost' (Using password: NO) in
/home/web/html/mysqltest.php3
on line 2
```

This constitutes a security breach, because it reveals your MySQL username and whether or not you use a password. In PHP4, MySQL error messages are no longer displayed by default. Two new functions, `mysql_errno()` and `mysql_error()`, allow you to opt for error codes or text warnings — but now you have to deliberately choose to ask for the information. Because, in most cases, you can opt for the more configurable `die()` instead or remove error messages after debugging, it's still not a good idea to use `mysql_error` on a public production server unless you scrupulously send messages to error logs using the `error_log()` function rather than to standard output.

Use two layers of password protection

Belt and suspenders types can apply even another layer of protection to their most sensitive PHP scripts by means of another round of usernames and passwords stored in the database itself, which you can check directly from the PHP script. So you would have your system login/password, plus database user permissions stored in a non-Web-accessible directory, plus a PHP name/passphrase testing script with values entered by hand just before the script is run.

This is a typical login form that checks a password against the database:

```
<HTML>
<BODY>
<FORM METHOD=POST ACTION="form_check.php">
<P>Username:  <INPUT TYPE="TEXT" SIZE=20 NAME="try_user"></P>
<P>Password:  <INPUT TYPE="PASSWORD" SIZE=10 NAME="try_pass"></P>
<P>Date:  <INPUT TYPE="TEXT" SIZE=10 NAME="try_date"></P>
<P>Entry:<BR>
<TEXTAREA COLS=50 ROWS=10 NAME="try_entry"></TEXTAREA></P>
<P><INPUT TYPE="SUBMIT"></P>
</BODY>
</HTML>
```

This file is the form handler mentioned in the ACTION attribute of the preceding form, named form_check.php.

```
<?php
// Check Unix user
if ($REMOTE_ADDR != '127.0.0.1') {
  die;
}

// Check database user
// Webvars.inc is a file with $host, $db_user, and $password values in
it
include("/home/phpuser/Webvars.inc");
mysql_connect($hostname, $db_user, $password) or die("You are not the
database user I'm looking for");
mysql_select_db("captainslog");

// Check form user
$post_try_user = $_POST['try_user'];
$post_try_date = $_POST['try_date'];
$post_try_entry = $_POST['try_entry'];
$query = "SELECT password
          FROM finalcheck
          WHERE user='$post_try_user'";
$result = mysql_query($query);
$passcheck = mysql_fetch_array($result);
```

```
if($passcheck[0] == $_POST['try_pass']) {
  // Enter new entry.
  $query = ("INSERT INTO captainslog (ID, date, entry) VALUES(NULL,
'$post_try_date', '$post_try_entry')");
  $result = mysql_query($query);
  print("New entry result is $result.");
} else {
  mail("security@localhost", "Database alert", "Someone from
$REMOTE_ADDR is trying to get into your captain's log.");
}
?>
```

As you can see from this example, this script will not insert anything into the database if a valid username and password are not provided or the user isn't logged into the localhost. You will also get an e-mail message warning you of a possible breach attempt.

Learn to make backups

And finally, the biggest part of database security may be backing up. Take an hour to learn the best way to back up data in your particular database (for example, via the mysqldump command in MySQL), and then schedule regular backups right away. Even better, with a little foresight you can also set up an automatic database backup schedule.

Summary

SQL is not rocket science. The four basic data manipulation statements supported by essentially all SQL databases are SELECT, INSERT, UPDATE, and DELETE. SELECT gets data out of the database, INSERT puts in a new entry, UPDATE edits pieces of the entry in place, and DELETE gets rid of an entry.

Designing databases is where most of the difficulty lies. Not all Web developers will be asked to do this. The designer must think long and hard about the best way to represent each piece of data and relationship for the intended use. Well-designed databases are a pleasure to program with, while poorly designed ones can leave you pulling your hair out while contemplating numerous connections and icky joins.

SQL databases are created by so-called data structure statements. The most important of these are CREATE, ALTER, and DROP. As one would expect, CREATE TABLE defines a new table within a database. ALTER changes the structure of a table. DROP is the nuclear bomb of SQL commands because it entirely deletes tables or sometimes even whole databases.

Good database design is also a security issue. By employing reasonable prophylactic measures, a SQL database can enhance the security of your site. The best defense against intrusion, of course, is maintaining a strict backup schedule — so every new SQL maintainer should learn the most efficient way to make backups.

Chapter 18

PHP/MySQL Database Functions

In This Chapter

- ♦ Connecting to MySQL
- ♦ Making queries
- ♦ Fetching data
- ♦ Getting data about data
- ♦ Using multiple connections
- ♦ Error checking
- ♦ Creating databases

After you've designed and set up your MySQL database, you can begin to write PHP scripts that interact with it. Here we will try to explain all the basic functions that enable you to pass data back and forth from Web site to database.

Connecting to MySQL

The basic command to initiate a MySQL connection is:

```
mysql_connect($hostname, $user, $password);
```

if you're using variables; or

```
mysql_connect('localhost', 'root', 'sesame');
```

if you're using literal strings.

The password is optional, depending on whether this particular database user requires one (it's a good idea). If not, just leave that variable off. You can also specify a port and socket for the server ($hostname:port:socket), but unless you've specifically chosen a nonstandard port and socket, there's little to gain by doing so.

Next, you'll want to choose a database to work on:

```
mysql_select_db($database);
```

if you're using variables; or

```
mysql_select_db('phpbook');
```

if you're using a literal string.

> **TIP:** You will sometimes see these two functions used with an @ prepended, such as
> `@mysql_select_db($database)`. This symbol denotes *silent mode*, meaning the function will not
> return any message on failure, as a security precaution.

You must select a database each time you make a connection, which means at least once per page or every time you change databases. Otherwise, you'll get a `Database not selected` error. Even if you've only created one database per daemon, you must do this, because MySQL also comes with default databases (called `mysql` and `test`) you might not be taking into account.

> **CAUTION:** Before PHP 4.0.6, you could skip this step and select a database by using
> `mysql_db_query()`. This function has now been deprecated.

Now that you've established a connection, you're ready to make a query.

Making MySQL Queries

A database query from PHP is basically a MySQL command wrapped up in a tiny PHP function called `mysql_query()`. This is where you use the basic SQL workhorses of `SELECT`, `INSERT`, `UPDATE`, and `DELETE` that we discussed in the previous Chapter. The MySQL commands to `CREATE` or `DROP` a table (but *not*, thankfully, a database) can also be used with this PHP function if you do not wish to make your databases using the MySQL client.

You could write a query in the simplest possible way, as follows:

```
mysql_query("SELECT Surname FROM personal_info WHERE ID<10");
```

PHP would dutifully try to execute it. However, there are very good reasons to split up this and similar commands into two lines with extra variables, like this:

```
$query = "SELECT Surname FROM personal_info WSHERE ID<10";
$result = mysql_query($query);
```

The main rationale is that the extra variable gives you a handle on an extremely valuable piece of information. Every MySQL query gives you a receipt whether you succeed or not — sort of like a cash machine when you try to withdraw money. If things go well, you hardly need or notice the receipt — you can throw it away without a qualm. But if a problem occurs, the receipt will give you a clue as to what might have gone wrong, similar to the "Is the machine not dispensing or is your account overdrawn?" type of message that might be printed on your ATM receipt.

Another advantage of assigning the query string to a variable is that you can more easily view the query if you run into an error. Of course, you would accomplish this by writing the variable out to an error log — never by dumping it out to the browser!

The function `mysql_query` takes as arguments the query string (which should not have a semicolon within the double quotes) and optionally a link identifier. Unless you have multiple connections, you don't need the link identifier. It returns a `TRUE` (nonzero) integer value if the query was executed successfully *even if no rows were affected.* It returns a `FALSE` integer if the query was illegal or not properly executed for some other reason.

If your query was an `INSERT`, `UPDATE`, `DELETE`, `CREATE TABLE`, or `DROP TABLE` and returned `TRUE`, you can now use `mysql_affected_rows` to see how many rows were changed by the query. This function optionally takes a link identifier, only necessary if you are using multiple connections. It *does not* take the result handle as an argument! You call the function like this, without a result handle:

```
$affected_rows = mysql_affected_rows();
```

If your query was a `SELECT` statement, the integer returned will have a slightly different meaning: Instead of being `TRUE` or `FALSE`, it returns an integer called a *result identifier.* This is a unique identifier for each `SELECT`, generally incremented from 1 beginning with the first such statement in each script. You cannot use the `mysql_affected_rows` function with a `SELECT`, because no rows were changed. Instead, you can use `mysql_num_rows($result)` to find out how many rows were returned by a successful `SELECT`.

Fetching Data Sets

One thing that often seems to temporarily stymie new PHP users is the whole concept of fetching data from PHP. It would be logical to assume the result of a query would be the desired data, but that is not correct. As we discussed in the previous section, the result of a PHP query is an integer representing the success or failure or identity of the query.

What actually happens is that a `mysql_query()` command pulls the data out of the database and sends a receipt back to PHP reporting on the status of the operation. At this point, the data exists in a purgatory that is immediately accessible from neither MySQL nor PHP — you can think of it as a staging area of sorts. The data is there, but it's waiting for the commanding officer to give the order to deploy. It requires one of the `mysql_fetch` functions to make the data fully available to PHP.

The fetching functions are as follows:

♦ `mysql_fetch_row`: Returns row as an enumerated array.

♦ `mysql_fetch_object`: Returns row as an object.

♦ `mysql_fetch_array`: Returns row as an associative array.

♦ `mysql_result`: Returns one cell of data.

> **CAUTION:** In our humble opinions, the functions `mysql_fetch_field` and `mysql_fetch_lengths` are misleadingly named. They both provide information *about* database entries rather than the entry values themselves. For instance, one might expect a function named `mysql_fetch_field` to be a quick way to fetch a single-field result set (the ID associated with a particular username, for instance), but that is not the case at all. The actual purpose of these functions is explained in Table 18-1 — but for the moment, the point is not to be misled into thinking these functions will return database values.

The difference between the three main fetching functions is small. The most general one is `mysql_fetch_row`, which can be used something like this:

```
$query = "SELECT ID, LastName, FirstName FROM users WHERE Status = 1";
$result = mysql_query($query);
while ($name_row = mysql_fetch_row($result)) {
  print("$name_row[0] $name_row[1] $name_row[2]<BR>\n");
}
```

This code will output the specified rows from the database, each line containing one row or the information associated with a unique ID (if any).

> **CAUTION:** In an enumerated array, the integers in brackets are called *field offsets*. Remember that they always begin with the integer zero. If you start counting at 1, you will miss the value of your first column.

The function `mysql_fetch_object` performs much the same task, except the row is returned as an object rather than an array. Obviously, this is helpful for those among the PHP brethren who utilize the object-oriented notation:

```
$query = "SELECT ID, LastName, FirstName FROM users WHERE Status = 1";
$result = mysql_query($query);
while ($row = mysql_fetch_object($result)) {
  echo "$row->ID, $row->LastName, $row->FirstName<BR>\n";
}
```

The most useful fetching function, `mysql_fetch_array`, offers the choice of results as an associative or an enumerated array — or both, which is the default. This means you can refer to outputs by database field name rather than number:

```
$query = "SELECT ID, LastName, FirstName FROM users WHERE Status = 1";
$result = mysql_query($query);
while ($row = mysql_fetch_array($result)) {
  echo "$row['ID'], $row['LastName'], $row['FirstName']<BR>\n";
}
```

Remember that `mysql_fetch_array` can *also* be used exactly the same way as `mysql_fetch_row` — with numerical identifiers rather than field names. By using this function, you leave yourself the option. If you want to specify offset or field name rather than making both available, you can do it like this:

```
$offset_row = mysql_fetch_array($result, MYSQL_NUM);
or
$associative_row = mysql_fetch_array($result, MYSQL_ASSOC);
```

It's also possible to use MYSQL_BOTH as the second value, but because that's the default, it's redundant.

In early versions of PHP3, mysql_fetch_row was considered to be significantly faster than mysql_fetch_object and mysql_fetch_array, but this is no longer an issue, as the speed differences have become imperceptible. The PHP junta now recommends use of mysql_fetch_array over mysql_fetch_row because it offers increased functionality and choice at little cost in terms of programming difficulty, performance loss, or maintainability.

Last and least of the fetching functions is mysql_result(). You should only even *consider* using this function in situations where you are positive you need only one piece of data to be returned from MySQL. An example of its usage:

```
$query = "SELECT count(*) FROM personal_info";
$db_result = mysql_query($query);
$datapoint = mysql_result($db_result, 0, 0);
```

The mysql_result function takes three arguments: *result identifier, row identifier*, and (optionally) *field*. Field can take the value of the field offset as above, or its name as in an associative array ("Surname"), or its MySQL field-dot-table name ("personal_info.Surname"). Use the offset if at all possible, as it is substantially faster than the other two. Even better, don't use this function with any frequency.

> **CAUTION:** You should never use mysql_result() to return information that is available to you through a predefined PHP-MySQL function. The classic no-no is inserting a row and then selecting out its ID number (extra demerits if you select on MAX(ID)!). Wicked bad style — use mysql_insert_id() instead.

A special MySQL function can be used with any of the fetching functions to more specifically designate the row number desired. This is mysql_data_seek, which takes as arguments the result identifier and a row number and moves the internal row pointer to that row of the data set. The most common use of this function is to reiterate through a result set from the beginning by re-setting the row number to zero, similar to an array reset. This obviates another expensive database call to get data you already have sitting around on the PHP side. Here is an example of using mysql_data_seek():

```
<?php
echo("<TABLE>\n<TR><TH>Titles</TH></TR>\n<TR>");
$query = "SELECT title, publisher FROM books";
```

```
$result = mysql_query($query);
while ($book_row = mysql_fetch_array($result)) {
  echo("<TD>$book_row[0]</TD>\n");
}
echo("</TR></TABLE><BR>\n");
echo("<TABLE>\n<TR><TH>Publishers</TH></TR>\n<TR>");
mysql_data_seek($result, 0);
while ($book_row = mysql_fetch_array($result)) {
  echo("<TD>$book_row[1]</TD>\n");
}
echo("</TR></TABLE><BR>\n");
?>
```

Getting Data about Data

You only need four PHP functions to put data into or get data out of a preexisting MySQL database: mysql_connect, mysql_select_db, mysql_query, and mysql_fetch_array. Most of the rest of the functions in this section are about getting information about the data you put into or took out of the database, or about the construction of the database itself. PHP offers built-in functions to help you learn the name of the table in which your data resides, the data type handled by a particular column, or the number of the row into which you just inserted data.

Obviously you don't want J. Random Cracker to be able to find out everything about the structure and contents of your database for the asking. If you have scripts that use these functions extensively — for instance, some kind of Web database-administration tool — you need a higher level of security. Make sure only the root MySQL user can use these tools, and preferably use forms to pass in a password every time, or use one of the methods to limit usage to certain IP addresses.

The MySQL metadata functions fall into two major categories:

♦ Functions that return information about the previous operation only.

♦ Functions that return information about the database structure in general.

A very commonly used example of the first type is mysql_insert_id(), which returns the autoincremented ID assigned to a row of data you just inserted. A commonly used example of the second type is mysql_field_type(), which reveals whether a particular database field's data must be an integer, a varchar, text, or what have you.

Most of the data-about-data functions are pretty self-explanatory. There are a couple of things to keep in mind when using them, though. First, most of these functions are only effective if used in the proper combination — don't try to use a mysql_affected_rows after a SELECT query and then wonder what went wrong. Second, be careful about security with the functions that return information about your database structure. Knowing the name and structure of each table is very valuable to a cracker. And finally, be aware that some of these functions are shopping baskets full of simpler functions. If you need several pieces of information about a particular result set or database, it could be faster to use `mysql_fetch_field` than all the `mysql_field` functions one after the other.

Multiple Connections

Unless you have a specific reason to require multiple connections, you only need to make one database connection per PHP page. Even if you escape into HTML many times within the page, your connection is still good (assuming it was good in the first place). You do not want to make multiple connections if you don't have to, because that is one of the most costly and time-consuming parts of most database queries.

Conversely, there's no easy way to keep your connection open from page to page —because PHP and MySQL would never know for sure when to close it after visitors wander off. Therefore, your connection is closed at the end of each script unless you use persistent connections.

The main reason you would need to use different connections is if you're querying two or more completely separate databases. The most common situation in which you might do this is when you're using MySQL in a replicated situation. MySQL replication is accomplished through a master-slave setup, where you might get reads from the slave and make writes to the master.

To use multiple connections, you simply open connections to each database as needed, and make sure to hang on to the right result sets. PHP will help you do this by utilizing the result identifiers discussed in the "Making MySQL Queries" section above. You pass them along with each MySQL function as an optional argument. If you're completing all your queries on one connection before moving on to the next, you don't even need to do this; PHP will automatically use the last link opened.

In this example, we are using connections from three different databases:

```php
<?php
$link1 = mysql_connect('host1', 'me', 'sesame');
mysql_select_db('userdb', $link1);
$query1 = "SELECT ID FROM usertable WHERE username = '$username'";
$result1 = mysql_query($query1, $link1);
$array1 = mysql_fetch_array($result1);
$usercount = mysql_num_rows($result1);
mysql_close($link1);

$today = '2002-05-01';
$link2 = mysql_connect('host2', 'myself', 'benne');
mysql_select_db('inventorydb', $link2);
$query2 = "SELECT sku FROM widgets WHERE ship_date = '$today'";
$result2 = mysql_query($query2, $link2);
$array2 = mysql_fetch_array($result2);
$widgetcount = mysql_num_rows($result2);
```

```
mysql_close($link2);

if ($usercount > 0 && $widgetcount > 0) {
  $link3 = mysql_connect('host3', 'I', 'seed');
  mysql_select_db('salesdb', $link3);
  $query3 = "INSERT INTO saleslog (ID, date, userID, sku) VALUES (NULL,
'$today', '$array1[0]', '$array2[0]')";
  $result3 = mysql_query($query3, $link3);
  $insertID = mysql_insert_id($link3);
  mysql_close($link3);
  if ($insertID >= 1) {
    print("Perfect entry");
  }
  else {
    print("Danger, danger, Will Robinson!");
  }
} else {
  print("Not enough information");
}
?>
```

In this example we have deliberately kept the connections as discrete as possible for clarity's sake, even going to the trouble to close each link after we use it. Without the `mysql_close()` commands, we would be running multiple concurrent connections – which you may want to do. There's nothing stopping you from doing so. Just remember to pass the link value carefully from one function to the next, and you should be fine.

Building in Error-Checking

This section could have been titled "Die, die, die!" because the main error-checking function is actually called `die()`. There was something about that title that failed to reinforce the warm, hospitable learning environment we cherish, so we went with the more prosaic subheading.

`die()` is not a MySQL-specific function — the PHP manual lists it in "Miscellaneous Functions." It simply terminates the script (or a delimited portion thereof) and returns a string of your choice.

```
mysql_query("SELECT * FROM mutual_funds WHERE code = '$searchstring'")
or die("Please check your query and try again.");
```

Notice the syntax: the word `or` (you could alternatively use `||`, but that isn't as much fun as saying `or die`) and only one semicolon per pair of alternatives.

Until quite recently, MySQL via PHP returned very insecure and unenlightening (except to crackers) error messages upon encountering a problem with a database query. die() was often used as a way to exert control over what the public would see on failure. Now that no error messages are returned at all, `die()` may be even more necessary — unless you want your visitors to be left wondering what happened.

Other built-in means of error-checking are error messages. These are particularly helpful during the development and debugging phase, and they can be easily commented out in the final edit before going live on a production server. As mentioned, MySQL error messages no longer appear by default. If you want them, you have to ask for them by using the functions `mysql_errno()` (which returns a code number for each error type), or `mysql_error()` (which returns the text message). Then you can send them to a custom error log by using the `error_log()` function.

```
if (!mysql_select_db($bad_db)) {
  print(mysql_error());
}
```

Creating MySQL Databases with PHP

You can, if you wish, actually create your databases with PHP rather than using the MySQL client tool. This practice has potential advantages — you can use an attractive front end that may appeal to those who find the MySQL client horribly plain or finicky to use — counterbalanced by one big disadvantage, which is security.

To create a database from PHP, the user of your scripts will need to have full CREATE/DROP privileges on MySQL. That means anyone who can get hold of your scripts can potentially blow away all your databases and their contents with the greatest of ease. This is not such a great idea from a security standpoint. Furthermore, most external Web hosts very sensibly won't let you do it on their servers anyway.

If you're even considering creating databases with PHP, do yourself a big favor and at least don't store the database username and password in a text file. Make yourself type your database username and password into a form and pass the variables to the inserting handler each and every time you use this script. This is one case where keeping the variables in an `include` file outside your Web tree is not sufficient precaution.

For those who like to live dangerously, the relevant functions are:

 ♦ `mysql_create_db()`: Creates a database on the designated host, with name specified in arguments.

 ♦ `mysql_drop_db()`: Deletes the specified database.

 ♦ `mysql_query()`: Pass table definitions and drops in here.

A bare-bones database-generation script might look like this:

```
<?php
$linkID = mysql_connect('localhost', 'root', 'sesame');
mysql_create_db('new_db', $linkID);
mysql_select_db('new_db');
$query = "CREATE TABLE new_table (id INT NOT NULL AUTO_INCREMENT PRIMARY
KEY, new_col VARCHAR(25))";
$result = mysql_query($query);
```

```
$axe = mysql_drop_db('new_db');
?>
```

There are also prefab tools that do much of this for you in a pretty way. You simply fill out a Web form, and the PHP script on the back end will create the database according to your specifications. In many cases, the tool will also enable you to perform other administrative tasks, such as checking the sizes of your databases or backing them up. This is even less secure than doing it yourself (insofar as you probably won't check over every line of the code with an eye to security), but apparently people do use these tools without incident.

A highly attractive and popular Web database admin tool specifically for MySQL is phpMyAdmin, originated by Tobias Ratschiller, which you can try out and download from:

```
www.phpmyadmin.net
```

Several other GUI tools are available that are not database-specific but will probably work with MySQL.

> **CAUTION:** If you insist on using a Web GUI tool to design your databases, at least minimize the security hazards by only using it on a development machine inside the firewall. After you've fiddled with the database design to your heart's content, you can initiate a database dump and then move the entire structure and code over to a production database server. Do not use MySQLAdmin or any other Web GUI in production.

MySQL Functions

Table 18-1 includes a recap the MySQL functions. All arguments in brackets are optional.

Table 18-1: PHP-MySQL Functions

Function name	Usage
mysql_affected_rows([link_id])	Use after a nonzero INSERT, UPDATE, or DELETE query to check number of rows changed.
mysql_change_user(user, password[, database][, link_id])	Changes MySQL user on an open link.
mysql_close([link_id])	Closes the identified link (usually unnecessary).
mysql_connect([host][:port][:socket][, username][, password])	Opens a link on the specified host, port, socket; as specified user with password. All arguments are optional.
mysql_create_db(db_name[, link_id])	Creates a new MySQL database on the host associated with the nearest open link.
mysql_data_seek(result_id, row_num)	Moves internal row pointer to specified row number. Use a fetching function to return data from that row.

`mysql_drop_db(`*`db_name`*`[,` *`link_id`*`])`	Drops specified MySQL database.
`mysql_errno([`*`link_id`*`])`	Returns ID of error.
`mysql_error([`*`link_id`*`])`	Returns text error message.
`mysql_fetch_array(`*`result_ id`*`[,` *`result_type`*`])`	Fetches result set as associative array. Result type can be MYSQL_ASSOC, MYSQL_NUM, or MYSQL_BOTH (default).
`mysql_fetch_field(`*`result_ id`*`[,` *`field_offset`*`])`	Returns information about a field as an object.
`mysql_fetch_lengths(`*`resul t_id`*`)`	Returns length of each field in a result set.
`mysql_fetch_object(`*`result _id`*`[,` *`result_type`*`])`	Fetches result set as an object. See `mysql_fetch_array` for result types.
`mysql_fetch_row(`*`result_id`*`)`	Fetches result set as an enumerated array.
`mysql_field_name(`*`result_i d`*`,` *`field_index`*`)`	Returns name of enumerated field.
`mysql_field_seek(`*`result_i d`*`,` *`field_offset`*`)`	Moves result pointer to specified field offset. Used with `mysql_fetch_field`.
`mysql_field_table(`*`result_ id`*`,` *`field_offset`*`)`	Returns name of specified field's table.
`mysql_field_type(`*`result_i d`*`,` *`field_offset`*`)`	Returns type of offset field (for example, TINYINT, BLOB, VARCHAR).
`mysql_field_flags(`*`result_ id`*`,` *`field_offset`*`)`	Returns flags associated with enumerated field (e.g., NOT NULL, AUTO_INCREMENT, BINARY).
`mysql_field_len(`*`result_id`*`,` *`field_offset`*`)`	Returns length of enumerated field.
`mysql_free_result(`*`result_ id`*`)`	Frees memory used by result set (usually unnecessary).
`mysql_insert_id([`*`link_id`*`])`	Returns AUTO_INCREMENTED ID of INSERT; or FALSE if insert failed or last query was not an insert.
`mysql_list_fields(`*`databas e`*`,` *`table`*`[,` *`link_id`*`])`	Returns result ID for use in `mysql_field` functions, without performing an actual query.
`mysql_list_dbs([`*`link_id`*`])`	Returns result pointer of databases on mysqld. Used with `mysql_tablename`.
`mysql_list_tables(`*`databas`*	Returns result pointer of tables in database. Used

e[, *link_id*])	with `mysql_tablename`.
`mysql_num_fields(`*result_i d*`)`	Returns number of fields in a result set.
`mysql_num_rows(`*result_id*`)`	Returns number of rows in a result set.
`mysql_pconnect([`*host*`][:`*po rt*`][:`*socket*`][,` *username*`][,` *password*`])`	Opens persistent connection to database. All arguments are optional. Be careful — `mysql_close` and script termination will not close the connection.
`mysql_query(`*query_string*`[ ,` *link_id*`])`	Sends query to database. Remember to put the semicolon outside the double-quoted query string.
`mysql_result(`*result_id*`,` *row_id*`,` *field_identifier*`)`	Returns single-field result. Field identifier can be field offset (0), field name (`FirstName`) or table-dot name (`myfield.mytable`).
`mysql_select_db(`*database*`[ ,` *link_id*`])`	Selects database for queries.
`mysql_tablename(`*result_id* `,` *table_id*`)`	Used with any of the `mysql_list` functions to return the value referenced by a result pointer.

Summary

PHP's MySQL functions are easy to use, if sometimes named confusingly. Each instance of a PHP-MySQL interaction must have a connection, a database select, and a query or command which returns a result identifier. The result identifier is like an ATM receipt that reports on the success or failure of an operation.

If data is returned after a SELECT statement, one of the PHP-MySQL fetching functions must also be employed. Data pulled from a MySQL database exists in a kind of limbo until one of the fetching functions is applied to the result set. If you wish to loop through the result set again, you can use `mysql_data_seek()` to reset the row pointer back to zero.

PHP also has a large number of functions that return data about the database itself or about a particular operation. Two of the most common are `mysql_num_rows()`, which returns the number of rows in a result set; and `mysql_insert_id()`, which returns the ID of the proximate INSERT operation.

PHP handles much of the MySQL connectivity for you without requiring specific link identifiers or result pointers. The exception comes when you need multiple database connections on the same Web page. In this case, you use exactly the same functions and syntax but simply pass the correct link identifier with most commands.

Chapter 19

Oracle Functions

In This Chapter

♦ When do you need Oracle?

♦ Oracle and Web architecture

♦ Using Oracle functions

♦ Project: Point editor

♦ Project: Batch editor

Oracle databases are extremely powerful, reliable, and fast for certain kinds of queries. They are also a testament to the power of marketing, as they enjoy a mystique unmatched by any other data storage product. In this chapter, we try to cut through the hype and give you a practical foundation in using Oracle with PHP.

> **TIP:** Much of the information in this chapter is also applicable to IBM DB2, which PHP connects to using the ODBC interface, InterBase, and similar products. Much of Oracle's functionality is also duplicated by PostgreSQL, although this open source database, unfortunately, has a considerably different API than any other database. The point of this chapter is not to push Oracle over another product; it is to introduce a market-leading commercial database to those who want to learn how to use it. Feel free to mentally substitute *DB2* or *PostgreSQL* for every instance of *Oracle* in the following section.

When Do You Need Oracle?

We have never had a prospective employer or client for a PHP job who did not, at least, mention the possibility of using Oracle. Ironically, the one organization that really needed this type of functionality was very slow to adopt it; whereas everyone else didn't need Oracle at all, but wanted to architect current development around the theoretical possibility that they might need it later. In an anecdotal way, this experience testifies to the niche Oracle Corporation has managed to carve out in the mindshare of the entire software industry.

Through a powerful marketing machine (and, of course, a fine product), Oracle has managed to make its name synonymous with size, scale, and (by implication) success. Therefore, every businessperson who dreams of making it big in any business having to do with data has a fantasy that someday he or she will need and be able to afford an Oracle installation. When the humble PHP developer says, "You don't need Oracle," this is too often taken as equivalent to saying, "You're never going to amount to anything." — in other words, a big splash of cold water right in the face of the entrepreneur or manager. This does not tend to endear the humble PHP developer to the person writing the checks, even if your motivation is to save money and trouble for the businessperson. Sometimes reality cannot compete with fantasy, even in the supposedly hard-headed world of business.

So how do you realistically decide whether you need Oracle (or a workalike) or not? Certain well-understood factors are tripwires. If you are in one of these situations, your pondering is done. If not, the chances are very high that your needs could be met perfectly well — perhaps even better — by a cheaper, easier to use database.

Money

If you keep track of money or anything that can be converted to money (credit card charges, equities, airline miles, royalty payments, vacation time), you need the transactional model. Done, end of story, move on to the next thing. Not only are these things important to track end to end, but people tend to get very annoyed when you fail to do this correctly. You do not want to be matching up failed charge attempts or stock purchases programmatically.

The only exception is if you do not handle the financial part of the transaction yourself. It's fairly common these days for even fairly large Web sites to route their fulfillment transactions through some third party. If you are willing to send a customer off to your fulfillment partner, and then take its word for it whether the transaction was completed successfully or not, you can offload the transactional database requirements on it.

Other rivalrous resources

If you track other kinds of rivalrous resources on a large scale — airline tickets, concert tickets, inventory — you very likely need a transactional database. Note that the operative term is *large scale*. This feature only applies if you are in imminent danger of having colliding writes — if the chances are good that, between the time you check if a resource is available and the time you write it into another table, someone else may have claimed it. In other words, this stricture applies to computer-scale time. If you run a Web site which takes a couple hundred new registrations a day, you are not going to run into this kind of problem except as a rare fluke.

Huge data sets

Again, *huge* is the key. Millions of rows is not huge. If you will never realistically get past tens of millions of rows, you don't need Oracle for sheer scalability.

Lots of big formulaic writes or data munging

Oracle's stored procedures can increase speed immensely in situations where you have the same kind of big write or data processing happening all the time. Stored procedures amount to moving part of the code into the database itself. Processes that use these stored procedures will get done faster than processes that don't, because you've already told the database exactly what to do in a certain situation. Databases without stored procedures require all instructions to come from the PHP program, which is far slower in loops than simply handing off the input data and letting the database run with it.

For instance, if you run an e-commerce site that just takes inputs from one kind of order form and nothing else, you'll get increased overall speed from a stored procedure. The database will not have to finish one step and then wait for the program to tell it the next step or to feed it the next bit of data. PHP will simply open up the connection, shovel some data down the pipe as fast as it can, kick off the stored procedure, and possibly wait for a response.

Stored procedures obviously add extra value in cases where there is massive data munging happening on the database side. For instance, if you have a big data warehouse which takes a described data set and performs lots of analytical operations on it, then returns the results of those operations, you will very likely get much improved performance from a stored procedure.

Remember that stored procedures don't help you in cases where there is variability in the process. For instance, if you make ad-hoc queries on a data warehouse all the time, those queries will be extremely slow compared to a query that you make every day using a stored procedure. Also, you have to use stored procedures pretty often to choose a database on this basis. A whole infrastructure needs to be in place for you to derive benefits from stored procedures, and you need to decide whether it's worth the very real costs to build this infrastructure.

Triggers

Triggers are just what they sound like: The database keeps track of state; and when some kind of triggering event happens, it kicks off one or more stored procedures. You need them if you need to respond to certain well-defined data events in real time and are willing to give up global performance to do it. If your changes do not have to occur instantly — if, for instance, they can happen once an hour — you are probably better off without triggers as you can schedule stored procedures to run periodically. This is a pretty rare feature for a Web architecture, which usually requires many more reads than writes, so think hard about whether you need triggers.

Legal liability

Finally, there are non-technical reasons why you might need Oracle — one of which is legal liability. Imagine that you run a business that is in the some kind of personal information space — credit reports or medical records, perhaps. If somehow two records get mixed up, you would face significant legal liability for this most private type of information. One line of defense is to assert that you followed industry standard practices to safeguard data integrity, including use of the industry-leading database system. The tens of thousands of dollars you spend on an Oracle installation may seem cheap in this circumstance.

Bottom line: Two-year outlook

Even if you don't need any of these features now, it behooves you to think whether you might need them sometime in the foreseeable future. But don't try to build a Web architecture for the ages — new things happen so fast on the Internet that cathedral-builders are made fools of daily.

In general it seems like a two-year window is about right unless your needs are changing exceptionally quickly or slowly. If you don't see any of the preceding conditions looming on your horizon within two years or so, don't worry too much about switching to Oracle.

On the other hand, if you meet any of the preceding criteria, don't waste time — you need Oracle or one of its functional competitors.

Oracle and Web Architecture

Having an Oracle database on your back end implies certain things about your architecture and your Web development team. Do not think you can finesse these issues. If you're not ready to accept them, you're not ready for Oracle.

Specialized team members

The minute you have an Oracle installation, you need at a minimum a DBA and a PL/SQL programmer. Do not think that it's at all reasonable to expect Web developers or binary programmers to take over any of these tasks, as they often are expected to do with simpler data stores. Database tasks such as installation, tuning, refreshing, setting indexes, maintaining hot backups, and writing complex stored procedures are very highly specialized skills, which require specialized training.

One of us once worked in a situation where (mercifully briefly) a team of programmers tried to get a database installed and running with help from a couple of contractors rather than full-time Oracle professionals. This was an indescribably miserable experience for everyone concerned, with data corruption and bizarre server issues on a daily basis. The minute a real DBA and PL/SQL programmer came in, the situation improved immeasurably — ten-second queries became half-second queries, and so on. There's a reason that these professionals make the big bucks, and we can assure you that you don't want to learn why the hard way.

Shared development databases

Due to the cost and complexity of the database, you will almost certainly need to limit the number of separate development instances in the office. This means that if all your developers are working against one development database that gets corrupted or otherwise goes down, the whole team will be out of commission until the problem can be resolved. On the other hand, MySQL and SQL Server make it easy for every developer to run a local instance if necessary.

And don't even *think* about cheating on your licenses — an Oracle software license audit is nothing you want to experience.

Limited schema changes

Lighter-weight databases make it possible to make schema changes on-the-fly — even in production. In Oracle, this is not a good idea. It's more difficult to add new database-driven features quickly because of the time and planning necessary to successfully create schema changes. With Oracle you really need to design the entire schema in advance, as you're supposed to do but never quite take the time to complete.

Tools (or lack thereof)

Be prepared to invest significantly in tools. Almost no tools are available on the market to help you with Oracle from a PHP platform specifically. More generally, Oracle is not interested in data sets smaller than a few tens of thousands of records; and many of the tools available are not really worth running on data sets smaller than that.

Replication and failover

Some database servers, like MySQL, work best in clusters with one master handling writes while a bunch of slaves serve up reads. This means that, for maximum efficiency, MySQL code should be written to take advantage of multiple connections on a single page — each MySQL function specifying a particular resource handle, for instance.

Oracle, however, works best in a single monolithic instance. Remember that eBay grew to be one of the biggest sites on the Web, and suffered many costly site failures, before even beginning to move away from a monolithic database instance. This tends to create a single point of failure model which affects all aspects of deployment — after all, what's the point in having massive redundancy in Web servers when all of them could be struck down by a single hardware problem on the database server? Most importantly for PHP developers, writing code for Oracle will not require you to juggle multiple connections on a per-page basis as there is little to be gained by this practice.

Data caching

One piece of good news is that Oracle can be configured to cache data. This means that if you make the same query over and over for awhile — for instance, you validate the user against the database on every page load — the database will only actually perform the query the first time. On subsequent requests, it will just serve up the result from some cache memory, for a much faster result. This means that you will not have to implement a custom data-caching scheme of your own, which is a very expensive and tricky task.

However, we should mention that lighter-weight databases are rapidly catching up to Oracle's data caching capabilities for small queries. Microsoft SQL Server is reported to have excellent data caching; and MySQL implements it for the first time in version 4.0.1 (in alpha at press time).

Using OCI8 Functions

PHP has two Oracle extensions: Oracle, and OCI8. The Oracle extension is deprecated for versions of Oracle after 7 and should be avoided if at all possible. The OCI8 extension is literally dozens to hundreds of times faster at most queries, and also allows much better handling of cursors. We will not be describing the Oracle extension at all; use OCI8 from the beginning.

If you walk through a couple of typical Oracle queries step by step, you can see that the procedure is a bit different than that for MySQL or SQL Server:

```php
$name = str_replace("'", "''", $name);
$query = "SELECT product_id FROM product WHERE product_name = '$name'";
$stmt = OCIParse($conn, $query);
OCIExecute($stmt, OCI_DEFAULT);
$err_array = OCIError($stmt);
if ($err_array) {
   $err_message = $err_array['message'];
   $$error_str = $err_message;
   OCIFreeStatement($stmt);
} else {
   OCIFetchStatement($stmt, $res, OCI_RETURN_NULLS);
   OCIFreeStatement($stmt);
}
$product_id = $res['PRODUCT_ID'][0];
```

Right away you will notice differences such as string escaping, parsing and executing, memory management, and fetching data sets. We explain these differences in more detail in the sections that follow. Please refer to the preceding code block for all references which do not have their own code examples.

Escaping strings

Remember that Oracle uses Sybase-style string escaping — in other words, it escapes single quotes with a single-quote, not with a backslash. This means that you will have to manually escape every string, since `magic_quotes` has the wrong effect; or you have to set Sybase style magic quotes in your `php.ini` file.

Parsing and executing

In many other databases, you send a SQL query over and pipe, and it returns either a value or an error message. In Oracle, you have an intermediate step where you parse the query for correctness; if your SQL is bad, the query will never be sent to the database. An invalid SQL query will return an Oracle error code via `OCIError()`.

In most cases, you'll move right to executing the query. This is your opportunity to specify a mode for your query, either OCI_COMMIT_ON_SUCCESS or OCI_DEFAULT, which does not auto-commit. We generally do not auto-commit because we like to know when a rollback is necessary, but this is largely a matter of preference. Of course for SELECT statements it doesn't matter which mode you choose because no commitment or rollback is happening anyway. See the section on transactions later in this chapter.

Error reporting

Oracle error reporting is also unique. For one thing, you can specify whether you're asking for a *global-*, *connection-*, or *statement-level* error. A global error is failure to get a connection. A connection error is an invalid SQL statement that chokes at the parse stage — remember, it isn't a statement yet, so it can't be a statement-level error. A statement error involves a problem with a properly parsed statement.

The product of OCIError() is an associative array, where code is the error code and message is a text string.

Memory management

In Oracle, you are expected to do some memory management manually. In particular, it's a good idea to free statement memory when you're done with the statement handle, and cursor memory when you're done with the cursors. Theoretically, all the memory will be reclaimed at the end of every script, but if your scripts are big you might want to do it as you go.

Ask for nulls

If you want null values in your data set, you have to ask for them in the fetch function. Otherwise, Oracle will not return the field name as part of its associative array, and thus an array member you expect to see will not exist. Many other databases will automatically return the null values.

Fetching entire data sets

Oracle has four fetching functions: OCIResult, OCIFetch, OCIFetchInto, and OCIFetchStatement. The first three correspond fairly straightforwardly to the single-column, row, and array fetching functions enjoyed by all other PHP database extensions — but the last is unique to Oracle. It fetches the entire result set into one big array. This can mean less looping and faster access to your data. Of course, you should make sure you are returning a reasonably small result set; otherwise, you can bring PHP to its knees.

All caps

Oracle column names, which become associative array indices, are in all capital letters. You can ask for the field in lowercase, but by the time it comes back from the database it will be in all caps.

```
$query = "SELECT product_name, modified, created FROM product
          WHERE product_id = 1";
$stmt = OCIParse($conn, $query);
OCIExecute($stmt, OCI_DEFAULT);
$err_array = OCIError($stmt);
if ($err_array) {
   $err_message = $err_array['message'];
   $error_str = $err_message;
   OCIFreeStatement($stmt);

} else {
   OCIFetchStatement($stmt, $res)
   OCIFreeStatement($stmt);
   $product_name = $res['PRODUCT_NAME'][0];
   $modified = $res['MODIFIED'][0];
   $created = $res['CREATED'][0];
}
```

Transactionality

Oracle's famous transactionality implies that all INSERT, UPDATE, and DELETE statements
must be committed or rolled back before they will really be stored in the database. You can
commit automatically during the OCIExecute() step, but if you really want an entire string
of queries to succeed or fail together — the essence of transactionality — it's better to commit
by hand when all of them are complete.

```
$query = "DELETE FROM product WHERE product_name = '$product_name'";
$stmt = OCIParse($conn, $query);
OCIExecute($stmt, OCI_DEFAULT);
$err_array = OCIError($stmt);
if ($err_array) {
   $err_message = $err_array['message'];
   $error_str = $err_message;
   OCIFreeStatement($stmt);
   OCIRollback($conn);
} else {
   OCIFreeStatement($stmt);
}

$query = "INSERT INTO product (product_name, modified, created) VALUES
('$product_name', SYSDATE, SYSDATE)";
$stmt = OCIParse($conn, $query);
OCIExecute($stmt, OCI_DEFAULT);
$err_array = OCIError($stmt);
if ($err_array) {
   $err_message = $err_array['message'];
   $error_str = $err_message;
   OCIFreeStatement($stmt);
```

```
   OCIRollback($conn);
} else {
   OCIFreeStatement($stmt);
}

OCICommit($conn);
```

The net effect of this code block will be to ensure that there is only, at most, one row in the database for each product name. If either the DELETE or the INSERT fails, the state of the database will not be changed. You will never have a situation where you have zero or two rows with the same product name. Note the second argument to OCIExecute() is OCI_DEFAULT, which means that statements will not be auto-committed and must, therefore, be committed by hand.

> **CAUTION:** It's very important to remember that commits and rollbacks occur on a *connection*, not on a statement. Everything since the last commit or rollback will be entered into the database when you call OCICommit() or OCIRollback(). You may call it as many times during a script as you like, but generally all the parts of a transaction are committed or rolled back together.

Stored procedures and cursors

Stored procedures are programs that execute on the database. They move some of the programming into the database layer rather than the PHP layer. PHP merely sends data to the function and handles any returned values.

Because you are connecting to a particular compiled program on the database server, you need to establish a more specific kind of connection to the stored procedure. This connection is called a *cursor*, and the process of designating variables for use by the stored procedure is called *binding to a cursor*. Basically you are taking a PHP variable and transforming it into a variable on the Oracle side, or creating a PHP variable, which will contain data from Oracle. Cursors must be executed separately from ordinary Oracle statements.

The code block that follows shows a simple example of stored procedure calling from PHP. In this case, we are executing the stored procedure named get_categories(), which takes no inputs and returns one output, OUT1, which we are binding to the PHP variable name $cursor1.

```
// Call stored procedure get_categories
$request = "begin DEV.get_categories(:OUT1); end;";
$cursor1 = OCINewCursor($conn);
$stmt = OCIParse($conn, $request);
OCIBindByName($stmt, ":OUT1", &$cursor1, -1, OCI_B_CURSOR);
OCIExecute($stmt);
OCIExecute($cursor1);
$err_array = OCIError($conn);
if ($err_array) {
   $err_message = $err_array['message'];
```

```
    echo $err_message;
    OCIFreeCursor($cursor1);
    OCIFreeStatement($stmt);
    OCILogoff($conn);
    exit;
}
while (OCIFetchInto($cursor1, &$cat_array)) {
    $opt_str .= "<OPTION
VALUE=\"".$cat_array[0]."\">".$cat_array[1]."</OPTION>\n";
}
OCIFreeCursor($cursor1);
OCIFreeStatement($stmt);
OCILogoff($conn);
```

It's possible to kick off a stored procedure or Oracle function and walk away, but more often you will be waiting for a result. This result will come on one or more cursors. These cursors, and possibly any other variables that come back to PHP, need to be created by OCINewCursor() and bound to PHP variables using OCIBindByName(). They are not immediately available to PHP otherwise. After that, they can be treated much like statements — their contents can be fetched, and their memory must be freed.

Project: Point Editor

The *product point editor* is a very simple Oracle tool that allows you to edit the data associated with a single item in a product catalog (as for an e-commerce site). Not only does it fetch information that all products share, such as product name and SKU; but it also automatically sweeps up product attribute data for editing. This is data associated with each item, such as price, manufacturer, size, color, and so forth.

Because the attribute information you wish to save for each product varies with the product category — for books you might want to know the author and number of pages, whereas for toys you might want to know recommended age — you cannot simply save this information in the product table, even if it would normally be one-to-one data. To maintain flexibility, each product category (books, toys, and so on.) has a number of attributes associated with it; and then each product is associated with a number of attribute values. The relationships look schematically like this:

```
Category
  category_id
  category_name

Product
  product_id
  product_name
  category_id

Attribute
```

```
  attribute_id
  attribute_name
  category_id

Attribute_value
  attrib_val_id
  attrib_val
  attribute_id

Product_attribute
  product_id
  attrib_val_id
```

The product point editor will query the database for all attributes associated with this product, and construct a series of pull-down menus with all possible attribute values neatly laid out for the editor to select from. If an attribute value is already associated with this product, that value will be pre-selected in the HTML form field.

Listing 19-1 is a file of functions that are used in both the product point editor and the product batch editor in the next section. This file should be saved under the name oci8_funcs.php.

Listing 19-1: Oracle functions for use in other listings (oci8_funcs.php)

```php
<?php

/************************************
 * Functions for Oracle-based tools *
 ************************************/

putenv("ORACLE_HOME=/tools/oracle");


// Use when fetching data from the db
function unescape_quotes($str
{
   $esc_str = str_replace("''", "'", $str);
   $esc2_str = str_replace("\"\"", "\"", $esc_str);
   return $esc2_str;
}


// Use when inserting data into the db
function escape_sq($str)
{
   $esc_str = str_replace("'", "''", $str);
   return $esc_str;
}
```

```php
function escape_html($str)
{
    $gt_str = str_replace("&gt;", ">;", $str);
    $lt_str = str_replace("&lt;", "<", $gt_str);
    $dq_str = str_replace("&quot;", "\"", $lt_str);
    $esc_str = str_replace("&amp;", "&", $dq_str);
    return $esc_str;
}


// Use this one for INSERTs, UPDATEs, and DELETEs
function parse_exec_free($conn, $query, &$error_str)
{
    $stmt = OCIParse($conn, $query);
    OCIExecute($stmt, OCI_DEFAULT);
    $err_array = OCIError($stmt);
    if ($err_array) {
        $err_message = $err_array['message'];
        $$error_str = $err_message;
        OCIFreeStatement($stmt);
        $stmt = FALSE;
    } else {
        OCIFreeStatement($stmt);
        $stmt = TRUE;
    }
    return $stmt;
}


// Use this one for SELECTs
function parse_exec_fetch($conn, $query, &$error_str, &$res, $nulls=0)
{
    $stmt = OCIParse($conn, $query);
    OCIExecute($stmt, OCI_DEFAULT);
    $err_array = OCIError($stmt);
    if ($err_array) {
        $err_message = $err_array['message'];
        $$error_str = $err_message;
        OCIFreeStatement($stmt);
        $stmt = FALSE;
    } else {
        if ($nulls == 1) {
            OCIFetchStatement($stmt, $res, OCI_RETURN_NULLS);
        } else {
            OCIFetchStatement($stmt, $res);
        }
    }
    return $stmt;
}
```

```
// For batch_upload.php, which writes a separate error log
function choke_and_die($conn, $fp, $error_str)
{
   OCIRollback($conn);
   OCILogoff($conn);
   $error_line = $error_str."<BR>\n";
   echo $error_line;
   fwrite($fp, $error_line);
   fwrite($fp, "</HTML>\n");
   fclose($fp);
   exit;
}


// For all nonlogwriting uses (which is most of them)
function die_silently($conn, $error_str)
{
   OCIRollback($conn);
   OCILogoff($conn);
   // You can uncomment these when debugging
   //$error_line = $error_str."<BR>\n";
   //echo $error_line;
   exit;
}


// Excel sometimes adds random quotes around field contents
function unquote($str)
{
   $pos = strpos($str, "\"");
   if ($pos === 0) {
      $qstr = substr($str, 1, -1);
      return trim($qstr);
   } else {
      return trim($str);
   }
}


// Excel sometimes doubles double-quotes in an attempt to close them
function strip_db($str)
{
   $esc_str = str_replace("\"\"", "\"", $str);
   return $esc_str;
}

?>
```

Listing 19-2 is the actual product point editor itself.

Listing 19-2: Product point editor (prod_point.php)

```php
<?php

/*******************************************************
 * This is the product point editor.               *
 * The purpose of this tool is to edit all the data  *
 * associated with a single product.  It will mostly *
 * be used for trivial fixes (e.g., spelling errors) *
 *******************************************************/

include("oci8_funcs.php"); //common functions for Oracle-based tools
$thisDB = "dev";
$thisDBuser = "oci_user";
$thisDBpassword = "sesame";

// ----------------
// EDIT PRODUCT DATA
// ----------------
if($_POST['submit'] == "Submit") {
   // Get a timestamp
   $begin_time = time();
   // Open the pipe
   $conn = OCILogon($thisDBuser, $thisDBpassword, $thisDB) or die("Can't
get a database connection.");

   // UPDATE PRODUCT TABLE
   $product_id = $_POST['product_id'];
   $product_name = escape_sq($_POST['product_name']);
   $sku = escape_sq($_POST['sku']);
   $itemurl = escape_sq($_POST['itemurl']);
   $itemimage = escape_sq($_POST['itemimage']);
   $desc_text = escape_sq($_POST['desc_text']);

   $query = "UPDATE product
            SET product_name = '$product_name',
                sku = '$sku',
                itemurl = '$itemurl',
                itemimage = '$itemimage',
                desc_text = '$desc_text',
                modified = SYSDATE
            WHERE product_id = $product_id";
   $stmt = parse_exec_free($conn, $query, &$error_str);
   if (!$stmt) {
      die_silently($conn, $error_str);
   }
```

```
   // UPDATE PRODUCT_ATTRIB_VAL TABLE
   // First blow away all existing rows for this product
   $query = "DELETE FROM product_attrib_val
           WHERE product_id = $product_id";
   $stmt = parse_exec_free($conn, $query, &$error_str);
   if (!$stmt) {
      die_silently($conn, $error_str);
   }
   if (is_array($_POST['attrib']) && count($_POST['attrib']) > 0) {
      foreach ($_POST['attrib'] as $attrib_id=>$av_id_array) {
         if (is_array($av_id_array) && count($av_id_array) > 0) {
            foreach ($av_id_array as $attrib_val_id) {
               // If attrib value is not Delete All, add new rows
               if ($attrib_val_id != -1) {
                  $query = "INSERT INTO product_attrib_val
(attrib_val_id, product_id, modified, created)
                            VALUES($attrib_val_id, $product_id, SYSDATE,
SYSDATE)";
                  $stmt = parse_exec_free($conn, $query, &$error_str);
                  if (!$stmt) {
                     die_silently($conn, $error_str);
                  }
               }
            }
         }
      }
   }

   OCICommit($conn);
   OCILogoff($conn);

   /*
   // Uncomment this block for debugging
   // Get a second timestamp, and do the math
   $end_time = time();
   echo "DONE!  This operation took ".($end_time - $begin_time) ."
seconds to complete.";
   exit;
   */

   // Redisplay the form
   header("Location:  $PHP_SELF?url=$prod_url");
}


// ---------
// SHOW FORM
// ---------
elseif (!isSet($_POST['submit']) || $_POST['submit'] != "Submit") {
```

```
   set_time_limit(0);
   // Get a timestamp
   $begin_time = time();
   // Open the pipe
   $conn = OCILogon($thisDBuser, $thisDBpassword, $thisDB) or die("Can't
get a database connection.");

   // Get the product data based on a unique URL passed in the GET vars
   $url = $_GET['url'];
   if ($url == "") {
      // If a URL isn't passed, spit out a message and quit
      echo "<HTML>\n<BODY>";
      echo '<P>You need to designate a product to edit by passing a url
like this:
http://localhost/tools/prod_point.php?url=book_PHP4_Bible.</P>';
      echo "</BODY>\n</HTML>";
      exit;
   }
   $query = "SELECT product_id, name, sku, itemurl, itemimage,
desc_text, category_id
            FROM product
            WHERE url = '$url'";
   $stmt = parse_exec_fetch($conn, $query, &$error_str, &$res);
   if (!$stmt) {
      die_silently($conn, $error_str);
   } else {
      OCIFreeStatement($stmt);
      $product_id = $res['PRODUCT_ID'][0];
      $product_name = $res['PRODUCT_NAME'][0];
      $sku = $res['SKU'][0];
      $itemurl = $res['ITEMURL'][0];
      $itemimage = $res['ITEMIMAGE'][0];
      $desc_text = $res['DESC_TEXT'][0];
      $category_id = $res['CATEGORY_ID'][0];
   }


   // Get attributes for all products in this category
   $query = "SELECT attribute_id, attribute_name
            FROM attribute
            WHERE category_id = $category_id";
   $stmt = parse_exec_fetch($conn, $query, &$error_str, &$res1);
   if (!$stmt) {
      die_silently($conn, $error_str);
      exit;
   } else {
      OCIFreeStatement($stmt);
   }
```

```
    if (is_array($res1['ATTRIBUTE_ID']) && count($res1['ATTRIBUTE_ID']) >
0) {
        foreach ($res1['ATTRIBUTE_ID'] as $key=>$attrib_id) {
            $attrib_name = $res1['ATTRIBUTE_NAME'][$key];
            // Get attrib values for this product
            $query = "SELECT product_attrib_val.attrib_val_id
                    FROM product_attrib_val, attrib_val
                    WHERE product_attrib_val.attrib_val_id =
attrib_val.attrib_val_id
                    AND attrib_val.attrib_id = $attrib_id
                    AND product_attrib_val.product_id = $product_id";
            $stmt = parse_exec_fetch($conn, $query, &$error_str, &$res2);
            if (!$stmt) {
                die_silently($conn, $error_str);
            } else {
                OCIFreeStatement($stmt);
                // Get all possible attribute values for this attribute
                // and construct nice pulldown lists
                $query = "SELECT attrib_val_id, name
                        FROM attrib_val
                        WHERE attrib_id = $attrib_id
                        ORDER BY name";
                $stmt = parse_exec_fetch($conn, $query, &$error_str,
&$res3);
                if (!$stmt) {
                    die_silently($conn, $error_str);
                } else {
                    OCIFreeStatement($stmt);
                    // This stuff is for Case 2 below
                    $is_vals = $res2['ATTRIB_VAL_ID'];
                    $num_is_vals = count($is_vals);
                    $poss_vals = $res3['ATTRIB_VAL_ID'];
                    $num_poss_vals = count($poss_vals);
                    $nonmatching = array_diff($poss_vals, $is_vals);

                    if ($num_poss_vals > 0) {
                        foreach ($poss_vals as $av_key=>$avalue_id) {
                            $av_name = $res3['NAME'][$av_key];
                            // Existing values are selected in this list.
                            // Case 0:  if no existing value than don't
highlight any
                            if (!is_array($is_vals) || $num_is_vals == 0) {
                                $av_str .= "<OPTION
VALUE=\"$avalue_id\">$av_name</OPTION>\n";
                            }
                            // Case 1:  single attrib value
                            elseif ($num_is_vals == 1) {
                                if ($is_vals[0] == $avalue_id) {
```

```
                                    $av_str .= "<OPTION VALUE=\"$avalue_id\"
SELECTED>$av_name</OPTION>\n";
                    } else {
                        $av_str .= "<OPTION
VALUE=\"$avalue_id\">$av_name</OPTION>\n";
                    }
                }
                // Case 2:  multiple attrib values
                // A bit messy because I have to avoid multiple
                // nonmatching options.
                elseif ($num_is_vals > 1) {
                    foreach ($is_vals as $avid) {
                        if ($avid == $avalue_id) {
                            $av_array[] = "<OPTION
VALUE=\"$avalue_id\" SELECTED>$av_name</OPTION>";
                        }
                    }
                    if (count($nonmatching) > 0) {
                        foreach ($nonmatching as $avid){
                            if ($avid == $avalue_id) {
                                $av_array[] = "<OPTION
VALUE=\"$avalue_id\">$av_name</OPTION>";
                            }
                        }
                    }
                    $av_str = implode("\n", $av_array);
                }
            }
        }
    }
    $attrib_str .= "$attrib_name ($num_is_vals):  <SELECT
NAME=\"attrib[$attrib_id][]\" SIZE=5 MULTIPLE>\n<OPTION VALUE='-
1'>Delete All</OPTION>\n$av_str</SELECT><BR><BR>\n";
    unset($av_array);
    unset($av_str);
    }
    }
}
OCILogoff($conn);


// ------------
// DISPLAY FORM
// ------------
$php_self = $_SERVER['PHP_SELF']; // Superglobals don't work with
heredoc
$form_str = <<< EOFORMSTR
<HTML>
<HEAD>
```

```
<TITLE>Product Point Editor</TITLE>
<STYLE>
<!--
.header     {font-family: verdana, arial, sans-serif; font-size: 14pt;
font-weight: bold; color: #000000; text-align: left}
.subheader    {font-family: verdana, arial, sans-serif; font-size: 12pt;
font-weight: bold; color: #000000; background: #ebeef1; text-align:
left}
-->
</STYLE>
</HEAD>

<BODY BGCOLOR="#FFFFFF">
<P class="header">Product point editor</P>

<P>The database is <B>$thisDB</B></P>

<P><B>PRODUCT DATA</B></P>
<FORM ACTION="$php_self" METHOD="post">
<INPUT TYPE=HIDDEN NAME="product_id" VALUE="$product_id">
Name:  <INPUT TYPE=TEXT NAME="product_name" SIZE=30
VALUE="$product_name"><BR><BR>
SKU #:  <INPUT TYPE=TEXT NAME="sku" SIZE=70 VALUE="$sku"><BR><BR>
Item URL:  <INPUT TYPE=TEXT NAME="itemurl" SIZE=70
VALUE="$itemurl"><BR><BR>
Item Image:  <INPUT TYPE=TEXT NAME="itemimage" SIZE=70
VALUE="$itemimage"><BR><BR>
Description:  <TEXTAREA NAME="desc_text" COLS=50
ROWS=5>$desc_text</TEXTAREA><BR><BR>

<P><B>ATTRIBUTES</B></P>
$attrib_str
<INPUT TYPE=SUBMIT NAME="submit" VALUE="Submit">
</FORM>
</BODY>
</HTML>
EOFORMSTR;
   echo $form_str;

   // Get a second timestamp, and do the math
   $end_time = time();
   echo "DONE!  This operation took ".($end_time - $begin_time) ."
seconds to complete.<BR>\n";
}

?>
```

For single product editing, a PHP form that makes a direct connection to the Oracle database is not noticeably slower than one that employs a stored procedure. This tool also has the advantage that it can be altered by a PHP developer alone, whereas use of a stored procedure usually also requires time from a PL/SQL programmer.

Project: Batch Editor

To edit data for more than one product at a time, you might want to use stored procedures. This tool, the *product batch editor*, has two main parts. A script called header_download.php downloads the attributes for a particular category to a spreadsheet. A corresponding script called batch_upload_new.php allows the user to upload data from a spreadsheet to the server, where it is loaded into the database. This is the simplest use of stored procedures.

This is the first stored procedure called in header_download.php. It is called get_categories.sql, and it merely downloads a complete list of all the product categories in this schema.

Listing 19-3: Stored procedure (get_categories.sql)

```
CREATE OR REPLACE PROCEDURE get_categories(
  category_list_out OUT pack.my_targets)
IS

BEGIN
  OPEN category_list_out FOR
    SELECT category_id, category_url
    FROM CATEGORY
    ORDER BY category_url;
END;
/
show errors
```

After you use the form to select a category, header_download.php calls the stored procedure called get_cat_header shown in the file that follows. This takes the category ID as an input and returns two cursors: one consisting of some common product fields, and the other consisting of attribute types associated with this category.

Listing 19-4: A second stored procedure (header_download.php)

```
create or replace procedure get_cat_header(
    category_id_in INTEGER,
    cat_header_out OUT pack.my_targets,
    cat_attrib_out OUT pack.my_targets,
IS
    v_action VARCHAR2(2) := '01';
BEGIN
    IF category_id_in is NULL THEN
      OPEN cat_header_out for select NULL from DUAL;
      OPEN cat_attrib_out for select NULL from DUAL;
```

```
    END IF;

    open cat_header_out for
      SELECT
      column_name,
      column_display_name,
      column_order
      FROM
      event_table_columns
      WHERE
      table_name = 'product'
      ORDER BY column_order;

  open cat_attrib_out for
    SELECT attribute_id, attribute_name
    FROM attribute
    WHERE category_id = category_id_in;
END;
/
show errors
```

This is `header_download.php`, which shows the form to call both stored procedures.

Listing 19-5: Form to call stored procedures (header_download.php)

```php
<?php

/*********************************************
 * New product download attributes script. *
 * The purpose of this tool is to download  *
 * a spreadsheet with the product data       *
 * header.  Editors will use this to add     *
 * new items to a category.  Use script      *
 * batch_upload_new.php to upload data.       *
 *********************************************/

include("oci8_funcs.php"); //common functions for Oracle tools
$thisDB = "dev";
$thisDBuser = "oci_user";
$thisDBpassword = "sesame";

// Open the pipe
$conn = OCILogon($thisDBuser, $thisDBpassword, $thisDB);


// ----------------------
// GET THE CATEGORY HEADER
// ----------------------
if ($_POST['submit'] == "Add") {
   // Call stored procedure for this category
   $cat_id_in = $_POST['cat_id'];
```

```php
    $request = "begin DEV.get_cat_header($cat_id_in, :OUT1, :OUT2);
end;";
    $cursor1 = OCINewCursor($conn);
    $cursor2 = OCINewCursor($conn);
    $stmt = OCIParse($conn, $request);
    OCIBindByName($stmt, ":OUT1", &$cursor1, -1, OCI_B_CURSOR);
    OCIBindByName($stmt, ":OUT2", &$cursor2, -1, OCI_B_CURSOR);
    OCIExecute($stmt);
    OCIExecute($cursor1);
    OCIExecute($cursor2);
    $err_array = OCIError($conn);
    if ($err_array) {
        $err_message = $err_array['message'];
        echo $err_message;
        OCIFreeCursor($cursor1);
        OCIFreeCursor($cursor2);
        OCIFreeStatement($stmt);
        OCILogoff($conn);
        exit;
    }
    while (OCIFetchInto($cursor1,&$data1)) {
        $p_array[] = $data1[1];
    }
    while (OCIFetchInto($cursor2,&$data2)) {
        $a_array[] = $data2[1]."|".$data2[0];
    }
    OCIFreeCursor($cursor1);
    OCIFreeCursor($cursor2);
    OCIFreeStatement($stmt);
    OCILogoff($conn);
    // ASSEMBLE THE DOWNLOAD
    $init_p_str = implode("\t", $p_array);
    $p_str = str_replace("CATEGORY_ID", $cat_id_in, $init_p_str);
    if (count($a_array) > 0) {
        $a_str = implode("\t", $a_array);
    }
    $full_header = implode("\t", array($p_str, $a_str));

    // SEND THE FILE
    $header_file = 'header.xls.Z';
    $zp = gzopen($header_file, "w+");
    gzwrite($zp, $full_header);
    gzclose($fp);
    header("Location:  header.xls.Z");
    // For IE5.x, this is the correct way to trigger a file download
    // -- by simply directing the browser to download a file type
    // that the browser cannot open
}
```

```php
// ----------------
// CHOOSE A CATEGORY
// ----------------
elseif (!isSet($_POST['submit'])) {
   // Call stored procedure get_categories
   $request = "begin DEV.get_categories(:OUT1); end;";
   $cursor1 = OCINewCursor($conn);
   $stmt = OCIParse($conn, $request);
   OCIBindByName($stmt, ":OUT1", &$cursor1, -1, OCI_B_CURSOR);
   OCIExecute($stmt);
   OCIExecute($cursor1);
   $err_array = OCIError($conn);
   if ($err_array) {
       $err_message = $err_array['message'];
       echo $err_message;
       OCIFreeCursor($cursor1);
       OCIFreeStatement($stmt);
       OCILogoff($conn);
       exit;
   }
   while (OCIFetchInto($cursor1, &$cat_array)) {
       $opt_str .= "<OPTION
VALUE=\"".$cat_array[0]."\">".$cat_array[1]."</OPTION>\n";
   }
   OCIFreeCursor($cursor1);
   OCIFreeStatement($stmt);
   OCILogoff($conn);


   // CHOOSE CATEGORY FORM
   $php_self = $_SERVER['PHP_SELF']; // Superglobals don't work with
heredoc
   $form_str = <<< EOFORMSTR
<HTML>
<HEAD>
<TITLE>Batch Editor New: Download</TITLE>
<STYLE>
<!--
.header    {font-family: verdana, arial, sans-serif; font-size: 14pt;
font-weight: bold; color: #000000; text-align: left}
.subheader    {font-family: verdana, arial, sans-serif; font-size: 12pt;
font-weight: bold; color: #000000; background: #ebeef1; text-align:
left}
.ftrnote    {font-family: verdana, arial, sans-serif; font-size: 8pt;
color: #000000; text-align: left}
LI    {line-height:200%}
-->
</STYLE>
```

```
</HEAD>

<BODY BGCOLOR="#FFFFFF">
<P class="header">Batch editor new:  download</P>

<P>The database is <B>$thisDB</B></P>

<FORM ACTION="$php_self" METHOD="POST">
<SELECT NAME="cat_id" SIZE=1>
<OPTION VALUE="-1" SELECTED>Choose one</OPTION>
$opt_str
</SELECT><BR>
<INPUT TYPE=SUBMIT NAME="submit" VALUE="Add">
</FORM>
</BODY>
</HTML>
EOFORMSTR;

    echo $form_str;
}
?>
```

The result of `header_download.php` is a zipped spreadsheet with one row. It resembles the first row of the image in Figure 19-1 that follows:

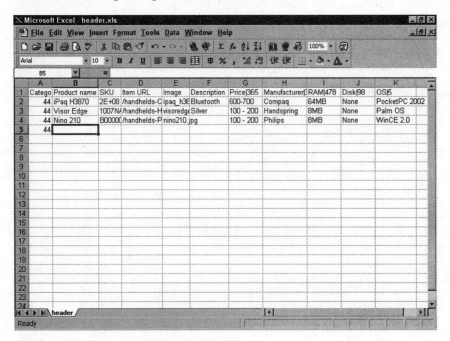

Figure 19-1: Category header with some data filled in

We have filled in some data in the preceding figure, using the header row as a guide.

Note that the attributes at the top have names like "`Price|376`". The number is the attribute ID, which will be used when we upload data with Listing 19-6, `batch_upload_new.php`. This script enables the user to upload a spreadsheet to the server, using the normal HTML file upload capability of his browser. The server will then convert the spreadsheet into rows of data, which are inserted into the database.

Listing 19-6: Spreadsheet upload script (batch_upload_new.php)

```php
<?php

/*******************************************
 * New product batch upload script. The   *
 * purpose of this tool is to upload a     *
 * spreadsheet with new product data.      *
 * Editors will use this to add new items *
 * to a category.  Use script              *
 * header_download.php to get attributes. *
 *******************************************/

include("oci8_funcs.php"); //common functions for Oracle tools
$thisDB = "dev";
$thisDBuser = "oci_user";
$thisDBpassword = "sesame";


// HEADER
$header_str = <<< ENDOFHEADER
<HTML>
<HEAD>
<TITLE>Batch Editor New: Upload</TITLE>
<STYLE>
<!--
.header    {font-family: verdana, arial, sans-serif; font-size: 14pt;
font-weight: bold; color: #000000; text-align: left}
.subheader    {font-family: verdana, arial, sans-serif; font-size: 12pt;
font-weight: bold; color: #000000; background: #ebeef1; text-align:
left}
-->
</STYLE>
</HEAD>

<BODY BGCOLOR="#FFFFFF">
<P class="header">Batch editor new: upload</P>

<P>The database is <B>$thisDB</B></P>
ENDOFHEADER;
echo $header_str;
```

```
// ADD NEW PRODUCTS
if($_POST['submit'] == "Upload") {
   set_time_limit(0);
   echo "<P>Check the error log (<A
HREF\"upload_log.html\">upload_log.html</A>) for problems.</P>";

   // Copy uploaded file to a specific directory
   $tempfile = $HTTP_POST_FILES[file][tmp_name];
   $localfile = $HTTP_POST_FILES[file][name];
   if(!copy($tempfile, "/tmp/$localfile")) {
      echo "<P>Error writing file to upload directory.
Quitting.</P>\n";
      exit;
   }

   // Start an error log
   $error_log = 'upload_log.html';
   $fp = fopen($error_log, "w+") or die("Can't open error log.");
   fwrite($fp, "<HTML>\n");

   // Open the pipe
   $conn = OCILogon($thisDBuser, $thisDBpassword, $thisDB) or die("Can't
get a database connection.  Whine at a webdev.");

   // Get a timestamp
   $begin_time = time();

   // Read in the data file as an array
   $uarray = file("/tmp/$localfile");

   // Parse the header for cat_id and attributes
   $header = array_shift($uarray);
   $harray = explode("\t", $header);
   $num_ha = count($harray);
   $cat_id = $harray[0];
   $attrib_array = array();
   for($i = 6; $i <= ($num_ha - 1); $i++) {
      $a_array = explode("|", $harray[$i]);
      $attrib_array[] = $a_array[1];
   }
   $num_attribs = count($attrib_array);

   $error_str = "";
   $res = array();
   // Get all the attrib values and stick them in a multidimensional
array
   foreach($attrib_array as $attrib) {
```

```
      $query = "SELECT attrib_value_id, name
                FROM attrib_value
                WHERE attrib_id = $attrib";
      $stmt = parse_exec_fetch($conn, $query, &$error_str, &$res);
      if (!$stmt) {
         choke_and_die($conn, $fp, $error_str);
      } else {
  foreach($res['NAME'] as $key => $val) {
     $ava[$attrib][$val] = $res['ATTRIB_VALUE_ID'][$key];
  }
         OCIFreeStatement($stmt);
      }
   }
   reset($attrib_array);

   // Shove the data down the pipe.
   foreach ($uarray as $valrow) {
      // Get a fresh product id from Oracle
      $query = "begin :new_id := newid('product'); end;";
      $sth = OCIParse($conn, $query);
      OCIBindByName($sth, ":new_id", &$new_id, 200);
      OCIExecute($sth);
      if (!$sth) {
         choke_and_die($conn, $fp, $error_str);
      } else {
         $rowid = $new_id;
         OCIFreeStatement($sth);
      }

      // Format new product data.
      $val_array = explode("\t", $valrow);
      $prod_name = unquote($val_array[1]);
      $prod_name = strip_db($prod_name);
      $prod_name = escape_sq($prod_name);
echo "Working on $prod_name<BR>\n";
      $sku = unquote($val_array[2]);
      $itemurl = unquote($val_array[3]);
      $itemimage = unquote($val_array[4]);
      $desc = unquote($val_array[5]);
      $desc = escape_sq($desc);

      // PRODUCT
      $query = "INSERT INTO product (product_id, name, sku, itemurl,
itemimage, desc, created, modified, category_id) VALUES ($rowid,
'$prod_name', '$sku', '$itemurl', '$itemimage', '$desc', SYSDATE,
SYSDATE, $cat_id)";
      $stmt = parse_exec_free($conn, $query, &$error_str);
      if (!$stmt) {
         choke_and_die($conn, $fp, $error_str);
```

```php
    }

    // PRODUCT_ATTRIB_VALUE
    for ($i = 6; $i <= (6 + $num_attribs - 1); $i++) {
        $av = unquote($val_array[$i]);
        if($av != "") {
            $temp_q = explode("|", $av);
            foreach($temp_q as $av) {
                $av = unasterisk($av);
                $av = escape_sq($av);
                $akey = $i - 6;
                $attrib_id = $attrib_array[$akey];
                if($ava[$attrib_id][$av]) {
                    $pav = $ava[$attrib_id][$av];
                    $query = "INSERT INTO product_attrib_value
(attrib_value_id, product_id, created, modified) VALUES($pav, $rowid,
SYSDATE, SYSDATE)";
                    $stmt = parse_exec_free($conn, $query, &$error_str);
                    if (!$stmt) {
                        choke_and_die($conn, $fp, $error_str);
                    }
                }
            }
        } else {
            //echo "Null attrib value.<BR>\n";
        }
    }
}

    // Get a second timestamp, and do the math
    $end_time = time();
    echo "DONE!  This operation took ".($end_time - $begin_time) ."
seconds to complete.";

    OCICommit($conn);
    OCILogoff($conn);
    fwrite($fp, "</HTML>\n");
    fclose($fp);
}


// SHOW FILE UPLOAD FORM
elseif($_POST['submit'] != "Upload") {
    $upload_str = <<< ENDOFUPLOAD
<P>Upload new product data:</P>
<FORM ACTION="$PHP_SELF" METHOD="post" ENCTYPE="multipart/form-data">
<INPUT TYPE=HIDDEN NAME="max_file_size" VALUE="1000000">
<INPUT TYPE=FILE NAME="file" SIZE=50><BR><BR>
```

```
<INPUT TYPE=SUBMIT NAME="submit" VALUE="Upload">
</FORM>
ENDOFUPLOAD;
    echo $upload_str;
}

?>
</BODY>
</HTML>
```

Notice particularly in this script how we call for a new product ID using Oracle's incrementor (search for the comment `// Get a fresh product id from Oracle`). This is in marked contrast to, for instance, MySQL where the auto-incrementor is generally built into a column's definition and can be kicked off by merely entering a null value in that column.

Summary

Oracle is, for better or worse, the biggest name in enterprise databases. The PHP OCI8 extension is quite fast and powerful, offering some functionality not found in most other database extensions. However, the use of Oracle has many implications and should not be undertaken lightly.

There are significant differences in the syntax of Oracle functions versus those of lighter-weight databases. These differences include so-called Sybase-style string escaping, separate parsing and execution steps, manual memory management, cursors, transactionality, and the capability to fetch data sets into one big array. We demonstrate the use of all these Oracle features in two examples: a single-product data editor and a mass data-entering tool.

## Chapter 20

Displaying Queries InTables

In This Chapter

♦ Mapping database tables to HTML tables

♦ Reusable functions for table display using SELECT

♦ Displaying complex relational table data

♦ Creating relational data using INSERT

Much of the point of PHP is to help you translate between a back-end database and its front-end presentation on the Web. Data can be viewed, added, removed, and tweaked as a result of your Web user's keystrokes and mouse clicks.

For most of this chapter, we restrict ourselves to ways to use PHP to *look* at the contents of a database without altering it, using only the SELECT statement from SQL and displaying the results in HTML tables. We use a single database example to show different strategies, including some handy reusable functions. Finally, we look at code to create the sample data shown in the display examples, using the INSERT statement.

The two big productivity points from this chapter are:

♦ *Reuse functions* in simple cases. The problem of database table display shows up over and over in database-enabled site design. If the display is not complicated, you should be able to throw the same simple function at the problem rather than reinventing the wheel with each PHP page you write.

♦ *Choose between techniques* in complex cases. You may find yourself wanting to pull out a complex combination of information from different tables (which, of course, is part of the point of using a relational database to begin with). You may not be able to map this onto a simple reusable function, but there aren't that many novel solutions either — get to know the alternatives, and you can decide how to trade off efficiency, readability, and your own effort.

NOTE: This chapter uses the MySQL database and functions exclusively, but the display strategies should be directly transferable to almost any SQL-compliant database supported by PHP.

HTML Tables and Database Tables

First of all, some terminology — unfortunately, both relational databases and HTML scripting use the term *table*, but the term means very different things in the two cases. A *database table* persistently stores information in columns, which have predefined names and types so that the information in them can be recovered later. An *HTML table* is a construct that tells the browser to lay out the table's arbitrary HTML contents in a rectangular array in the browser window. We'll try to always make it clear which kind of table we are talking about.

One-to-one mapping

HTML tables are really constructed out of rows (the `<TR></TR>` construct), and columns have no independent existence — each row has some number of table datum items (the `<TD></TD>` construct), which will produce a nice rectangular array only if there are the same number of TDs for every TR. (There is no corresponding `<TC>` construct that lets you display by column first.) By contrast, *fields* (a.k.a. *columns*) in database tables are the more primary entity — defining a table means defining the fields, and then you can add as many rows as you like. In this chapter, we will focus on printing out tables and queries in such a way that each database field prints in its own HTML column, simply because there are usually more database rows than database fields, and people are more used to up-and-down scrolling than left-to-right scrolling. If you find yourself wanting to map database fields to HTML rows, it is a simple inversion exercise.

The simplest case of display is where the structure of a database table or query *does* correspond to the structure of the HTML table we want to display — the database entity has m columns and n rows, and we'd like to display an m-by-n rectangular grid in the user's browser window, with all the cells filled in appropriately.

Example: A single-table displayer

So let's write a simple translator that queries the database for the contents of a single table and displays the results on screen. Here's the top-down outline of how the code will get the job done:

1. Establish a database connection.
2. Construct a query to send to the database.
3. Send the query and hold on to the result identifier that is returned.
4. Using the result identifier, find out how many columns (fields) there are in each row.
5. Start an HTML table.
6. Loop through the database result rows, printing a `<TR></TR>` pair to make a corresponding HTML table row.
7. In each row, retrieve the successive fields and display them wrapped in a `<TD></TD>` pair.

8. Close off the HTML table.

9. Close the database connection.

Finally, we'd like to wrap all the preceding steps up into a handy function that we can use whenever we want to. Also, for reasons of efficiency, we don't want to include the first and last steps of creating and closing the database connection in the function — we may want to use such a function more than once per page, and it wouldn't make sense to open and close the connection each time. Instead, we'll assume we have a connection already and pass the connection to the function along with the table name.

Such a function is shown in Listing 20-1, embedded in a complete PHP page that uses the function to display the contents of a couple of tables.

Listing 20-1: A table displayer

```php
<?php
include("/home/phpbook/phpbook-vars.inc");
$global_dbh = mysql_connect($hostname, $username, $password);
mysql_select_db($db, $global_dbh);

function display_db_table($tablename, $connection)
{
  $query_string = "select * from $tablename";
  $result_id = mysql_query($query_string, $connection);
  $column_count = mysql_num_fields($result_id);

  print("<TABLE BORDER=1>\n");
  while ($row = mysql_fetch_row($result_id))
    {
      print("<TR ALIGN=LEFT VALIGN=TOP>");
      for ($column_num = 0;
           $column_num < $column_count;
           $column_num++)
        print("<TD>$row[$column_num]</TD>\n");
      print("</TR>\n");
    }
    print("</TABLE>\n");
}
?>


<HTML>
<HEAD>
<TITLE>Cities and countries</TITLE>
</HEAD>
<BODY>

<TABLE><TR><TD>
<?php display_db_table("country", $global_dbh); ?>
```

```
</TD><TD>
<?php display_db_table("city", $global_dbh); ?>
</TD></TR></TABLE></BODY></HTML>
```

Some things to notice about this script:

♦ Although the script refers to specific database tables, the `display_db_table()` function itself is general. You could put the function definition in an `include` file and then use it anywhere on your site.

♦ The first thing the script does is load in an `include` file that contains variable assignments for the database name, database username, and database password. It then uses those variables to connect to MySQL and then to choose the desired database. (The fact that this file is located outside the publicly available Web hierarchy makes it *slightly* more secure than just including that information in your code.)

♦ In the function itself, we chose to use a `while` loop for printing rows, and a `for` loop to print the individual items. We could as easily have used a bounded `for` loop for both and recovered the number of rows with `mysql_num_rows()`.

♦ *The main `while` loop reflects a very common idiom, which exploits the fact that the value of a PHP assignment statement is the value assigned. The variable $row is assigned to the result of the function `mysql_fetch_row()`, which will be either an array of values from that row or a false value if there are no more rows. If we're out of rows, then $row is false, which means the value of the whole expression is false, which means that the `while` loop terminates.

♦ *We put line breaks (\n) at the end of selected lines, so that the HTML source would have a readable structure when printed or viewed as source from the browser. Notice that these breaks are not HTML line breaks (<BR>) and do not affect the look of the resulting Web page. (In fact, if you want to make it annoying for someone else to scrutinize the HTML you generate, don't put breaks in at all!)

The sample tables

To see the Listing 20-1 script in action, see Figure 20-1, which shows the displayed contents of the Country and City sample tables. These tables have the following structure:

```
Country:
    ID int (auto-incremented primary key)
    continent varchar(50)
    countryname varchar(50)
City:
    ID int (auto-incremented primary key)
    countryID int
    cityname varchar(50)
```

Think of these tables as being a rough draft of the database for an eventual online almanac. They employ our usual convention of always having one field per table called ID, which is a primary key and has successive integers assigned to it automatically for each new row. Although you can't tell for sure from the preceding description, the tables have one "relation" embodied in their structure — the `countryID` field of the `City` table is matched up with the `ID` field of the `Country` table, representing which country the city belongs to. (If you were designing a real almanac database, you would want to take this one step further and break the `Country` table into a relational pair of `Country` and `Continent` tables.)

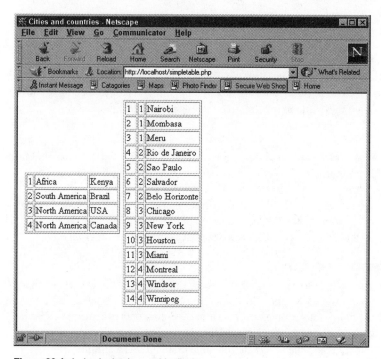

Figure 20-1: A simple database table display

> **CROSS-REFERENCE:** To see how we created these tables and populated them with sample data, see the "Creating the Sample Tables" section at the end of this chapter.

Improving the displayer

Our first version of this function has some limitations: It works with a single table only, does no error-checking, and is very bare-bones in its presentation. We'll address these problems one by one and then fix them in one fell revision. (If you want to look ahead, the new-and-improved version of the function is in Listing 20-2.)

Displaying column headers

Our first version of a database table displayer simply displays all the table cells, without any labeling of what the different fields are. It's conventional in HTML to use the <TH> element for column and/or row headers — in most browsers and styles, this displays as a bold table cell. One improvement we can make is to optionally display column headers that are based on the names of the table fields themselves. To actually retrieve those names, we can use the function mysql_field_name().

Error-checking

Our original version of the code assumes that we have written it correctly, and also that our database server is up and functioning normally — if either of these is not the case, then we will run into puzzling errors. We can partially address this by appending a call to die() to the actual database queries — if they fail, an informative message will be printed.

Cosmetic issues

Another source of dissatisfaction with our simple table-displayer is that it always has the same look. It would be nice, at a minimum, to control whether table borders are displayed. The simple solution we will use in our new function is just to permit passing in a string of arguments that will be spliced into the HTML table definition. This is a pretty crude form of style control that style-sheet proponents would discourage, but it will permit us to directly specify some elements of the table's look without writing an entirely new function.

Displaying arbitrary queries

Finally, it would be nice to be able to exploit our relational database and display the results of complex queries rather than just single tables. Actually, our single-table displayer has an arbitrary query embedded in it — it just happens that it is hard-coded as select * from table, where table is the supplied table name. So let us transform our simple table-displayer into a query-displayer and then recreate the table displayer as a simple wrapper around the query displayer. These two functions, complete with the cosmetic improvements and better error-checking, are shown in Listing 20-2.

Listing 20-2: A query displayer

```php
<?php
include("/home/phpbook/phpbook-vars.inc");
$global_dbh = mysql_connect($hostname, $username, $password)
              or die("Could not connect to database");

mysql_select_db($db, $global_dbh)
  or die("Could not select database");

function display_db_query($query_string, $connection,
                          $header_bool, $table_params)
{
```

```
  // perform the database query
  $result_id = mysql_query($query_string, $connection)
              or die("display_db_query:" . mysql_error());

  // find out the number of columns in result
  $column_count = mysql_num_fields($result_id)
                  or die("display_db_query:" . mysql_error());

  // TABLE form includes optional HTML arguments passed
  //   into function
  print("<TABLE $table_params >\n");

  // optionally print a bold header at top of table
  if ($header_bool)
  {
    print("<TR>");
    for ($column_num = 0;
         $column_num < $column_count;
         $column_num++)
    {
      $field_name =
          mysql_field_name($result_id, $column_num);
      print("<TH>$field_name</TH>");
      }
      print("</TR>\n");
  }
  // print the body of the table
  while ($row = mysql_fetch_row($result_id))
  {
    print("<TR ALIGN=LEFT VALIGN=TOP>");
    for ($column_num = 0;
         $column_num < $column_count;
         $column_num++)
    {
        print("<TD>$row[$column_num]</TD>\n");
      }
    print("</TR>\n");
  }
  print("</TABLE>\n");    }

function display_db_table($tablename, $connection,
                          $header_bool, $table_params)
{
  $query_string = "select * from $tablename";
  display_db_query($query_string, $connection,
                  $header_bool, $table_params);
}
?>
```

```
<HTML><HEAD><TITLE>Countries and cities</TITLE></HEAD>
<BODY>
<TABLE><TR><TD>
<?php display_db_table("country", $global_dbh,
                       TRUE, "BORDER=2"); ?>
</TD><TD>
<?php display_db_table("city", $global_dbh,
                       TRUE, "BORDER=2"); ?>
</TD></TR></TABLE></BODY></HTML>
```

The result of using this code on the same database contents is shown in Figure 20-2. The only visible difference is the column header. Splitting the functions apart means that we also have a new function in our bag of tricks — we could do the same kind of display with an arbitrary query string that joins data from different tables.

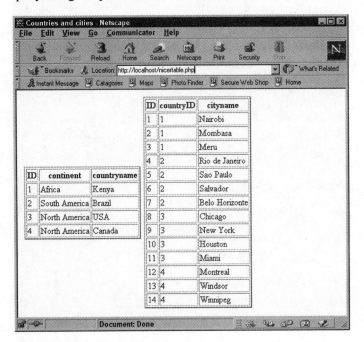

Figure 20-2: Using the query displayer

Complex Mappings

So far in this chapter, we've enjoyed a very nice and simple-minded correspondence between query result sets and HTML tables — every row in the result set corresponds to a row in the table, and the structure of the code is simply two nested loops. Unfortunately, life isn't often this simple, and sometimes the structure of the HTML table we want to display has a complex relationship to the relational structure of the database tables.

VIEWS AND STORED PROCEDURES

Our query-displayer assumes a particular division of labor between the PHP code and the database system itself — the PHP code sends off an arbitrary query string, which the database responds to by setting up a result set. In particular, this means that the database system has to parse that query and then figure out the best way to go about retrieving the results. This is part of what can make querying a database a mildly expensive operation.

In cases where your code may construct novel queries on-the-fly, this is the best you can hope for. However, Some databases offer ways to set up queries in advance, which gives the database system a chance to preoptimize how it handles the query. One such construct is called a *view* under MS SQL Server and some other RDMSs — after you have set up a query as a named view, it can be treated just like a real table. A related idea is the *stored procedure*, which is like a view that also accepts runtime arguments that are spliced into the query. In general, if you realize that you are suffering from slow query performance, you may want to investigate what optimizations like this your particular RDBMS makes available.

Multiple queries versus complex printing

Let's say that, rather than displaying our sample `City` and `Country` tables individually, we want to match them up in a tabular display.

We can easily write a `SELECT` statement that joins these tables appropriately:

```
select country.continent, country.countryname,
       city.cityname
from country, city
where city.countryID = country.ID
order by continent, countryname, cityname
```

Now, this would be a handy place to use our query-displayer function — all we have to do is send it the preceding statement as a string, and it will print out a table of cities matched up with their continents and countries. However, if we do this, we will see an individual HTML table row for each city, and the continent and country will print each time — for example, we'll see `North America` printed several times. Instead, what if we want one name matched with many titles? This is a case where the structure of what we print differs from the structure of the most convenient query.

If we want to do a more complex mapping, we have a choice: We can throw database queries at the problem, or we can write more complex display code. Let's look at each option in turn. (For each of these examples, we'll be moving away from the reusable generality of the functions we wrote earlier, toward functions that address a particular display problem.)

A multiple-query example

If we want to print just one HTML row per country, we can make a query for the countries, and then make another query for the relevant cities in each trip through a country row. A function written using this strategy is shown in Listing 20-3.

Listing 20-3: A display with multiple queries

```php
<?php
include("/home/phpbook/phpbook-vars.inc");
/* open database connection */
$global_dbh = mysql_connect($hostname, $username, $password)
            or die("Could not connect to database");
mysql_select_db($db, $global_dbh)
  or die("Could not select database");

function display_cities($db_connection)
{
  /* Displays table of cities and countries */
  $country_query = "select id, continent, countryname
                    from country
                    order by continent, countryname";
  $country_result =
    mysql_query($country_query, $db_connection);

  /* begin table, print hard-coded table header */
  print("<TABLE BORDER=1>\n");
  print("<TR><TH>Continent</TH><TH>Country</TH>
          <TH>Cities</TH></TR>");

  /* loop through countries */
  while ($country_row = mysql_fetch_row($country_result))
    {
      /* set up country info */
      $country_id = $country_row[0];
      $continent = $country_row[1];
      $country_name = $country_row[2];

      print("<TR ALIGN=LEFT VALIGN=TOP>");
      print("<TD>$continent</TD>");
      print("<TD>$country_name</TD>");

      /* begin table cell for city list */
      print("<TD>");
      $city_query = "select cityname from city
                     where countryID = $country_id
                     order by cityname";
      $city_result =
        mysql_query($city_query, $db_connection)
```

```
          OR die(mysql_error());
    /* loop through cities */
    while ($city_row = mysql_fetch_row($city_result))
      {
        $city_name = $city_row[0];
        print("$city_name<BR>");
      }
    /* close city cell and country row */
    print("</TD></TR>");
    }
  print("</TABLE>\n");
}
?>

<HTML>
<HEAD>
<TITLE>Cities by Country</TITLE>
</HEAD>
<BODY>
<?php
  display_cities($global_dbh);
?>
</BODY>
</HTML>
```

The strategy is appealingly simple: There is an outer loop that uses one query to proceed through all the countries, saving the country's name and the primary ID field of each country row. Then for each country, the ID field is used to look up all the cities belonging to that country. Notice the trick of embedding the $countryid variable in the inner query — the query string sent is actually different on each iteration through the country loop.

Simple? Yes. Efficient? Probably not. This code makes a *separate* city query for each country. If there are 500 countries in the database, this function will make 501 separate database queries (the extra one being the enclosing country query).

Your mileage will vary according to how efficient your particular database is in parsing queries and planning query retrieval, but the sum of these queries will certainly take more time than the simple query we started this section with.

A complex printing example

Now let's solve exactly the same problem, but using a different strategy. Instead of multiple queries, we will make a single query and print the resulting rows selectively, so that each HTML table row corresponds to more than one database row (see Listing 20-4). The resulting browser display is exactly the same as in the previous example.

Listing 20-4: A complex display with a single query

```php
<?php
include("/home/phpbook/phpbook-vars.inc");
/* open a single DB connection for this page */
$global_dbh = mysql_connect($hostname, $username, $password)
            or die("Could not connect to database");
mysql_select_db($db, $global_dbh)
            or die("Could not select database");

function display_cities($db_connection)
{
  /*  print table of countries and their cities,
      selectively printing only one HTML table row
      per country */
  $query = "select country.id,
                   country.continent, country.countryname,
                   city.cityname
                   from country, city
                   where country.id = city.countryID
                   order by country.continent,
                            country.countryname,
                            city.cityname";
  $result_id =
     mysql_query($query, $db_connection)
       OR die(mysql_error($query));

  /* begin table, print hard-coded table header */
  print("<TABLE BORDER=1>\n");
   print("<TH>Continent</TH><TH>Country</TH>
           <TH>Cities</TH></TR>");

  /* Initialize the ID for the "previous" country.
     We will rely on the fact that Country.ID is
     numbered beginning with 1, so a previous ID
     value of zero means that the current country
     is the first */
  $old_country_id = 0;

  /* loop through result rows (one per city) */
  while ($row_array = mysql_fetch_row($result_id))
    {
      $country_id = $row_array[0];
      /* if we have a new country */
      if ($country_id != $old_country_id)
        {
          /* set up country info */
          $continent = $row_array[1];
          $country_name = $row_array[2];
```

```
                /* if there was a previous country
                   close the city datum and country row */
                if ($old_country_id != 0)
                  print("</TD></TR>\n");

                /* start a row for the new country,
                   and begin the city table datum */
                print("<TR ALIGN=LEFT VALIGN=TOP>");
                print("<TD>$continent</TD>");
                print("<TD>$country_name</TD><TD>");

                /* the new country is no longer new */
                $old_country_id = $country_id;
              }
          /* the only thing that is printed for every result
             row is the name of a city */
          $city_name = $row_array[3];
          print("$city_name<BR>");
        }
      /* close off final country and table */
      print("</TD></TR></TABLE>");
}
?>
<HTML><HEAD><TITLE>Cities by Country</TITLE></HEAD>
<BODY>
<?php display_cities($global_dbh);
 ?>
</BODY></HTML>
```

This code is somewhat tricky — although it goes through the result rows in order, and everything it prints is grabbed from the current row, it only prints countries when their values have changed (Continents are still printed redundantly).

The change in a country is detected by monitoring the ID field of the country row. A country change is also a signal to print out the HTML necessary to close off the preceding table row and start a new one. Finally, the code must handle printing out the HTML necessary to start the first row and end the last one.

Creating the Sample Tables

Now we will show you the PHP/MySQL code we actually used to create the sample tables. (Such data might more normally be created by interacting only with MySQL, but we decided to respect our book's title by doing it from PHP.) The code (shown in Listing 20-5) is a special-purpose, one-time hack, not a model of style, but it has useful examples of using the SQL INSERT statement.

Listing 20-5: Creating the sample tables

```php
<?php
include("/home/phpbook/phpbook-vars.inc");
$global_dbh = mysql_connect($hostname, $username, $password)
            or die("Could not connect to database");
mysql_select_db($db, $global_dbh)
            or die ("Could not select databased");

function add_new_country($dbh, $continent, $countryname,
                            $city_array)


{
  $country_query =
    "insert into country (continent, countryname)
     values ('$continent', '$countryname')";
  $result_id =  mysql_query($country_query)
               OR die($country_query . mysql_error());
  if ($result_id)
    {
      $countryID = mysql_insert_id($dbh);
      for ($city = current($city_array);
          $city;
          $city = next($city_array))
        {
          $city_query =
            "insert into city (countryID, cityname)
                    values ($countryID, '$city')";
          mysql_query($city_query, $dbh)
            OR die($city_query . mysql_error());
        }
    }
}

function populate_cities_db($dbh)
{
  /* drop tables if they exist -- permits function to be
     tried more than once */
  mysql_query("drop table city", $dbh);
  mysql_query("drop table country", $dbh);

  /* create the tables */
  mysql_query("create table country
                (ID int not null auto_increment primary key,
                 continent varchar(50),
                 countryname varchar(50))",
              $dbh)
              OR die(mysql_error());
  mysql_query("create table city
```

```
                    (ID int not null auto_increment primary key,
                     countryID int not null,
                     cityname varchar(50))",
                $dbh)
                OR die(mysql_error());

   /* store data in the tables */
   add_new_country($dbh, 'Africa', 'Kenya',
           array('Nairobi','Mombasa','Meru'));
   add_new_country($dbh, 'South America', 'Brazil',
           array('Rio de Janeiro', 'Sao Paulo',
                   'Salvador', 'Belo Horizonte'));
   add_new_country($dbh, 'North America', 'USA',
           array('Chicago', 'New York', 'Houston', 'Miami'));
   add_new_country($dbh, 'North America', 'Canada',
           array('Montreal','Windsor','Winnipeg'));

   print("Sample database created<BR>");
}
?>


<HTML><HEAD><TITLE>Creating a sample database</TITLE></HEAD>
<BODY>
<?php populate_cities_db($global_dbh); ?>
</BODY></HTML>
```

You should be able to use this code to recreate the sample database on your development machine, assuming that you have PHP and MySQL configured, and an appropriately located file called phpbook-vars.inc containing username, password, and database-name strings.

Just as in the display examples, this code sends off query strings (with embedded variables), but this time the queries are INSERT statements, which create new table rows. For the most part, the data inserted is just string data passed in to the function, although we chose to pass in an arbitrary number of cities per country by using an array.

The only tricky thing in creating these sample tables is setting up the relational structure. We want each city row to have an appropriate countryID, which should be equal to the actual ID of the appropriate row from the country table. However, these country IDs are automatically assigned in sequence by MySQL and are not under our control. How can we know the right countryID to assign? The answer is in the incredibly handy function mysql_insert_id(), which recovers the ID associated with the last INSERT query made via the given database connection. We insert the new country, recover the ID of the newly created row, and then use that ID in our city insertion queries.

Summary

Database interaction is one of the areas where PHP really shines. One very common use for database-enabled Web code is simply to display database contents attractively. One approach to this kind of display is to map the contents of database tables, or SELECT statements, to corresponding HTML table elements.

When the mapping is simple enough you can employ reusable functions that take arbitrary table names, or SELECT statements, and display them as a grid. When you need a more complicated combination of information from relational tables, you probably need a special-purpose function, but certain tricks recur there as well. One such trick is to craft a SQL statement that returns all the information you need, in the order you want, and selectively print only the nonredundant portions.

Near the end of this chapter, we saw a quick example of populating a set of database tables using INSERT statements. Aside from that, all the techniques in this chapter were read-only, and do not modify the contents of databases at all. In Chapter 21, we'll see how you can get a more intimate connection to your database by combining SQL queries with HTML forms.

Chapter 21

Building Forms from Queries

In This Chapter

♦ HTML forms for use with databases

♦ Basic form submission to a database

♦ Self-submission

♦ Editing data with an HTML form

♦ Data-driven forms

Form handling is one of PHP's very best features. The combination of HTML to construct a data-input form, PHP to handle the data, and a database server to store the data lies at the heart of all kinds of supremely useful Web tasks.

HTML Forms

You already know most of what you need to make good forms to be handled by PHP and a database. There are a few PHP-specific points to brush up on:

♦ Always, always, *always* use a NAME for every data entry element (INPUT, SELECT, TEXTAREA, and so on). These NAME attributes will become PHP variable names — you will not be able to access your values if you do not use a NAME attribute for each one. If your WYSIWYG editor doesn't allow you to do this, you'll need to remember to add these NAME attributes by hand.

♦ A form field NAME does not need to be the same as the corresponding database field name, but it's often a good idea.

♦ You can (and usually should) specify a VALUE rather than let HTML send the default value. Consider substituting a numerical value for a text value if possible, because the database is much slower at matching strings than integers.

♦ The VALUE can be set to data you wish to display in the form.

♦ Remember that you can pass hidden variables from form to form (or page) using the HIDDEN data entry elements. This practice may have negative security implications, but it's often no worse than storing the data in a cookie.

♦ Remember that you can pass multiple variables in an array — but you need to inform the user that this is a possibility.

CROSS-REFERENCE: See Chapter 9 for more information on how to format an HTML form for use with PHP.

Basic Form Submission to a Database

Submitting data to a database via an HTML form is straightforward if the form and form-handler are two separate pages.

Figure 21-1 shows the result of the following code sample, a basic form to insert data into a database.

Figure 21-1: A form to insert data into a database

Listing 21-1, `newsletter_signup.html`, is a simple form with only one input field:

Listing 21-1: A simple form (newsletter_signup.html)

```
<HTML>
<HEAD>
<STYLE TYPE="text/css">
<!--
BODY, P       {color: black; font-family: verdana; font-size: 10 pt}
H1          {color: black; font-family: arial; font-size: 12 pt}
-->
</STYLE>
</HEAD>


<BODY>
<TABLE BORDER=0 CELLPADDING=10 WIDTH=100%>
```

```
<TR>
<TD BGCOLOR="#F0F8FF" ALIGN=CENTER VALIGN=TOP WIDTH=17%>
</TD>
<TD BGCOLOR="#FFFFFF" ALIGN=LEFT VALIGN=TOP WIDTH=83%>
<H1>Newsletter sign-up form</H1>
<P>Enter your email address and we will send you our weekly
newsletter.</P>
<FORM METHOD="post" ACTION="formhandler.php">
<INPUT TYPE="text" SIZE=25 NAME="email">
<BR><BR>
<INPUT TYPE="submit" NAME="submit" VALUE="Submit">
</FORM>
</TD>
</TR>
</TABLE>

</BODY>
</HTML>
```

You enter the data in the database and acknowledge receipt in the form handler in Listing 21-2, which (with great originality) we are calling `formhandler.php`.

Listing 21-2: form handler for newsletter_signup.html (formhandler.php)

```
<HTML>
<HEAD>
<STYLE TYPE="text/css">
<!--
BODY, P      {color: black; font-family: verdana; font-size: 10 pt}
H1           {color: black; font-family: arial; font-size: 12 pt}
-->
</STYLE>
</HEAD>


<BODY>
<TABLE BORDER=0 CELLPADDING=10 WIDTH=100%>
<TR>
<TD BGCOLOR="#F0F8FF" ALIGN=CENTER VALIGN=TOP WIDTH=17%>
</TD>
<TD BGCOLOR="#FFFFFF" ALIGN=LEFT VALIGN=TOP WIDTH=83%>
<H1>Newsletter sign-up form</H1>
<?php

if (!$_POST['email'] || $_POST['email'] == "" || strlen($_POST['email'])
> 30) {
  echo '<P>There is a problem.  Did you enter an email address?</P>';
} else {
  // Open connection to the database
```

```
  mysql_connect("localhost", "phpuser", "sesame") or die("Failure to
communicate with database");
  mysql_select_db("test");

  // Insert email address
  $as_email = addslashes($_POST['email']);
  $tr_email = trim($as_email);
  $query = "INSERT INTO mailinglist (ID, Email, Source)
          VALUES(NULL, '$tr_email',
'www.example.com/newsletter_signup.html')
          ";
  $result = mysql_query($query);
  if (mysql_affected_rows() == 1) {
    echo '<P>Your information has been recorded.</P>';
  } else {
    error_log(mysql_error());
    echo '<P>Something went wrong with your signup attempt.</P>';
  }
}
?>
</TD>
</TR>
</TABLE>
</BODY>
</HTML>
```

Having a separate form and form handler is a very clean design which can potentially be easier to maintain. However, there are quite a few things you might want to do that you can't do easily with this model, caused by the difficulty of going back to the form from the form handler and the fact that variables are not available to both at the same time.

For one thing, if something goes wrong with the submission, it's very difficult to redisplay the form with the values you just filled in. This is particularly important with something like a user registration form, where you might want to check for unique e-mail addresses or matching passwords, and reject the entire registration with an error message if it doesn't pass the tests. People are going to be very annoyed if one little typo causes them to lose all the data that they just filled in — and after one or two go-rounds, they will simply stop trying to register.

Another situation in which self-submission is a win is when you need to submit the same form more than once. Say you are applying for auto insurance online, and you need to give the particulars of three or four different cars. It's extra work for the user to submit the form, get a success message, and then have to click a button to go back to the form for car #2. This kind of navigation problem has no perfect solution, but in situations where there's a high probability of multiple submissions, self-submission causes fewer clickthroughs for your Web users.

Finally, the separate form and form handler make it difficult to pull data from the database, edit it, and submit it – repeating the process however many times it takes for the user to be satisfied. A common example of this usage is a form to allow users to change their personal information, such as photos and bios, which people often like to fiddle with until they look exactly like the users want. If you want to make five small incremental edits to your user profile, you aren't going to want to go back and forth between form and form-handler ten times.

The first step to solving all these problems is to combine form and handler into one self-submitting PHP script.

Self-Submission

Self-submission is not a new form of autoeroticism. It simply refers to the process of combining one or more forms and form-handlers in a single script, using the HTML FORM standard to submit data to the script one or more times. Self-submission is accomplished by the simplest of means: specifying the same script name as the ACTION target in the FORM element like this:

```
<FORM METHOD="POST" ACTION="myself.php">
```

Or, using a built-in feature unique to PHP:

```
<FORM METHOD="POST" ACTION="<?php echo $_SERVER['PHP_SELF']; ?>">
```

> **TIP:** Although you always have the option to just use the file's URL, the built-in $_SERVER['PHP_SELF'] variable is preferable in Unix. Then the file will continue to be handled correctly if you rename or move it (into a PHP-enabled directory, needless to say). On the other hand, there have been reports of problems with this predefined variable on Windows. $_SERVER['PHP_SELF'] is the replacement for $PHP_SELF, which was available from all PHP scripts until version 4.2.0.

The single most important thing to remember about self-submitting forms is: *The logic comes before the display.* If you're used to writing separate forms and handlers, this may seem a little counterintuitive at first —but think of it this way: Because your form will look different or display variables based on interactions with the database, obviously these interactions must happen before the HTML for the page is output to the browser. After you construct a few self-submitting forms, logic-before-display will seem totally natural and painless.

> **CAUTION:** To use self-submission with controls, you will need to employ a more programmatic PHP-writing style — what in Chapter 14 we term the *maximum* or *medium* style. Beginners may find this somewhat more difficult than a clear division between the functions of HTML (form display) and PHP (form handling). This can be mitigated somewhat by using the *heredoc* syntax, as we do in many of our examples.

If you're a think-ahead type, by now you're wondering: "BUT if the logic comes before the display, won't my script try to do the database operations before showing me the HTML form in the first place?" Good question — and an indication that we need some way to tell the script either "We want to see the form now," or "We want to insert data into the database now." This "What am I supposed to be doing now?" bit is called a *stage variable*. It lets you keep track of how many times the form has submitted values to itself and, therefore, which stage of a multistep process you have reached.

The cheapest stage variable to test for is the Submit button. You can name your Submit button and give it a value, which will be set as a PHP value only after the form is submitted at least once. The easiest way to demonstrate what we're talking about is by rewriting the previous form and form-handler as one self-submitting form, as we do in Listing 21-3.

Listing 21-3: unified form and form-handler (newsletter_signup.php)

```php
<?php

if ($_POST['submit'] == 'Submit') {
  if (!$_POST['email'] || $_POST['email'] == "" ||
strlen($_POST['email'] > 30)) {
    $message = '<P>There is a problem.  Did you enter an email
address?</P>';
  } else {
    // Open connection to the database
    mysql_connect("localhost", "phpuser", "sesame") or die("Failure to
communicate with database");
    mysql_select_db("test");

    // Insert email address
    $as_email = addslashes($_POST['email']);
    $tr_email = trim($as_email);
    $query = "INSERT INTO mailinglist (ID, Email, Source)
              VALUES(NULL, '$tr_email',
'www.example.com/newsletter_signup.html')
              ";
    $result = mysql_query($query);
    if (mysql_affected_rows() == 1) {
      $message = '<P>Your information has been recorded.</P>';

      $noform_var = 1;
    } else {
      error_log(mysql_error());
      $message = '<P>Something went wrong with your signup
attempt.</P>';
    }
  }

  // Show the form in every case except successful submission
  if (!$noform_var) {
    $thisfile = $_SERVER['PHP_SELF'];
    $message .= <<< EOMSG
<P>Enter your email address and we will send you our weekly
newsletter.</P>
<FORM METHOD="post" ACTION="$thisfile">
```

```
<INPUT TYPE="text" SIZE=25 NAME="email">
<BR><BR>
<INPUT TYPE="submit" NAME="submit" VALUE="Submit">
</FORM>
EOMSG;
    }
}
?>


<HTML>
<HEAD>
<STYLE TYPE="text/css">
<!--
BODY, P      {color: black; font-family: verdana; font-size: 10 pt}
H1           {color: black; font-family: arial; font-size: 12 pt}
-->
</STYLE>
</HEAD>

<BODY>
<TABLE BORDER=0 CELLPADDING=10 WIDTH=100%>
<TR>
<TD BGCOLOR="#F0F8FF" ALIGN=CENTER VALIGN=TOP WIDTH=17%>
</TD>
<TD BGCOLOR="#FFFFFF" ALIGN=LEFT VALIGN=TOP WIDTH=83%>
<H1>Newsletter sign-up form</H1>
<?php echo $message; ?>
</TD>
</TR>
</TABLE>

</BODY>
</HTML>
```

The first time you load up this page, you should see a normal HTML form exactly like the one in Figure 21-1. If you submit it without any data or with a string that's too long (often a sign of a cracking attempt), you'll see an error message and the form again. If something goes wrong with the database INSERT, you'll see an error message and the form again. Only if the INSERT completes successfully will you not see the form again — which is the navigation we want because we don't want people to sign up for the newsletter more than once.

In the example above, we only need to check for two states of the form (unsubmitted or submitted) so we can use the Submit button as our stage variable. But what if you want to check for more than one state? You need a variable that is capable of taking more than one value. You could either give your Submit button different values, which would show up as different labels in the button itself; or you could set a hidden variable which is capable of taking more than one value depending on the state. We demonstrate the technique in Listing 21-4, which collects some information and then allows you to rate your boss anonymously.

Listing 21-4: a three-part form (rate_boss.php)

```php
<?php

// First set the form strings, which will be displayed
//in various cases below
$thisfile = $_SERVER['PHP_SELF']; //Have to set this for heredoc

$reg_form = <<< EOREGFORM
<P>We must ask for your name and email address to ensure that no one
votes more than once, but we do not associate your personal information
with your rating.</P>
<FORM METHOD="post" ACTION="$thisfile">
Name: <INPUT TYPE="text" SIZE=25 NAME="name"><BR><BR>
Email: <INPUT TYPE="text" SIZE=25 NAME="email">
<INPUT TYPE="hidden" NAME="stage" VALUE="register">
<BR><BR>
<INPUT TYPE="submit" NAME="submit" VALUE="Submit">
</FORM>
EOREGFORM;

$rate_form = <<< EORATEFORM
<P>My boss is:</P>
<FORM METHOD="post" ACTION="$thisfile">
<INPUT TYPE="radio" NAME="rating" VALUE=1> Driving me to look for a new
job.<BR>
<INPUT TYPE="radio" NAME="rating" VALUE=2> Not the worst, but pretty
bad.<BR>
<INPUT TYPE="radio" NAME="rating" VALUE=3> Just so-so.<BR>
<INPUT TYPE="radio" NAME="rating" VALUE=4> Pretty good.<BR>
<INPUT TYPE="radio" NAME="rating" VALUE=5> A pleasure to work
with.<BR><BR>
Boss's name: <INPUT TYPE="text" SIZE=25 NAME="boss"><BR>
<INPUT TYPE="hidden" NAME="stage" VALUE="rate">
<BR><BR>
<INPUT TYPE="submit" NAME="submit" VALUE="Submit">
</FORM>
EORATEFORM;

if (!$_POST['submit']) {
  // First time, just show the registration form
  $message = $reg_form;

} elseif ($_POST['submit'] == 'Submit' && $_POST['stage'] == 'register')
{
  // Second time, show the registration form again on error,
  // rating form on successful INSERT
```

```php
   if (!$_POST['name'] || $_POST['name'] == "" || strlen($_POST['name'] >
30) || !$_POST['email'] || $_POST['email'] == "" ||
strlen($_POST['email'] > 30)) {
     $message = '<P>There is a problem.  Did you enter a name and email
address?</P>';
     $message .= $reg_form;
   } else {
     // Open connection to the database
     mysql_connect("localhost", "phpuser", "sesame") or die("Failure to
communicate with database");
     mysql_select_db("test");

     // Check to see this name and email have not appeared before
     $as_name = addslashes($_POST['name']);
     $tr_name = trim($as_name);
     $as_email = addslashes($_POST['email']);
     $tr_email = trim($as_email);
     $query = "SELECT sub_id FROM raters
               WHERE Name = '$tr_name'
               AND Email = '$tr_email'
              ";
     $result = mysql_query($query);
     if (mysql_num_rows($result) > 0) {
       error_log(mysql_error());
       $message = 'Someone with this name and password has already rated
 . If you think a mistake was made, please email help@example.com.';
     } else {
       // Insert name and email address
       $query = "INSERT INTO raters (ID, Name, Email)
                 VALUES(NULL, '$tr_name', '$tr_email')
                ";
       $result = mysql_query($query);
       if (mysql_affected_rows() == 1) {
         $message = $rate_form;
       } else {
         error_log(mysql_error());
         $message = '<P>Something went wrong with your signup
attempt.</P>';
         $message .= $reg_form;
       }
     }
   }

} elseif ($_POST['submit'] == 'Submit' && $_POST['stage'] == 'rate') {
  // Third time, store the rating and boss's name

  // Open connection to the database
  mysql_connect("localhost", "phpuser", "sesame") or die("Failure to
communicate with database");
```

```
  mysql_select_db("test");

  // Insert rating and boss's name
  $as_boss = addslashes($_POST['boss']);
  $tr_boss = trim($as_boss);
  $rating = $_POST['rating'];
  $query = "INSERT INTO ratings (ID, Rating, Boss)
            VALUES(NULL, '$rating', '$tr_boss')
          ";
  $result = mysql_query($query);
  if (mysql_affected_rows() == 1) {
    $message = '<P>Your rating has been submitted.</P>';
  } else {
    error_log(mysql_error());
    $message = '<P>Something went wrong with your rating attempt.  Try
again.</P>';
    $message .= $rate_form;
  }
}
?>


<HTML>
<HEAD>
<STYLE TYPE="text/css">
<!--
BODY, P      {color: black; font-family: verdana; font-size: 10 pt}
H1        {color: black; font-family: arial; font-size: 12 pt}
-->
</STYLE>
</HEAD>


<BODY>
<TABLE BORDER=0 CELLPADDING=10 WIDTH=100%>
<TR>
<TD BGCOLOR="#F0F8FF" ALIGN=CENTER VALIGN=TOP WIDTH=17%>
</TD>
<TD BGCOLOR="#FFFFFF" ALIGN=LEFT VALIGN=TOP WIDTH=83%>
<H1>Rate your boss anonymously</H1>
<?php echo $message; ?>
</TD>
</TR>
</TABLE>

</BODY>
</HTML>
```

Figure 21-2 shows the rating form after an error has occurred.

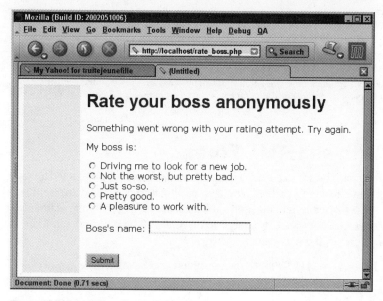

Figure 21-2: A multiple self-submitting form

Some of you might be thinking, "Hey wait! You said logic always comes before display — but then you started this script with a bunch of HTML." Very perspicacious — but not quite right. Look closely and you will realize that we are merely setting a bunch of text to a couple of variable strings ($reg_form and $rate_form). In the entire PHP section, we actually don't display anything. We merely construct a string, $message, which will be plugged in to the HTML at the bottom. If we took away the HTML, you would see a blank page in the browser. So it's OK to assemble the text you're going to want to display in the logic part; just don't echo it out to the browser until the end.

Another issue with self-submitted forms is navigation. With the traditional HTML form, navigation is strictly one-way: form to handler to whatever navigational device (if any) the designer decrees. Self-submitted forms need not conform to this rule, however. In each individual instance, you need to decide:

♦ Whether the form can be resubmitted multiple times by the user, in whole or in part.

♦ Whether the user decides when to move on by clicking a link or the form moves users along automatically.

♦ Whether you need to pass variables on to the next page, hidden or in plain view.

♦ Whether you want to control where the user can go next or if you want to give users multiple choices.

CROSS-REFERENCE: All these techniques are most commonly used in user-management functions — registration, login, and editing user information — which are demonstrated realistically in Chapter 38.

The answers to these questions will determine whether you need a control, another form, a simple link or button, or multiple links.

> **TIP:** Whatever you decide about navigation, remember to provide plenty of text that clearly explains what's going to happen at every step. Because PHP gives you so much flexibility with forms, new users' default expectations may be crossed up, and they could end up uncertain whether they accomplished their mission with your form.

Editing Data with an HTML Form

PHP is brilliant at putting variables into a database, but it really shines when taking data from a database, displaying it in a form to be edited, and then putting it back in the database. Its HTML-embeddedness, easy variable-passing, and slick database connectivity are at their best in this kind of job. These techniques are extremely useful, because you will find a million occasions to edit data you're storing in a database.

Let's look at the specific kinds of HTML FORM data elements and how they are handled.

TEXT and TEXTAREA

TEXT and TEXTAREA are the most straightforward types because they enjoy an unambiguous one-to-one relationship between identifier and content. In other words, there is only one possible VALUE per NAME. You just pull the data field from the database and display it in the form by referencing the appropriate array value, as shown in Figure 21-3.

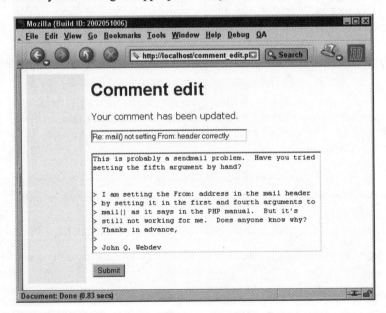

Figure 21-3: Displaying text for editing

Listing 21-5, `comment_edit.php`, takes a comment out of the database and allows you to edit it.

> **TIP:** You may need to use the `stripslashes` function when displaying TEXTAREA and TEXT if there's any chance the values might have single quotes or apostrophes and `magic_quotes_gpc` is on. Watch out for people with apostrophed names like O'Malley or D'Nesh!

Listing 21-5: editing data from database (comment_edit.php)

```php
<?php

// Open connection to the database
mysql_connect("localhost", "phpuser", "sesame") or die("Failure to
communicate with database");
mysql_select_db("test");

if ($_POST['submit'] == 'Submit') {
  // Format the data
  $comment_id = $_POST['comment_id'];
  $comment_header = $_POST['comment_header'];
  $as_comment_header = addslashes($comment_header);
  $comment = $_POST['comment'];
  $as_comment = addslashes($_POST['comment']);


  // Update values
  $query = "UPDATE comments
            SET comment_header = '$as_comment_header',
            comment = '$as_comment'
            WHERE ID = $comment_id";
  $result = mysql_query($query);
  if (mysql_affected_rows() == 1) {
    $success_msg = '<P>Your comment has been updated.</P>';
  } else {
    error_log(mysql_error());
    $success_msg = '<P>Something went wrong.</P>';
  }
} else {
  // Get the comment header and comment
  $comment_id = $_GET['comment_id'];
  $query = "SELECT comment_header, comment
            FROM comments
            WHERE ID = $comment_id";
  $result = mysql_query($query);
  $comment_arr = mysql_fetch_array($result);
  $comment_header = stripslashes($comment_arr[0]);
  $comment = stripslashes($comment_arr[1]);
}
```

```
$thispage = $_SERVER['PHP_SELF']; //Have to do this for heredoc

$form_page = <<< EOFORMPAGE
<STYLE TYPE="text/css">
<!--
BODY, P      {color: black; font-family: verdana; font-size: 10 pt}
H1           {color: black; font-family: arial; font-size: 12 pt}
-->
</STYLE>
</HEAD>

<BODY>
<TABLE BORDER=0 CELLPADDING=10 WIDTH=100%>
<TR>
<TD BGCOLOR="#F0F8FF" ALIGN=CENTER VALIGN=TOP WIDTH=17%>
</TD>
<TD BGCOLOR="#FFFFFF" ALIGN=LEFT VALIGN=TOP WIDTH=83%>
<H1>Comment edit</H1>

$success_msg
<FORM METHOD="post" ACTION="$thispage">
<INPUT TYPE="text" SIZE="40" NAME="comment_header"
VALUE="$comment_header"><BR><BR>
<TEXTAREA NAME="comment" ROWS=10 COLS=50>$comment</TEXTAREA><BR><BR>
<INPUT TYPE="hidden" NAME="comment_id" VALUE="$comment_id">
<INPUT TYPE="submit" NAME="submit" VALUE="Submit">
</FORM>

</TD></TR></TABLE>
</BODY>
</HTML>
EOFORMPAGE;
echo $form_page;
?>
```

> **TIP:** Remember that in an HTML form integers and doubles must use the TEXT or TEXTAREA type, as there is no specifically numeric HTML form field type.

CHECKBOX

The CHECKBOX type has only one possible value per input: off (unchecked) or on (checked). The database field which records this information is almost always going to be a small integer or bit type with values 0 and 1 corresponding to unchecked or checked check boxes. Figure 21-4 shows a common type of check box being edited.

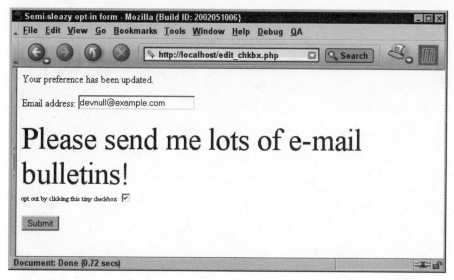

Figure 21-4: A prepopulated check box

Listing 21-6 demonstrates how to use a check box to display and change a Boolean value:

Listing 21-6: checkbox displaying boolean data from database (optout.php)

```php
<?php

// Open connection to the database
mysql_connect("localhost", "phpuser", "sesame") or die("Failure to
communicate with database");
mysql_select_db("test");

// If the form has been submitted, record the preference and redisplay
if ($_POST['submit'] == 'Submit') {
  $email = $_POST['email'];
  $as_email = addslashes($_POST['email']);
  if (isSet($_POST['OptOut'] && $_POST['OptOut'] == 1) {
    $optout = 1;
  } else {
    $optout = 0;
  }

  // Update value
  $query = "UPDATE checkbox
            SET BoxValue = $optout
            WHERE BoxName = 'OptOut'
            AND email = '$as_email'";
  $result = mysql_query($query);
  if (mysql_error() == "") {
```

```php
    $success_msg = '<P>Your preference has been updated.</P>';
  } else {
    error_log(mysql_error());
    $success_msg = '<P>Something went wrong.</P>';
  }
  // Get the value
  $query = "SELECT BoxValue FROM checkbox WHERE BoxName = 'OptOut' AND
email = '$as_email'";
  $result = mysql_query($query);
  $optout = mysql_result($result, 0, 0);

  if ($optout == 0) {

    $checked = "";
  } elseif ($optout == 1) {
    $checked = 'CHECKED';
  }
}


// Now display the page
$thispage = $_SERVER['PHP_SELF']; //Have to do this for heredoc

$form_page = <<< EOFORMPAGE
<HTML>
<HEAD>
<TITLE>Semi-sleazy opt-in form</TITLE>
</HEAD>

<BODY>
$success_msg
<FORM METHOD=POST ACTION="$thispage">
Email address:  <INPUT TYPE="text" NAME="email" SIZE=25
VALUE="$email"><BR><BR>
<FONT SIZE=+4>Please send me lots of e-mail bulletins!</FONT><BR>
<FONT SIZE=-2>opt out by clicking this tiny checkbox</FONT>
<INPUT TYPE="checkbox"  NAME="OptOut" VALUE=1 $checked><BR><BR>
<INPUT TYPE="submit" NAME="submit" VALUE="Submit">
</FORM>

</BODY>
</HTML>
EOFORMPAGE;
echo $form_page;

?>
```

Although each check box is only capable of expressing a fixed chunk of data, check boxes are often used in bunches to convey more complex aggregate meanings. Look at this check box grouping in Figure 21-5:

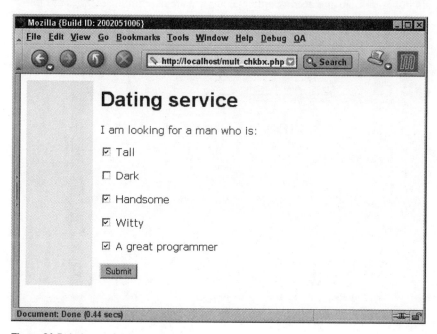

Figure 21-5: A cluster of check boxes

Forms with large numbers of check boxes like this are more work for the Web development team, but they have a nice interface for the user. The code for this page is very similar to that of the previous example, with more variables. You can download it from the Web site for our book at www.troutworks.com/phpbook/ch21/.

RADIO

RADIO data elements allow for a one-to-many relationship between identifier and value. In other words, they have multiple possible values, but only one can be predisplayed or selected. They are best for small sets of options, generally between 2 and 10, which need more than a word or two of text to identify themselves.

Unfortunately, it's somewhat more difficult to represent stored data in a radio button than in a check box or text field. This is because there is only one possible value for a text or textarea, and only two possible values for a check box — but radio buttons can have more than two possible values. Therefore, you will have to output part of the actual form with PHP. This looks a little bit less neat than the styles we employed previously, so you have to go to a little more trouble to have an easily readable script. Again, the user interface experience allowed by radio buttons is worth the extra trouble it gives to the Web developer.

In the example in Figure 21-6 and accompanying code, we are assembling a series of radio buttons that display preference data from the database.

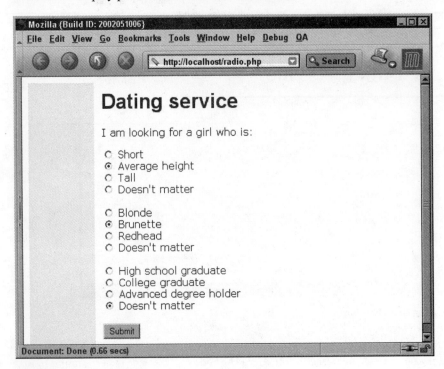

Figure 21-6: Prepopulated radio buttons

Listing 21-7 shows the code for Figure 21-6, which shows how to edit forms with radio buttons:

Listing 21-7: radio buttons displaying boolean data from database (date_prefs.php)

```php
<?php

// Subscriber ID is stored in a cookie on the user's browser
$sub_id = $_COOKIE['userID'];

// Open connection to the database
mysql_connect("localhost", "mysqluser", "sesame") or die("Failure to
communicate with database");
mysql_select_db("test");

// If the form has been submitted, record the preferences
```

```php
if ($_POST['submit'] == 'Submit') {
  $height = $_POST['height'];
  $haircolor = $_POST['haircolor'];
  $edu = $_POST['edu'];

  // Update value
  $query = "UPDATE qualities
           SET height = $height, haircolor = $haircolor, edu = $edu
           WHERE subscriber = $sub_id";
  $result = mysql_query($query);
  if (mysql_affected_rows() == 1) {
    $success_msg = '<P>Your preferences have been updated.</P>';
  } else {
    error_log(mysql_error());
    $success_msg = '<P>Something went wrong.</P>';
  }

}

// Get the values
$query = "SELECT height, haircolor, edu FROM qualities WHERE subscriber
= $sub_id";
$result = mysql_query($query);
$pref_arr = mysql_fetch_array($result);
$height = $pref_arr[0];
$haircolor = $pref_arr[1];
$edu = $pref_arr[2];

// Assemble the radio button part of the form
if ($height == 1) {
  $radio_str .= "<INPUT TYPE=RADIO NAME=\"height\" VALUE=1 checked>
Short<BR>\n";
} else {
  $radio_str .= "<INPUT TYPE=RADIO NAME=\"height\" VALUE=1>
Short<BR>\n";
}
if ($height == 2) {
  $radio_str .= "<INPUT TYPE=RADIO NAME=\"height\" VALUE=2 checked>
Average height<BR>\n";
} else {
  $radio_str .= "<INPUT TYPE=RADIO NAME=\"height\" VALUE=2> Average
height<BR>\n";
}
if ($height == 3) {
  $radio_str .= "<INPUT TYPE=RADIO NAME=\"height\" VALUE=3 checked>
Tall<BR>\n";
} else {
  $radio_str .= "<INPUT TYPE=RADIO NAME=\"height\" VALUE=3> Tall<BR>\n";
}
```

```
if ($height == 0) {
  $radio_str .= "<INPUT TYPE=RADIO NAME=\"height\" VALUE=0 checked>
Doesn't matter<BR><BR>\n";
} else {
  $radio_str .= "<INPUT TYPE=RADIO NAME=\"height\" VALUE=0> Doesn't
matter<BR><BR>\n";
}

if ($haircolor == 1) {
  $radio_str .= "<INPUT TYPE=RADIO NAME=\"haircolor\" VALUE=1 checked>
Blonde<BR>\n";
} else {
  $radio_str .= "<INPUT TYPE=RADIO NAME=\"haircolor\" VALUE=1>
Blonde<BR>\n";
}
if ($haircolor == 2) {
  $radio_str .= "<INPUT TYPE=RADIO NAME=\"haircolor\" VALUE=2 checked>
Brunette<BR>\n";
} else {
  $radio_str .= "<INPUT TYPE=RADIO NAME=\"haircolor\" VALUE=2>
Brunette<BR>\n";
}
if ($haircolor == 3) {
  $radio_str .= "<INPUT TYPE=RADIO NAME=\"haircolor\" VALUE=3 checked>
Redhead<BR>\n";
} else {
  $radio_str .= "<INPUT TYPE=RADIO NAME=\"haircolor\" VALUE=3>
Redhead<BR>\n";
}
if ($haircolor == 0) {
  $radio_str .= "<INPUT TYPE=RADIO NAME=\"haircolor\" VALUE=0 checked>
Doesn't matter<BR><BR>\n";
} else {
  $radio_str .= "<INPUT TYPE=RADIO NAME=\"haircolor\" VALUE=0> Doesn't
matter<BR><BR>\n";
}

if ($edu == 1) {
  $radio_str .= "<INPUT TYPE=RADIO NAME=\"edu\" VALUE=1 checked> High
school graduate<BR>\n";
} else {
  $radio_str .= "<INPUT TYPE=RADIO NAME=\"edu\" VALUE=1> High school
graduate<BR>\n";
}
if ($edu == 2) {
  $radio_str .= "<INPUT TYPE=RADIO NAME=\"edu\" VALUE=2 checked> College
graduate<BR>\n";
} else {
```

```
   $radio_str .= "<INPUT TYPE=RADIO NAME=\"edu\" VALUE=2> College
graduate<BR>\n";
}
if ($edu == 3) {
  $radio_str .= "<INPUT TYPE=RADIO NAME=\"edu\" VALUE=3 checked>
Advanced degree holder<BR>\n";
} else {
  $radio_str .= "<INPUT TYPE=RADIO NAME=\"edu\" VALUE=3> Advanced degree
holder<BR>\n";
}
if ($edu == 0) {
  $radio_str .= "<INPUT TYPE=RADIO NAME=\"edu\" VALUE=0 checked> Doesn't
matter<BR><BR>\n";
} else {
  $radio_str .= "<INPUT TYPE=RADIO NAME=\"edu\" VALUE=0> Doesn't
matter<BR><BR>\n";
}


// Now display the page
$thispage = $_SERVER['PHP_SELF']; //Have to do this for heredoc

$form_page = <<< EOFORMPAGE
<HTML>
<HEAD>
<STYLE TYPE="text/css">
<!--
BODY, P     {color: black; font-family: verdana; font-size: 10 pt}
H1        {color: black; font-family: arial; font-size: 12 pt}
-->
</STYLE>
</HEAD>


<BODY>
<TABLE BORDER=0 CELLPADDING=10 WIDTH=100%>
<TR>
<TD BGCOLOR="#F0F8FF" ALIGN=CENTER VALIGN=TOP WIDTH=17%>
</TD>
<TD BGCOLOR="#FFFFFF" ALIGN=LEFT VALIGN=TOP WIDTH=83%>
<H1>Dating service</H1>
$success_msg
<P>I am looking for a girl who is:</P>
<FORM METHOD=POST ACTION="$thispage">
$radio_str
<INPUT TYPE=SUBMIT NAME="submit" VALUE="Submit">
</FORM>

</TD>
</TR>
```

```
</TABLE>
</BODY>
</HTML>
EOFORMPAGE;
echo $form_page;

?>
```

SELECT

The SELECT field type is perhaps the most interesting of all. It can handle the largest number of options, and it also allows the user to select multiple options that can be passed back to the database using arrays.

> **CROSS-REFERENCE:** See Chapter 28 for ideas about using JavaScript to make even more interesting SELECT forms.

In Figure 21-7, we are using the SELECT form element with multiple options. In PHP, this is done by creating an array of the multiple selected option values to pass to the form handler. You set up the array in the HTML form by declaring the MULTIPLE attribute of the SELECT element, and by naming the SELECT element something like $val[] — in other words, appending a set of square brackets to the variable name. This will indicate to PHP that it's dealing with an array rather than a single variable, and it will construct the array appropriately with the multiple selected values. When the array gets to the form handler, you will need to deal with the values as you would any array's values — by dereferencing, or by listing out the contents of the array.

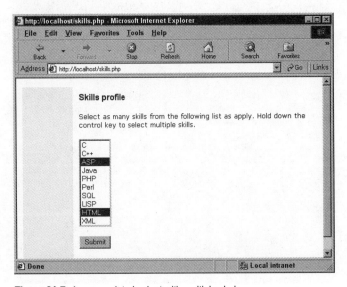

Figure 21-7: A prepopulated select with multiple choice

Listing 21-8 shows the code for Figure 21-7, which demonstrates how to display and edit a select list with multiple options:

Listing 21-8: select list displaying database values (skills_profile.php)

```php
<?php

$user_id = $_COOKIE['user_id'];

// Open connection to the database
mysql_connect("localhost", "mysqluser", "sesame") or die("Database
error!");
mysql_select_db("test");

if ($_POST['submit'] == 'Submit') {

  // Delete this user's skills
  $query2 = "DELETE FROM user_skill
            WHERE user_id = $user_id";
  $result2 = mysql_query($query2);

  foreach ($_POST['skills'] as $val) {
    $query = "INSERT INTO user_skill (ID, user_id, skill_id) VALUES
(NULL, $user_id, $val)";
    $result = mysql_query($query);
    if (mysql_affected_rows() == 1) {
      continue;
    } else {
      error_log(mysql_error());
      $error_msg = '<P>Something went wrong</P>';
      break;
    }
  }
}

// Get all the results
$query = "SELECT * FROM skills";
$result = mysql_query($query);

// Download this user's skills
$query1 = "SELECT skill_id
          FROM user_skill
          WHERE user_id = $user_id";
$result1 = mysql_query($query1);
while ($user_skill = mysql_fetch_array($result1)) {
  $skill_id = $user_skill[0];
  $user_skill_arr[$skill_id] = $skill_id;
}
```

```
while ($skills = mysql_fetch_array($result)) {
  $key = $skills[0];
  if ($key == $user_skill_arr[$key]) {
    $select_str .= "<OPTION VALUE=\"$key\" SELECTED>$skills[1]\n";
  } else {
    $select_str .= "<OPTION VALUE=\"$key\">$skills[1]\n";
  }
}


$thispage = $_SERVER['PHP_SELF']; //Have to do this for heredoc
$form_str = <<< EOFORMSTR
<HTML>
<HEAD>
<STYLE TYPE="text/css">
<!--
BODY, P      {color: black; font-family: verdana; font-size: 10 pt}
H1       {color: black; font-family: arial; font-size: 12 pt}
-->
</STYLE>
</HEAD>

<BODY>
<TABLE BORDER=0 CELLPADDING=10 WIDTH=100%>
<TR>
<TD BGCOLOR="#F0F8FF" ALIGN=CENTER VALIGN=TOP WIDTH=17%>
</TD>
<TD BGCOLOR="#FFFFFF" ALIGN=LEFT VALIGN=TOP WIDTH=83%>
<H1>Skills profile</H1>
<P>Select as many skills from the following list as apply.  Hold down
the control key to select multiple skills.</P>
$error_msg

<FORM METHOD=POST ACTION="$thispage">
<SELECT NAME="skills[]" SIZE=10 MULTIPLE>
$select_str
</SELECT>
<BR><BR>
<INPUT TYPE="submit" NAME="submit" VALUE="Submit">
</FORM>

</TD></TR></TABLE>
</BODY></HTML>
EOFORMSTR;
echo $form_str;

?>
```

Summary

PHP is an extremely powerful form-handling tool, especially in conjunction with a database. You can use PHP to display database-stored data as form values, and of course, you can also store form-generated data in the database.

To prepare your HTML forms to work smoothly with PHP, you need to follow a few simple rules. First and foremost, remember to always name every single form element — the HTML standard itself doesn't require this, but PHP does because the element names will become variable names in the form handler. A good idea is to make the form element name the same as the corresponding database field name so they are easy to match. PHP also allows you to make clever use of hidden form inputs and of multiple SELECT options, which should be delineated with square brackets (denoting an array) after the element name.

You have the choice with PHP to have separate HTML forms and PHP form handlers or to commingle the two in a single self-submitting PHP script. The latter option is perhaps the more powerful, but it can also be more difficult to work with. You will need to set a variable within the form to indicate whether the entries have been submitted; and the PHP logic should be placed before the HTML display. You can even have multiple forms on one page that are handled by the same PHP script.

Chapter 22
Weblogs

Small standalone PHP applications, such as polls and email forms, are all very useful; but complete content sites are where PHP really shines. Here we give complete instructions for developing the simplest type of stand-alone site, which is the Weblog.

Why Weblogs?

A *Weblog* is the simplest kind of dynamic site. It can be thought of as a dynamic version of the personal home page: a content site organized by chronology with frequently updated posts. Most Weblogs do not create all their own content in the sense of writing full news stories or producing a trove of artwork; they instead exist to comment on other people's content and events of the day, or to provide a venue for personal thoughts and reflections. On the high end of the genre, public Weblogs like Slashdot can become extremely popular meeting places for online communities to chew the fat of their common interests.

If you are a newcomer to server-side scripting, we encourage you to immediately start a personal Weblog as your first major project. Nothing helps you learn faster than running an actual complete site of your own, where you can try out a range of new techniques and ideas in context. Especially because PHP and other open source technologies grow and change so quickly, it's well-nigh essential to have a preexisting test bed always available to doodle around on.

Weblogs are also just fun and, therefore, worthwhile even for those who also use PHP in more serious contexts. There's no pleasure quite like that of conducting an intellectual debate, an argument, or a romance by Weblog. Forget movies, pop music, and TV — the Weblog is the true medium of the age, baby!

The Simplest Weblog

The main goal of this section is to introduce you to the layout and display aspects of building a dynamically generated site. In later sections, we will refine our techniques for handling the data-related aspects. At the end of this chapter, you should have the ability to make and maintain a simple data-driven site of your own. Conceptually, even the most complicated dynamic content sites are just bigger versions of the concepts you will learn by building a personal Weblog.

The easiest Weblog is just a PHP template and some included text files. It's limited to local development only — in other words, you won't be able to make entries via HTTP but only by creating text files while logged into the PHP server as a trusted user (or copying text files to the server, which amounts to the same thing). You also won't be able to assign different levels of permissions very effectively, so this style of Weblog is most appropriate for a purely personal single-author site.

We decided to use the most basic type of navigation, Previous and Next text links that we'll maintain by hand. This gives you the maximum flexibility to decide how often you want to change the front page of your Weblog — we'll do it daily, but you may prefer a weekly, monthly, or irregular changeover depending on how much you have to write about. We'll also include an old reliable left-side navbar with links to standalone pages, such as About Me and Favorite Things information. A finished Weblog page is shown in Figure 22-1.

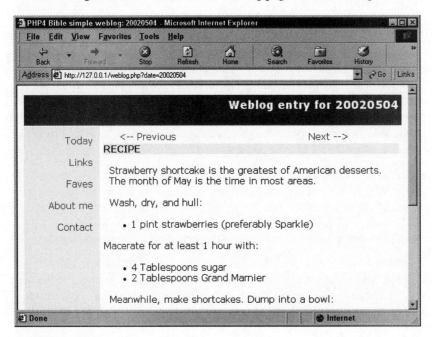

Figure 22-1: A Weblog page

It is assembled from these files:

- `weblog.php`: Main display page template

- `20000101.txt`, `20000102.txt`: Weblog entries (changed daily)

- `default.txt`: Default text entry for days when there is no new content

- `favorites.php`, `links.php`, `aboutme.php`: Semistatic pages (changed infrequently)

- `header.inc`: Header and navigation bar on every page

- `footer.inc`: Footer on every page

- `style.inc`: Internal style sheet

You can grab all this code from our Web site:www.troutworks.com/php4book/ to save having to retype it.

> **CAUTION:** You must change the variable `$initial_entry_date` in `weblog.php` to the date of your first entry, or you may start an infinite loop that will eat up all your server cycles! You must also check all the paths to included files and change them to real paths.

Listings 22-1 through 22-7 are the code for a simple Weblog. Instead of using a database to store your entries, the data will be stored in text files on your filesystem.

Listing 22-1: Main Weblog template (`weblog.php`)

```php
<?php

// -------------------------------
// GET YOUR VARIABLES ALL LINED UP
// -------------------------------
// Change this to the date of your first log entry.
$initial_entry_date = 20000101;

$today = date('Ymd');
if (isSet($_GET['date'])) {
  if ($_GET['date'] < $initial_entry_date) {
    // Go to first entry if the specified date is earlier than range
    $date = $initial_entry_date;
  } elseif ($_GET['date'] > $today) {
    // Go to last entry if specified date is later than range
    $date = $today;
  } else {
    $date = $_GET['date'];
  }
} else {
  $date = $today;
}
```

```php
$title_msg = $date;
$header_msg = "Weblog entry for $date";

// Assemble the Previous/Next links
$prevdate = $date - 1;
$nextdate = $date + 1;
if ($date == $initial_entry_date) {
  $flipbar = "\n<P CLASS=\"next\"><A
HREF=\"$PHP_SELF?date=$nextdate\">Next --&#62;</A></P>\n";
} elseif ($date == $today) {
  $flipbar = "\n<P CLASS=\"previous\"><A
HREF=\"$PHP_SELF?date=$prevdate\">&#60;-- Previous</A></P>\n";
} else {
  $flipbar = "\n<TABLE BORDER=0><TR><TD WIDTH=\"50%\"
ALIGN=\"left\"><SPAN CLASS=\"previous\"><A
HREF=\"$PHP_SELF?date=$prevdate\">&#60;-- Previous</A></SPAN></TD><TD
WIDTH=\"50%\" ALIGN=\"right\"><SPAN CLASS=\"next\"><A
HREF=\"$PHP_SELF?date=$nextdate\">Next --
&#62;</A></SPAN></TD></TR></TABLE>\n";
}



// --------------------
// NOW ASSEMBLE THE PAGE
// --------------------
include_once('header.inc');

echo $flipbar;
// Include the specified text file, or a default message
// Replace the fake path below with a real one
if (file_exists($DOCUMENT_ROOT."/path/to/entries/subdir/$date.txt")) {
  // Replace the fake path below with a real one
  include($DOCUMENT_ROOT."/path/to/entries/subdir/$date.txt");
} else {
  include("default.txt");
}
echo $flipbar;

include_once('footer.inc');
?>
```

Listing 22-2: A dated entry (`20000101.txt`)

```html
<DIV CLASS="topic">HOLIDAY</DIV>
<P>This is the Year No Techies Were Hungover On New Year's. We were all
sleeping under our desks to reassure the stockholders that the bossman
is On Top of Y2K.</P>
```

```
<P>My New Year's Resolutions are:
<UL>
<LI>No Win2K in Y2K! Fight the power.</LI>
<LI>Contribute to OSS project.</LI>
<LI>Take full 2 weeks vacation (dude ranch?).</LI>
`<LI>Be less snide.</LI>
</UL>
</P>
```

Listing 22-3: Default message (`default.txt`)

```
<P>Sorry, nothing new today!  Check back tomorrow.</P>
```

Listing 22-4: A static page (`favorites.php`)

```
<?php
$title_msg = 'favorites';
$header_msg = 'My favorite things';

include_once('header.inc')
?>

<P>These are a few of my favorite things.</P>

<DIV CLASS="topic">BOOKS</DIV>
<DL>
<DT>Cryptonomicon, by Neal Stephenson</DT>
<DD>The techie masterpiece -- it's our life, put in the blender of a
massive inventiveness. Be sure to also download the essay "In the
beginning was the command line" from his site, www.crytonomicon.com
.</DD>
</DL>

<DIV CLASS="topic">MUSIC</DIV>
<DL>
<DT>When The Pawn..., by Fiona Apple</DT>
<DD>Just another bubblegum Latin pop entry. Merengue, anyone?</DD>
</DL>
<?php include_once('footer.inc'); ?>
```

Listing 22-5: Included header file (`header.inc`)

```
<HTML>
<HEAD>
<TITLE>PHP4 Bible simple weblog: <?php echo $_GET['date']; ?></TITLE>
<?php include("style.inc"); ?>
</HEAD>

<BODY BGCOLOR="#FFFFFF">
<TABLE BORDER="0" CELLPADDING="5" WIDTH="100%">
```

```
<!-- Title box -->
<TR WIDTH="100%" BGCOLOR="#822222">
  <TD WIDTH="100%" ALIGN="right" COLSPAN="2"><H1><?php echo $header_msg;
?></H1></TD>
</TR>
<!-- End Title box -->

<!-- Begin main body -->
<TR WIDTH="100%">
  <TD WIDTH="20%" VALIGN="top" BGCOLOR="#FFFECC">
    <!-- Navbar -->
    <P CLASS="sidebar"><A HREF="weblog.php">Today</A></P>
    <P CLASS="sidebar"><A HREF="links.php">Links</A></P>
    <P CLASS="sidebar"><A HREF="favorites.php">Faves</A></P>
    <P CLASS="sidebar"><A HREF="aboutme.php">About me</A></P>
    <P CLASS="sidebar"><A HREF="mailto:me@localhost">Contact</A></P>
    <!-- End Navbar -->
  </TD>
  <TD WIDTH="80%">
```

Listing 22-6: Included footer (`footer.inc`)

```
<!-- End of main body -->
</TD></TR>
</TABLE>
<P CLASS="footer">Copyright Troutworks, Inc. 2000 - 20002</P>
</BODY>
</HTML>
```

Listing 22-7: Included stylesheet (`style.inc`)

```
<STYLE TYPE="text/css">
<!--
BODY, P, LI   {font-family: verdana, arial, sans-serif; font-size:
12pt; color: #000000; text-align: left; margin-left:10px}
H1     {font-family: verdana, arial, sans-serif; font-size: 14pt;
color: #FFFFFF}
A:link, A:visited {font-family: verdana, arial, sans-serif; font-size:
12pt; color: #822222; text-decoration:none}
.sidebar {font-family: verdana, arial, sans-serif; font-size: 12pt;
color: #822222; text-align:right; margin-top:10; margin-right:7}
.topic   {font-family: verdana, arial, sans-serif; font-size: 12pt;
font-weight: bold; color: #000000; background: #FFFECC; text-align:
left}
.footer  {font-family: verdana, arial, sans-serif; font-size: 9pt;
color: #808080; text-align:right}
.previous {font-family: verdana, arial, sans-serif; font-size: 12pt;
color: #808080; text-align:left; margin-left:25; margin-right:100}
.next  {font-family: verdana, arial, sans-serif; font-size: 12pt; color:
#808080; text-align:right; margin-left:100; margin-right:25}
```

```
-->
</STYLE>
```

To use the simple Weblog, place all the files in a PHP-enabled directory on your Web server. Create a subdirectory for your daily entries (for example,. `20000101.txt`, `20020504.txt`), otherwise you'll quickly end up with dozens of files cluttering up your main directory. The files in this subdirectory need to be writable by you and readable by all.

When you're ready to make an entry, log into your Web server, fire up a text editor like `vi`, and write an HTML-formatted text file for each day you want to post, naming it according to the date convention we've established. Alternatively, instead of logging into your Web server you can write up your daily text file on a local client copy, and then use `scp` to upload it to your Web server. Obviously, you can edit this file however many times you like, if you have multiple things to say per day. As long as the files have the correct names, locations, and permissions, this code should run smoothly for you. This type of Weblog is self-archiving, so you don't need to do anything special with old entries — they'll just stay around forever if you have a big enough hard disk.

> **NOTE:** If you still use FTP to upload files, please take an hour to learn how to use `scp` instead. A fine command-line Windows client called `pscp` is available for free download at `www.chiark.greenend.org.uk/~sgtatham/putty/`. A even easier GUI Windows client called `WinSCP` is available for free download at `http://winscp.vse.cz/eng/`. FTP should only be used for file download, as in anonymous FTP servers, because it has caused so many security problems on file upload. One of the reasons to avoid the otherwise fine Weblog-publishing applications like Movable Type and Blogger is that they rely on FTP to write files to your Web server.
>
> We promise that `scp` is just as easy to use if not easier — instead of typing **ftp myserver.mydomain.com** and **put myfile.php**, you combine both commands into a simple **pscp myfile.php me@myserver.mydomain.com:myfile.php**. The only even slightly tricky part is generating a public key and having it put in your server's key file — you may be forced to use FTP or e-mail to accomplish this – but after that chore, with which any sysadmin will be happy to help you, you will be home free.
>
> If you really can't make up your mind to learn `scp`, it might be safer to use an HTTP-based editing tool as detailed in the next section

Adding an HTML Editing Tool

This simple Weblog is quite adequate for many purposes, but it has one big disadvantage: You can't write up your daily entries using the Web itself. Instead, you must create each entry using a text editor like emacs or Notepad and save it to your Web server's `docroot`. This can be a significant issue over time, especially if you are not allowed telnet/ssh/FTP access to your server or aren't comfortable with the process. HTTP is the next logical step for many users, and is probably no less safe than using FTP.

This process has one big problem: You need to give read/write permissions to the HTTP user (usually Nobody or Everybody) in a particular directory. This is an inherently insecure process, and we do not recommend it in the long run. We'll describe the HTTP tools here so that you can become comfortable with the new aspects before moving on to a better solution, which is using a database instead of separate include() files for each entry. We'll also try to keep the security problems to a minimum, employing a password and letting you send mail to yourself if an unauthorized person tries to log in.

The files you need for an HTML-based file-writing tool are:

♦ login.php

♦ logentry.php

♦ logentry_handler.php

♦ password.inc

Put password.inc in a directory outside the Web tree, such as /home/htmluser. This will ensure that your passwords cannot be read via the Web without being processed by PHP first. The directory must be world-executable and the document must be readable by the httpd user (Nobody). If you have root access on this server, you could chown it to belong to the httpd user; if not, you may have to make the file world-readable, which is a security breach. Be sure to use a password that is not your system user password, just in case it's compromised.

Listings 22-8 through 22-10 are the files you need for an HTML form to edit Weblog entries.

Listing 22-8: Weblog entry login screen (login.php)

```
<HTML>
<HEAD>
<TITLE>Weblog login screen</TITLE>
</HEAD>

<P><B>Supply a username and password.</B></P>
<FORM METHOD=POST ACTION="logentry.php">
<P>USERNAME:<INPUT TYPE=TEXT NAME="test_username" SIZE=20></P>
<P>PASSWORD:<INPUT TYPE=PASSWORD NAME="test_password" SIZE=20></P>
<P>BLOG ENTRY:<BR><TEXTAREA NAME="logtext" COLS=75 ROWS=20
WRAP="VIRTUAL"></TEXTAREA></P>
<P><INPUT TYPE="SUBMIT" VALUE="SUBMIT">
</FORM>
</BODY>
</HTML>
```

Listing 22-9: Included password file (password.inc)

```
<?php
$username = "logwriter";
$password = "logpass";
?>
```

Listing 22-10: Weblog data entry script (`logentry.php`)

```php
<?php
$date = date("Ymd");
include("/home/htmluser/password.inc");

if($_POST['test_username'] == $username && $_POST['test_password'] ==
$password) {
  $fp = fopen("/entries/$date.txt", "w");
  $try_entry = fwrite($fp, $_POST['logtext']);
  if ($try_entry > -1) {
    print("Weblog entry for $date written to disk.");
  } elseif ($try_entry == -1) {
    print("Weblog entry write failed.");
  }
} else {
  mail("me@localhost", "Weblog snoop alert", "Someone from $REMOTE_ADDR
is trying to get into your weblog entry handler.");
}
?>
```

Adding Database Connectivity

Once you see how HTTP data entry is effected using the PHP file writing function, it's a short step to keeping your entries in a database rather than in discrete text files. This is neater — important as your site grows — and considerably more secure. Furthermore, you can give different database permissions to different users, enabling multiple content developers to work on the site safely.

By using a database, you get three more bonuses. First, you can write a script to edit your previous journal entries using a Web form, as well as just enter them. Even better, you can now classify and search your entries. And finally, you are no longer required to have entries every day — now you can do it as frequently or infrequently as you want without having a bunch of blank pages.

Although they have similar names and functions, the files shown in the following listings are somewhat different from the preceding set. You also need a script called `weblog_db_create.php` to create the database (unless you'd rather do it using the MySQL command line tool); and if you want to edit previous entries, you have to add a script called `db_logedit.php`.

> **CAUTION:** Most of these scripts will not fail gracefully if the database has no data in it, particularly usernames and passwords in the `login` table. Because the whole thing is designed to be nonfunctional until you enter at least one entry into these tables, and we want you to focus on the main functionality rather than error-checking, there didn't seem to be a lot of point in testing for empty tables. If it's important to you, feel free to alter the code below.

Listings 22-11 through 22-16 are the files you need for a database-enabled Weblog.

Listing 22-11: Included database password file (`db_password.inc`)

```php
<?php
$hostname = "localhost";
$user = "dbuser";
$password = "dbpass";
?>
```

Put `db_password.inc` somewhere outside your Web tree, such as in your home directory. This will prevent your database passwords from being visible in a Web page or available to anyone who can get into your Web directory.

Listing 22-12: Database creation script (`weblog_db_create.php`)

```php
<?php
// You'll probably have to be the root MySQL user to run this script.
// If you can't get that permission, you could alter the script below
// to create tables in your pre-existing database.
include("/home/htmluser/db_password.inc");

mysql_connect($hostname, $user, $password) or die("Failure to
communicate");
$try_create = mysql_create_db("weblogs");
if ($try_create > 0) {
  echo ("Successfully created database.<BR>\n");
  mysql_select_db("weblogs");
  $query = "CREATE TABLE login (ID SMALLINT NOT NULL AUTO_INCREMENT
PRIMARY KEY, username VARCHAR(20), password VARCHAR(20))";
  $result = mysql_query($query);
  // Since we're not using the standard MySQL
  // date format, store date as an integer
  $query2 = "CREATE TABLE mylog (ID SMALLINT NOT NULL AUTO_INCREMENT
PRIMARY KEY, date INT(8), blogtext TEXT)";
  $result2 = mysql_query($query2);
  mysql_close();
  if ($result > 0 && $result2 > 0) {
    echo ("Successfully created tables<BR>\n");
  } else {
    echo ("Unable to create tables.");
  }
} else {
  echo ("Unable to create database");
}
?>
```

After creating the database as the MySQL root user, you can grant a more restrictive permissions package to some other MySQL user and then run the following scripts as that user.

Listing 22-13: Database Weblog login screen (`db_login.php`)

```
<HTML>
<HEAD>
<TITLE>Weblog login screen</TITLE>
</HEAD>

<P><B>Use this login to add a new entry.</B></P>
<FORM METHOD=POST ACTION="db_logentry.php">
<P>USERNAME:<INPUT TYPE=TEXT NAME="test_username" SIZE=20></P>
<P>PASSWORD:<INPUT TYPE=PASSWORD NAME="test_password" SIZE=20></P>
<P><INPUT TYPE="SUBMIT" VALUE="SUBMIT">
</FORM>

<P><B>Use this login to edit a previous entry.</B></P>
<FORM METHOD=POST ACTION="db_logedit.php">
<P>USERNAME:<INPUT TYPE=TEXT NAME="test_username" SIZE=20></P>
<P>PASSWORD:<INPUT TYPE=PASSWORD NAME="test_password" SIZE=20></P>
<P>EDIT DATE:<INPUT TYPE=TEXT NAME="edit_date" SIZE=8></P>
<P><INPUT TYPE="SUBMIT" VALUE="SUBMIT">
</FORM>
</BODY>
</HTML>
```

Listing 22-14: Database Weblog data entry screen (`db_logentry.php`)

```
<?php
include("/home/htmluser/db_password.inc");
mysql_connect($hostname, $user, $password);
mysql_select_db("weblogs");

// Validate this user
$test_username = $_POST['test_username'];
$query = "SELECT password
          FROM login
          WHERE username = '$test_username'";
$result = mysql_query($query);
if (mysql_num_rows($result) != 1) {
  echo "Something is wrong";
  exit;
}
$password_row = mysql_fetch_array($result);
$db_password = $password_row[0];

if ($_POST['test_password'] == $db_password && $_POST['test_password']
!= "") {
  if ($_POST['Submit'] == 'Enter') {
    // Enter new entry
    $date = date('Ymd'); // Remember, date is an integer type
    $blogtext = $_POST['blogtext'];
```

```
    $query = "INSERT INTO mylog (ID, date, blogtext) VALUES(NULL, $date,
'$blogtext')";
    $result = mysql_query($query);
    if (mysql_affected_rows() == 1) {
      header("Location: db_login.php");
    } else {
      echo "There was a problem inserting your text.";
      exit;
    }
  } else {
    // Show the form
    $php_self = $_SERVER['PHP_SELF'];
    $test_password = $_POST['test_password'];
$form_str = <<< EOFORMSTR
<HTML>
<HEAD>
<TITLE>Weblog data entry screen</TITLE>
</HEAD>
<BODY>
<FORM ACTION="$php_self" METHOD="POST">
<P>Text:<BR><TEXTAREA NAME="blogtext" COLS=75 ROWS=20
WRAP="VIRTUAL"></TEXTAREA></P>
<INPUT TYPE="hidden" NAME="test_username" VALUE="$test_username">
<INPUT TYPE="hidden" NAME="test_password" VALUE="$test_password">
<P><INPUT TYPE="SUBMIT" NAME="Submit" VALUE="Enter"></P>
</FORM>
</BODY>
</HTML>
EOFORMSTR;
    echo $form_str;
  }
} else {
  mail("me@localhost", "Weblog snoop", "Someone from $REMOTE_ADDR is
trying to get into your weblog entry screen.");
}
?>
```

Listing 22-15: Database Weblog data edit screen (`db_logedit.php`)

```
<?php
include("/home/htmluser/db_password.inc");
mysql_connect($hostname, $user, $password);
mysql_select_db("weblogs");

// Validate this user
$test_username = $_POST['test_username'];
$query = "SELECT password
          FROM login
          WHERE username = '$test_username'";
```

```
$result = mysql_query($query);
if (mysql_num_rows($result) != 1) {
  echo "Something is wrong";
  exit;
}
$password_row = mysql_fetch_array($result);
$db_password = $password_row[0];

if ($_POST['test_password'] == $db_password && $_POST['test_password']
!= "") {
  if ($_POST['Submit'] == 'Enter') {
    // Insert edited entry
    $edit_date = $_POST['edit_date'];
    // Escape single-quotes and apostrophes
    $blogtext = addslashes($_POST['blogtext']);
    $query = "UPDATE mylog SET blogtext = '$blogtext' WHERE date =
$edit_date";
    $result = mysql_query($query);
    if (mysql_affected_rows() == 1) {
      header("Location: db_login.php");
    } else {
      echo "There was a problem inserting your text.";
      exit;
    }
  } else {
    // Show the form with the appropriate entry filled in
    $php_self = $_SERVER['PHP_SELF'];
    $test_password = $_POST['test_password'];
    $edit_date = $_POST['edit_date'];
    $query = "SELECT blogtext FROM mylog WHERE date = $edit_date";
    $result = mysql_query($query);
    if (mysql_num_rows($result) == 0) {
      echo "No entry matches that date";
      exit;
    }
    $entry_row = mysql_fetch_array($result);
    // When you get text from a SQL database,
    // you may need to strip backslashes from single-quotes.
    $blogtext = stripslashes($entry_row[0]);

$form_str = <<< EOFORMSTR
<HTML>
<HEAD>
<TITLE>Weblog data edit screen</TITLE>
</HEAD>
<BODY>
<FORM ACTION="$php_self" METHOD="POST">
<P>Text:<BR><TEXTAREA NAME="blogtext" COLS=75 ROWS=20
WRAP="VIRTUAL">$blogtext</TEXTAREA></P>
```

```
<INPUT TYPE="hidden" NAME="test_username" VALUE="$test_username">
<INPUT TYPE="hidden" NAME="test_password" VALUE="$test_password">
<INPUT TYPE="hidden" NAME="edit_date" VALUE="$edit_date">
<P><INPUT TYPE="SUBMIT" NAME="Submit" VALUE="Enter"></P>
</FORM>
</BODY>
</HTML>
EOFORMSTR;
    echo $form_str;
  }
} else {
  mail("me@localhost", "Weblog snoop", "Someone from $REMOTE_ADDR is
trying to get into your weblog entry screen.");
}
?>
```

Listing 22-16: Main database Weblog template (`db_weblog.php`)

```
<?php

/**************************************************************
 * This page has 4 possible cases:                           *
 * 1.  You're viewing this page without a supplied date,     *
 * so default to Case 4.                                     *
 *                                                            *
 * 2.  There is a date.  This is neither the first nor       *
 * the last entry in the db.                                 *
 *                                                            *
 * 3.  There is a date.  This is the first entry in the db.  *
 *                                                            *
 * 4.  There is a date.  This is the last entry in the db.   *
 **************************************************************/

// Open database connection
include("/home/htmluser/db_password.inc");
mysql_connect($hostname, $user, $password);
mysql_select_db("weblogs");

// Identify the latest entry
$query = "SELECT MAX(ID) FROM mylog";
$result = mysql_query($query);
$lastID_row = mysql_fetch_array($result);
$last_ID = $lastID_row[0];

// Get specified weblog entry
if ($_GET['date'] != "") {
  $entry_date = $_GET['date'];
  $query1 = "SELECT * FROM mylog WHERE date = $entry_date";
} else {
```

```
  $query1 = "SELECT * FROM mylog WHERE ID = $last_ID";
}
$result1 = mysql_query($query1);
$row_test_num = mysql_num_rows($result1);
if ($row_test_num > 0) {
  $entry_row = mysql_fetch_array($result1);
  $entry_ID = $entry_row[0];
  $entry_date = $entry_row[1];
  $entry = stripslashes($entry_row[2]);
} else {
  // If someone enters a bad date, redirect to homepage
  header("Location: /index.php");
}

// Get previous date for Cases 2 and 4
if ($entry_ID > 1) {
  $prev_ID = $entry_ID - 1;
  $query2 = "SELECT date FROM mylog WHERE ID = $prev_ID";
  $result2 = mysql_query($query2);
  $prevdate_row = mysql_fetch_array($result2);
  $prev_date = $prevdate_row[0];
} else {
  $prev_date = "";
}

// Get next date for Cases 2 and 3
if ($entry_ID != $last_ID) {
  $next_ID = $entry_ID + 1;
  $query3 = "SELECT date FROM mylog WHERE ID = $next_ID";
  $result3 = mysql_query($query3);
  $nextdate_row = mysql_fetch_array($result3);
  $next_date = $nextdate_row[0];
} else {
  $next_date = "";
}

// Assemble the Previous/Next links
// Case 2
if ($next_date != "" && $prev_date != "") {
  $flipbar = "\n<TABLE BORDER=0><TR><TD WIDTH=\"50%\"
ALIGN=\"left\"><SPAN CLASS=\"previous\"><A
HREF=\"$PHP_SELF?date=$prev_date\">&#60;-- Previous</A></SPAN></TD><TD
WIDTH=\"50%\" ALIGN=\"right\"><SPAN CLASS=\"next\"><A
HREF=\"$PHP_SELF?date=$next_date\">Next --
&#62;</A></SPAN></TD></TR></TABLE>\n";
}
// Case 3
elseif ($next_date != "" && $prev_date == "") {
```

```
  $flipbar = "\n<P CLASS=\"next\"><A
HREF=\"$PHP_SELF?date=$next_date\">Next --&#62;</A></P>\n";
}
// Case 4
elseif($next_date == "" && $prev_date != "") {
  $flipbar = "\n<P CLASS=\"previous\"><A
HREF=\"$PHP_SELF?date=$prev_date\">&#60;-- Previous</A></P>\n";
}


// --------------------
// NOW ASSEMBLE THE PAGE
// --------------------
$title_msg = $entry_date;
$header_msg = "Weblog entry for $entry_date";
include_once('header.inc');

echo $flipbar;
// Include the specified entry text
echo $entry;
echo $flipbar;

include_once('footer.inc');
?>
```

Changes and Additions

Things you might want to immediately change, add, or alter in this codebase include:

♦ Alter colors, styles, layout.

♦ Change frequency of expected update (weekly, monthly).

♦ Change to calendar-based navigation rather than Next/Previous links.

♦ Change to topic-based rather than date-based navigation.

♦ Stop automatic entry changeover by date.

♦ Allow future entries in database.

♦ Allow multiple authors/editors with different permissions.

Besides a personal Weblog, you could use this code for any simple, chronological note taking, such as:

♦ A vacation journal

♦ A project log

♦ The story of your vast weight loss through heroic diet and exercise

♦ A chronicle of your pregnancy and baby's development

Summary

Although it's handy for small, standalone projects such as polls, PHP's most impressive use is in developing complete data-driven content sites. The easiest such site to develop is the personal Weblog. We encourage every PHP user to keep one, if only as a handy testbed for new ideas and techniques.

If you wish, you can store your data in ordinary text files, using PHP to plug these files into a template based on a criterion such as date. This will save a certain amount of formatting-related repetition at the cost of somewhat decreased security. Far better in every way is to keep the data in a database.

The Weblog format is very flexible. It can scale up to a major public site like Slashdot, with tens of thousands of contributors and a steady stream of new content upon which to comment. Or you can keep a little secret diary on your own laptop, reading it in a browser window on the sly. The important point is that once you've made a complete data-driven site with PHP, you'll never go back to static Web pages.

## Chapter 23

Case Study: A User-Rating System

In This Chapter

- Designing a rating system
- Collecting votes
- Counting and displaying results
- Extensions of the design

In this chapter, we look at a very common use of database-driven PHP code: presenting content to users and encouraging them to give it a quality rating.

In the first edition's version of this chapter, we used sample user ratings code that we had extracted from a site of our own. Although "realistic" in some sense, the resulting code samples could not be usefully run without the rest of that Website's code base. This time around, we've gone entirely in the other direction, creating a complete mini-site that forefronts the capability to rate content. Our hope is that it will be straightforward to adapt the rating code to your own site.

Initial Design

We will design our mini-site from the ground up, but bear in mind that the part we really care about is the code relevant to user ratings. In a moment, we will zero in on a particular example content site, but first let's lay out the site characteristics that our ratings code will assume. We assume that:

- The site presents content items to users (books, movies, consumer goods, politicians — anything that could conceivably be rated).
- The site presents one such item per dynamically generated page.
- Each item is stored in a database table or set of tables with a unique database key.

Our ratings code will inevitably be interwoven with the particular content site we choose, but with minimal changes it ought to work with any content site that has these characteristics.

Domain: A quotation site

For our example domain, we'll create a site that displays amusing quotes from famous and not-so-famous people. All we want to present to the user on each quotation page is a pithy quote and an attribution. To store these quotations, we'll make a MySQL database for our entire project and then create a quotation table:

```
create database user_ratings;
use user_ratings;
create table quotations (ID int primary key auto_increment,
                         quotation varchar(255),
                         attribution varchar(255));
```

All this amounts to is two pieces of text (the quotation itself and an attribution) per row, with an automatically assigned identification number. Note that we plan for the quotes to be very pithy indeed — no more than 255 characters. If you want longer quotes, you should make the quotation field a larger type, say type text.

Possible ratings

Working from the other end, let's design another table that specifies the rating values that users can choose between when rating quotations. This is an equally simple MySQL schema:

```
create table rating_values (ID int primary key auto_increment,
                            rank int not null default 0,
                            rating_text varchar(255));
```

As always, the ID field is the unique identifier we rely on. The rank field we intend for ordering the rating values — if you choose a "scale of 1 to 10" style of rating, you want ten rows in the table, with ranks ranging from 1 to 10. (You could make the ID field do double duty here and play the role of the rank field, if you are careful with order of entry; but this seems like more trouble than it's worth.) Finally, the text field contains the explanation of the choice that will be shown to the voter.

While we're at it, let's populate this table with a particular rating scheme.

```
insert into rating_values (rank, rating_text)
  values (5, "5 - Excellent");
insert into rating_values (rank, rating_text)
  values (4, "4 - Very good");
insert into rating_values (rank, rating_text) values (3, "3 - Good");
insert into rating_values (rank, rating_text)
  values (2, "5 - Mediocre");
insert into rating_values (rank, rating_text) values (1, "1 - Poor");
```

Note that the redundancy of including the rank in the text is only necessary if the rank will not be displayed along with the text.

Linking ratings with content

So now we have a table representing possible ratings, and a table representing the content to be rated. How shall we associate them?

We've already made a decision of sorts by making two separate tables. If each piece of content only received one rating, we could have added the rating value as a column in the content table. Similarly, if each rating were applied to only one piece of content (as with finishing order in a race), we could have made the content ID a column in the ratings table. As it is though, we have multiple pieces of content, which different users will associate with different ratings. This is a many-to-many relationship, so we will need a third table to capture the associations.

We want each row in this `ratings` table to represent an instance of a content item receiving a rating. At a minimum, then, we need to identify both the content and the rating in each row. We'll do this by using the primary keys from each table. In addition, we'll throw in a few columns that we have found to be useful, even if we won't be using them much in this chapter's code.

```
create table ratings (ID int primary key auto_increment,
                       rating int,
                       rated_id int,
                       rating_date timestamp,
                       user_ip varchar(30),
                       bogus_bit tinyint default 0);
```

The first three columns are the minimum we need: our usual auto-incremented primary key, and the IDs from the two tables we are associating. The next two will be used to capture some information about the rating event: the time it happened, and the IP address of the user doing the rating. (This last one we include not for any evil, privacy-invading purpose, but just because it turns out to be useful in combating mass ballot stuffing. If you receive a negative review for an item once every two seconds, it can be useful to know that all those votes are coming from the same place.) Finally, we include a bit we can flip if we conclude that large number of rows are bogus — without deleting them, we can write code to screen them out of vote totals and displays.

Now we have designed our three tables and have populated only one of them (`rating_values`). It seems wasteful to print out sample quotes that make up the entries for the quotations table (although we will include them in the database dump for this chapter found at `http://www.troutworks.com/phpbook`). Finally, we have not yet populated the ratings table, because that is something that our users should do.

Collecting Votes

To let our users vote on our content, we need to display that content alongside some kind of form that lets them express their feelings. In this section, we'll create a content page that displays one item and encourages the user to rate it. The code for this page is shown in Listing 23-1. This is a high-level code file, which includes other function files, which in turn do most of the work.

> **NEW FEATURE:** As with much of the code in this edition, we are assuming the existence of the new
> superglobal variables, which only became part of PHP as of version 4.1. The code in this chapter will not
> work in any earlier version, although it should be fairly easy to modify for previous versions. To retrofit this
> code for earlier versions of PHP, look for any variables that start with $_ (such as $_GET, $_POST, and
> $_SERVER), and see Chapter 9 for a discussion of what should replace them.

All the display code is predicated on knowing a database key for the content that will be rated.
This identifier will arrive either as a GET variable or a POST variable. (If a user is arriving for
the first time, we choose a content ID somewhat arbitrarily.) Then this top-level page creates
both the quotation content and the ratings form based on two pieces of information: the current
page name (used for both form submission and previous/next navigation) and the ID of the
current quote. One view of this top-level page is shown in Figure 23-1 — the content is on the
left, and the solicitation to rate is on the right.

Figure 23-1: Displaying a quotation for rating

The code that produced Figure 23-1 is shown in Listing 23-1.

Listing 23-1: `rated_display.php`

```php
<?php
include_once("db_connection.php");
include_once("rating_functions.php");
include_once("content_functions.php");

if (isSet($_GET['RATED_ID'])) {
  $rated_id = $_GET['RATED_ID'];
}
```

```
else if (isSet($_POST['RATED_ID'])) {
  $rated_id = $_POST['RATED_ID'];
}
else {
  $rated_id = 1;
}

// create the quote content
$content_box =
  make_content_box($_SERVER['PHP_SELF'],
                   $rated_id);

// create the navigation links
$nav_box =
  make_next_prev_box($_SERVER['PHP_SELF'],
                     $rated_id);

// create the self-submitting ratings box
// (also handles submissions)
$submission_box =
  make_ratings_box($_SERVER['PHP_SELF'],
                   $rated_id);

// create the link to the main ratings page
$ratings_link =
  "<A HREF=\"all_ratings.php\">See
   other ratings</A>";

// create the actual page
$page_string = <<<EOP
<HTML><HEAD><TITLE>Sample ratable page</TITLE></HEAD>
<BODY>
<CENTER><H2>Quote of the moment</H2></CENTER>
<TABLE WIDTH=500 VALIGN=TOP CELLPADDING=20>
<TR VALIGN=TOP>
<TD VALIGN=TOP COLSPAN=50%>
$content_box
<CENTER>$nav_box</CENTER>
</TD><TD ALIGN=TOP COLSPAN=50%>
$submission_box
<BR>$ratings_link
</TD></TR></TABLE>
</BODY></HTML>
EOP;
echo $page_string;
?>
```

As with many code files in this book, the very first file included (db_connection.php, shown in Listing 23-2) is one that handles all the details of making a MySQL database connection, including the loading of another file (not shown), which sets the database login and passwords appropriately. All the subsequent database interactions implicitly use this connection and (in this chapter) do not explicitly use a connection identifier.

Listing 23-2: `db_connection.php`

```php
<?php
include("../dbvars.php"); // sets $host, $user, $pass
mysql_connect($host, $user, $pass)
  or die("Could not connect to database");
mysql_select_db("user_ratings");
?>
```

As we've said, in this chapter our focus is on the content rating mechanism, and the content itself is there merely so we have something to rate. So as much as possible, we have separated the content-related code from the ratings-related code (and also make no claims for the beauty of our layout or design). Most of the code for presenting the quotations' content is in the form of functions loaded from the file `content_functions.php` (shown in Listing 23-3).

Listing 23-3: `content_functions.php`

```php
<?php

function make_content_box($current_page, $content_id) {
  $query =
    "select quotation, attribution from quotations
       where ID = $content_id";
  $result = mysql_query($query) or die(mysql_error());
  if ($row = mysql_fetch_row($result)) {
    $quotation = $row[0];
    $attribution = $row[1];
    $return_string .=
      "<table align=top><tr align=top>
       <td>\"$quotation\"<br>
       --- $attribution</td></tr></table>";
    return($return_string);
  }
  else {
    return("No content in database");
  }
}

function make_next_prev_box ($current_page, $current_id) {
  $prev_id = prev_content_id($current_id);
  $next_id = next_content_id($current_id);
  return("<TABLE><TR><TD>
          <A HREF=\"$current_page?RATED_ID=$prev_id\">Prev quote</A>
          </TD><TD>
          <A HREF=\"$current_page?RATED_ID=$next_id\">Next quote</A>
```

```
                     </TD></TR></TABLE>");
}

function next_content_id ($current_id) {
  $query = "select ID from quotations
              where ID > $current_id
              order by ID asc";

  $result = mysql_query($query)
    or die("MySQL rejected query $query" . mysql_error());
  if (mysql_num_rows($result) > 0) {
    $row = mysql_fetch_row($result) or die(mysql_error());
    $id = $row[0];
  }
  else {
    $query = "select min(ID) from quotations";
    $result = mysql_query($query) or die(mysql_error());
    $row = mysql_fetch_row($result) or die(mysql_error());
    $id = $row[0];
  }
  return($id);
}

function prev_content_id ($current_id) {
  $query = "select ID from quotations
              where ID < $current_id
              order by ID desc";
  $result = mysql_query($query)
     or die("MySQL rejected query $query" . mysql_error());
  if (mysql_num_rows($result) > 0) {
    $row = mysql_fetch_row($result) or die(mysql_error());
    $id = $row[0];
  }
  else {
    $query = "select max(ID) from quotations";
    $result = mysql_query($query) or die(mysql_error());
    $row = mysql_fetch_row($result) or die(mysql_error());
    $id = $row[0];
  }
  return($id);
}

function truncate_quotation ($quotation) {
  if (strlen($quotation) < 40) {
    return($quotation);
  }
  else {
    $broken_by_punctuation =
      strtok($quotation, ".,!?");
```

```
      return("$broken_by_punctuation ...");
  }

}

?>
```

The only content functions used directly by the `rated_display.php` page are `make_content_box()` (which retrieves a quotation/attribution pair from the database and displays them, wrapped up in an HTML table) and `make_next_prev_box()` (which determines a next and previous quotation ID and creates appropriate navigation links). Finally, there's a utility function (`truncate_quotation()`), which we'll use later in a "top ten" page.

The center of the ratings action is in the file `ratings_function php`, and, in particular, in the top-level function `make_ratings_box()`, which either creates a form as a rating opportunity or thanks the user for having submitted a rating, depending on the presence of POST arguments.

If a rating has been submitted via POST variables, the ratings code puts together an INSERT statement, which records the current content item ID, the ID of the rating that was chosen, and the IP address (if available) of the user's machine. Because the `rating_date` column is a timestamp variable, the time of insertion is recorded without any work on our part. Finally, after handling the submitted rating, the ratings box returned contains a simple thank-you with no immediate opportunity to vote again. (See the "Extensions and Alternatives" section at the end of the chapter for more discussion about how to prevent voting multiple times for the same item.) Figure 23-2 shows the page after a rating has been submitted.

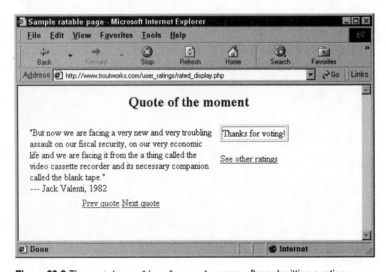

Figure 23-2: The `rating_display.php` page after submitting a rating

If no rating has been submitted, the ratings box is a constructed form, which offers all the values found in the ratings_values table. The form sends the ID of the quote as a hidden variable (RATED_ID), and sends the ID of the rating itself as a radio-button variable (RATING_ID).

Listing 23-4: `rating_functions.php`

```php
<?php

function rating_types_as_array () {
  $return_array = array();
  $result =
    mysql_query("select ID, rating_text from rating_values
                 order by rank desc")
    or die(mysql_error());
  while ($row_array = mysql_fetch_array($result)) {
    $id = $row_array['ID'];
    $text = $row_array['rating_text'];
    $return_array[$id] = $text;
  }
  return($return_array);
}

function maybe_handle_new_rating() {
  if (isSet($_POST['RATING_ID'])) {
    $new_rating = $_POST['RATING_ID'];
    $rated_id = $_POST['RATED_ID'];
    $user_ip = $_SERVER['REMOTE_ADDR'];
    handle_new_rating($new_rating, $rated_id,
                      $user_ip);
    return(true);
  }
  else {
    return(false);
  }
}

function handle_new_rating($new_rating, $rated_id,
                           $user_ip) {
  $query = "insert into ratings
            (rating, rated_id, user_ip)
            values ($new_rating, $rated_id,
                    '$user_ip')";
  mysql_query($query) or
    die("Could not insert due to: " . mysql_error());
}

function make_ratings_box ($target_page, $rated_id) {
  $new_rating_handled = maybe_handle_new_rating();
```

```
  if ($new_rating_handled) {
    return(make_ratings_receipt_box());
  }
  else {
    return(make_ratings_submission_box($target_page,
                                       $rated_id));
  }
}

function make_ratings_receipt_box () {
  return("<TABLE BORDER=1><TR><TD>Thanks for voting!".
         "</TD></TR></TABLE>");
}

function make_ratings_submission_box
  ($target_page, $rated_id) {
  $rating_array = rating_types_as_array();
  // Beginning of HTML table
  $return_string =
    "<TABLE BORDER=1><TR><TD>What did you think?</TD></TR>".
    "<TR><TD ALIGN=LEFT><FORM METHOD=POST ACTION=\"$target_page\">";
  foreach ($rating_array as $id => $text) {
    $return_string .=
       "<BR><INPUT TYPE=RADIO NAME=RATING_ID VALUE=\"$id\">" .
       "  $text</INPUT>";
  }
  $return_string .=
    "<INPUT TYPE=HIDDEN NAME=RATED_ID VALUE=$rated_id>";
  $return_string .=
    "<BR><CENTER><INPUT TYPE=SUBMIT
    NAME=SUBMIT VALUE=\"Submit\"></CENTER>";
  $return_string .= "</FORM></TD></TR></TABLE>";
  return($return_string);
}

?>
```

Aggregating Results

Finally, we offer a simple page that shows a "top ten" ranking of the quotations that have been rated. Code for this is shown in Listing 23-5, and a browser view of the generated page is shown in Figure 23-3.

Listing 23-5: `all_ratings.php`

```
<?php
include_once("db_connection.php");
include_once("rating_functions.php");
include_once("content_functions.php");
```

```
$query_best =
  "select quotations.ID,
          quotations.quotation,
          quotations.attribution,
          avg(rating_values.rank) as avg_rank
   from quotations, ratings, rating_values
   where ratings.rated_id = quotations.id
         and ratings.rating_id = rating_values.id
   group by quotations.id
   order by avg_rank desc limit 10";
$result = mysql_query($query_best)
  or die(mysql_error());

$table_rows_string =
"<TR><TH>Quote</TH><TH>Attribution</TH><TH>Average rating</TH></TR>";
while ($row_array = mysql_fetch_array($result)) {
  $quotation_id = $row_array['ID'];
  $quotation_text = $row_array['quotation'];
  $truncated_quotation = truncate_quotation($quotation_text);
  $quotation_attribution = $row_array['attribution'];
  $avg_rank = $row_array['avg_rank'];
  $rounded_avg_rank = sprintf("%.1f", $avg_rank);

  $table_rows_string .=
    "<TR><TD><A HREF=\"rated_display.php?RATED_ID=$quotation_id\">
     $truncated_quotation</A></TD>
     <TD>$quotation_attribution</TD>".
    "<TD>$rounded_avg_rank</TD></TR>";
}

// lay out the page
$title = "Ratings page for quotes";
$page_string = <<<EOP
<HTML><HEAD></HEAD><BODY>
<CENTER><H2>$title</H2></CENTER>
<TABLE BORDER=1>
<H2>Top ten most popular quotes</H2>
$table_rows_string
</TABLE>
</BODY>
</HTML>
EOP;

echo $page_string;
?>
```

The aggregated page is pretty much just a sorted and aggregated view of the underlying ratings table, with some tricks to make the display more concise. (We round the averaged ratings to a reasonable precision and truncate the quotes at the first sign of punctuation.) The aggregation happens as a result of grouping the ratings rows (of which there are many per quotation) by quotation in the SQL statement and averaging the ranks. We also turn the truncated quotations into links back to the display pages, using the ID of the content as a GET argument. (Note that although this is a top-ten list, there are only eight quotations in our sample dataset.)

Figure 23-3: A top-ten view of the rated quotations

The analysis this page provides is a direct product of the SQL statement it displays. Rather than displaying the most highly-rated items, it would be easy to display the most poorly-rated, or the items with the most ratings overall, or any number of other analyses, simply by varying the SQL statement and the title.

What about performance? We don't have any hard data, but you can look at http://www.mysteryguide.com/readerratings.html, which uses roughly these techniques, and see how such a page performs with three "best of" analyses on approximately 30,000 individual ratings. As you may be able to tell, it's just beginning to slow up perceptibly, taking a second or two to respond under typical conditions on our Web host.

Extensions and Alternatives

We have tried to make this example as bare bones as possible, focusing on the ratings code while also retaining the minimum functionality to make a functioning mini-site. There are several ways in which you could improve or extend the code if you feel so moved.

For one thing, we don't like the fact that you have to do two things to submit a rating (choose a radio button and then click Submit) rather than one. Long before we were aware of any "one-click" patent controversy, we had a "one-click" version of such a rating system on the MysteryGuide site (www.mysteryguide.com) — this made each voting alternative into its own Submit button, so that only one user action was needed. The problem with this is that, although the radio-button code in this chapter manipulates three different values (the variable name, the corresponding submitted value, and the text displayed in association with the button), you really only have two alternatives with a Submit button: the name of the variable and the value (which will also be the text displayed in the button). There is no good way, for example, to display meaningful text and actually submit something else when clicked (like a database ID). The alternatives are 1) resort to Javascript, 2) to use radio buttons instead (as in this chapter), or 3) to somehow map from submitted text back to the value you really want to send (as we do on the MysteryGuide site). Probably Javascript is the way to go.

Another improvement that our rating system needs is better prevention of ballot stuffing. In this chapter, we present the weakest defense to multiple voting for the same item: The ratings form disappears in response to detecting a ratings submission, so the user cannot simply click a button on the same page over and over. However, nothing stops our user from hitting the Back button or typing in the original URL to get the form back again, and repeating *ad nauseum*. Any better technique needs to start with identifying multiple requests as actually coming from the same person — see Chapter 27 for a discussion of how to do this.

Summary

In this chapter, we have shown you a system that lets users rate your pages, and we have taken you through how it hooks up to a minimal "content site." The code lets users rate items, and it displays a summary page of votes. We also discussed some ways in which you could take this code and extend it to make it more useful and interesting. We hope we've made it easy to detach it from our sample content domain (a small set of quotations) and to snap it back on to some content you care about.

Chapter 24

PHP/Database Efficiency and Style

In This Chapter

♦ Using database resources efficiently

♦ Making the database work for you

♦ Timestamping insertions and updates

This quick chapter is for people making database-enabled PHP Web sites who suspect that they are doing things awkwardly or inefficiently. Maybe you are new to databases, or maybe you know there must be a way to speed things up just because your pages are loading unacceptably slowly.

We offer some tips and tricks for making things run faster, and we show you some common ways that database systems can save you from writing unnecessary PHP code. As usual, some of our code examples will use MySQL functions, although the lessons are mostly general and independent of particular database implementations.

> **CROSS-REFERENCE:** This chapter will do little to help you get your database-enabled code working in the first place. For a guide to common errors, gotchas, and problems with PHP/database code, see Chapter 25.

Connections — Reduce, Reuse, Recycle

One important thing to realize is that establishing an initial connection with a database is never a cheap operation. Unless your PHP script is doing some unusually computationally-intensive work, the overall database interaction will be the most time- and resource-intensive part of your code, and it is frequently true that the establishment of a connection is the most expensive part of code that interacts with a database, even if the connection is only established once in serving the page.

You have two potentially competing goals here. On the one hand, you want to minimize the number of times your code makes the expensive and time-consuming call to open an entirely new database connection. This argues for leaving connections open during the course of page execution, rather than closing and reopening. On the other hand, there are sometimes hard limits on the number of simultaneous connections that a database program can support. This might argue for closing connections whenever possible, in hopes that less connected time per script might allow more scripts to execute simultaneously.

In our experience, however, most Web scripts are evanescent enough that it is never worth the overhead to close and reopen a database connection within one page's execution. If you want to minimize total time connected, open the connection immediately before the first call to the database, and close it immediately after the last one.

A bad example: One connection per statement

Our first bad example seems stylistically reasonable in one sense because it uses a function to eliminate repetitive code.

```php
<?php
function box_query ($query, $user, $pass, $db)
{
  $my_connection =
    mysql_connect('localhost', $user, $pass)
    or die("Couldn't connect to database");;
  mysql_select_db($db, $my_connection)
    or die("Couldn't select database");
  $result_id = mysql_query($query, $my_connection)
    or die(mysql_error());
  print("<H3>Results for query:  $query</H3>");
  print("<TABLE>");
  while ($row = mysql_fetch_row($result_id))
  {
    print("<TR>");
    $row_length = mysql_num_fields($result_id);
    for ($x = 0; $x < $row_length; $x++)
    {
      $entry = $row[$x];
      print("<TD>$entry</TD>");
    }
    print("</TR>\n");
  }
  print("</TABLE>");
  mysql_close($my_connection);
}
/* code that uses box_query() */
?>
```

The idea is that we take a function that packages up an arbitrary MySQL query and displays the returned data in an attractive HTML table. The main virtue of this function as defined is that it is very self-contained — it opens its own database connection for its own purposes, and then it disposes of that connection when the function is done.

The preceding code is fine if we expect to display only one such table per page. If we use this function more than once per page, however, we will find ourselves opening and closing connections every time the function is invoked, which is bound to be more inefficient than leaving the connection open. The general rule is to leave a single connection open for as long as it is needed in the execution of a single page's script. Applying this rule to the preceding function would mean rewriting it so that it takes a connection as argument (or implicitly uses a connection opened at the beginning of the script) and then opening a single connection per page.

Multiple results don't need multiple connections

One thing that surprised us the very first time we saw Web-database scripting was that, with many database programs, it is possible to retain the results from more than one query at once, even though only one connection has been opened. For example, with a MySQL database you can do something like this:

```
mysql_connect('localhost', $user, $pass); //opens connection
mysql_select_db('scienceguide');
$author_result = mysql_query("select ID from author")
                 or die(mysql_error());
while ($author_row = mysql_fetch_row($author_result))
{
  $book_result =
    mysql_query("select title from book
                 where authorID = $author_row[0]")
      or die(mysql_error());
  while ($book_row = mysql_fetch_row($book_result))
    {
      $title = $book_row[0];
      print("$title<BR>");
    }
}
```

This would print out titles of books after retrieving them from the book table, using IDs from rows retrieved from the author table. Now, this is in fact an extremely inefficient way to retrieve the data (see "Make the Database Work for You" below), but it illustrates that two different result sets (identified by the variables $author_result and $book_result) can be actively used at the same time, after having been retrieved over a single connection.

Persistent connections

Finally, if you become convinced that the sheer overhead of opening new database connections is killing your performance, you might want to investigate opening *persistent* connections. Unlike regular database connections, these connections are not automatically killed when your page exits (or even when mysql_close() is called) but are saved in a pool for future use. The first time one of your scripts opens such a connection, it is opened in the same resource-intensive way as with a regular database connection. The next script that executes, however, might get that very same connection in response to its request, which saves the cost of reopening a fresh connection. (The previous connection will be reused only if the parameters of the new request are identical.)

> **NOTE:** Persistent database connections only work in the module installation of PHP. If you ask for a persistent connection in the CGI version, you will simply get a regular connection.

The PHP function to request such a persistent connection for MySQL is mysql_pconnect(), which is used in exactly the same way as mysql_connect(). This naming convention seems to be stable across PHP functions for the different databases — if you use a particular DB connect function, you should consult the documentation to see if a pconnect version exists.

> **NOTE:** Other than offering a particular kind of increased efficiency, persistent database connections do not provide any functionality beyond that of regular database connections. In particular, you should not expect persistent connections to have any "memory" of previous queries or of variables from previous page executions.

Make the Database Work for You

Just as when you write code in a programming language, writing code that interacts with a database is an exercise in appropriate division of labor. People who write programming languages and databases have agreed to automate, standardize, and optimize certain tasks that come up over and over again in programming, so that programmers don't have to constantly reinvent the wheel when making their individual applications. The very general rule is that, unless you're willing to spend a lot of energy in optimizing code for your special case, you are better off using a database-provided facility than trying to invent your own solution for the same task.

It's probably faster than you are

Database programs are judged partly on their speed, and so database programmers devote a large proportion of their effort toward ensuring that queries execute as quickly as possible. In particular, any searching or sorting of the contents of a database is best done within that database (if possible), rather than by your own code.

A bad example: Looping, not restricting

For example, take the following code fragment (and please don't laugh — we have actually seen code like this):

```
function print_first_name_bad ($lastname, $dbconnection)
{
  $query = "select firstname, lastname from author";
  $result_id = mysql_query($query, $dbconnection)
```

```
    or die(mysql_error());
  while ($row = mysql_fetch_array($result_id))
  {
    if ($row['lastname'] == $lastname)
      print("The first name is " . $row['firstname']);
  }
}
```

When this code is handed a last name string and a database connection, it will print out associated first names, if any, in the "author table" of the database. For example, A call to print_first_name_bad('Sagan', $dbconnection) might produce the output

```
The first name is Carl
```

If there were multiple authors in that table with the same last name, then multiple lines would be printed.

The problem here is that we don't need to grab all the data in this table, pull it through the narrow pipe of a connection, and then pick and choose from it on our side of the pipe. Instead, we should restrict the query with a "WHERE" clause:

```
function print_first_name_better ($lastname, $dbconnection)
{
  $query = "select firstname, lastname from author
            where lastname = '$lastname'";
  $result_id = mysql_query($query, $dbconnection)
      or die(mysql_error());
  while ($row = mysql_fetch_array($result_id))
  {
      print("The first name is " . $row['firstname']);
  }
}
```

The WHERE clause ensures that only the rows we care about are selected in the first place. Not only does this cut down on the data passed over the SQL connection, but the code used to locate the correct rows on the database side is almost certainly quicker than your PHP code.

Sorting and aggregating

Exactly the same argument applies if you find yourself writing code to sort results that have been returned from your database, or to count, average, or otherwise aggregate those results. In general, the ORDER BY syntax in SQL will allow you to presort your retrieved rows by any prioritized list of columns in the query, and that sort will probably be more efficient than either homegrown code or the PHP array-sorting functions. Similarly, rather than looping through DB rows to count, sum, or average a value, investigate whether the syntax of your particular DB's flavor of SQL supports the GROUP BY construct, and in-query functions like count(), sum(), and average(). In general, executing a query like:

```
$query = "select count(ID) from author";
```

will be a radically more efficient approach to counting table rows than selecting them and iterating through them with a PHP looping construct.

Use MIN or MAX rather than sorting where possible

Although it's good to let the database system do your sorting for you, it's even better to not have to sort at all. One task that is often addressed by unnecessary sorting is finding the minimum or maximum value in a set of result rows. You may see code like this:

```
$query = "select ID from author order by ID limit 1;  // inefficient
```

This query will return a single ID from the author table after having sorted it in ascending order — in other words, the minimum ID. It does have the virtue that the actual result set returned is small, and so it is a better approach for finding the minimum than using the same query without the limit clause and picking off the desired value from the top of that large result set. But if all we are interested in is the minimum (or maximum) value, there is no need to require the DB to figure out the rank order of all the other IDs that we are not interested in. A better solution is:

```
$query = select min(ID) from author; // efficient
```

The difference between these approaches will be imperceptible when your tables only have tens or hundreds of rows in them, but will begin to matter as your tables grow to thousands or tens of thousands of rows in size.

Creating date and time fields

It is very common to want to associate a date and/or time with a row's worth of data. For instance, your table rows might represent requests made by your Web site users, and the associated date/time is the time that that request hit your database.

Now, one way to insert or update date fields is to include a string that represents the desired date in a format parsable by your database. For example, if you want to set the `mydate` datetime field of all rows of `mytable` to a particular date, you might set up a query like this one:

```
$query = "update mytable set mydate = '2003-11-24'";
```

and then send that query off for evaluation. (Unfortunately, the exact standards of readable date formats vary quite widely from one SQL database system to another. This particular date string means November 24, 2003 as far as MySQL is concerned.)

The preceding approach is fine, as long as you take care that the particular date string you send is, in fact, readable as a date by your DB. Things get more complicated if you need to construct such a string on-the-fly to represent a date that depends on the value of variables in your script.

The main thing to remember is that, with most database systems, there is no need to go through such contortions to set a field to the current date or time. Many have a current-date function that can be embedded directly in your query. For example, A MySQL version of the preceding query that sets the relevant date/time field to the current instant looks like this:

```
$query = "update mytable set mydate = now()";
```

(Note that the call to now() is not enclosed in single quotes because it's a call to database function, rather than a string to be interpreted by the database as data.) The analogous query for Microsoft SQL Server looks like:

```
$query = "update mytable set mydate = getdate()";
```

Finally, even if the time you want stored is not that of the instant of execution, there may still be better alternatives than constructing readable date strings in your script. In addition to functions returning the current date, many versions of SQL offer functions for performing date arithmetic — start with a particular date/time, and then add or subtract years, months, or hours. In MySQL, these functions are:

♦ date_add(*date, date-interval*)

♦ date_sub(*date, date-interval*)

Here *date-interval* is a string that includes a number of time units and the type of unit. A MySQL query to set all rows to a time a week from now might look like this:

```
$query = "update mytable set mydate = date_add(now(), INTERVAL 7 DAY)";
```

Finding the last inserted row

Another surprisingly helpful capability offered by some database systems is finding the ID of the last row inserted.

This problem arises when you are trying to create a new database entry that is distributed across several database tables, each of which has an automatically incremented primary key. As an example, take the tables created by the following MySQL statements:

```
create table author (ID int primary key auto_increment,
                    lastname varchar(75),
                    firstname varchar (75));
create table book (ID int primary key auto_increment,
                    authorID int,
                    title varchar(100));
```

One intent of these statements is that the book table is linked to the author table by joining them so that book.authorID = author.ID. Another intent is that we don't have to worry about assigning unique ID fields for either table — the database will automatically assign them. Unfortunately, the combined intent leads to a problem. How do we write code that will gracefully insert a linked book-author pair, when both the author and the book are new to the database? If we insert a new author, the ID field of the inserted row will be automatically created by the database and so will not be a part of our SQL insert statement. How can we give the correct `authorID` to our new `book` row?

One possible strategy is to do something like the following (in MySQL):

```
$author_lastname = 'Feynman';
$author_firstname = 'Richard';
$book_title = 'The Character of Physical Law';
$author_insert = "insert into author (lastname, firstname)
      values ('$author_lastname','$author_firstname')";
mysql_query($author_insert) OR die(mysql_error());
$author_id_query =
  "select ID from author
   where lastname = '$author_lastname'
   and firstname = '$author_firstname'";
$author_id_result =
  mysql_query($author_id_query) OR die(mysql_error());
if (mysql_num_rows($author_id_result) <= 0)
  die("Inserted author not found!");
else
  $author_row = mysql_fetch_row($author_id_result);
$authorID = $author_row[0];
$book_insert = "insert into book (authorID, title)
                values ($authorID, $book_title)";
mysql_query($book_insert) OR die(mysql_error());
```

In this code we create a new author row, use the last name and first name of the author to select the row we have just created, pull out the unique ID of that newly created row, and then incorporate that ID in a statement inserting a new row into the `book` table. This code would probably work in this particular instance, if we assume that the author's last name and first name are sufficient for unique identification. But for many databases, we will not be able to make such an assumption, which is, of course, why the convention of unique IDs developed in the first place.

A similar approach that is sometimes used is to insert a row (for example, into the `author` table) and then select the maximum ID from that table, on the theory that the highest row ID will be the one most recently inserted. If the most recently inserted row is, in fact, the one we just inserted, this will work like a charm. Unfortunately, this is exactly the kind of approach that appears to work when tested by a solitary user/programmer and then breaks when used with a real database server that is dealing with requests from multiple connections at the same time. The problem is that an insertion from another connection might well arrive in between our own insertion and the statement we send to retrieve the maximum ID to date, with the result that our second insertion is matched with an inappropriate ID.

The best solution, when it is available, is to have the database itself keep track of the last inserted ID in a retrievable way, and do this tracking on a *per-connection* basis, so that there are no worries about the synchronization issues in the previous paragraph. For MySQL users,

PHP offers the function `mysql_insert_id()`, which takes a connection ID as argument and returns the autoincremented ID of the last inserted row. We can use it to rewrite our previous code example:

```
$author_lastname = 'Feynman';
$author_firstname = 'Richard';
$book_title = 'The Character of Physical Law';
$author_insert = "insert into author (lastname, firstname)
        values ('$author_lastname', '$author_firstname')";
mysql_query($author_insert) OR die(mysql_error());
$authorID = mysql_insert_id();
$book_insert = "insert into book (authorID, title)
            values ($authorID, '$book_title')";
mysql_query($book_insert) OR die (mysql_error());
```

As with many PHP/MySQL functions, the connection argument to `mysql_insert_id()` is actually optional and defaults to the most recently opened connection.

In some other database systems, the ID of the most recent autoincrement is available (per-session) as a "special" variable that can be embedded in the next query. In Microsoft SQL Server, for example, the variable is `%%identity`, which can be embedded in a query as follows to retrieve the last insert ID:

```
$query = "select @@identity";
```

Summary

Because database-related functionality is among the most resource-intensive things that PHP can do, you can become a hero by giving just a little thought to efficient coding practices. Particularly if your data-driven PHP scripts are sluggish, you want to learn to work with the database instead of against it.

The basic principles of database-intensive coding are simple. It costs a lot to open a connection to a database, so don't turn the tap on and off unnecessarily. Remember the pipe is narrow — you want to transport the bare minimum of data you need for each page. And take the time to learn all the functionality your particular database can offer you. SQL is really good at sorting, filtering, restricting, numbering, and grouping — use these powers rather than doing it less well and more slowly with PHP.

In the next chapter, we move from these tips and stylistic concerns to problems and gotchas that can actually break your database code or give you unintended results.

## Chapter 25

PHP/Database Gotchas

In This Chapter

♦ No connection

♦ Problems with privileges

♦ Unescaped quotes

♦ Broken SQL statements

♦ Too little data, too much data

♦ Specific SQL functions

♦ Debugging and sanity checking

This chapter details some of the common difficulties that arise with using PHP and databases. The goal is to help you diagnose and solve problems more quickly and with less frustration. As usual, our specific code and function references are to MySQL (with one exception), although the set of gotchas is fairly independent across different databases.

> **CROSS-REFERENCE:** This chapter is about diagnosing and fixing PHP/database code that is genuinely broken — that is, it is not successfully retrieving data, or it is producing error messages. If your scripts are working, but too slowly, see Chapter 24.

No Connection

If you have a database call in your PHP script and the connection can't be opened, you will see a version of one of these two warning screens (depending on how high your error reporting levels are cranked up, and, to some extent, the precise cause of the problem).

The first possibility is the No Connection warning, as shown in Figure 25-1.

This option indicates a problem either with the MySQL server itself or with the path to `mysqld`. In its own special way, PHP is telling you that it knows about MySQL but can't hook up to it. This is the error you will see on a working PHP-MySQL installation if the database server crashes.

If the problem is on the PHP side, your error screen will look more like the one shown in Figure 25-2.

Figure 25-1: A No Connection warning

Figure 25-2: An undefined function fatal error

This means PHP doesn't know about MySQL at all.

Of the two, the fatal error is much more straightforward to fix. Clearly if you're running into an undefined function that is supposed to be in the PHP function set, you can be pretty sure you simply forgot to build that module into your installation. So on the Unix side, you will need to recompile with the —with-mysql option. On the Windows side, MySQL should be precompiled into the binary for you and immediately available. In the case of any other supported database or a version of PHP older than 4.1, you merely need to uncomment the `extension=php_[database].dll` line in your `php.ini` to be ready to go, unless you put your MySQL executable in a very, very strange place (which you shouldn't do unless you're prepared to handle the consequences, including fatal errors).

The innocuous-looking No Connection error is actually a little harder to diagnose because there are several possible causes. They fall into two main categories:

♦ The MySQL daemon isn't running.

♦ The MySQL socket isn't where PHP is looking for it.

It's easy to check whether `mysqld` is running, so you may as well do that first. Just use whatever method you prefer to check running processes. On Windows, this means it's time for the old `Ctrl+Alt+Delete` action to bring up the Task Manager. On Unix, where freedom of choice is the watchword, you can check the system processes by means of `ps` or a graphical system monitoring utility or even by querying `mysqladmin` directly.

If `mysqld` is down, perhaps you have merely forgotten to (re)start it (Don't laugh. It happens). If it's been running continuously for 143 days before suddenly quitting in the middle of an operation, your problem is beyond the scope of this book. We can only direct you to the MySQL Web site (at `www.mysql.com`) with our deepest sympathies and most fervent hopes that you've maintained a good backup schedule.

The socket problem usually arises the first time you fire up MySQL on a new server. It's rather uncommon for this problem to occur in a long-running site, although it does happen. For instance, we recently had a Web host move our MySQL daemon to another server on short notice, at which point all our scripts that used the hostname `localhost` immediately crashed.

The solution to your database connection problems is generally to be found in the `php.ini` file. There's a section of MySQL variables that you must carefully check against whatever hostname, port, and socket you're specifying in your PHP scripts. You want to ensure you're not inadvertently directing PHP to look for MySQL on an odd port or at the wrong default host. On Unix, you can also check the `/etc/services` file for a different socket address, and the `/etc/hosts` file for an unexpected server alias. In general, you should leave these variables open unless you have a specific reason to set them.

Problems with Privileges

Error messages caused by privilege problems look a lot like the connection errors described previously. You will see a No Connection error that looks like Figure 25-3:

Figure 25-3: Privilege problems

The key differentiator is that little piece about the user and password.

> **CAUTION:** Because of the security issues caused by these failure messages, which include the database username and host and whether you're using a password or not, it's best to use silent mode on a production site. You do this by putting the character @ in front of the functions `mysql_connect` and `mysql_select_db`.

These errors are many in number but fall into pretty clear major types:

♦ Mistyping usernames/passwords.

♦ Failing to use a necessary password.

♦ Trying to use a nonexistent password.

♦ Trying to use your system's username/password instead of the MySQL username/password.

♦ Employing a database username that lacks the necessary permissions for the task.

♦ Logging in from a location or client that the MySQL database does not allow for a particular user

♦ PHP being unable to open the database-password `include` file due to incorrect file permissions. (It must be a world-readable file in a world-executable directory.)

♦ The database root user having deliberately changed permissions on you.

These are not structural problems but usually just simple slips of memory that result in miscues or misrecollections. They are very common. We aren't too proud to confess that we've fallen victim to all of them — and not just once, but over and over. They should be trivial to fix in the vast majority of situations.

Unescaped Quotes

Quotes can cause many small but annoying buglets between PHP and MySQL. The crux of the issue is that PHP evaluates within double quotes and largely ignores single quotes, whereas MySQL evaluates within single quotes and largely ignores double quotes. This can lead to situations where you have to think hard about the purpose of each quotation mark. An example is:

```
mysql_query("INSERT INTO book (ID, title, year, ISBN) VALUES(NULL,
'$title', '$year', '$ISBN')");
```

In most of PHP, variables within single quotes are not expanded, whereas variables in double quotes or unquoted variables are — so this query looks a bit strange. But if you think about it, the statement is valid in both languages. The single quotes exist within double quotes, so PHP takes them as literal characters; and the variables are actually within double quotes, so PHP replaces them with their values. You can think of the division of labor this way: In a database query, PHP does its thing on the stuff between double quotes (treating single quotes literally), and MySQL later deals with the stuff left over within single quotes.

Obviously you'll need to exercise some care when writing these statements. This is one of the reasons why it's preferable to break up your MySQL queries into two parts, a query string and a `mysql_query()` function, like so:

```
$query = "INSERT INTO book (ID, title, year, ISBN) VALUES(NULL,
'$title', '$year', '$ISBN')";
$result = mysql_query($query);
```

This style also eliminates the double parentheses that account for common PHP errors.

Even greater issues arise with strings that use single quotes and double quotes within the text. Remember that apostrophes and single quotes are the same thing for PHP and MySQL — they have no smart-quoting feature (not that most smart quotes are all that smart anyway). So this insertion query will break as follows if any of your lastname entries ever has an apostrophe in it (for example, O'Hara, D'Souza, and M'Naughten):

```
$query = "INSERT INTO employee (ID, lastname, firstname) VALUES(NULL,
'$lastname', '$firstname')";
$result = mysql_query($query);
```

Other very common problems are caused by names of businesses with apostrophes in them, such as Rosalita's Bar and Grill or Yoshi's Hair Salon, and by any string that might have a contraction or possessive in it (such as can't, what's, or Mike's).

The parallel issue on the PHP side is a string with a double quote in it. This construction will definitely not work as intended:

```
$string = "He said, "I'm not angry," but I knew he was.";
$statement = mysql_query("INSERT INTO diary (ID, entry) VALUES(NULL,
'$string')";
```

> **CAUTION:** In very long text entries, a quote problem may present as a partial string being inserted; or it may appear as a complete failure; or it may seem as though only short entries are being accepted while longer entries fail.
>
> If you're using an HTML form with values, and only the first word of your string is being inserted, the problem is likely to be that you forgot to quote the form value properly. In other words, your form field says `<INPUT TYPE="text" VALUE=quoted string>` rather than `<INPUT TYPE='text' VALUE="quoted string">`.

The following list reviews the three ways of dealing with quoting issues:

♦ In cases where the string is directly stated within the code, you can escape the necessary characters with a backslash.

```
$query = "INSERT INTO employee (ID, lastname, firstname) VALUES(NULL,
'O\'Donnell', 'Sean')";
```

♦ In cases where the string is represented by a variable, you can use `addslashes()`, which will automatically add any necessary backslashes.

```
$string =
addslashes("He said, 'I'm not angry,' but I knew he was.");
$statement = mysql_query("INSERT INTO diary (ID, entry) VALUES(NULL,
'$string')";
```

♦ You can build PHP with the `--with-magic-quotes` option, and/or set magic-quotes to on in the `php.ini` file, or use the `set_magic_quotes_runtime(1)` function. This will add slashes without your needing to specify `addslashes()` each time. If your ISP controls the `php.ini` file, you should still be able to set these variables by changing your own `.htaccess` file.

For some murky psychological reason, many PHP users seem exceedingly averse to using `addslashes()` and its partner, `stripslashes()`. People will tie themselves in knots using single quotes when they really shouldn't, just so they don't have to escape double quotes. This practice is bad style at any time but is especially dangerous when using a database.

You need to add slashes when inserting values into a database; and conversely you'll need to strip out the slashes when pulling strings from a database (unless you have magic quotes turned on).

```
$query = "SELECT passphrase FROM userinfo WHERE username='$username'";
$result = mysql_query($query);
$query_row = mysql_fetch_array($result);
$passphrase = stripslashes($query_row[0]);
```

If you fail to do this, more and more slashes will be added each time you reenter the data into MySQL! This is an issue that is very frequently encountered with editable Web forms that redisplay values pulled from a database, as shown in Figure 25-4.

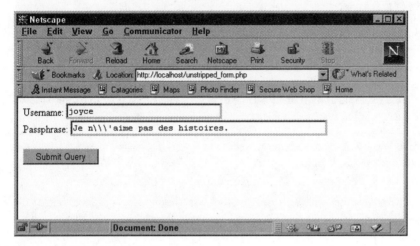

Figure 25-4: Unstripped slashes in a form

Broken SQL Statements

In addition to quoting problems, there are a number of easy ways to send a "bad" query to the database. That query might be syntactically malformed, have the right syntax but refer to tables that do not exist, or have any of a number of problems that make the database unable to handle it properly. A typical error message is shown in Figure 25-5.

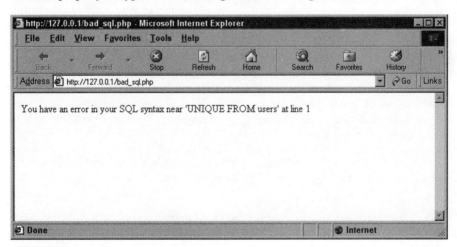

Figure 25-5: A bad SQL statement error

> **CAUTION:** A MySQL error (such as the one shown in Figure 25-5) is different from a connection or link error, which looks something like Figure 25-1. A MySQL error is the error returned from the database when you try to do something that it doesn't like. It is not automatically echoed to the screen; you need to call `mysql_error()` to see any output. A connection error is a message that PHP is sending to you when an expected connection or link is not present. It is automatically echoed to the screen and must be silenced by being prepended with a `@`.

Older versions of PHP used to automatically `echo` an error statement in these circumstances. Now, if you wish to find out what the problem is, you must manually call `mysql_error()` (as we've done in the example above) or `mysql_errno()`. The safest way to capture these errors is to send them to a log file by using `error_log()`.

> **NOTE:** A broken or invalid SQL query is not the same thing as a query that returns no rows. You can write a perfectly fine SQL query like the following:
>
> `$query = "select ID from cust where name = 'nonexistent'";`
>
> You send it to your DB and get back a perfectly valid result set, which happens to contain exactly 0 rows. Among other things, this means that error-trapping that catches query failures will not help you detect the case of zero rows. For MySQLers, a helpful function is `mysql_num_rows()`, which is called on the query result ID and returns an integer.

Exactly how a bad SQL problem will present itself in your browser depends on your PHP version, your database version, your error settings, and how much error-checking code you yourself have incorporated in your script. Just as with other kinds of malignancy, early detection of a failed query is key.

Your new best friend for making MySQL queries looks like this:

```
$result = mysql_query($query) or error_log(mysql_error());
```

Because `mysql_query()` will return a false value if it fails, the `error_log()` portion will be executed only if a failure occurs. The low operator precedence of the `or` operator ensures that the `error_log()` call also plays no role in the assignment statement — if the assignment succeeds, it is as if the `error()` portion did not exist. Failure leads to the script exiting just as soon as it has printed the most informative error message that the MySQL designers could concoct. If your particular database lacks such an error variable in PHP, you might want to simply call `error_log($query)`. Often the problem is obvious after you see the query that is actually being sent.

If you have not incorporated error-checking into your query calls, you will get the first bad news when you try to use the query result ID in subsequent database code. The typical pattern is:

```
$my_result = mysql_query($bad_query);
$row = mysql_fetch_row($my_result); // error shows up here
```

The typical error message for MySQL is `0 is not a mysql result identifier in [`*`some row`*`]`. This is because, rather than detecting the `0` value that `mysql_query()` returns when it fails, you have tried to use that value as if it were a valid identifier for a result set.

> **TIP:** Although a bad query is by far the most common way of producing the `0 is not a valid result identifier`, message, it is not the only way. You would also get that message if you misspelled the name of the result identifier variable (and it was, therefore, unbound) or if the query statement had never actually executed (with the same result). Again, it is much easier to distinguish these problems if you trap the errors early on.

Misspelled names

The sad truth is that for every bug that plumbs the depths of programming esoterica, there are a gazillion cheap mistakes that seem obvious once you've discovered them. The former may break your brain, but afterward you feel a certain exhilaration at testing your skills against a really hard nut. The latter just leave you feeling empty and regretful at the time you wasted on something so trivial.

So let us start with the single most common error: simple misspelling of table, column, and value names. It doesn't help that PHP and MySQL are both case sensitive. Ask for `'mytable'` instead of `'MyTable'`, and you can expect a quick return of *el número céro*. No force on earth can prevent you from doing this once in awhile, and the error messages will be uninformative at best. So what can we say? Remember that even the most experienced programmers do it too.

Comma faults

Remember to put the comma *outside* the single quotes within a SQL statement. This will not work:

```
$query = "UPDATE book SET title='$title,' subtitle='$subtitle,'
ISBN='$ISBN'";
```

But this will:

```
$query = "UPDATE book SET title='$title', subtitle='$subtitle',
ISBN='$ISBNisbn'";
```

Think of the single quotes as part of the variable itself rather than following common American-English typographical practice, which often puts a comma inside a quote.

Unquoted string arguments

Any values that should be treated by the database as string data types typically need to be single-quoted within a SQL statement. For example, this query has the correct syntax:

```
$query = "select * from author where firstname = 'Daniel'";
```

By contrast, if we make a `mysql_query()` call using the following query, we should expect an error:

```
$query = "select * from author where firstname = Daniel";
```

The actual error returned by the database may be deceiving, though — quite likely the complaint will be about an unknown column named 'Daniel'. This is because unquoted strings are assumed to name columns, as in:

```
$query = "select * from author where firstname = lastname";
```

This would be a perfectly acceptable way to search our database for Humbert Humbert and Lisa Lisa, but it won't work for people with more ordinary names.

Unbound variables

One of the sneakier ways to break a SQL statement is to interpolate an unbound variable into the middle of it.

When it works, the automatic splicing of variables into double-quoted strings is a perfect match for a SQL-based dialog with your database. Your code can determine values, for example, that are used to restrict the scope of a query made to the DB, as in this snippet:

```
$customerID = find_customer_id(); //returns int
$result_id = mysql_query("select from customers where ID =
$customer_ID"); //BUG
$row = mysql_fetch_row($result_id);   //CRASH
```

Because this code makes no attempt to trap query errors, you will again see a complaint about the fact that 0 is not a valid MySQL result identifier. It's possible (for us anyway) to stare at code like this for quite a while without seeing anything wrong (although the good PHP coders who habitually crank error reporting up to `E_ALL` will be rewarded with the cause of the error in a warning message). The problem, of course, is that we assigned a variable (`$customerID`) and then embedded a different one (`$customer_ID`) in our SQL statement. The latter variable is unbound and so behaves like an empty string when interpreted by the double-quote parsing. The result is that the database sees the following query, which is not valid SQL:

```
select from customers where ID =
```

This kind of problem is one reason why it is often a good idea to construct your query and assign it to a variable in a separate statement, like this:

```
$my_query = "select from customers where ID = $customer_ID";
```

Then make a distinct subsequent call to `mysql_query($my_query)`. If you do this, it is very easy to add printing or logging statements that show you the actual query you are sending.

Too Little Data, Too Much Data

Finally, you may find that your PHP/database script is working apparently without error but is displaying no data from the database, or far more than you expected. As a vague and general rule, if your query function is returning successfully (and your code checks that), your suspicions might rightly turn to the SQL itself. Recheck the logic, particularly of WHERE clauses. It is easy, for example, to write a query like:

```
"select * from families where kidcount = 1 and kidcount = 2";
```

In this query, you are really intending an or rather than an and, with the result that zero rows will be returned regardless of the contents of your database.

If your script is iterating through database rows and displaying them and you find that you have far, far too many of those rows, the problem is very often a SQL join that has too few restrictions. As a general rule, the number of restrictions in a WHERE clause should not be fewer than the number of tables joined minus one. For example, the following query has three tables but only one joining restriction:

```
"SELECT book.title FROM book, author, country WHERE author.countryID =
country.ID"
```

It is likely to return every possible book/author pair, without reference to whether the author wrote the book, which is probably not what was intended.

Specific SQL Functions

A few specific functions seem to cause a higher than normal number of problems, especially in the learning phase. These functions can send even the experienced PHP developer running to the online manual to check the arguments and returned data types time and time again.

mysql_affected_rows() vs. mysql_num_rows()

Both of these functions tell you how many rows of data your last SQL statement touched. However, mysql_num_rows() works only on SELECT statements, while mysql_affected_rows() works only on INSERT, UPDATE, and DELETE statements. The way to think about it is that SELECTs do not affect (meaning change) any data that exists in the database.

Furthermore, mysql_affected_rows() takes an optional link identifier as the argument, whereas mysql_num_rows() takes a non-optional result resource. This means that you can only get a valid result from mysql_affected_rows() until the moment you call another INSERT, UPDATE, or DELETE. In contrast, if you use different variable names for your result resources, you can use mysql_num_rows() anytime in the script. This code will help clarify the differences:

```
$link_id = mysql_connect($host, $user, $pass);
```

```
mysql_select_db($database, $link_id);

$query = "INSERT INTO mytable VALUES(NULL, '$myval')";
$result_resource = mysql_query($query);
$test_insert = mysql_affected_rows(); //This should work and return 1

$query1 = "SELECT * FROM mytable";
$result_resource1 = mysql_query($query1);
$test_select = mysql_num_rows($result_resource1);

$query2 = "DELETE FROM mytable";
$result_resource2 = mysql_query($query2);
$test_select2 = mysql_num_rows($result_resource2); //Will not work
$test_delete = mysql_affected_rows(); //This will return the number of
rows in the table; at this point you can no longer get the old result of
1
$test_select_again = mysql_num_rows($result_resource1); //Should be the
same as $test_select
```

mysql_result()

This function, which returns one value at a time from the database, is now used rather rarely. Unlike `mysql_fetch_row()` and `mysql_fetch_array()`, you need to specify the row and field of the value you're fetching as well as the result resource. Thus, you cannot do this:

```
// This won't work
while (mysql_result($result_resource)) {
  // Some loop
}

// This will
$firstname = mysql_result($result_resource1, 0, 'firstname');
```

You should really only use this function when you know you'll be fetching one or two pieces of data (a user's first name, for instance). Otherwise, the others are much faster.

OCIFetch()

When users of MySQL or SQL Server switch over to Oracle, they often have trouble with the OCI fetching functions — particularly this one. Unlike most other database row-fetching functions, you don't immediately access the result of `OCIFetch()` via echo or some other PHP function. This function fetches the result of a SQL statement into a result buffer —where it can be accessed via `OCIResult()`.

```
$query = "SELECT * from mytable";
$stmt = OCIParse($conn, $query);
$exec_result = OCIExecute($stmt, OCI_DEFAULT);
$row2buffer = OCIFetch($stmt);
$myval = OCIResult($stmt, "MYCOLUMN");
```

```
echo $myval;
```

This function should probably be thought of as analogous to `mysql_result()` rather than `mysql_fetch_row()`, or at best occupying a middle ground between the two. Similarly, it should only be used when you are sure you will be fetching very small data sets. Otherwise, use `OCIFetchInto()` or `OCIFetchStatement()`, both of which return arrays.

Debugging and Sanity Checking

If you are nearing your wit's end in trying to debug query-related errors and misbehavior, it can be extremely useful to actually compare the results of your PHP-embedded queries with the same queries made directly to the database. If your technical setup permits actually running a SQL client directly (for example, the `mysql` or Oracle command-line clients), as well as cross-program cutting and pasting, try this two-step process:

1. Insert a debugging statement in your PHP script that prints the query itself immediately before it is actually used in a DB query call (for example, `echo $query`).

2. Directly paste that query from your browser output (or the HTML source) into your SQL client.

> **CAUTION:** Obviously this advice only applies to code under development, not code you are running in production. It might be OK to echo errors to the browser while you're developing something for the first time; but when it's ready to go into production, you should make sure all your `echo()` statements are replaced with `error_log()` functions.

If the query looks reasonable to you, but it breaks both in the SQL program and in PHP, then there is some syntax or naming error in that SQL statement itself that you are missing, and your PHP code is not to blame (unless, of course, your code constructed that query in the first place). Similarly, with a dearth or overabundance of rows — if the behavior is the same in both places — the query is to blame. If, on the other hand, the behavior in the SQL interpreter looks like what you wanted, then the query is fine, and your suspicion should turn to your PHP code that actually sends that query and processes the results.

One final and general tip is to study any error messages very carefully, paying attention to phrases like `link identifier` and `result resource identifier`. In MySQL, the former means an identifier of a database *connection*, and the latter identifies the set of rows returned by a particular *query*. It is easy to confuse the two, as in the following code:

```
$my_connection = mysql_connect('localhost', $myname, $mypass);
mysql_select_db('MyDB');
$result = mysql_query($my_query, $my_connection);
while ($row = mysql_fetch_row($my_connection)) {
  // LOOP
}
```

This code will probably yield an error that contains the words not a valid result identifier. The problem is that we are using the connection ID where the result ID should be. The resulting error message is justified yet opaque.

Summary

PHP/database bugs are often not very deep or subtle but can still be difficult to diagnose. In general, the earlier in a script you can detect trouble, the easier the diagnosis will be. Especially when you are debugging, every statement that interacts with the database should have an associated error_log() clause, containing an informative error message.

By far, the most common cause of database connection problems is incorrect arguments to the connection function (hostname, username, password). The most common causes of failed queries are quote faults, unbound variables, and simple misspellings.

If you have repeated failures with database queries that seem like they should be working, have your code print out the query that it is sending to the DB; if possible, try making that very query to the database directly. If the problem persists when PHP is out of the loop, you can safely restrict your attention to database design and your understanding of SQL queries.

Part III

Advanced Techniques

Chapter 26

Object-Oriented Programming with PHP

In This Chapter

♦ What is object-oriented programming?

♦ The basics of PHP OOP

♦ Advanced topics: serialization and introspection

♦ Troubleshooting and style issues

There are many possible audiences for this chapter, including people who know basic PHP but nothing about object-oriented programming (OOP), and people who know all about OOP and nothing about PHP. As usual, we aim to please everyone all at once, but be warned that you may want to pick and choose from the sections depending on who you are.

We start with a quick and very general introduction to object-oriented programming for those who are completely unfamiliar with it. If you are already comfortable with OOP from another language, please skip this section -- it will not enlighten you (and might well enrage you). The following section ("PHP Constructs for OOP") gets into the meat of the basic syntax and behavior of PHP objects. Later in the chapter, we delve into more extended examples and cover some of the more obscure issues and gotchas around objects in PHP. Along the way, we offer a couple of sidebar meta-discussions, about the merits of object-oriented PHP and the extent to which PHP should be considered to be OOP.

> **NEW FEATURE:** In general in this chapter, we discuss OOP programming constructs as they are implemented in PHP 4.2, which uses Zend Engine 1 as its parser. Zend Engine 2, however, extends the OOP syntax in several ways, and (at this writing) ZE2 is bundled with the development version of PHP 4.3 for alpha testing. We will occasionally mention OOP limitations that will go away when ZE2 is eventually incorporated into PHP releases, and we also have a "Zend Engine 2" section near the end of the chapter.

What Is Object-Oriented Programming?

So what is object-oriented programming (OOP) all about anyway? OOP turns out to be a very simple idea, which (when taken seriously and built into the structure of programming languages) leads to all sorts of more complicated elaborations.

The simple idea

The simple idea is this: Rather than creating data structures on the one hand and code on the other, suppose we reorganize everything so that associated pieces of code and data are bundled together?

The procedural approach

For example, imagine a conventional procedural (non-object-oriented) program for manipulating personal calendars, with the capability to display, update, and edit calendars. Somewhere in the code for such a program, we would find the actual data definitions for representing someone's appointments for a particular month; somewhere else we would find code that did the right things to manipulate that data. Typically, the only connection between the datatype definitions and the manipulation code is that a clever programmer has made sure that they get matched up appropriately.

Now, imagine combining our calendar program with a recipe program (say that we want to plan our meals in detail for an entire year). Again, there will be data structures somewhere that represent the contents of the calendar, and other data structures that represent the contents of the recipes. The data structures will use the basic datatypes of the programming language; for all we know, the top-level type of a calendar might be an array, and the top-level type of a recipe might also be an array. Somewhere else in the program there is code for digging into the data structures that represent calendars and recipes and doing the right things with them. What is the connection between the data structures and the code? Only that a careful programmer has made sure that the arrays that represent calendars and the arrays that represent recipes get fed to the appropriate manipulation code. (Otherwise, we might find ourselves trying to schedule an appointment in Beef Stroganoff rather than in March 2006.)

If we think of procedural code as being outlined like a book, the outline for the code we're talking about might look like:

- ◆ 1) Data definitions
  - • 1a) Data definitions for calendars
  - • 1b) Data definitions for recipes
- ◆ 2) Data manipulation code
  - • 2a) Code for calendars
  - • 2b) Code for recipes

The object-oriented approach

The most basic version of OOP reorganizes the procedural approach by grouping associated pieces of code and data together into conceptual units. This means that we replace the outline in the preceding subsection with:

- ◆ 1) Calendars

- 1a) Data definitions
- 1b) Manipulation code

♦ 2) Recipes

- 2a) Data definitions
- 2b) Manipulation code

This organizational inversion is the heart of object-oriented programming.

But so what (we can hear you say)? If we're just talking about a way to organize code, we could do that without any special terminology or programming languages. In normal procedural code, we can organize function definitions and datatype definitions in any order we want to. For example, we could put all the datatype definition code into one directory and all the manipulation code into another (a procedural organization); or we could put all the calendar code into one directory and all the recipe code into another (an object-oriented organization).

Object-oriented programming begins to be interestingly different from procedural programming, however, once the programming language itself is set up to make it easy to organize things in an object-oriented way. (See the sidebar "Do Web-Scripting Languages Really Need OOP," for a discussion of how useful this organization is in languages like PHP.) The most basic form this takes is that data objects can be built out of local functions as well as local data. For example, as we build a data structure that represents a calendar, we can include the data members that are needed (structures to represent days, months, years, appointments), but also the functions that will be needed (`new_appointment()`, `calendar_display()`, and so forth). These functions are (in some sense) stored locally in the object definition itself. A calendar doesn't have an ingredient list, and a recipe doesn't have 31 days; similarly, a calendar object doesn't have a `print_ingredients()` function, and a recipe doesn't have a `new_appointment()` function. Finally, of course, the data members in an object may themselves be objects of a different type.

Bundling code and data together into units is the basic idea, and OOP languages always offer some support for this kind of bundling. However, most OOP languages take things further, and offer one or more of the following elaborations that give OOP even more leverage. (See the sidebar "How OOP Is PHP" for a discussion of the extent to which PHP itself has these features.)

Elaboration: Objects as datatypes

In addition to allowing us to store functions in our data, a good OO programming language lets us define these combinations as genuinely new datatypes that the language supports like any other type.

DO WEB-SCRIPTING LANGUAGES REALLY NEED OOP?

The object-oriented revolution has not been without controversy. Although many programmers embraced OOP quickly, others preferred the procedural approach they were used to, and wondered aloud if the extra machinery needed to support OOP wasn't more trouble than it was worth. Still, there's no doub t that the revolution has largely succeeded. Most of the popular programming languages in use today are either fully object-oriented or have object-oriented extensions. Also, at least some of the promises about improved productivity and increased code reuse seem to have been realized, as design methodologies like UML and patterns gain greater influence, and as people get more used to subclassing as a standard way to reuse and extend vendor-supplied libraries.

We feel that the benefits of OOP for "major" (that is, compiled) programming languages like Java and C++ are clear. On the other hand, we feel that the benefits of OOP for scripting languages (like Perl and PHP) are less obvious and are most debatable in the case of Web-scripting (PHP).

How is Web scripting different from other kinds of programming tasks? The most obvious difference is simply that Web scripts typically execute quickly and then go away. In other programming situations, you may have RAM-resident objects that live for hours or days and undergo complex evolutions of state which affect their behavior. A typical Web script, on the other hand, might execute for half a second, as it serves up a particular page, and then dies happy. You may knit these scripts together to provide a more extended user experience (using databases, sessions, cookies), but often such efforts are all about making the experience outlive any PHP objects that may or may not be created. More generally, scripting languages like PHP and Perl typically have a less thoroughgoing implementation of OOP than languages like Java, C++, and Smalltalk, and the limitations of implementation make these OOP extensions less attractive. (For more detail, see the sidebar "How OOP is PHP?," later in this chapter.)

This is not to say that there aren't still benefits of OOP in PHP. In addition to the conceptual benefits that may result from structuring code in an object-centered way, there are two good reasons to use PHP objects: 1) It's a good way to distribute third-party code for reuse. 2) Many programmers, who are used to OO syntax from other languages, won't feel comfortable unless they can use the same idioms in PHP.

But our main point is that use of PHP constructs for OOP is a very "tradeoffy" and pragmatic decision, which we have often seen made more on the basis of religion or fashion. If you are comfy with OO, this kind of syntax is there for you; and if you work in a group that has decided to write in that style, you may want to let the majority rule. If you decide not to go OO, however, be strong — we urge you not to be swayed by the moral-superiority arguments you may hear from people who disdain your five-line procedural script in favor of their ten-line OO script which does exactly the same task.

After such a type is defined, we can create as many such objects as we like, just as we can create as many integers as we like given the integer type. In object-oriented terminology, the term *class* is used to refer to the general type definition, which specifies the data members and member functions that each instance of that class should have.

The term *object* (or *instance*) refers to any individual instance of the type. For instance, after we define a class called Calendar (which specifies the different kinds of data and functions that every self-respecting calendar should have), we can make any number of Calendar objects (which might be associated with individual people).

Elaboration: Inheritance

After we've written a program that uses the class Calendar, we might want to make a more specific version of the program for a particular purpose. What we would really like to do is copy most of the code from the Calendar class, but change it in just a few places, so that it prints differently, or has a culturally appropriate set of holidays, or allows us to schedule appointments to the second rather than to the hour.

This desire is common enough that OOP offers a mechanism to support it called *inheritance*. The basic idea is that you can define a class in terms of another class, and then specify only the things that you want to be different in your own class. If you view the original class as the parent, the default is that both function definitions and data definitions are *inherited* by your child class unless you specify otherwise. This turns out to be a powerful technique for reusing class definitions. (As we will see in the "Basic PHP Constructs for OOP" section, OOP in PHP supports inheritance.)

Elaboration: Encapsulation

Part of the point of segregating both data and functions into objects is to reduce the complexity of programming by reducing unnecessary interactions. There is no reason why calendars should have to know about the internals of cooking recipes, or vice versa. So some OOP languages actually enforce information barriers between objects — after the programmer has defined which parts of recipes and calendars are purely internal and private to those classes, the language actually forbids code that is external to an object from messing with an object's internal workings. This kind of information-hiding is called *encapsulation*, and although this sounds restrictive, it can be a good source of clarity. In particular, if the programmer who designed a particular class knows that some parts of its workings have been designed to be private in this sense, the programmer also knows that those parts can be redesigned without checking with everyone who might be using that class's code. (PHP with Zend Engine 1 does not offer any particular support for encapsulation, but future releases with ZE2 will support it See the New Feature icon at the very beginning of this chapter and the Zend Engine 2 section at the very end.)

Elaboration: Constructors and destructors

After you have defined a class, you can make as many instances of it as you like. Each time you create such an instance, your favorite OOP language allocates memory to store the instance in, and gives you some way to refer to that instance later in the program. There are frequently a number of initialization steps you want to take every time you make an object of that class. *Constructor* functions offer a way to build that set of steps into the class definition. The standard way to create a new instance is to call a constructor function (which usually has the same name as the class and which you can customize to do all the necessary initialization).

Destructors are the opposite of constructors and specify all the cleanup actions that should happen when an object is dispensed with. PHP 4.2 (with Zend Engine 1) offers constructors as part of its OOP support, but does not offer destructors because deallocation of memory is usually handled by PHP itself rather than by the programmer. True destructors will be offered as part of Zend Engine 2 in future releases of PHP.

Terminology

There are some standard terms in OOP parlance for all the concepts we have talked about thus far, and we will be using them for the rest of the chapter. (Several of these terms have alternate names, which we include in parentheses.)

♦ **Class:** This is a programmer-defined datatype, which includes local functions as well as local data.

♦ **Object:** (Also known as *object instance*, or *instance*.) An individual instance of the data structure defined by a class. You define a class once and then make many objects that belong to it.

♦ **Member variable:** (Also known as *property* or *attribute*.) One of the component pieces of data in a class definition.

♦ **Member function:** (Also known as *method*.) A member that happens to be a function.

♦ **Inheritance:** The process of defining a class in terms of another class. The new (child) class has all the member data and member function definitions from the old (parent) class by default but may define new members or "override" parent functions and give them new definitions. We say that class A *inherits from* class B if class A is defined in terms of class B in this way.

♦ **Parent class** (or **superclass** or **base class**): A class that is inherited from by another class.

♦ **Child class** (or **subclass** or **derived class**): A class that inherits from another class.

HOW OOP IS PHP?

How "object-oriented" is PHP? Your answer to that question probably depends on your particular litmus tests for object-orientedness. In this sidebar, we offer a whirlwind tour of features that typically show up in OOP languages and briefly discuss the extent to which PHP supports them. Some of these issues are explored more broadly in the section "Advanced OOP Features," later in this chapter. (Note: This sidebar is really only of interest to developers who are coming to PHP from a different OO language; everyone else may want to skip this game of buzzword bingo.)

Single inheritance

PHP allows a class definition to inherit from another class, using the `extends` clause. Both member variables and member functions are inherited.

Multiple inheritance

PHP offers no support for multiple inheritance and no notion of interface inheritance as in Java. Each class inherits from, at most, one parent class.

Constructors

Every class can have one constructor function, which in current (Zend Engine 1) versions of PHP has the same name as the class. In future versions of PHP, which include the Zend Engine 2 parser, the constructor function in each class will be called `__construct()`. Constructors of parent classes are not automatically called but must be invoked explicitly.

Destructors

Current versions of PHP (with Zend Engine 1) offer no destructors, largely because deallocation of memory in PHP is not under the programmer's control. Future versions with Zend Engine 2 will include destructors.

Encapsulation/access control

There is no support for encapsulation in PHP with Zend Engine 1. All member variables and member functions are public. Zend Engine 2 will offer private member variables.

Polymorphism/overloading

PHP supports polymorphism in the sense of allowing instance of subclasses to be used in place of parent instances. The correct member function will be dispatched to at runtime. There is no support for method overloading, where dispatch happens based on the method's signature — each class only has one member function of a given name. However, PHP's weak typing and support for variable numbers of arguments makes workarounds possible. See the section "Simulating polymorphism," later in this chapter (in "Advanced OOP Features").

Early vs. late binding

Two equally good answers are: 1) The question doesn't arise, due to PHP being loosely typed, and 2) All binding is late. In PHP values are typed but variables are not, so there is no question about what method to call when the variable is of a different type than the value.

> **Static (or class) functions**
>
> There is no explicit support for class functions, but it is possible to call member functions via the `Classname::function()` syntax, without reference to an instance. Such a function can be treated as a class function as long as it does not refer to member variables.
>
> **Introspection**
>
> PHP offers a wide variety of functions here, including the capability to recover class names, member function names, and member variable names from an instance. (See the section "Introspection Functions," later in this chapter.)

Basic PHP Constructs for OOP

In this section, we cover the basic PHP syntax for OOP from the ground up, with some simple examples.

Defining classes

The general form for defining a new class in PHP is as follows:

```php
class myclass extends myparent {
  var $var1;
  var $var2 = "constant string";
  function myfunc ($arg1, $arg2) {
    [..]
  }
  [..]
}
```

The form of the syntax is as described, in order, in the following list:

♦ The special form `class`, followed by the name of the class that you want to define.

♦ An optional extension clause, consisting of the word `extends` and then the name of the class that should be inherited from.

♦ A set of braces enclosing any number of variable declarations and function definitions. Variable declarations start with the special form `var`, which is followed by a conventional $ variable name; they may also have an initial assignment to a constant value. Function definitions look much like standalone PHP functions but are local to the class.

As an example, consider the simple class definition in Listing 26-1, which prints out a box of text in HTML.

Listing 26-1: TextBox.php

```php
class TextBoxSimple {
  var $body_text = "my text";
```

```
function display() {
   print("<TABLE BORDER=1><TR><TD>$this->body_text");
   print("</TD></TR></TABLE>");
}
}
```

This is an extremely simple class definition. It has no parent (and, therefore, no extends clause). It has a single member variable (the variable $body_text), and a single member function (the function display()). The display function simply prints out the text variable, wrapped up in an HTML table definition.

Accessing member variables

In general, the way to refer to a member variable from an object is to follow a variable containing the object with ->, and then the name of the member. So if we had a variable $box containing an object instance of the class TextBox, we could retrieve its body_text variable with an expression like:

```
$text_of_box = $box->body_text;
```

However, when we are writing code within a member function, we haven't yet created the object instance, and so we have no variable like $box to refer to. The answer is the magic variable $this, which (when used inside a member function of a class) refers to the object instance itself. Note that this is how the display() function in Listing 26-1 retrieves the text it displays ($this->body_text).

This syntax can be a little counterintuitive. You might think that we could simply refer to $body_text in functions within our TextBox class because we have declared it in the class definition, but in fact the only way to get to members from within a member function definition is via $this. Notice also that the syntax for this access does not put a $ before the member variable name itself, only the $this variable.

Creating instances

After we have a class definition, the default way to make an instance of that class is by using the new operator. If we have already defined the class TextBox as in Listing 26-1, we can make an instance of it, and then use it, like so:

```
$box = new TextBoxSimple;
$box->display();
```

The result of evaluating this code will be to print an HTML fragment containing a table definition enclosing the text my text. (Not especially useful, but it's a start.)

Constructor functions

One way in which our TextBox class is not very useful is that its instances do not contain any data when they are created, except for the static initialization of the variable $body_text.

The point of such a class would be to display arbitrary pieces of text, not the same message every time. It's true that we could make an instance, and then install the right data in the instance's internal variables, like so:

```
$box = new TextBoxSimple;
$box->body_text = "custom text";
$box->display();
```

But that would be cumbersome and error-prone as we build more complex objects.

The correct way to arrange for data to be appropriately initialized is by writing a constructor function — a special function with the same name as the class, which will be called automatically whenever a new instance is created.

> **NOTE:** In PHP4 (with Zend Engine 1), a constructor function for a class is a function with the same name as the class that is defined within the class. Such constructor functions (if defined) are automatically called when a new instance of their class is created. This fixes the somewhat buggy behavior of PHP 3, which treated a function with the same name as a class as a constructor for that class, even if it happened to be defined within a different class. In future versions of PHP that include the Zend Engine 2 parser (no earlier than PHP 4.3 and probably later), the constructor function will be called `__construct()`, rather than having the same name as the class.

Modifying our previous example to include a constructor function gives us Listing 26-2.

Listing 26-2: TextBox redefined

```
class TextBox {
  var $body_text = "my text";
  // Constructor function
  function TextBox ($text_in) {
    $this->body_text = $text_in;
  }
  function display() {
    print("<TABLE BORDER=1><TR><TD>$this->body_text");
    print("</TD></TR></TABLE>");
  }
}
// creating an instance
$box = new TextBox("custom text");
$box->display();
```

As the preceding code is executed, the output is an HTML table enclosing the text `custom text`.

> **NOTE:** There should be only one constructor function per class definition. Defining more than one such function is legal, but only the definition that occurs last will be in effect. If you'd like to have different constructors to handle different numbers and types of input arguments, see the section "Simulating Polymorphism," later in this chapter.

Inheritance

PHP class definitions can optionally *inherit* from a parent class definition by using the extends clause. The syntax is as follows:

```
class Child extends Parent {
 <definition body>
}
```

The effect of inheritance is that the child class (or subclass or derived class) has the following characteristics:

- Automatically has all the member variable declarations of the parent class (or superclass or base class).

- Automatically has all the same member functions as the parent, which (by default) will work the same way as those functions do in the parent.

In addition, the child class can add on any desired variables or functions simply by including them in the class definition in the usual way.

In Listing 26-2, we defined a class called TextBox; now we'll define a class called TextBoxHeader that extends TextBox (see Listing 26-3). TextBoxHeader has two member variables: one ($body_text) that it receives through inheritance from TextBox, and another ($header_text) that it defines itself. Like TextBox, it has a constructor function and a function called display. This function definition overrides the display function in TextBox.

Listing 26-3: TextBoxHeader

```php
class TextBoxHeader extends TextBox
{
  var $header_text;

  // CONSTRUCTOR
  function TextBoxHeader($header_text_in,
                   $body_text_in) {
    $this->header_text = $header_text_in;
    $this->body_text = $body_text_in;
  }

  // MAIN DISPLAY FUNCTION
  function display() {
    $header_html =
      $this->make_header($this->header_text);
    $body_html = $this->make_body($this->body_text);
    print("<TABLE BORDER=1><TR><TD>\n");
    print("$header_html\n");
    print("</TD></TR><TR><TD>\n");
    print("$body_html\n");
```

```
    print("</TD></TR></TABLE>\n");
  }

  // HELPER FUNCTIONS
  function make_header ($text) {
    return($text);
  }
  function make_body ($text) {
    return($text);
  }
}
```

Overriding functions

Function definitions in child classes *override* definitions with the same name in parent classes. This just means that the overriding definition in the more specific class takes precedence and will be the one actually executed. In the example in Listing 26-3, the `TextBoxHeader` class defines a function called `display()`, which means that executing the following code:

```
$text_box_header = new TextBoxHeader("The Header", "The Body");
$text_box_header->display();
```

will result in a call to TextBoxHeader's `display()` function, not the `display()` function in TextBox. The resulting HTML output prints a box with a header of `The Header` and a body of `The Body`. The more specific `display()` function takes total responsibility here; there is no call, either explicit or implicit, to the `display()` function defined in the `TextBox` class. (Although PHP makes no such implicit calls, it is possible to explicitly call functions that have been defined in a parent class — see "Calling parent functions" in the "Advanced OOP Features" section later in the chapter.)

The flip side of overriding functions, however, is that whenever a subclass does not override a parental definition, the parent's definition will be in effect. Note that the "helper" functions in the definition of `TextBoxHeader` don't really do anything interesting, and you might wonder why we bothered to separate them out. The answer is that this provides an opportunity for an inheriting class to do something interesting with those functions by selectively overriding them — or not, as they see fit.

Chained subclassing

PHP does not support multiple inheritance, but does support *chained subclassing*. This is a fancy way of saying that, although each class can have only a single parent, classes can still have a long and distinguished ancestry (grandparents, great-grandparents, and so on). Also, there's no restriction on family size; each parent class can have an arbitrary number of children.

As example, see Listing 26-4, where our definition of `TextBoxBoldHeader` inherits from `TextBoxHeader`, which in turn inherits from `TextBox`.

Listing 26-4: TextBoxBoldHeader

```
class TextBoxBoldHeader extends TextBoxHeader {

  // CONSTRUCTOR
  function TextBoxBoldHeader($header_text_in,
                  $body_text_in) {
    $this->header_text = $header_text_in;
    $this->body_text = $body_text_in;
  }

  // HELPER FUNCTIONS
  // make_header overrides parent
  function make_header ($text) {
    return("<B>$text</B>");
  }
}
```

This definition of `TextBoxBoldHeader` is very minimal; it defines no new member variables and defines only one function besides its constructor. That new function (`make_header()`) overrides the definition in its parent. Now what happens when we actually use this definition in the usual way?

```
$text_box_bold_header =
  new TextBoxBoldHeader("The Header", "The Body");
$text_box_bold_header->display();
```

It's worth looking in a bit of detail to see exactly what happens when we make these two function calls.

First, when we call the constructor (`TextBoxBoldHeader()`), the constructor sets variables that were defined in the grandparent (`TextBox`) and the parent (`TextBoxHeader`), respectively, and returns a new instance of `TextBoxBoldHeader`.

Secondly, when we call `$text_box_bold_header->display()`, the call sequence is as follows:

1. No `display()` function is found in `TextBoxBoldHeader`, so the version from `TextBoxHeader` is called.

2. The first function call in that version of `display()` is to `$this->make_header()`. Remember that `$this` refers to the object instance that we started with, which happens to be an instance of `TextBoxBoldHeader`, so PHP looks first of all for a definition from that class. It finds one and uses it to return the header string wrapped up in the HTML bold text construct (`<B></B>`).

3. The second function call is to `$this->make_body()`. This time, though, there is no overriding definition in `TextBoxBoldHeader`, so the version from `TextBoxHeader` is used.

The upshot is that, in defining `TextBoxBoldHeader`, we mostly exploited the behavior of the parent class, but were able to change its behavior slightly by overriding a single member function.

Modifying and assigning objects

Modifying an object instance turns out to be trickier than it looks. The problem is that objects are silently copied whenever an object is assigned to a variable and also whenever an object is passed to a function (at least, if references are not used).

> **NEW FEATURE:** The problems we discuss in this section should largely go away when Zend Engine 2 is officially incorporated into PHP. This is because objects will be referred to via handles and will no longer silently be copied when assigned to a variable or passed to a function. ZE2 will not be included until PHP 4.3 at the very earliest, however, and probably not until a much later version.

For example, consider the following pseudocode:

```
$my_instance = new MyObject();
$other_instance = $my_instance;
$other_instance->member_var = "something completely different";
```

In this example, there are really two object instances, because of the implicit copying of `$my_instance` that happens as `$other_instance` is assigned. In the third line, `$other_instance` is changed, but `$my_instance` will not reflect this change. (This may or may not be what you intended.)

There are two reasons why you might not have to worry about this issue:

♦ If you never directly modify the data in your objects, don't worry. Many OOP programs do wonderful things simply by creating objects (with constructors) and not changing the internal data thereafter. If this is true of your code, and your objects are not so large and numerous that the overhead of copying is burdensome, you can happily forget that any copying is taking place at all.

♦ If you never reassign objects to new variables or pass them to functions, don't worry. If you create an object and leave it in the same variable all the time, you can freely change its member variables whenever you want to.

If you are still reading this section, we assume that it is because you are still worried. The answer to the problem is to use references whenever you want to ensure object identity. This can be accomplished at assignment time by assigning a reference rather than a value:

```
$other_instance = &$my_instance;
```

It can also be accomplished for function calls either by passing a reference:

```
my_function(&$my_instance);
```

or by modifying the formal parameters in the function definition itself:

```
function my_function (&$my_argument) {
  ..
}
```

The bottom line is that, if you want only a single copy of a modifiable object to exist, you must ensure an unbroken chain of references rather than value assignments.

> **CROSS-REFERENCE:** For more on assignments, references, and call-by-value versus call-by-reference, see Chapter 8.

Scoping issues

Before we move onto the more advanced features of PHP's version of OOP, it's important to nail down issues of scope — that is, which names are meaningful in what way to different parts of our code. It may seem as though the introduction of classes, instances, and member functions have made questions of scope much more complicated. Actually, though, there are only a few basic rules we need to add to make OOP scope sensible within the rest of PHP:

♦ Names of member variables and member functions are never meaningful to calling code on their own — they must always be reached via the -> construct (or, as we'll see in the "Advanced OOP Features" section, the :: construct). This is true both outside the class definition and inside member functions.

♦ The names visible within member functions are exactly the same as the names visible within global functions — that is, member functions can refer freely to other global functions, but can't refer to normal global variables unless those variables have been declared global inside the member function definition.

These rules, together with the usual rules about variable scope in PHP, are respected in the intentionally confusing example in Listing 26-5. What number would you expect that code to print when executed?

Listing 26-5: Confusing scope

```
$my_global = 3;

function my_function ($my_input) {
  global $my_global;
  return($my_global * $my_input);
}

class MyClass {
  var $my_member;
  function MyClass($my_constructor_input) {
    $this->my_member =
      $my_constructor_input;
  }
  function myMemberFunction ($my_input) {
```

```
    global $my_global;
    return($my_global *
           $my_input *
           my_function($this->my_member));
  }
}

$my_instance = new MyClass(4);
print("The answer is: " .
      $my_instance->myMemberFunction(5));
```

The answer is: 180 (or 3 * 5 * (3 * 4)). If any of these numerical variables had been undefined when multiplied, we would have expected the variable to have a default value of 0, making the answer have a value of 0 as well. This would have happened if we had:

♦ Left out the global declaration in my_function()

♦ Left out the global declaration in myMemberFunction()

♦ Referred to $my_member rather than $this->my_member

Advanced OOP Features

In the previous section, we presented a minimal subset of PHP's object-oriented constructs that let you use the most basic OOP techniques. In this section we look at some of the slightly more unusual constructs, techniques, and gotchas that can get you into more trouble. (We defer any discussion of the functions that give meta-information about classes and objects to the section "Introspection Functions," later in this chapter.)

Simulating class functions

Some other OOP languages make a distinction between *instance* member variables, on the one hand, and *class* or *static* member variables on the other. Instance variables are those that every instance of a class has a copy of (and may possibly modify individually); class variables are shared by all instances of the class. Similarly, instance functions depend on having a particular instance to look at or modify; class (or static) functions are associated with the class but are independent of any instance of that class.

In PHP, there are no declarations in a class definition that indicate whether a function is intended for per-instance or per-class use. But PHP does offer a syntax for getting to functions in a class even when no instance is handy. The :: syntax operates much like the -> syntax does, except that it joins classnames to member functions rather than instances to members. For example, in the following implementation of an extremely primitive calculator, we have some functions that depend on being called in a particular instance, and one function that does not:

```
class Calculator
{
```

```
  var $current = 0;
  function add($num) {
    $this->current += $num;
  }
  function subtract($num) {
    $this->current -= $num;
  }
  function getValue() {
    return($current);
  }
  function pi() {
    return(M_PI); // the PHP constant
  }
}
```

We are free to treat the `pi()` function as either a class function or an instance function, and access it using either syntax:

```
$calc_instance = new Calculator;
$calc_instance->add(2);
$calc_instance->add(5);
print("Current value is " .
       $calc_instance->current ."<BR>");
print("Value of pi is " .
       $calc_instance->pi() . "<BR>");
print("Value of pi is " .
       Calculator::pi() . "<BR>");
```

This means that we can use the `pi()` function even when we don't have an instance of `Calculator` at hand.

Calling parent functions

Due to the way overriding works, asking an instance to call a function will always result in the most specific version of that function being called. If the function exists in the instance's class, the parent's version of that function will not be executed.

Sometimes it is handy for code in a subclass to explicitly call functions from the parent class, even if those names have been overridden. It's also sometimes useful to define subclass functions in terms of superclass functions, even when the name is available.

Calling parent constructors

In the section "Inheritance," earlier in this chapter, we showed you code (Listing 26-3) where both subclass and superclass had constructors, and both constructors set a variable that was defined by the superclass. This might be stylistically dodgy but, more important, we would like to avoid duplicating work across the two constructors, especially if a lot of code is involved.

Instead of writing an entirely new constructor for the subclass, let's write it by calling the parent's constructor explicitly and then doing whatever is necessary in addition for instantiation of the subclass. Here is a simple example:

```
class Name
{
  var $_firstName;
  var $_lastName;
  function Name($first_name, $last_name)
  {
    $this->_firstName = $first_name;
    $this->_lastName = $last_name;
  }
  function toString() {
    return($this->_lastName .
          ", " .
          $this->_firstName);
  }
}

class NameSub1 extends Name
{
  var $_middleInitial;
  function NameSub1($first_name, $middle_initial,
                    $last_name) {
    Name::Name($first_name, $last_name);
    $this->_middleInitial = $middle_initial;
  }
  function toString() {
    return(Name::toString() . " " .
          $this->_middleInitial);
  }
}
```

In this example, we have a parent class (Name), which has a two-argument constructor, and a subclass (NameSub1), which has a three-argument constructor. The constructor of NameSub1 functions by calling its parent constructor explicitly using the :: syntax (passing two of its arguments along), and then setting an additional field. Similarly, NameSub1 defines its non-constructor toString() function in terms of the parent function that it overrides.

It might seem strange to call Name::Name() here, without reference to $this. The good news is that both $this and any member variables that are local to the parent are available to a parent function when invoked from a child instance.

The special name parent

There is a stylistic objection to the previous example, which is that we have hardcoded the name of a parent class into the code for a subclass. Some would say that this is bad style because it makes it harder to revise the class hierarchy later. A fix is to use the special name parent, which when used in a member function, always refers to the parent class of the current class. Here is a revised version of the example using parent rather than Name:

```
class NameSub2 extends Name
{
  var $_middleInitial;
  function NameSub2($first_name, $middle_initial,
                    $last_name) {
    $parent_class = get_parent_class($this);
    parent::$parent_class($first_name, $last_name);
    $this->_middleInitial = $middle_initial;
  }
  function toString() {
    return(parent::toString() . " " .
           $this->_middleInitial);
  }
}
```

Notice that we've swapped in parent for all instances of Name whenever it's used as the name of a class. We had to do a little bit of extra work, though, when finding a replacement for the call Name::Name() because the second name in that call is actually the name of a constructor function. PHP does not accept parent as the name of a function , so we retrieve the constructor name using the function get_parent_class() (which we cover in the section "Introspection Functions," later in this chapter).

This replacement version could be attached to a different parent class simply by changing the class named in the extends clause (as long as the parent constructor is expecting the same two arguments!).

Automatic calls to parent constructors

In a sense, constructor functions in a subclass override the constructors in superclasses. (We say "in a sense" because we usually only say that one function overrides another if the two functions have the same name; a subclass constructor and a superclass constructor always have different names.)

As you saw in the previous section, if you want both the subclass constructor and the superclass constructor to be called, you must include code in the subclass to call the superclass code explicitly. But in PHP4 (and not in PHP 3), if a subclass lacks a constructor function and a superclass has one, the superclass's constructor will be invoked. The most specific constructor that can be found (if any) will be called — anything else is up to the programmer.

Simulating method overloading

One neat trick offered by some OOP languages (and not offered by PHP) is automatic overloading of member functions. This means that you can define several different member functions with the same name but different signatures (number and types of arguments). The language itself takes care of matching up calls to those functions with the right version of the function, based on the arguments that are given.

PHP does not offer such a capability, but the loose typing of PHP lets you take care of one half of the overloading equation — you can define a single function of a given name that behaves differently based on the number and types of arguments it is called with. The result looks like an overloaded function to the caller (but not to the definer).

Here's an example of an apparently overloaded constructor function:

```
class MyClass
{
var $string_var = "default string";
var $num_var = 42;

  function MyClass ($arg1) {
    if (is_string($arg1)) {
      $this->string_var = $arg1;
    }
    elseif (is_int($arg1) ||
            is_double($arg1)) {
      $this->num_var = $arg1;
    }
  }
}

$instance1 = new MyClass("new string");
$instance2 = new MyClass(5);
```

The constructor of this class will look to its caller as though it is overloaded, with different behavior based on the type of its inputs. You can also vary behavior based on the number of arguments by testing the number of arguments supplied by the caller.

CROSS-REFERENCE: For information on writing functions with variable numbers of arguments, see Chapter 8. The techniques work the same way with member functions in classes as they do with standalone user-defined functions.

Serialization

Serialization of data means converting it into a string of bytes in such a way that you can produce the original data again from the string (via a process known, unsurprisingly, as *unserialization*). After you have the ability to serialize/unserialize, you can store your serialized string pretty much anywhere (a system file, a database), and recreate a copy of the data again when needed.

PHP offers two functions, `serialize()` and `unserialize()`, which take a value of any type (except type `resource`), and encode the value into string form and decode again, respectively. The PHP 3 implementation of object serialization wasn't very useful because member function definitions didn't survive the serialization/unserialization process; the PHP 4 implementation, however, robustly recreates all important aspects of the instance from the string, as long as the class definition is available to the code where unserialize() is called.

Here is a quick example, which we'll extend later in this section:

```
class ClassToSerialize {
  var $storedStatement = "data";
  function classToSerialize ($statement) {
    $this->storedStatement = $statement;
  }
  function display ()
  {
    print($this->storedStatement . "<BR>");
  }
}

$instance1 =
  new ClassToSerialize("You're objectifying me!");
$serialization = serialize($instance1);
$instance2 = unserialize($serialization);
$instance2->display();
```

This class has just one member variable and a couple of member functions, but it's sufficient to demonstrate that both member variables and member functions can survive serialization. We create an object, convert it to a serialized string, convert it back to a new instance, and the printed result is the accurate complaint (You're objectifying me!).

Of course, there is no point in serializing and unserializing an object in the same script; all that will accomplish will be to make a copy of an object instance, which (as we saw in the section "Modifying and assigning objects," earlier in the chapter) happens every time you assign an object to a variable anyway (in current PHP versions using Zend Engine 1 as the parser). Serialization is only worthwhile when we expect the serialized string to outlive the script (and the variable) that it currently lives in and be reincarnated in another execution. This may be because we store the serialization in a file or a database and read it back in again. It can also happen automatically as a result of PHP's session mechanism — variables that are registered as belonging to a session will be serialized and unserialized from page to page.

> **CROSS-REFERENCE:** For more on how the session mechanism uses serialization, see Chapter 27.)

Sleeping and waking up

PHP provides a hook mechanism so that objects can specify what should happen just before serialization and just after unserialization. The special member function __sleep() (that's *two* underscores before the word sleep), if defined in an object that is being serialized, will be called automatically at serialization time. It is also required to return an array of the names of variables whose values are to be serialized. This offers a way to not bother serializing member variables that are not expected to survive serialization anyway (such as database resources) or that are expensive to store and can be easily recreated. The special function __wakeup() (again, two underscores) is the flip side — it is called at unserialization time (if defined in the class) and is likely to do the inverse of whatever is done by __sleep() (restore database connections that were dropped by __sleep() or recreate variables that __sleep() said not to bother with).

You may wonder why these functions are necessary — couldn't the code that calls serialize() also just do whatever is necessary to shut down the object? Actually, it's very much in keeping with OOP to include such knowledge in the class definition rather than expecting code using the objects to know about their special needs. Also the calling code may have no knowledge of the object's internals at all (as in the code that serializes all session objects). The author of the class is uniquely qualified to say what should happen when an instance is sent away or revived.

As an example of how to use these functions, here is the previous serialization example, augmented with an extra variable, and the __sleep() and __wakeup() functions.

```
class ClassToSerialize2 {
  var $storedStatement = "data";
  var $easilyRecreatable = "data again";
  function classToSerialize2 ($statement) {
    $this->storedStatement = $statement;
    $this->easilyRecreatable =
      $this->storedStatement . " Again!";
  }
  function __sleep() {
    // Could include DB cleanup code here
    return array('storedStatement');
  }
  function __wakeup() {
    // Could include DB restoration code here
    $this->easilyRecreatable =
      $this->storedStatement . " Again!";
  }
  function display ()
  {
    print($this->easilyRecreatable . "<BR>");
  }
}

$instance1 =
  new ClassToSerialize2("You're objectifying me!");
$serialization = serialize($instance1);
$instance2 = unserialize($serialization);
```

```
$instance2->display();
```

The variable called $easilyRecreatable is meant to stand in for a piece of data that is 1) expensive to store, and 2) is implied by the other data in the class anyway. The definition of __sleep() does no cleanup itself, but it returns an array that contains only one variable name, and does not include easilyRecreatable. At serialization time, only the value of the variable storedStatement is included in the string. When the object is recreated, the __wakeup() function assigns a value into $this->easilyRecreatable, which is then displayed: You're objectifying me! Again!

Serialization gotchas

The serialization mechanism is pretty reliable now (that is, in PHP 4) for objects, but there are still a few things that can trip you up:

♦ The code that calls unserialize() must also have loaded the definition of the relevant class. (This is also true of the code that calls serialize() too, of course, but that will usually be true because the class definition is needed for object creation in the first place.)

♦ Object instances can be created from the serialized string only if it is really the same string (or a copy thereof). A number of things can happen to the string along the way, if stored in a database (make sure that slashes aren't being added or subtracted in the process), or if passed as url or form arguments. (Make sure that your URL-encoding/decoding is preserving exactly the same string, and that the string is not long enough to be truncated by length limits.)

♦ If you choose to use __sleep() make sure that it returns an array of the variables to be preserved; otherwise no variable values will be preserved. (If you do not define a __sleep() function for your class, all values will be preserved.)

Introspection Functions

While PHP lacks some features of full OO languages like Java or C++, it is surprisingly good in the esoteric area of *introspection*. (It's The classes and objects that get introspective here, not the programmer.) Introspection allows the programmer ask objects about their classes, ask classes about their parents, and find out all the parts of an object without have to crunch the source code to do it. Introspection also can help you to write some surprisingly flexible code, as we will see.

Function overview

Most of this section will be example-driven, but we begin by looking at the introspection functions provided by PHP. Table 26-1 summarizes these functions, what they do, and what version of PHP introduced them. (This table is essentially a reframing of information from the on-line manual; we offer it here mainly because it highlights features that we found somewhat confusing the first time we studied the manual.)

Table 26-1: Class/Object Functions

Function	Description	Operates on class names	Operates on instances	As of PHP version
Get_class()	Returns the name of the class an object belongs to	No	Yes	4.0.0
Get_parent_class()	Returns the name of the parent class of the given instance or class	Yes (as of PHP v.4.0.5)	Yes	4.0.0, 4.0.5
Class_exists()	Returns TRUE if the string argument is the name of a class, FALSE otherwise	Yes	No	4.0.0
Get_declared_classes()	Returns an array of strings representing names of classes defined in the current script.	N/A	N/A	4.0.0
is_subclass_of()	Returns TRUE if the class of its first argument (an object instance) is a subclass of the second argument (a class name), FALSE otherwise	No	Yes	4.0.0
is_a()	Returns TRUE if the class of its first argument (an object instance) is a subclass of the second argument	No	Yes	4.2.0(?) (CVS only)

	(a class name), or is the same class, and FALSE otherwise			
Get_class_vars()	Returns an associative array of var/value pairs representing the name of variables in the class and their default values. Variables without default values will not be included.	Yes	No	4.0.0
get_object_vars()	Returns an associative array of var/value pairs representing the name of variables in the instance and their default values. Variables without values will not be included.	No	Yes	4.0.0
method_exists()	Returns TRUE if the first argument (an instance) has a method named by the second argument (a string) and FALSE otherwise.	No	Yes	4.0.0

`get_class_methods()`	Returns an array of strings representing the methods in the object or instance	Yes	Yes (as of v4.0.6)	4.0.0, 4.0.6
`call_user_method()`	Takes a string representing a method name, an instance that should have such a method, and additional arguments. Returns the result of applying the method (and the arguments) to the instance.	No	Yes	3.0.3, 4.0.0
`call_user_method_array()`	Same as `call_user_method()`, except that it expects its third argument to be an array containing the arguments to the method.	No	Yes	4.0.5

These functions break down into the following four broad categories:

- Getting information about the class hierarchy
- Finding out about member variables
- Finding out about member functions
- Actually calling member functions

The first group of functions (`get_class()` through `is_a()`) deal with discovering what classes exist, asking an object about its class, and discovering class inheritance relationships.

Some of these functions start with an instance of an object, some start with the class name as a string, and some are happy with either one. (We've included columns in the table to try to clarify this.) Note that after we have the get_class() function, it's easy to satisfy functions that require a class as input; for example, if get_parent_class() insists on a class name, and we want to know the parent class of an object instance, we could just wrap it like this:

```
$parent_class = get_parent_class(get_class($my_instance));
```

Going in the other direction (trying to satisfy a function that wants an instance when all we have is a class) would be more problematic because you don't want to instantiate a class just to ask questions of it.

The second group of functions (get_class_vars(), get_object_vars()), return an associative array containing member variables and their values. The keys of these arrays are the names of the variables as strings (without leading $ symbols), and the array values are the values of those variables in the object or class. In both cases (for reasons unknown to your authors), only member variables that actually have a value are returned.

The difference between get_class_vars() and get_object_vars() is subtle, but it's more than just a question of what type of input they prefer. The get_class_vars() function returns information about variables and default values as they exist in the class definition itself, independent of any instance; get_object_vars() returns information about the current state of a particular instance. For example, consider this class definition and use:

```
class Example {
  var $var1 = "initialized";
  var $var2 = "initialized";
  var $var3;
  var $var4;
  function Example () {
    $this->var3 = "set";
    $this->var1 = "changed";
  }
}

$example = new Example();
print_r(get_class_vars("Example"));
print_r(get_object_vars($example));
```

For the first call (to get_class_vars()), we should expect to find var1 and var2 both bound to "initialized" as in the class definition itself. The second call (to get_object_vars()) should return bindings of var1, var2, and var3 to "changed", "initialized", and "set", respectively. In neither case will either function retrieve var4.

The third group of functions (`method_exists()`, `get_class_methods()`) manipulate member function names as strings. The first allows you to ask an instance if it contains a given function, and the second recovers all function names from an instance or class. (Notice that we don't need two separate functions as we did with `get_class_vars()` and `get_object_vars()` because PHP doesn't offer you a way to add or delete member functions from instances on-the-fly.)

Finally, the fourth group lets you apply method names (presumably recovered using functions from the third group) to instances. But these are probably best explained by example, so let's dive in.

Example: Class genealogy

Consider the following, somewhat confusing class hierarchy.

```
class Color {}
class Control extends UIelement {}
class Widget extends Control { }
class Button extends Widget {}
class Pulldown extends Widget {}
class Clicker extends Button {}
class Blue extends Color {}
class Displayer extends UIelement {}
class UIElement {}
class LightBlue extends Blue {}
```

Now imagine that we'd like to have a better visualization of this tangle, just for purposes of documentation. For starters, it's pretty easy to use the `get_parent_class()` function to figure out the classes that a given class descends from:

```
function print_ancestry($class_name) {
  print("Class ancestry: ");
  print_ancestry_aux($class_name);
  print("<BR>");
}

function print_ancestry_aux ($class_name) {
  print("$class_name");
  if ($parent = get_parent_class($class_name)) {
    print(" => ");
    print_ancestry_aux($parent);
  }
}
print_ancestry("Clicker");
```

Which gives us the somewhat informative output:

```
Class ancestry: Clicker => button => widget => control => uielement
```

(Notice that our retrieved class names have become lowercase. This happens to user-defined classes, whereas built-in classes should have their capitalization intact.)

Getting a view of the entire class tree is a little bit harder, because PHP doesn't offer a straightforward way to retrieve child classes given a parent class. Our recourse is the `get_declared_classes` function, which tells us all the classes that are defined in the current script — we can then somewhat inefficiently do paternity tests on all known classes to discover the children of a given class (see Listing 26-6).

Listing 26-6: Class genealogy

```
function same_class_name ($string1, $string2) {
  return ((strtolower($string1)) ==
          (strtolower($string2)));
}

function get_child_classes ($parent) {
  $all_classes = get_declared_classes();
  $children = array();
  foreach ($all_classes as $candidate) {
    if (same_class_name($parent,
          get_parent_class($candidate)) &&
        !same_class_name($parent, $candidate)) {
      array_push($children, $candidate);
    }
  }
  return($children);
}

function print_class_tree () {
  $all_classes = get_declared_classes();
  print("<PRE>");
  print("CLASS HIERARCHY:\n");
    foreach ($all_classes as $candidate) {
      if (!get_parent_class($candidate)) {
        print_class_tree_aux($candidate, 0);
      }
    }
  print("</PRE>");
}

function print_class_tree_aux ($parent, $level) {
  for ($x = 0; $x < $level; $x++) {
    print("    ");
  }
  print("$parent<BR>");
  $children = get_child_classes($parent);
  foreach ($children as $child) {
    print_class_tree_aux($child, $level + 1);
```

```
  }
}
print_class_tree();
```

We start off this listing by defining what it means for two class names to be the same. This may be overkill, but converting every name to lowercase before comparison lets us stop worrying about whether we'll be tripped up by case issues. Then we define a general function to retrieve child classes (inefficiently, but it should make no difference unless your class hierarchy grows to be very very large). The `print_class_tree()` function essentially recovers all *orphans* or *roots* (classes without parents) and prints each one individually as a tree. The auxiliary function handles printing a rooted tree — first the parent and then indented children. Finally, we wrap the whole thing in a `<PRE></PRE>` construct so we can just use spaces for indenting The result looks like this:

```
CLASS HIERARCHY:
stdClass
__PHP_Incomplete_Class
OverloadedTestClass
Directory
color
    blue
        lightblue
uielement
    control
        widget
            button
                clicker
            pulldown
    displayer
```

The first few classes printed are unfamiliar and not defined in your code file. These either belong to the PHP implementation itself or to auxiliary packages that you have compiled — the precise classes that you see when you execute this code may vary.

Example: Matching variables and DB columns

One frequent use for PHP objects in database-driven systems is as a wrapper around the entire database API. The theory is that the wrapper insulates the code from the specific database system, which will make it trivial to swap in a different RDBMS when the technical needs change. (We've never seen it work out quite this way in practice, but . . . don't get us started.) Another use that is almost as common (and that your authors like better) is to have object instances correspond to database result rows. In particular, the process of reading in a result row looks like instantiating a new object that has member variables corresponding to the result columns we care about, with extra functionality in the member functions. As long as the fields and columns match up (and as long as you can afford object instantiation for every row), this can be a nice abstraction away from the database.

A repetitive task that arises when writing this kind of code is assigning database column values to member variables, in individual assignment statements. This feels like it should be unnecessary, especially when the columns and the corresponding variables have exactly the same names. In this section, we write a hack to automate this process.

For concreteness, let's start with an actual database table. Following are the MySQL statements necessary to create a simple table and insert one row into it:

```
mysql> create table book
  (id int not null primary key auto_increment,
   author varchar(255), title varchar(255),
   publisher varchar(255));
mysql> insert into book (author, title, publisher)
       values ("Robert Zubrin", "The Case For Mars",
               "Touchstone");
```

Because the id column is auto-incremented, it will happen to have the value 1 for this first row.

Now, let's say that we want a Book object that will exactly correspond to a row from this table, with fields corresponding to the DB column names. There's no way around actually defining the variable names (because PHP doesn't let us dynamically add variables to classes), but we can at least automate the assignment.

The code in Listing 26-7 assumes a database called oop with the table created as above, and also that we have a file called dbconnect_vars that sets $host, $user, and $pass appropriately for our particular MySQL setup. There is also little or no error-checking (the code assumes the connection works, that the row was retrieved successfully, and so on). The main point we want to highlight is the hack in the middle of the Book constructor.

Listing 26-7: Matching variables and columns

```php
<?php
include_once("dbconnect_vars.php");

class Book
{
var $id;

// variables corresponding to DB columns
var $author = "DBSET";
var $title = "DBSET";
var $publisher = "DBSET";

  function Book ($db_connection, $id) {
    $this->id = $id;
    $query = "select * from book " .
             "where id = $id";
    $result = mysql_query($query, $db_connection);
```

```
    $db_row_array =
      mysql_fetch_array($result);
    $class_var_entries =
      get_class_vars(get_class($this));
    while ($entry = each($class_var_entries)) {
      $var_name = $entry['key'];
      $var_value = $entry['value'];
      if ($var_value == "DBSET") {
        $this->$var_name =
          $db_row_array[$var_name];
      }
    }
  }

  function toString () {
    $return_string = "BOOK<BR>";
    $class_var_entries =
      get_class_vars(get_class($this));
    while ($entry = each($class_var_entries)) {
      $var_name = $entry['key'];
      $var_value = $this->$var_name;
      $return_string .=
        "$var_name: $var_value<BR>";
    }
    return($return_string);
  }
}
$connection =
  mysql_connect($host, $user, $pass)
  or die("Could not connect to DB");
mysql_select_db("oop");
$book = new Book($connection, 1);
$book_string = $book->toString();
?>
<HTML><HEAD></HEAD><BODY>
<?php echo $book_string ?>
</BODY></HTML>
```

The database query returns all columns from the book table, and the values are indexed in the result array by the column names. The constructor then uses get_class_vars() to discover all the variables that have been set in the object, tests them to see if they have been bound to the string "DBSET", and then sets those variables to the value of the column of the same name.

The result is the output:

```
BOOK
Author: Robert Zubrin
Title:  The Case For Mars
```

Publisher: Touchstone

If we add fields to the database table definition, the only change we will need to make to Listing 26-7 is to add appropriately named variables to the class definition and initialize them to `"DBSET"`. (We use this initialization to be clear about which variables should be overwritten, but also because we cannot retrieve the variables at all unless they have been initialized.)

Example: Generalized test methods

As a final introspection example, suppose we are working on a large OOP project, with complex objects that need to maintain a lot of internal state. Testing is extremely important, because bugs will creep in and waste our time if we don't catch them early on.

So let's adopt some testing conventions for this project. As one of them, let's agree that any class in our system can (optionally) define a member function called `selfTest()`. The point of this function is to test the object instance it is called on to make sure the data in the object is valid and consistent across the instance. The `selfTest()` function should always return FALSE if everything is okay and a diagnostic string if something is wrong. The coders of the objects agree that they will write these tests in such a way that a test can potentially be applied at any time during execution.

If we agree on such a framework, we can write a general object tester. The tester simply calls `selfTest()` on any object it is pointed at, if such a method has been defined for that object. To make it easier to apply, we'll also make the object tester accept arrays of objects, and test each component object individually. Such an object tester is in Listing 26-8, along with some sample class definitions that have `selfTest()` defined.

Listing 26-8: ObjectTester

```php
class Namestring {
  var $name;
  var $nameLength;
  var $checksum;

  function Namestring ($string_in) {
    $this->name = $string_in;
    $this->nameLength = strlen($string_in);
    $this->checksum =
      $this->computeChecksum($string_in);
  }

  function setName ($new_string) {
    $this->name = $new_string;
    $this->nameLength = strlen($new_string);
    $this->checksum =
      $this->computeChecksum($new_string);
  }
```

```
  function computeChecksum ($string) {
    // not a good checksum in practice
    $sum = 0;
    for ($x = 0;
         $x < strlen($string);
         $x++) {
      $sum += ord($string[$x]);
    }
    return($sum % 100);
  }

  function selfTest () {
    // returns FALSE if everything is OK
    if ($this->nameLength !=
        strlen($this->name)) {
      return("Name $this->name not of ".
             "length $this->nameLength!");
    }
    elseif
      ($this->checksum !=
         $this->computeChecksum($this->name)) {
      return("Name $this->name fails checksum!");
    }
    else {
      return(FALSE);
    }
  }
}

class NonTestingObject {
}

class ObjectTester {
  function ObjectTester() {
    // empty constructor
  }

  function test ($thing) {
    if (is_object($thing)) {
      if (method_exists($thing, 'selfTest')) {
        $this->handleTest(
          call_user_method('selfTest', $thing));
      }
    }
    elseif (is_array($thing)) {
      foreach ($thing as $component) {
        $this->test($component);
      }
```

```
      }
      // ignore if not an array or object
    }
    function handleTest ($result) {
      if ($result) {
        print("Warning: $result");
      }
    }
  }
}
```

The Namestring object in Listing 26-8 has several pieces of data, which must be kept consistent with each other. Using the constructor to build an instance of Namestring keeps them consistent, as does changing the name with setName. Namestring also defines selfTest(), which cross-checks the name, the length of the name, and a primitive checksum.

Now let's see how to use the ObjectTester class with some sample Namestring data:

```
$object_list = array();
array_push($object_list, new Namestring("Jordan"));
array_push($object_list, new Namestring("Rodman"));
array_push($object_list, new NonTestingObject);
array_push($object_list, new Namestring("Pippen"));

$tester = new ObjectTester($object_list);

print("Running test..<BR>");
$tester->test($object_list);

print("Changing name..<BR>");
$current_object = &$object_list[0]; // note reference!
$current_object->setName("Michael");
print("Running test..<BR>");
$tester->test($object_list);

print("Changing name..<BR>");
$current_object = &$object_list[1]; // note reference!
$current_object->name = "Jordan";

print("Running test..<BR>");
$tester->test($object_list);
```

The results of running this code are:

```
Running test..
Changing name..
Running test..
Changing name..
Running test..
```

```
Warning:  Name Jordan fails checksum!
```

This warning resulted because we messed with the object's data directly the second time, rather than using the approved method for changing the name.

We've used toy self-testing classes here, but the basic approach extends easily to more complex classes. Among possible extensions are more interesting handling of the warning messages (and possibly interrupting execution). Another extension would be to use introspection on member variables themselves, as well as array components, to find contained objects and test those. This would mean defining the test runner recursively so that a thing passes a `selfTest()` if 1) its own `selfTest()` method (if it exists) finds no problem, and 2) any components (member variables, array slots) also pass `selfTest()`. (Watch out for circularities though! If the tester is ever called on objects that mutually refer to each other, it would have to be rewritten to track the identities of previously seen objects and would only test each object once.)

Extended Example: HTML Forms

All the OOP code we've seen so far in this chapter has been fairly short, so in this chapter we present an extended piece of code for your enjoyment, shown in Listing 26-9.

The point of this class is to semi-automate the production of HTML forms, which one of your authors has always found to be a bit of a pain to generate. The top-level class represents a form, while other classes represent inputs, text areas, and hidden variables (just the ones that your author uses most frequently). The idea is that you can make a form by adding input fields to an existing object and display the form upon request. The resulting form will be not be especially pretty (every element is displayed sequentially down the left-hand side of the page), but it's good enough for situations where, say, you want to enter some information into your own database yourself.

Listing 26-9: form_printer.php

```php
<?php

// ---- The form class itself ---

class HtmlForm {

  // suitable for generating quick&dirty forms

  var $actionTarget; // path to receiving page
  var $inputForms;   // array of HtmlFormInput
  var $hiddenVariables; // associative name/val

  // CONSTRUCTOR
  function HtmlForm ($action_target) {
    $this->actionTarget = $action_target;
```

```php
    $this->inputForms = array();
    $this->hiddenVariables = array();
}

// PUBLIC METHODS
function toString () {
  $return_string = "";
  $return_string .=
      "<FORM METHOD=\"POST\" ".
      "ACTION=\"$this->actionTarget\">\n";
  $return_string .= $this->inputFormsString();
  $return_string .= $this->hiddenVariablesString();
  $return_string .= "<BR>\n";
  $return_string .= $this->submitButtonString();
  $return_string .= "</FORM>";
  return($return_string);
}

// adding elements to form

function addInputForm ($input_form) {
  if (!isSet($input_form) ||
      !is_object($input_form) ||
      !is_subclass_of($input_form,
                'htmlforminput')){
    die("Argument to HtmlForm::addInputForm ".
        "must be instance of HtmlFormInput.".
        "  Given argument is of class " .
        get_class($input_form));
  }
  else {
    array_push($this->inputForms, $input_form);
  }
}

function addInputButton ($input_button) {
  if (!isSet($input_button) ||
      !isObject($input_button) ||
      !is_a($input_button, 'HtmlInputButton')){
    die("Argument to HtmlForm::addInputButton ".
        "must be instance of HtmlInputButton");
  }
  else {
    array_push($this->inputButtons, $input_button);
  }
}

function addHiddenVariable ($name, $value) {
  if (!isSet($value)) {
```

```
      die("HtmlForm::addHiddenVariable requires ".
        "two arguments (name and value)");
    }
  else {
    $this->hiddenVariables[$name] = $value;
  }
}

function inputFormsString () {
  $return_string = "";
  $form_array = $this->inputForms;
  foreach ($form_array as $input_form) {
    $return_string .=
      "<B>$input_form->heading</B>";
    if ($this->headingElementBreak()) {
      $return_string .= "<BR>";
    }
    $return_string .= $input_form->toString();
    $return_string .= "<BR>\n";
  }
  return($return_string);
}

function hiddenVariablesString () {
  $return_string = "";
  while ($hidden_var =
          each($this->hiddenVariables)) {
    $var_name = $hidden_var['key'];
    $var_value = $hidden_var['value'];
    $return_string .=
      "<INPUT TYPE=HIDDEN " .
      "NAME=$var_name ".
      "VALUE=$var_value >";
      $return_string .= "\n";
  }
  return($return_string);
}

function headingElementBreak () {
  // override to disable breaks after headings,
  // or to do more complicate layout
  return(TRUE);
}

function submitButtonString () {
  $return_string = "<INPUT TYPE=Submit " .
                  " VALUE=Submit >\n";
  return($return_string);
}
```

```php
}

// ---- Classes for parts of a form ----

class HtmlFormInput {
  var $name; // The variable name for form submission
  var $heading; // The visible label on form
  function HtmlFormInput () {
    die("Class HtmlFormInput intended only " .
        "to be subclassed");
  }
  function toString () {
    die("Subclass of HtmlFormInput missing " .
        "definition of toString()");
  }
}

class HtmlFormSelect extends HtmlFormInput
{
  var $_valueArray = array();
  var $_selectedValue;

  function HtmlFormSelect ($name, $heading,
                           $value_array,
                           $selected_value=NULL) {
    if (!isSet($value_array)) {
      die("HtmlFormSelect needs a minimum of two " .
          "arguments: a name, and value array");
    }
    elseif (!is_array($value_array)) {
      die("Third argument to HtmlFormSelect()" .
          "should be array where keys are values " .
          "submitted, and values are display values");
    }
    else {
      // actual initialization
      $this->name = $name;
      $this->heading = $heading;
      $this->_valueArray = $value_array;
      $this->_selected_value = $selected_value;
    }
  }

  function toString () {
    $return_string = "";
    $return_string .=
      "<SELECT NAME=\"$this->name\">";
    while ($var_entry =
              each($this->_valueArray)) {
```

```
       $submit_value = $var_entry['key'];
       $display_value = $var_entry['value'];
       if ($submit_value == $this->_selected_value) {
         $return_string .=
           "<OPTION VALUE=${submit_value} SELECTED >";
       }
       else {
         $return_string .= "<OPTION VALUE=${submit_value}>";
       }
       $return_string .= $display_value;
     }
     $return_string .=
       "</SELECT>";
     return($return_string);
   }
}

class HtmlFormText extends HtmlFormInput
{
  var $initial_value;

  function HtmlFormText ($name,
                         $heading,
                         $initial_value="")
  {
    // Initialization of member vars
    if (!isSet($name) ||
        !isSet($heading)) {
      die("HtmlFormText constructor needs " .
          "at least two arguments (name, heading)");
    }
    $this->name = $name; // name defined in parent
    $this->heading = $heading; // defined in parent
    $this->initial_value = $initial_value;
  }

  function toString () {
    $return_string = "";
    $return_string .= "<INPUT TYPE=TEXT ";
    $return_string .= "NAME=\"$this->name\" ";
    $return_string .=
        "VALUE=\"$this->initial_value\" ";
    $return_string .= " >";
    return($return_string);
  }
}

class HtmlFormTextArea extends HtmlFormInput {
  var $initial_value;
```

```php
var $rows;
var $cols;
var $wrapType;

function HtmlFormTextArea ($name,
                           $heading,
                           // optional args:
                           $initial_value="",
                           $rows=1, $cols=60,
                           $wrapType="VIRTUAL")
{
  // Initialization of member vars
  if (!isSet($name)) {
    die("HtmlFormTextArea constructor needs " .
        "at least two arguments (name, heading)");
  }
  $this->name = $name; // name defined in parent
  $this->heading = $heading; // name defined in parent
  $this->initial_value = $initial_value;
  $this->rows = $rows;
  $this->cols = $cols;
  $this->wrapType = $wrapType;
}

function toString ()
{
  $return_string = "";
  $return_string .= "<TEXTAREA ";
  $return_string .= "NAME=\"$this->name\" ";
  $return_string .= "ROWS=$this->rows ";
  $return_string .= "COLS=$this->cols ";
  $return_string .= "WRAP=$this->wrapType ";
  $return_string .= $this->additionalAttributes();
  $return_string .= ">";
  $return_string .= $this->initial_value;
  $return_string .= "</TEXTAREA>";
  return($return_string);
}

function additionalAttributes () {
  // OVERRIDE THIS to return a string with
  // TextArea attributes other than
  // NAME, ROWS, COLS, and WRAP
  return("");
}
}
?>
```

The basic design for all these objects includes a constructor function with default arguments, and a `toString()` method that returns HTML for the form or piece thereof. Forms store pieces of input (which might conceivably be reordered or laid out by a more sophisticated version), and recursively call `toString()` on these pieces. The HTML form elements that are supported are: TEXTAREA, TEXT, and SELECT.

Here is an example of calling this code to generate a simple form page:

```
<HTML><HEAD></HEAD><BODY>
<?php include("form_printer.php");
$my_form = new HtmlForm($PHP_SELF);
$my_form->addInputForm(
        new HtmlFormText("firstname",
                        "First Name"));
$my_form->addInputForm(
        new HtmlFormText("lastname",
                        "Last Name"));
$my_form->addInputForm(
        new HtmlFormSelect(
            "age",
            "Age",
            array(0 => "0 - 9",
                  1 => "10 - 19",
                  2 => "20 - 29",
                  3 => "Senior citizen"),
            2));
$my_form->addInputForm(
        new HtmlFormTextArea(
            "feedback",
            "What's on your mind?",
        "[Please fill in your own personal rant]",
            5));
print($my_form->toString());
?>
</BODY>
</HTML>
```

Much of the form-producing code is straightforward and is concerned with churning out various kinds of HTML syntax. There are two interesting things to notice from the point of view of OOP-in-PHP, however.

The first is that the `HtmlFormInput` class is purely *abstract* or *virtual*, as some other OOP languages might term it. That is, it exists not to be instantiated, but only to be inherited from. PHP does not offer a way to enforce this at compilation time, but (at least) any attempts to instantiate it directly should error out at runtime because the constructor function intentionally dies.

The second point of interest is that the `HtmlForm` class has an array that is intended to hold `HtmlFormInput` objects. Of course, because PHP is loosely typed, we cannot enforce that in any way at compile time, and even at runtime nothing stops other code from directly manipulating the storage array to insert inappropriate things (because there is no distinction between public and private members). But the manufacturer-approved way to insert new forms (`addInputForm()`) does some type-checking on insertion. If users of this class rely only on this method, we can be assured that everything that ends up in that array will be a instance of `HtmlFormInput` (or subclass thereof) and so should be a well-behaved form element when display time comes around.

Zend Engine 2

The syntax for object-oriented programming is somewhat limited as of PHP 4.2 and lacks features that OOP developers who are experienced in other languages have come to expect. Unfortunately, these features turn out to be impossible to add without reworking the parsing code at the core of PHP, known as the Zend Engine. In part because of this, there is a new version of this engine currently under development, known as Zend Engine 2.

The new features in ZE2 are not limited to OOP, but the behavior of objects will be somewhat different, and the OOP syntax will be extended considerably. Among the planned changes:

- Member variables can be marked `private`, as in languages like C++ and Java. (Interestingly, attempts to access private variables will not result in either compilation or runtime errors, but will simply return an empty value.)

- Constructor functions for a class will be called `__construct()` rather than having the same name as the class, and there will also be analogous destructor functions (called `__destruct()`).

- Objects will be referred to by handles, which implies that they will not be implicitly copied when assigned to variables or passed to functions.

When will ZE2 become a part of PHP? There is an alpha version of ZE2 bundled with the development version of PHP 4.3, but it is not clear at this writing what version of PHP will include the first official release of the engine.

Gotchas and Troubleshooting

In the spirit of Chapter 15, we offer in the following sections the top-three most likely symptoms of problematic OOP code, along with the most likely cause.

Symptom: Member variable has no value in member function

This could have many causes, of course, but the most common is simply just a confusion about the right way to refer to member variables. The syntax is:

```
$this->member_name
```

If, instead, your function simply refers to $member_name, that will usually be an unbound variable and, at any rate, will never succeed in referring to the member variable. Similarly, if your function refers to $this->$member_name, you are asking for the field named by the string in the variable $member_name (which is probably unbound).

Symptom: Parse error, expecting T_VARIABLE ...

There are of course many ways to munge a class definition so that PHP will complain when it tries to parse it. One of the most common errors again has to do with placement of those $ symbols. A class declaration like the following:

```
class MyClass {
  var my_var;   // WRONG
}
```

inevitably gives you a parse error of some sort because the syntax requires a $ before my_var.

Symptom: Change to object's data seems to have no effect

Ask yourself whether the object you are inspecting is exactly the same object that was modified, keeping in mind that variable assignments and passing objects to functions result in object copying. (See the section "Modifying and assigning objects," earlier in this chapter, in "Basic OOP Constructs.")

OOP Style in PHP

The topic of OOP programming style is a huge one (because it includes OOP design!) and is well beyond the scope of this book. In the spirit of Chapter 14, however, we offer in the following sections some brief notes on writing readable, maintainable PHP OOP code.

Naming conventions

In this section, we simply pass along the parts of the PEAR coding style that pertain to objects.

> **CROSS-REFERENCE:** For more information on the PEAR project and the PEAR coding style, see Chapter 14 or the PEAR Web site (at http://php.pear.net).

PEAR recommends that class names begin with an uppercase letter and (if in a PEAR-approved directory hierarchy of packages) have that inclusion path in the class name, separated by underscores. Presumably the parts of the name that are not so separated have their component words separated by capitalization. (This is not entirely clear from the PEAR naming standards page at this writing.) So your class that counts words, and which belongs to a PEAR package called TextUtils, might be called TextUtils_WordCounter. If building large OOP packages, you may want to emulate this underscore convention with your own package names; otherwise you can simply give your classes names like WordCounter.

Member variables and member function names should have their first real letter be lowercase, and have "word" boundaries be delineated by capitalization. In addition, names that are intended to be private to the class (that is, they are used only within the class, and not by outside code) should start with an underscore. So the variable in your WordCounter class that holds the count of words might be called wordCount (if intended to be messed with from the outside) or _wordCount (if intended to be private to the class).

As we have said, PHP (with Zend Engine 1) doesn't offer any way to enforce privacy of object members, so any naming scheme that marks variables as private is simply documenting the intent of the author. If you follow the underscore naming convention, however, it becomes very easy to see when the intent is being violated. For example, it is easy to see that the following code does not respect the convention:

```
class Customer
{
    var name;
    var _creditCardNumber;
}
$customer = new Customer;
print($customer->_creditCardNumber);   // violation of privacy!
```

It fails simply because the variable immediately before the ->_ is not $this.

Accessor functions

Another style of documenting your intent about use of internal variables is to have your variables be marked as private, in general, and provide "getter" and "setter" functions to outside callers. For example, we might rewrite and augment the preceding class definition like this:

```
class Customer
{
    var _name;
    var _creditCardNumber;
    var _rating;

    function getName ()
    {
        return($this->_name);
    }

    function getRating ()
    {
        return($this->_rating);
    }
```

```
    function setRating($rating)
    {
        $this->_rating = $rating;
    }
    [... more functions ]
}
```

This class definition has three private variables: one (`_creditCardNumber`) that should neither be set nor retrieved from outside code, another (`_name`) that outside code should be able to retrieve but not set, and a third (`_rating`) that outside code should feel free to both get and set.

Although PHP class syntax lets you interleave variables with function definitions, it's a good idea, in general, to organize your code so that similar items with similar usage intent are together in the class definition. For example, you might develop the habit of laying out class functions like this:

```
class myClass
{
// Public variables:
..
// Private variables
..
// Constructor

// Public functions
..
// Private functions
..
}
```

Designing for inheritance

The question of exactly how to design a class hierarchy is, as we've said, a vast area of study unto itself, and we're not about to try to contribute to it here. Just as a stylistic matter, though, it's worth thinking about whether you intend your class to be inherited from, and then try to indicate your decision, either with comments or in the structure of the definition.

For example, you may intend that your class should never breed, in which case you might just indicate that in comments, and then stop worrying about inheritance issues. (There is currently no way in PHP to enforce that a class cannot be inherited from.) At the other end of the spectrum, you might have all or part of your class intended only for inheritance. You can indicate this in comments, or you can use the trick we used in the definition of `HtmlFormInput` in Listing 26-9: Provide methods that die informatively when called directly in the base class. Finally, of course, you may have some methods that can be called directly in the base class, but are especially intended for overriding. You may want to group these "hook" methods together in a clearly marked section of your class definition, so that the later writer of a derived class can quickly figure out what options are available for specializing the class's behavior. (Remember that that clueless coder of the future that you are helping may well be yourself.)

Summary

PHP provides the basics to support object-oriented programming. Among other things, the OOP syntax in PHP allows for programmer-defined classes with member variables and member data and offers single inheritance, constructor functions, object serialization, and functions for introspection. Nothing in PHP requires that you write in an object-oriented style, but if you prefer that style you can write almost all your code that way.

The object-oriented part of PHP is, frankly, an add-on; PHP was not originally intended to be an object-oriented language, and developers with OOP experience will miss some aspects of more mature OOP languages. On the other hand, the OOP extension is usable, fairly mature, pretty stable, and widely used. It provides an extra layer of organization that can be helpful when maintaining complex code and offers a nice way to package code for distribution and reuse.

Chapter 27

Sessions, Cookies, and HTTP

In This Chapter

♦ Why do you need sessions?

♦ How PHP sessions are implemented?

♦ Cookies and their use

♦ Sending HTTP headers directly using PHP

This chapter might as well have been called "Keeping Track," because the theme throughout is the problem of tracking interactions with users over longer periods of time than it takes to generate a single Web page. We explain the extent of PHP support for extended user sessions and for setting and checking cookies, and then, finally, we cover a couple of related techniques involving directly sending HTTP headers.

Sessions and cookies are closely allied concepts in PHP and in Web programming more generally, largely because the best way to actually implement sessions is by using cookies. Sessions are a higher-level concept than cookies, and for this chapter, we plan to start at the top and work our way down.

What's a Session?

What do we mean by a *session*? Informally, a session of Web browsing is a period of time during which a particular person, while sitting at a particular machine, views a number of different Web pages in his or her browser program and then calls it quits, either for the night or because the person in question actually has a life. If you run a Web site that this person visits during that time, for your purposes the session runs from that person's first download of a page from your site through the last. For example, a Caribbean hotel's Web site might enjoy a session of five pages duration in the middle of a real user's session that began with a travel portal and ended with that user booking his or her vacation with a competitor.

So what's the problem?

Why is the idea of a session tricky enough that we're just talking about it now, even though PHP is at version 4 already? It's because the HTTP protocol by which browsers talk to Web servers is *stateless,* with the result that your Web server has less long-term memory than your housecat. That is, your Web server reacts independently to each individual request it receives and has no way to link requests together even if it is logging requests. If I sit at my computer in Chicago, and you sit at yours in Monterey, and we both ask for page 1 and then page 2 of the Caribbean hotelier's site, the HTTP protocol offers no help toward figuring out that two people looked at two pages each — what it sees is four individual requests for pages, with various information attached to each request. Not only does this information not identify you personally (by name, email address, phone number, or any other traceable identification), it also offers nothing reliable to identify your two page requests as being from the same person.

Why should you care?

If our Web site's only mission in life is to offer various pages to various users, we may, in fact, not care at all where sessions begin and end. On the other hand, there are a number of reasons why we might in fact care. For example:

♦ We want to customize our users' experiences as they move through the site, in a way that depends on which (or how many) pages they have already seen.

♦ We want to display advertisements to the user, but we do not want to display a given ad more than once per session.

♦ We want the session to accumulate information about users' actions as they progress — as in an adventure game's tracking of points and weapons accumulated, or an e-commerce site's shopping cart.

♦ We are interested in tracking how people navigate through our site in general — when they visit that interior page, is it because they bookmarked it, or did they get there all the way from the front page?

For all of these purposes, we need to be able to match up page requests with the sessions they are part of, and for some purposes it would be nice to store some information in association with the session as it progresses. PHP sessions solve both of these problems for us.

Home-Grown Alternatives

Before we look at PHP's treatment of sessions, let's look at a few alternative ways the problem can be handled. As we'll see, the PHP treatment combines a couple of these techniques.

IP address

Web servers usually know either the Internet host name or the IP address of the client that is requesting a page. In many configurations of PHP, these show up for free as variables — $REMOTE_HOST and $REMOTE_ADDR, respectively. Now you might think that the identity of the machine at the other end is a reasonable stand-in for the person at the other end, at least over the short term. If you get two requests in quick succession from the same IP address, your code can safely conclude that the same person followed a link or form from one of your site's pages to another.

Unfortunately, the IP address your browser knows about may not belong to the machine your user is browsing from. In particular, AOL and other large operations employ proxy servers, which act as intermediaries. Your user's browser actually requests a URL from the proxy server, which in turn requests the page from your server and then forwards back the page to the user. The result is that many different AOL users might be browsing your site simultaneously, all apparently from the same address. IP addresses are not unique enough to form a basis for session tracking.

Hidden variables

Every HTTP request is dealt with independently, but each time your user moves from page to page within your site, it is usually via either a link or a form submission. If the very first page a user visits can somehow generate a unique label for that visit, then every subsequent "handoff" of one page to another can pass that unique identifier along.

For example, here is a hypothetical code fragment that you might include near the top of every page on your site:

```
if (!IsSet($my_s_id))
  $my_session_id =
    generate_session_id(); // warning! hypothetical function
```

This fragment checks to see if the $my_s_id variable is bound — if it is, we assume that it has been passed in, and we are in the middle of a session. If it is not, we assume that we are the first page of a new session, and we call a hypothetical function called generate_session_id() to create a unique identifier.

After we have included the preceding code, we assume that we have a unique identifier for the session, and our only remaining responsibility is to pass it along to any page we link or submit to. Every link from our page should include the $my_s_id as a GET argument, as in:

```
<A HREF="next.php?my_s_id=<?php echo $my_s_id;?>">Next</A>
```

And every form submission should have a hidden POST argument embedded in it, like this:

```
<FORM ACTION=next.php METHOD=POST>
body of form
<INPUT TYPE=HIDDEN NAME=my_s_id
       VALUE="<?php echo $my_s_id;?>" >
</FORM>
```

What's wrong with this technique? Nothing. It works just fine as a way to keep different sessions straight (as long as you can generate unique identifiers). And once we have unique labels for the sessions, we can use a variety of techniques to associate other kinds of information with each session, such as using the session ID as a key for database storage. However, this approach to sessions is a pain to maintain — you must make sure that *every* link and form submission propagates the information as described, or the session identifier will be dropped. Also, if you send the information as GET arguments, your session-tracking machinery will be visible in the Web-address box of your user's browser, and such arguments are easily edited by the user.

Cookies

Another approach to session tracking is to use a unique session identifier as in the previous section, but perform the "handoff" by setting or checking a cookie.

A cookie is a special kind of file, located in the file system of your user's browsing computer, that Web servers can read from and write to. Rather than checking for a passed GET/POST variable (and assigning a new identifier if none is found), your script checks the user's machine for a previously written cookie file and stores a new identifier in a new cookie file if none is found. This method has some benefits over using hidden variables: The mechanism works behind the scenes (typically, not showing any trace of its activity in the browser window), and the code that checks or sets the cookie can be centralized (rather than affecting every form and link).

What's the drawback? Some very old browsers do not support cookies at all, and more recent browsers allow users to deny cookie-setting privileges to Web servers. So, although cookies make for a smooth solution, we can't assume that they are always available.

> **NOTE:** There is a subtle difference in the "coverage" of cookie-based sessions and that of sessions based on GET/POST variables. A variable-based session will only maintain its identity as long as your user stays within your site, following intrasite links or form postings. However, there are any number of ways that a user might go away and come back again within a short period of time — by visiting a site that your site links to, which in turn links back, or by wandering away and then finding your site again with a search engine. Cookie-based approaches will treat returns from these little detours as a continuation of the same session, whereas variable-propagation approaches have to treat them as new visits.

We cover cookies in more detail in the "Cookies" section later in the chapter.

How Sessions Work in PHP

Good session support takes care of the following two things:

♦ Session tracking (that is, detecting whether two separate script invocations are, in fact, part of the same user session).

♦ Storing information in association with a session.

Obviously, you need the first capability before you can hope to have the second.

PHP session tracking works by a combination of the hidden variables method and the cookie method described in the last section. Because of the advantages of cookies, PHP will use them when the user's browser supports them and, otherwise, will have recourse to stashing the session ID in a GET and POST argument. Fortunately, though, the session functions themselves operate at a more abstract level and take care of checking for cookie support all by themselves. If your version of PHP 4 has been appropriately configured for sessions, you should be able to use the session functions without worrying which method is being used.

> **NOTE:** If you want PHP to transparently handle passing session variables for you when cookies are not available, you need to have configured PHP with both the `--enable-trans-sid` and `--enable-track-vars` options. If PHP is not handling this for you, you must arrange to pass a GET or POST argument, of the form *session_name=session_id,* in all your links and forms. When a session is active, PHP provides a special constant, SID, which contains the right argument/value pair. Following is an example of including this constant in a link:
>
> `<A HREF="my_next_page.php?<?php echo(SID);?>">Next page</A>`

Making PHP aware of your session

The first step in a script that uses the session feature is to let PHP know that a session may already be in progress so that it can hook up to it and recover any associated information. This is done by calling the function session_start(), which takes no arguments. (If you want every script invocation to look for a session without having to call this function, set the variable session.auto_start to 1 in your php.ini file [The usual default is 0]). Also, any call to session_register() causes an implicit initial call to session_start().

The effect of session_start() depends on whether PHP can locate a previous session identifier, as supplied either by HTTP arguments or in a cookie. If one is found, the values of any previously registered session variables are recovered. If one is not found, then PHP assumes that we are in the first page of a new session, and generates a new session ID.

Propagating session variables

Changes in PHP's treatment of global and external variables starting with version 4.1 have made certain things more inconvenient. (See Chapter 9 for more detail on these changes.) In our view, though, these changes will also remove a lot of potential confusion about sessions. Accordingly, we'll list two approaches to propagating variables in sessions: one, which is simple and works in PHP version 4.1 or later, and another which is more complicated and works only in PHP version 4.1 or *earlier* (unless you re-enable the register_globals setting). (You can guess which one we recommend.)

The simple approach (using $_SESSION)

The simple approach is this: Assuming that you've made a call to session_start() (as early in your script as possible), use the $_SESSION superglobal array as your suitcase for storing anything that you want to retrieve again from a later page in the same session. Assume that any other variables will be left behind when you leave this page, and that everything in that suitcase will be there when you arrive at the next page.

So, session code to propagate a single numerical variable can be as simple as this:

```php
<?php
session_start();

$temporary_number = 45;
$save_this_one = 19;
$another_temporary = 33;

$_SESSION['save_this'] = $save_this_one;
?>
```

The receiving code can be as simple as the following example:

```php
<?php
session_start();
$saved_from_prev_page = $_SESSION['save_this'];
[..]
$temporary_number = 45;
$another_temporary = 33;
[..]
?>
```

That's all there is to it. Assignment into the $_SESSION superglobal array implicitly does any registration necessary for the new value to be carried forward to the next page.

Note that we could have given the same name to both the global variable ($save_this) and the corresponding $_SESSION index (save_this_one), because the two have nothing to do with one another.

For this simple approach, we assume that 'register_globals' has been turned off (as it is by default in versions 4.2 and later), so that no session variables are being automatically promoted into global variables. Or, more precisely, we don't care whether it is turned on or not because the code will work in either situation.

> **NOTE:** The $_SESSION array is one of the new superglobal variables introduced in PHP 4.1. The *superglobal* adjective means that it can be referenced anywhere in PHP code, even within functions. If you are using an earlier version you can use $HTTP_SESSION_VARS in exactly the same way (assuming that the track_vars configuration variable is enabled), but you will have to declare it as global within any functions that refer to it.

The complex approach (registering variables)

In the more complex approach, you have decided for reasons of your own that you want to have session variables become regular global page variables automatically. To do this, you must have the configuration directive register_globals enabled. (It is turned off by default in PHP 4.2 and later so, if you are using a recent PHP version, you will have to edit your php.ini file to turn it on again.)

When using register_globals, variables from previous pages that were registered as session variables will show up as regular global variables in your script as soon as the session is discovered. For example, if a previous page in a session has registered the variable $city and assigned it the value 'Chicago', then our script can take advantage of it simply by calling session_start():

```
session_start();
print("$city, $city, that toddlin' town<BR>");
```

The lyric will be as we expect. If no such variable has been previously registered and assigned, or if we forget the call to session_start(), the variable will act as though it is unbound.

> **NOTE:** Pulling session bindings into a page by calling session_start() will overwrite any variable bindings with the same name that already exists at that point in the script. In particular, this means that if a given variable is passed by GET/POST and there is also a cookie-based, session-level binding, the session binding will "win." under the default setting for the configuration directive 'variables_order'. This becomes a non-issue if you can use the "simple" approach and refer to superglobals only for session, GET, and POST variables.

If PHP cannot find a previous session identifier, the call to session_start() actually does start a new session. The main effect of this is that a new unique identifier is created, which can now be used to register variables, and a cookie will be sent containing this new session identifier.

Registering variables in sessions

Calling session_start() takes care of "importing" any variables from the session context to our current script — now all we have to worry about is "exporting" them again, to see that they make it to later pages in the same session. This is done with the function session_register(). As it turns out, the import business is wholesale (one call to session_start() does it), but the export business is retail (we have to name each registered variable individually).

Say that, as in the previous example, a previous page has set the value of $city to be 'Chicago', and had already called session_register($city). Here's how we take advantage of it and set it up (or change it) for later pages as well:

```
session_start();
print("$city, $city, that toddlin' town<BR>");

print("$city, $city, I'll show you around<BR>");
$city = 'San Mateo';
```

The session_start() call pulls in the binding of $city to 'Chicago' as before, so it can be used in the first print statement. From then on, $city would normally be treated just like any other global page variable. The previous page's call to session_register(), however, has put the session mechanism on notice that the 'city' variable is to be exported again out to session-world, and that later pages in the same session should receive whatever binding $city has at the end of this script. In the preceding excerpt, the value gets changed to 'San Mateo', so future pages should expect to do their toddlin' there.

> **NOTE:** Variable names given as arguments to session_register shouldn't include the leading $.

If we had forgotten the session_start() call, the first print line would have empty strings in place of the $city variable. The second print line would look good even so, because calling session_register() causes an implicit call to session_start(), if such a call has not already been made. Finally, if we had omitted the session_register() call, everything on this page would look fine, but subsequent pages would not receive any session variable called 'city'.

> **NOTE:** Registration of a variable is entirely independent of assigning a value to it. You can assign a value to a variable without registering it (in which case, it will simply be a normal page variable that is not propagated to other pages), or you can register a variable without assigning it a value (in which case, it will show up in later pages as unset).

Where is the data really stored?

There are two things that the session mechanism must hang onto: the session ID itself and any associated variable bindings.

As we have seen, either the session ID is stored as a cookie on the browser's machine, or it is incorporated into the GET/POST arguments submitted with page requests. In the latter case, there is really no storage happening — the ID is submitted as part of a request and is returned folded into HTML code for links and forms, which may generate the next request. The browser and server pass this vital information back and forth like a hot potato, and the session is effectively over if either side drops it.

By default, the contents of session variables are stored in special files on the server, one file per session ID. (It's already slightly rude to store the session ID as a client-side cookie — it would be even more rude to store session variable data on the client disk when it's not necessary.) Doing this kind of storage requires the session code to serialize the data, which means turning it into a linear sequence of bytes that can be written to a file and read back to recreate the data.

It's possible to configure PHP to store the contents of session variables in a server-side database, rather than in files. For more information, see the section "Configuration Issues" later in this chapter.

> **CROSS-REFERENCE:** In the first edition of this book, we warned you that serialization support for objects was still problematic, and so we didn't recommend trying to store object variables in sessions. Fortunately, in PHP version 4.1 and later, session serialization seems to be stable. See Chapter 26 for more about object serialization and Chapter 39 for an extended example of storing objects in sessions.

Sample Session Code

In Listing 27-1, we show a short code file, which really has a dual purpose. The first purpose is to provide an example of a full (short) script that successfully uses session functions; the second is to provide a test script that you can use to make sure that you have session support and that it is doing what you expect.

In this listing, we perform the following tasks:

- Initiate a session (or pick up an existing one) by using `session_start()`.

- Check for the existence of a pre-existing entry in `$_SESSION`. If not present, we assume that the session is new.

- Increment a counter that tracks how many times that the user has visited this page.

- Store the incremented counter back in `$_SESSION`.

- Provide a link back to the page itself, embedding the session ID as an argument if it is found.

Listing 27-1: Test script using `$_SESSION`

```php
<?php
session_start();
?>

<HTML><HEAD><TITLE>Greetings</TITLE></HEAD>
<BODY>
<H2>Welcome to the Center for Content-free Hospitality</H2>
<?php

if (!IsSet($_SESSION['visit_count'])) {
  print("Hello, you must have just arrived.  Welcome!<BR>");
  $_SESSION['visit_count'] = 1;
}
else {
  $visit_count = $_SESSION['visit_count'] + 1;
  print("Back again are ya?  That makes $visit_count times now ".
        "(not that anyone's counting)<BR>");
  $_SESSION['visit_count'] = $visit_count;
}

$self_url = $_SERVER['PHP_SELF'];
```

```
$session_id = SID;
if (IsSet($session_id) &&
    $session_id) {
  $href = "$self_url?$session_id";
}
else {
  $href = $self_url;
}
print("<BR><A HREF=\"$href\">Visit us again</A> sometime");
?>
</BODY></HTML>
```

This code should be available at www.troutworks.com/phpbook and is suitable for your use in testing your session support if you are using PHP 4.1 or later. (See Listing 27-2, a little later in this section, if you are using a pre-4.1 version or if you prefer the register_globals style of using sessions.) After obtaining the code, you should first simply test that it loads without errors. The page you see should look something like that shown in Figure 27-1. After that, to see if cookie-based session support is working, try simply reloading or refreshing the page in your browser. You should see a page that looks something like Figure 27-2.

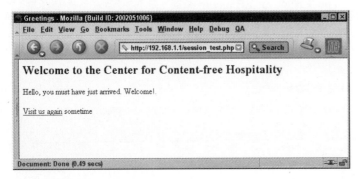

Figure 27-1: Session test page

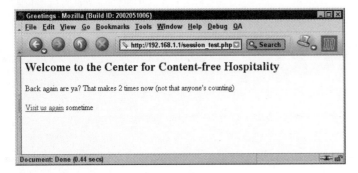

Figure 27-2: Session test page, second visit

If the result of your second visit is Figure 27-2, then cookie-based session support is working. If instead it still looks like Figure 27-1, then PHP did not detect your session. Make sure that the browser you are testing with is configured to accept cookies and take a look at the section "Gotchas and Troubleshooting," at the end of this chapter.

The second half of Listing 27-1 is about constructing a self-link that will propagate session information even without cookie support. You can test it by turning off cookies in your test browser. (This is usually an Advanced or Security option in your browser's preferences or options.) After cookies have been turned off, you should be treated as a first-time visitor when you reload the page. However, with cookies off, the SID constant should now contain the session ID name and value, which our code embeds in the link's URL as a GET argument. Clicking on this link should increment the visit count appropriately, and thereafter either clicking the link or reloading should increment it again (because the session ID should now be in the URL that is being reloaded).

This embedding of the session ID in the URL is exactly what should be unnecessary if PHP has been compiled with `--enable-trans-sid`. In this case, you should be able to add another self-link to this page, without embedding anything extra in the URL, and PHP should take care of it for you.

Listing 27-2 shows the same test script as in Listing 27-1, except that it does not use superglobal variables and assumes that the `register_globals` directive has been turned on. It's appropriate if you happen to be using PHP version 4.0.*x*, or if you prefer the `register_globals` style.

Listing 27-2: Test script assuming `register_globals`

```php
<?php
session_start();
session_register('visit_count');
?>

<HTML><HEAD><TITLE>Greetings</TITLE></HEAD>
<BODY>
<H2>Welcome to the Center for Content-free Hospitality</H2>
<?php
if (!IsSet($visit_count)) {
  print("Hello, you must have just arrived.  Welcome!<BR>");
  $visit_count = 1;
}
else {
  $visit_count++;
  print("Back again are ya?  That makes $visit_count times now ".
        "(not that anyone's counting)<BR>");
}

$self_url = $PHP_SELF;
```

```
$session_id = SID;
if (IsSet($session_id) &&
    $session_id) {
  $href = "$self_url?$session_id";
}
else {
  $href = $self_url;
}
print("<BR><A HREF=\"$href\">Visit us again</A> sometime");
?>
</BODY></HTML>
```

Session Functions

Table 27-1 lists the most important session-related functions, with descriptions of what they do. Note that in some cases the behavior of these functions depends on configuration options that we detail in the "Configuration Issues" section.

Table 27-1: Session Function Summary

Function	Behavior
session_start()	Takes no arguments and causes PHP either to notice a session ID that has been passed to it (via a cookie or GET/POST) or to create a new session ID if none is found.
	If an old session ID is found, PHP retrieves the assignments of all variables that have been registered and makes those assigned variables available as regular global variables.
session_register()	Takes a string as argument and registers the variable named by the string — for example, session_register('username'). (*Note:* The variable-name string should not include the leading $.) It can also be passed an array of string arguments to register multiple variables at once.
	The effect of registering a variable is that subsequent assignments to that variable will be preserved for future sessions. (After a script completes, the registered variables and their values are serialized and propagated in such a way that later calls to session_start() can recreate the bindings.)
	If session_start() has not yet been called, session_register will implicitly call it before executing.

`session_unregister()`	Takes a string variable name as argument and unregisters the corresponding variable from the session. As a result, the variable binding will no longer be serialized and propagated to later pages. (The variable-name string should not include the leading $.)
`session_is_registered()`	Takes a variable-name string and tests whether a variable with a given variable name is registered in the current session, returning `TRUE` if so and `FALSE` if not.
`session_destroy()`	Calling this function gets rid of all session variable information that has been stored. (Note: A browser's session ID may still be the same after this function call.) It does not unset any variables in the current script.
`session_name()`	When called with no arguments, returns the current session-name string. This is usually `'PHPSESSID'` by default.
	When called with one string argument, `session_name()` sets the current session name to that string. This name is used as a key to find the session ID in cookies and GET/POST arguments — for successful retrieval, the session name must be the same as it was when the values were serialized and stored. Note that there is no reason to change the session name unless you have some need to distinguish session types that are being served by the same Web server (such as in the case of multiple sites that each track sessions). The session name is reset to the default whenever a script executes, so any name change must happen in every script that uses the name, and before any other session functions are called.
`session_module_name()`	If given no arguments, returns the name of the module that is responsible for handling session data. This name currently defaults to `'files'`, meaning that session bindings are serialized and then written to files in the directory named by the function `session_save_path()`.
	If given a string argument, changes the module name to that string. (This could presumably be, for example, `'user'` for a user-defined session database, but it should not be changed unless you know what you are doing.)
`session_save_path()`	Returns (or sets, if given an argument) the pathname of the directory to which session variable-binding files will be written (which typically defaults to `/tmp` on Unix systems). This directory needs to exist and have appropriate permissions for PHP to write files to it.

`session_id()`	Takes no arguments and returns a string, which is the unique key corresponding to a particular session. If given a string argument, will set the session ID to that string.
`session_encode()`	Returns a string encoding of the state of the current session, suitable for use by `string_decode()`. This can be used for saving a session for revival at some later time, such as by writing the encoded string to a file or database.
`session_decode()`	Takes a string encoding as produced by `session_encode()` and reestablishes the session state, turning session bindings into page bindings as `session_start()` does.

Configuration Issues

The variables in Table 27-2 are settable in the `php.ini` file and viewable by calling `phpinfo()`. We offer descriptions and the "typical" default values. (Some defaults are platform-dependent.)

Table 27-2: Session Configuration Variables

Php.ini Variable	*Typical Value*	*Description*
`session.save_path`	`/tmp` under Unix systems	Pathname for the server-side folder where session variable-binding files will be written.
`session.auto_start`	0	When 1, sessions will initialize automatically every time a script loads. When 0, no session code will be code unless there is an explicit call to either `session_start()` or `session_register()`.
`session.save_handler`	`'files'`	String that determines underlying method for saving session variable information. Changing this is not recommended for the casual user.

| session.cookie_lifet ime | 0 | Specifies how long session cookies take to expire and, consequently, the lifetime of a session. The default of 0 means that sessions last until the browser is closed — any other value indicates the number of seconds the session is allowed to live. |
| session.use_cookies | 1 | If 1, the session mechanism will attempt to propagate the session ID by setting/checking a cookie. (If the browser refuses the cookie, then GET/POST vars may be used.) If this variable is 0, no attempt to use cookies is made. |

Cookies

CROSS-REFERENCE: Many uses of cookies amount to session-tracking — keeping track of some piece of information as a single user navigates through your site. If you are tempted to use cookies for a purpose like this, and you are using PHP 4, you might want to consider simply using the built-in session functions that are covered in the section "Cookies," earlier in this chapter. Not only do they offer a nicer level of abstraction, but they also have a built-in fallback mechanism that deals with refusal of cookies by propagating the information via GET/POST arguments instead.

A *cookie* is a small piece of information that is retained on the client machine, either in the browser's application memory or as a small file written to the user's hard disk. It contains a name/value pair — *setting a cookie* means associating a value with a name and storing that pairing on the client side. *Getting* or *reading* a cookie means using the name to retrieve the value. (See the sidebar "Cookies and Privacy," a little later in this chapter, for a summary of the controversy surrounding the use of cookies.)

NOTE; As a general rule, you only want to store information in a client-side cookie when storing it on the server is not an option. This is partly simple politeness, but it is also because there are constraints that prevent server abuses of the client's hard disk (Typically one Web server can store a maximum of 20 cookies per client, for example). If you need to store a lot of info, consider developing a scheme where the cookie file contains an ID that enables you to look up the rest of that information on the server.

In PHP, cookies are set using the setcookie() function, and cookies are read nearly automatically. In PHP 4.1 and later, names and values of cookie variables show up in the superglobal array $_COOKIES, with the cookie name as an index, and the value as the value it indexes.

The setcookie() function

There is just one cookie-related function, called setcookie(). Table 27-3 shows its arguments, in order, all but the first of which are optional:

Table 27-3: Arguments to setcookie()

Argument Name	Expected Type	Meaning
name	string	The name of your cookie (analogous to the name of a variable).
value	string	The value you want to store in the cookie (analogous to the value you would assign to a variable). If this argument is not supplied, the cookie named by the first argument is deleted.
expire	int	Specifies when this cookie should expire. A value of 0 (the default) means that it should last until the browser is closed. Any other integer is interpreted as an absolute time (as returned by the function mktime()) when the cookie should expire.
path	string	In the default case, any page within the Web root folder would see (and be able to set) this named cookie. Setting the path to a subdirectory (for example, "/mysteryguide") allows distinguishing cookies that have the same name but are set by different "sites" or subareas of the Web server.
domain	string	In the default case, no check is made against the domain requested by the client. If this argument is nonempty, then the domain must match. For example, If the same server serves mysteryguide.com and sciencebookguide.com, then one site's code can ensure that the other site does not read (or set) its cookies by including this argument as "mysteryguide.com."
secure	int (0 or 1)	Defaults to 0. If this argument is 1, the cookie will only be sent over a secure (HTTPS) connection. Note that a secure connection must already be running for such a cookie to be set in the first place.

CROSS-REFERENCE: For details about the representation of time used by the expire argument, see Chapter 13 — specifically, the discussions of the functions time() and mktime().

> **CAUTION:** Calling `setcookie()` results in sending HTTP header information, which cannot be done after you have already sent some regular PHP output (even if that output consists of a single space or blank line!).

Examples

This section provides some example calls to `setcookie()`, along with comments, such as the following:

```
setcookie('membername', 'timboy');
```

This sets a cookie called `membername`, with a value of `timboy`. Because there are no arguments except for the first two, the cookie will persist only until the current browser program is closed, and it will be read on subsequent page requests from this browser to this server, regardless of the domain name in the request or where in the Web root file hierarchy the page is served from. The cookie will also be read regardless of whether the Web connection is secure. For example, consider the following call:

```
setcookie('membername', 'troutgirl', time() + (60 * 60 * 24),
          "/", "www.troutworks.com", 1);
```

> **NOTE:** If you want to specify later arguments to `setcookie()` while leaving the earlier ones with their default values, it is best to give the empty string (`" "`) for the domain argument, a string containing a slash character (`"/"`) for the path argument, and `0` for the expiration.

This sets the cookie to have the value `'troutgirl'` and would overwrite the previous example's value if it had been set by a previous page. The expiration time is set to 86,400 seconds (or 1 day) after the current time. The path argument is given the most inclusive path possible (`"/"`), so this cookie will still be read regardless of where it is in the Web directory hierarchy. The host argument is set to `'www.troutworks.com'`, which means that subsequent page views will not cause the cookie to be read unless the user actually is making a request of that host. Finally, the last argument specifies that this cookie will only be read or written over a secure connection. (If the very connection used by this page is not secure, then presumably the cookie will not be set at all.)

> **CAUTION:** Multiple calls to `setcookie()` will typically be interpreted in the opposite order that they appear in your PHP script, although not every browser version does this. The best rule is to never send two different values for the same cookie from a single page execution. (Sending more than one is pointless anyway because one of them will always overwrite the other.)

COOKIES AND PRIVACY

Cookies have always been controversial from a privacy point of view, and that controversy heats up again periodically. As we wrote the first edition, DoubleClick (an Internet advertising agency) was being flamed for its announcement that it planned to cross-correlate cookie information with a very large database of consumer names, addresses, and buying habits (in an apparent reversal of earlier promises about such behavior).

The worry was that, after a consumer reveals his or her identity on a site by filling out a form and accepting a cookie, any other site that compares notes with the original site could conceivably know the true identity of the user (and lots of other information as well). If this practice became widespread, every e-commerce site you visit might be able to figure out not only your name, address, and buying habits, but also a list of other pages you have visited on the Web.

So, cookies worry some people, but at the same time they are also a reasonable and benign workaround to the statelessness of the HTTP protocol. There are plenty of good reasons to want a Web client/server interaction to coherently span a few page requests in a row, rather than covering just a single request. As a Web designer, you might well decide to use cookies for such a purpose, comfortable in the knowledge that there is no substantive invasion of privacy occurring.

Your comfort is not the same as the user's comfort, however, and many users have set up their browsers to refuse all cookies, as is their right. (Remember that what is at issue here is not only the user's privacy, but also the use of his own personal hard disk!) Any server-side code you write should gracefully handle a cookie refusal from the client side, and any Web sites you design should have easily found privacy policies, so that your users know what they are getting into. This does not mean, though, that you are obligated to provide the same level of service to users that refuse cookies; there are some kinds of functionality that are just too painful to write without them, and deciding that cookie cooperation is a prerequisite to using a privately provided site seems perfectly legitimate.

Deleting cookies

Deleting a cookie is easy. Simply call `setcookie(cookie_name)`, with no second argument for the value. This does not set the cookie's value to an empty string — it actually removes the cookie.

Reading cookies

Cookies that have been successfully set in a browser or user's machine will automatically be read on the next request from that browser. This has the following effects:

- ◆ In PHP 4.1 and later, the cookie's name/value pair will be added to the superglobal array `$_COOKIE`, as though we had evaluated `$_COOKIE['name'] = value`.

- In both current and earlier versions of PHP, the name and value will also be added to the merely global array $HTTP_COOKIE_VARS, at least if the track_vars directive is enabled.

- If the register_globals directive is turned on, a regular page-level global variable will be set to the cookie's value, named the same as the cookie's name. Because register_globals is turned off by default starting with PHP 4.2, this feature is not available in 4.2 or later, unless either you or your ISP's administrator has changed the configuration.

So, for example, you can set a cookie as follows:

```
setcookie('membername', 'timboy');
```

This means that, on a *later* page access, you might be able to print out the value again as easily as this:

```
$membername = $_COOKIE['membername'];
print("The member name is $membername<BR>");
```

And, if register_globals has been turned on, the later page's use of the cookie becomes even simpler:

```
print("The member name is $membername<BR>");
```

> **NOTE:** If you set a cookie in a given script, it won't be set on the client until that page (and its HTTP headers) are sent off to the client, which is too late for you to be able to take advantage of it in that very script. This means that the corresponding global variable won't be available to you until the next page request.

The following, typically, does not work as you might expect:

```
setcookie('membername', 'timboy');
print("I set a cookie!  Now I will grab the value<BR>");
// (WRONG - the following membername will most likely be blank)
$membername = $_COOKIE['membername'];
print("The member name is $membername<BR>");
```

This is because, as the preceding Note points out, the cookie will not be set until the current page's worth of HTTP headers arrives at the client. Because that has not yet happened in this example, and the variable $membername has not been otherwise set, that variable will probably produce an empty string in the preceding print statement.

The following gets it right:

```
$cookievalue = 'timboy';
setcookie('membername', $cookievalue);
print("I set a cookie for the benefit of future pages<BR>");
// (RIGHT - only print variables that this page actually set)
print("Its name is membername, its value is $cookievalue<BR>");
```

Any subsequent scripts that are loaded into the same browser can now refer to $membername.

> **CROSS-REFERENCE:** We have already noted some privacy risks to users of accepting cookies from servers. It's worth noting that there are risks that go the other way as well. If you write scripts that depend on the integrity of data that you include in cookies, you should remember that a clever end user can edit those cookies and install arbitrary values in them. See Chapter 36 for techniques for encrypting sensitive data, even inside cookies.

register_globals and variable overwriting

Just as with sessions, we believe that use of the superglobal variables is the way to go, both because it eliminates certain kinds of confusion and because the PHP developers have clearly indicated that register_globals is going away. So we recommend that any time you want to reach into the cookie jar and get some information, you do it by directly referring to $_COOKIE. If you are using PHP 4.0.x, and $_COOKIE is not available, then we urge to you refer to $HTTP_COOKIE_VARS.

If you must rely on the register_globals functionality, and want cookie variables to automatically become global page variables, it's worth noting that such global variables arrive from several different sources, and that this can cause name conflicts. Say that you refer to one of your own pages with the URL http://mysite.org/mypage.php?id=4, indicating that you intend to serve up page four of your content, but you also set a cookie variable named id, which you intend to be your reader's account number. Now, what's going to happen when you refer to $id in your script?

The PHP directive that controls this behavior is called variables_order, and its default value is EGPCS. This encodes the different sources for global variables by their first letters — *e*nvironment, GET, POST, *c*ookie, *s*erver — and determines their overwriting order. Being late in this ordering means having higher priority, since later values overwrite the earlier values. If 'EGPCS' is in effect, then cookie variables overwrite POST variables that happen to have the same name.

You can change this ordering by changing the value of 'variables_order' in your PHP initialization file. You can also drop any of the letters, meaning that you don't want the corresponding globals to be created at all. If you change the value of 'variables_order' to be 'CG', it means that the automatically created global variables will be derived first from cookies and then from GET variables (possibly overwriting cookie-derived variables of the same name) and that no other kinds of auto-globals will be made.

Cookie pitfalls

It is hard to do much wrong with cookies purely at the PHP level. After all, setting a cookie involves only one function (set_cookie()), and reading cookies involves no functions at all. What could be easier than that? The problems that typically arise are those imposed by the HTTP protocol itself.

Sending something else first

The single most common error in using cookies is trying to set a cookie after some regular HTML content has already been generated. (We may be repeating ourselves here, but we will also repeat it in the "Sending HTTP Headers" section later in the chapter, because this fact applies to other direct HTTP protocol manipulations in addition to cookies and is the cause of a great deal of debugging confusion.)

The reason this doesn't work is that the HTTP protocol requires headers to be sent before the content of the HTML page itself — they can't be intermixed. As soon as any regular content is generated, PHP figures that it must already know about all headers of interest, and so it sends them off and then begins the transmission of HTML content. If it encounters a cookie (or other header information) later on, it is too late, and an error is generated.

It's surprisingly easy to write code that violates this prohibition. Consider the following:

```php
 <?php /* A subtle, insidious cookie error */
setcookie('mycookie', 'myvalue');
?>
<HTML><HEAD>
<TITLE>A seemingly benign cookie-setting page</TITLE>
</HEAD><BODY>
  <H3>This page is so simple it absolutely must be right</H3>
</BODY></HTML>
```

When we load this script, we get browser output indicating "cannot add header information." The culprit is the very first character in the file: the space before <?php. Because PHP files start off in HTML mode by default, this file causes one space's worth of generated content to be sent to the client before PHP mode kicks in, and the attempt is made to set the cookie.

A similar way to accidentally send header information too early is to load an include file that includes blank lines at the end after the closing PHP tag. Finally, of course, you can violate the prohibition entirely in PHP mode, but only if you include something like a print or echo statement.

If you ever run into this kind of error, it is relatively easy to debug if you are methodical about it. Try moving HTTP-related code toward the beginning of the script file first — if you still get the error after that, then trace backward from the offending line toward the beginning of the file. Somewhere between the beginning and the failing statement you either have some characters that are being interpreted in HTML mode, or else you have a PHP printing construct. If you have any included PHP files before the offending statement, make sure that there are no characters at all before the start tags or after the end tags.

Reverse-order interpretation

As with most HTTP commands, calls to setcookie() may actually be executed in the opposite order from how they appear in your PHP script, but it depends on the particular browser your user is running. This means that a pair of successive statements like the following probably have the counterintutive result of leaving the "mycookie" cookie with no value, because the unsetting statement is executed second.

```
setcookie("mycookie");// get rid of the old value (WRONG)
setcookie("mycookie", "newvalue");// set the new value (WRONG)
```

> **TIP:** There is no need to remove a cookie before setting it to a different value — simply set it to the desired new value. Among other things, this means that the confusing reverse order of interpretation of setcookie() calls should not usually matter — if the effect depends on the order, it may mean that you are doing something wrong (or at least something unnecessary).

Cookie refusal

Finally, be aware that setcookie() makes no guarantees that any cookie data will, in fact, be accepted by the client browser — setcookie() just agrees to try, by sending off the appropriate HTTP headers. What happens after that is up to the client, and the client may be an older browser that does not accept cookies or a browser whose user has intentionally disabled cookies.

The setcookie() function does not even return a value that indicates acceptance or refusal of the cookie. If you think about it, this is imposed by the timing of the script execution and the HTTP protocol. First, the script executes (including the setcookie() call), with the result that a page complete with HTTP headers is sent to the client machine. At this point, the client browser decides how to react to the cookie-setting attempt. Not until the client generates another request can the server receive the cookie's value and detect whether the cookie-setting attempt was successful. The implication of this for scripting is that you must always ensure that something reasonable happens, even in cases where setcookie() is called without success. One common technique is to set a test cookie with the name CookiesOn, and then check on a subsequent page load if the $CookiesOn variable has been set.

Sending HTTP Headers

The setcookie() call provides a wrapper around a particular usage of HTTP headers. In addition, PHP offers the header() function, which you can use to send raw, arbitrary HTTP headers. You can use this function to roll your own cookie function if you like, but you can also use it to take advantage of any other kind of header-controlled functionality.

The syntax of header() is as simple as it can be: It takes a single string argument, which is the header to be sent.

> **CAUTION:** All the Cautions from earlier in this chapter (about sending HTTP before any real page content) apply to the header() function as well.

Example: Redirection

One useful kind of HTTP header is `"Location:"`, which can act as a redirector. Simply put a fully qualified URL after the `"Location:"` string, and the browser will start over again with the new address instead. An example:

```
<?php
  if (IsSet($gender) && ($gender == "female"))
    {
      header(
"Location: http://www.troutworks.com/phpbook/ch27/secret.php");
      exit;
    }
?>
<HTML><HEAD><TITLE>The inclusive page</TITLE></HEAD></HTML>
<BODY>
<H3>Welcome!</H3>
We welcome anyone to this page, even men!  Talk amongst yourselves.
</BODY></HTML>
```

If we simply enter the URL for this page
(`www.troutworks.com/phpbook/inclusive.php`), we will see the rendering of the HTML at the bottom. On the other hand, if we include the right GET argument
(`www.troutworks.com/phpbook/inclusive.php?gender=female`), we find ourselves redirected to a different page entirely. Note that this is significantly different from selectively importing contents with the `"include"` statement — we actually end up browsing a different URL than the one we typed in, and that new Web address is what shows up in the Location or Address bar of your browser.

This kind of redirection can be useful when you want the structure of your Web site to conditionally branch without having to make the user explicitly choose different links.

Example: HTTP authentication

Another useful thing you can do with HTTP is ask the browser to ask the user for a username and password, via a pop-up window. This is done with the `WWW-Authenticate` header, as in the following example:

```
<?php
  $the_right_user = 'user';  // example only! not recommended
  $the_right_password = 'password';  // example only!

  if(!isset($PHP_AUTH_USER)) {
    Header("WWW-Authenticate: Basic realm=\"PHP book\"");
    Header("HTTP/1.0 401 Unauthorized");
    echo "Canceled by user\n";
    exit;
  } else {
```

```
   if (($PHP_AUTH_USER == 'user') &&
       ($PHP_AUTH_PW == 'password')) //see caution below
     print("The realm is yours<BR>");
   else
     print("We don't need your kind<BR>");
 }
?>
```

If we visit this script for the first time (and are using the appropriate browser and server versions), we will get a pop-up window. After the user enters the information into the pop-up box, the script is automatically called again with new variables $PHP_AUTH_USER (set to the user string entered), $PHP_AUTH_PASSWD (set to the password string entered), and $PHP_AUTH_TYPE (which will be "Basic" until such time as another type of authentication is supported). The nice thing about this is that these variables will continue to be set by the browser on each request, and you do not need to do anything in your scripts to propagate them — one verification of identity per session should suffice.

CAUTION: The preceding code is the bare minimum necessary to demonstrate the HTTP authentication mechanism and is not a model for how user/password combinations should really be verified! Our code fragment simply compares the values of the variables delivered to hard-coded strings, which is a bad idea for several reasons. To make this part of a real verification system, you probably want to compare the result of encrypting the password to a similarly encrypted version in a database or password file. See Chapter 36 for more on encryption and real security measures.

In addition to redirection and authentication, the capability to send real HTTP headers offers finer control of many aspects of the HTTP client/server relationship, which usually are set by default. For example, You can explicitly set the expiration and caching behavior of your page, or send return status codes that tell the client whether whatever is returned should be considered a success or not. Because PHP is just acting as a channel to the underlying HTTP protocol, most of these techniques are beyond the scope of PHP documentation and this book.

NOTE: The WWW-Authenticate mechanism only works under the Apache Web Server, with PHP as a module. It does not currently work in the CGI version or under IIS/PWS.

Header gotchas

As we have said innumerable times by now, the header() function is subject to the same restriction as the setcookie() function: No headers may be sent after regular page content is generated, unless you are using a post-beta 3 release of PHP 4 that has output buffering enabled.

More generally, be aware that using the header capability requires not only some knowledge of the HTTP protocols, but also some knowledge of the extent to which different browser versions conform to them. Unless you are writing for a known population of users that all use the same browser, you will probably need to do more cross-browser testing than with vanilla HTML-generating scripts.

> **TIP:** Most browsers can be set to warn you whenever they are about to accept a cookie. Although this can be annoying when viewing benign yet cookie-intensive sites, it can also be a great debugging tool when writing your own cookie-setting code.

Gotchas and Troubleshooting

If you are having trouble with sessions, first make sure that your session support exists and is doing what you think it is. Try downloading the sample session code from www.troutworks.com/phpbook and debugging it from the earliest error, if any.

If sessions are not working or are giving errors, check the pathname returned by session_save_path(), and make sure that it exists and is PHP writable. If not, you should either make it so or change the value of 'session.save_path' in php.ini.

Remember that session functions that have variable names as arguments do not expect a leading $ in the name.

If you ever run into a complaint that refers to already having sent HTTP headers, it may be that your script is sending some text (even blank lines) before the session_start() or session_register() functions. Scrutinize any included files for blank lines or move the session functions to the very beginning of your file.

When testing session-related code, remember to try it out both with a browser that accepts cookies and with a browser that is set up to refuse them. If you see no session name in the URL of a link (such as, 'PHPSESSID') with a cookie-refusing browser, then either sessions are not working or your version of PHP is not configured to transparently pass session IDs in the GET/POST arguments. It's also informative to try session and cookie code with a browser that is configured to alert the user whenever it is setting a cookie.

Summary

Sessions are useful for tracking a user's behavior over interactions that last longer than one script execution or page download. If what you present to the user depends on which previous pages they have seen or interacted with, your code must store or propagate that information in a way that distinguishes one user from another. Because the HTTP protocol is stateless, this inevitably entails some kind of workaround technique — usually either *hidden variables* (which impose maintenance headaches) or *cookies* (which are not universally supported by client browsers).

The PHP implementation of sessions encapsulates these messy issues and presents a clean layer of abstraction to the scripter. Unique session identifiers are automatically created and propagated, and a variables can be passed from page to page by storing them in the superglobal $_SESSION array. Aside from one's having to connect to a session initially and store (or register) the variables that should persist beyond the current page, session use is virtually transparent to the programmer.

PHP offers several ways to use the capabilities of the HTTP protocol, in addition to the obvious one of constructing HTML pages that are transmitted via HTTP. The setcookie() function allows you to set and delete cookies in your user's browser, the values of which show up in subsequent page views as ordinary global variables.

The header() function allows you to send arbitrary HTTP headers. Among other things, header() can be useful for authentication and page-level redirection.

The HTTP functions in PHP are very simple, and the main complexities that arise are a consequence of the HTTP protocol itself. One such complication is the fact that that HTTP requires all headers to be sent before any page content is sent.

Chapter 28
PHP and JavaScript

In This Chapter

♦ Outputting JavaScript with PHP

♦ PHP as a backup for JavaScript

♦ Static versus dynamic JavaScript

♦ Dynamic form generation

In this chapter, we try to get the best of both client-side and server-side scripting by combining PHP with JavaScript. We briefly touch upon the question of when to use which scripting language, and stylistic points that may be helpful when writing the code. Then we move on to pragmatic examples of the type you might see on a real-world PHP site.

> **TIP:** If you've never worked with JavaScript before, you won't learn how just by reading this chapter. We will only touch on aspects of JavaScript that materially impinge upon PHP. If you're wondering what an `onBlur` event is, we recommend Danny Goodman's superlative *JavaScript Bible* (Wiley, 2001).

Outputting JavaScript with PHP

Because PHP is server-side and JavaScript is client-side, you may expect to have problems using both on the same page. In actuality, it's the difference that makes them such a good match.

Although PHP offers plenty of power for creating dynamically generated Web pages, it is strictly a server-side language. There's a common category of Web site tasks that perhaps don't require all the processing power of a server and would best be done quickly — for instance, changing the look of a button on mouseover. JavaScript, a purely client-side language (there's a server-side version, but we're assuming you've already chosen PHP on that end), can be easily integrated into PHP to fill in many of these gaps.

On the other hand, client-side JavaScript (a.k.a. Javascript, JScript, ECMAScript) itself has many limitations. For example, because it can't communicate directly with a database, JavaScript cannot update itself on-the-fly. Even worse, it's impossible to depend on client-side technologies, because they may not be present in a visitor's browser or may be disabled. Conscientious client-side Web developers must either decide to code probabilistically (and accept complaints from minority-browser users) or maintain several versions of a site at the same time. (Nonconscientious developers simply adapt themselves to the market-leading browser's full capabilities and damn the torpedoes . . . but that's another story.) PHP can help to mitigate the effects of client-side indeterminacy.

Dueling objects

Perhaps the biggest divergence between JavaScript and PHP is in the area of object models. The two are quite divergent conceptually, and they use different styles of notation. Some people consider this a good thing, because at least there's no chance of mixing up objects that look similar (as there is with, say, ASP and JavaScript). Probably just as many consider it a pain, an incompatibility, or a design flaw. In any case, there is no chance you can access the same object with both PHP and JavaScript — so forget it.

JavaScript is consistently object-oriented from top to bottom. Every statement requires an object and a method or function to be specified and may also have event handlers. JavaScript uses the so-called "dot" object notation (`object.method`), which is similar to that of other common programming languages such as C, Java, and Microsoft's VBScript.

The downside is that JavaScript's document object model has been shakily standardized: Although, in theory, ECMA and the W3C shepherd the international standard, in practice the various browser manufacturers violate/add to this core at their whim. Proficient JavaScripters spend a good deal of energy keeping track of incompatibilities and workarounds for various browsers and platforms.

As we discuss elsewhere in this book (notably Chapter 26), PHP's classes are more of an add-on, retrofit, or convenience than an essential part of the language. The notation is the "arrow" or "pointer" style that is sometimes seen in C++ code (`$this->variable`). There is no mechanism in place to use a "dot" style. Honesty compels us to admit that PHP classes probably don't ever add up to anything like a thoroughgoing object model. Not that we ever wanted one anyway — and who are you calling defensive?

PHP doesn't care what it outputs

The main thing to keep in mind is that PHP doesn't know or care what it returns. You can (and people do) use PHP to write out plaintext, HTML, XHTML, DHTML, JavaScript, XML, MathML, various graphical formats, CSS, XSL, or even (for the ironic ironists among us) ASP. No real technical barrier exists to having PHP output C code, although it's probably not a usage whose popularity is going to sweep the nation. Remember, PHP does not always output PHP — its ultimate end product is usually code that will be run by another application, usually a browser.

There are a couple of ways to write out the JavaScript with PHP. The simplest is to escape from PHP whenever you get the urge to go client-side. This is accomplished in precisely the same way you would escape from HTML.

```
<?php
echo("Imagine tons of complex PHP code in this block.");
?>
<script language="JavaScript">
<!-- Hide from JavaScript disabled browsers
document.write("Strict separation of client-side and server-side code is
a good thing.")
// end hiding -->
</script>
<?php
echo("More PHP in this block.");
?>
```

Even this example doesn't show the fullest extent of PHP/JavaScript separation. A lot of JavaScript is actually defined within the `<HEAD>` element of an HTML page and simply called in the `<BODY>`, whereas PHP is generally used in the latter.

As with HTML, there are occasions when you don't want to escape from PHP — or this style may just be your personal preference. In that case, you can use PHP's `echo` or `print` statements to output JavaScript.

```
<?php
echo("This is some complex PHP code.");
echo("<script language=\"JavaScript\">\n");
echo("<!-- Hide from JavaScript disabled browsers\n");
echo("document.write(\"Strict separation of client-side and server-side
code is a good thing.\\n\")");
echo("// end hiding -->\n");
echo("</script>\n");
echo("More PHP in this block.");
?>
```

> **CAUTION:** You may run into trouble if you use script tags (for instance, `<script language="PHP">`) to delineate PHP chunks — the PHP parser may have a hard time figuring out which `</script>` tag goes with what `<script>` tag.

This style is not at all incorrect, but it can be considerably harder to keep everything straight. Unless you're an experienced programmer, you might want to limit this style to occasions in which you simply call predefined JavaScript functions, such as `onSubmit` events.

> **TIP:** Remember to escape double-quotes in JavaScript sections if using `echo`/`print` to output code. See Line 3 of the preceding snippet.

Where to use JavaScript

Client-side JavaScript doesn't do heavy lifting, but it is faster at certain tasks and also allows for some effects that you can't easily duplicate with PHP. Some places you should definitely consider replacing or enhancing PHP with JavaScript include:

♦ Simple arithmetic in forms and calculators (such as shopping-cart running total, mortgage calculator).

♦ Browser sniffing.

♦ Simple form validation (such as making sure e-mail addresses have @ symbols).

♦ Site navigation (such as pull-down navigation menus).

♦ Pop-ups (alerts, search boxes).

♦ Mouseover and on-click events.

PHP as a Backup for JavaScript

The flip side of our "where to use JavaScript" advice is that PHP can help caulk the cracks in JavaScript. Sometimes you can seamlessly implement both client-side and server-side methods of doing a task. If a visitor's browser is JavaScript-enabled, fine —visitors will be able to take advantage of the zippier method, generally without even noticing that they've had a choice. If not, at least you won't suffer the ignominy of totally locking them out of your site's functionality.

A perfect example is the double-barreled pull-down menu for site navigation. JavaScript gives you an instant redirect, whereas PHP provides the same result after a longer wait for those without JavaScript-enabled browsers. This trick takes advantage of the fact that JavaScript has event handlers (for example, onChange) that work off the structure of HTML forms without requiring an actual button-clicking submission. Therefore, the Submit button can be reserved for PHP's use. Listing 28-1 shows an HTML page that uses a JavaScript onChange redirect and, if that doesn't work, a PHP form handler.

Listing 28-1: A JavaScript and PHP navigation form (navigation.html)

```
<html>
<head>
<title>Navigation pulldown</title>
<script language="JavaScript">
<!--
function Browse(form, i){
  var site = form.elements[i].selectedIndex;
  if(site > 0){
    top.location = form.elements[i].options[site].value
  }
}
}
// -->
```

```
</script>
</head>

<body>
<form method="post" action="redirect.php">
<select name="category" onChange="Browse(this.form,0)">
<option selected value=0>Choose a Category</option>
<option value="desktop.php">Desktops</option>
<option value="laptop.php">Laptops</option>
<option value="monitor.php">Monitors</option>
<option value="input.php">Input devices</option>
<option value="storage.php">Storage devices</option>
</select>
<input type="submit"">
</form>
</body>
</html>
```

The PHP form handler file, called `redirect.php`, need only have two lines:

```
<?php $category = $_POST['category'];
header("Location: $category"); ?>
```

You could use a similar division of labor with form validation. If JavaScript is enabled, you can use it to make sure zip codes have 9 digits, phone numbers have 10 digits, and e-mail addresses have both an @ and a .. If JavaScript is not enabled, you can write a little PHP script that will do the same things when the form is submitted and return the form with warnings if the values are bad.

> **CAUTION:** JavaScript form validation should be relied on only for quick convenience reminders, never for data sanitization. See Chapter 36 for more information.

Another kind of form is basically arithmetic — a shopping cart with running totals or a mortgage payment calculator. Again, you can combine both JavaScript and PHP in an arithmetic form to cover all the bases.

Finally, there is one use where PHP is so much faster that you might want to replace JavaScript altogether: browser sniffing. This is done to send different versions of a file (for instance, a stylesheet) to a visitor depending on which browser she's using. Server-side browser sniffing is vastly more efficient than client-side because no text is sent until the sniffing has occurred. A JavaScript browser sniff can amount to hundreds of lines of JavaScript, which must be sent on every download whether the correctly browser version has been detected or not. Listing 28-2 shows a very simple server-side browser sniff:

Listing 28-2: A server-side browser sniff (browsersniff.php)

```
<?php
if (strpos($HTTP_USER_AGENT, 'MSIE') > 0) {
```

```
   header("Location: index_ie.html");
} elseif (strpos($HTTP_USER_AGENT, 'Gecko') > 0) {
   header("Location: index_moz.html");
}
?>
```

Static Versus Dynamic JavaScript

Although the static JavaScript-PHP form in Listing 28-1 is handy for many applications, there's one big problem with it: You have to maintain it by hand. Every time you decide to add a new page to your site, you'll have to remember to manually add it to the drop-down list. Big deal, you're thinking — but these are the little things that become time-sucking nightmares when you're running a huge and high-traffic site.

With PHP and a database, you can update some of your JavaScript automatically — or, as we might say, *dynamically*. You want to take this option whenever possible, as it will help you save time in the long run. Listing 28-3 is how you'd rewrite the form in Listing 28-1 for even better client/server integration:

Listing 28-3: Dynamic JavaScript and PHP form (dyn_navigation.html)

```
<html>
<head>
<title>Navigation pulldown</title>
<script language="JavaScript">
<!--
function Browse(form, i){
  var site = form.elements[i].selectedIndex;
  if(site > 0){
     top.location = form.elements[i].options[site].value
    }
}
// -->
</script>
</head>

<body>
<form method="post" action="redirect.php">
<select name="category" onChange="Browse(this.form,0)">
<option selected value=0>Choose a Category</option>
<?php
mysql_connect("localhost", "user", "password");
mysql_select_db("site_db");
$query = "SELECT filename, my_text FROM categories WHERE display = 1";
$result = mysql_query($query);
while (list($filename, $my_text) = mysql_fetch_array($result)) {
   print("<option value=\"$filename\"> $my_text</option>\n");
}
```

```
?>
</select>
<input type="submit">
</form>
</body>
</html>
```

You will doubtless have realized by now that a similar technique would be valuable even if you were making a straight JavaScript form (such as by using the `onSubmit` event handler rather than `onChange`). It would enable you to make a basic JavaScript function more flexible by allowing PHP to change variable values within the function before it was sent to the browser. So feel free to use PHP to output straight JavaScript using variables from a data source, if you like.

Dynamically generated forms

You can usefully extend this train of programming thought even further, by setting up a series of dynamic drop-downs that change according to previous form inputs. PHP will fetch all the data from a database and load it into the HTML page; whereas JavaScript will decide which data set should be visible under various conditions.

In this example, we want to help users find information on specific cars. The list of the model of every car made by every manufacturer is dauntingly large, too long for even a well-designed drop-down list. Furthermore, car names tend to be eerily similar to each other, like the first names of a large family of sisters in a Swedish farming village — Integra, Sentra, Jetta, Elantra, Sephia, and so forth. So one way to narrow things down logically is to have the user pick a manufacturer from a pull-down menu, which would narrow the list to only models made by that company.

The database table we need looks like this (actually it probably doesn't if you're using a relational database — but here we want to focus on the JavaScript part, not the database part):

```
---------------------------
| make     | model       |
---------------------------
| Audi     | A4          |
| Audi     | A6          |
| Audi     | A8          |
| Audi     | Quattro     |
| Chrysler | Cirrus      |
| Chrysler | Concorde    |
| Chrysler | PT Cruiser  |
| Toyota   | Camry       |
| Toyota   | Corolla     |
| Toyota   | Rav4        |
---------------------------
```

Using this database table and server-side PHP scripts, you would be limited to two suboptimal choices. You could opt for one extremely large list (either drop-down or full-page) of manufacturers and models; or you could make the visitor go through two sequential forms. But after we add JavaScript to the mix, we can start a page with two drop-downs and have the contents of the second list change depending on what is selected in the first.

Our double drop-down design is based on Andrew King's very clever JavaScript code, available at www.webreference.com under the Gnu General Public License. We used PHP simply to connect to the database and fetch data to populate the two-dimensional arrays from which the JavaScript works. All of the interesting functionality here is provided by the JavaScript portion (Listing 28-4).

Listing 28-4: A two-dimensional dynamic dropdown (double_drop.html)

```
<HTML>
<HEAD>
<META NAME="save" CONTENT="history">
<STYLE>
  .saveHistory {behavior:url(#default#savehistory);}
</STYLE>

<SCRIPT LANGUAGE="JavaScript">
<!--
v=false;
//-->
</SCRIPT>

<SCRIPT LANGUAGE="JavaScript1.1">
<!--
if (typeof(Option)+"" != "undefined") v=true;
//-->
</SCRIPT>

<SCRIPT LANGUAGE="JavaScript">
<!--
// Universal Related Select Menus - cascading popdown menus
// by Andrew King. v1.34 19990720
// Copyright (c) 1999 internet.com LLC. All Rights Reserved.
// Modified by Joyce Park 20000703
//
// This program is free software; you can redistribute it
// and/or modify it under the terms of the GNU General Public
// License as published by the Free Software Foundation; either
// version 2 of the License, or (at your option) any later
// version.
//
// This program is distributed in the hope that it will be
// useful, but WITHOUT ANY WARRANTY; without even the implied
```

```
// warranty of MERCHANTABILITY or FITNESS FOR A PARTICULAR
// PURPOSE.  See the GNU General Public License for more
// details.
//
// You should have received a copy of the GNU General Public
// License along with this program; if not, write to the Free
// Software Foundation, Inc., 59 Temple Place, Suite 330,
// Boston, MA  02111-1307  USA
//
// Originally published and documented at www.webreference.com
// see www.webreference.com/dev/menus/intro2.html for changelog

if(v){a=new Array(22);}

function getFormNum (formName) {
  var formNum =-1;
  for (i=0;i<document.forms.length;i++){
    tempForm = document.forms[i];
    if (formName == tempForm) {
      formNum = i;
      break;
    }
  }
  return formNum;
}

function jmp(form, elt) {
// The first parameter is a reference to the form.
  if (form != null) {
    with (form.elements[elt]) {
      if (0 <= selectedIndex)
        location = options[selectedIndex].value;
    }
  }
}

var catsIndex = -1;
var itemsIndex;

if (v) { // ns 2 fix
function newCat(){
  catsIndex++;
  a[catsIndex] = new Array();
  itemsIndex = 0;
}

// Andrew chose to name this function "O", presumably standing
// for "Option".  It's not a zero, here or in the array below!
function O(txt,url) {
```

```
  a[catsIndex][itemsIndex]=new myOptions(txt,url);
  itemsIndex++;
}

function myOptions(text,value){
  this.text = text;
  this.value = value;
}

// fill array
<?php
mysql_connect("localhost", "db_user");
mysql_select_db("auto_db");
// Get the makes
$i = 0;
$make_query = "SELECT DISTINCT make FROM cars";
$make_result = mysql_query($make_query);
while ($make_row = mysql_fetch_array($make_result)) {

  $make[$i] = $make_row[0];
  // Now fill the array with models for each make
  echo "newCat();\n";
  $model_query = "SELECT model FROM cars WHERE make = '$make[$i]' ORDER
BY model";
  $model_result = mysql_query($model_query);
  while(list($model) = mysql_fetch_array($model_result)) {
    echo "O(\"$model\", \"/$model.php\")\n";
  }
  echo "\n";
  $i++;
}
?>
} // close if (v)

function relate(formName,elementNum,j) {
if(v){
var formNum = getFormNum(formName);
  if (formNum>=0) {
    formNum++; // reference next form, assume it follows in HTML
    with (document.forms[formNum].elements[elementNum]) {
      for(i=options.length-1;i>0;i--) options[i] = null; // null out in
reverse order (bug workarnd)
      for(i=0;i<a[j].length;i++){
        options[i] = new Option(a[j][i].text,a[j][i].value);
      }
      options[0].selected = true;
    }
  }
} else {
```

```
    jmp(formName,elementNum);
  }
}

// BACK BUTTON FIX for ie4+- or
// MEMORY-CACHE-STORING-ONLY-INDEX-AND-NOT-CONTENT
// see www.webreference.com for full comments
function IEsetup(){
  if(!document.all) return;
  IE5 = navigator.appVersion.indexOf("5.")!=-1;
  if(!IE5) {
    for (i=0;i<document.forms.length;i++) {
      document.forms[i].reset();
    }
  }
}

window.onload = IEsetup;

//-->
</SCRIPT>
</HEAD>
<BODY BGCOLOR="#ffffff">


<CENTER>
<TABLE BGCOLOR="#DDCCFF" BORDER="0" CELLPADDING="8" CELLSPACING="0">
<TR VALIGN="TOP">
<TD>Choose a make:<BR>
<FORM NAME="f1" METHOD="POST" ACTION="redirect.php" onSubmit="return
false;">
<SELECT NAME="m1" ID="m1" CLASS=saveHistory
onChange="relate(this.form,0,this.selectedIndex)">
<?php
while (list($key, $val) = each($make)) {
  echo "<OPTION VALUE=\"/$val.php\">$val</OPTION>\n";
}
?>
</SELECT>
<INPUT TYPE=SUBMIT VALUE="Go" onClick="jmp(this.form,0);">
</FORM>
</TD>

<TD BGCOLOR="#FFFFFF" VALIGN=MIDDLE><B>---&gt;</B></TD>

<TD>Choose a model:<BR>
<FORM NAME="f2" METHOD="POST" ACTION="redirect.php" onSubmit="return
false;">
<SELECT NAME="m2" ID="m2" CLASS=saveHistory onChange="jmp(this.form,0)">
// These are placeholder values for the first time the page is
```

```
// loaded.  They will not change when the form values change.
// If you delete them, the forms will still work, but the
// second select menu would come up empty until changed.
// These values could be generated dynamically, but we wanted
// to show them in place.
<OPTION VALUE="/A4.php">A4</OPTION>
<OPTION VALUE="/A6.php">A6</OPTION>
<OPTION VALUE="/A8.php">A8</OPTION>
<OPTION VALUE="/Quattro">Quattro</OPTION>
</SELECT>
<INPUT TYPE=SUBMIT VALUE="Go" onClick="jmp(this.form,0);">
<INPUT TYPE="hidden" NAME="baseurl" VALUE="http://localhost">
</FORM>
</TD>
</TR>
</TABLE></CENTER>

</BODY>
</HTML>
```

If you were to add to or change any of the data in the database, the JavaScript would change automatically. Dynamic integration of new data makes this a very powerful tool and keeps page maintenance to a minimum.

Passing data back to PHP from JavaScript

Finally, we close the data loop by passing form values back to PHP with JavaScript. Listings 28-5, 28-6, and 28-7 use JavaScript to force at least one check box to be checked at all times. In addition, it passes an array to a PHP script. We've chosen to use frames here to maximize the speed of the changes; and we wrote all values out by hand for clarity, rather than assembling them dynamically from a data source:

Listing 28-5: Frameset (sandwich_frames.html)

```
<HTML>
<HEAD>
<FRAMESET ROWS="50%, 50%" FRAMEBORDER="no" BORDER=0>
<FRAME SRC="sandwichorder.html" NAME="main" SCROLLING="auto">
<FRAME SRC="results.php" NAME="results" SCROLLING="auto">
</FRAMESET>
</HEAD>
<BODY></BODY>
</HTML>
```

Listing 28-6: Form page (sandwichorder.html)

```
<HTML>
<HEAD>
<SCRIPT LANGUAGE="JavaScript">
```

```
<!--

function deselectAllOthers(boxVals) {
  for (var x = 1; x < boxVals.length; x++) {
    boxVals[x].checked=false;
  }
}

function confirmOne(boxVals) {
  var count = 0;
  for (var x = 1; x < boxVals.length; x++) {
    if (boxVals[x].checked == false) {
      count++;
    }
  }
  if (count == (boxVals.length - 1)) {
    boxVals[0].checked = true;
  } else {
    boxVals[0].checked = false;
  }
}

function toArray(boxVals) {
  for (var x = 0; x < boxVals.length; x++) {
    var valArray = boxVals[x].name+"[]";
    boxVals[x].name = valArray;
  }
}

// -->
</script>
</HEAD>

<BODY BGCOLOR=#FCFCF0 onLoad="document.selector.submit();">

<TABLE CELLPADDING=20>
<TR>
<TD VALIGN="top">
<B>Order a sandwich with...</B>
<BR><BR>
<FORM NAME="selector" TARGET="results" METHOD="post"
ACTION="results.php">
<B>Fillings (check one or more)</B><BR><BR>
<INPUT TYPE="checkbox" name="filling" value="everything" checked
onClick="deselectAllOthers(document.selector.filling);
confirmOne(document.selector.filling);
toArray(document.selector.filling); submit();"> Everything
<BR>
```

```
<INPUT TYPE="checkbox" name="filling" value="turkey"
onClick="confirmOne(document.selector.filling);
toArray(document.selector.filling); submit();"> Turkey
<BR>
<INPUT TYPE="checkbox" name="filling" value="roastbeef"
onClick="confirmOne(document.selector.filling);
toArray(document.selector.filling); submit();"> Roast beef
<BR>
<INPUT TYPE="checkbox" name="filling" value="pastrami"
onClick="confirmOne(document.selector.filling);
toArray(document.selector.filling); submit();"> Pastrami
<BR>
<INPUT TYPE="checkbox" name="filling" value="eggplant"
onClick="confirmOne(document.selector.filling);
toArray(document.selector.filling); submit();"> Eggplant
<BR>
</TD>
<TD VALIGN="top"><BR><BR>
<B>Cheese</B><BR><BR>
<SELECT NAME="cheese" onChange="submit();">
<OPTION VALUE="none">None</OPTION>
<OPTION VALUE="cheddar">Cheddar</OPTION>
<OPTION VALUE="swiss">Swiss</OPTION>
<OPTION VALUE="camembert">Camembert</OPTION>
<OPTION VALUE="bleu">Blue</OPTION>
<OPTION VALUE="cottage">Cottage</OPTION>
</SELECT>
<BR><BR>
</TD>
<TD VALIGN="top"><BR><BR>
<B>Bread</B><BR><BR>
<SELECT NAME="bread" onChange="submit();">
<OPTION VALUE="white">White</OPTION>
<OPTION VALUE="wheat">Wheat</OPTION>
<OPTION VALUE="rye">Rye</OPTION>
<OPTION VALUE="kaiser">Kaiser roll</OPTION>
<OPTION VALUE="onion">Onion roll</OPTION>
<OPTION VALUE="dutch">Dutch crunch</OPTION>
</SELECT>
</FORM>
<BR><BR>
</TD>
</TR></TABLE>
</BODY>
</HTML>
```

Listing 28-7: Results listing (results.php)

```
<HTML>
<HEAD></HEAD>

<BODY BGCOLOR=#666680 TEXT=#ffffff>
<TABLE CELLPADDING=30><TR><TD>
<B>Da Results</B><BR><BR>
<?php
$filling = $_POST['filling'];
$cheese = $_POST['cheese'];
$bread = $_POST['bread'];

if ($filling) {
  if (is_array($filling)) {
    reset($filling);
    while (list($key, $value) = each($filling)) {
      echo("$value<BR>\n");
    }
  } else {
    echo($filling);
  }
}
?>
<BR><BR></TD>
<TD VALIGN=top><BR><BR>
<B>Cheese</B><BR><BR>
<?php echo($cheese); ?>
<BR><BR></TD>
<TD VALIGN=top><BR><BR>
<B>Bread</B><BR><BR>
<?php echo($bread); ?>
</TD></TR>
</TABLE>
</BODY>
</HTML>
```

This form admittedly doesn't actually do very much yet — but the point is that it would obviate one or two trips from client to server and back. It also demonstrates another of the interesting effects PHP developers can get by experimenting with JavaScript.

Summary

JavaScript is a client-side scripting language that is highly efficient at many tasks that do not require server-side processing. Not everyone will want to use JavaScript, which has longstanding usability and security issues; but for those who do, the combination of client-side and server-side programming languages can offer an attractive combination of functionalities.

PHP and JavaScript have different object notations. JavaScript uses the so-called "dot" notation, whereas PHP uses the "arrow" or C++ style notation. JavaScript is thoroughly object-oriented, whereas PHP treats objects as an optional feature. The good news is that you'll never confuse a JavaScript object for a PHP object, or vice versa. The bad news is that you cannot access the same object from both languages.

It's often possible to implement a feature in both a client-side and a server-side way. Users with JavaScript-enabled browsers can enjoy greater speed and convenience, whereas those without can still get the functionality. This makes it possible to consider using JavaScript without its greatest drawback, which is unpredictability leading to alienation of segments of the userbase.

Perhaps the greatest service PHP can perform for JavaScript is to enable database connectivity — resulting in what we might call *Dynamic JavaScript*. JavaScript, being purely a client-side technology, cannot query a server-side database for variable data with which to dynamically generate content. Without a server-side helper like PHP, JavaScripts must be updated by hand whenever variable data is changed. PHP's capability to pass in up-to-date variables from a data store can make it considerably less labor-intensive to maintain JavaScript-enabled forms and functions.

## Chapter 29

E-mail

In This Chapter

♦ Understanding e-mail

♦ Receiving e-mail with PHP

♦ Sending e-mail with PHP

♦ More e-mail applications

♦ E-mail gotchas

This chapter is all about using PHP (and, in some cases, databases) to send and receive e-mail. It assumes a very basic familiarity with e-mail systems and protocols such as POP, IMAP, and SMTP.

Understanding E-mail

E-mail is obviously one of the killer apps of the Internet, and it's been around in basically the same form for years. But judging from postings to the PHP and other mailing lists, there are few more misunderstood or frustrating topics even now. Because recent developments, such as cheaper connectivity, free server operating systems, and the explosion of new domains, have made it possible for everyone and his grandmother to run their own mail servers, there's a lot of frustration to go around.

We don't have the space or the expertise to explain every detail of e-mail. If you become fascinated with the topic after our necessarily short synopsis, you will want to immediately visit the Web site of the International Mail Consortium, at www.imc.org, which will explain in dizzying detail every abstruse jot and tittle of Internet mail that the most exacting computer scientist's heart could desire. In the meantime, we'll stick to the quickest and dirtiest of conceptual explanations.

To help you visualize the considerable number of moving parts involved, we're going to build a simple model mail server.

This explanation will mostly use Unix terms, for the simple reason that the vocabulary of e-mail was perfected long before Microsoft or Lotus came along. Exchange Server is quite likely very similar underneath — it even has a daemon called sendmail — but who knows for sure, because we can't lift the hood. Vendors of proprietary software also have the annoying habit of making up their own terminology for things rather than using the names everyone knows already, a practice that considerably hinders anyone trying to understand these systems in an abstract, cross-platform way. Finally, most proprietary mail systems these days are incorporated into very powerful groupware packages that confuse the issue even more. For these reasons, Unix mail servers are undoubtedly easier to learn from and implement.

We are mentioning specific products so that you can contact them directly to learn more about these pieces of the puzzle. This does not constitute a recommendation. We have deliberately chosen to list only products that are available without monetary cost.

The major parts of our model e-mail system are as follows:

♦ TCP/IP server

♦ Mail Transfer Agent (MTA), a.k.a. SMTP server

♦ Mail spool

♦ Mail User Agent (MUA, a.k.a. mail client)

♦ Mail retrieval program, a.k.a. POP/IMAP server

♦ Mailing list manager (MLM)

Let's examine these in greater detail. We're going to use a cheesy but apt metaphor to help you remember who does what: Mail Server Mansion.

TCP/IP server

A good way to visualize a *TCP/IP server* is to think of it as the footman who answers every knock at the front door of Mail Server Mansion. Actually, if you think of every separate port as a door, maybe the TCP/IP server is more like a security guard who sits in a cubbyhole and monitors a bank of video cameras pointed at multiple avenues of ingress and egress. In any event, it's simpler and more picturesque just to think of an old-fashioned single footman at a single door.

The footman does not actually speak to any visitors. He simply opens the door when he hears a knock, recognizes the type of interaction this will be, and calls the correct person (say a butler or a bouncer) to handle the request. This second person, who has a speaking role, will take over to find out what the visitor wants.

The point is not to open the door — it is to know there is a door to be opened. A TCP/IP server maintains a list of several services for which it is responsible, and it answers each request by invoking the proper daemon — in the case of mail, either `sendmail` or a POP/IMAP authenticator. This saves resources because a single daemon monitors all the requests and the other daemons are only invoked on an "as needed" basis.

Well-known TCP/IP servers include:

- GNU `inetd`, the TCP/IP super server usually found by default on Unix setups (`www.gnu.org/software/inetutils/inetutils.html`)

- `xinetd`, a secure replacement for inetd (`www.xinetd.org`)

- Dan Bernstein's `tcpserver`, often used with qmail (`http://cr.yp.to/ucspi-tcp.html`)

Mail Transfer Agent, a.k.a. SMTP server

The *Mail Transfer Agent (MTA)* is the heart of any mail server, and the part whose workings we are most radically simplifying in this discussion.

The most important task of an MTA is to accept e-mail from another SMTP server and deliver it to the correct addressee's mail spool. A lot more is involved in this than one might think, but we can't get into it here. Also, the MTA will collect outgoing e-mail and try to send it to other SMTP servers.

So the MTA is roughly in the position of the butler at Mail Server Mansion. He is called by the footman to deal with mail and to inquire of the visitor (with the utmost politeness, of course): "Who are you, and what do you want?" If the visitor happens to be a known spammer, for instance, the butler might outright refuse delivery of any letters from that address. If the visitor is not recognized as a spammer, the butler will check the envelope to see if the intended recipient is, in fact, a resident of Mail Server Mansion. If not, he will write "Return to sender, undeliverable as addressed," on the envelope and drop it in the outgoing mailbag. Finally, if the addressee is recognized and the message is good, the butler will put the letter on a silver platter and carry it up to the resident's sitting room (actually their home directory or other mail spool location) and leave it there.

The actual SMTP protocol — the dialogue by which one server asks another, "Who are you, and what do you want?" — goes something like this (`sendhost` and `receipthost` are dummy server names):

```
220 receipthost ESMTP
HELO
250 receipthost
MAIL From:<sender@sendhost>
250 ok
RCPT To:<receiver@receipthost>
250 ok
DATA
354 Go ahead
Body of message.
.
250 Message accepted for delivery
QUIT
221 receipthost closing connection
```

Well-known MTAs — along with their corresponding URLs — include:

sendmail   `www.sendmail.org`

qmail   `www.qmail.org`

zmailer   `www.zmailer.org`

Mail spool

The silver platter on which the butler places the letters is analogous to a *mail spool* or *mailbox*. Different mail systems use different types of mail stores. At the level we're discussing, the main difference is whether a new message simply goes on the end of a single long spool (like a single roll of paper with the text of all the mail you've ever received transcribed on it, in order of time of receipt) or whether each message becomes its own text file inside a directory.

Some well-known mailbox formats are:

mbox   Used by many Unix mail clients

maildir   Closely associated with qmail

mbx   Microsoft proprietary format

Mail User Agent, a.k.a. local mail client

So the letter is lying on a silver platter in the recipient's sitting room, which is actually his or her home directory. When a resident of Mail Server Mansion decides she wants to read her mail, she sends a maid to go to the sitting room, collect the silver platter full of letters left there by the butler, return to the boudoir with them, open them, and hold them up to the light so she can read them more stylishly. This maid is the *Mail User Agent*.

> **TIP:** Mail user agents are a very "Unixy" concept, and may have little relevance for those whose mail clients are mostly on other operating systems. See the next section below for more information about POP and IMAP remote mail clients.

Popular MUAs and their URLs include:

pine   `www.washington.edu/pine`

elm   `www.instinct.org/elm`

mutt   `www.mutt.org`

In many cases, the choice of MUA will be closely tied to the choice of mailbox format. For instance, `mutt` makes it especially easy to use `qmail`'s maildir format, and it seems to be the MUA of choice for the `qmail` community.

Mail-retrieval program, a.k.a. POP/IMAP server

Sending the maid to the sitting room to fetch the mail works fine if you happen to be at home in your local domain. But let's say the residents of Mail Server Mansion travel a lot to remote domains. (Remember, a remote domain can be in the same room — as long as it's not local in the sense of being one of the domains handled by this particular mail server, it's remote.) How will they get their mail?

The short answer is that they will send a request to Mail Server Mansion periodically, and another butler will forward any letters that have collected on the addressee's silver platter since the last time. This butler does not accept mail at all — he only forwards mail. He is the *mail retrieval program.*

This second butler needs to be very security-conscious. It's one thing for the SMTP butler to send and receive letters for people he knows to be in residence in the household; but anyone can send a request for mail to be forwarded to some distant address. Therefore, Butler Number Two has arranged a secret password with each resident of Mail Server Mansion, and no mail will be forwarded without that password.

These e-mail messages can then be read on remote mail clients — more and more of which are Web-based and/or no-cost — such as:

Microsoft Outlook Express   `www.microsoft.com/windows/ie`

Mozilla mail/news   `www.mozilla.org`

Qualcomm Eudora Light   `www.eudora.com`

Hotmail   `www.hotmail.com`

AOL mail client   `www.aol.com`

One of the consequences of implementing a mail retrieval program is that now clients on every platform can receive mail from a Unix server. MUAs are limited to Unix clients, and preferably local Unix clients.

A diversity of mail retrieval protocols exist; and a large number of products (often of wildly varying design) implement those protocols. The most popular are called *POP3* and *IMAP.*

A *POP server* (sometimes called a *POP toaster*) simply verifies a name, password, and mailspool location by having this little dialog with a remote mail client:

```
user peter
+OK
pass rabbit
+OK
data
```

checking the answers in a file, and looking up where this user's mailbox is located. If there are new messages there, it will forward them to the client. Some POP systems can be configured to save a copy of every message forwarded to a client, some will allow clients to delete messages remotely, but most will just forward and forget. A user can take as much time as necessary to read and respond to messages offline, and then connect to the SMTP server to send replies.

POPular POP servers include:

Qualcomm qpopper   www.eudora.com/qpopper/index.html

qmail-pop3d   www.qmail.org

IMAP is a newer and more powerful mail retrieval protocol. Instead of forwarding and forgetting, IMAP allows for a simulacrum of the local client/server experience. The potential downside is that, unlike in a relatively quick POP3 data dump, each client must maintain a connection to the IMAP server as long as the user is reading and responding to e-mail — so the process is quite resource-intensive. An IMAP server is also somewhat more difficult to learn, install, configure, and maintain.

The most popular IMAP servers are:

Washington IMAP   www.washington.edu/imap

Cyrus   http://asg.web.cmu.edu/cyrus

> **TIP:** A great guide to understanding the differences between POP and IMAP is Terry Gray's paper "Messaging Access Paradigms and Protocols," available at:
> http://www.imap.org/papers/imap.vs.pop.html.

There is also a category of programs called a *mail retrieval utility*. The most famous of these is Eric Raymond's Fetchmail (http://www.tuxedo.org/~esr/fetchmail), which is particularly useful with dial-up connections. It implements POP, IMAP, and other protocols.

Mailing list manager

Finally, a mail server is hardly complete without a *mailing list manager*. This is a software package that helps send large volumes of e-mail automatically. Think of this program as the social secretary of Mail Server Mansion: Her job is to send out invitations to the endless parties given by the Mansion's residents. Needless to say, she must write out copy after copy after copy of each invitation — and then drop batches of them into the outgoing mailbag. She also handles all responses according to a standard set of scripts, analogous to handling RSVP acceptance notes.

Common MLMs include:

Majordomo	`www.greatcircle.com/majordomo`
MailMan	`www.list.org`
ezmlm (for qmail)	`www.ezmlm.org`

So there you have our model mail server. Now that you have a firm grasp on the basic architecture of e-mail, the rest is cake.

Receiving E-mail with PHP

Web-based e-mail clients — which download mail from the POP/IMAP server and relay outgoing mail through the SMTP server — are taking over a larger and larger slice of the market because of their convenience and platform independence. Furthermore, for those who habitually use shared or public computers, Webmail is the best way to ensure private communications. PHP is one of the tools that can be used to develop these most useful applications.

Say you want to make your own custom POP or IMAP client. You now have every development option from writing-from-scratch to choosing a different theme or skin from a drop-down menu. We discuss the main ones below, in order of most to least work.

Implementing from scratch

In a word: Don't. We're not joking. The only conceivable reason to re-implement from scratch at this point is for a university project, in which case you don't need someone to explain how to do it because you want to think through it for yourself.

Free Webmail providers all over the world will practically pay you to use their services, which you can configure to connect to any POP server anywhere. Also, many ISPs now provide Webmail along with connectivity. Extremely secure Web mail applications, such as Hushmail, are also starting to show up on the market at no cost to the consumer. We are personally more than happy to let the hardworking engineers at a major Web portal handle our personal e-mail accounts for us.

Even if you're determined to build your own custom Web-based e-mail app, there are now so many complete PHP Webmail clients free for the taking with their source code, you would have to go out of your way to avoid doing things (as the immortal Tina Turner says) nice . . . and easy.

Modifying other people's PHP

If you have some pressing reason why you need to write your own mail client in PHP, make it a little easier on yourself by using the power of *the Source* — the open source, that is. At least consider looking the code over to see if there's something you just haven't thought about yet — this is frequently the case with consumer apps, given the randomness of user behavior.

For those who want just a minimum of help, start with a look at Manuel Lemos's e-mail classes. The author, a well-known PHP community member, offers one for POP3, a couple for SMTP, and one for composing MIME messages. Put some nice screens on top of these, and you're halfway home. You can find them at:

```
www.phpclasses.org
```

There's no canonical URL for this site because it's mirrored at locations around the world. You will have to go to the above URL and click through to a specific mirror, then to the "E-mail" section. Be careful about using any code that isn't produced by a known-good developer like Manuel or Richard Heyes.

For those who want to start with the source code for a full-featured, Web-based e-mail client, there are many good ones now available.

An amazingly full-featured, stylish, and well-supported IMAP and POP3 client named *IMP* is available under the GPL from those fun-loving systems guys at Horde.org:

```
www.horde.org/imp
```

Another popular choice is *SquirrelMail*, an HTML4-compliant IMAP client with a cool plug-in system for add-ons like a clock module or POP3 fetching. This is now one of the top five open source Webmail projects.

```
http://squirrelmail.org
```

A quick search of SourceForge will reveal several other candidates, each with its own advantages and philosophy. For instance, JAWmail (`http://jawmail.sourceforge.net`) offers a WAP client and support for the Slovene language. NOCC (`http://nocc.sourceforge.net`) does not require a database or cookies. There's even an embryonic PHP-GTK mail client called Teak (`http://teak.sourceforge.net`). Look around. You're sure to find some project that's already going in the direction you want.

Cosmetic changes

Finally, rememberthat many open source programs make it very easy to grab some code and slap a coat of makeup on it, or redesign the user interface altogether. If you want to design a mail page that looks like a paper letter, a TV screen, or the command deck of the starship Enterprise — grab your copy of the GIMP and a CSS manual and go to it. Let a thousand cosmetic changes bloom!

This is particularly helpful to those who would like to put out a branded Web mail client, as many ISPs do. But remember it's not cool to implicitly take credit for work you haven't done — a little acknowledgment, in the form of a small logo or link, goes a long way in the open source community. Some Webmail clients explicitly leave room in their design for you to add your company logo.

More and more Web-based apps are using themes or skins, which are basically style sheets plus graphic elements, to allow the quickest changes to their look and feel. Many apps are now shipping with user-contributed themes, and sometimes the developer's work simply consists of selecting a theme from a pull-down menu — it doesn't get any easier than that.

Sending E-mail with PHP

Sending mail is where PHP really comes into its own with e-mail. But before you can send any mail from your server, you need to tweak the configuration file a little.

Windows configuration

You need to set two variables in the `php.ini` file:

- `SMTP`: A string containing the DNS name or IP address of an SMTP server that relays for the Windows machine on which PHP is installed. If it is on the PHP server, specify `localhost`.

- `sendmail_from`: A string containing the e-mail address of your default PHP mail sender (for example, `mailbot@example.com`).

> **TIP:** IIS4+ has an SMTP server built in, which is lighter than Exchange Server, if you don't need the power of the latter.

Unix configuration

You need to check and possibly change one variable in the `php.ini` file if you're using Unix: `sendmail_path`, a string containing the full path to your sendmail program (usually `/usr/sbin/sendmail` or `/usr/lib/sendmail`), a replacement, or a wrapper (such as `/var/qmail/bin/sendmail`).

If you are not using `sendmail`, and you do not reset this configuration directive to the correct alternative daemon, your mail transfer may be very slow, as several alternative programs are tried and allowed to time out before the correct one is found.

Be aware that PHP 4+ designates the user me as the default mail sender on a Unix system. PHP 3 used the PHP user (generally nobody), but apparently too many servers were rejecting mail from this account; early versions of PHP 4 used the root user, but this is a seriously bad idea because the Unix root user should never send mail.

> **CAUTION:** In some mail systems, notably qmail, there is no mail account for root because the writers of the program want to discourage the practice of sending mail as the root user. You'll need to specify a "From," "Reply-to," and/or "Bounce-to" address in each outgoing mail message when using PHP to send mail.

The mail function

Only one real mail sending function exists in PHP: mail(). This function, which returns a Boolean, attempts to send one message using the data within the parentheses and returns 0 or 1. The simplest use of this function (keeping in mind that this is a dummy address and should not be used for testing purposes) is:

```php
<?php
mail('receiver@receipthost.com', 'A Sample Subject Line', "Body of e-
mail\r\nwith lines separated by the newline character.");
?>
```

This is the default and minimum format: address of recipient, subject line, body. In this case, PHP will automatically add a From: me@sendhost line to each message header.

> **CAUTION:** Even though e-mail has been around in substantially the same form for decades, there is still no universal format for messages that is guaranteed readable by all MTAs or mail clients. Some clients require a carriage return plus a newline ("\r\n") instead of just a newline character. Some will choke on multiple addresses separated by commas. Some will not deliver e-mails without a proper date. There's really not a lot you can do to ameliorate this situation, except try as hard as you can to cover all the ground.

You can also, as always, use variables instead of hard-coded values:

```php
<?php
$address = 'santa@claus.com';
$subject = 'All I want for Christmas';
$body = "Is my two front teeth.\r\nSincerely, Joey";
$mailsend = mail($address, $subject, $body);
echo $mailsend;
?>
```

Multiple recipients all go into the address field, with commas separating them (this feature is not supported by all MTAs; if you want to be sure, use cc: instead):

```php
<?php
$address1 = 'receiver@receipthost';
$address2 = 'jane@hotmail.com';
$address3 = 'john@aol.com';
```

```
$all_addresses = "$address1, $address2, $address3";
$subject = 'A Sample Subject Line';
$body = "Body of e-mail\r\nwith lines separated by the newline
character.";

$mailsend = mail($addresses, $subject, $body);
echo $mailsend;
?>
```

Remember to ensure that the multiple addresses are one string, as in the preceding . You do *not* want to do this:

```
<?php
$address1 = 'receiver@receipthost';
$address2 = 'jane@hotmail.com';
$address3 = 'john@aol.com';
$subject = 'A Sample Subject Line';
$body = "Body of e-mail\r\nwith lines separated by the newline
character.";

// This is wrong, don't do it!
$mailsend = mail($address1, $address2, $address3, $subject, $body);
echo $mailsend;
?>
```

Most people would like more control over the addresses, appearance, and format of their e-mails. You can do that too, by adding an additional header *after* the three default headers.

```
<?php
$address = 'receiver@receipthost';
$subject = 'A Sample Subject Line';
$body = "Body of e-mail\r\nwith lines separated by the newline
character.";
$extra_header_str = "From: me@sendhost\r\nbcc: phb@sendhost\r\nContent-
type: text/plain\r\nX-mailer: PHP/" . phpversion();

$mailsend = mail($address, $subject, $body, $extra_header_str);
echo $mailsend;
?>
```

This "additional header" field is somewhat odd because it crams in several types of information that would normally be given their own fields. Ours is not to wonder why, ours is but to explain the kinds of things you might want to put in this field:

- ◆ Your name
- ◆ Your e-mail address
- ◆ A reply-to or bounce-to address
- ◆ X-mailer and version number

- ◆ MIME version
- ◆ Content-type
- ◆ Charset (which uses a = to assign a value and not a : like the other headers)
- ◆ Content-transfer-encoding
- ◆ Copy (cc:) and blind-copy (bcc:) recipients

> **CAUTION:** The mail() function returns 1 (TRUE) *when PHP believes it has successfully sent mail.* This has no relationship to any mail actually being sent or received. There are still an endless number of things that can go wrong: bad e-mail address, SMTP daemon incorrectly designated or configured, local Internet conditions, and so on. Think of 1 as a message meaning no more than "PHP has applied the function to the inputs without a big choke."

More Fun with PHP E-mail

Besides using PHP to construct full-blown mail clients, it's quite common to use the mail() function to send occasional mail when a particular event occurs on your Web site.

Sending mail from a form

Sending mail from a form is quite likely the single most popular application of PHP's mail() function. It's a functional alternative to HTML's mailto link tag, which of course results in e-mail being sent from the client machine's mail program.

Why use a server-side method rather than a client-side method of sending mail? After all, in many cases it's slower and more awkward, and it's certainly more work for you, the overburdened Web developer. Some reasons that might make you decide to choose this method include:

- ◆ A significant proportion of your audience uses public browsers or Web mail or both.
- ◆ You want to impose tighter syntax on the messages that you receive.
- ◆ You want to put the contact information into a database as well as send mail.
- ◆ You want to reduce unwanted messages (spam).
- ◆ You want to obviate the need for SMTP relaying from your main mail account.

This type of form-based, mail-sending page can be useful for many purposes, such as requesting quotes, reporting bugs, and getting technical support.

Listing 19-1 is a simple example form of the type that often sends e-mail.

Listing 19-1: e-mail form (titlehelp.html)

```
<html>
<head>
```

```
<title>titlehelp.html</title>
</head>

<body>
<center>
<table width="550">
<tr bgcolor= #FF9933><td align="center"><BR><H3>The
ThrillerGuide.com<BR>"What was the name of that thriller?"<BR>
Form</H3></td></tr>
<tr><td>
Did you once read an unforgettable thriller, but now you can't remember
the name?  Fill out as many of the fields below as you can, press the
button to submit, and we'll search our sources and e-mail you back.
</td></tr></table>
</center>

<FORM METHOD=post ACTION="TitleHelp.php">
<P>First name: <input type="text" size=30 name="FirstName">
<P>Last name: <input type="text" size=30 name="LastName">
<P>Your Email Address: <input type="text" size=30 name="Email">
<P>In approximately what year did the action of the book occur? <input
type="text" size=4 name="Year">
<P>Can you remember any settings from the book? <input type="text"
size=30 name="Setting">
<P>The gender of the protagonist(s) was: <br>
<ul>
<input TYPE="radio" NAME="Gender" VALUE=1>Female<br>
<input TYPE="radio" NAME="Gender" VALUE=2>Male<br>
<input TYPE="radio" NAME="Gender" VALUE=3>One of each<br>
<input TYPE="radio" NAME="Gender" VALUE=4>Two males<br>
<input TYPE="radio" NAME="Gender" VALUE=5>Two females<br>
</ul>
<P>When the book first came out, it was: <br>
<ul>
<input TYPE="radio" NAME="Status" VALUE=1>A bestseller<br>
<input TYPE="radio" NAME="Status" VALUE=2>A critic's darling<br>
<input TYPE="radio" NAME="Status" VALUE=3>Neither<br>
<input TYPE="radio" NAME="Status" VALUE=4>I don't know<br>
</ul>
<P>Please tell us anything else you can remember about this title (plot,
characters, settings, cover, movie versions, etc.):
<br><textarea NAME="Other" ROWS=6 COLS=50></textarea>
<P><input type="submit" name="Submit">
</body>
</html>
```

Listing 19-1 submits to a form handler, shown in Listing 19-2.

Listing 19-2: E-mail form handler (titlehelp.php)<html>

```
<head>
<title>titlehelp.php</title>
</head>

<body>
<?php
// If you wished, you could also save this information to a database
$LastName = $_POST['LastName'];
$FirstName = $_POST['FirstName'];
$Year = $_POST['Year'];
$Setting = $_POST['Setting'];
$Gender = $_POST['Gender'];
$Status = $_POST['Status'];
$Other = $_POST['Other'];

$formsent = mail('help@example.com', 'What was the name of that
thriller?', "Request from: $LastName $FirstName\r\nYear:
$Year\r\nSetting(s): $Setting\r\nProtagonist gender: $Gender\r\nBook
status: $Status\r\nOther identifying characteristics: $Other", "From:
$Email\r\nBounce-to: help@example.com");
if ($formsent) {
  echo "<P>Hi, $FirstName.  We have received your request for help, and
will try to respond within 24 hours.  Thanks for visiting
ThrillerGuide.com!";
} else {
  echo "I'm sorry, there's a problem with your form.  Please try
again.";
)
?>
</body>
</html>
```

Sending mail from a database

It's probably not a very good idea to send batch mail from PHP rather than using a mailing list manager for the task. It's definitely a very bad idea if you have a large, active list to serve. However, programmatic people may just feel more comfortable with a function than a special-purpose tool — and in the right situation, the PHP `mail()` function can work as well as a mailing list manager.

> **CAUTION:** How many e-mails are too many? Probably about a couple hundred is the maximum you'd want to send with PHP mail from a Web script, maybe 500 from a command-line call of a binary version of PHP.

Listing 19-3 is a PHP script you can use to send e-mail to everyone on a mailing list. Keep in mind you should not use this script if your list is not quite short.

Listing 19-3: Mailing list script (mailinglist.php_)

```
<html>
<head>
<title>ThrillerGuide: Site update notification</title>
</head>
<body>
<?php
mysql_connect('localhost', 'root');
mysql_select_db('thrillerguide');

$query = "SELECT email FROM mailinglist";
$result = mysql_query($query);
while ($MailArray = mysql_fetch_array($result)) {
  $formsent = mail($MailArray[0], "2000.1.23 ThrillerGuide update",
"This is to inform you that ThrillerGuide has recently been
updated.\r\n\r\nYou requested these e-mail notifications. If you do not
wish to receive them, reply to this mail with \"Cancel\" in the subject
line.", "From: mailinglist@thrillerguide.com\r\nReply-to:
help@example.com");
  echo "The result is $formsent.\n";
}
?>
</body>
</html>
```

Sending attachments with MIME mail

> **NOTE:** What is a *MIME* anyway? It stands for *M*ultipurpose *I*nternet *M*ail *E*xtensions and is a code to
> specify the media type (beyond plain old US-ASCII) of your file. For instance, even though HTML is actually
> just text, you often want some programs to "know" that they should treat a file as an HTML file rather than
> plain text — render it instead of printing it out literally, for instance. A MIME header ensures this. For the
> purposes of e-mail, MIME types are relevant for HTML-format mail (which we discourage), multipart mail
> (such as mail with embedded graphics, which we also discourage), and attachments.

Sending attachments with the PHP `mail()` function used to be a bit more complicated, but
lately a truly humanitarian PHP developer named Richard Heyes has made things super easy
by promulgating his MIME mail classes. You have two options: If you have simple needs and
don't care too much about licensing issues, you can get his HTML MIME mail class from his
own site:

```
www.phpguru.org/mime.mail.html
```

Or, if you want finer-grained control and/or a clearer license, you can use the Pear MIME class
developed by Heyes and Tomas V. V. Cox. This is shipped with the PHP distribution:

```
/php4.x.x/pear/Mail/mime.php
```

> **CROSS-REFERENCE:** Not only do these classes make sending attachments a snap, but they're an exemplary usage of PHP's OOP capabilities. This is a situation where a natural "bundle" of code plus data exists: The number of necessary functions is limited, the data elements are well-understood and stable, and the object notation makes usage easier rather than more difficult. Even a hardened skeptic would have to admit that, in this case, OOP is a clear win. For more about PHP's OOP capabilities and when to use them, see Chapter 26.

For the most common task, simply sending mail with an attachment, the original HTML MIME mail class is much simpler to use than the one shipped in the PEAR repository of the PHP distribution. This is the one we are using in the example that follows.

In Listing 19-4, we'll send a license file for an evaluation software download to anyone who requests one via a Web form.

Listing 19-4: Send e-email with a text attachment (send_license.php)

```php
<?php

/*************************************************************
 * This file initially shows a form to input an email address. *
 * Once submitted, it sends e-mail with a license file attached.*
 * The text of the e-mail is contained in a text file named     *
 * license_mail.txt.                                            *
 *************************************************************/

if ($_POST['submit'] == 'Send my license!') {
  // Make sure it's not some kind of attack
  if (strlen($_POST['email']) > 40) {
    echo 'Bad string';
    exit;
  }

  include('class.html.mime.mail.inc');

  $mail = new html_mime_mail(array('X-Mailer: Html Mime Mail Class'));
  $attachment = $mail->get_file('eval_license.lic');
  $mailbody = $mail->get_file('license_email.txt');

  $mail->add_text($mailbody);
  $mail->add_attachment($attachment, 'eval_license.lic', 'text/plain');
  $mail->build_message();
  $mail->send('Evaluator', $_POST['email'], 'mailbot@example.com',
'mailbot@example.com', 'Evaluation license');
} else {
  $form_str = <<< EOFORM
<HTML>
<BODY>
<FORM METHOD="post" ACTION="$PHP_SELF">
```

```
<INPUT TYPE="text" NAME="email" SIZE=25>
<INPUT TYPE="submit" NAME="submit" VALUE="Send my license!">
</FORM>
</BODY>
</HTML>
EOFORM;

  echo $form_str;
}
?>
```

A custom PHP mail application

Various organizations have their own special needs, for which you might be called upon to design a custom gizmo. For instance, here is a not-uncommon situation in which a custom mail application might be appropriate:

♦ The client wants to send personalized e-mail messages, each containing a password, to several hundred people.

♦ The client will enter each name and e-mail address by hand into a form from hardcopy. The program will insert this data into a database, along with passwords generated by PHP.

♦ PHP will compose and send a batch of e-mail using boilerplate text.

Listings 19-5, 19-6, and 19-7 show the code for a sample application to meet these specs. It combines the functionality of the two previous code samples and adds a couple of twists such as arrays and a random password generator (based on an example from Chapter 12).

Listing 19-5 is the entry form, `address_entry.php`:

Listing 19-5: Batch e-mail entry form (address_entry.php)

```
<HMTL>
<HEAD>
<TITLE>address_entry.php</TITLE>
</HEAD>

<BODY>
<CENTER><TABLE WIDTH=550><TR><TD>
Enter the names and e-mail addresses of recipients on this page. You do
not have to complete all 25 entries. When you are ready to actually send
the e-mails, click the Submit button at the bottom of the page.<BR><BR>
</TD></TR></TABLE></CENTER>

<FORM METHOD=post ACTION="email_send.php">
<?php
/* To keep the page sizes and mail batches to a manageable size, we will
arbitrarily limit each batch to 25 names. If anything goes wrong -- the
client accidentally closes the browser window before submitting, the PHP
```

```
module isn't working, whatever -- the maximum number of entries that
must be retyped is 25. To alter the batch size, change the number in the
while loop below; and also in the form handling script. */

for ($batch_size = 0; $batch_size <= 25; $batch_size++) {
  print("<P>First name: <input type=\"text\" size=30
name=\"FirstName[]\">\<BR>\nLast name: <input type=\"text\" size=30
name=\"LastName[]\">\<BR>\nE-mail Address: <input type=\"text\" size=30
name=\"Email[]\"\n>");
}
?>
<BR><BR>
<P><INPUT TYPE="Submit" NAME="SUBMIT">
</FORM>
</BODY>
</HTML>
```

Listing 19-6 is the form handler, email_send.php:

Listing 19-6: Batch e-mail form handler (email_send.php)

```
<html>
<head>
<title>email_send.php</title>
</head>

<body>
<?php
/* This screen enters the names, addresses, and passwords into a
database and sends the e-mails off into the wild black yonder of
cyberspace. */

include("password_maker.inc");

mysql_connect('localhost', 'root');
mysql_select_db('mailinglist');

$list_length = 0;
// Includes a test to stop the loop sooner if
// fewer than 25 names have been entered.
for ($list_length = 0 && strlen($_POST['Email'][$list_length] > 0;
$list_length <= 24 && strlen($_POST['Email'][$list_length]) > 0;
$list_length++) {
  // 8 is the number of characters desired in each password.
  $Password = random_string($charset, 8);
  $FirstName = $_POST['FirstName'][$list_length];
  $LastName = $_POST['LastName'][$list_length];
  $Email = $_POST['Email'][$list_length];
```

```
  $query = "INSERT INTO recipient (FirstName, LastName, Email, Password)
VALUES('$FirstName', '$LastName', '$Email', $Password)";
  $result = mysql_query($query);
  $formsent = mail($Email, "Login and password info", "Your login is:
$FirstName $LastName.\r\nMake sure there is only one space between the
two words when you log in.\r\nYour password is: $Password.\nGood luck!",
"From: mailinglist@sendhost\r\nReply-to: help@sendhost");
  echo "The result is $formsent for $list_length.<BR>\n";
}


?>
</body>
</html>
```

Listing 19-7 is the password generation file, `password_maker.inc`:

Listing 19-7: Random password generation functions (password_maker.inc)

```
<?php
// random_string is the function you actually call,
// and it in turn uses random_char

function random_char($string)
{
$length = strlen($string);
$position = mt_rand(0, $length - 1);
return($string[$position]);
}

function random_string ($charset_string, $length)
{
$return_string = random_char($charset_string);
for ($x = 1; $x < $length; $x++)
$return_string .= random_char($charset_string);
return($return_string);
}

// magic line to seed random generator
mt_srand((double)microtime() * 1000000);

$charset = "abcdefghijklmnopqrstuvwxyz";
?>
```

Sending mail from a cronjob

In the examples above, mail is triggered by the action of a human being interacting with a Web form. Sometimes, though, you want to send a batch of e-mail periodically and automatically. This is where Unix comes in handy — just set up a `cronjob` with PHP. It is a very happy feeling to drift off to sleep knowing that your little automatons are still working hard for you.

A very common use of a cronjob is to send a batch of e-mail in the middle of the night. Not only does this mean your mail will be waiting for the user at the top of the queue in the morning, but the dark hours before dawn are the traditional and best time to schedule batch processes that might slow down your servers.

To schedule a cronjob, first you write a script in the language of your choice. In this case, we are going to use the binary version of PHP — the one that is not a module of any Web server. The script (nagmail.php) sends out a reminder to everyone who downloaded an evaluation license 45 days ago.

Listing 19-8: Mail script for cron (nagmail.php)

```php
<?php

/***********************************************************
 * This script is intended to run once per day as a cron. *
 * It will query the database and send nagmail to people   *
 * who got evaluation licences 45 days before.             *
 ***********************************************************/

$db = mysql_connect("localhost", "root");
mysql_select_db("evaluators");

// Format date for query
// Actually the afternoon of 46 days ago
$now = time();
$fortyfive_days_ago = $now - 3888000 - 43200;

$target_date = date('Y-m-d', $fortyfive_days_ago);
$send_info_email_arr = array();

$query = "SELECT email
          FROM sent_licenses
          WHERE sent_date >= '$target_date 00:00:00'
          AND sent_date <= '$target_date 23:59:59'
          ";
$result = mysql_query($query,$db);

if (mysql_num_rows($result) > 0) {
  while ($email_arr = mysql_fetch_array($result)) {
    $to = $email_arr[0];
    $from = 'mailbot@example.com';
    $subject = 'Evaluation software license expires';
    $msg    = 'You downloaded our evaluation software 45 days ago.
Now you should pay us, or it will self-destruct.';
    $mailsend = mail($to, $subject, $msg, "From: $from");
    $send_info_email_arr .= "\n".$to."\n";
  }
```

```
  // Send me some email to let me know what happened
  $info_msg .= "I sent mail to the following evaluators
today:<BR><BR>\n";
  $info_msg .= print_r($send_info_email_arr);
  $info_mail = mail('webdev@example.com', "Cron job for $target_date",
$info_msg, "From: cronjob@example.com");

} else {
  // If there were no recipients today, let me know that
  $info_msg = "I didn't find anyone to send mail to today.";
  $info_mail = mail('webdev@example.com', "Cron job for $target_date",
$info_msg, "From: cronjob@example.com");

}
?>
```

Save this file in a location and with permissions that allow the PHP binary user to run it.

Now you need to schedule your `cronjob`. Say we want to send this mail out once a day at 3:15 a.m., the slowest hour of the day for your Web servers. Open up your `crontab` (type **crontab -e** in a shell) and enter this line (make sure your Unix user can execute the PHP binary):

```
15 03 * * * /usr/local/bin/php /home/phpcrons/nagmail.php
```

Reading from left to right, the various notations stand for minute, hour, day, month, day of week, and the command to be executed. (Asterisks are wildcards.) So this line tells the `cron` daemon to wake up and tap the PHP binary to run the `nagmail.php` script at 3:15 a.m. every morning of the year.

> **CAUTION:** So sad for Windows users, but this is not possible with PHP in your operating system. Unix has a lot of functionality in the system layer that Windows tends to put in the application layer — so for instance Unix programmers constantly use the "`grep`" utility to search for a string in a set of files, which Windows programmers accomplish in the IDE. Similarly, scheduling a repetitive task like sending automatic e-mail is done in Outlook on Windows or as a trigger from SQL Server, rather than via a `cronjob`.

E-mail Gotchas

Given that there are so few mail-related functions in PHP, and these are very straightforward, e-mail related issues are highly likely to be caused by problems with the mail servers or even with the protocols themselves. In our experience, there is little a PHP developer can do to fix mail problems that suddenly arise in a working PHP installation.

If you experience a mail-related error message in PHP, the first thing you want to do is send and receive mail using the `sendmail` server that your PHP installation points to – just to eliminate the possibility that your SMTP server is totally hosed.

Next, make sure that you have set the sendmail or SMTP path in your configuration files correctly. Remember that you will have to do this every time you upgrade your PHP and/or Web server binary. Even if you're positive you did it correctly, it doesn't hurt to check again. Remember that there may be multiple configuration files — for instance, php.ini and Apache's httpd.conf can both be used to set the sendmail path.

If you don't see an error message and some of your e-mails are getting through, see if you can find a common denominator in the failure cases. For instance, it's quite common for well-managed mail servers to refuse delivery of e-mail from servers that do not pass a reverse-DNS lookup check. If your sendmail aliasing is configured incorrectly, the name or private-network IP address of a non-public machine inside your firewall might be making it into your mail headers — leading to a quick bounce from some of the better-administered SMTP servers (typically corporations and the more technical universities). Another common problem can occur when you forget to change the default PHP mail sending user, or have it set to a user such as "nobody" or "root" — many well-managed SMTP servers will refuse mail from these users.

If your problem is with POP or IMAP accounts accessed via a PHP client, try waiting awhile to see if matters improve on the server end. These servers are notoriously flaky, and not only crash a lot, but require an unusual amount of scheduled maintenance. This is frustrating but totally outside the realm of anything most Web developers are responsible for.

Finally, if you are having problems with sending attachments with PHP, check out the documentation (including code comments) that shipped with the MIME mail class you're using. Fiddly little issues with things like line breaks and timestamps and multiple addresses may be causing you problems.

Summary

E-mail is one of the most useful and attractive functions of the Internet. PHP gives you the ability to both send and receive e-mail from a Web page. However, PHP is not a specialized e-mail program and will not cope gracefully with large quantities of messages.

Unfortunately, e-mail is one of the more complicated services in most domains, with a large number of moving parts and a surprising lack of standardization for such a relatively long-established functionality. Do not blame this on PHP — it's inherent in e-mail itself.

One of the most common uses of PHP's mail function is to send an e-mail (often to yourself) with values generated from a Web form. This is more reliable and spam-resistant than a mailto link, and it allows you to impose more structure on the data. You can also use PHP to send off small batches of e-mail using data from a database. However, large batches require a mailing-list manager or other solution.

## Chapter 30

Regular Expressions

In This Chapter

♦ What are regular expressions good for?

♦ POSIX versus Perl-compatible regular expressions

♦ Regular expression functions in PHP

♦ Using regex to extract links from Web pages

Regular expressions are patterns that match to strings. They are used not only to create complex true/false tests on strings, but also to extract substrings and make complex substitutions. A full treatment of regular expressions is well beyond our scope in this chapter. Instead, we will explain what regular expressions are good for, what varieties of regex are offered by PHP. We also give some examples of their uses.

Why Regular Expressions?

The string-comparison and substring-finding functions we saw in Chapter 10 are fine as far as they go, but they are on the literal-minded side. As an example of their weakness, let's say that you want to test strings to see if they are a particular kind of Web hostname: addresses that start with `www.` and end with `.com`, and have one lowercase alphabetic word in the middle. For example, these are strings we want:

```
'www.ibm.com'
'www.zend.com'
```

And the following are not:

```
'java.sun.com'
'www.java.sun.com'
'www.php.net'
'www.IBM.com'
'www.Web addresses can't have spaces.com'
```

With a little thought, it's obvious that there is no convenient way to simply use string and substring comparison to build the test that we want. We can test for the presence of `www.` and `.com`, but it is difficult to enforce what should be happening in between them. This is what regular expressions are good for.

Regex in PHP

Regular expressions (or *regex*, pronounced with a soft *g* by your authors, but with no consensus pronunciation) are patterns for string matching, with special wildcards that can match entire portions of the target string. There are two broad classes of regular expression that PHP works with: *POSIX* (extended) regex and *Perl-compatible* regex. The differences mostly have to do with syntax, although there are some functional differences, too.

POSIX-style regular expressions are ultimately descended from the regex pattern-matching machinery used in Unix command-line shells; Perl-compatible regex is a more direct imitation of regular expressions in Perl.

An example of POSIX-style regex

Here are a few of the rules for POSIX-style regular expressions, simplified:

♦ Characters that are not "special" get matched literally. The letter a in a pattern, for example, matches the same letter in a target string.

♦ The special character ^ matches the beginning of a string only, and the special character $ matches the end of a string only.

♦ The special character . matches any character.

♦ The special character * matches zero or more instances of the previous regular expression, and + matches one or more instances of the previous expression.

♦ A set of characters enclosed in square brackets matches any of those characters — the pattern [ab] matches either a or b. You can also specify a range of characters in brackets by using a hyphen — the pattern [a-c] matches a, b, or c.

♦ Special characters that are escaped with a backslash (\) lose their special meaning and are matched literally.

Now we can use the preceding rules to construct an expression that matches the kind of Web address we want in the section, "Why Regular Expressions," earlier in this chapter. Our chosen expression is:

```
^www\.[a-z]+\.com$
```

In this expression we have the '^' symbol, which says that the www portion must start at the beginning of the string. Then comes a dot (.), preceded by a backslash that says we really want a dot, not the special . wildcard character. Then we have a bracket-enclosed range of all the lowercase alphabetic letters. The following + indicates that we are willing to match any number of these lowercase letters in a row, as long as we have at least one of them. Then another literal ., the com, and the special $ that says that com is the end of it.

Now let's use that expression as an argument to the function `ereg()`, which takes as arguments a pattern string and a string to match against. We can use an `ereg()` call to build a test function for our kind of Web address.

```
function simple_dot_com ($url)
{
  return(ereg('^www\\.[a-z]+\\.com$', $url));
}
```

Confusingly, we have to put two backslashes in the pattern string, because PHP treats the first slash as an escape character for the second backslash. (You can get away with just one backslash, but that behavior is not guaranteed to continue in future versions of PHP.) The second backslash (escaped by the first), in turn, is a regex escape character for the following character.

This function will return TRUE or FALSE, depending on whether it succesfully matches our pattern. Now we can use our function to test some of the addresses listed earlier.

```
$urls_to_test =
    array('www.ibm.com', 'www.java.sun.com',
          'www.zend.com', 'java.sun.com',
          'www.java.sun.com', 'www.php.net',
          'www.IBM.com',
          'www.Web addresses can\'t have spaces.com');
while($test = array_pop($urls_to_test)){
  if (simple_dot_com($test))
    print("\"$test\" is a simple dot-com<BR>");
  else
    print("\"$test\" is NOT a simple dot-com<BR>");

}
```

The results of our tests are as follows:

```
"www.Web addresses can't have spaces.com" is NOT a simple dot-com
"www.IBM.com" is NOT a simple dot-com
"www.php.net" is NOT a simple dot-com
"www.java.sun.com" is NOT a simple dot-com
"java.sun.com" is NOT a simple dot-com
"www.zend.com" is a simple dot-com
"www.java.sun.com" is NOT a simple dot-com
"www.ibm.com" is a simple dot-com
```

This is the kind of discriminating behavior we are looking for.

> **TIP** On many Unix systems, typing **man 7 regex** will lead you to a guide to POSIX regular expressions. If that does not work, try **man regex** and follow any pointers to related pages.

Regular expression functions

The POSIX-style regular expression functions in PHP are summarized in Table 30-1.

> **TIP:** If you find yourself using a regular expression function with a "pattern" that has no special characters, you are probably using an expensive tool where a cheap one would do. If you are trying to match a simple string to a simple string, you need only one of the more basic (and faster) functions that we cover earlier in this chapter.

Table 30-1: POSIX Regular Expression Functions

Function	Behavior
ereg()	Takes two string arguments and an optional third-array argument. The first string is the POSIX-style regular expression pattern, and the second string is the target string that is being matched. The function returns TRUE if the match was successful, and FALSE otherwise. In addition, if an array argument is supplied and portions of the pattern are enclosed in parentheses, the parts of the target string that match successive parenthesized portions will be copied into successive elements of the array.
ereg_replace()	Takes three arguments: a POSIX regular expression pattern, a string to do replacement with, and a string to replace into. The function scans the third argument for portions that match the pattern and replaces them with the second argument. The modified string is returned.
	If there are parenthesized portions of the pattern (as with ereg()), the replacement string may contain special substrings of the form \\$digit$ (that is, two backslashes followed by a single-digit number), which will themselves be replaced with the corresponding piece of the target string.
eregi()	Identical to ereg(), except that letters in regular expressions are matched in a case-independent way.
eregi_replace()	Identical to ereg_replace(), except that letters in regular expressions are matched in a case-independent way.
split()	Takes a pattern, a target string, and an optional limit on the number of portions to split the string into. Returns an array of strings created by splitting the target string into chunks delimited by substrings that match the regular expression. (Note that this is analogous to the explode() function, except that it splits on regular expressions rather than literal strings.)
spliti()	Case-independent version of split().

Perl-Compatible Regular Expressions

Perl-compatible regex in PHP has a completely distinct set of functions and a slightly different set of rules for patterns.

Perl-compatible regex patterns are always bookended by one particular character, which must be the same at beginning and end, indicating the beginning and end of the pattern. By convention, this is most often the / character, although you can use a different character if you so desire. The Perl-compatible pattern:

```
/pattern/
```

matches any string that has the string (or substring) pattern in it. To make things slightly more complicated, these patterns are typically strings, and PHP needs its own quotes to recognize such strings. So if you are putting a pattern into a variable for later use, you might well do this:

```
$my_pattern = '/pattern/';
```

This variable $pattern would now be suitable for passing off to a Perl-compatible regex function that expects a pattern as argument.

Although we don't have time or space to cover Perl-compatible regex patterns in detail, Table 30-1 shows a list of the most commonly used constructs.

Table 30-2: Common Perl-Compatible Pattern Constructs

Construct	Interpretation
Simple literal character matches	If the character involved is not special, Perl will match characters in sequence. The example pattern /abc/ matches any string that has the substring 'abc' in it.
Character class matches: [<*list of characters*>]	Will match a single instance of any of the characters between the brackets. For example, / [xyz] / matches a single character, as long as that character is either x, y, or z. A sequence of characters (in ASCII order) is indicated by a hyphen, so that a class matching all digits is [0-9].
Predefined character class abbreviations.	The patterns \d will match a single digit (from the character class [0-9]), and the pattern \s matches any whitespace character.
Multiplier patterns	Any pattern followed by * means: "Match this pattern 0 or more times."
	Any pattern followed by ? means: "Match this pattern exactly once."
	Any pattern followed by + means: "Match this pattern 1 or more times."

Anchoring characters	The caret character ^ at the beginning of a pattern means that the pattern must start at the beginning of the string; the $ character at the end of a pattern means that the pattern must end at the end of the string. The caret character at the beginning of a character class [^abc] means that the set is the complement of the characters listed (that is, any character that is not in the list).
Escape character '\'	Any character that has a special meaning to regex can be treated as a simple matching character by preceding it with a backslash. The special characters that might need this treatment are: `. \ + * ? [ ] ^ $ ( ) { } = ! < >	:`
Parentheses	A parenthesis grouping around a portion of any pattern means: "Add the substring that matches this pattern to the list of substring matches."

Take, as an example, the following pattern:

```
/phone number\s+(\d\d\d\d\d\d\d)/
```

It matches any string that contains the literal phrase phone number, followed by some number of spaces (but at least one), followed by exactly seven digits (no spaces, no dash). In addition, because of the parentheses, the seven-digit number is saved and returned in an array containing substring matches if it is called from a function that returns such things.

The Perl-compatible functions are summarized in Table 30-3.

Table 30-3: Perl-Compatible Regular Expression Functions

Function	Behavior
preg_match()	Takes a regex pattern as first argument, a string to match against as second argument, and an optional array variable for returned matches. Returns 0 if no matches are found, and 1 if a match is found. If a match is successful, the array variable contains the entire matching substring as its first element, and subsequent elements contain portions matching parenthesized portions of the pattern.
preg_match_all()	Like preg_match(), except that it makes all possible successive matches of the pattern in the string, rather than just the first. The return value is the number of matches successfully made. The array of matches is not optional (If you want a true/false answer, use preg_match()). The structure of the array returned depends on the optional

	fourth argument (either the constant `PREG_PATTERN_ORDER`, or `PREG_SET_ORDER`, defaulting to the former). (See further discussion following the table.)
`preg_split()`	Takes a pattern as first argument and a string to match as second argument. Returns an array containing the string divided into substrings, split along boundary strings matching the pattern. (Analogous to the POSIX-style function `split()`.) An optional third argument (*limit*) controls how many elements to split before returning the list; `-1` means no limit.
`preg_replace()`	Takes a pattern, a replacement string, and a string to modify. Returns the result of replacing every matching portion of the modifiable string with the replacement string. An optional limit argument determines how many replacements will occur (as in `preg_split()`).
`preg_replace_call back()`	Like `preg_replace()`, except that the second argument is the name of a callback function, rather than a replacement string. This function should return the string that is to be used as a replacement.
`preg_grep()`	Takes a pattern and an array and returns an array of the elements of the input array that matched the pattern. Surviving values of the new array have the same keys as in the input array.
`preg_quote()`	A special-purpose function for inserting escape characters into strings that are intended for use as regex patterns. The only required argument is a string to escape; the return value is that string with every special regex character preceded by a backslash.

The most widely used of these functions are probably `preg_match()`, and `preg_match_all()`. The first is best for simply answering whether a pattern matches a string, and the latter is best for either counting matches or collecting portions that match.

The optional fourth argument to `preg_match_all()` requires a little more explanation. The array that contains the returned matches is going to be two levels deep, with one level being the iteration of the match (the first match, the second, and so on), and the other level being the position of the match in the pattern. (The entire match is always first, then any parenthesized subpatterns in order.) The question is: Which level is on top? Will the array be a list of positions, each of which contains a list of iterations, or the other way around? If the argument is `PREG_PATTERN_ORDER`, the first element will contain all matches of the entire pattern, the second element will contain all matches of the first parenthesized pattern, and so forth. If the argument is `PREG_SET_ORDER`, the first argument will be all the substrings from the first match (first the total match, then parenthesized bits in order), the second element will contain all the substrings from the second match, and so on. (See the example following to clarify.)

Example: A Simple Link-Scraper

As an example of what regex can do for us, let's write a simple function to grab and print links from an arbitrary Web page. The input will be a URL for the page we're interested in analyzing; the output will be a printed list of the links on the page, split into the target URL for the link and the descriptive text that appears in the link (the *anchortext*). We will do this using Perl-compatible regex functions.

Such a function might be the very first step in writing a Web-crawler for a search engine. Search engines download the contents of Web pages to analyze and index them, but they also need to discover links to other pages, if only to discover new content.

The regular expression

The heart of our little function will be the regular expression itself. What we need to do is design an expression that will match HTML links (and nothing else) and that is suitable for using to extract pieces of such links.

HTML links generally look something like this:

```
<A HREF="http://mysite.com/mypage.php">My cool page on my cool site</A>
```

That is, an anchor tag that has an HREF attribute, and which encloses the anchortext between the start tag (<A>) and the end tag (</A>. We'll construct a pattern to match this simplified view of an anchortext. (This won't capture everything that the HTML spec permits as legal anchor links — in particular, you are allowed attributes in anchors other than HREFs, but we will ignore that for our purposes.)

Now, regular expressions are famously unreadable when considered all at once. So we will grow this one in several drafts as we explain what's going on.

First, let's start with a minimal expression to catch a beginning anchor tag. Our first draft looks like this:

```
/<A\sHREF="[^"]+">/     // first draft of a pattern to match anchor links
```

In English, our first-draft definition of an anchor tag is: left-angle bracket, followed by A, followed by a space, followed by the string HREF=, followed by a double-quote sign, followed by any number of characters that are not quote signs, followed by a closing quote sign, followed by a right angle bracket. Then the whole expression is enclosed in a pair of slashes, indicating to the regex engine the start and end of the expression.

The [^"]+ construction in the middle of this expression breaks down like this: The brackets indicate a character set, and the caret (^) immediately after the left bracket indicates that we are negating the set — that the set contains every character that is *not* in the subsequent list. Finally, the + after that bracketed class means that we expect at least one nonquote character.

As we've said, we're not trying to capture the precise syntax prescribed by the HTML specification. But there are a couple of ways that we can make this expression less strict. For one thing, as far as we know there may be spaces between the initial < character and the A tag. Similarly, there may be an arbitrary number of spaces between the A and the HREF, or the closing double-quote and the right angle-bracket. Adding these, the expression becomes:

```
/<\s*A\s*HREF="[^"]+"\s*>/     // second draft, allowing more spaces
```

Here, \s* means zero or more spaces.

Now we add the anchortext itself and the closing </A> tag.

```
/<\s*A\s*HREF="[^\"]+"\s*>[^>]*<\/A>/  // third draft, with text and
close tag
```

We are allowing the anchor text to be anything up until a closing anchor tag, so we make an anything-but-right-angle-bracket character class ([^>]), and indicate that it can repeat zero or more times. Finally, we add the subpattern to match the closing anchor tag (<\/A>).

This is fine as far as it goes, but it will only match anchors where the tag name (A) and attribute (HREF) are in uppercase. Lowercase tags should be legal as well, so we add an i modifier after the entire expression, to specify case-independent matching.

```
/<\s*A\s*HREF="[^\"]+"\s*>[^>]*<\/A>/i  // fourth draft, case-
independent
```

This draft is nearly final and could be used to give true/false answers to the question of whether a page contains the kind of links we like. But we want to go further and extract certain portions of any string that does match. We signify this by adding parentheses to enclose the portions we're interested in:

```
/<\s*A\s*HREF="([^\"])+"\s*>([^>]*)<\/A>/i  // final draft, extracts
portions
```

They may be hard to see by this point, but we've added a pair of parentheses to enclose the target of the HREF (between the quotes) and another pair around the anchortext area (between the tags). These parentheses tell the calling function to save the string portion that matches the enclosed area, so that it can be added to the return array.

Using the expression in a function

With an anchor-tag-matching expression in hand, our goal now is to write a function to scrape links from an HTML page. We'll need to:

♦ Take a URL as argument.

♦ Open up an HTTP connection to the URL and grab its contents as a string.

♦ Iterate through the string, applying our regex pattern wherever we can, saving what matches.

♦ Print out the extracted portions (target URL and anchortext).

Such a function is shown in Listing 30-1.

Listing 30-1: A print_links function

```php
<?php

function print_links ($url)
{
  $fp = fopen($url, "r")
    or die("Could not contact $url");
  $page_contents = "";
  while ($new_text = fread($fp, 100)) {
    $page_contents .= $new_text;
  }
  $match_result =
    preg_match_all('/<\s*A\s*HREF="([^\"]+)"\s*>([^>]*)<\/A>/i',
              $page_contents,
              $match_array,
              PREG_SET_ORDER);

  foreach ($match_array as $entry) {
    $href = $entry[1];
    $anchortext = $entry[2];
    print("<B>HREF</B>: $href;
          <B>ANCHORTEXT</B>:  $anchortext<BR>");
  }
}
?>
```

This function is easier to write than you might expect because PHP takes care of several parts of it for us. We do not need to write anything special to make an HTTP connection to download a Web page because fopen() will accept a URL as argument and do the right thing. All we need to do after calling fopen() on the URL is to read characters until we are out of them, appending what we get onto a constructed string.

The iteration through the HTML page's contents is taken care of by preg_match_all(), which applies the regex pattern as many times as possible, starting from the previous match each time, and saving the matches in $match_array. We chose to have the array arranged by PREG_SET_ORDER, meaning that each entry in the top-level array is the portions from a particular match in the iteration, rather than across matches.

Applying the function

The only argument the function requires is a URL. In testing the function before including it in the book, we pointed it at link-rich, top-level pages like `http://slashdot.org`, `http://www.cnn.com`, and `http://www.php.net`. Those results would be fun to display, but all of those sites have copyright notices, and publishers are understandably wary of allowing authors to put other people's copyrighted material into their copyrighted book without permission. So, instead, we pointed it at the top-level placeholder page for our own vanity site (`www.troutworks.com`), like this:

```
print_links("http://www.troutworks.com/");
```

You get the following result (approximately):

```
HREF: http://www.mysteryguide.com; ANCHORTEXT: MysteryGuide
HREF: http://www.sciencebookguide.com; ANCHORTEXT: ScienceBookGuide
HREF: /Joycelog/joycelog.php; ANCHORTEXT: Troutgirl weblog
HREF: /Timlog/timlog.php; ANCHORTEXT: Timboy weblog
HREF: http://www.amazon.com/exec/obidos/ASIN/076454716X/;
   ANCHORTEXT: PHP 4 Bible
```

Just because we didn't feel that we could print the results of the links from those more interesting sites doesn't mean that you can't apply this code to them (however, see the warnings in the section entitled "Writing well-behaved spiders").

Extending the code

As we've said, code like Listing 30-1 is the very beginning of writing a Web-search spider. If you want to make it more real, you could:

♦ Convert the relative links to absolute (`http://`) links by remembering the URL that you are scraping and splicing that base URL appropriately with the relative path.

♦ Add a more graceful way to bounce back from an unreachable site rather than immediately dying.

♦ Expand the regex pattern to match HREFs that have quotes around the URL as well as HREFs that do not.

♦ Add capability for recursive calls so that, rather than simply printing a child link, you apply the same function again to it and explore its own links.

Writing well-behaved spiders

A note of caution, however (informed by the experience of one of your authors in the search-engine business). There is absolutely no reason you shouldn't feel free to point this code at `www.cnn.com/` to view the links on that front page — after all, it's exactly what happens when your own browser contacts that site, and certainly the people at CNN won't be able to tell the difference between those two contacts.

There are two rules that you should observe, though, before writing any kind of spider that does more automated crawling. When you crawl any site, you should:

♦ Check to see if there is a `robots.txt` file (at `http://sitename/robots.txt`). If there is no such file, the site owners are implicitly saying the site is okay to crawl. If there is such a file, you should either not crawl the site or, if you do, you should make sure that you are not crawling pages that match the patterns laid out in that file. (For more on this, do a Web search for "robot exclusion standard").

♦ Make sure that you don't request files from any particular site too frequently. A decent interval to wait between requests is ten seconds or so. (You can implement this delay on a per-site basis, or simply by sleeping for ten seconds between every request.) It is not OK to simply create a recursive version of the preceding code, and then unleash it on a large site, grabbing new links and pages as fast as your code can loop. Remember: One man's search engine is another's denial-of-service attack.

Summary

Simple string matching is all very well, but when you need industrial-strength pattern matching, nothing less than regex will do. PHP offers not only full regular-expression functionality, but two flavors of it to choose from. Our personal preference is for the Perl-compatible regex functions, but you can use whichever flavor suits you best.

Chapter 31

PHP and XML

In This Chapter

♦ What is XML?

♦ Working with XML

♦ Documents and DTDs

♦ SAX versus DOM

♦ DOM

♦ SAX

♦ Sample XML application

XML is one of the hottest buzzwords in the software business today; but what does it mean for Joe or Jane Average PHP Developer? Well, it could very well be the necessary precondition for a better Internet — one that is faster to develop, more interactive, less junky, and more accessible to a larger audience. With PHP, you're already in an excellent position to smoothly integrate XML into your Web development arsenal as the technology matures.

What Is XML?

XML stands for *eXtensible Markup Language*. XML is a form of *SGML*, the *S*tandard *G*eneralized *M*arkup *L*anguage, but you don't need to know anything about SGML to use XML. It defines a syntax for structured documents that both humans and machines can read.

> **NOTE:** Our explanation of XML will necessarily be extremely brief (because this is a book about PHP rather than XML). For those who want to learn more, we highly recommend Elliotte Rusty Harold's *XML Bible, 2nd. Edition* (Wiley, 2001). Although this book is neither short nor a specific guide to programming XML-based applications, it will give you a firm conceptual grasp of XML that should set you up nicely for any particular XML-based task.

Perhaps the easiest way to understand XML is to think about all the things HTML can't do. HTML is also a markup language, but HTML documents are anything but structured. HTML tags (technically known as elements) and attributes are just simple identification markers to the browser. For instance, a pair of matched <H1> and </H1> tags designate a top-level heading. Browsers interpret this to mean you want heading text to be displayed in a really big, bold, possibly italicized font. HTML does not, however, indicate whether the text between those tags is the title of the page, the name of the author, an invitation to enter the site, an apposite quotation, a promise of special sale prices, or what. It's just some text that happens to be big.

One implication of HTML's lack of structure is that search engines have little built-in guidance about what's important on each page of your site or what each chunk of text means in relation to the others. They use various methods to guess, none of which are foolproof. <META> tags are notoriously prone to abuse — porn sites often load popular but irrelevant search terms into their headers to fool unwary Web surfers — and spiders can end up giving too much weight to portions of the page that designers might think are unimportant. If XML becomes ubiquitous, it could eliminate many of these problems and lead the way to much more meaningful Web searching.

Now let's say you work for a content Web site which has just signed a major distribution deal with a top-five portal. After you wake up from the champagne hangover, you're faced with the hard question of how you plan to deliver the content. HTML isn't going to do the job: Obviously the portal's page design and Web serving technology are different from your site's, and they won't be able to just plug your HTML into theirs. Just to make things really interesting, let's presume you and Big Portal Company use different programming languages, different data stores, different HTML editors, different style sheets — in short, different everything. The necessary bridge is a data-exchange format which is easy for you to output with your technical setup, clearly understood by both parties with existing software, and equally easy for the Big Portal Company to convert to its own purposes and designs. XML promises to be that data-exchange format.

You could, of course, write a script to dump data from your data store into a tab-delimited file. Then you could write out the details of your custom data format and send it with the tab-delimited file to Big Portal Company. There one of its engineers would try to figure out your schema and write code to transform your data into its format. However, anyone who has actually done this knows how much fiddly work it is, how many tests need to be performed, how much time even the tiniest error can suck up. On the other hand, you could just output your data in XML, and the Big Portal Company engineer could write a very short script — perhaps just three functions long — to transform your XML tags to its corresponding XML tags. Then Big Portal Company could treat the data just like its own data. XML is an attempt to move towards a common language and set of methods for performing tasks like these, instead of having data-exchange involve a series of custom jobs each time.

Hopefully these examples begin to answer the "Why XML?" question. If you forget the hype and focus on what problems XML might begin to solve, you'll be in a much better position to assess whether it can help you today or sometime in the future. In the simplest terms, XML is a flexible data-exchange format that is not dependent on any particular software or domain, can be parsed easily by both machines and humans, and allows content providers to include information about the structure of the data along with the data itself.

The next question about XML is typically, "What does XML look like anyway?" Actually, XML looks a lot like HTML. A simple XML file, such as the one shown in Listing 31-1, is easy for HTML-users to understand:

Listing 31-1: A simple XML file

```
<?xml version="1.0"?>
<book>
 <publisher>IDG Books</publisher>
 <title>PHP4 Bible</title>
 <chapter title="PHP and XML">
  <section title="What is XML?">
   <paragraph>
If you know HTML, you're most of the way to understanding XML.
   </paragraph>
   <paragraph>
They are both markup languages, but XML is more structured than HTML.
   </paragraph>
  </section>
 </chapter>
</book>
```

As you can see, XML has tags and attributes and the hierarchical structure that you're used to seeing in HTML. In XML, each pair of tags (`<paragraph></paragraph>`) is known as an *element*. Actually, this is true in HTML, too, but most people strongly prefer the term *tag* (the construction that marks an element) over *element* (the conceptual thing that is being marked by a tag) — we're not picky. Use whatever term you want as long as you know what you mean. The biggest difference is that XML tags are self-defined; and they carry absolutely no display directive to the Web browser or other viewing application.

XML makes the following minimal demands:

♦ There must be a single root element that encloses all the other elements, similar to `<HTML></HTML>` in HTML documents. This is also sometimes called the *document element*.

♦ Elements must be hierarchical. That is, `<X> <Y> </Y> </X>` is allowed, but `<X> <Y> </X> </Y>` is not. In the first example, `<X>` clearly contains all of `<Y>`. In the second example, `<X>` and `<Y>` overlap. XML does not allow overlapped tags.

♦ All elements must be deliberately closed (in contrast to HTML, which allows some unclosed elements such as `<OPTION>` or `<LI>`). This can be accomplished with a closing tag (`<title></title>`) as in HTML or by using an XML feature with no HTML equivalent called a *self-closing element* (`<logo href="graphic.jpg"/>`). A self-closing element is also known as an *empty element*.

♦ Elements can contain elements, text, and other data. If an element encloses something that looks like it might be XML — such as `<hello>` — but isn't, or if you don't want something parsed, it must be escaped.

> **CAUTION:** The &, <, >, ', and " characters are all restricted in XML. You can use them in your data by *escaping* them — using codes such as & and < — or by putting them in CDATA sections, which we discuss in the section "Documents and DTDs," later in this chapter.

In addition to these mandatory requirements for what is called *well-formedness*, the XML standard also suggests that XML documents should start with an identifying XML declaration. This is a processing instruction giving the MIME type and version number, such as <?xml version="1.0"?>. This is not required, but some parsers complain if it isn't present. Also, XML is case sensitive; and some variants, such as XHTML, require lowercase tags and attributes. Lowercase tags are not absolutely required by the XML standard itself, but unless you have a good reason to do otherwise you should use lowercase tags and attributes.

> **NOTE:** It's the XML declaration, and other processing instructions with the same format, that prevent you from using PHP's short tags with XML. Because the two tag styles are identical (<? ?>), it would be unclear whether this character sequence set off a PHP block or an XML processing instruction.

XML documents are usually text. They can contain binary data, but they aren't really meant to. If you want to put binary data in your XML documents, you have to encode it first and then decode it later. Note that including binary data may break some of the platform-independence of pure XML.

Working with XML

By now you may or may not think XML is the greatest thing since cinnamon toast; but in either case you're probably asking yourself, "OK, but what can I actually *do* with it?" This is actually not such an easy question to answer. In theory, you can do three main things with XML: manipulate and store data; pass data around between software applications or between organizations; and display XML pages in a browser or other application using style sheets to apply display directives.

In practice, almost no one actually uses XML as a primary data store when SQL is so ubiquitous. It's possible, although still difficult, to manipulate data using XML — for instance, to edit documents by creating and manipulating XML nodes rather than straight text — but again many users don't see a tremendous amount of extra value to this practice. A great deal of progress has been made in displaying XML in the browser, generally in the form of XHTML, in the last couple of years; but there are still significant issues with this practice. For more information about displaying XML, see the sidebar "The Promises and Pitfalls of Displaying XML," at the end of this section.

This leaves one main job for XML right now: exchanging data between applications and organizations. This happens to be the area in which PHP can have the most immediate impact. For instance, a C program might perform some operations on data from a data store and then output the results in XML, which PHP could transform into HTML for display in a browser or other application.

THE PROMISES AND PITFALLS OF DISPLAYING XML

XML attempts to do something that HTML has only very imperfectly accomplished: enforce real separation between content and display. XML tags contain no display-oriented meaning whatsoever — so an element called <header></header> in XML does not imply anything about large bold text, and, we hope, never will. All display information will be applied through style sheets. These can be either Cascading Style Sheets, which are already familiar to many HTML developers, or *XSL* (e*X*tensible *S*tyle *L*anguage), which is the next-generation style sheet.

A single XML document will, in theory, be displayable in any number of ways simply by applying a different style sheet. The promise is that you will be able to take an XML document and, by simply swapping in various XSL templates, be able to create a version of the page for very large screens, a version for cellular phones, a version for the visually handicapped, a version with certain lines highlighted in red, and so forth.

The reality of the situation right now is not that rosy. The XSL standard is still notoriously shaky, and it seems to be resisting wide adoption. Cascading Style Sheets have been around since 1997 and browser support for them remains so problematic that most major Web sites still use font tags — indicating that XSL has quite a way to go before it gains wide acceptance. It's a perfect example of the truism that "worse is better" — people have been complaining about HTML's limitations almost since it was invented; but a technology which is better yet harder to implement, like XML, might not have so quickly acquired such a large user base.

In the meantime, XML must be transformed into HTML on the server side. It is possible to do this using XSL itself, but so far relatively few sites have chosen this option. Among other discouraging factors, XSL transformations can only result in HTML that still meets the requirements for XML well-formedness, also known as XHTML. It's far more common at this point to use some other program, such as PHP, to translate the XML into HTML.

This data flow actually makes sense if substantial amounts of computation need to happen behind the scenes because you do not want to have a big program both performing complex operations and outputting HTML if you can possibly help it.

PHP can also read in data from a data store and write XML documents itself. This can be helpful when transferring content from one Web site to another, as in syndicating news stories. You can also use this functionality to help non-technical users produce well-formed XML documents with a Web-form front-end. At the moment, writing XML might well be the most common category of XML-related PHP task.

Finally, data is beginning to be manipulated and exchanged across human and non-human endpoints via the Internet itself. This technology is called "Web services," and it is the subject of Chapter 32.

Documents and DTDs

As we explained earlier, the requirements for a well-formed XML document are fairly minimal. However, XML documents have another possible level of "goodness," which is called *validity*. A valid XML document is one that conforms to certain stated rules that together are known as a *document type definition*, or *DTD*.

To get in the mood to understand the value of DTDs, imagine that you are the head of an open source project that exists to make books and other documents freely available in electronic form on the Internet. You're very excited about XML from the moment you learn about it because it seems to meet your need for a data exchange format that can adapt easily to new display technologies as they evolve. Your group members vote to encode all the project's books and documents in XML, and soon the XMLized documents start to pour in.

But when you look at the first couple of submissions, you get a rude shock. One of them is in the same format as Listing 31-1, earlier in this chapter; but one of them looks like what you see in Listing 31-2:

Listing 31-2: A book in XML format

```
<?xml version="1.0"?>
<book title="PHP4 Bible">
 <publisher name="Wiley Publishing"/>
 <chapter number="31">
  <chapter_title>PHP and XML</chapter_title>
  <p>
    <sentence>If you know HTML, you're most of the way to understanding
XML.</sentence>
    <sentence>They are both markup languages, but XML is more structured
than HTML.</sentence>
  </p>
 </chapter>
</book>
```

The two XML files express similar, but not identical, hierarchical structures using similar but not identical tags. This is the potential downside of the self-defined markup tags that XML enables: random variation that makes it difficult to match up similar kinds of information across files. You quickly realize that you will need to implement some rules about what kinds of information should be in a book file and what the relationships between these elements will be. You've just realized you need a DTD.

A document type definition, or DTD, describes the structure of a class of XML documents. A DTD is a kind of formal constraint, guaranteeing that all documents of its type will conform to stated structural rules and naming conventions. A DTD enables you to specify exactly what elements are *allowed*, how elements are *related*, what *type* each element is, and a *name* for each element. DTDs also specify what attributes are required or optional, and their default values. You could of course just write down these rules in a text file:

```
The top-level object of this document is a BOOK
A BOOK has one and only one TABLE OF CONTENTS
A BOOK has one and only one TITLE
A BOOK is composed of multiple CHAPTERS
CHAPTERS have one and only one CHAPTERTITLE
All CHAPTERTITLEs are listed in the TABLE OF CONTENTS
etc.
```

You could give a copy of the list to anyone who might need it. A DTD is just a more concise, well-defined, generally agreed upon grammar in which to do the same thing. It's a useful discipline to apply to XML documents, which can be chaotic because of their entirely self-defined nature. Furthermore, if you can get a group of people to agree on a DTD, you are well on the way to having a standard format for all information of a certain type. Many professions and industries, from mathematicians to sheet-music publishers to human-resources departments, are eager to develop such domain-specific information formats.

In our imaginary previous example, which uses XML to store books electronically, your group members may have to argue for months before hashing out the details of a DTD that perfectly describes the relationships between the table of contents, chapters, titles and headings, indexes, appendices, sections, paragraphs, forwards, epilogues, and so on. You can, of course, iterate on DTDs as frequently as necessary.

But after your DTD is finalized, you can enjoy another value-add of XML. You can now run any XML document through a so-called "validating parser" which will tell you whether it's meeting all the requirements of its DTD. So instead of a human editor having to read each electronic book submission to see whether it has the required elements and attributes in the correct relationship, you can just throw them all into a parser and let it do the formal checking. This won't tell you anything about the quality of the content in the XML document, but it will tell you whether the form meets your requirements.

Honesty compels us to admit that PHP does not (exactly) support a validating XML parser. However, you will still need to learn about the basic structure of DTDs and the XML documents they describe whether you choose to validate or not.

The structure of a DTD

A *document type definition* is a set of rules that defines the structure of a particular group of XML documents. A DTD can be either a part of the XML document itself (in which case it is an *internal DTD*); or it can located externally, in another file on the same server or at a publicly available URL anywhere on the Internet (in which case, it is an *external DTD*).

> **NOTE:** Although a DTD can be internal (part of the XML document itself), making it external (a separate file) is usually better. DTDs are meant to define a class of documents, so separating them from the XML saves you from editing every XML document of that class if you need to change the DTD later on. Because demonstrating on an internal DTD is easier for readers to follow in a book format, however, we use both as examples in this chapter.

You can start by looking at a simple XML document with an internal DTD in Listing 31-3.

Listing 31-3: An XML document with internal DTD (`recipe.xml`)

```
<?xml version="1.0"?>

<!DOCTYPE recipe [
<!ELEMENT recipe (ingredients, directions, servings)>
<!ATTLIST recipe name CDATA #REQUIRED>
<!ELEMENT ingredients (#PCDATA)>
<!ELEMENT directions (#PCDATA)>
<!ELEMENT servings (#PCDATA)>
]>

<recipe name ="Beef Burgundy">
 <ingredients>Beef</ingredients>
 <ingredients>Burgundy</ingredients>
 <directions>
 Add beef to burgundy. Serve.
 </directions>
 <servings>12</servings>
</recipe>
```

We've divided the XML document into three subsections for easier reading. The first section is the standard one-line XML declaration that should begin every XML document. The second section is the internal DTD, marked by lines beginning with the < ! sequence. The third section is the XML itself, strictly speaking. For the moment, we are focusing on the second section, the DTD. In our example, the stuff outside the square brackets is a *document type declaration* (not to be confused with *document type definition*): < !DOCTYPE recipe [...]>. The document type declaration gives information about the DTD this document is using. Because this is an internal DTD, we simply give the name of the root element (recipe) and then include the rest of the definition within square brackets. If you are using an external DTD, however, you use the document type declaration to state the type and location of the DTD. Two example document type declarations referring to external DTDs are as follows:

```
<!DOCTYPE recipe SYSTEM "recipe.dtd">
<!DOCTYPE HTML PUBLIC "-//W3C//DTD HTML 4.01 Transitional//EN"
"http://www.w3.org/TR/html4/loose.dtd">
```

External document type declarations give a root element name, the type (SYSTEM, meaning on the server, or PUBLIC, meaning a standardized DTD) and the location where it can be found. You are doubtless familiar with document type declarations because, without exception, you always include one, like the preceding example, in every single HTML or XHTML document you write — right?

The DTD proper consists of the lines inside the square brackets. These lay out the elements, element types, and attributes contained in the XML document.

♦ **Element:** A start and end tag pair — for example, `<b>` *something* `</b>` — or an empty element (`<br/>`). Elements have types and sometimes content and attributes.

♦ **Element Type:** A constraint on the content and attributes of an element. A type can be used to specify what kind of data it can contain and to specify what attributes it can have.

♦ **Attribute:** A name and value pair associated with an element, in the form `<element attributename="attributevalue">`.

In the example DTD in Listing 31-3, we've declared that our root element, `recipe`, contains three child elements — `ingredients`, `directions`, and `servings` — and has one required attribute, `name`. Each child element is of the parsed character data type, and the attribute is of the character data type.

If you wanted to split up Listing 31-3 into an XML document and an external DTD, it would look much the same, except that, instead of providing the definition in square brackets, you would give a reference to the external DTD file. The result would look like Listings 31-4 and 31-5:

Listing 31-4: An XML document with external DTD (`recipe_ext.xml`)

```
<?xml version="1.0"?>
<!DOCTYPE recipe SYSTEM "recipe.dtd">

<recipe name ="Beef Burgundy">
 <ingredients>Beef</ingredients>
 <ingredients>Burgundy</ingredients>
 <directions>
 Add beef to burgundy. Serve.
 </directions>
 <servings>12</servings>
</recipe>
```

Listing 31-5: An external DTD (`recipe.dtd`)

```
<!ELEMENT recipe (ingredients, directions, servings)>
<!ATTLIST recipe name CDATA #REQUIRED>
<!ELEMENT ingredients (#PCDATA)>
<!ELEMENT directions (#PCDATA)>
<!ELEMENT servings (#PCDATA)>
```

Because the XML used in both examples conforms to the internal and external DTDs, both documents should be declared valid by a validating parser.

You could learn a lot more about the specifics of DTDs and XML documents, but these basics should enable you to understand most of PHP's XML functions.

Validating and nonvalidating parsers

XML parsers come in two flavors: *validating* and *nonvalidating*. Nonvalidating parsers care only that an XML document is well formed — that it obeys all the rules for closing tags, quotation marks, and so on. Validating parsers require well-formed documents as well, but they also check the XML document against a DTD. If the XML document doesn't conform to its DTD, the validating parser outputs specific error messages explaining what has gone wrong.

PHP 4's SAX parser, `expat`, is nonvalidating. That doesn't mean that you should ignore DTDs. Going through the process of creating a DTD for each of your document types is a good design practice. It forces you to think out the document structure very carefully. And if your documents ever need to go through a validating parser, you're covered. In fact, many experts recommend that you put all XML documents through a validating parser even if you never plan to use one again.

Most validating parsers are written in Java and are a pain to set up and use. The easiest way to validate your XML is to use an online validator. A well-known one is the STG validator at the following URL:

`www.stg.brown.edu/service/xmlvalid`

Actually, using Gnome `libxml` to validate an XML document is possible — but it takes some work. Examples of validation using C are on the `libxml` Web site (at `www.xmlsoft.org`).

SAX versus DOM

There are two common APIs for handling XML and XML documents: the *Document Object Model* (DOM) and the *Simple API for XML* (SAX). PHP 4 has one module for each API. The SAX module is now included by default in all PHP distributions; the DOM XML module is optional.

You can use either API to parse and change an XML document. To create or extend an XML document entirely through the PHP interface (in other words, without writing any of it by hand), you must use the DOM. Each API has advantages and disadvantages.

SAX

SAX is much more lightweight and easier to learn, but it basically treats XML as flowthrough string data. So if, for instance, you want to parse a recipe, you could whip up a SAX parser in PHP, which might enable you to boldify the ingredient list. Adding a completely new element or attribute would be very difficult, however; and even changing the value of one particular ingredient would be laborious.

SAX is very good for repetitive tasks that can be applied to all elements of a certain type — for instance, replacing a particular element tag with HTML tags as a step toward transforming

XML into HTML for display. The SAX parser passes through a document once from top to bottom — so it cannot "go back" and do things based on inputs later in the document.

DOM

.PHP's DOM extension reads in an XML file and creates a "walkable" object tree in memory. Starting with a document or an element of a document (called *nodes* in the DOM), you can get or set the children, parents, and text content of each part of the tree. You can save DOM objects to containers as well as write them out as text. DOM XML works best if you have a complete XML document available. If your XML is streaming in very slowly or you want to treat many different XML snippets as sections of the same document, you want to use SAX. Because the DOM extension builds a tree in memory, it can be quite the resource hog with large documents.

DOM

The Document Object Model is a complete API for creating, editing, and parsing XML documents. The DOM is a recommendation of the World Wide Web Consortium. You can read all about it in the W3's inimitable prose, at:

```
www.w3.org/DOM/
```

Basically the idea is that every XML document can be viewed as a hierarchy of nodes resembling leaves on a tree. Starting with the root element, of which all other elements can be expressed as children, any program should be able to build a representation of the structure of a document. Attributes and character data can also be attached to elements. This "tree" can be read into memory from an XML file, manipulated by PHP, and written out to another XML file, or stored in a container.

The parser behind the scenes in PHP's DOM extension is *gnome-libxml* (a.k.a. Gnome *libxml*), which is supposedly less memory-intensive than others. This is available at the following Web site:

```
www.xmlsoft.org
```

DOM XML is the only entirely object-oriented API in PHP, so some familiarity with object-oriented programming helps when using it. However, there are a limited number of objects and methods, so you do not need any particularly deep knowledge of Object-Oriented Programming to use DOM XML.

Using DOM XML

How you use the DOM will depend on your goals, but these steps are common:

1. Open a new DOM XML document, or read one into memory.
2. Manipulate the document by nodes.

3. Write out the resulting XML into a string or file. This also frees the memory used by the parser.

The simple example in Listing 31-6 shows some basic DOM XML functions in use.

Listing 31-6: A simple DOM XML example (`dom_example.php`)

```php
<?php
$doc = domxml_new_doc("1.0");
$root = $doc->create_element("HTML");
$root = $doc->append_child($root);
$body = $doc->create_element("BODY");
$body = $root->append_child($body);
$body->set_attribute("bgcolor", "#87CEEB");
$graff = $doc->create_element("P");
$graff = $body->append_child($graff);
$text = $doc->create_text_node("This is some text.");
$text = $graff->append_child($text);
$doc->dump_file("test_dom.xml", false, true);
?>
```

DOM functions

Table 31-1 lists the most common DOM functions. You must call one of these functions before you can use any of the other DOM XML functions!

> **CAUTION:** The DOM XML functions changed considerably in PHP 4.3.0. Functions that worked in previous versions may have been deprecated.

Table 31-1: DOM XML Top-Level Function Summary

Function	Behavior
`domxml_open_mem(string)`	Takes a string containing an XML document as an argument. This function parses the document and creates a Document object.
`domxml_open_file(filename)`	Takes a string containing an XML file as an argument. This function parses the file and creates a Document object.
`domxml_xmltree(string)`	Takes a string containing an XML document as an argument. Creates a tree of PHP objects and returns a DOM object. *Note:* The object tree returned by this function is read-only.
`domxml_new_doc(version)`	Creates a new, empty XML document in memory. Returns a Document object.

Table 31-2 lists the most important classes of the DOM API.

Table 31-2: XML DOM Class Summary

Class	Behavior
Document	This class encapsulates an XML document. It contains the root element and a DTD if any.
Node	Encapsulates a node, a.k.a. an element. A node can be the root element or any element within it. Nodes can contain other nodes, character data, and attributes.
Attribute	This class encapsulates a node attribute. An *attribute* is a user-defined quality of the node.

Table 31-3 lists the most important methods of the Document class.

Table 31-3: Document Class Summary

Method	Behavior
create_element(*na me*)	Creates a new element whose tag is the passed string. You must append this element to another element using DomNode->append_child().
create_text_node(*character_data*)	Creates a new text node (DomText object). You must append this node to another node using DomNode->append_child();
dump_file(*filenam e [, compressionmode, format]*)	Dumps XML from memory to a designated file. Optional second parameter is a Boolean designating compression or not; optional third parameter is a Boolean designating whether output should be neatly formatted or not.
dump_mem([*format*])	Dumps XML from memory to a string. Optional parameter is a Boolean designating whether output should be neatly formatted or not.

Table 31-4 lists the most important methods of the Node class.

Table 31-4: Node Class Summary

Method	Behavior
append_child(newn ode)	Attaches a node to another node.
attributes()	Returns an associative array of attribute names and their values.
child_nodes()	Returns a complete list of the node's children.
get_content()	Returns content of the node; for instance, character data.
parent_node()	Returns the node's parent node or false if this node is the root node.
remove_child(chil d)	Removes the child node.

Table 31-5 lists the most important methods of the Attribute class.

Table 31-5: Attribute Class Summary

Method	Behavior
name()	Returns an attribute name.
value()	Returns the value of an attribute.

SAX

The Simple API for XML is widely used to parse XML documents. It is an event-based API, which means that the parser calls designated functions after it recognizes a certain trigger in the event stream.

SAX has an interesting history, especially in contrast to the DOM. The SAX API is not shepherded by an official standardizing body. Instead, it was hammered out by a group of programmers on the XML-DEV mailing list, many of whom had already implemented their own XML parsers (in Java first!) without a standard API. You can learn more at the Web sites of SAX team members, such as the following site:

```
www.saxproject.org
```

SAX works from a number of *event hooks* supplied by you via PHP. As the parser goes through an XML document, it recognizes pieces of XML such as elements, character data, and external entities. Each of these is an event. If you have supplied the parser with a function to call for the particular kind of event, it pauses to call your function after it reaches that event. The parsed data associated with an event is made available to the called function. After the event-handling function finishes, the SAX parser continues through the document, calling functions on events, until it reaches the end. This process is unidirectional from beginning to end of the document — the parser cannot back up or loop.

A very simple example is an event hook that directs PHP to recognize the XML element `<paragraph></paragraph>` and substitute the HTML tags `<p></p>` around the character data. If you wrote this event hook, you could not specify a particular paragraph — instead, the function is called for every instance of this event.

The parser behind the scenes in the PHP SAX extension is James Clark's `expat`, a widely used (and supposedly the world's fastest) XML parser toolkit. More information about expat can be found on Clark's Web site:

```
www.jclark.com/xml/
```

The expat parser is now included, by default, in all versions of PHP.

> **CAUTION:** Unfortunately, the term *parser* can refer either to a software library such as `expat`, or to a block of XML-handling functions in PHP. Verbs such as *create* and *call* indicate the latter, more specific meaning. Any PHP XML function that uses the term *parser* also refers to the latter meaning.

Using SAX

How you use the SAX will depend on your goals, but these steps are common:

1. Determine what kinds of events you want to handle.
2. Write handler functions for each event. You almost certainly want to write a character data handler, plus start element and end element handlers.
3. Create a parser by using xml_parser_create() and then call it by using xml_parse().
4. Free the memory used up by the parser by using xml_parser_free().

The simple example in Listing 31-7 shows all the basic XML functions in use.

Listing 31-7: A simple XML parser (`simpleparser.php`)

```php
<?php
$file = "recipe.xml";

// Call this at the beginning of every element
function startElement($parser, $name, $attrs) {
```

```
    print "<B>$name =></B>  ";
}

// Call this at the end of every element
function endElement($parser, $name) {
    print "\n";
}

// Call this whenever there is character data
function characterData($parser, $value) {
    print "$value<BR>";
}

// Define the parser
$simpleparser = xml_parser_create();
xml_set_element_handler($simpleparser, "startElement", "endElement");
xml_set_character_data_handler($simpleparser, "characterData");

// Open the XML file for reading
if (!($fp = fopen($file, "r"))) {
  die("could not open XML input");
}

// Parse it
while ($data = fread($fp, filesize($file))) {
if (!xml_parse($simpleparser, $data, feof($fp))) {
  die(xml_error_string(xml_get_error_code($simpleparser)));
  }
}

// Free memory
xml_parser_free($simpleparser);
?>
```

SAX options

The XML parser in the SAX API has two configurable options: one for case folding and the other for target encoding.

Case folding is the residue of a series of past decisions and may not be relevant now that XML has been definitely declared case sensitive. Early versions of SGML and HTML were not case sensitive and, therefore, employed case folding (making all characters upper- or lowercase during parsing) as a means of getting a uniform result to compare. This is how your browser could tell match up a <P> tag with a </p> tag. Case folding fell out of favor due to problems with internationalization, so after much debate XML was declared case sensitive. When case folding is enabled, node names passed to event handlers are turned into all uppercase characters. A node named mynode would be received as MYNODE. When case folding is disabled, a <paragraph> tag will not match a </PARAGRAPH> closing tag.

> **NOTE:** Case folding is enabled by default, which violates the XML 1.0 specification. Unless you disable it by using `xml_parser_set_option() as explained below,` your event handlers receive tags in uppercase letters.

Event handlers receive text data from the XML parser in one of three encodings: *ISO-8859-1, US-ASCII,* or *UTF-8.* The default is ISO-8859-1. The encoding of text passed to event handlers is known as the *target encoding.* This is by default the same encoding as in the source document, which is known as the *source encoding.* You can change the target encoding if you need to process the text in an encoding other than the encoding it was stored in.

> **NOTE:** Computer programs store letters as integers, which they convert back to letters according to *encodings.* Early programs used English, which conveniently needs only one byte (actually only seven bits) to represent all the common letters and symbols. This encoding standard was promulgated in 1968 as ASCII (*American Standard Code for Information Interchange*).
>
> However, programmers soon found that English has an unusually small number of characters, and thus the only languages that can be expressed with any completeness in ASCII are Hawaiian, Kiswahili, Latin, and American English. Ever since then, programmers concerned with internationalization have tried to promote encoding standards that promise to assign a unique integer to every one of the letters of every one of the world's alphabetical languages. The result of this effort is referred to as *Unicode.*
>
> The three encodings supported by PHP's XML extension are *ISO-8859-1, US-ASCII,* and *UTF-8.* US-ASCII is the simplest of these, a slight renaming of the original 7-bit ASCII set. *ISO-8859-1* is also known as the Latin1, Western, or Western European encoding. It can represent almost all western European languages adequately. *UTF-8* allows the use of up to 6 bytes to represent as many of the world's languages as possible. If your XML document is written in Han-gul or Zulu, you have no choice but to use UTF-8.

These options are retrieved and set with the functions `xml_parser_get_option()` and `xml_parser_set_option()`. Case folding is controlled by using the constant `XML_OPTION_CASE_FOLDING`, and target encoding by using the constant `XML_OPTION_TARGET_ENCODING`.

In the following example, we create an XML parser that reads in data as ASCII, turns off case folding, and then spits out the output as UTF-8.

```php
$new_parser = xml_parser_create('US-ASCII');
$case_folding = xml_parser_get_option(XML_OPTION_CASE_FOLDING);
echo $case_folding;
$change_folding = xml_parser_set_option($new_parser,
XML_OPTION_CASE_FOLDING,0);

$target_encoding = xml_parser_get_option(XML_TARGET_ENCODING);
echo $target_encoding;
$change_encoding = xml_parser_set_option($new_parser,
XML_OPTION_TARGET_ENCODING, 'UTF-8');
```

SAX functions

Table 31-6 lists the most important SAX functions, with descriptions of what they do.

Table 31-6: XML SAX Function Summary

Function	Behavior
xml_parser_create([enc oding])	This function creates a new XML parser instance. You may have several distinct parsers at any time. The return value is an XML parser or false on failure. Takes one optional argument, a character-encoding identifier (such as UTF-8). If no encoding is supplied, ISO-8859-1 is assumed.
xml_parser_free(parser)	Frees the memory associated with a parser created by xml_parser_create().
xml_parse(parser, data[, final])	This function starts the XML parser. Its arguments are a parser created by using xml_parser_create(), a string containing XML, and an optional finality flag. The finality flag indicates that this is the last piece of data handled by this parser.
xml_get_error_code(par ser)	If the parser has encountered a problem, its parse fails. Call this function to find out the error code.
xml_error_string(error code)	Given an error code returned by xml_get_error_code(), it returns a string containing a description of the error suitable for logging.
xml_set_element_handle r(parser, start_element_handler, end_element_handler)	This function actually sets two handlers, which are simply functions. The first is a start-of-element handler, which has access to the name of the element and an associative array of its elements. The second is an end-of-element handler, at which time the element is fully parsed.
xml_set_character_data _handler(parser, cd_handler)	Sets the handler function to call whenever character data is encountered. The handler function takes a string containing the character data as an argument.
xml_set_default_handle r(parser, handler)	Sets the default handler. If no handler is specified for an event, the default handler is called if it is specified. Takes as arguments the parser and a string containing unhandled data, such as a notation declaration or an external entity reference.

A Sample XML Application

This series of scripts will write out XML to a file by using data from an HTML form, and then will allow you to edit the values in that file.

Listing 31-8 is an HTML form that can be used by non-technical users to define forms. They don't need to care that this data will be formatted and stored in XML. Listing 31-9 is a script to write out the XML file.

Listing 31-8: A form to collect values for an XML file (`pollform.php`)

```
<HTML>
<HEAD>
<TITLE>Make-a-poll</TITLE>
</HEAD>

<BODY>
<CENTER><H3>Make-a-poll</H3></CENTER>

<P>Use this form to define a poll:</P>
<FORM METHOD="post" ACTION="writepoll.php">

<P>Give this poll a <B>short</B> name, like <FONT COLOR="red">Color
Poll</FONT>.<BR>
<INPUT TYPE=TEXT NAME="PollName" SIZE=30>
</P>

<P>This poll should <B>begin</B> on this date (MM/DD/YYYY):
<INPUT TYPE=TEXT Name="Poll_Startdate" SIZE=10>
</P>

<P>This poll should <B>end</B> on this date (MM/DD/YYYY):
<INPUT TYPE=TEXT NAME="Poll_Enddate" SIZE=10>
</P>

<P>This is the poll question (<FONT COLOR="blue">e.g. Why did the
chicken cross the road?</FONT>):
<INPUT TYPE=TEXT NAME="Poll_Question", size=100>
</P>

<P>These are the potential answer choices you want to offer (<FONT
COLOR="darkgreen">e.g. Yes, No, Say what?</FONT>).  Fill in only as many
as you need.  Keep in mind that brevity is the soul of good poll-
making.<BR>
<INPUT TYPE=TEXT NAME="Raw_Poll_Option[]" SIZE=25><BR>
<INPUT TYPE=TEXT NAME="Raw_Poll_Option[]" SIZE=25><BR>
<INPUT TYPE=TEXT NAME="Raw_Poll_Option[]" SIZE=25><BR>
<INPUT TYPE=TEXT NAME="Raw_Poll_Option[]" SIZE=25><BR>
<INPUT TYPE=TEXT NAME="Raw_Poll_Option[]" SIZE=25><BR>
```

```
<INPUT TYPE=TEXT NAME="Raw_Poll_Option[]" SIZE=25><BR>
</P>

<INPUT TYPE="submit" NAME="Submit" VALUE="Add a poll">
</FORM>

</BODY>
</HTML>
```

Listing 31-9: A script to write out an XML file (`writepoll.php`)

```
<html>
<head>
<title>Write an XML file</title>
</head>

<body>
<?php

$pollfile = "poll.xml";



// Reading in the xml file as a string
$fd = fopen($pollfile, "r") or die("Can't open file.");
$fstr = fread($fd, filesize($pollfile)) or die("Can't read file, check
permissions.");
fclose($fd);

// Format response sets.
$PollName = str_replace("\'", "", $PollName);
$PollName = str_replace(" ", "_", $PollName);

for ($r=0; $r<=5; $r++) {
  if (!empty($Raw_Poll_Option[$r])) {
    $Poll_Option[$r] = "$PollName-".str_replace("'", "",
$Raw_Poll_Option[$r]);
    $Poll_Option[$r] = "$PollName-".str_replace(" ", "_",
$Raw_Poll_Option[$r]);
    $RespSet .= "\t<response
id=\"$Poll_Option[$r]\">$Raw_Poll_Option[$r]</response>\n";
  }



}

//Add new poll data
```

```
$separator = "</PollList>";
$divide = explode($separator, $fstr);
$glue =
"\t<Poll name=\"$PollName\"/>
</PollList>

<Poll id=\"$PollName\">
\t<StartDate>$Poll_Startdate</StartDate>
\t<EndDate>$Poll_Enddate</EndDate>
\t<name>$PollName</name>
\t<text>$Poll_Question</text>
\t<display type=\"Bar-Graph\"/>
\t<responseSet resource=\"$PollName-responseSet\"/>
</Poll>

<responseSet id=\"$PollName-responseSet\">
$RespSet</responseSet>
";


$newxml = implode($glue, $divide);

//Write to file
$fd = fopen($pollfile, "w") or die("Can't open file for writing; check
file permissions");
$writestr = fwrite($fd, $newxml);

//Message
echo "Wrote $writestr chars to $pollfile.";
?>

</body>
</html>
```

Listing 31-10 shows the XML file where our polls are stored, with one poll already defined for you. If you add a new poll, it will be appended near the top of this file and its name will be added to the PollList.

Listing 31-10: An XML file (poll.xml)

```
<?xml version="1.0"?>

<PollDefs>
<PollList id="default-PollList">
  <Poll name="Best_Text_Editor" />
</PollList>

<Poll id="Best_Text_Editor">
```

```
<StartDate>09/01/2002</StartDate>
<EndDate>10/01/2002</EndDate>
<name>Best Text Editor</name>
<text>Which is the best programmer's editor</text>
<display type="Bar-Graph"/>
<responseSet resource="Best_Text_Editor-responseSet"/>
</Poll>

<responseSet id="Best_Text_Editor-responseSet">
<response id="Best_Text_Editor-emacs">emacs</response>
<response id="Best_Text_Editor-vi">vim</response>
<response id="Best_Text_Editor-notepad">notepad</response>
<response id="Best_Text_Editor-Kate">Kate</response>
<response resource="Best_Text_Editor-BBEdit">BBEdit</response>
</responseSet>

</PollDefs>
```

Listing 31-11 shows a script that will allow you to edit the XML file in Listing 31-10 using DOM XML.

Listing 31-11: XML editor (`dom_polledit.php`)

```
<html>
<head>
<title>Poll XML editor</title>
</head>

<body>
<?php

$pollfile = "poll.xml";

if ($_POST['stage'] == 1) {
  // Reading in the XML file as a DOM object
  if (!$doc = domxml_open_file($pollfile)) {
    echo "Cannot read XML file.";
    exit;
  }

  // Once a poll is created, the user will only be able to change
  // the StartDate, EndDate, Text, and response values.  We are
  // going to simply replace the node values, without taking the
  // time to figure out if anything has changed.

  // Figure out which poll we're editing
  $pollname = $_POST['poll_name'];
  $responseSet_name = $pollname.'-responseSet';
  $startdate = $_POST['Poll_Startdate'];
```

```php
    $enddate = $_POST['Poll_Enddate'];
    $question = $_POST['Poll_Question'];


    // Replace the StartDate, EndDate, and text values
    $poll_list = $doc->get_elements_by_tagname('name');
    foreach ($poll_list as $poll_obj) {
      $pollname_value = $poll_obj->get_content();
      if ($pollname_value == $pollname) {
        $poll = $poll_obj->parent_node();
        $children = $poll->child_nodes();
        foreach ($children as $key=>$child_obj) {
          $node_name = $child_obj->node_name();
          if ($node_name == "StartDate") {
            $old_startdate = $child_obj->child_nodes();
            $new_startdate = $doc->create_text_node($startdate);
            $new_startdate = $old_startdate[0]-
>replace_node($new_startdate);
          }
          if ($node_name == "EndDate") {
            $old_enddate = $child_obj->child_nodes();
            $new_enddate = $doc->create_text_node($enddate);
            $new_enddate = $old_enddate[0]->replace_node($new_enddate);
          }
          if ($node_name == "text") {
            $old_text = $child_obj->child_nodes();
            $new_text = $doc->create_text_node($question);
            $new_text = $old_text[0]->replace_node($new_text);
          }
        }
      }
    }


    // Delete the responses and add new ones
    $responseSet_list = $doc->get_elements_by_tagname('responseSet');
    foreach ($responseSet_list as $responseSet_obj) {
      $responseSetname = $responseSet_obj->attributes();
      if ($responseSetname[0]->name == "id" && $responseSetname[0]->value
== $responseSet_name) {
        $old_responses = $responseSet_obj->child_nodes();
        foreach ($old_responses as $delete_responses) {
          $delete = $responseSet_obj->remove_child($delete_responses);
        }
        foreach ($_POST['response'] as $val) {
          $resp_elem = $doc->create_element("response");
          $resp_elem = $responseSet_obj->append_child($resp_elem);
          $id_val = str_replace("'", "", $val);
          $id_val = "$pollname-".str_replace(" ", "_", $id_val);
          $resp_elem->set_attribute("id", $id_val);
          $new_response = $doc->create_text_node($val);
```

```
            $new_response = $resp_elem->append_child($new_response);
        }
    }
}

    // Write out the file
    $doc->dump_file("poll.xml", false, true);

}


// Reading in the XML file as a DOM object
// Must read fresh every time
if (!$doc = domxml_open_file($pollfile)) {
    echo "Cannot read XML file.";
    exit;
}

// Get a list of the polls in this XML document
$poll_list = $doc->get_elements_by_tagname('Poll');
foreach ($poll_list as $poll_obj) {

    // Get data for each poll
    $children = $poll_obj->child_nodes();
    foreach ($children as $key=>$child_obj) {
        $node_name = $child_obj->node_name();
        if ($node_name != "#text" && $node_name != 'responseSet') {
            $content_str = $child_obj->get_content();
            $poll_array["$node_name"] = $content_str;
        } elseif ($node_name == 'responseSet') {
            // Get the response set name, and find the matching response set
            $responseSet_name_obj = $child_obj->attributes();
            $responseSet_name = $responseSet_name_obj[0]->value();

            $responseSet_list = $doc->get_elements_by_tagname('responseSet');
            foreach ($responseSet_list as $rSl_obj) {
                $responseSet_attr = $rSl_obj->attributes();
                if ($responseSet_attr[0]->name == "id" && $responseSet_attr[0]-
>value == $responseSet_name) {
                    $response_obj = $rSl_obj->child_nodes();
                    foreach ($response_obj as $responses) {
                        $response_attr_obj = $responses->attributes();
                        $response_name = $response_attr_obj[0]->value;
                        if ($response_name != "") {
                            $response_array[] = $responses->get_content();
                        }
                    }
                }
            }
        }
```

```php
    }
  }
  // Arrange all the data nicely
  $poll_startdate = $poll_array['StartDate'];
  $poll_enddate = $poll_array['EndDate'];
  $poll_name = $poll_array['name'];
  $poll_question = $poll_array['text'];
  $poll_question = stripslashes($poll_question);
  foreach ($response_array as $key=>$val) {
    $resp_str .= "Option:  <INPUT TYPE=\"text\" SIZE=25
NAME=\"response[$key]\" VALUE=\"$val\"><BR>\n";
  }

  // Display form with old values
  $php_self = $_SERVER['PHP_SELF'];
$form = <<< EOFORM
<FORM METHOD="post" ACTION="$php_self">
Start Date:  <INPUT TYPE="text" SIZE=10 NAME="Poll_Startdate"
VALUE="$poll_startdate"><BR>
End date:  <INPUT TYPE="text" SIZE=10 NAME="Poll_Enddate"
VALUE="$poll_enddate"><BR>
Poll question:  <INPUT TYPE="text" SIZE=100 NAME="Poll_Question"
VALUE="$poll_question"><BR>
$resp_str
<INPUT TYPE="hidden" NAME="poll_name" VALUE="$poll_name">
<INPUT TYPE="hidden" NAME="stage" VALUE=1><BR>
<INPUT TYPE="submit" VALUE="Presto-chango">
</FORM>


EOFORM;
  echo $form;
  unset($resp_str);
  unset($response_array);
}
?>

</body>
</html>
```

Gotchas and Troubleshooting

The DOM and SAX parsers will only parse a well-formed XML document. If the parser rejects your XML, make sure it is well formed. If it looks good to your eye, run it through a different validating parser or an online XML checker, such as the one at http://www.xml.com/xml/pub/tools/ruwf/check.html.

If you cannot read and write XML documents to disk, check that the Web server process has permission to do so.

If the DOM API returns a fatal *function not found* error, the DOM XML module may not be installed. Use the `phpinfo()` function to check for a `domxml` entry. If it isn't there, you will have to recompile PHP with the DOM XML module (on Unix) or uncomment the `php_domxml.dll` line in `php.ini` (on Windows).

The DOM API is new in PHP 4, and substantially changed in PHP 4.3.0, so all the kinks may not be worked out yet. Keep this in mind and check the bug databases if you encounter problems.

```
http://bugs.php.net/
```

Remember that you're supposed to make a strenuous effort to search the mailing-list archives before you search the bugs database. Please make sure that your problem is really a bug and has not been resolved before filing it as a bug. If any doubt is in your mind, read the "Dos and Don'ts" document attached to the bugs database.

Summary

XML is an application-independent data-exchange format that promises to make Web development faster and easier in the future. XML and HTML are both descended from SGML, accounting for their close resemblance at first glance. Both have tags and attributes, although XML's are self-defined and structured whereas HTML's are defined by the HTML standard and contain no information about document structure.

XML has only a few minimal requirements for well-formedness. These include closed tags, no overlapping tags, escaped special characters, and the presence of a single root element for each document. XML can also be valid, however, in the sense of conforming to a formal declaration of its structure in a document type definition or DTD. DTDs can be internal or external to the XML document and even located on another server. They contain declarations of the type, attributes, and names of the various elements within the XML file.

For the present, few prefabricated tools are available to help you write, edit, and display XML. You can use one of the two PHP XML APIs, SAX or DOM, to write your own tools. The two APIs have different tradeoffs and uses. SAX is an event-based parser, whereas DOM XML creates an object tree in memory.

At the moment, PHP with the SAX extension can be used to write out well-formed XML from values entered into a Web form, and to edit XML documents. DOM XML can be used to create complete XML documents programmatically. The SAX parser is also commonly employed to transform XML into HTML for less problematic display in current Web browsers. Another possible task for PHP's XML extensions is to pull data from a data store and write it out as XML for exchange with another organization.

Chapter 32
Web Services

In This Chapter

♦ The end of programming as we know it

♦ REST, XML-RPC, SOAP, .NET

♦ Current issues with Web services

♦ Project: A REST client

♦ Project: A SOAP server and client

Web services is an emerging field of programming that may threaten to turn traditional programming upside down. PHP, which has already proven itself as a core "glue" component of the Web, has the opportunity to grab even more market share in the Web services arena. As is true of other hot technologies such as XML and Java, however, a world of hype surrounds Web services. Here we try to cut through the buzzwords and analyst predictions to look at what Web services means to the average PHP developer.

The End of Programming As We Know It

The title of this section is a bit of a joke — one of us works in the Web services field and often hears presentations that assert things such as: "In 10 years, we will have no more need for programmers because Web services will eliminate duplication of effort." Many people have thought that programming was about to die out, and all of them have been wrong so far — but hope springs eternal in the pundit's breast. Notching down the hyperbole to manageable levels, we can say that Web services could make some common but hard tasks in commercial computer programming a lot easier.

The ugly truth about data munging

Joking aside, Web services do solve some problems, at the moment largely in the realm of moving data around. Later in this chapter, for example, we offer code for a client to the Amazon Associates REST service. This code enables you to grab the latest data about a given product or group of products — photos, current prices, availability, and so on — several times a day via an automatic process.

If you're a first-time author who has a small informational site with one link to Amazon, this isn't really going to help you much. But there are Amazon Associates who link to thousands or even millions of products. They do so now by horrible hacks involving downloading all those Web pages and using some kind of string or XPATH parsing to pick out the three or four pieces of data they want from each page. Furthermore, each client organization now must do all this work for itself — because, among other things, this is a totally unauthorized use of Amazon's copyrighted material, so they can hardly expect Amazon to help them. Harvesting data from full HTML pages is tremendously wasteful and expensive for both Amazon and the Associate — so much so that it's a good way to get banned from Amazon altogether. Slamming the door on requests from a particular IP block is almost the only way to control access to a public Web server.

Even if an organization wants to give you large amounts of information in a data feed, the mechanics right now are not very elegant. We are aware of many large and well-respected data-related businesses who move data around in text files (or spreadsheets) that are downloaded via some mechanism such as FTP (or email) and parsed on both ends by custom Perl code (or by hand). Often there is no way to send only data that has changed — the feeds are dumped out and processed in a dumb way every so often, rather than updating only if and when changes occur. Obviously, these are all batch processes, which have no possibility of working in real-time. XML-based Web services promise to offer a common language, a common transport mechanism, a common authentication and authorization method, and potentially common code for organizations to access Amazon's data.

If Web services were just about moving data around, the idea would be extremely useful but not at all sexy. What excites everyone about Web services is the promise that it can help solve the hardest problems of distributed computing once and for all.

Brutal simplicity

Think back, if you can, to the bad old days before the Web. If you can go back far enough, think back to the days when the Internet itself was a rarity and networking something limited to high-end universities (it may help to remember that for a long time one of Apple's selling points in college computer labs was AppleTalk).

Back in those dark days, my children, things such as operating systems and programming languages were major barriers to integration — they were little islands in the sea of incompatibility. If you were going to write an application, you were specifically writing it for a particular platform and language — sometimes even for a particular version of a compiler. It was very, very hard to make one program talk to another program. If you wrote a COBOL program on a VAX, that was where it was going to stay. With a great deal of effort you could get one program to send something simple, such as ASCII data, to another — but any little thing could mess up your interapp communication. If you changed anything on one side, it might mean that you had to change a bunch of stuff on the other side, too. These programs were said to be *tightly coupled*.

This meant a lot of duplication of effort. Porting was technically difficult, and the market was fragmented. So a team that wrote an application — say an accounting program — for Minicomputer X was not necessarily going to have the resources to do the same for Microcomputer Y. Lots of teams wrote lots of accounting programs, and all the formats were proprietary. None of them could exchange data with each other, much less share tasks easily.

Slowly, mankind groped toward a way to make programs talk to each other. The blanket term for this activity was *distributed computing*. It took until the mid-1990s for these methods to reach the common programmer, in the form of standards such as DCOM, CORBA, and Java RMI. These standards enabled all programs that shared a common architecture to call each other's methods and send data back and forth. When you are able to embed a spreadsheet inside a word processor document, it's via the magic of DCOM.

These common object models, however, had three major problems. They were still more or less tied to particular platforms or programming languages; they were considered difficult to learn; and they reached general usability at the same moment that the Web arrived to tantalize us with the possibility of Internet-scale loosely coupled, distributed computing based on open standards.

The Web is the biggest, most open, most loosely coupled — and most successful — distributed architecture of all time. With few exceptions, no Web server cares which Web browser is asking it for a page, or what operating system that browser is running on, or what chip is running the hardware on which that operating system lives. The application asking for the page doesn't even need to be a browser — it may be a spider from a search engine, it may be an `fopen()` call from a PHP command-line script, or it may be a cellular phone. The HTML it sends may not render nicely on every device, but that has nothing to do with whether Apache or IIS is serving up the page.

There are a lot of reasons why the World Wide Web has taken off as it has, but one of them is certainly a factor that computer scientists semi-affectionately refer to as "worse is better." This philosophy, which exists in contrast to the lofty perfectionism of "the right thing," means that in many circumstances it is the very junkiness of a thing that leads to its success. Certainly if all HTML had been forced to meet the standards of well-formedness that some Web pundits now want to impose, the Web would still be the province of a few physicists trying to distribute their academic papers via plain grey home pages. On a more fundamental level, HTTP and other Internet protocols grew on the back of TCP/IP — which itself is a notoriously "worse is better" design. TCP/IP never guarantees you an entire message in a timely manner. It tries really hard to make that happen, via methods such as replication — but we're just going to say that one of us once got an email two and a half years after it was sent.

Applying the lessons of the Web to applications, you come up with something quite a lot like Web services. The beauty of Web services is its brutal simplicity, which squashes everything down to a lowest common denominator. A Web services architecture doesn't care about the benefits of any particular platform, and it doesn't care about the pitfalls. Those are your problems. All that matters to the outside world is that a program can send and receive text messages across HTTP or SMTP, and that these text messages can trigger computational actions.

An archetypal Web service would be something like a Japanese-to-English translation service. It lives somewhere on the Internet, on some unknown platform and is written in some unknown programming language. You don't need to know or care about that stuff. All you care about is that your browser or your mail client knows that you only read English — so every time you get a Web page or an email in Japanese, these applications automatically send their contents to this translation service and then display the translated results to you. You don't ever see or care that part of the processing is happening at some remote location — to you, the end user, it just looks as though your application is handling it seamlessly.

of effort. Instead of your Web browser using Babelfish to translate Japanese to English, and your mail client having a little built-in dictionary, and your local department store's inventory management system using a third-party program that runs only on Solaris — all of them can just call this translation Web service.

Web services should also enable much easier integration. Say that you work for a university alumni office, which is still using an alumni database written in COBOL on a VAX. (You may laugh, but Y2K wouldn't have been such a big deal if there weren't so many legacy systems lying around.) It works perfectly well, and you don't have budget to replace it — but those VAX terminals are getting old. It would sure be great if you could query your alumni database via an ordinary Web browser — but there's no way you're ever going to be able to squeeze a full Web server onto that old VAX, even if someone wrote one. With Web services, if you can get the VAX to understand just a little bit of XML and spit out its data as XML, you're all set. You can exchange instructions and data via XML by using some other machine that does have a Web server, and that other machine can communicate with the rest of the world. Someday when you are ready to replace that VAX with a newer machine and a different programming language, no one need ever know. As long as the service is reachable at the same address by using the same method invocations, it doesn't matter whether it's a VAX or a PC, whether the application was written in COBOL or whether it's just a thin shell of PHP on top of a database.

Integration between businesses particularly benefits the smaller parties involved. Web services are easy to implement because corporate firewalls already have holes punched through them for HTTP and SMTP and because they can be implemented by using inexpensive software such as PHP. Say that you run a small business that makes widgets. You want your widgets distributed by a large retailer, Humongous Widget Depot. Until recently, for you (and the gazillions of other manufacturers who supply goods to Humongous Widget Depot) to provide real-time inventory information to the retailer entailed tremendous expense as you bought a large software package such as SAP and integrated it on a private network. Now, in theory, each small manufacturer can merely expose its inventory information via a Web service, and Humongous Widget Depot's humongous IT department merely points a Web services client at them.

That, in a nutshell, is the dream and the promise of Web services. We are quite a way from the actuality, but the outlines of a solution are firming up.

REST, XML-RPC, SOAP, .NET

For Web services to work, every application and many servers need to speak a common language. Everyone agrees that the common language is XML, but there are some philosophical differences about the implementation details. The three main Web services standards are *REST*, *XML-RPC*, and *SOAP*.

REST

REST is an acronym for *RE*presentational *S*tate *T*ransfer. The concept is based on a dissertation by Roy Fielding, and its main point is that we already have everything we need to implement Web services — in HTTP itself. So all REST services must be reachable by normal URIs, and they return XML without any special coded wrapping. For all intents and purposes, a REST service is just an XML page on the Web, although usually not one that is intended to be read by a human being using a browser.

REST is particularly valuable for content-focused services. You can build an XML document on-the-fly, and your users can access it reliably as a URI. In theory, REST should also be easier for lightly technical users to deal with. On the other hand, REST doesn't have built-in support for complex types — because there's no shared "vocabulary," there's no particular way to designate an array versus a string.

You can learn more about REST at the RESTWiki:

```
http://internet.conveyor.com/RESTwiki/moin.cgi/FrontPage
```

and at the Website of Paul Prescod, REST's most tireless promotor:

```
www.prescod.net
```

XML-RPC

XML-RPC refers to a spec for making remote procedure calls over HTTP by using XML encoding. An XML-RPC server takes an input that consists of a simple XML encoding of a method call sent as an HTTP POST. An example is as follows:

```
POST /xmlrpc-epi/xmlrpc-php-epi/sample/server.php HTTP/1.0
User-Agent: xmlrpc-epi-php/0.2 (PHP)
Host: localhost:80
Content-Type: text/xml
Content-Length: 191

<?xml version='1.0' encoding='iso-8859-1' ?>
<methodCall>
<methodName>greeting</methodName>
```

```
<params>
  <param>
    <value>
      <string>World</string>
    </value>
  </param>
</params>
</methodCall>
```

Assume that `greeting()` is a function that takes a string input and returns a string output consisting of the string "Hello, " prepended to the input string. It returns a response that is formatted in a similar way. An example is the following:

```
<?xml version='1.0' encoding='iso-8859-1' ?>
<methodResponse>
<params>
  <param>
    <value>
      <array>
        <data>
          <value>
            <string>Hello, World</string>
          </value>
        </data>
      </array>
    </value>
  </param>
</params>
</methodCall>
```

Notice that unlike REST, you are not simply asking for data back — you are calling a specific function on another machine. This particular function happens to simply return data, but that is entirely arbitrary — any method the server owner is willing to expose as a Web service is fair game. Also unlike REST, XML-RPC supports all PHP native types, except objects and resources, and also a couple that PHP doesn't have (structs, date-time, base-64 binary).

XML-RPC can be seen as a compromise between the complexity of SOAP and the simplicity of REST. It is so similar to SOAP, however, that it may simply be absorbed wholesale into the more vendor-friendly concept. As you will see, the PHP XML-RPC server can also deliver SOAP responses.

Learn more about XML-RPC at the following URL:

`www.xmlrpc.org`

SOAP

SOAP may or may not stand for Simple Object Access Protocol — some members of the committee dispute this — but so many people have said it now that it's become true through usage. SOAP is a proposal of the W3C, written by a committee that is largely controlled by Big Software — of the eight principal authors, four are from Microsoft, one is from Lotus, one from IBM, and two represent everyone else. This is the upside and the downside of SOAP: Adoption by other software makers has been swift since Microsoft and IBM threw their support behind SOAP; but there is the constant threat of an open standard being turned into a mechanism for vendor lock-in.

SOAP, as does XML-RPC, sends messages in XML wrappers with a fairly strict vocabulary. A SOAP request may look as follows:

```
POST /xmlrpc-epi/xmlrpc-php-epi/sample/server.php HTTP/1.0
User-Agent: xmlrpc-epi-php/0.2 (PHP)
Host: localhost:80
Content-Type: text/xml
Content-Length: 530

<?xml version='1.0' encoding=''iso-8859-1' ?>
<SOAP-ENV:Envelope
  xmlns:SOAP-ENV="http://schemas.xmlsoap.org/soap/envelope/"
  xmlns:xsi="http://www.w3.org/1999/XMLSchema-instance"
  xmlns:xsd="http://www.w3.org/1999/XMLSchema">
<SOAP-ENV:Header>
...
</SOAP-ENV:Header>
<SOAP-ENV:Body>
  <greeting>
    <xsd:string>World</xsd:string>
  </greeting>
</SOAP-ENV:Body>
</SOAP-ENV:Envelope>
```

The response may be something like the following:

```
<?xml version='1.0' encoding=''iso-8859-1' ?>
<SOAP-ENV:Envelope
  xmlns:SOAP-ENV="http://schemas.xmlsoap.org/soap/envelope/"
  xmlns:xsi="http://www.w3.org/1999/XMLSchema-instance"
  xmlns:xsd="http://www.w3.org/1999/XMLSchema">
<SOAP-ENV:Header>
...
</SOAP-ENV:Header>
<SOAP-ENV:Body>
  <greetingResponse>
    <SOAP-ENC:Array SOAP-ENC:arrayType="xsd:string[1]">
      <xsd:string>Hello, World</xsd:string>
    </SOAP-ENC:Array>
  </greetingResponse>
</SOAP-ENV:Body>
</SOAP-ENV:Envelope>
```

SOAP offers you even more data types than XML-RPC. You must, however, specify a lot more, too. Other than that, the two protocols are very similar. Obviously SOAP also enjoys greater acceptance from Big Software.

Learn more about SOAP at the following URL:

```
www.soapware.org/bdg
```

.NET services

.NET can seem to mean almost anything. Is .NET a programming language, a virtual machine, a set of Web services, a specific service for transparent user identification across the Internet, a marketing slogan — or all the preceding?

The part that we care about is .NET XML Web Services. Basically this just means that Microsoft is in the middle of a huge drive to make all Windows applications expose themselves as Web services. .NET services are implemented within the MS development framework, and they all speak SOAP.

To date the issue is that some interoperability problems have arisen with non-Microsoft clients interacting with .NET services. Interop is a big area of concern among all Web service developers, so expect much discussion and, we hope, some move by Microsoft towards a truly common standard for SOAP.

Current Issues with Web Services

By now, you're probably thinking, "Okay, if Web services is so great, why aren't we using it everywhere?" Well, there are still many issues to be worked out. Web services is in its infancy, and it is likely to be years before we live in a totally Web-serviced world.

Fat and slow

SOAP, in particular, is fat, verbose, graceless, and heavy-handed. This drives binary programmers especially crazy, accustomed as they are to apps talking to each other in compact binary formats. To a large extent, people just need to get over this; but there are still many situations where data storage, memory, and bandwidth are issues — in cellular phones, for instance.

Potentially heavy load

So far there is no standard way to cache the results of RPC calls. Even if 80 percent of your clients are asking for the exact same response and, therefore, you can't save resources —every request must handled *de novo*.

REST enables caching via all the methods by which HTML can be cached.

Standards

Before Web services can really take off, applications need to handle their results transparently. Because the Web services standards are still somewhat in flux, and there are multiple candidates with competing strengths, this has not yet happened. For smallish Web applications, it's not that big a deal if some service changes one of its API methods — but for a big app like Lotus Notes, it's a major investment of resources to transparently deal with SOAP.

Hide and seek

The ultimate goal of Web services is to have the application transparently find all the resources it needs. Say that you get an email in Japanese — your mail server or client should be smart enough to find the translation service it needs, get your document translated, and show the final result to you.

To accomplish this, we need some kind of directory system and a standard way for servers to describe themselves. WSDL and UDDI are the technologies that can make this possible. *WSDL* (*W*eb *S*ervices *D*escription *L*anguage) describes a Web service interface; while *UDDI* (*U*niversal *D*escription, *D*iscovery, and *I*ntegration) is a registry for Web services. Learn more about UDDI and WSDL respectively at the following URLs:

```
www.uddi.org
www.w3.org/TR/wsdl
```

We are a long way, however, from automatic discovery and communication by applications. In fact, many businesses that deploy Web services deliberately do so under a veil — for example, FedEx, which needed to take down its public SOAP server after it was used for fraud by crackers. Web services is growing most quickly in the realm of semi-private transactions — companies set up Web services that are only meant to be accessed by authenticated and authorized business partners.

In the meantime, if you want to play with Web services now, you can find some at the following sites:

```
www.syndic8.com (news feeds, site written in PHP!)
www.xmlrpc.com/directory/1568/services
www.xmethods.com (some of these use scraped data from copyrighted sites)
```

Who pays and how?

Ultimately, the biggest question about public Web services is: Who pays for them, and how? So far most of the Web services that you can access are things such as Weblog entries and simple currency calculators — services for which you normally would not expect to pay. Big Software's answer is to create huge private networks of Web services, similar to those of Hailstorm or the Liberty Alliance. This has serious implications for privacy and open architecture.

Unless and until Web services finds a way to pay for itself, it is likely to continue to be deployed mostly inside corporate firewalls and in nonprofit situations.

Project: A REST Client

Listing 32-1 is a basic client script for Amazon's elegantly simple REST service, which has been available to Amazon Associates since spring of 2002. You feed it a search string at the top, and it outputs a CSS-formatted box at the end containing information about the first-listed paperback edition of the book in question.

This service clearly demonstrates the biggest advantage of REST: You can work with it by using the HTTP concepts — and the PHP functions — you're already familiar with. For all intents and purposes, you are simply asking for a Web page by using `http fopen()`. It happens to be well-formed XML — but that is incidental to the transport mechanism.

We chose to parse the XML by using PHP's DOM XML extension, which so far has found relatively few real-world uses (see Chapter 31 for discussion of the DOM). Many other PHP-literate Amazon Associates have produced scripts that use other types of parsing, such as string parsing and regex, to extract the desired information — but we want to show you the power of using XML itself.

We should warn you, however, that this type of solution does not scale — DOM XML is a notorious memory hog. (We've heard credible reports that a 1,000-line XML document read into the DOM results in 1MB of memory being appropriated.) However, the Amazon Associates interface will only return 15 items max at this time, so DOM XML is an appropriate technology for this purpose.

Listing 32-1: REST client for Amazon Associates service (rest_client.php)

```php
<?php

// Get the xml
$file =
"http://rcm.amazon.com/e/cm?t=XXXXX&l=st1&search=Pollan+Botany+Desire&mo
de=books&p=102&o=1&f=xml"; //Replace X's with your Associates ID
// Or replace this entire URL with a path to am_botany.xml below
$fp = fopen($file, "r");
$xml_array = file($file);
fclose($fp);
$xml_str = implode("", $xml_array);

// Write the xml to a file
$writefile = 'am_botany.xml';
$fp2 = fopen($writefile, "w");
$fw_return = fwrite($fp2, $xml_str);
fclose($fp2);
```

```php
// Load up the xml file into memory
if (!$dom = domxml_open_file($writefile)) {
  echo "Cannot open xml file";
}


// Look for a paperback edition
$formats = $dom->get_elements_by_tagname("binding");
foreach ($formats as $format_obj) {
  $format_str = $format_obj->get_content();
  if ($format_str == 'Paperback') {
    // Get all the information for this book
    $book_array = array();
    $parent_node = $format_obj->parent_node();
    $children = $parent_node->child_nodes();
    foreach($children as $child_obj) {
      $node_name = $child_obj->node_name();
      if ($node_name != "#text") {
        $content_str = $child_obj->get_content();
        $book_array["$node_name"] = $content_str;
      }
    }
    continue;
  } else {
    // Non-paperbacks get ignored
  }
}

//print_r($book_array);
$title = $book_array['title'];
$author = $book_array['author'];
$url = $book_array['tagged_url'];
$price = $book_array['our_price'];



// Format a nice box
$box_str = <<< EONICEBOX
<HTML>
<HEAD>
<STYLE>
#content {
 float: left;
 padding: 10px;
 margin: 10px;
 background: #FFFFFF;
 border: 4px solid #008000;
 width: 400px; /* ie5win fudge begins */
 voice-family: "\"}\"";
```

```
 voice-family:inherit;
 width: 200px;
 }
html>body #content {
 width: 370px; /* ie5win fudge ends */
 }
p {
        font-family: Verdana, Arial, sans-serif;
 font-size: 12px;
 line-height: 22px;
 margin-top: 3px;
 margin-bottom: 2px;
 }

</STYLE>
</HEAD>
<BODY>
<div id="content">
<P><A HREF="$url">$title</A>
<BR>$author
<BR>$price</P>
</BODY>
</HTML>
EONICEBOX;
echo $box_str;
?>
```

Those of you who do not have Amazon Associates accounts can use Listing 32-2 for testing, which you should save as am_botany.xml somewhere under your Web tree.

Listing 32-2: XML sample (am_botany.xml)

```
<?xml version="1.0" encoding="ISO-8859-1"?>
<!DOCTYPE catalog [<!ENTITY pound "£">]>
<catalog>

<keyword>Pollan+Botany+Desire</keyword>
<product_group>Books</product_group>

<product>
   <ranking>1</ranking>
   <title>The Botany of Desire: A Plant's-Eye View of the World</title>
   <asin>0375760393</asin>
   <author>Pollan, Michael</author>

<image>http://images.amazon.com/images/P/0375760393.01.MZZZZZZZ.jpg</ima
ge>
```

```
<small_image>http://images.amazon.com/images/P/0375760393.01.TZZZZZZZ.jp
g </small_image>
   <our_price>$9.72</our_price>
   <list_price>$13.95</list_price>
   <release_date>20020528</release_date>
   <binding>Paperback</binding>
   <availability> </availability>
   <tagged_url>
http://www.amazon.com:80/exec/obidos/redirect?tag=XXXXX&amp;creative=944
1&amp;camp=1793&amp;link_code=xml&amp;path=ASIN/0375760393</tagged_url>
</product>
<product>
   <ranking>2</ranking>
   <title>The Botany of Desire: A Plant's-Eye View of the World</title>
   <asin>0375501290</asin>
   <author>Pollan, Michael</author>

<image>http://images.amazon.com/images/P/0375501290.01.MZZZZZZZ.jpg</ima
ge>

<small_image>http://images.amazon.com/images/P/0375501290.01.TZZZZZZZ.jp
g </small_image>
   <our_price>$16.48</our_price>
   <list_price>$24.95</list_price>
   <release_date>20010508</release_date>
   <binding>Hardcover</binding>
   <availability> </availability>
   <tagged_url>
http://www.amazon.com:80/exec/obidos/redirect?tag=XXXXX&amp;creative=944
1&amp;camp=1793&amp;link_code=xml&amp;path=ASIN/0375501290</tagged_url>
</product>
<product>
   <ranking>3</ranking>
   <title>The Botany of Desire: A Plants-Eye View of the World (G K Hall
Large Print Nonfiction Series)</title>
   <asin>0783896417</asin>
   <author>Pollan, Michael</author>

<image>http://images.amazon.com/images/P/0783896417.01.MZZZZZZZ.jpg</ima
ge>

<small_image>http://images.amazon.com/images/P/0783896417.01.TZZZZZZZ.jp
g </small_image>
   <our_price>$30.95</our_price>
   <release_date>20011200</release_date>
   <binding>Hardcover</binding>
   <availability> </availability>
```

```
   <tagged_url>
http://www.amazon.com:80/exec/obidos/redirect?tag=XXXXX&amp;creative=944
1&amp;camp=1793&amp;link_code=xml&amp;path=ASIN/0783896417</tagged_url>
</product>
<product>
   <ranking>4</ranking>
   <title>The Botany of Desire</title>
   <asin>B00005MLJW</asin>
   <author>Random House</author>

<image>http://images.amazon.com/images/P/B00005MLJW.01.MZZZZZZZ.jpg</ima
ge>
   <small_image>
http://images.amazon.com/images/P/B00005MLJW.01.TZZZZZZZ.jpg</small_imag
e>
   <our_price>$11.00</our_price>
   <release_date>20010600</release_date>
   <binding>Digital</binding>
   <availability> </availability>
   <tagged_url>
http://www.amazon.com:80/exec/obidos/redirect?tag=XXXXX&amp;creative=944
1&amp;camp=1793&amp;link_code=xml&amp;path=ASIN/B00005MLJW</tagged_url>
</product>
<product>
   <ranking>5</ranking>
   <title>The Botany of Desire</title>
   <asin>B00005N5LA</asin>
   <author>Random House</author>

<image>http://images.amazon.com/images/P/B00005N5LA.01.MZZZZZZZ.jpg</ima
ge>

<small_image>http://images.amazon.com/images/P/B00005N5LA.01.TZZZZZZZ.jp
g </small_image>
   <our_price>$11.00</our_price>
   <release_date>20010600</release_date>
   <binding>Digital</binding>
   <availability> </availability>
   <tagged_url>
http://www.amazon.com:80/exec/obidos/redirect?tag=XXXXX&amp;creative=944
1&amp;camp=1793&amp;link_code=xml&amp;path=ASIN/B00005N5LA</tagged_url>
</product>
</catalog>
```

The result of the REST client script is shown in Figure 32-1 below:

Figure 32-1: A REST client gets XML and outputs the HTML box.

As you can see from the XML sample, there is a lot of potential data from the Web service that we didn't use — pictures of the book cover, suggested price, and so on. This demonstrates how easy it is to pick out just the data you want from the feed using DOM XML. According to the current Amazon Associates rules, you could poll its Web service for fresh XML every hour, so you could keep this part of your information very fresh.

> **CAUTION:** As we go to press, the Amazon Associates REST service is in beta flux. By the time this book comes out, it may no longer be available or the API may have changed significantly.

Project: An XML-RPC/SOAP Server and Client

Here we have an extremely simple Web service and a matching client script. It uses functions from Dan Libby's `xmlrpc-epi-php` package — his C implementation is the basis of the official PHP XMLRPC extension. You can get `xmlrpc-epi-php` at the following URL:

```
http://sourceforge.net/projects/xmlrpc-epi/
```

You do not need the "base" file, which is now distributed as part of PHP, just the PHP utilities. You should already have built PHP with XML-RPC and `expat`.

XML-RPC and SOAP Web services have two major parts: the actual programming logic and the mechanism by which the program is exposed or turned into a Web service. The latter includes tasks such as encoding the request from a function to XML, actually sending the request as an HTTP `POST`, and decoding the response. In Perl, this is accomplished by using a package such as `SOAP::Lite`. Server-side Java programmers often use the Apache SOAP toolkit (aka `Axis`). ASP now uses the .NET framework. PHP does not yet have an "official" package that does all this for you, partly because it can all be accomplished by using basic PHP functions. One package that is easy to use is NuSoap by Dietrick Ayala, which you can find here:

```
http://dietrich.ganx4.com/nusoap/index.php
```

But here we are trying to give you a conceptual understanding of PHP Web services by showing you the bare functions involved, so we've decided not to use a nice cushy class — but for real Web services, it would save a lot of work.

This Web service basically distributes recipes. Any client can come along and request a particular recipe in either XML-RPC or SOAP format. The recipes themselves happen to be written in XML, but that doesn't matter — they could just as easily be in HTML, plain text, or whatever. After you have the recipe data, you can do whatever you want with it — format it for display in a Web page, use it in an XML application, or (as we chose to do in our client) write out a shopping list. Listing 32-3 is a sample recipe that lives on the server:

Listing 32-3: Sample XML recipe (mapo_tofu.xml)

```
<?xml version='1.0' encoding="iso-8859-1" ?>
<recipe>
<recipe_name>Mapo tofu</recipe_name>
<ingredient>1 T peanut oil</ingredient>
<ingredient>2 oz minced pork</ingredient>
<ingredient>14 oz firm tofu, cut in cubes</ingredient>
<ingredient>2 T garlic chili paste</ingredient>
<ingredient>1 T black bean paste</ingredient>
<ingredient>1 T sherry</ingredient>
<ingredient>1 T rice vinegar</ingredient>
<ingredient>10 oz frozen peas and carrots</ingredient>
<ingredient>1 T. chopped green onion</ingredient>
<instruction>Brown the pork in the peanut oil.  Add all the rest of the
ingredients except the green onion.  Braise for 15 minutes or until the
tofu loses that icky raw taste.  Garnish with green onion and serve
hot.</instruction>
</recipe>
```

Listing 32-4 is the code for the XML-RPC or SOAP service. Invoking it is very similar to invoking an XML parser in PHP. There are four main steps: Create the server, register methods on the server, call those methods, and destroy the server. In this case, all four happen each time a request comes in, but that is not necessary.

Listing 32-4: An XML-RPC and SOAP server (recipe_server.php)

```
<?php

// some utilities
include("/xmlrpc-php-epi/sample/xmlrpc_utils.php"); // In the xmlrpc-
epi-php package
```

```php
// ensure extension is loaded.
xu_load_extension();


// Get pre-encoded request from POST
$request_xml = $HTTP_RAW_POST_DATA;
if(!$request_xml) {
  $request_xml = $HTTP_POST_VARS[xml];
}


// This is the function that does the action we want
function getRecipe($method_name, $params, $app_data) {
    $recipe_name = $params[0];
    $file = "$recipe_name.xml";
    $fp = fopen($file, 'r');
    $recipe_str = fread($fp, filesize($file));
    fclose($fp);

    return $recipe_str;
}


// Create, register, call, and destroy
$xmlrpc_server = xmlrpc_server_create();

if($xmlrpc_server) {
    if(!xmlrpc_server_register_method($xmlrpc_server, "getRecipe",
"getRecipe")) {
     die("<h2>method registration failed.</h2>");
    }

    // Serve up either XML-RPC or SOAP
    if (strstr($request_xml, 'SOAP-ENV')) {
     $result = xmlrpc_server_call_method($xmlrpc_server, $request_xml,
$response, array(output_type => "xml", version => "soap 1.1"));
     echo $result;
    } else {
     $result = xmlrpc_server_call_method($xmlrpc_server, $request_xml,
$response, array(output_type => "xml", version => "xmlrpc"));
     echo $result;
    }

    $success = xmlrpc_server_destroy($xmlrpc_server);
}
?>
```

As you can see, the client can request results in either XML-RPC or SOAP format; this server will handle both types of requests transparently. Our client script, which is implemented as an ordinary PHP page in the browser, asks for XML-RPC. After it gets the results back, it writes the ingredients out to a text file on the client as shown in Listing 32-5.

Listing 32-5: XML-RPC and SOAP client script (recipe_client.php)

```php
<?php

include_once("/xmlrpc-php-epi/sample/utils/utils.php");

// Get the XML results
$recipe = $_GET['recipe'];

$result = xu_rpc_http_concise(array(method => "getRecipe",
                                    args => array(0 => "$recipe"),
                                    host => "localhost",
                                    uri => "/xmlrpc-epi/xmlrpc-php-
epi/sample/recipe_server.php",
                                    port => "80",
                                    debug => 1,
                                    output => array(version => "xmlrpc")
                                    )
                             );
// If you want SOAP output, change the output['version'] to "soap 1.1"
//echo $result;



// Fire up Expat to make a shopping list
// ------------------------------------

$ingred_arr = array('types' => array(), 'values' => array());
$i = 0;
$e = -1;
// There is an element without a value, the recipe element
// so I'm jiggering this offset to match

function startElement($parser, $name, $attrs)
{
  global $ingred_arr, $e;
  if ($name != 'INGREDIENT' && $name != 'RECIPE_NAME' && $e > 0) {
    $ingred_arr[types][$e] = 1;
  }
  $e++;
}



function endElement($parser, $name)
```

```
{
  // Just need to define an endElement function for the parser
}


function characterData($parser, $value)
{
  global $ingred_arr, $i;
  if (strlen($value) > 1) {
    $ingred_arr[values][$i] = $value;
    $i++;
  }
}

// Run through the XML and stick the values in an array
// Also note if any of the elements are not recipe names or ingredient
$simpleparser = xml_parser_create();
xml_set_element_handler($simpleparser, "startElement", "endElement");
xml_set_character_data_handler($simpleparser, "characterData");

if (!xml_parse($simpleparser, $result, strlen($result))) {
  die(xml_error_string(xml_get_error_code($simpleparser)));
}
xml_parser_free($simpleparser);

// Get rid of any values that aren't ingredients or recipe name
foreach ($ingred_arr['values'] as $key=>$val) {
  if ($ingred_arr['types'][$key] == 1) {
    $ingred_arr['values'] = array_slice($ingred_arr['values'], 0, $key);
  }
}
$shopping_list = implode("\n", $ingred_arr['values']);

// Write it out to a file
$file = '/home/me/shoppinglist.txt';
$fp = fopen($file, "a+");
$write_int = fwrite($fp, $shopping_list);
fclose($fp);

// If you want, mail it to yourself instead
// mail('me@example.com', 'Shopping list', $shopping_list);
?>
```

To use this script, you call it with the name of the recipe as the GET var, as follows:

```
recipe_client.php?recipe=mapo_tofu
```

The script calls a PHP function, `xu_rpc_http_concise()`, which is defined in the `xmlrpc-epi-php` package `utils.php` file. This function takes some inputs and formats a nice XML HTTP POST request to the Web service. Figure 32-2 shows the request:

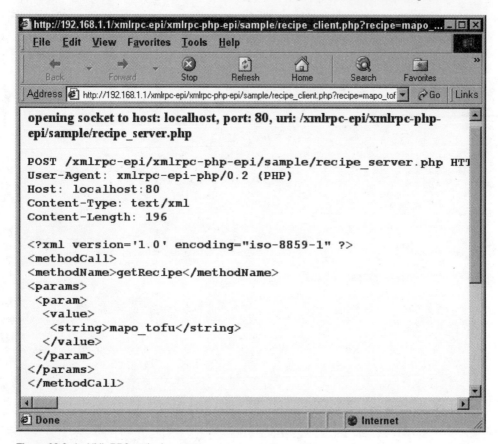

```
opening socket to host: localhost, port: 80, uri: /xmlrpc-epi/xmlrpc-php-
epi/sample/recipe_server.php

POST /xmlrpc-epi/xmlrpc-php-epi/sample/recipe_server.php HT1
User-Agent: xmlrpc-epi-php/0.2 (PHP)
Host: localhost:80
Content-Type: text/xml
Content-Length: 196

<?xml version='1.0' encoding="iso-8859-1" ?>
<methodCall>
<methodName>getRecipe</methodName>
<params>
 <param>
  <value>
   <string>mapo_tofu</string>
  </value>
 </param>
</params>
</methodCall>
```

Figure 32-2: An XML-RPC method request

Because this is a synchronous request-response model, the client blocks and waits for a response. The response may come in either an XML-RPC version (see Figure 32-3) or a SOAP format (see Figure 32-4) depending on which you've requested.

After the response comes, the `xu_rpc_http_concise()` function picks out the payload from the XML-RPC format and delivers it neatly as a PHP variable suitable for further processing. We wanted to do something besides displaying the recipe in a browser, so we used PHP's SAX parser to write out the ingredients to a text file as a shopping list.

Figure 32-3: Raw XML-RPC response

Figure 32-4: Raw SOAP response

You may have noticed that, ultimately, both the REST example in the previous section of this chapter and the XML-RPC example here do pretty much exactly the same thing: return a chunk of XML. In the REST example, we go on to munge it by using the DOM; in this one, we run it through a SAX parser. This goes to show two things: For simple Web services like this one, the REST and SOAP are functionally equivalent; and XML gives you basic building blocks that you can use in many ways.

Summary

Web services is an emerging field of programming. Web services offers immediate payoffs in data transfer, especially for Web applications, and may finally unlock the promise of distributed computing. Although there is a lot of hype and misinformation out there about the technologies, and although much of the action is happening inside intranets and in semiprivate transactions, you can start familiarizing yourself with PHP to both create and consume Web services.

The three main Web services standards in discussion now are REST, XML-RPC, and SOAP. REST is the most lightweight and easy to use, but offers the least functionality. SOAP is the most complicated and, as a consequence, has the most interoperability problems; but large vendors like Microsoft and IBM have thrown their support behind it. XML-RPC offers a nice blend of power and simplicity, but lacks big-vendor support.

PHP can be used to create servers and clients in REST, XML-RPC, and SOAP. However, particularly with SOAP, the syntax is so complex that a third-party package may be highly useful for help with the serialization, type-shuffling, and request-creation steps required by Web services.

## Chapter 33

Graphics

In This Chapter

♦ Overview of images in Web scripting

♦ Creating graphics in HTML

♦ Introduction to the gd image manipulation library

♦ An extended database-visualization example

♦ Troubleshooting image creation code

In this chapter, we delve into how to use PHP to create graphics of your own and display them to the user. Although we spend a little bit of time on pure HTML "graphics," our primary focus is on creating images on-the-fly by using the gd library. This library helps you create images such as PNGs and JPEGs, which you can then link to from dynamically generated HTML pages or send to the user as standalone Web pages.

Overview

One of the pleasures (and headaches) of writing about PHP is that, as a glue language, PHP touches so many other areas of programming beyond pure Web scripting. This is fun because there is so much that you can do by using PHP. To authors, however, it poses a challenge. No one (and certainly not us) has the expertise to write in depth about all the areas that PHP connects to: database design, cryptography, text analysis, arbitrary-precision arithmetic, graphics, XML, javascript, email, and so on. Even assuming the requisite expertise, doing justice to all those topics would yield a 20,000-page book rather than the mere 1000 pages or so we must work with in the Bible format.

That said, though, we think it's cheating to merely describe PHP's interface to a completely different body of code and practice, without describing what that code and practice is — instead of just pointing to the door, we should at least go through the door and walk around a little. So in this chapter, we plan to be largely example-driven as we write about creating images, while choosing examples that, we hope, point out interesting possibilities for PHP programmers.

Your options

Just to see where image creation fits into the Web-scripting world, look at the following spectrum of choices, in order of increasing dynamicness:

♦ You can have no graphics at all and display purely textual information.

♦ You can embed static images in your HTML, whether created by yourself or by other people.

♦ You can write programmatically generated HTML pseudographics.

♦ You can embed static image graphics (or even image animations, if you insist) in your HTML pages, but display different ones conditionally.

♦ You can use gd to pregenerate static graphics for all the cases that may possibly arise from your code, store them in files, and display them conditionally.

♦ You can create graphic images on demand in response to user input.

We start off with the third option (HTML graphics) and then devote most of the rest of the chapter to the last one, which is the most interesting case.

Image formats and browsers

PHP/gd programming involves creating images via gd, transforming them into some well-known image format, and sending them down the pipe to the user for display (or storing them in a file for later display). This is substantially different from our usual practice in this book, which is to use PHP to generate HTML.

The three image formats we talk about at all seriously are: GIF, JPEG, and PNG, although for examples we focus mostly on the last of these (for reasons that we explain in the "gd library" section). (We have reluctantly decided not to cover Flash in this book, although we may have some Flash-related material on our Web site at www.troutworks.com/phpbook).

The GIF and PNG formats essentially exist to describe a grid of colored cells corresponding to pixels, with a few complications. The first complication is that the cells may contain actual color values or they may contain indexes in a table of color values. (The former is more expressive because any number of different colors may be used, and the latter is more compact.)

Compression

Another complication is that, although the conceptual representation of GIFs and PNGs is fairly simple, in practice they are always read, written, and transferred in compressed form. Compression is necessary because a grid of cells is a costly thing to specify. A simple 500 x 400 pixel image is 200,000 pixels — if each pixel needs three bytes to specify, then we're over half a megabyte already. Compression is a large and abstruse topic, but most compression algorithms take advantage of redundancy in the image to make it smaller. (There are more concise ways to say that every pixel is green than specifying every pixel's green color value individually.) Unfortunately, there is a lot more to compression algorithms than that — enough so that the compression algorithm used for writing GIFs is patented.

Early browsers were written using GIF as the graphics format of choice, and it wasn't until that practice had been underway for a while that it became clear that the patent holder was going to insist on going after people who used the compression algorithm. This left Web graphics in a bit of a bind — GIF was the *lingua franca*, but you couldn't legally create such graphics, at least without paying a license fee. The PNG format has come to the rescue in a sense — recent versions of major browsers support it, and with that support it plays much the same role as GIF.

Compression is different in the case of JPEGs, as well, although not for legal reasons. Compression for GIFs and PNGs is lossless, meaning that if you compress and then uncompress an image, you should have exactly your original image back. The JPEG compression, on the other hand is lossy. Essentially, if redundancy helps compression, JPEG compression tries to introduce a little bit of extra redundancy into the image before compression, mostly in ways that the human eye won't notice. This is particularly effective with photographic images, but it does mean that sometimes the compression/uncompression cycle doesn't leave you with exactly what you started with.

The gd library

Much of this chapter is devoted to using the gd library to create images. Although this library (a public service from the Boutell company) was not created specifically for PHP, a PHP interface has been written to it. In this library, you can create graphics in an internal format, write to them, modify them, and then ship them off in a variety of formats. Among formats offered are JPEG and PNG, although GIF has been discontinued for the legal reasons listed in the "Compression" section. Because JPEG is better for photographic images than the kinds of images we're making, and because deciding on the export format is a final step anyway, we've decided to focus on PNG graphics exclusively. If you would rather produce JPEGs, it is a simple matter to change the export functions appropriately.

Before we start making these images, we make a brief digression to talk about how far you can get by using HTML alone.

HTML Graphics

You know those sideways colored bar graphs you see all over the Web, especially in connection with poll results? It looks as though some graphics is being done in creating these graphs, but in truth there's just a couple of canned color images and the magic of image scaling in HTML. This graphing technique is actually very useful, and we include it here because it's very easy to create graphs like this dynamically from PHP.

Before we get into this data visualization technique, we need some data. Listing 33-1 shows a small sample dataset, which we imagine has been produced from a survey of programmers asked about their favorite languages and operating systems. The data is stored in a MySQL database, in a single table, with the following definition:

```
CREATE TABLE programmers (
  id int(11) NOT NULL auto_increment,
  sex char(1) default NULL,
  age int(11) default NULL,
  language varchar(30) default NULL,
  os varchar(30) default NULL,
  country varchar(30) default NULL,
  continent varchar(30) default NULL,
  PRIMARY KEY  (id)
);
```

Listing 33-1: Sample dataset

id	sex	age	language	os	country	continent
1	F	33	PHP	Linux	USA	North America
2	M	41	Java	Solaris	USA	North America
4	M	31	C++	Solaris	USA	North America
5	M	45	Lisp	MacOS	USA	North America
6	M	25	C	Solaris	Antarctica	Antarctica
7	F	17	PHP	Linux	Denmark	Europe
8	M	21	Perl	Linux	UK	Europe
9	M	14	PHP	Linux	UK	Europe
10	F	21	Perl	Linux	Germany	Europe
11	F	38	PHP	Linux	Germany	Europe
12	M	26	C++	Windows	USA	North America
13	M	22	PHP	Windows	France	Europe
14	M	17	PHP	Linux	Japan	Asia
15	F	38	C	Solaris	South Korea	Asia
16	F	19	PHP	Linux	Canada	North America
17	F	32	Perl	Linux	France	Europe
18	M	32	Java	Solaris	Mexico	North America
19	F	23	PHP	Solaris	Brazil	South America
20	F	19	PHP	Linux	Finland	Europe
21	M	21	PHP	Linux	Brazil	South America
22	M	51	Java	Linux	UK	Europe
23	M	29	Java	Linux	Japan	Asia
24	M	29	Java	Solaris	China	Asia
25	M	21	C++	MacOS	Germany	Europe
26	M	21	Perl	Solaris	France	Europe
27	M	27	PHP	Linux	India	Asia
28	M	31	Perl	Linux	India	Asia
29	M	17	C	Linux	Pakistan	Asia
30	M	45	PHP	Windows	USA	North America
31	F	22	Java	Windows	Italy	Europe

```
| 32 | F    |  33  | C        | Linux    | Spain        | Europe          |
+----+------+------+----------+----------+--------------+-----------------+
```

We use the data for this example but also come back to it for a much more extended example in the section "Example: Data Visualization with Venn Diagrams," later in the chapter.

So say that our goal is to visualize counts of the distribution of values for different columns — we want to not only know how many of our respondents list this or that programming language, but also to see comparisons graphically.

Although our data is in a MySQL database, the display portion of this code need not be tied to that. We may want to use it for a different purpose entirely. So we break out a separate function that produces a bar graph from an array in a particular format, and only later hook that up to code that produces the requisite array via SQL queries. The code to translate an array into a bar graph is shown in Listing 33-2.

Listing 33-2: `bar_graph.php`

```php
<?php

function array_to_bar_graph ($array, $max_width) {
  // expects as input an array where the keys
  //    are string labels and the values are
  //    numbers.  Values must be non-negative
  // returns an HTML bar graph as a string
  // assumes bar[1-5].gif, located in images/

  foreach ($array as $value) {
    if ((IsSet($max_value) &&
        ($value > $max_value)) ||
        (!IsSet($max_value))) {
      $max_value = $value;
    }
  }
  $pixels_per_value = ((double) $max_width)
                      / $max_value;

  $string_to_return = "<TABLE CELLPADDING=5>";
  $counter = 0;
  foreach ($array as $name => $value) {
    $bar_width = $value * $pixels_per_value;
    $image_no = ($counter % 5) + 1;
    $string_to_return .=
    "<TR><TD>$name ($value)</TD>
     <TD><IMG SRC=\"images/bar$image_no.gif\"
            WIDTH=$bar_width
            HEIGHT=10>
     </TD></TR>";
    $counter++;
```

```
  }
  $string_to_return .= "</TABLE>";
  return($string_to_return);
}
?>
```

The bar graph code is extremely simple — it iterates through an array, which is assumed to have names for keys and quantities for values. It normalizes the maximum value to a fixed width bar and calculates the width of all the other bars proportionally. Finally, it displays bars by using the scaling parameters in the <IMG> tag to give each variable a fixed height and an appropriate width. It cycles through a list of five images, which are pre-made one-color GIFs (which could as well be PNGs) and could be created by using your favorite graphics program. As long as these images are monocolor, their size and shape are irrelevant. (If you don't have any such images handy, you can find the ones we used at the code download site: www.troutworks.com/phpbook/.)

Now that we can display names and associated values in a bar graph, we can hook that up to the database via a Web form and an SQL query. Code for this is shown in Listing 33-3.

Listing 33-3: `bar_graph_form.php`

```
<?php
include_once("dbconnect.php");
include_once("bar_graph.php");

if (IsSet($_POST['COLUMN_NAME'])) {
  $column_name = $_POST['COLUMN_NAME'];
  $query = "select $column_name, count(*)
            from programmers
            group by $column_name";
  $result = mysql_query($query)
            or die("Error in database interaction<BR>".
                    mysql_error());
  $array_collection = array();
  while ($row = mysql_fetch_row($result)) {
    $name = $row[0];
    $count = $row[1];
    $array_collection[$name] = $count;
  }
  $bar_graph =
    array_to_bar_graph($array_collection,
                        300);
}
else {
  $bar_graph = "";
}

$self = $_SERVER['PHP_SELF'];
```

```
$form = <<<EOT
<FORM METHOD=POST ACTION="$self">
<H3>Choose a table column for graphing</H3>
<SELECT NAME=COLUMN_NAME>
<OPTION VALUE=os>os
<OPTION VALUE=language>language
<OPTION VALUE=continent>continent
<OPTION VALUE=sex>sex
</SELECT>
<INPUT TYPE=SUBMIT NAME=SUBMIT>
</FORM>
EOT;

$page = <<<EOT
<HTML><HEAD><TITLE>Survey data</TITLE></HEAD>
<BODY>
$form
<BR>
$bar_graph
</BODY></HTML>
EOT;

echo $page;
?>
```

The form is self-submitting and loads a file called dbconnect.php, which we assume takes care of a call to mysql_connect(), with appropriate login, password, and database name.

All that is supplied by the form submission is the name of the column. Starting with that, the code submits an SQL statement to count all the distinct values that occur for that column and then creates an array by using names and the corresponding counts. What remains is to feed the resulting array to the bar-graph code from Listing 33-1 and to do some layout. The results for two different columns are shown in Figures 33-1 and 33-2. (Since this is a grayscale book, you won't see interestingly different colors in the diagram, but you should at least see bars of different sizes.)

The gd Library

Having mostly exhausted the graphic possibilities afforded by vanilla HTML, let's turn our attention to creating real standalone graphics by using the gd library.

What is gd?

What is gd, anyway? The gd toolkit is a C code library for creating and manipulating images, which was created by the kind and clever people at Boutell.com (at www.boutell.com). gd is not a graphics or paint program in and of itself, as it has no standalone application or GUI. Instead, it provides functions that programs can call to do these manipulations, and any C program that wants to can link against that library to use the routines. The PHP developers have done this and, in fact, have written a set of interface functions that make it easy to call gd routines from PHP. But nothing in gd is specific to PHP, and there are interfaces to it from several other languages and environments, including Perl, Tcl, Pascal, Haskell, and REXX.

Figure 33-1: HTML bar graph

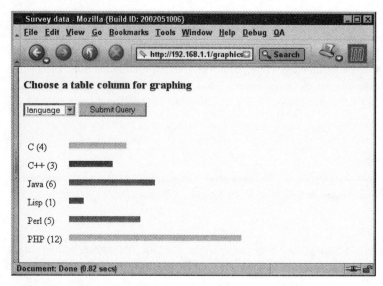

Figure 33-2: HTML bar graph 2

gd lets you call functions to create images (initially blank, like a clean sheet of paper), draw and paint on those images in various ways, and ultimately convert the image from gd's internal image format to a standard image format, and send it off to its ultimate fate (display in a browser, or storage in a file or database). And because all this is under programmatic control rather than human control, these created images can be arbitrarily complex, and they can depend on anything in your program that you would like to have them depend on.

Installation

Installing gd and getting it to work with PHP is, frankly, a pain. This is not because of any weakness in either the PHP codebase or the gd codebase, but is all about configuration issues: sorting out the likely and actual locations of the libraries gd depends on, and making sure that everything can build and link appropriately. So the happiest situation possible is to find out that gd is already installed, and PHP already has gd support enabled (whether that's due to the diligence of your Webhost or because the PHP you installed by yourself had it included).

So the zeroth step in installing gd is: Check to see if it's already been installed. Whether you are running via a Webhost or are in command of your own installation, start off as always by putting the following into a file and viewing the result in a browser:

```
<?php
phpinfo();
?>
```

After you have the displayed page, just do a text search for gd in the browser window — you may find a subsection that describes to what extent gd is enabled in your PHP installation. If you only want to produce certain kinds of images (PNGs, for example) and phpinfo() tells you that support for that image type is enabled, then you may be good to go.

If this fails, and if you are in control of your PHP installation, you will have to install and configure gd. (If, instead, your PHP installation is run by a hosting company, your options may be reduced to asking them to provide gd support, or to switching Webhosts.) As of this writing, the place to start is www.boutell.com/gd/. (This may or may not change after this writing, because there is now talk on the PHP developers' mailing list about possibly forking the gd codebase and making it part of PHP. If that happens (at the earliest imaginable time, as part of version 4.3), some of these configuration headaches may go away.)

The gd library itself depends on several other libraries: libpng (for manipulating PNG images), zlib (used in compression), and jpeg-6b or later (if you want to manipulate JPEG images). Only gd, libpng, and zlib are necessary for the examples in this chapter.

The best place to start is from the documentation links at www.boutell.com/gd — the documentation explains the library dependencies and the best places to get current versions of zlib and libpng. After you have installed the libraries you will need to rebuild PHP, by using the configuration option --with-gd or else by using --with-gd=gdpath if you want to specify a particular location for gd.

Choosing versions

As of this writing, the two versions of gd that are available from www.boutell.com/gd are 1.8.4 and 2.0.1 (beta). Which should you choose? If you do not need any 2.0.1-specific features, then for stability reasons you are probably better off with the former. If, however, you need support for color transparency, or truecolor support (more than 256 possible colors), or lines with varying thickness, then you need version 2.0.1 or higher. (See the documentation at www.boutell.com/gd for the complete details on features supported by different versions.)

gd Concepts

While an image is being constructed or manipulated in the gd toolkit, it is stored in a gd-specific format that doesn't correspond to any conventional image type. Images can in theory be exported in this gd format, but it's unusual to do so because the resulting image is not compressed and cannot be displayed in a browser or conventional graphics program.

An image in the gd toolkit has a width, a height, and color information for all the *width x height* many pixels. (See the Colors section below for more detail on how colors are stored.) Usually a program starts off its interaction with gd by either creating a new blank image (which is drawn and painted on), or by importing an image from a file. The next steps are typically: 1) allocate colors in the image, 2) draw, paint, or otherwise transform the image, 3) translate the image to a conventional format (for example, PNG, JPEG), and send it to output.

Colors

The representation of colors in pre-2.0 gd was very simple, but gd 2.0 and later offer many more color options. Especially because none of the code in this chapter uses features from gd 2.0, we describe the earlier palette-based system in detail and then briefly mention the additional options available in gd 2.x.

Colors in palette-based images

Colors are specified in a red-green-blue (RGB) format, with three numbers between 0 and 255. The color specified by (255, 0, 0), for example, is bright red; (0, 255, 0) is green; (0, 0, 255) is blue; (0, 0, 0) is black; (255, 255, 255) is white; and (127, 127, 127) is gray. You can tweak these values to your heart's content to design new colors.

Any drawing into an image must be done in a particular color, and colors must be allocated in an image before they are used. Also, the first color allocated into an image automatically becomes the background color. So, colors are not optional in any sense, and usually color allocation is the first thing you do after creating a new blank image.

Colors in palette-based images are created by using imagecolorallocate(), which takes as arguments an (already created) image, and three integers specifying the proportion of red, green, and blue. The return value is an integer, which specifies the index of the new color in the image's internal palette. You must hang on to this return value in a variable, because you need the index value for any future drawing using that color. Palette-based images can have a maximum of 256 colors. (It may or may not be obvious what's going on under the hood here, but every pixel in a palette-based image is actually a single byte, which stores an index into the 256-color palette.)

Note that the index returned by allocating a color in an image only makes sense for that image. If you assign an allocated color to the PHP variable $black, it won't work to use that variable as the color input for a drawing command called on a different image.

Truecolor and transparency

In gd 2.0 and later, you can also create images that are not palette-based, where every pixel stores an individual RGB color value. In this truecolor format, the number of colors is essentially unlimited. This can be useful not only for the free range of your artistic expression, but for faithfully representing truecolor PNGs and JPEG images that have been loaded into gd.

In addition, gd version 2 supports transparency in the form of an *alpha value* (addition to the red, green, blue values) that specifies how transparent the given color is.

Drawing coordinates and commands

After you create an image within gd, you have an implicit coordinate system for drawing on it, determined by the width and height you specified.

In this coordinate system, the origin (0, 0) is at the top-left corner of the image, and the positive direction for x values is to the right, whereas the positive direction for y values is down. (This is often true of computer graphics coordinate systems, but you may be more accustomed to a lower-left origin if you learned analytic geometry in school.)

There are many drawing commands, including but not limited to drawing line segments, rectangles, arcs, and setting particular pixel values. Note that the end effect of all these painting and drawing commands is to set the value of pixels. There is no memory retained of the commands that changed the pixels and, therefore, no way to undo drawing commands or separate out the effects of distinct commands.

Nothing stops you from drawing outside the bounds of the image you have specified, but such drawing has no visible effect. A rectangle with coordinate values that are all negative, for example, is not visible.

Format translation

All this drawing and image manipulation is done on the image in its gd-internal format. After your script is done, it can use one of the translation-and-output commands (imagetopng, imagetojpeg, and so on.) to translate the image to the desired graphics format and echo it out to the user's browser (or to a file).

Freeing resources

After you have sent a translation of your completed gd image off to the user, you are done with the internal version and should dispose of it. The right way to do this is to call imagedestroy() with the image as an argument.

This is slightly less necessary in PHP 4 than in previous versions because the image is of type resource, and so should automatically be freed whenever PHP gets around to it. Freeing images yourself is a good habit to get into — there's no reason to hold onto memory that you know you have no further use for.

Functions

We are not planning to individually list and describe all the functions in PHP's gd interface in this chapter; for that, we refer you to the "Image Functions" section of the manual at www.php.net/. Most of the gd functions are in one of the categories shown in Table 33-1. Note that the function names in this table have internal capital letters at word breaks for clarity, but we may not always observe this when writing code because PHP function names are not case sensitive.

Table 33-1: Breakdown of gd Functions

Type	*Examples*	*Notes*
Image-creation functions	ImageCreate(), ImageCreateTruecolor(), ImageCreateFromgd(), ImageCreateFromJpeg()	These functions return a new gd image. ImageCreate() takes a width and height as arguments; others take a filepath, URL, or string containing a pre-existing image to load in and convert to gd.
Color functions	ImageColorAllocate(), ImageColorDeallocate(), ImageColorClosest()	ImageColorAllocate() (the most important one) takes an image and the desired red, green, and blue color values and creates a new color-palette entry in the image, returning its index. Some of the other functions translate between RGB values and indexes in the palette; ImageColorClosest(), for example, takes red, green, and blue color arguments and finds the closest matching color in the palette.

Line-drawing functions	`ImageLine()`, `ImageRectangle()`, `ImageArc()`	These functions draw lines or curves in the specified shapes. Usually the first argument is an image, the last argument is a color, and the intermediate arguments are x- and y-coordinates.
Pen-setting functions for line drawing	`ImageSetStyle()`, `ImageSetThickness()`	These functions alter settings that affect the lines created by later line-drawing commands. (Some of these are available only with gd 2.0.1 or later.)
Painting and filling functions	`ImageFilledRectangle()`, `ImageFilledArc()`, `ImageFill()`	Usually analogous to corresponding line-drawing functions but with areas filled rather than outlined. The `ImageFill()` function "flood fills" outward from a specified x-y coordinate with a given fill color. (Some of these functions require gd 2.0.1 or later).
Exporting functions	`ImagePng()`, `ImageJpeg()`	These functions convert the internal gd image to the relevant image format and then send to output. If only one argument (an image) is given, the image is echoed to the user; if an additional path name argument is given, the destination is a file.
Image-destruction function	`ImageDestroy()`	Takes an image argument and frees all resources associated with the image

Images and HTTP

Before the user's browser can display an image appropriately, it has to know that an image is coming, and what the image format is. So it is, unfortunately, not sufficient to simply embed a call to `ImageToPng()` in your generated HTML and have an image show up. You essentially have three choices in regard to intermixing images with PHP-generated HTML.

Full-page images

You can make the entire generated page an image. In this case, you need to send an HTTP header before the image data, announcing that an image of a certain type is on the way. You may, for example, have lines such as the following near the end of your script:

```
// ... code to create image in $image
header("Content-type: image/png");   // announcement to browser
imagepng($image);   // sending actual PNG-converted image data
imagedestroy($image);   // freeing resources
```

This approach has the benefit that you can use any kind of information, including POST arguments, to decide what the image should contain. The downside is that the resulting page can't contain any conventional HTML. In fact, you need to be careful that no textual output is sent from your scripts before the header and image because this causes content to be sent prematurely. In this case, you get a Headers already sent . . . error.

Embedded images from files

Of course, HTML has had the <IMG> tag for a long time. This enables you to embed an image by specifying its file path or URL, like this:

```
<IMG SRC="my_png.png">
```

This works with static image files, but there is no reason why the image can't have been recently created. So you can have a script that 1) creates an image, 2) writes the image data to a local file, and then 3) produces HTML with an appropriate <IMG> tag referring to the file that you just made.

The only drawbacks to this approach are 1) that you're introducing file writes, which may be time-consuming, into the page-generation process, and 2) you need to figure out what to do with the files after you are done with them. There is one situation this approach is perfect for, however, which is creating and caching images that represent a finite set of possibilities. In this case, you have some way to map from a situation to an image filename. Whenever a display situation arises, you check to see if you already have the appropriate file — if you do, you simply refer to it by using an <IMG> tag, and if not, you create the image, write it out to a file, and then refer to it. Eventually, you should need to do no more creation.

You can see a page created this way at a just-for-fun site that we made a few years ago. In www.sciencebookguide.com/sizescales.html, there is a bar graph in the top part of the page, and then a scale legend at the bottom, which was a gd-generated GIF. The text and tick marks of the scale legend depend on the exact bar-graph data that is being displayed, but there are only a limited number of cases. So, long ago, we auto-cached all the possible images, and ever since the displays have been static. (This is a good thing, of course, since gd quite rightly no longer supports the GIF format. Sometime soon we may get around to replacing the GIFs with PNGs.)

Embedded images from scripts

Finally, there is no reason why you cannot have a standalone generated image, as in the preceding section,"Full-page images," but, in turn, embed that URL in a different dynamic page via an <IMG> tag. The only difficulty lies in how to communicate necessary data to the dependent page. You may, for example, have an embedded image tag like this:

```
<IMG SRC="ballpage.php?ball_color=green&ball_position=5>
```

where `ballpage.php` happened to return PNG images of colored balls in various positions in the image.

There is a gotcha lurking here because both Web servers and browsers sometimes pay attention to the suffix of the served file, and in different ways. You may need the suffix of `ballpage` to be `.php` to let Apache (for example) know that the server-side code should be interpreted as PHP (although this behavior can be controlled with configuration files). Some broken browsers, however, may insist that a file that ends in `.php` cannot be an image despite the headers we are sending. This technique requires some cross-browser testing to make sure that your intended users are seeing the same thing you are.

Now it's high time to move on to an example of using `gd` to create images.

Example: Fractal images

There's a fine tradition of livening up the potentially unexciting topic of line drawing by using fractals as examples, and your authors are not about to mess with tradition. In addition to showing how you can produce a complex image programmatically, this kind of example is also a good fit for PHP because its arrays and loose datatypes make it very easy to build complex data structures corresponding to fractal images, without a lot of declarations.

What's a fractal? It's a shape that is self-similar, in that the parts of a fractal have a shape similar to the shape of the whole, and the parts of those parts have a similar shape, and so on.

In theory, you can keep zooming into ever-smaller pieces of an ideal fractal, and keep finding the same patterns repeated. In practice, computer-generated fractals bottom out after some limited number of generations into nonfractal shapes like simple curves and line segments.

An example of the kind of image we're going to create is shown in Figure 33-3. Although it may not look like it, this image is simply a lot of small line segments with endpoints connected into a path.

Our job is to calculate the endpoints of all those line segments and then display them appropriately as a PNG image. We're going to be slightly more ambitious than simply creating a one-off piece of fractal display code and construct a little framework that makes it easy to vary the fractal parameters and to generate new kinds of displays.

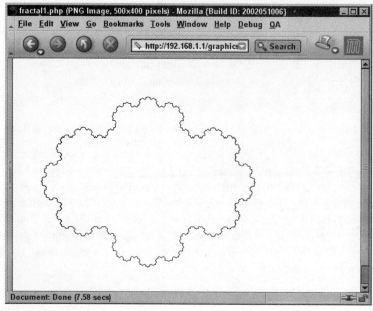

Figure 33-3: Fractal 1

To start with, we build some data structures to represent the complex shapes that we are displaying. We use these data structures both in our intermediate calculations and for drawing the end result. Let's say somewhat arbitrarily that:

♦ A coordinate point is a pair of numbers.

♦ A path is a list of points.

We end up drawing paths by drawing line segments between all the points in a path. If we want to draw a simple line segment, we draw a path that has two points in it; if we want to draw a rectangle, then we draw a path that has five points in it (with the starting point repeated to close off the rectangle). (We could have made a line segment a primitive entity here, but paths seemed more concise for our fractal purposes.)

Now, how shall we represent points and paths? The easiest way to make lists of things in PHP is to use arrays. So we declare that a point is an array that happens to contain two numbers, and a path is an array that happens to contain a sequence of points. The resulting structures are multidimensional PHP arrays, but if we define well-named constructor and accessor functions, we can forget about that and just write code that acts as though these things are genuine datatypes.

Listing 33-4 shows such code, which defines the datatypes in terms of functions to create them (starting with make_), functions to access their parts, and functions to draw them into an image (starting with `display_`). Points cannot be drawn and have no display function; paths are drawn by drawing lines between successive pairs of points.

Listing 33-4: `path_display.php`

```php
<?php

// --- points ----

// A point is just a pair of numerical coordinates

function make_point ($x, $y) {
  return(array($x, $y));
}

function point_x ($point) {
  return($point[0]);
}

function point_y ($point) {
  return($point[1]);
}

// --- paths ---

// A path is a list of points

function make_path () {
  return array();
}

function add_point_to_path ($path, $point) {
  $path[] = $point;
  return($path);
}

function display_path ($image, $path, $color) {
  static $line_count = 0;
  $prev_point = NULL;
  foreach ($path as $point) {
    if ($point && $prev_point) {
      $line_count++;
      imageline($image,
                point_x($prev_point),
                point_y($prev_point),
                point_x($point),
                point_y($point),
                $color);
    }
```

```
      $prev_point = $point;
  }
}

?>
```

Listing 33-5 shows a single function, which, among other arguments, takes the name of a function name to apply. (This function is in its own file because our original version of this code had more complex transformation functions for more complex fractal examples, removed for reasons of space. We may restore these examples to the code on the Web site at www.troutworks.com/phpbook.)

The function transform_path takes an input path as first argument, and as second argument it takes the name of a function that, in turn, is expected to take a path as argument and return a path as a result. The third argument to transform_path() is a number of times that the path-to-path function should be successively applied to create a new path. The reason that this kind of second-order function is useful is that, otherwise, we may find ourselves writing a new looping function every time we wanted to build a new fractal. With this approach, we can bundle the varying part of the fractal code into a function that we pass into transform_path and avoid duplicating work.

Listing 33-5: path_tranform.php

```php
<?php


function transform_path ($path_input,
                         $function_name,
                         $iterations) {
  // Expects a path, a path-to-path function
  //  and a number of times to apply the
  //  function.
  // Returns a path
  $path_to_return = $path_input;
  for ($i = 0; $i < $iterations; $i++) {
    $path_to_return = $function_name($path_to_return);
  }
  return($path_to_return);
}

?>
```

What we have so far is a way to represent and draw paths composed of line segments, and also functions that can repeatedly apply transformation functions to these paths. What we need now is the transformation functions themselves — the functions that we pass in that actually twiddle the locations of points in the data structures.

Listing 33-6 shows a set of such functions. The `spike` function takes a path as argument and returns a path where every two-point line segment has been replaced by a five-point line segment with a spike in the middle. The `top-hat` function does something similar, except that six points are involved, and the spike is rectangular. We also include a couple of functions to create rectangular paths of standard sizes, to use as starting points.

Listing 33-6: `path_manipulation.php`

```php
<?php

include_once("path_display.php");

function spike ($path) {
  // Takes a path and returns a path
  $path_to_return = make_path();
  $prev_point = NULL;
  foreach ($path as $point) {
    if ($point && $prev_point) {
      $path_to_return =
          add_point_to_path($path_to_return,
                            $prev_point);
      $path_to_return =
          add_point_to_path($path_to_return,
            point_along_segment($prev_point,
                            $point,
                            0.25));
      $path_to_return =
          add_point_to_path($path_to_return,
            point_off_segment($prev_point,
                            $point,
                            0.5, 0.23));
      $path_to_return =
          add_point_to_path($path_to_return,
            point_along_segment($prev_point,
                            $point,
                            0.75));
      $path_to_return =
          add_point_to_path($path_to_return,
                            $point);
    }
    $prev_point = $point;
  }
  return($path_to_return);
}

function top_hat ($path) {
```

```
// Takes a path and returns a path
$path_to_return = make_path();
$prev_point = NULL;
foreach ($path as $point) {
  if ($point && $prev_point) {
    $path_to_return =
        add_point_to_path($path_to_return,
                          $prev_point);
    $path_to_return =
        add_point_to_path($path_to_return,
          point_along_segment($prev_point,
                              $point,
                              0.35));
    $path_to_return =
        add_point_to_path($path_to_return,
          point_off_segment($prev_point,
                            $point,
                            0.35, 0.24));
    $path_to_return =
        add_point_to_path($path_to_return,
          point_off_segment($prev_point,
                            $point,
                            0.65, 0.24));
    $path_to_return =
        add_point_to_path($path_to_return,
          point_along_segment($prev_point,
                              $point,
                              0.65));
    $path_to_return =
        add_point_to_path($path_to_return,
                          $point);
  }
  $prev_point = $point;
}
return($path_to_return);
}


function point_along_segment ($first_point,
                              $second_point,
                              $proportion)
{
  $delta_x = (point_x($second_point) -
            point_x($first_point));
  $delta_y = (point_y($second_point) -
            point_y($first_point));
  return(make_point(point_x($first_point) +
                  $proportion * $delta_x,
```

```
                      point_y($first_point) +
                      $proportion * $delta_y));
}

function point_off_segment ($first_point,
                            $second_point,
                            $proportion,
                            $proportional_distance)
{
  $delta_x = (point_x($second_point) -
              point_x($first_point));
  $delta_y = (point_y($second_point) -
              point_y($first_point));
  return(make_point(point_x($first_point) +
                    $proportion * $delta_x -
                    $proportional_distance *
                    $delta_y,
                    point_y($first_point) +
                    $proportion * $delta_y +
                    $proportional_distance *
                    $delta_x));
}

function make_small_rectangle () {
  $path = make_path();
  $path = add_point_to_path ($path, make_point(75, 275));
  $path = add_point_to_path ($path, make_point(375, 275));
  $path = add_point_to_path ($path, make_point(375, 125));
  $path = add_point_to_path ($path, make_point(75, 125));
  $path = add_point_to_path ($path, make_point(75, 275));
  return($path);
}

function make_large_rectangle () {
  $path = make_path();
  $path = add_point_to_path ($path, make_point(5, 5));
  $path = add_point_to_path ($path, make_point(495, 5));
  $path = add_point_to_path ($path, make_point(495, 395));
  $path = add_point_to_path ($path, make_point(5, 395));
  $path = add_point_to_path ($path, make_point(5, 5));
  return($path);
}

?>
```

Now we can combine all these elements and actually make images. Listing 33-7 shows the file that produced our original example in Figure 33-3. After loading all the functions from the included files, this code creates a gd image of specific height and width and allocates colors into that image. (The background is white, and the lines are black.)

The fractal creation code starts off by creating a standard rectangular path (containing five points and, therefore, four (implicit) line segments). It then passes this off to the transform_path function, asking it to return the path that results from applying the spike() function to the rectangle four times. The rectangle path starts with four line segments, and every segment is itself replaced by four segments. So the four successive iterations have 16 segments, 64 segments, 256 segments, and 1024 segments, respectively.

Then all that remains is to display the complicated path that we've generated. We call our own function display_path() to draw all the lines into the image, send off an HTTP header announcing a PNG, call imagepng() for the conversion and output, and then dispense with the internal gd image.

Listing 33-7: fractal1.php

```php
<?php
include_once("path_display.php");
include_once("path_transform.php");
include_once("path_manipulation.php");

$IMAGE_WIDTH = 500;
$IMAGE_HEIGHT = 400;

$image = imagecreate($IMAGE_WIDTH, $IMAGE_HEIGHT)
  or die("Could not create image");
$background_color = ImageColorAllocate($image, 255, 255, 255);
$drawing_color = ImageColorAllocate($image, 0, 0, 0);

$path = make_small_rectangle();
$path = transform_path($path, 'spike', 4);
display_path($image, $path, $drawing_color);

header("Content-type: image/png");
imagepng($image);
imagedestroy($image);
?>
```

Although we won't show it as a separate listing, we took a copy of Listing 33-7, changed the function name argument from spike to top-hat, and renamed the file fractal2.php. The resulting image is shown in Figure 33-4.

> **CAUTION:** Creating and displaying these images can be time-consuming and the more so the more line segments are created. Your Web server may time out while the creation is happening. Your options then are to decrease the number of generations in the fractal code or to raise the timeouts in your Web server or PHP configuration files.

Tweaking fractal code is definitely an art, and your humble authors are not particularly good artists. We wish you luck in improving on our images.

Figure 33-4: Fractal 2

Example: Data Visualization with Venn Diagrams

Now we get a little bit more ambitious and move on to a longer, more challenging example. In this section we build a complete system that starts with a MySQL database and uses the gd library to produce a particular kind of visualization of that database.

Scaled Venn diagrams

The visualization we have in mind is something like the Venn diagram. If you've ever been in an academic setting where set intersection was being discussed, then you've probably seen these diagrams — they're the circles that may or may not have overlapping portions representing intersections.

We say "something like" the Venn diagram, because scale has no significance in a traditional Venn diagram. If you want to illustrate the fact that there are people who use both BeOS and Windows, then you might draw two circles of equal size (representing Windows users and BeOS users) that happen to have a region of overlap. In our version, which you might call a *scaled* or *proportional* Venn diagram, the sizes of both circles and intersections matter; the Windows/BeOS example would become one large circle and one much smaller circle, with an overlap area proportional to the number of people in both sets.

The task

The job of our code is to start with a database, provide a way to query that database about sets and their overlap, and then display the results as a scaled Venn diagram, generated by using the gd library. As a sample database, we use the pseudosurvey dataset that we used in the section "HTML Graphics," earlier in the chapter for HTML bar graphs.

If we're going to offer a way to query the database, then it may as well be via a Web form. So the end-to-end view of our task is that we start with a Web form and end up with a picture to display. Let's start the design by enumerating the things that need to happen for this to come about. We'll need to:

1. Generate (or at least present) the Web form itself.
2. Receive the submitted form data and transform it into appropriate SQL queries for submission to the database.
3. Receive results from the SQL queries.
4. Use the SQL results to decide on the locations and sizes of all the elements in our graphic.
5. Actually generate the graphic and send it back to the user.

Outline of the code

To do this, we write the following code files:

♦ **visualization_form.php:** This is essentially a hardcoded form that enables the user to choose two different restrictions on the data in our table. The restrictions chosen map directly to where clauses loaded from an auxiliary file called query_clauses.php.

♦ **db_visualization.php:** This code handles the form data sent by visualization_form.php and builds three SQL statements: one with only the first where clause, one with the second where clause, and a third with both clauses joined by an and. It collects resulting three counts and displays the numbers in a graphic by calling functions loaded from venn.php.

♦ **venn.php:** This actually produces the Venn diagram graphic and ships it back to the user. Its primary function takes as input the three amounts (the sizes of the two sets and their intersection), decides the sizes and locations of corresponding circles, and does all the drawing and shading necessary. For the complicated case of sets that actually have an overlapping area, it uses functions loaded from trig.php to calcuate areas.

♦ **trig.php:** This code actually calculates the intersection area whenever circles overlap.

We discuss these code files in reverse order, from the bottom up. By the way, although we like this example, we don't want to give the impression that you need to do trigonometry to do computer graphics in PHP, or even vector graphics in PHP. If you want to understand every bit of this example, then you need to go through the trig, but we encourage those who don't care to skip the next section ("Necessary Trigonometry"). The core of the graphics code itself is in venn.php, and that example code really is important to understand if you want to do gd-based graphics in PHP.

Necessary trigonometry

Let's get the math out of the way first. Unavoidably, because we're talking about circles and areas, we're going to be talking about trigonometry. (As we've said, though, if you're not interested and are willing to trust us that we have code to calculate the area of circle intersections, please do skip ahead to the section "Planning the Display," later in this chapter).

The eventual task for our system is to start with three quantities (items in set A, items in set B, and items in the intersection) and produce a diagram containing two circles, with areas proportional to the set sizes, and positioned so that the area of overlap is proportional to the size of the intersection. For this section, we go in the other direction, and calculate intersection area from given circles. Our starting information will be: the radii of the two circles and the distance between their centers.

With reference to Figure 33-5, say that our circles have centers at points C and D, respectively, and that we know the radius of the circle on the left (segment CA or segment CB) and the radius of the circle on the right (DA or DB). What we'd like to know is the size of that odd lens-shaped object in the middle.

Area of intersecting circles

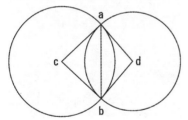

Figure 33-5: Area of intersection

The lens-shaped intersection area is split into two "halves" by segment AB (not quite halves because the circle sizes may be different), and we can calculate the area of each half independently. The crucial thing to notice is that the area of each of these half-lenses is the area that you get after you subtract the area of a triangle from the area of a pizza-slice-shaped sector of a circle. The right-hand lens half, for example, has an area equal to the sector of the left-hand circle determined by angle ACB, minus the area of the triangle ACB.

So if we can calculate the areas of sectors and triangles, then we are nearly done. The area of a sector is straightforward — it's just the area of the circle multiplied by the fraction of that circle that the angle of the sector sweeps over.

It takes a little more work and trigonometry to get the areas of the triangles. In our code, we make the job more straightforward by drawing a line from point C to point D, and considering only the half of the diagram above that line — then at the end, we multiply by two to get the real area. If we say that the intersection of segments AB and CD is point E, what we eventually care about is the area of triangles CAE and DAE. We start by calculating the angles of triangle CDA (whose side lengths are known to us) and, by using that information, determining the lengths of CE, DE, and AE. After we know these lengths, we know the bases and heights, and the areas of the right triangles CAE and DAE are just 1/2 (*base* x *height*).

The code in Listing 33-8 shows code to do this kind of area calculation. Its main "public" function is `circle_intersection_area()`, which expects as arguments the radii of two circles and the distance between them. The simplest case is where the distance is greater than the sum of the radii: The circles do not touch; there is no intersection, and the answer is zero.

Listing 33-8: `trig.php`

```php
<?php

function angle_given_sides ($opposite, $other_1, $other_2) {
   if (($opposite <= 0) ||
       ($other_1 <= 0) ||
       ($other_2 <= 0) ||
       ($opposite >= ($other_1 + $other_2)) ||
       ($other_1 >= ($opposite + $other_2)) ||
       ($other_2 >= ($other_1 + $opposite))) {
     die("Triangle with impossible side lengths in ".
         "angle_given_sides: $opposite, $other_1, $other_2");
   }
   else {
     $numerator =
       ((($other_1 * $other_1) +
          ($other_2 * $other_2)) -
         ($opposite * $opposite));
     $denominator = 2 * $other_1 * $other_2;
     return(acos($numerator / $denominator));
   }
}

function area_to_radius ($area) {
  return (sqrt ($area / M_PI));
}

function circle_intersection_area ($radius_left,
                                   $radius_right,
                                   $distance) {
  if ($radius_right + $radius_left <= $distance) {
    return(0);
  }
```

```
else {
  // first, we find the angle measures of a triangle
  //   formed by the two radii and the distance
  //   between them
  $left_sector_angle =
    angle_given_sides($radius_right, $radius_left,
                      $distance);
  $right_sector_angle =
    angle_given_sides($radius_left, $radius_right,
                      $distance);

  // test for obtuseness --- the sector angle can
  // be obtuse, but the triangle angle should not
  // be.  Also save the result as a sign for the
  // eventual area calculation

  if ($left_sector_angle < M_PI / 2) {
    $left_triangle_angle = $left_sector_angle;
    $left_triangle_sign = 1;
  }
  else {
    $left_triangle_angle = M_PI - $left_sector_angle;
    $left_triangle_sign = -1;
  }
  if ($right_sector_angle < M_PI / 2) {
    $right_triangle_angle = $right_sector_angle;
    $right_triangle_sign = 1;
  }
  else {
    $right_triangle_angle = M_PI - $right_sector_angle;
    $right_triangle_sign = -1;
  }

  // next, find the height of that triangle, assuming
  //   the distance is the base

  $height = ($radius_left / sin(M_PI_2)) *
            sin($left_triangle_angle);
  $base_left = ($radius_left / sin(M_PI_2)) *
               sin(M_PI_2 - $left_triangle_angle);
  $base_right = ($radius_right / sin(M_PI_2)) *
                sin(M_PI_2 - $right_triangle_angle);

  // finally find triangle and sector areas, and
  // subtract (or add) appropriately to get the
  // intersection area.  Multiply by 2 to reflect
  // areas on both sides of the segment connecting
  // the circle centers
```

```
    $left_triangle_area = $base_left * $height / 2;
    $right_triangle_area = $base_right * $height / 2;
    $left_sector_area =
        ($left_sector_angle / (2 * M_PI)) *
        (M_PI * $radius_left * $radius_left);
    $right_sector_area =
        ($right_sector_angle / (2 * M_PI)) *
        (M_PI * $radius_right * $radius_right);

    $intersection_area = 2 *
        (($left_sector_area -
            ($left_triangle_sign * $left_triangle_area)) +
         ($right_sector_area -
            ($right_triangle_sign * $right_triangle_area)));

    return($intersection_area);
    }
}

?>
```

Note that all the angle calculations are in radians, rather than degrees. In radians, a right angle is pi/2, and a complete revolution around a circle is 2 x pi. We tend to use PHP constants for these values whenever we can; in particular M_PI (the value of pi), and M_PI_2 (pi/2).

There's one final wrinkle that we've ignored in our discussion so far, but which we had to deal with in the code. The problem is that it's possible for either angle ACE or angle ADE (as we call them in Figure 33-5) to be obtuse — that is, more than 90 degrees in size. To see this, look at that diagram and imagine what happens as you make the circle on the right smaller, and move its center D progressively closer to C. At some point D actually moves to the left of segment AB. In this case, the circle intersection area to the left of AB is actually the sum of a sector and a triangle rather than a difference. The sector determined by DA and DB sweeps out more than half of the circle centered at D, and the remaining portion we want to include is the area of the triangle ADB. We handle this in the code by testing if the angles are obtuse, and multiplying the triangle areas by either 1 or -1, depending on the result of the test.

Planning the display

Now we pop up a couple t of levels and think about actually generating a diagram. We assume that we have as input three numbers (size of set 1, size of set 2, and size of intersection), along with some textual labels. We want to scale and locate these circles so that everything has the right area, labels get associated with the right circles, and everything fits within the size of the diagram we're creating.

Simplifying assumptions

We start off with some totally arbitrary decisions that, after being made, simplify everything. We decree that:

- All the images that we generate are the same size, and that size is 300 pixels high and 600 pixels wide.

- The centers of the circles are always on the same horizonal line. This means that their y-coordinate is decided in advance, and we change the area of intersection just by changing the x-coordinates.

- The circles always fit within the top two-thirds of the diagram (reserving the lower third for labels). So put the y-coordinate of the centers one third of the way down the image from the top. And because the circles may not intersect at all, they shouldn't be larger than half of the width of the image, so we have room to display two of them. We also make sure that the circles are no greater than 90% of the room available given everything we've said so far, so that they don't touch the image borders. Finally, we decide that, regardless of the actual numbers as input, the larger of the two circles is as large as it can be. (Scale is consistent within the diagram, but not between diagrams.)

Determining size and scale

Now we have nearly all the information needed to create a visualization, and the pieces we are lacking, of course, depend on the input values we are going to receive. We use the sizes of the actual sets to determine the radii of the circles for display. We want the larger of the two set counts to correspond to the largest circle we can afford to display, and then scale everything else appropriately. (We do all this in the code in Listing 33-9 (venn.php) — you may want to look ahead to that code as we lay out what we need to do in it.)

It's actually easiest for us to calculate the largest radius we can afford: Given the constraints we've already listed, the larger radius should be 90 percent of 1/4 of the image width, or 90 percent of 1/3 of the image height, whichever is smaller. So we calculate this maximum radius, assume that the larger set size is proportional to the area of a circle with this radius, and come up with a general conversion for mapping from input numbers to area as measured in pixels. We use this to decide on the areas of the circles and of the intersection area we want.

What numbers should we know at this point? We know:

- The radius of the bigger circle. (It's the largest radius that fits our constraints.)

- The area of the bigger circle (calculated as pi x r^2).

- The radius of the smaller circle (from the ratio of the input set sizes treated as area ratios and then mapped back to a radius).

- The area of the smaller circle (calculated).

- The area of intersection (scaled the same way as other areas, from the input numbers).

- The y-coordinate of the circle centers. (We decreed that it be the line that's one-third of the way down the image.)

What are we missing before we can display our circles? The only thing that we're missing is the x-coordinates of the centers.

The easy cases

Where we decide to put the circle centers depends on the extent to which our sets overlap. There are some cases that we can dispense with, that don't need all this trigonometry we've been spending our time on. Those are:

♦ *No items are in the intersection.* In this case, we don't want the circles to touch at all. We simply locate the centers at default locations in the middles of the two halves of the diagram. Because of the way that we limited the maximum radius, the circles are completely separated.

♦ *One set is completely contained in the other* — that is, one of the sets has the same size as the intersection. For this case, we just choose to put the center of the larger circle in the middle of the diagram and the middle of the other circle offset a bit from it but not so much that any of the smaller circle is outside the larger one.

♦ *The two sets are the same* (and all three input numbers are the same). For this, we just draw one circle with an x-coordinate right in the middle of the picture.

The hard case

Now the hard one: If the sets only partially overlap, where should we put the circle centers? At this point, we have some math in our pocket from the "Necessary trigonometry" section: Given two circles and the distance between their centers, we can figure out the area of overlap. Unfortunately, this is not the direction we need the calculation go in — we start with the desired area of intersection, and we must work backwards to the desired locations of the circle centers.

Now if we were good and diligent mathematicians but lazy programmers, we would just invert the trigonometric equations we used in `trig.php`, to solve for center distance rather than for intersection area. As it is, though, we're enthusiastic programmers, and if we're any kind of mathematician at all we're definitely the lazy kind. So what we're going to do instead is search for the answer. The function `find_circle_centers()` in Listing 33-9 implements a binary search for the answer: It starts with a middling distance, asks our trigonometry code what the resulting area would be, and successively refines the distance to zero in on the desired area.

Listing 33-9: `venn.php`

```php
<?php
include_once("trig.php");

$IMAGE_WIDTH = 600;
$IMAGE_HEIGHT = 300;
$CENTER_FINDING_ITERATIONS = 20;

function imagecircle ($image, $center_x, $center_y,
                $radius, $color)
{
```

```
    $diameter = $radius * 2;
    imagearc($image, $center_x, $center_y,
      $diameter, $diameter, 0, 360,
            $color);
}

function venn_visualization
  ($left_amount, $left_name,
   $right_amount, $right_name,
   $intersection_amount)
{
  global $IMAGE_HEIGHT, $IMAGE_WIDTH,
         $CENTER_FINDING_ITERATIONS;
  // --- create the image and allocate colors
  $image = imagecreate($IMAGE_WIDTH, $IMAGE_HEIGHT)
    or die("Could not create image");
  $background_color = ImageColorAllocate($image, 255,255,255);
  $left_color = ImageColorAllocate($image, 100, 100, 200);
  $right_color = ImageColorAllocate($image, 200, 100, 100);
  $intersection_color = ImageColorAllocate($image, 225, 225, 225);
  $black_color = ImageColorAllocate($image, 0,0,0);

  // --- decide how big the circles should be
  $max_radius = min((($IMAGE_HEIGHT * 0.9) / 3),
            (($IMAGE_WIDTH * 0.9) / 4));
  $center_y = $IMAGE_HEIGHT / 3.0;
  $default_center_x_left = $IMAGE_WIDTH / 4.0;
  $default_center_x_right = (3 * $IMAGE_WIDTH) / 4.0;
  $middle_x = $IMAGE_WIDTH / 2.0;
  $radius_left_side_raw =
    area_to_radius($left_amount);
  $radius_right_side_raw =
    area_to_radius($right_amount);
  $intersection_radius_raw =
    area_to_radius($intersection_amount);
  $scale_factor = $max_radius /
                  (max($radius_left_side_raw,
                      $radius_right_side_raw));
  $radius_left_side = $radius_left_side_raw * $scale_factor;
  $radius_right_side = $radius_right_side_raw * $scale_factor;
  // (it's convenient to pretend that the intersection area
  //  has a radius (although it's not circular) just so we can
  //  calculate things the same way as the circles)
  $intersection_radius = $intersection_radius_raw * $scale_factor;
  $area_left_side = M_PI *
                    $radius_left_side * $radius_left_side;
  $area_right_side = M_PI *
                    $radius_right_side * $radius_right_side;
  $intersection_area = M_PI *
```

```
                    $intersection_radius * $intersection_radius;

// We now have all necessary info except where to locate the
//   centers of the circles.
// Four cases:
// 1) no intersection, 2) partial intersection
// 3) left is strict subset of right,
// 4) right is subset of left.

if ($intersection_amount == 0) {
  // No intersection
  $center_x_left = $default_center_x_left;
  $center_x_right = $default_center_x_right;
  $left_fill_x = $center_x_left;
  $right_fill_x = $center_x_right;
  $intersection_fill_x = -1;
}
else if (($intersection_area < $area_left_side) &&
         ($intersection_area < $area_right_side)) {

  // The complicated case --- we must decide where the
  //   circle centers should be so that the overlap is
  //   proportional to the set intersection
  // First, we call a function that decides how far apart
  //   the circle centers need to be.
  $center_distance =
    find_center_distance($radius_left_side, $radius_right_side,
                         $intersection_area,
                         $CENTER_FINDING_ITERATIONS);

  // Once we know the distance, we place the circle centers
  //   approximately in the middle of the image
  $center_x_left = $middle_x  // left/right middle of image
                   - ($center_distance *
                     ($radius_left_side /
                       ($radius_left_side +
                         $radius_right_side)));
  $center_x_right = $middle_x  // left/right middle of image
                    + ($center_distance *
                      ($radius_right_side /
                        ($radius_left_side +
                          $radius_right_side)));

  // we have decided the sizes and centers of the circles.
  //   Now, we must determine good points to start a
  //   "flood fill" coloring of the three different regions
  $left_fill_x =
    (($center_x_left - $radius_left_side) +
     ($center_x_right - $radius_right_side))
```

```
      / 2.0;
    $right_fill_x =
      (($center_x_left + $radius_left_side) +
       ($center_x_right + $radius_right_side))
       / 2.0;
    $intersection_fill_x =
        (($center_x_right - $radius_right_side) +
         ($center_x_left + $radius_left_side))
         / 2.0;
}
else if (($intersection_area == $area_left_side) &&
         ($intersection_area < $area_right_side)) {
    // The right set completely contains the left set
    //    We need to place the left circle somewhere
    //    inside the right circle.
    $center_x_right = $middle_x;
    $center_x_left = $middle_x -
      ($radius_right_side - $radius_left_side) / 2;
    $left_fill_x = -1;
    $right_fill_x =
      (($center_x_left + $radius_left_side) +
       ($center_x_right + $radius_right_side))
       / 2.0;
    $intersection_fill_x = $center_x_left;
}
else if ($intersection_area == $area_right_side) {
    $center_x_left = $middle_x;
    $center_x_right = $middle_x +
      ($radius_left_side - $radius_right_side) / 2;
    $right_fill_x = -1;
    $left_fill_x =
      (($center_x_left - $radius_left_side) +
       ($center_x_right - $radius_right_side))
       / 2.0;
    $intersection_fill_x = $center_x_right;
}

// now, actually draw and fill regions
imagecircle($image, $center_x_left, $center_y,
          $radius_left_side, $black_color);
imagecircle($image, $center_x_right, $center_y,
        $radius_right_side, $black_color);
if ($left_fill_x > 0) {
  imagefill($image, $left_fill_x,
          $center_y, $left_color);
}
if ($right_fill_x > 0) {
  imagefill($image, $right_fill_x,
          $center_y, $right_color);
```

```php
  }
  if ($intersection_fill_x > 0 ) {
     imagefill($image, $intersection_fill_x,
             $center_y, $intersection_color);
  }
  $left_hand_text = "$left_name ($left_amount)";
  $right_hand_text = "$right_name ($right_amount)";
  $intersection_text = "Intersection: $intersection_amount";
  left_label($image, $left_hand_text, $left_color);
  right_label($image, $right_hand_text, $right_color);
  intersection_label($image, $intersection_text, $black_color);

  // send off the image
  header("Content-type: image/png");
  imagepng($image);
  imagedestroy($image);
}

function left_label ($image, $label_string, $color) {
  global $IMAGE_WIDTH, $IMAGE_HEIGHT;
  imagestring($image, 5,
              ($IMAGE_WIDTH / 4.0 -
                (imagefontwidth(5) * strlen($label_string))
                / 2),
              $IMAGE_HEIGHT - 55.0,
              $label_string, $color);
}

function right_label ($image, $label_string, $color) {
  global $IMAGE_WIDTH, $IMAGE_HEIGHT;
  imagestring($image, 5,
              ($IMAGE_WIDTH * 3 / 4.0 -
                (imagefontwidth(5) * strlen($label_string))
                / 2),
              $IMAGE_HEIGHT - 55.0,
              $label_string, $color);
}

function intersection_label ($image, $label_string, $color) {
  global $IMAGE_WIDTH, $IMAGE_HEIGHT;
  imagestring($image, 2,
              ($IMAGE_WIDTH / 2.0  -
                (imagefontwidth(2) * strlen($label_string))
                / 2),
              $IMAGE_HEIGHT - 30.0,
              $label_string, $color);
}

function find_center_distance ($r1, $r2, $desired_area,
```

```
                              $iterations) {
  // The greatest possible distance is r1 + r2, and
  //  the smallest is abs(r1 - r2) Let's start in the middle.
  $distance_guess = (($r1 + $r2) + abs($r1 - $r2)) / 2.0;
  $distance_increment = (($r1 + $r2) - abs($r1 - $r2)) / 4.0;
  for ($x = 0; $x < $iterations; $x++) {
    $calculated_area =
      circle_intersection_area($r1, $r2, $distance_guess);
    if ($calculated_area < $desired_area) {
      // move centers closer
      $distance_guess -= $distance_increment;
      $distance_increment *= 0.5;
    }
    else if ($calculated_area > $desired_area) {
      // move centers apart
      $distance_guess += $distance_increment;
      $distance_increment *= 0.5;
    }
    else {
      // unlikely, but ya never know
      break;
    }
  }
  return($distance_guess);
}
?>
```

Display

Now we know exactly where we want to put our circles, and how large they should be. What remains is the graphics code to actually make the display happen. This is also in Listing 33-9 (venn.php). (We are actually committing a stylistic error here, in that the code that decides on sizes and shapes is in the same file and function as the code that actually draws those shapes. We apologize and, of course, urge you to do as we say, not as we do.)

To produce the graphic, we go through the following steps by using the gd library:

1. We create an image by using ImageCreate(). (At this point, the image is not any particular image format, such as PNG or JPEG, but just an internal gd image.)

2. We allocate colors within the image by using ImageColorAllocate(). We care about five colors: the background color (white), a color for borders and regular text (black), a color for the interior of the left hand circle (which we decide is bluish), a color for the interior of the right-hand circle (reddish), and a color for the intersection (gray). All these colors are specified by using a red-green-blue scale of 0 to 255.

3. We draw the circles in black by using a function of our own, imagecircle(), that takes as arguments the image, the radius, the location of the centers, and a color. (See the "Notes on circles" section about drawing circles in gd.)

4. Now, we want to fill in the three areas (the intersection and the two non-intersection portions of the circles) with the appropriate colors. We use `ImageFill()` for this, which *flood-fills* outward from a specified point until the fill encounters previously drawn lines. Choosing the starting points for the fills is somewhat tricky because it depends on the different intersection cases. In general, though, we start with a y-coordinate that is the same as the circle centers and calculate an x-coordinate that's right in the middle of the area we are trying to color.

5. We use `ImageString()` to draw the appropriate labels for each circle, centering each one in the middle of the lower-third of the image and in the middle of the appropriate left-right half. We also create and display a count label for the intersection and display it in the middle of the image.

6. Now, we have a complete gd image, and what remains is to ship it off to the user. We send an HTTP header advising the browser that a PNG image is on the way. Then we use `ImagePng()` to convert the gd image to PNG and send it off.

7. Finally, we call `ImageDestroy()` to free any resources associated with the temporary image we created. More recent versions of PHP should be handling this already, assuming that the image is of type `resource`, but either way calling `ImageDestroy()` does no harm.

Notes on circles

One thing that puzzles people sometimes, if confronted with the gd functions, is that there seems to be no way to draw a circle (or at least there is no function name with `circle` in its name). This is because there are at least two functions that generalize circle-drawing: `imageellipse()` (available only with gd 2.0.1 and later), and `imagearc`. The former draws an ellipse (which can be a circle if the width and height are the same), and the latter draws a circular arc portion (which can be a circle if you specify a full 360 degrees of arc). In our code we chose the latter because we were using a pre-2.0.1 version of gd.

Notes on centering text

As we wrote textual labels in the image code, we actually didn't bother centering the text around any horizontal axis, but we did do some left-right centering. We simply used a built-in numbered font from gd, calculated the width of our text as displayed by that font (by using `imagefontwidth()`), and ensured that the left-hand starting point for the text was our desired center minus half the width of the text. This was easy, in part because the built-in fonts we used were monospace, and so `imagefontwidth()` was able to calculate width by referring only to the length of the string. Things get slightly more complicated if you're using a variable-width font — any calculation of string width then needs to know the actual string that is printed, not just the number of characters in it.

Visualizing a database

We can now produce these Venn-like diagrams on demand, given some numbers and text to start with. Our final task is to hook this up appropriately to a database via a Web form. We use exactly the same small MySQL database that we use in the section on HTML bar graphs, earlier in this chapter.

The goal is to let the user choose exactly two restrictions on our database's table, extract counts corresponding to how many rows survive each restriction, count how many rows survive both restrictions, and then pass the results off to our diagramming code.

Listing 33-10 shows code for a form designed around our particular database, mostly just hardcoded HTML. It loads an auxiliary file called `query_clauses.php` (shown in Listing 33-11), which is extremely hard-coded. This file lists and numbers all the restrictions that we want to offer to users, in the form of both an SQL `where` clause and in an English translation.

Listing 33-10: `visualization_form.php`

```
<HTML><HEAD><TITLE>DB Visualization</TITLE></HEAD>
<BODY>

<B>Choose one from each column, and we'll<B>
display the intersection from the survey data:<BR>
<FORM METHOD=POST ACTION="db_visualization.php"
      TARGET=_new >
<TABLE>

<?php
include("query_clauses.php");
for ($x = 0; $x < count($QUERY_CLAUSES); $x++) {
  print("<TR><TD><INPUT
            TYPE=RADIO NAME=\"left_clause\"
            VALUE=$x>".
            $QUERY_DESCRIPTION[$x] ."</TD>
        <TD><INPUT
            TYPE=RADIO NAME=\"right_clause\"
            VALUE=$x>".
            $QUERY_DESCRIPTION[$x] ."</TD></TR>");
}
?>

</TABLE>
<INPUT TYPE=HIDDEN NAME="table" VALUE="programmers">
<INPUT TYPE=SUBMIT NAME=SUBMIT>
</FORM>

</BODY>
</HTML>
```

Notice that this form is not self-submitting. For this example, we've chosen to completely separate PHP-generated HTML pages from PHP-generated PNG pages and avoid the complexity of embedding images in HTML. We've also chosen a _new target type for the form submission so that the image appears in a new browser window.

Listing 33-11: `query_clauses.php`

```php
<?php

$QUERY_CLAUSES = array();
$QUERY_DESCRIPTION = array();

$QUERY_CLAUSES[0] = "sex = 'F'";
$QUERY_DESCRIPTION[0] = "Female";

$QUERY_CLAUSES[1] = "sex = 'M'";
$QUERY_DESCRIPTION[1] = "Male";

$QUERY_CLAUSES[2] = "language = 'PHP'";
$QUERY_DESCRIPTION[2] = "likes PHP";

$QUERY_CLAUSES[3] = "language = 'Java'";
$QUERY_DESCRIPTION[3] = "likes Java";

$QUERY_CLAUSES[4] = "language = 'Lisp'";
$QUERY_DESCRIPTION[4] = "likes Lisp";

$QUERY_CLAUSES[5] = "language = 'C'";
$QUERY_DESCRIPTION[5] = "likes C";

$QUERY_CLAUSES[6] = "language = 'Perl'";
$QUERY_DESCRIPTION[6] = "likes Perl";

$QUERY_CLAUSES[7] = "os = 'Linux'";
$QUERY_DESCRIPTION[7] = "uses Linux";

$QUERY_CLAUSES[8] = "os = 'Solaris'";
$QUERY_DESCRIPTION[8] = "uses Solaris";

$QUERY_CLAUSES[9] = "os = 'MacOS'";
$QUERY_DESCRIPTION[9] = "uses MacOS";

$QUERY_CLAUSES[10] = "os = 'Windows'";
$QUERY_DESCRIPTION[10] = "uses Windows";

$QUERY_CLAUSES[11] = "age < 20";
$QUERY_DESCRIPTION[11] = "is less than 20 years old";

$QUERY_CLAUSES[12] = "age > 30";
$QUERY_DESCRIPTION[12] = "is over 30 years old";
```

```
$QUERY_CLAUSES[13] = "continent = 'North America'";
$QUERY_DESCRIPTION[13] = "lives in North America";

$QUERY_CLAUSES[14] = "continent = 'South America'";
$QUERY_DESCRIPTION[14] = "lives in South America";

$QUERY_CLAUSES[15] = "continent = 'Antarctica'";
$QUERY_DESCRIPTION[15] = "lives in Antarctica";

$QUERY_CLAUSES[16] = "continent = 'Asia'";
$QUERY_DESCRIPTION[16] = "lives in Asia";

$QUERY_CLAUSES[17] = "continent = 'Europe'";
$QUERY_DESCRIPTION[17] = "lives in Europe";
?>
```

A screenshot of the form itself is shown in Figure 33-6.

One last code file and we're done. We have our image creation code and a form for requesting an image. The last piece of the puzzle is code to handle the form submission, perform the appropriate counts on the database, and call the image code. This code is shown in Listing 33-12.

Figure 33-6: DB visualization Web form

Listing 33-12: `db_visualization.php`

```php
<?php
include_once("dbconnect.php");
include_once("query_clauses.php");
include_once("venn.php");

if (IsSet($_POST['table']) &&
    IsSet($_POST['left_clause']) &&
    IsSet($_POST['right_clause'])) {
  $table = $_POST['table'];
  $left_clause_id = $_POST['left_clause'];
  $right_clause_id = $_POST['right_clause'];

  $left_clause = $QUERY_CLAUSES[$left_clause_id];
  $right_clause = $QUERY_CLAUSES[$right_clause_id];

  visualize_intersection ($table, $left_clause,
                                  $right_clause);
}
else {
  print("Form submission not handled correctly.<BR>".
      "Did you choose all options?");
}

function visualize_intersection ($table, $left_clause,
                                  $right_clause)
{

  $left_query = "select count(*) from $table
              where $left_clause";
  $right_query = "select count(*) from $table
              where $right_clause";
  $intersection_query =
              "select count(*) from $table
              where $left_clause and $right_clause";

  $result = mysql_query($left_query)
    or die("Query was $left_query:" . mysql_error());
  $row = mysql_fetch_row($result);
  $left_count = $row[0];

  $result = mysql_query($right_query)
    or die(mysql_error());
  $row = mysql_fetch_row($result);
  $right_count = $row[0];

  $result = mysql_query($intersection_query)
    or die(mysql_error());
```

```
$row = mysql_fetch_row($result);
$intersection_count = $row[0];

venn_visualization($left_count, $left_clause,
                   $right_count, $right_clause,
                   $intersection_count);
}
?>
```

The submission form passes in index numbers of SQL clauses, rather than the clauses themselves, so we don't need to worry about escape characters in the submission. The form-handling code includes the same query_clauses.php file, so the index numbers should always agree. The form handler collects the two clauses, creates three SQL statements out of them, executes the statements to get counts, and uses the results as arguments to the venn_visualization() function.

Trying it out

Now that our system is complete, let's give it a spin. Bringing up visualization_form.php, we choose the first option from the left-hand column (Female), and the second option from the right-hand column (Male), and submit. The result is shown in Figure 33-7 — two separate circles because, given the database schema, it's impossible for anyone to be both male and female. (Please, no e-mails about the narrowness of our views — it's just an example!)

Figure 33-7: No intersection

On a color monitor the left-hand circle is bluish while the right-hand circle is reddish. Because this is a grayscale book, though, you probably see two gray or black circles.

Now a different query: uses Solaris on the left, and lives in Antarctica on the right. (We chose this deliberately, knowing that our lone South Pole correspondent sees only one kind of Sun during the winter.)

The result is shown in Figure 33-8: one small gray circle inside a larger blue one, indicating that all Antarcticans are Solaris users but not vice versa.

Figure 33-8: Subset

Finally, for the more typical case, let's choose likes PHP from the left, and uses Linux from the right.

The result, in Figure 33-9, is two mostly-overlapping circles. (Again, please no letters — we have no idea if these proportions match the world as it is or just the world as we would like it to be.)

Figure 33-9: Partial intersection

Extensions

This example is a complete, working, end-to-end system, but as always there are countless ways in which it could be tweaked, improved, and especially extended. Naturally, there is a lot you could do to change the cosmetics of the images or to make the look more configurable.

The weakest part right now in our view is the form submission, which is hard-coded to pertain only to a particular known MySQL table. Much cooler would be code that, armed only with a table (or view) name and the appropriate login, would quiz the database about column names and types and the distribution of values, and then develop such a form on its own.

One extension that may immediately occur to you doesn't work, unfortunately, at least without substantial changes to the display code. There is no good way to involve a third set (and circle) in the diagram, cover all the cases, and be assured that all the shapes can still be circular. If you have any doubt about this, try diagramming the following three sets: people who were born in Europe, people who currently live in Europe, and people who currently live in a continent different from the one they were born in.

Gotchas and Troubleshooting

Code to produce images can be especially difficult to debug, because some of the simplest tricks (for example, diagnostic print statements) can't be used as easily. What follows is a list of symptoms you may encounter in running gd-enabled PHP code, and some things you can try to correct them.

Symptom: Completely blank image

Sometimes your code runs without incident or apparent error, but the image that results is a blank slate, although you expected it to be full of graphic wonders. Some things to check (some obvious, some not):

♦ Are you drawing outside the bounds of the image? (If your image is 100 x 100, a small circle drawn at (200, 200) cannot be seen)

♦ Are you drawing infinitesimally small graphics? (A circle with a center in range of the image with a radius of zero or near-zero may be completely undetectable.)

♦ Are you drawing by using the background color? (White-on-white is the same as white.)

Symptom: Headers already sent

This is almost always due to printing text to output before the header call that announces a graphic image. Just as with other HTTP headers (such as those setting cookies), you must ruthlessly root out any printing of text before that call, even if that text is composed of blank lines or spaces.

One common pattern is to see something such as the following in your browser as you test:

```
Warning:  Division by zero in
/usr/local/apache/htdocs/graphics/fractal1.php on line 18
Warning:  Cannot add header information - headers already sent by
(output started at /usr/local/apache/htdocs/graphics/fractal1.php:18) in
/usr/local/apache/htdocs/graphics/fractal1.php on line 19)
PNG
IHDR [trailing off into binary gibberish]
```

The binary gibberish is, of course, your image data, which is being printed as text in your browser resulting in nonsense characters. The reason you're seeing it as text is that the image announcement headers could not be sent, because some text was sent before those headers were encountered. And that text that was sent, in turn, was probably just (in this case) the text of the division-by-zero warning itself. Fixing the division-by-zero problem (or whatever the error or warning is in your case) may eliminate the printed error, which may make the header-sending statement happy, which may mean a successful image display.

If, instead, the very first thing you see is the warning about headers, you may be sending blank lines or spaces before the header without being aware of it. Look for any print statements, any included HTML, and (especially) any space at the beginning or end of files that have been included or required. If an included PHP file so much as ends with '?> ' rather than '?>', you may be sending a space's worth of HTML, which would cause text headers to be sent before the image headers are seen.

Symptom: Broken image

How exactly this displays depends on your browser program — some display a sad, visibly broken image icon, while Mozilla may politely inform you that your image can't be displayed because it contains errors. Either way, though, the problem is that your browser cannot read the data in the image format you said you were sending. Some possible causes:

♦ The flip side of the previous Headers already sent problem: You may be printing random text without being aware of it but, in this case, *after* the image header has already been sent rather than before. This text is munging up the stream of image data.

♦ You have misspelled the variable of containing your image — for example imagepng($imag) where you meant imagepng($image). You are actually calling the convert-and-send function on nothing at all.

♦ Your convert-and-send function is actually producing a text error rather than a graphic image (possibly because you don't actually have support for that image type compiled into PHP).

♦ You have actually somehow screwed up your internal gd image well before trying to send it off. One very common cause of this is failure to allocate colors in a palette-based image or to use color indexes that haven't been allocated.

♦ Your gd library is producing in good faith, and your browser is receiving in good faith, but they disagree about what a valid image format looks like. (This is generally about the last explanation you should consider, although we did see it happen once.) With some (but not all) PNG images, Mozilla RC2 wouldn't display apparently valid PNGs generated by gd 1.8.4, although other browsers had no problem. (Mozilla RC1 and 1.0 did just fine.)

In our experience, the best way to debug this sort of problem is simply to comment out the PHP statement that sends the header announcing an image, and then look at the output as text in your browser. If everything were working perfectly, you would expect to see your binary image data as text, which would mean a lot of strange-character gibberish, possibly starting with a short amount of recognizable text (like PNG). If you see a PHP warning or error instead of the image data, or in addition to the image data, you can proceed to debug that. If you see nearly nothing, not much of an image is being sent — this may imply problem #2 or #4 above. If you see what looks like a reasonable amount of pure image data, you may need to look at your code very carefully for small amounts of text (like spaces) that you may have introduced.

If all else fails, you can reluctantly consider explanations such as #5, or other kinds of browser, gd, or PHP bugs, which you may want to test by using different image formats or different browsers. But remember that explaining things that way breaks the cardinal rule of code debugging which is: It's always your fault.

Summary

If you create on-the-fly graphic images by using PHP, you're creating something completely different from the usual HTML that PHP generates — a completely different format, and a completely different look. Although there are hassles associated with getting the gd image library working, after you get past those you have quite a rich set of image-manipulation functions to work with. You can create Web pages that are all image, or pages that have <IMG> tags that link to dynamic images, or you can start building a library of image files for display later on. Either way you go, you have a richer vocabulary to work with than with pure HTML, and (even if many situations don't require dynamic images) you have another type of tool in your kit.

## Chapter 34

Converting Static HTML Sites

In This Chapter

♦ Planning the big upgrade

♦ Redesigning the UI

♦ Designing a new schema

♦ Dumping data into a database

♦ Templating

♦ Performance and caching

Almost everything we've discussed in this book so far assumes that you are designing your PHP-enabled site from scratch, including any database schemas that may be required. The truth, however, is that many of the most common and valuable PHP projects involve converting a pre-existing HTML site to a more maintainable PHP version. Here we describe in detail how this is accomplished, using a real site as an example.

The information in this chapter may also be valuable if you need to transfer data from one format to another (tab-delimited file to database, one database to another) or if you want to take a bunch of text files and turn them into a Web site.

Planning the Big Upgrade

Our example site, MysteryGuide.com (at www.mysteryguide.com), is one we've run since about 1996. If you can think back that far in the history of the Internet, most people and companies were barely experimenting with HTML, much less technologies for creating dynamic Web sites. PHP was then still a CGI tool; MySQL had just gotten off the ground — and we hadn't heard of either of them.

We originally kept our data in FileMaker, therefore, and wrote it out to static HTML files by using another, little-known computer language. Although the site kept growing over time, we never quite got the motivation or time to upgrade our backend systems — among other things, we were writing the first and second editions of this book and thus heroically sacrificing our own projects to share our knowledge with you, dear Reader. In any case, after a few years, we had a site that consisted of almost 1000 separate HTML files, which were a growing nightmare to maintain. The hardware and software on which we developed the site were old and prone to breakage, and upgrading didn't seem an option for various reasons. (It was all Macintosh OS 8, for one thing.) It became almost impossible to add new titles to our review database because of the large amount of work entailed by every new addition. And, of course, we had the extra shame and humiliation of being the writers of a book about creating dynamic Web sites by using PHP — while our own site was minimally dynamic! It's only after years of therapy that we can confess this to you, dear Reader, in the hope that it may help you find the inner strength to clear up the ugly, static HTML sites in your own life.

The baby and the bathwater

The first step to recoding a site is to step back and take inventory of what is working well and what the most important fix-it items may be. Our experience has been that teams often skip this step through impatience and live to regret it later when they are confronting huge, difficult-to-reverse architectural issues. You already have a lot of good things going for you, and you know a lot of invaluable information about your needs and your audience — make sure you capture this information in a usable format.

As we took stock of MysteryGuide's code, content, and mission, this is what we found.

Audience characteristics:

♦ Audience is comprised of all ages and an equal gender split.

♦ No internationalization needs — all visitors can be assumed to read English competently.

♦ Unusually large percentage of older people and a heavy number of readers with poor vision.

♦ New visitors may land on any page because most come from search engines.

♦ Fairly large and vocal percentage of Macintosh users.

♦ MysteryGuide does not collect user data.

♦ Users often print out pages for offline viewing (for example, taking to library, sharing with friends).

Things that are working well:

♦ Navigation scheme (for example, dividing books into subgenres).

♦ Reviews and other data.

♦ Features (for example, book ratings, games, interviews).

♦ Heavily crawled by search engines.

Things that need work:

♦ Very difficult to change page layouts.

♦ Database is offline, non-relational, and can't be searched by users.

◆ Forums — not much traffic, spam magnet.

◆ Some users can't find the author or book they're looking for.

◆ Need tools to add and edit data.

◆ Site design lacks professional look.

What does all this stock-taking tell us? Actually the news is very good in this case. Basically the content is fine, and the big-picture navigation is working for now. In this case, our three major goals are very clear:

◆ Move data into a new database.

◆ Create dynamic page-generation with PHP and database.

◆ Initiate a cosmetic look-and-feel upgrade.

If we accomplish these three tasks and also drop the forum (which is an entirely separate subsystem), we can be in a good technical position to add new features desired by our users, such as search and printable versions of the book reviews.

Technical assessment

In addition to strategic insights about the site, we should assess the logical, physical, and software requirements of MysteryGuide.com and consider whether we need to upgrade them too.

Site architecture

MysteryGuide currently consists of approximately 900 pages, of which the vast majority (about 800) could be made dynamic. There are actually only a few types of pages:

◆ Front page

◆ Complete author list

◆ Genre pages

◆ Genre history pages

◆ Book pages

◆ Feature pages (interviews, games, and so forth)

◆ Miscellaneous pages (top rated books, FAQ, and so forth)

Of these, by far the most numerous and important are the book pages. We expect to spend at least half the time required by the whole project on just the book page template; the big data dump we plan is almost all for the book pages. After that, the genre page is the most important; and then the front page. Feature pages and single pages are the least important, and if push comes to shove, we could launch the redesigned site without them.

Hardware and software requirements

Obviously we're using PHP for the scripting language, and Apache for the Web server (because we run on Unix). For a purpose like this, moving from a static HTML site, MySQL is a no-brainer as the database. All we care about are very fast reads and the ability to scale to thousands of rows per table because we don't collect user data and perform writes only very occasionally (essentially just when someone reviews a book). If you needed to make a lot of writes, and especially if you needed rollbacks and triggers, you would have to evaluate other databases. (See Chapter 16 for more information on choosing a database.)

Because we're already using all these programs for the current version of MysteryGuide.com, we require no new hardware or software. After the upgrade is complete, we will actually be using fewer system resources and less disk space than before. Our upgrade actually makes the site (marginally) cheaper to run and more portable, as well as much more maintainable and scalable.

> **TIP:** You need a binary version of PHP to perform some of the tasks described in this section. If you don't have one already, compile and install it now. Refer to Chapter 4 for instructions.

Redesigning the UI

You want to get your designers working on the new look and feel as soon as possible, because they need some lead time to iterate on their ideas, and little UI code can be usefully written before they deliver their piece of the puzzle. If you don't know any good designers, finding some should be your first priority. If you're lucky enough to be in this position, having a usability team contribute from the beginning can also be helpful.

Our experience has been that most designers do best if you (or your usability people) give them the basic layout you want on each page — in the case of a working site, they can simply look at the old site or you can draw a little wireframe. You should also explain clearly any special factors that must be taken into account, such as (in our case) the stricture against tiny or light-colored fonts. You're actually helping them do their jobs more efficiently by imposing some structure at the beginning, and you have only yourself to blame if you give a designer carte blanche and end up with some bizarre art-school production.

We were very lucky to work with a designer, Mimi Yin of Mydesignco.com, who is deeply interested in data-rich sites, has a knack for using shape to add movement and interest to the page, and believes in getting client feedback early and often. She started working on the most important and pressing parts of the site (book and genre pages) and then harmonized the rest of the site to match. This is exactly what you want — the designer should not automatically begin working on the most visually appealing or prominent parts of the site (for example the front page or splash screen) just because that is the most interesting piece for him or her. She or he should work on the part that is most important for the site.

These are before and after screenshots of a MysteryGuide.com book page. As we noted in the "Site architecture" section above, the book page is the most important and numerous of our types of pages. Figure 34-1 shows the old design. (Keep a kind thought — it was designed in 1997.)

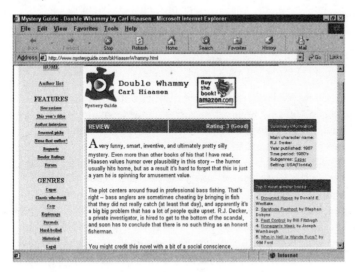

Figure 34-1: MysteryGuide.com book page before

Figure 34-2 shows the new design in the mockup phase. Notice how cleverly our designer has framed the various elements to set them off visually.

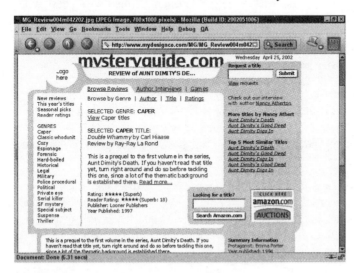

Figure 34-2: MysteryGuide.com book page after (mockup)

Even at this early stage, one thing is immediately obvious: If we go with this design, we are very likely to need to use a table layout and some spacer images. This kind of design is difficult (verging on impossible if you're not a DHTML master) to lay out nicely with "pure" XHTML and CSS. Few organizations really care about this distinction; but as a professional Web developer, it's your job to think about the ramifications of such a decision. If, for example, you're developing a new site for an IT consultancy, it may negatively affect their professional image to be seen using Web techniques that are not state-of-the-art. In our case, we feel that the attractiveness of the design is worth the tradeoff; and, in any case, we haven't taken a strong position in the great HTML 4 versus XHTML debate.

The important point is that you, as the Web developer, need to work with your designer to ensure that the look and feel you end up with melds smoothly with the technology you want to use. You can't necessarily expect designers to know or care about how the design is implemented. For example, the designer selects a font that he or she feels best expresses the mission of your site; but the Web developer is usually the one who decides whether to use <FONT> tags or cascading style sheets. He is also definitely the one who needs to test the design in different browsers with different settings. Sometimes the Web developer has to be the person to say, "This design looks incredibly crummy on a Macintosh," or "This design only works if JavaScript is on," or "This design loads incredibly slowly on a modem, leading to unacceptable latency on our servers." So trust your designers, treasure their talents, let them express their ideas — but remember that ultimately their deliverable is a mockup, whereas yours is an actual working site.

Planning a New Database Schema

As your designers are iterating away, you need to do some design of your own — designing a database schema, that is. If you already have a workable database, feel free to skip to the "Templating" section below.

> **CROSS-REFERENCE:** For basic information on working with SQL, see Chapter 17.

Besides the book reviews, MysteryGuide's main feature is a book recommendation system. This subsystem depends upon a questionnaire that our reviewers fill out for each book, detailing such things as the settings in which the action took place, the name of the protagonist, and how violent the book was. It is this data that we are seeking to represent in a SQL format.

Although we previously kept our data in a database, it was not truly relational. Each book had one big monolithic database record that listed everything that we wanted to know about that book. Relationality didn't matter that much for one-to-one fields, such as year of first publication — every book is only published for the first time once, after all. But for many-to-one fields, such as setting, we were forced to make some awkward compromises. Basically these boiled down to two methods. The first was setting a fixed number of fields of a certain type (for example: Subgenre1, Subgenre2, Subgenre3), which may or may not be filled in for any given book. The second was enabling multiple entries to be placed in a single field, separated by commas (for example: "UK, Germany, Switzerland" as the setting of one book). These multiple fields had to be untangled and redrawn as many-to-many SQL relationships in the new database.

Furthermore, a non-relational database inevitably has repetition that can be eliminated in a relational database. We want to know, for example, the name, sex, and nationality of each author. There are some authors whom we've reviewed multiple times, and this information is entered separately in each book's record. Besides causing inefficiency and duplication of effort, this practice resulted in a higher incidence of mistakes.

Our old non-relational database table looked something like this:

```
Title
Author name
Author gender
Author nationality
Year of first publication
Subgenre1
Subgenre2
Subgenre3
Settings (multiple)
Time period (multiple)
Rating
Protagonist name
Protagonist gender
Protagonist age
Protagonist nationality
Protagonist occupation
Protagonist organization
Action (1 - 5)
Humor (1 - 5)
Romance (1 - 5)
Sex (1 - 5)
Violence (1 - 5)
Type of crime (multiple)
Reviewer
Number of pages
Review completion date
Book ISBN
Movies (multiple)
Awards (multiple)
Review
Blurb
Author interview
```

Starting from this schema, it's pretty easy to divide these fields into three main buckets: Author, Protagonist, and Book information. The new Author table follows. Notice that we changed the field names to a more SQL-like naming style

```
A_id
A_firstname
A_lastname
A_gender
A_nationality
A_interview
```

The Protagonist table looks like this:

```
P_id
P_firstname
P_lastname
P_gender
P_age
P_nationality
P_occupation
P_organization
```

The main Book table contains these fields:

```
B_id
B_title
B_year
B_rating
B_action
B_humor
B_romance
B_sex
B_violence
B_reviewer
B_pages
B_reviewdate
B_ISBN
B_movie
B_awards
B_review
B_blurb
```

Notice that we have removed most of the multiple-entry fields, which must now get their own definition tables and also tables relating them to books. Subgenre information, for example, is now be stored in a simple table:

```
Sub_id
Sub_name
```

A matching table, Book_Subgenre, is required to store the relationships:

```
BSub_id
B_id
Sub_id
```

Settings, time periods, and type of crimes would also need similar new tables.

We decided, however, not to make new tables for Movies and Awards. Although a given book can have several film adaptations — for instance, *The Maltese Falcon* was filmed at least three times and won several awards — these are many-to-one relationships and treated by MysteryGuide basically as strings rather than categorizable information.

Now that you've worked out your schema on paper, go implement it as a bunch of SQL commands. You could also write a PHP script to do this, but a SQL file is actually much easier after you're comfortable with the concept. A SQL file is just a text file that strings together a bunch of SQL commands so you don't need to enter them one by one on the command line — instead you can read the whole file into MySQL with a single command. Listing 34-1 creates a database definition file.

Listing 34-1: Database definition file (newmg_structure.sql)

```
# MySQL dump file
# MysteryGuide SQL structure only


#
# Table structure for table 'author'
#
CREATE TABLE author (
  A_id int(11) DEFAULT '0' NOT NULL auto_increment,
  A_firstname tinytext,
  A_lastname tinytext,
  A_gender tinyint(4),
  A_nationality tinytext,
  A_interview tinytext,
  PRIMARY KEY (A_id)
);


#
# Table structure for table 'book'
#
CREATE TABLE book (
  B_id int(11) DEFAULT '0' NOT NULL auto_increment,
  B_title tinytext,
  B_year year(4),
  B_rating tinyint(4),
  B_action tinyint(4),
  B_humor tinyint(4),
  B_romance tinyint(4),
  B_sex tinyint(4),
  B_violence tinyint(4),
```

```
  B_reviewer tinytext,
  B_pages smallint(6),
  B_reviewdate date,
  B_ISBN tinytext,
  B_movie text,
  B_awards text,
  B_review text,
  B_blurb text,
  PRIMARY KEY (B_id)
);


#
# Table structure for table 'book_author'
#
CREATE TABLE book_author (
  BA_id int(11) DEFAULT '0' NOT NULL auto_increment,
  B_id int(11),
  A_id int(11),
  PRIMARY KEY (BA_id)
);


#
# Table structure for table 'subgenre'
#
CREATE TABLE subgenre (
  Sub_id int(11) DEFAULT '0' NOT NULL auto_increment,
  Sub_name tinytext,
  PRIMARY KEY (Sub_id)
);


#
# Table structure for table 'book_subgenre'
#
CREATE TABLE book_subgenre (
  BSub_id int(11) DEFAULT '0' NOT NULL auto_increment,
  B_id int(11),
  Sub_id int(11),
  PRIMARY KEY (BSub_id)
);
...
```

Whenever you're ready, you can dump this file into a MySQL database by typing the following commands (plus the password, when you're prompted for it) on the command line:

```
mysqladmin -u root -p create mysteryguide
mysql -u root -p mysteryguide < newmg_structure.sql
```

If you make a mistake, don't panic! You can keep dropping the database, fixing your SQL errors in the file, re-creating the database, and reloading.

Remember to grant privileges for this database to non-root MySQL users as soon as you finish creating the database permanently. The principle to follow is to give each database user the lowest level of privileges necessary to get the job done. In this case, your default MySQL user only needs read privileges because ordinary visitors do not write to our database. You must create a different MySQL user with write privileges for reviewers, and possibly another for editors or administrators. These come into play in the section "Tools," later in this chapter.

Dumping Data Into a Database

Now that you have a nice fresh database, you're ready to dump information into it. We mainly assume that you are starting with another database (as we are) or possibly a spreadsheet. In the section "Harvesting data," later in this chapter, we discuss how to adapt these tasks if you're starting with multiple text files (for example, HTML files or Word documents) instead.

Data-massaging

So we begin by dumping the data from FileMaker (or any data store) into a tab-delimited file. Most small databases and spreadsheets have some way to do this automatically — the command may be called something such as Export or Dump. It's very important to write down or print out the order in which the fields exported, which may be considerably different from their display order.

At this point you should check over the tab-delimited file and make sure that the data is basically good. You may need to fix it up a little bit at this point. We needed to turn some old-style Macintosh linebreaks, for example, into Unix-compatible newlines. The easiest way to do so is to break out Perl regex on the command line:

```
perl -pi -e 's/\r/\n/g' tabdelimitedfile.txt
```

If you're going from Windows to Unix or Unix to Windows, you probably must do something similar. Windows to Unix is:

```
perl -pi -e 's/\r\n/\n/g' tabdelimitedfile.txt
```

Unix to Windows is:

```
perl -pi -e 's/\n/\r\n/g' tabdelimitedfile.txt
```

Converting from Macintosh or Unix to Windows is a bit more problematic because the toolkits are different. You may want to use something like Perl for Windows (ActiveState distributes a well-regarded version without cost, www.activestate.com/Products/ActivePerl). Alternatively, you could do the conversion on the Unix side before shipping over to Windows.

Another thing you may want to do at this point is cut up your data file into pieces. This is probably a good idea in any case, because you want to break off a chunk of data for testing anyway. Also, it's a lot easier to recoup from errors when working with a smaller data set — if your script chokes on some unexpected error, this may mean the difference between having to redo 100 entries and having to redo the entire data dump. You *must* cut up the file if your data file is more than 2GB large, because most Unix applications and utilities have a limited capability to deal with files greater than that size. You probably must use special 32-bit versions tools such as split or Perl to accomplish this task.

To cut up a file into manageable pieces, you want to use the Unix utility split like this:

```
split --lines=100 tabdelimitedfile.txt chunk_
```

This results in a bunch of 100-line files called chunk_aa, chunk_ab, chunk_ac, and so on. Obviously you can substitute a different integer value for the number of lines. If you leave off the final argument, the files are just called aa, ab, ac, and so on. Remember that these are 100 lines as Unix counts them, which means 100 units of text between (invisible) newline characters (\n). If you are using a Windows or Macintosh format file with different line breaks, they may look like line-breaks in the text file but are not necessarily counted correctly by split. If you have newlines within some field entry, split also gets confused.

Data dumping

Now you're ready to write a script to dump the data into the database. You have two choices: Either you can use the binary version of PHP, which is fast and does not time out; or you can use the normal module version in the browser, which may be easier for Windows users or anyone not comfortable with the command line. The actual scripts in binary or module versions are not hugely different. The biggest issue is probably that the module version can only handle smallish data sets because most Web servers are configured to timeout after 60 seconds or so. And the binary version must echo to the terminal in text, whereas the module version outputs to the browser in HTML.

Either way, the basic steps are clear:

1. Read in the data file.
2. Split it into an array, where each array element is one row of data.
3. Cycling through the array, split each row into fields.
4. Cycling through the array, arrange the field data into one or more SQL queries and send it to the database.
5. Repeat until all data is stored.

> **TIP:** Work with a test batch of representative data while you write and debug your script.

The following code, Listing 34-2, should be saved under some name like dumpdata.php. It runs in either the browser or on the command line (/usr/local/bin/php dumpdata.php). It inserts data into the database tables that we define in Listing 34-1.

Listing 34-2: Script to dump data ino MySQL (dumpdata.php)

```php
<?php

/***********************************************
 * Script to dump data into the MG database. *
 ***********************************************/


// Read in the file as an array
// ---------------------------
$filename = 'tabdelimitedfile.txt';
$farray = file($filename) or die("Can't read in file");


// Open up a database connection
$db = mysql_connect('localhost', 'editor', 'sesame') or die("Can't
connect to the database");
mysql_select_db('mg');


// Loop through each entry
// -----------------------
foreach ($farray as $val) {
  $l_arr = explode("\t", $val);
  print_r($l_arr);

  // Tidy up the entries
  // -------------------

  // Author info
  $Author = $l_arr[1];
  // Divide name into first and last
  $A_array = explode(', ', $Author);
  $A_firstname = addslashes($A_array[1]);
  $A_lastname = addslashes($A_array[0]);
  $A_gender = addslashes($l_arr[2]);
  if ($A_gender == 'F') {
    $A_gender = 0;
  } elseif ($A_gender == 'M') {
    $A_gender = 1;
  } else {
    echo "$A_firstname $A_lastname has gender issues";
  }
  $A_nationality = addslashes($l_arr[3]);
  $A_interview = addslashes($l_arr[31]);

  // Book info
  $B_title = addslashes($l_arr[0]);
```

```
$B_year = $l_arr[4];
$B_rating = $l_arr[10];
$B_action = $l_arr[17];
$B_humor = $l_arr[18];
$B_romance = $l_arr[19];
$B_sex = $l_arr[20];
$B_violence = $l_arr[21];
$B_reviewer = addslashes($l_arr[23]);
$B_pages = $l_arr[24];
$B_reviewdate = $l_arr[25];
// Reformat the review date from m/d/yy to yyyy-mm-dd
$date_arr = explode('/', $B_reviewdate);
$B_reviewdate = date('Y-m-d', mktime(12, 30, 0, $date_arr[0],
$date_arr[1], $date_arr[2]));
$B_ISBN = $l_arr[26];
$B_movie = addslashes($l_arr[27]);
$B_awards = addslashes($l_arr[28]);
$B_review = addslashes($l_arr[29]);
$B_blurb = addslashes($l_arr[30]);

// Subgenre info
$Subgenre[1] = addslashes($l_arr[5]);
$Subgenre[2] = addslashes($l_arr[6]);
$Subgenre[3] = addslashes($l_arr[7]);


// Enter data into database
// ------------------------

// Author data
// First see if this author is already in the database
$query = "SELECT A_id FROM author
          WHERE A_firstname = '$A_firstname'
          AND A_lastname = '$A_lastname'
          ";
$result = mysql_query($query);
if (mysql_num_rows($result) == 0) {
  // If not already there, add the author
  $query = "INSERT INTO author VALUES(
          NULL,
          '$A_firstname',
          '$A_lastname',
          $A_gender,
          '$A_nationality',
          '$A_interview'
          )";
  $result = mysql_query($query);
  if (mysql_affected_rows() != 1) {
    echo "Problem inserting author data for $A_firstname $A_lastname";
```

```php
  } else {
    $author_id = mysql_insert_id(); //Need this for book_author
  }
} else {
  $author_id = mysql_result($result, 0, 0);
}

// Book data
// We can assume each book is unique
$query = "INSERT INTO book VALUES(
        NULL,
        '$B_title',
        '$B_year',
        $B_rating,
        $B_action,
        $B_humor,
        $B_romance,
        $B_sex,
        $B_violence,
        '$B_reviewer',
        $B_pages,
        '$B_reviewdate',
        '$B_ISBN',
        '$B_movie',
        '$B_awards',
        '$B_review',
        '$B_blurb'
        )";
$result = mysql_query($query);
$book_id = mysql_insert_id(); //Need this for book_author
if (!$book_id || $book_id == "") {
  echo "Problem inserting book data for $B_title";
}

// Associate book and author
$query = "INSERT INTO book_author VALUES(
        NULL,
        $book_id,
        $author_id
        )";
$result = mysql_query($query);
if (mysql_affected_rows() != 1) {
  echo "Problem inserting book_author data for $B_title";
}

// Subgenres
for ($i = 1; $i <= 3; $i++) {
  if ($Subgenre[$i] == "") {
    continue;
```

```
    } else {
      // First see if this subgenre is already in the database
      $query = "SELECT Sub_id FROM subgenre
              WHERE Sub_name = '$Subgenre[$i]'
              ";
      $result = mysql_query($query);
      if (mysql_num_rows($result) == 0) {
        // If not already there, add the subgenre
        $query = "INSERT INTO subgenre VALUES(
                NULL,
                '$Subgenre[$i]'
                )";
        $result = mysql_query($query);
        if (mysql_affected_rows() != 1) {
          echo "Problem inserting subgenre $Subgenre[$i]";
        } else {
          $subgenre_id = mysql_insert_id();
        }
      } else {
        $subgenre_id = mysql_result($result, 0, 0);
      }

      // Now associate the subgenre with the book
      $query = "INSERT INTO book_subgenre VALUES(
              NULL,
              $book_id,
              $subgenre_id
              )";
      $result = mysql_query($query);
      if (mysql_affected_rows() != 1) {
        echo "Problem inserting book_subgenre data for $B_title and
$Subgenre[$i]";
      }
    }
  }
}

}

?>
```

Notice that we deal with several problematic but common situations in this script, such as:

♦ Changing strings (M/F) into integers (1/0) for more compact storage.

♦ Turning one field into two fields (Author_name into A_firstname and A_lastname).

♦ Handling duplicate information (same author for multiple books).

♦ Turning three different fields (`Subgenre1`, `Subgenre2`, `Subgenre3`) into three rows in the same table.

♦ Making a nonrelational database truly relational (`book_author` and `book_subgenre` tables).

Harvesting data

The code in the preceding section assumes that you want to transfer data from one database to another — but what if, instead, you need to dump data from a bunch of static HTML or text files into a database? In that case, you have to write yourself a little mini-spider.

Before you try this, you should know that harvesting data from existing documents is an inherently difficult task. If you've been maintaining 500 static HTML pages for any length of time, there's very likely to be some irregularities in the files that make it more difficult to pick out the pieces that you want. Sometimes even a simple typo or case change causes problems. Harvesting data this way could still save you some time, however, in certain circumstances.

Basically what you want to do is parse text by looking for unique patterns. You hope the information you want to harvest is identifiable by such a pattern. The process is very similar to navigating by landmarks, and only human labor can parse the structure of your documents well enough to pick out the patterns. After a person has clearly picked out a pattern, however, PHP can help you with the repetitive grunt-labor of applying this patterned searching to a whole bunch of documents.

Say, for example, that you have several hundred individual HTML press release pages that you now want to turn into a database. You analyze the pages and discover that the headline is always located inside `<H2>` tags, and is the only thing on each page marked by such tags. In this case, it would be very easy to pick out the headline from each page. Unfortunately this is a deliberately easy example — in many cases, the actual pattern you need to find is more likely to be something like "look for this string; then it is two paragraphs after that, between the third and fourth linebreaks."

Here is a sample snippet of HTML from the old MysteryGuide.com:

```
<html>
<head>
<title>Mystery Guide - The Man who Knew Too Much by G.K.
Chesterton</title>
<meta NAME="description" CONTENT="Mystery Guide review of The Man who
Knew Too Much by G.K. Chesterton">
<meta NAME="keywords" CONTENT="G.K. Chesterton, The Man who Knew Too
Much, Horne Fisher, Harold March, Classic whodunit, Political, West
Country, Ireland, Edwardian">
<!-- Review of The Man who Knew Too Much by G.K. Chesterton -->
</head>
<body TEXT="#000000" LINK="#006400" VLINK="#800080">
```

```
<table BORDER=1 RULES=NONE CELLPADDING=5>
<tr><td ALIGN=LEFT BGCOLOR="#A32242" WIDTH=50%>

<font SIZE=-1 FACE="ARIAL, GENEVA, SANS-SERIF"
COLOR="#FFFFFF"><b>REVIEW</b></font>
</td><td BGCOLOR="#A32242" WIDTH=50% ALIGN=RIGHT>
<font SIZE=-1 FACE="ARIAL, GENEVA, SANS-SERIF" COLOR="#FFFFFF">
<b>Rating: 4 (Very good)</b></font></td></tr>
</td></tr>
<tr><td colspan=2>
<font SIZE=+3 FACE="new york, palatino, times">C</font><font SIZE=-1
FACE="ARIAL, GENEVA, SANS-SERIF">hesterton's Man who Knew Too Much is a
long review in text here.
<p ALIGN=RIGHT><b>Reviewer:</b>  JP </font><br><br></td></tr></table>


<br><table BORDER=0 CELLPADDING=5>
<tr BGCOLOR="#A32242" WIDTH=100%><td>
<font SIZE=-2 FACE="ARIAL, GENEVA, SANS-SERIF"
COLOR="#FFFFFF"><b>Further reading</b></font>
</td></tr>
<tr BGCOLOR="#FFFECC" WIDTH=100%>
<td><font SIZE=-2 FACE="ARIAL, GENEVA, SANS-SERIF"><a
HREF="http://www.amazon.com/exec/obidos/ASIN/0898706297/troutworksmyster
/"> <P><b>Wisdom and Innocence:  a life of GK Chesterton</b></a> (1997)
by Joseph Pearce<BR>Bio focussing on Chesterton's
Catholicism.</td></tr></table>

<table BORDER=0 CELLPADDING=5><tr BGCOLOR="#A32242" WIDTH=100%>
<td>
<font SIZE=-2 FACE="ARIAL, GENEVA, SANS-SERIF" COLOR="#FFFFFF">
<b>Summary information</b></font>
</td></tr>
<tr BGCOLOR="#FFFECC" WIDTH=100%>
<td><font SIZE=-2 FACE="ARIAL, GENEVA, SANS-SERIF">
<b>Main character name:</b><br>  Horne Fisher<br>
<b>Year published:</b>  1922<br>
<b>Time period:</b>  1910's<br>
<b>Subgenres:</b>  <a HREF="classic-whodunit.html">Classic whodunit</a>,
<a HREF="political.html">Political</a><br>
<b>Setting:</b> UK(West Country), Ireland<br>
</font></td></tr></table>
<br>

<table BORDER=0 CELLPADDING=5><tr BGCOLOR="#A32242" WIDTH=100%>
<td>
<font SIZE=-2 FACE="ARIAL, GENEVA, SANS-SERIF" COLOR="#FFFFFF">
<b>Top 5 most similar books</b></font>
</td></tr>
```

```
<tr BGCOLOR="#FFFECC" WIDTH=100%>
<td><font SIZE=-2 FACE="ARIAL, GENEVA, SANS-SERIF">
1. <a HREF=bkCopperPons.html TARGET=_top><strong>The Further Adventures
of Solar Pons</strong></a> by Basil Copper and August] [Derleth <br>
2. <a HREF=bkOrczyCorner.html TARGET=_top><strong>The Old Man in the
Corner</strong></a> by Emma Orczy <br>

3. <a HREF=bkHareBodkin.html TARGET=_top><strong>With a Bare
Bodkin</strong></a> by Cyril Hare <br>
4. <a HREF=bkRossLove.html TARGET=_top><strong>Whom the Gods
Love</strong></a> by Kate Ross <br>
5. <a HREF=bkSayersBody.html TARGET=_top><strong>Whose
Body?</strong></a> by Dorothy L. Sayers <br>
</font></td></tr></table>
<br>

<table BORDER=0 CELLPADDING=5><tr BGCOLOR="#A32242" WIDTH=100%>
<td>
<font SIZE=-2 FACE="ARIAL, GENEVA, SANS-SERIF" COLOR="#FFFFFF">
<b>By the same author</b></font>
</td></tr>
<tr BGCOLOR="#FFFECC" WIDTH=100%>
<td><font SIZE=-2 FACE="ARIAL, GENEVA, SANS-SERIF">
<a HREF=bkChestertonThursday.html TARGET=_top><strong>The Man Who Was
Thursday</strong></a> (1908) <br>
</font></td></tr></table>
<br>

<table BORDER=0 CELLPADDING=5>
<tr BGCOLOR="#A32242" WIDTH=100%>
<td>
<font SIZE=-2 FACE="ARIAL, GENEVA, SANS-SERIF" COLOR="#FFFFFF">
<b>Movies</b></font>
</td></tr>
<tr BGCOLOR="#FFFECC" WIDTH=100%>
<td>
<font SIZE=-2 FACE="ARIAL, GENEVA, SANS-SERIF">Neither Alfred Hitchcock
movie of this title has any relation to the book
</td></tr></table>

<p ALIGN=RIGHT><font SIZE=-2 FACE="ARIAL, GENEVA, SANS-SERIF">&#169 1999
Troutworks, Inc.  All rights reserved. <br>Revised July 6,
1999</font></p></body></html>
```

Say that you want to harvest some information from this page — for example, information about movies that were made from this book. First, you'd probably want to divide up the page into chunks corresponding to tables. From here, there are many ways to accomplish your goal using string, array, and possibly regex functions.

> **CAUTION:** Do not let yourself be intimidated by people who write self-aggrandizing comments on PHP mailing lists or Websites claiming that all smart people use a certain method to perform these tasks! This type of grungy parsing is all about getting the job done and producing code you can read — it's not a programming style contest. It may be true that, in theory, you could use one line of regex instead of five lines of string functions, but who cares?

Listing 34-3 shows one straightforward method of getting the movie information you want.

Listing 34-3: Script to harvest data from HTML files (harvest.php)

```php
<?php

// harvest.php - get movie information from a MysteryGuide HTML file

$file = 'sample_HTML_for_harvesting.html';
$fp = fopen($file, "r");
$file_str = fread($fp, filesize($file));

// Divide the page into chunks corresponding to tables
$tables = explode('</td></tr></table>', $file_str);

// Not every page will have all tables, so we need to
// rename our array in a more informative way.  If all your
// pages have all identical sections, you don't need to do this.
foreach ($tables as $table_val) {
  if (strpos($table_val, 'SIZE=+3') > 30) {
    $chunk['review'] = $table_val;
  } elseif (strpos($table_val, '<b>Further reading</b>') > 1) {
    $chunk['further'] = $table_val;
  } elseif (strpos($table_val, '<b>Summary information</b>') > 1) {
    $chunk['summary'] = $table_val;
  } elseif (strpos($table_val, '<b>Top 5') > 1) {
    $chunk['top5'] = $table_val;
  } elseif (strpos($table_val, '<b>By the same') > 1) {
    $chunk['sameauthor'] = $table_val;
  } elseif (strpos($table_val, '<b>Movies</b>') > 1) {
    $chunk['movie'] = $table_val;
  }
}


// Now we'll get the movie information
if (isSet($chunk['movie'])) {
  // Get everything after the word "Movies"
  $movie_str = strstr($chunk['movie'], 'Movies');

  // Now get the actual string value of the movie data
  $movie_data_str = strstr($movie_str, '<font SIZE=-2 FACE="ARIAL,
GENEVA, SANS-SERIF">');
```

```
  $movie_data = substr($movie_data_str, 47); //get rid of the font tag
above
  //echo $movie_data;

  // Now you can escape this string and put it in a database or
whatever...
}

?>
```

You could use this same code with a few additions to harvest all the data on this page — just copy the movie part, and replace the array names and substrings you want to select on.

Now say that you want to harvest data from a whole bunch of HTML or text files. Copy them to an empty directory to minimize unintended consequences. Then you want to iterate over the files by wrapping the following cases around the preceding code:

```
$path = '/path/to/directory';
if ($dir_handle = opendir($path)) {
  while (false !== ($file = $path . readdir($dir_handle))) {
    if ($file != "." && $file != "..") {
      // Code from harvest.php above

    }
  }
}
```

This snippet opens a directory (which must have the proper read and execute permissions for the Web server user), iterates through all the files in that directory, and executes the `harvest.php` code on data from any file that isn't a special Unix directory file. You are almost certainly going to want to run a script such as this from the command line rather than the browser because iterating over a large number of files almost guarantees ugly timeouts.

Templating

Now comes the fiddly bit. This is the moment where you must take a mockup and a database, and turn them into a working Web page.

There are various methods to do this, including use of a full-templating extension such as Smarty templates. Our style, however, is to lay out the main HTML in heredoc syntax, with replacement variables defined on the same page. This is one of the fastest methods, and it still maintains satisfactory separation between logic and display.

Listing 34-4 shows a full-page template, in this case, the one for book reviews.

Listing 34-4: Book page template (review.php)

```
<?php
```

```php
/********************
* Book review page. *
********************/

// For now, pass in the id in the URI
$book_id = $_GET['book_id'];
if !isSet($book_id) || !isNumeric($book_id) {
  echo "You did not pass in a valid book ID";
  exit;
}


// ------------
// GET THE DATA
// ------------
$db = mysql_connect('localhost', 'mg_user', 'sesame');
mysql_select_db('mg');

// Book data
$query = "SELECT
            B_id,
            B_title,
            B_year,
            B_rating,
            B_movie,
            B_awards,
            B_review,
            B_similar
          FROM book
          WHERE B_id = $book_id";
$result = mysql_query($query);
if (mysql_num_rows($result) == 1) {
  $book_arr = mysql_fetch_array($result);
} else {
  echo mysql_error();
}
$title = stripslashes($book_arr['B_title']);
$year = $book_arr['B_year'];
$rating = $book_arr['B_rating'];
$movie = stripslashes($book_arr['B_movie']);
$awards = stripslashes($book_arr['B_awards']);
$review = stripslashes($book_arr['B_review']);
$review_words = explode(" ", $review);
$chunk = array_slice($review_words, 0, 200);
$review = implode(' ', $chunk);
$similar = stripslashes($book_arr['B_similar']);

// Author data
$query = "SELECT author.A_id, author.A_firstname, author.A_lastname
          FROM author LEFT JOIN book_author USING (A_id)
```

```php
          WHERE book_author.B_id = $book_id";
$result = mysql_query($query);
if (mysql_num_rows($result) == 1) {
  $author_arr = mysql_fetch_array($result);
  $author_id = $author_arr['A_id'];
  $a_firstname = stripslashes($author_arr['A_firstname']);
  $a_lastname = stripslashes($author_arr['A_lastname']);
  $author = "$a_firstname $a_lastname";
} else {
  echo mysql_error();
}

// Potential multiple other books by the same author
$query = "SELECT book.B_title
          FROM book LEFT JOIN book_author USING (B_id)
          WHERE book_author.A_id = $author_id
          AND book.B_id != $book_id";
$result = mysql_query($query);
if (mysql_num_rows($result) >= 1) {
  while ($titles_arr = mysql_fetch_array($result)) {
    $titles[] = stripslashes($titles_arr['B_title']);
  }
  $title_str = implode('<BR>\n', $titles);
} else {
  $title_str = 'None';
}

// Protagonist data
$query = "SELECT protagonist.P_firstname, protagonist.P_lastname
          FROM protagonist LEFT JOIN book_protagonist USING (P_id)
          WHERE book_protagonist.B_id = $book_id";
$result = mysql_query($query);
if (mysql_num_rows($result) == 1) {
  $prot_arr = mysql_fetch_array($result);
  $p_firstname = stripslashes($prot_arr['P_firstname']);
  $p_lastname = stripslashes($prot_arr['P_lastname']);
  $protagonist = "$p_firstname $p_lastname";
} else {
  echo mysql_error();
}

// Multiple subgenres
$query = "SELECT Sub_name
          FROM subgenre LEFT JOIN book_subgenre USING (Sub_id)
          WHERE book_subgenre.B_id = $book_id";
$result = mysql_query($query);
if (mysql_num_rows($result) >= 1) {
  while ($sub_arr = mysql_fetch_array($result)) {
    $sub_name[] = stripslashes($sub_arr['Sub_name']);
```

```php
  }
  $subgenre = implode(', ', $sub_name);
} else {
  echo mysql_error();
}

// Multiple settings
$query = "SELECT Set_name
          FROM setting LEFT JOIN book_setting USING (Set_id)
          WHERE book_setting.B_id = $book_id";
$result = mysql_query($query);
if (mysql_num_rows($result) >= 1) {
  while ($set_arr = mysql_fetch_array($result)) {
    $set_name[] = stripslashes($set_arr['Set_name']);
  }
  $setting = implode(', ', $set_name);
} else {
  echo mysql_error();
}


// ------------
// DISPLAY PAGE
// ------------
$php_self = $_SERVER['PHP_SELF']; //Superglobal arrays don't work with
heredoc
$page_str = <<< EOPAGESTR

<HTML>
<HEAD>
<STYLE>
TD.textblock {
  padding-left: 20;
  padding-top: 20;
  padding-right: 20;
}
P.td {
  font-family: arial, verdana, sans-serif;
  font-size: 8pt;
}
P.td_med {
  font-family: arial, verdana, sans-serif;
  font-size: 10pt;
  line-height:125%
}
P.title {
  font-family: arial, verdana, sans-serif;
  font-size: 10pt;
  font-weight: bold;
```

```
}
P.tab_links {
  font-family: arial, verdana, sans-serif;
  font-size: 10pt;
  margin-top: 17;
}
a {
  color:#006400;
  text-decoration:none;
  }
a:link {color:#006400;}
a:visited {color:#800080;}
</STYLE>
</HEAD>

<BODY BACKGROUND="background.gif">

<!-- Begin main table -->
<TABLE BORDER=0 WIDTH=815>
<TR>
<TD>
  <IMG SRC="spacer.gif" WIDTH=815 HEIGHT=8>
</TD>
</TR>
<TR>
<TD>
  <!-- Begin banner table -->
  <TABLE BORDER=0>
  <TR>
  <TD WIDTH=48 HEIGHT=90>
    <IMG SRC="spacer.gif" WIDTH=48 HEIGHT=90>
  </TD>
  <TD WIDTH=472 HEIGHT=90 ALIGN="center" VALIGN="middle"">
    <IMG SRC="red.png" WIDTH=460 HEIGHT=60>
  </TD>
  <TD WIDTH=14 HEIGHT=90>
    <IMG SRC="spacer.gif" WIDTH=14 HEIGHT=90>
  </TD>
  <TD WIDTH=292 HEIGHT=90 VALIGN="top" class="textblock">
    <P class="td">a Troutworks, Inc. site<BR>
    &#169; 1994 - 1999 Troutworks, Inc.</P>
    <P class="td">Last updated July 6, 1999</P>
  </TD>
  </TR>
  </TABLE>
  <!-- End banner table -->
</TD>
</TR>
<TR>
```

```
<TD>
  <!-- Begin title table -->
  <TABLE BORDER=0>
  <TR>
  <TD WIDTH=140 HEIGHT=30>
    <IMG SRC="spacer.gif" WIDTH=140 HEIGHT=30>
  </TD>
  <TD WIDTH=330 HEIGHT=30 ALIGN="center" VALIGN="bottom">
    <P class="title">$title</P>
  </TD>
  <TD WIDTH=345 HEIGHT=30>
    <IMG SRC="spacer.gif" WIDTH=345 HEIGHT=30>
  </TD>
  </TR>
  </TABLE>
  <!-- End title table -->
</TD>
</TR>
<TR>
<TD>
  <!-- Begin info table -->
  <TABLE BORDER=0>
  <TR>
  <TD WIDTH=135 HEIGHT=350 ROWSPAN=2 ALIGN="left" VALIGN="top"
style="padding-left:22; padding-top:40">
    <P class="td">
    <A HREF="newbooks.html">New Reviews</A><BR>
    <A HREF="readerratings.html">Reader ratings</A></P>

    <P class="td">
    GENRES<BR>
    <A HREF="caper.html">Caper</A><BR>
    <A HREF="classic-whodunit.html">Classic whodunit</A><BR>
    <A HREF="cozy.html">Cozy</A><BR>
    <A HREF="espionage.html">Espionage</A><BR>
    <A HREF="forensic.html">Forensic</A><BR>
    <A HREF="hard-boiled.html">Hard-boiled</A><BR>
    <A HREF="historical.html">Historical</A><BR>
    <A HREF="legal.html">Legal</A><BR>
    <A HREF="military.html">Military</A><BR>
    <A HREF="police-procedural.html">Police procedural</A><BR>
    <A HREF="political.html">Political</A><BR>
    <A HREF="private-eye.html">Private eye</A><BR>
    <A HREF="serial-killer.html">Serial killer</A><BR>
    <A HREF="sf-mystery.html">SF mystery</A><BR>
    <A HREF="special-subject.html">Special subject</A><BR>
    <A HREF="suspense.html">Suspense</A><BR>
    <A HREF="thriller.html">Thriller</A></P>
  </TD>
```

```
  <TD WIDTH=15 HEIGHT=350 ROWSPAN=2>
    <IMG SRC="spacer.gif" WIDTH=15 HEIGHT=350>
  </TD>
  <TD>
    <TABLE BORDER=0 WIDTH=665>
    <TR>
    <TD WIDTH=350 HEIGHT=240 ALIGN="left" VALIGN="top" style="padding-
left:11">
      <P class="tab_links">Read Reviews</P>
      <P class="tab_links">Browse by:    Genre    |    <A
HREF="authorlist.html">Author</A>    |    <A
HREF="authorlist.html">Title</A>    |    <A
HREF="readerratings.html">Ratings</A></P>
      <P class="tab_links">Author:  $author<BR>
      Protagonist name:  $protagonist<BR>
      Year published:  $year<BR>
      Subgenres:  $subgenre<BR>
      Setting:  $setting</P>
    </TD>
    <TD WIDTH=334 HEIGHT=240 ALIGN="left" VALIGN="top" style="padding-
left:13">
      <P class="td"><B>Other Reviewed Titles By This
Author</B><BR>$title_str
      </P>
      <P class="td"><B>Top 5 Most Similar Titles</B><BR>$similar
      </P>
      <P class="td"><B>Movie versions</B><BR>$movie</P>
    </TD>
    </TR>
    </TABLE>
  </TD>
  </TR>
  <TR>
  <TD WIDTH=665 HEIGHT=100>
    <TABLE BORDER=0 WIDTH=665>
    <TR>
    <TD WIDTH=250 HEIGHT=100 ALIGN="left" VALIGN="top" style="padding-
left:13">
      <P class="title">Our rating:  $rating
      <BR>Community rating:  $comm_rating</P>
      <P class="td_med"><B>Awards:</B>  $award</P>
    </TD>
    <TD WIDTH=415 HEIGHT=100 ALIGN="left" VALIGN="top" style="padding-
left:40; padding-top:7">
      <IMG SRC="red.png" WIDTH=350 HEIGHT=80>
    </TD>
    </TR>
    </TABLE>
  </TD>
```

```
  </TR>
  </TABLE>
  <!-- End info table -->
</TD>
</TR>
<TR>
<TD>
  <!-- Begin review table -->
  <TABLE BORDER=0>
  <TR>
  <TD WIDTH=40 HEIGHT=250>
    <IMG SRC="spacer.gif" WIDTH=40 HEIGHT=250>
  </TD>
  <TD WIDTH=560 HEIGHT=250 class="textblock">
    <P CLASS="td_med">$review <A
HREF="$php_self?format=review_only">...READ COMPLETE REVIEW...</A></P>
  </TD>
  <TD WIDTH=155 HEIGHT=250 ALIGN="left" VALIGN="top" style="padding-
left:10; padding-top:5">
    <P class="title">What did YOU think?</P>
    <P class="td">Read this book?  Rate it!</P>
    <FORM><INPUT TYPE="submit" VALUE="5 - Superb"></FORM>
    <FORM><INPUT TYPE="submit" VALUE="4 - Very Good"></FORM>
    <FORM><INPUT TYPE="submit" VALUE="3 - Good"></FORM>
    <FORM><INPUT TYPE="submit" VALUE="2 - Mediocre"></FORM>
    <FORM><INPUT TYPE="submit" VALUE="1 - Poor">
  </TD>
  <TD WIDTH=40 HEIGHT=250>
    <IMG SRC="spacer.gif" WIDTH=40 HEIGHT=260>
  </TD>
  </TR>
  </TABLE>
  <!-- End review table -->
</TD>
</TR>
<TR>
<TD>
  <!-- Begin credits table -->
  <TABLE BORDER=0 HEIGHT=65>
  <TR>
  <TD WIDTH=25>
    <IMG SRC="spacer.gif" WIDTH=25 HEIGHT=65>
  </TD>
  <TD WIDTH=790 HEIGHT=65 VALIGN="bottom" style="padding-
left:25;padding-bottom:28">
    <P class="td">FAQs | Team Trout | Privacy | Advertising |
Email Us</P>
  </TD>
  </TR>
```

```
  </TABLE>
  <!-- End credits table -->
</TD>
</TR>
</TABLE>
<!-- End main table -->
</BODY>
</HTML>
EOPAGESTR;
echo $page_str;
?>
```

The results of the preceding book review page are shown in Figure 34-3:

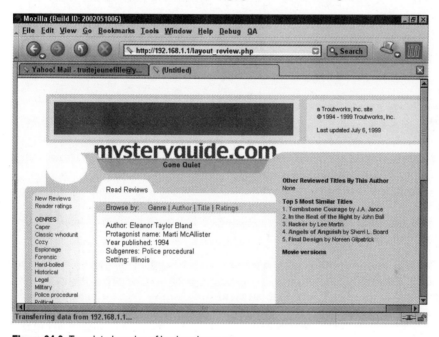

Figure 34-3: Templated version of book review page

If you compare this page to Figure 34-2, it is immediately obvious that we've simplified the elements somewhat. Inevitably, as you move toward a final layout in actual HTML, you find that not everything envisioned by the designer can be easily implemented. In this case, we found that the small visual elements such as the title area and "Browse By" navbar are extremely fiddly and difficult to lay out decent HTML without enormous overhead in pixel-level layout. It's difficult to know these things until you actually begin work on a production template. Your designers should be willing to work with you to make small tweaks at this point.

Performance and Caching

At this stage you should do some performance testing and evaluation. You want to get decent estimates of:

- ◆ **Server latency:** How long the code takes your server to produce.
- ◆ **Network latency:** How long it takes to get the code down the pipe to you.
- ◆ **Browser latency:** How long it takes a browser to completely render the page.

You can measure server latency by putting microtime() calls at the beginning and end of each page, like this:

```php
<?php

$begin_time = microtime();

// Your script here

$end_time = microtime();
$duration = $end_time - $begin_time;
echo $duration;
?>
```

This duration should average to less than one second on every page. If it's more than one second per page load, you have an architecture problem. Subseconds of latency are achieved by much larger and more complicated sites than yours. Make sure that you test this on a setup similar to your production environment — a production server can be several times faster than a development server, so unacceptable times in development can magically become acceptable in production.

The reason server latency is particularly bad is that it ends up costing you money to scale your site. Because your code hogs processor cycles, threads, database connections, and other resources longer than it should, you need to invest more in hardware than a zippier site with similar features. The cure for this type of performance problem is to simplify your architecture, particularly those features (templates, objects, message catalogs, and so on) that are known to add server latency.

Network latency is (insofar as Web developers can affect it) usually a function of how large your page is. To test this, you need to save an HTML page and all its attendant graphic files (including ads) and note their combined size. Divide by 40 kilobytes per second (a realistic estimate of the speed of a 56K modem) for a ballpark estimate of how long your data spends on the wire.

Heavy pages also cost you money, especially if you pay for metered bandwidth. Your Web servers can't take another request until they finish sending all the data from this one — and the longer it takes, the fewer available threads your Web servers have at any given time. You can sometimes finesse the fat-page problem temporarily by looking into transparent page compression — Apache, for example, can `gzip` any file before serving it up in a way that is totally invisible to the user — but in the long run you just need to make your pages lighter.

Finally, take a look at browser latency. The best way to do this is to get on a known slow browser — Internet Explorer 5.1 for Macintosh is supposedly the market leader in this category — and actually time how long it takes from the initial request to the moment you see a complete Web page in your browser. Because a lot of this is controlled by the particular browser, there's not much you can do — except to realize that complicated layouts featuring massive tables, immense amounts of non-breaking spaces, and hundreds of transparent single-pixels add to rendering time.

Caching

Besides the steps mentioned in the preceding section , another way you can make your site faster is to use *caching*. There are many types of caching, but the most important one for Web developers is HTML caching. Many "dynamic" sites, such as Slashdot and Epinions, are actually serving up mostly static pages that change every few minutes. Without this trick, few organizations could afford to scale a Web site.

The review page in Listing 34-4 is an interesting example, because although we're storing all the data in a database, the only thing on the whole page that is dynamic is the Community Rating score. The rest of the page only changes if updates are made to the database records. We could, therefore, easily write out the whole site as a series of static HTML pages with one PHP function embedded in the middle.

You're probably thinking, "That's nuts! I just went to all that work to turn my static HTML site into a dynamic, database-driven one — and now you're telling me to go back to static HTML?!?!" But if you think about it, you see a vast difference between a static site that you maintain by hand and a dynamic site that happens to update itself automatically whenever a meaningful change occurs. This scheme gives you the best of both worlds: the speed and scalability of static HTML plus the flexibility and maintainability of a database-driven PHP site.

We've written another code listing that takes all the entries in your database and writes them out to static HTML files. In the middle is a PHP snippet that includes a text file. This text file contains the Community Rating and is updated by a separate process every hour. You can see this listing at `www.troutworks.com/phpbook/ch34`.

If you want to make the Community Rating call on this page fully dynamic, instead of taking cached data from a flat file, you can do that too. But you will no longer be able to construct the entire page as a single heredoc block. The code to accomplish a static page with a dynamic code block is available at `www.troutworks.com/phpbook/ch34`.

The code to insert a dynamic PHP block into a static HTML page doesn't look as pretty as a plain HTML page, and you must be very careful about all the quoting and concatenating; but in the end, you have an automatically generated HTML file with chunks of PHP for the dynamic bits.

You could schedule this script to run on the command line once a day via a `cron` job. (You're definitely not going to be able to use the Web server module version of PHP for this task.) Or you could kick it off whenever you add new pages to the Web site. This has another security benefit: You do not need to maintain a full database in production, but can merely push flat files periodically (perhaps via some tool such as `rsync`) plus maintain a small database with data only for those fields you want to display dynamically.

Summary

PHP books usually assume that you are starting a site from scratch — but in the real world, another very common scenario is to upgrade an existing static site. PHP and a database can be used to take large, messy, hard-to-maintain HTML sites and make them dynamic. This makes the sites much easier to maintain, because they are assembled by PHP from data in a database. Instead of maintaining hundreds of HTML files, you can just work on one template and let PHP assemble the pages on-the-fly.

Before you do any work, you should take the time to assess your site's strategy and map out the goals you wish to accomplish. You should also gain a clear understanding of your site's structure, and the resources you will need to support your new design. After that, you must test your new design, create a new database, load data from possibly disparate sources into the database, and create PHP template pages. Finally, you should assess the performance of your new dynamic site, and possibly take steps to improve it.

Chapter 35

Other People's PHP

In This Chapter

♦ Laziness, impatience, and hubris

♦ Common integration projects

♦ Levels of integration

♦ Project: Integrating and customizing a bulletin board package

This chapter covers the process of integrating prefab PHP into your Web site. It covers the pleasures and pitfalls of tapping the source, describes what you want to look for in other people's code, and discusses various levels of integration. The rest of the chapter is then given over to a practical case study integrating a commercial PHP bulletin-board system into a typical business Web site.

Laziness, Impatience, and Hubris

Programmers, whose thinking often seems a bit orthogonal to that of the rest of the world, often like to slyly boast about virtues that other people consider flaws. Chief among these are laziness, impatience, and hubris. As Perl guru Larry Wall points out: Laziness makes you disinclined to do things over and over; impatience spurs you on to create systems that are better than what came before; and hubris makes you want to write code that your peers bow down before.

Those "virtues" clearly apply in situations where you are writing all the code yourself. But how do they speak to the issue of integration? Integration is an interesting tradeoff because it requires a programmer who is willing to sacrifice hubris to laziness and impatience by doing something faster and more repeatably rather than having the joy of creation. The reality of the situation is that, as Webdev matures into a discrete branch of professional programming, it is becoming more and more concerned with fitting pieces into a big picture — in other words, architecture — rather than painstakingly crafting everything from scratch. Integration requires someone who understands that there is craftsmanship both in building a new car on the assembly line and in customizing it with aftermarket parts and a unique paint job. Luckily, this attitude is built into the open source philosophy, which is about having the option to freely build upon the work of others rather than repeating their labors.

The advantages of buying (in the loosest sense of the term, because much PHP is actually available without monetary cost) rather than building include:

- Integration is usually much faster than construction.

- Prefab code is usually highly cost- and headcount-effective to implement.

- Packages come already QA-ed, often quite extensively.

- Many minds and skill sets applied to the problem for a long time result in more featureful code.

- It's often easier for clients or bosses to nail down their needs by critiquing a pre-existing product, rather than listing their demands from scratch.

- You maintain focus on your particular mission — serving a community, marketing a product, selling goods, or providing services — rather than getting caught up in the illusion that you're in the Web-app writing business.

- Because it's PHP, you can still customize it to your needs as much as you want.

Let's be clear though: Integration is still work — sometimes quite a lot of work (although rarely as much as making a large feature from scratch). It's also true that, for reasons that are difficult to change, the skills required to effectively absorb and improve someone else's code are rarer than those required to write functioning code in the first place. Linus Torvalds himself was recently quoted as saying, "The problem is that very few people want to just clean the stables and not do the big and 'exciting' stuff." So we should mention some reasons you may not want to adopt pre-fab PHP:

- You just need very basic functionality in some area.

- Your site is a labor of love and has no particular time constraints.

- This is a learning project or school assignment.

- Your site is so idiosyncratic in its architecture or needs that you can't integrate any new package without major pain.

If you're in one of these situations, it isn't worthwhile for you to think about integration.

But for developers who work in common business situations — where resources are limited and demands are relentless and you're judged on whether you achieved goals rather than how much fun you had getting there — the large base of cheap and well-tested pre-fab code is emerging as one of PHP's greatest advantages in the marketplace. If you never think about buying rather than building, you are probably not using your organization's resources to the fullest.

Common Integration Projects

A few types of Web functionality are widely applicable and highly useful, and for these reasons, they have attracted the attention of many programming teams. Unsurprisingly, PHP plus a database is the common thread in all the most popular packages. This makes it easy for us to demonstrate on one integration project, and have the principles carry over to others with the same kind of basic technical issues.

Forums

This is probably the most common type of integration project because almost any kind of site may need a *discussion forum* (also known as a *bulletin board*) for its users. PHP-based products are probably leading the forums market at this point, as Perl continues to lose ground as a Web-development technology. We discuss the leading products in this area in great detail in the section "Project," later in this chapter.

Forums are, unfortunately, perhaps the most difficult type of integration task because they usually require member registration to post messages. If you already have a registered userbase, you need to somehow deal with two competing user-registration systems, complete with their own database schemas. Luckily, we outline the entire procedure for you in the "Project" section of this chapter.

Bug trackers

Almost all software-producing organizations feature a bug-tracking system somewhere on their Web sites. The most popular product in this category by far is the Perl-based Bugzilla package (at `www.bugzilla.org`), which has been around pretty much as long as the commercial Web. (It was developed to track issues with the original Netscape browser.) This is one of the categories of software where the excellent no-cost alternatives came first and have prevented commercial products from really taking root.

PHP products in this category are still playing catch-up with the massive feature set of Bugzilla. They have one great advantage for public Web sites, however: Bugzilla does not boast the most attractive UI in the world (although, to be fair, at least one commercial product is even uglier), whereas the PHP alternatives tend to be fairly attractive. Some people also claim that the Bugzilla code base is a "hairball" that makes integration more difficult, whereas the PHP alternatives haven't yet been around long enough to develop serious cruft.

Many defect-tracking systems do not require pre-registration, but instead let any user file bugs with just an e-mail address for later notification purposes. Some, particularly the more popular ones, in order to cut down on spam and abuse, do now require registration – obviously, these are the harder integration jobs, especially if you have a database of pre-existing registered users.

Popular bug-tracking packages written in PHP include:

- **phpBugTracker** (`http://phpbt.sourceforge.net`): Database-neutral and template-based.
- **Mantis** (`http://mantisbt.sourceforge.net`): MySQL only.

Knowledgebases

Knowledgebases are searchable or otherwise easily navigable collections of topical information. So far, the most common use for them is to provide a store for answered technical support questions. Probably the most famous and largest knowledge base in the world is the one maintained by Microsoft to answer queries related to its software products (at `http://support.microsoft.com/default.aspx?scid=fh;en-us;kbinfo`).

Somewhat surprisingly, the PHP community has not paid much attention to knowledgebases to date. This may be because a truly useful knowledgebase must include a good search function (preferably with natural language support), which is not cheap or easy to implement from scratch. Regardless of the reason, PHP innovation in this area is rather low and tends to amount to copying functionality first deployed in Perl.

The Perl community came up with not one, but two brilliant concepts in the knowledgebase area: Jon Howell's Faq-O-Matic (at `http://faqomatic.sourceforge.net`) and Ward Cunningham's WikiWikiWeb (at `http://c2.com/cgi-bin/wiki?WikiWikiWeb`). The Faq-O-Matic concept makes it easier to maintain very large lists of frequently asked questions by subdividing them into smaller lists by topic. WikiWikiWeb is less structured but grows in an organic way, as the Web itself does, by using hyperlinks. Both of these architectures encourage contributions by multiple community members. Thus knowledge can be shared widely, and the store should grow quickly.

The functionality of the Faq-O-Matic has been duplicated and built upon by a commercial PHP product called *Knowledge E-gineer* (at `www.synop.com/document/index.phtml/id/16/topic_id/7`). Many open-source Wiki clones are written in PHP, such as PHPWiki (at `http://phpwiki.sourceforge.net`). You should keep in mind, however, that these products are meant to facilitate the sharing of information by a community rather than the "one-canonical-answer" style of question-answer (or issue-resolution) pairs commonly found on large commercial knowledgebases (a.k.a. self-serve customer relationship management, or CRM). We do not know of a PHP package in this category that is at all ready for prime time.

Photo albums

Photo albums are increasingly popular as more Web users become comfortable with digital cameras. They can be used in two ways: to enable your own nontechnical team members to prepare pages of photographs (for instance, pictures of your product or service in action) or to enable Web users to post their own snapshots on your site. The latter use, in particular, has many implications that should be carefully considered before slapping third-party photo-album software on your site.

Photo albums are one of the most inherently insecure Web packages, because they permit binary file uploads, which are among the most powerful ways to compromise a system. Anyone who voluntarily permits nontrusted users to write to disk is pretty literally asking for trouble and has no one else to blame if trouble arrives. We don't even permit *ourselves* to write to disk on our own public Web servers except via SSH! One thing that you can do to reduce some problems is use a database-backed package rather than one with only filesystem storage. Unfortunately, this slows your site performance somewhat and introduces its own (albeit a bit less serious) security issues.

Another issue with photo albums is that they often require extra libraries, some of which are not standard on a shared Webhost account. gd and ImageMagick are the two main packages for photo manipulation on the server. gd must be built into the PHP binary or module, which is not always possible if you aren't permitted to do your own building. ImageMagick is a binary — most Webhosts hate it if you run unauthorized binaries on their systems — and links to libraries that, again, are not necessarily available to you.

Finally, photo albums can be very resource intensive. They eat disk, bandwidth, and sometimes cycles (if you're creating thumbnails, for example) as few other PHP packages do. Be aware of the potential for your own costs to escalate quickly if you offer this type of functionality, and do everything you can to reduce the size of your graphics files.

Some of the more featureful photo album packages include:

♦ **Slooze** (`www.slooze.com`): Database or filesystem storage, no registration system, no thumbnails

♦ **MyPhotos** (`http://elmotheelk.xs4all.nl/myphotos/`): MySQL, permission system, rating system

♦ **phpGraphy** (`http://phpgraphy.sourceforge.net`): MySQL, user comments, private albums

Levels of Integration

Integration and customization can mean anything from changing the colors of hyperlinks on your site, to painstakingly knitting two or more software packages together in an attempt to make them essentially one. For our purposes, there are five main levels or types of integration, each of which has its own implications in practice. These are not mutually exclusive of each other, but present different buckets of problems.

Styles

Styles, in this context, refers to style and graphic elements set by the developers of a site. These are purely cosmetic alterations to the look and feel of a pre-fab package: changing the logo, the colors, the font, and perhaps a few graphic elements such as buttons. This is the easiest type of integration because it requires no structural changes whatsoever — you can just roll out the package, slap in your logo, tweak the hexadecimal color codes in the CSS files, and go.

Skins

Skins in the Web context are style sheets (which sometimes reference graphic elements) selected by the user and are easily hot-swappable. This is another fairly fast method of customization for the Web developer because all you need to do is offer a selection of style sheets and some stateful storing of each user's preference on every pageload (that is, cookies, sessions, or database fields with registered users). Some integration-friendly PHP packages come with several style alternatives that you can offer to your visitors and give you the option of downloading even more skins.

This type of customization, however, offers little real functionality gain and can potentially suck up lots of time while you tweak and test the various UI elements. Most Web developers want to maximize their control over how users see their site; but except for very simple pages, skins may throw off the layout of the site in unpredictable ways. Skins also require heavy use of CSS (and sometimes DHTML) that may negatively affect browser compatibility. For these reasons, skins are rarely appropriate for any type of business site, except possibly those advertising products or services involving design.

There's one exception to this rule: If your default site design tends toward the unreadable (as do, for example, many gaming sites, which favor tiny colored text on black backgrounds), you should prominently offer your visitors the option to apply a skin that is less "kewl-looking" but easier on the eyes.

Configuration options

Some of the more mature and featureful PHP packages, such as bulletin boards, are mindful of the fact that no single method is the only right way to do things — and they attempt to facilitate healthy diversity by building in the more common modifications as configuration directives. You, as the Web developer or administrator, for example, may be offered the option to use cookies or sessions; or perhaps you can enable posting by anonymous users; or you may be offered a choice of databases. By flipping a bit somewhere, often via a handy Web configuration tool, you can turn certain features on and off without doing any further work. This is a tremendous timesaver for the busy Web developer.

Built-in configuration flipping does, however, have a downside: The code is inevitably fatter and more complicated than an implementation that was designed specifically for your needs and your needs only. Some development groups also seem to deliberately choose a "make the easy mods easier and the hard mods harder" policy by building in lots of configuration directives but also by going out of their way to make further changes difficult. If you would actually rather not touch the code unless you must, and your desired functionality is within the capabilities of the configurator, this can be an excellent choice for your needs.

Separate user management

Many types of functionality are just naturally tied to user identities: anything involving e-mail, persistent communities, prizes, and so on. Totally read-only sites commonly decide to add a single subsystem with separate registration. A good example of this is the Internet Movie Database (www.imdb.com), which offers a tremendous amount of film information to all visitors but requires user registration to participate in its message boards and polls. Not only is a package with standalone user registration system a vast timesaver for sites that are lucky enough to be in this position; but it's great to know you can easily rip it out later if you have to, without affecting the rest of your site.

The implementation of a separate user management system is something of a gamble: You're taking the risk that you're never, in the future, likely to want to add another subsystem with user identities. So if you have a forum, you are positive that you're never going to want a bugtracker; or if you have a photo album, you're still sure you're never going to want an online chat room. After you go with a single-purpose user-registration system and accumulate data in it, you're running the risk of needing to make big changes to your schema or your site structure in the future to accommodate another subsystem or of taking on a lot of work to transfer data to a new setup.

Our advice is not to be too seduced by the idea of depending on a quick-and-dirty user-management system built into some package. Managing user data is really core functionality for any Web site that collects such data, and you may have business or even legal problems later if you choose a system without thinking through all the implications. It's like the difference between cleaning your kitchen versus cleaning your desk: You can hire someone to do the former, but no one else has the intimate knowledge of your mindset to do the latter for you. Some PHP packages that logically need user-management systems actually refuse to implement them on the grounds that any attempt to do so in a general way would just hinder integration with your own custom member-registration functions.

Combined user management

Finally, we come to the real issue: a combined, central user-management system. This means that you have only one canonical location for each piece of user information; you use only one database throughout your site for all user-related functions; you rely on one universal permissions scheme; and you use only one session or one (small) set of cookies to maintain state. All integration projects must fit into this centralized scheme on your site. This is, with few exceptions, the right way to do things — other alternatives represent more or less ugly, corner-cutting hacks. You can think of this method as full integration, whereas others are partial at best.

This is the type of integration project that causes the most problems but is also the one that gives you the most professional results. In the following sections, we walk you step by step through a sample combined integration project.

Project: Integrating a Bulletin Board

An enormous percentage of a major integration project consists of thinking and planning and communication, rather than simply opening up a text editor and hacking away. Because few people find integration inherently fun and exciting, most developers want to do things in the most efficient way possible — and that means taking the time to understand the process before writing a single line of code. In the following sections, we try to walk you through the entire life cycle of an integration project, from planning to release, by using a real-life example: a forum integration on a commercial Web site at `http://developer.knownow.com`.

Before the integration, this was a site that offered read-only access to unregistered users and downloads of evaluation software to registered users. It had a small homegrown message-posting area, but it lacked functionality and was tied to a certain design and navigation scheme. The main goal of the integration was to acquire a full-featured forum for users of KnowNow's software, as quickly as possible.

The functional spec

As Joe Jackson so cogently told us: You can't get what you want till you know what you want. In that spirit, it saves you a tremendous amount of future pain and aggravation if you sit down and enumerate the features you're looking for. If you get a fancy product manager to do it for you, you can call it a Products Requirements Definition (PRD); if you do it yourself, you may just call it a functional spec.

A spec is always a good idea — but on an integration project it is supremely necessary because the choice of product largely depends on the desired features. You need to have a clear idea, therefore, of what are the deal-breakers, what are the strongly desired but not absolutely necessary features, what are the nice-to-haves, and what are the features that you definitely do not want to have. List even the things that seem ridiculously obvious to you — it's better to look slightly overfussy in the beginning than to have your manager or client reject the whole project later because it doesn't look good on his or her new laptop (This is not as farfetched as it sounds.)

In this case, the PRD looked something like this:

Browsing

These are the read-only navigation and display features desired by the product manager in this case.

- ♦ Mandatory functions:
  - Read-only access to all boards, posts, and threads for unregistered users
  - Bookmarkable persistent URLs for all boards, posts, and threads
  - Search capability
  - Ability to print entire thread on one HTML page
- ♦ Nice to have:
  - Threaded and nonthreaded views
  - Ability to restrict read access in some areas of the forums

Posting

These are the write-access features desired by the product manager in this case.

- ◆ Mandatory:
  - Registration and login necessary to post
  - Forum topics (boards) created by admins rather than users
  - At least 30 separate forum topics (boards) possible
  - Moderated and unmoderated forums
  - Users can create new threads
  - Users can reply to other posts, potentially creating subthreads.
  - No practical limit to numbers of threads or posts per thread
  - Users can edit their own posts.
  - Users can use HTML-like formatting.
  - Users can preview posts.
  - Ability to restrict write access to some forums
  - Posts should not expire automatically.
- ◆ Nice to have:
  - Pruned posts should be disabled rather than deleted.

Notification

These are the remote user notification features desired by the product manager.

- ◆ Mandatory:
  - E-mail subscription per board — all posts to a board result in e-mail notification.
  - Customized e-mails
- ◆ Nice to have:
  - E-mail subscription per thread — all posts to a thread result in e-mail notification.

Browser support

All functionality must work correctly with these browsers.

- ◆ Mandatory:
  - Windows IE 5+, Macintosh IE 5
  - Windows Netscape 4, Solaris Netscape 4
- ◆ Nice to have:
  - Linux Netscape 4.7
  - Mozilla (all platforms)

User management

These are the user management features and tools requested by the product manager.

- ◆ Mandatory:
  - Integration with existing user database (MySQL)
  - Ability to block a user account
  - Pruned user accounts should be disabled rather than deleted.
  - User data-management forms (change password, change profile settings, and so on)
  - User can decide whether or not to display profile.
  - Single login — does not require separate login for forum versus main site.

Other

Finally, these are miscellaneous features requested by the product manager. Most of these are specific to this particular implementation; but almost all projects have analogous special requests.

- ◆ Mandatory:
  - Customizable style
  - Web-based administrator toolkit
  - 1,000 concurrent users
  - Save posts from old forum system
  - Less than one second of latency per page
  - Easy to integrate with KnowNow software

Do not need

Finally, remember to compile a list of features that have explicitly or implicitly been rejected. At a minimum, this list may come in handy as ammunition when some other project manager or executive demands some random feature just before you ship the project.

- ◆ Explicitly reject (turn off or rip out):
  - Private messages
  - Skins
  - Multilanguage support
  - Multidatabase support
  - COPPA support (special handling of users under age 13, required by law in USA)
  - Session support
  - Censor certain words
- ◆ Not necessary:

- Avatars
- Polls
- Rating threads or posts

The evaluation process

In this section, we walk you through the evaluation process for judging PHP packages. In larger companies you may be required to document this process; but even if you aren't, it's good to write up your thoughts as you test-drive the various products.

Bakeoff

Now that we have a clear idea what we're looking for, we can have a feature bakeoff. We quickly settled on four candidate forum packages, two open source and two commercial, all of which have large installed userbases and many enthusiastic users. The open source packages are:

- Phorum (www.phorum.org)

- phpBB (www.phpbb.org)

The commercial packages are:

- UBBThreads (www.infopop.com/products/ubbthreads/index.html)

- vBulletin (www.vbulletin.com)

Of these, the open-source packages obviously offer full source downloads. UBBThreads offers a full-featured trial version (with limited numbers of users, boards, and threads) for evaluation, whereas vBulletin offers a "lite" version with lots of missing functionality and an annoyingly buggy install process that is totally useless for evaluation purposes. (We purchased a vBulletin license in order to evaluate fairly and completely.)

In Table 35-1, we did not include desired features from the lists in the previous section that were common to all the candidates. These capabilities are for the program out of the box with only configuration options given by the package.

Table 35-1: Forum Features Comparison

Feature	Phorum	phpBB	UBBThreads	vBulletin
Print whole thread on one page	N	N	Y	N (multiple pages)
Restrict read access	N	Y	Y	Y
Users edit posts	N	Y	Y	Y

Users preview posts	N	Y	Y	Y
Posts disabled not deleted	Y (disables all children of disabled post)	N	N	N
Subcribe per board	N	N	Y (batch)	Y
Custom e-mail	N	N	N	N
Subscribe per thread (that user has posted to)	N	Y	Y (only direct replies)	Y
Expired users disabled	N	N	N	N
User displays profile	N (no profile)	N	N	N
Integrated login	N	N	N	N
Private message	N	Y	Y	Y
Skins	N	Y	Y	N
Multilanguage	Y (user-contributed packs)	Y (user-contributed packs)	Y	N
Multidatabase	N (MySQL)	Y	Y	N (MySQL)
COPPA	N	Y	Y	Y
Sessions	N (many cookies)	Y (and cookies)	Y (or cookies)	Y (or cookies)
Censor by word	N	Y	Y	Y

It's immediately obvious from this list that Phorum is out for our deployment — it would take way too much work to make it fit our requirements. This is not at all a general indictment of Phorum, however, so don't be too quick to dismiss it if your feature spec is significantly different from ours — especially if you want to have per-page forums rather than a separate forum area.

At this point, we have three candidate packages left. None of them is completely meeting our forum needs, but none of them have real deal-breakers either. The three are very similar in functionality and design, but at this point, the edge seems to be going to vBulletin for closest match to our particular desired functionality.

> **TIP:** Phorum has a unique architecture that is interestingly different from that of the other leading PHP forum packages. Most other forum packages are clearly meant to be deployed in a separate "forums" area of a Web site as a standalone feature. This is enforced by the fact that thread and post display are expansive and attractive, while actually posting to the forum requires clicking through to another page (or two). Phorum goes in the opposite direction: It puts the form to post a comment right on the display page, while displaying threads or posts in a condensed format (essentially zero or one message at a time).
>
> This makes Phorum uniquely suited to a particular use: having a small special-interest discussion on each page of a Web site. In other words, instead of having a separate forum area away from your content, you can have a smaller, more focused, deconstructed forum right on the same page as your article or other content. See any article on PHPBuilder.com or Zend.com for examples of this style of forum. (Both sites also have standalone forums.) Contrast this style to a centralized forum per article/column approach, such as the one employed on Slate (`http://slate.msn.com`).
>
> Phorum's architecture is a great example of one of the strengths of open source software: alternate architectures. In commercial software, companies are always jockeying to establish their design as "the standard" for that particular type of software, whether by having better code or simply by locking the user into a particular experience. After a company manages to establish a standard, generally alternate architectures find it difficult to find a niche. One of the beauties of open source is that different ways of doing the same thing are available for you to look at and choose among for your unique needs.

Licensing issues

One issue with PHP code that you shouldn't neglect is licensing. If you're like most people, you don't pay too much attention to the click-through licenses attached to most software packages — but in an integration situation, the license is just as important as any feature. Of our three remaining candidate packages, two are commercially licensed and one is open source.

The open source package, phpBB, is distributed under the Gnu General Public License. The GPL has rarely been tested in court, and it's not perfectly clear how it applies to Web sites. However, under one interpretation, if you came up with some particularly cool new feature for your deployment, the phpBB folks would have the right to demand that you contribute the code back to the community. At the extremes, they could ask that all your modifications be made public. These are issues you may need to discuss with your company's legal department before integrating open source code into your site.

The two commercial licenses are fairly similar. Obviously, they are more concerned with the cost-related issues such as number of processors in your cluster. One issue to watch out for: Generally with a commercial license you are required to display the logo and copyright notices of the forum package at a given level of prominence and frequency. Sometimes you can pay more to avoid this clause, but don't think you can just leave the logo off your pages.

A big issue for us is that we clearly need to alter some of the PHP source code in a commercial package — which sometimes voids the tech support agreement in theory. In practice, these suppliers are willing to work with you. You may want to discuss the issue with the company's support representatives before purchasing a license.

Integration-friendliness and ineffables

If the task were simply to roll out a full-featured forum as quickly as possible with only cosmetic changes, vBulletin would probably be our number one choice. It's very attractive, has almost all the features we require and the least number that we don't require, is less expensive than UBBThreads, and has been thoroughly QA-ed. The maker of the software, Jelsoft, also offers commercial support, which is a plus.

But although vBulletin is marginally the closest match to our functionality list, its architecture has one huge drawback for our purposes: Almost all the code is kept in the database itself. The company touts this as a feature rather than a bug — supposedly it prevents issues with file permissions — but let's get real. A file permissions issue rarely arises for an experienced Web development team, and if it does, it's a two-second fix. What seems far more likely is that the real advantage of this design for vBulletin is that it makes the code very difficult to view or alter. You'd probably need to write your own Web-based tool to make more than trivial changes, or pull all the code out and turn it into a file-based system. That's fine as a commercial policy but a drawback in this particular case because part of the goal is to eventually integrate KnowNow's software with the forum. The extensive use of OOP makes it even more difficult to figure out quickly what's going on — objects and templates divide things up in a different way than procedural code, which typically involves a steeper ramp-up although it may make long-term maintenance easier.

Also, vBulletin seems to be the slowest of the three finalists in page downloads. Most of this is probably attributable to its extensive (over)use of graphical elements instead of links; but the truth is that all the architectural choices made by that development team add latency — code-in-database, classes, message catalogs, and templates all pack on the milliseconds.

Of the three packages, UBBThreads has by far the cleanest, easiest code to integrate. In comparison, phpBB seems less focused as well as less functional. UBBThreads' style is exceptionally straightforward, confident, and mature. Instead of being hamstrung by theoretical issues, it makes a good cost-benefit analyses about where things such as OOP, functionalizing, and normalized data help and where they're more trouble than they're worth. Perhaps most important of all, the code is written in a beautiful style — the commenting alone is worth the price of admission.

> **TIP:** People can have very different ideas of what makes a code package easy to alter and maintain — but for us, one simple test is to look at any random file in the package and see how long it takes you to figure out exactly what that file does. Pick out one file from each package that you're evaluating, and time yourself while you apply the "sniff test" — write down what the file does, where it gets data from (if it does), where it sends data to (if it does), and how long it takes you to change one string. If it's taking more than a couple of minutes per file, think twice about using that code base.

One disappointing thing about all three packages: over-reliance on certain PHP and database configuration options. Every one of them, for example, uses `register_globals` to an unhealthy and unnecessary extent. Some set `magic_quotes` in either `php.ini` or during runtime, whereas others do the right thing in escaping all strings that are bound for the database. They make assumptions about what file extensions are parsed by PHP. Also, they all assume a Sendmail server is available. vBulletin scales by means of database replication, which is a less well-understood problem than simple PHP in most Webdev teams. Unfortunately if some of these configuration variables are unavailable because of the peculiarities of your setup, you immediately have problems running these packages.

It should be restated that all the candidates are excellent and would be appropriate in many situations. If fewer functional code changes were necessary, vBulletin would be our choice; if a simpler user experience or an open source package were the priority, phpBB would fit the bill nicely. Our choice of UBBThreads in this particular situation should not be interpreted as a claim that it is "the best" or even "better" in some global way. The best forum package is whichever is the best for you on any given project.

Step-by-step integration

Having decided on UBBThreads, these are the changes we made. They fall into three buckets: 1) setting things up to the point where we have a running installation we can test; 2) making display changes; and 3) making big backend changes.

> **CAUTION:** The changes in the following sections are based on the 5.4.6 version of UBBThreads. They may not be applicable to other versions. We do not intend the code in this chapter to be runnable unless you have the exact version and make the exact modifications we describe.

Checking global configuration

To use UBBThreads, you need to make sure that you have a few important configuration directives set the right way.

- You need to be positive that your database is correctly installed and accepting read and write connections from PHP.

- You do not need to have `magic_quotes` on because UBBThreads properly escapes data and, in fact, it's probably better to turn it off because you want to know if the escaping doesn't happen properly.

- You must make sure that PHP can send mail from this server; you may need to set the `sendmail_path` directive.

- You must make sure that PHP can include files from any directory in this tree; you may need to set the `include_path` directive.

- Finally (and unfortunately), at least at first, you need to have `register_globals` turned on. We return later to how you can turn this unsafe directive off, in the "Turn off register globals" section of this chapter.

Changing directory name

UBBThreads unpacks by default into a directory with the awkward name /ubbthreads-php — not exactly the URL you want to give out to your users. This would matter less if you were deploying the forum at the top level of your Web tree — if your site basically was a forum and nothing else — but in our case, we are deploying in a subdirectory. Our old forum lived in a directory called /forums, so the easiest thing for us was to rename the UBBThreads directory to that name. Even if we had chosen not to rename the directory, it would still be advisable to maintain a /forums directory with some mechanism (such as Apache mod_rewrite or a custom 404 page) to redirect visitors from the old URIs.

> **CAUTION:** Everything in the rest of this chapter assumes you also changed your directory name to /forums rather than /ubbthreads-php.

Adding index.html

Unaccountably, the UBBThreads package came without an index.html file and with an odd index.php file that displays a text link instead of redirecting to the actual front page of the forum (which is either ubbthreads.php or categories.php). This means that anyone who tries to reference http://developer.knownow.com/forums/ — a perfectly reasonable URL, and one supported by our old system — would get an ugly 404 or a Web server directory index (depending on your httpd configuration) instead of a redirect. Because we were sure that, sooner or later, we were going to get someone who tried this URL, we added a simple index.html file, which would redirect to the forum homepage. You would not need to do this if you don't support the .html file extension anywhere on your site. Listing 35-1 shows a redirect page.

Listing 35-1: A redirect page (index.html)

```php
<?php

/****************************************************
 * index.html                                      *
 * This file is a simple HTTP header redirect to    *
 * the forums front page, ubbthreads.php.           *
 ****************************************************/

header("Location: /forums/ubbthreads.php");
?>
```

You may also wish to replace /forums/index.php with a file such as this. If you choose to display categories on your main page (see the following section on configuration), you may want to redirect to categories.php instead.

Configuring the package

UBBThreads has two major configuration files, but it's not immediately clear why because one of them does nothing but include the other one. If you wanted, you could combine them, although it isn't really worth taking the trouble for a tiny gain in efficiency and transparency.

The one that is included from all the other forum files is main.inc.php. You need to set the path to your UBBThreads installation in here. It immediately turns around and includes a file that turns around and includes config.inc.php. You have an HTML form (/forums/admin/editconfig.php) to edit this second file — come to think of it, the two-file system is probably all about giving you the capability to use this form. We always prefer to edit configuration files by hand because it's a bad security mistake to make configuration files writable by the Apache user.

> **CAUTION:** To use the configuration forms to set your configuration directives, make them writable (chmod 666) by hand, use the form, and then immediately set them back to read-only (chmod 444).

One of the more important configuration questions is "What type of main page do you want to use? ". You can choose to either display all categories and forums, in which case your main page is ubbthreads.php, or just display the categories, in which case your main page is categories.php. For the rest of this section, we are assuming the former because, unless you have a tremendous number of forums, you probably don't want to select the latter. If you go for the category display option, you must copy all ubbthreads.php changes to categories.php where applicable.

Another issue is cookies versus sessions. We chose cookies because maintaining sessions for two pieces of information (username and password) seemed like such a waste of time; and because this is an integration to a pre-existing site, it needs to fit into our old method of maintaining state instead of introducing a new one. If you prefer sessions, some of the following may not apply to you.

Finally, it's a good idea to move your database password out of the Web tree entirely. Say you have a database password file like this, called forum_db_vars.inc (be sure to pick a file extension which is not parsed by PHP) in some location (which you may have to create) such as /usr/local/apache/protected:

```
<?php
$mysql_host = 'localhost';
$mysql_user = 'forumuser';
$mysql_pass = 'Myv3rYh4rd2gU3$$p4$$w0Rd';
?>
```

You make it readable only by the Apache user, which is Nobody; and you include the directory in your PHP include_path. Now you alter config.inc.php like so:

```
// Database Variables
require_once('/usr/local/apache/protected');
```

```
// Server hosting the database
  $config['dbserver'] = $mysql_host;

// Username that has permissions to the database
  $config['dbuser'] = $mysql_user;

// Password for the database
  $config['dbpass'] = $mysql_pass;
```

Now there is less chance that your database variables could ever be read, even if your HTTP document root is compromised.

Creating a new schema

Run `createtable.php` to create the necessary database tables and then move the file out of the Web tree. The script does not check for the existence of the table first before attempting to create it — a good safety measure, because it chokes on your database if the tables already exist rather than dropping them and recreating them (emptied of data). This means, however, that if you want to test schema creation multiple times, you must drop and create the tables multiple times by hand.

Everything in the rest of this chapter assumes that you created these tables in the same MySQL database as any other user data tables you may be using (if any). If this is not true, you need to account for the difference yourself in changing SQL queries throughout this chapter.

> **CAUTION:** Any files that can alter your database schema should be moved out of your Web tree at the earliest possible opportunity! It's a little disapointing that UBBThreads would put a whole bunch of schema-altering scripts in their main forums directory instead of in an administrator-only subdirectory, which could be quickly protected by basic auth. Get rid of them as soon as possible. Under no circumstances should they exist on your production server for any longer than it takes to do whatever they need to do.

Creating an administrator account

Now you need to go to `newuser.php` and set yourself up with a new user account. You must be the first and only user to do this, or you do not correctly receive administrator privileges. UBBThreads sends you a password by e-mail. The version of this password stored in the database is encrypted, so if you lose the e-mail, you are out of luck.

> **CAUTION:** UBBThreads' method of setting the initial administrator can introduce problems if you already have an existing user database. The issue is basically that it assumes the administrator is going to be the first user in the users database – identified by the value 1 in the `w3t_Users.U_Number` field. Unfortunately, we already had a user database of our own, with existing user IDs that we did not wish to change — and our administrator did not happen to have the user ID 1. As far as we can tell, the only way to fix this issue is to go into the MySQL database by hand after importing old user data (a process we describe in detail in the "Import pre-existing user data" section of this chapter), manually revoke the administrator permissions from the user with ID 1, and manually grant them to the real administrator.

Choosing a style sheet

Display preferences are set in the file `theme.inc.php`. You can use a form in the `admin` directory to edit this file — although again we do not necessarily recommend allowing your configuration files to be writable by the Apache user. The actual style sheets live in the subdirectory `/forums/stylesheets` by default.

We were very lucky to have a perfect fit with one of the stock style sheets right out of the box. The *Infopop* style, which is mostly greys, harmonized well with our bright orange and blue color scheme.

The Infopop theme, however, has one little problem: Logged out users see a small `Please register a username` message on the forums front page. The link starts out orange — but the visited link changes into the exact same color as its background, making it invisible. Oops. You can fix this by adding a line to the Infopop style sheet:

```
.welcome A:visited {
   color: #cc6600;
}
```

This keeps the link orange. If you want it to be white for better legibility, use `#FFFFFF` instead.

UBBThreads uses text links instead of the graphical elements favored by vBulletin and phpBB. This makes it faster to get a different look and faster to download. Just start with the style sheet that is closest to your desired look — and then, even if you don't know a lot about styles, fiddling around with them should be easy.

UBBThreads gives you the option of offering your visitors a choice of style sheet. If you want skins, this is the easiest way to do it. You can set this in the `theme.inc.php` file. We do not want to avail ourselves of this feature.

Deleting unused files

We no longer need these files, which represent three or four features of UBBThreads that we want to rip out (the feature we don't want is detailed in parentheses after each filename in the bulleted list below). Those files, therefore, were removed from the forums directory and checked into some other location in our version control source tree.

- `addaddress.php` (private messages)
- `adduser.php` (registration)
- `domailthread.php` (mail posts)
- `dopoll.php` (polls)
- `logout.php` (log out)
- `mailthread.php` (mail posts)

- ♦ `mess_handler.php` (private messages)

- ♦ `mess_reply.php` (private messages)

- ♦ `newuser.php` (registration)

- ♦ `removeaddress.php` (private messages)

- ♦ `sendmessage.php` (private messages)

- ♦ `sendprivate.php` (private messages)

- ♦ `showaddressbook.php` (address book)

- ♦ `showmembers.php` (member list)

- ♦ `start_page.php` (log in)

- ♦ `viewmessage.php` (private messages)

- ♦ `viewmessages.php` (private messages)

- ♦ `viewpoll.php` (polls)

- ♦ `altertable-*.php` (files to upgrade database schema)

- ♦ All non-English FAQs and message catalogs

- ♦ All unused style sheets

- ♦ All message catalogs corresponding to deleted files

By *message catalogs*, we mean the files that contain the string values for each page. Each page of UBBThreads has a matching file in the `/languages/[languagename]` subdirectory, which contains all the text strings used in that PHP script. They are obviously translated into all the languages supported by UBBThreads. This is an internationalization feature, and some people think it makes the system more maintainable because you do not have to hunt around in code just to make a string change.

Inflection point: Bucket-one tasks complete

At this point, the first bucket of integration tasks (setting things up to the point where we have a running installation we can test) is complete. You should have a working rough draft of a forum that pretty much does what you want. Make sure that you have administrator permissions in the `w3t_Users` table. Now you can add the custom features that make your forum different from all others — testing and commenting at every step as you go.

> **TIP:** An excellent way to learn the package quickly and a good idea, in general, is to add a block comment at the top of every page. Include, at least, what the file does, where it gets data from, and where it sends data to. In all the code listings in this chapter, you see that we've recommended every page at the top. We've also added comments to mark the areas where we made changes.

Adding custom header and footer files

These files already exist in the UBBThreads package as `/forums/includes/header.php` and `/forums/includes/footer.php`. This step consists mostly of replacing the placeholder header and footer HTML with our own.

However, there is one twist. UBBThreads wants to send the first few HTML tags on each page (essentially the HTML `<HEADER>` element) separately from most of the header. Probably this is all about wanting to control the sending of HTTP headers to manipulate redirects and `<TITLE>` tags. The reason this is undesirable is that the header for the rest of our site does not do this; it starts at `<HTML>`. Using UBBThreads' included header file, therefore, means maintaining two separate header files — one for forums, and one for the rest of the site. Generally, you want to avoid doing things such this, because they can too easily get unsynched.

Unfortunately, changing this design requires you to alter some pretty core code and is probably not worth the trouble. The main functionality you'd lose would be the specific mechanism used to redirect users after adding, deleting, or editing a post, adding or deleting a favorite forum or thread, or setting a subscription. UBBThreads accomplishes this by showing a message indicating the success of the action for five seconds and then by using an HTML `<META>` tag to reload the new page. You could instead choose to simply use a PHP `header()` redirect to that page on success.

Adding a terms-of-use statement

Because this is a commercial deployment for a software company, it's very important for us to include a link to the terms-of-use page from the main forum page.

The actual file, `forumstermsofuse.html`, is a simple text message in HTML format, with a header and footer. The more important part was adding a prominent link to this page from `ubbthreads.php` — which is a great introduction to working with UBBThreads' message catalogs.

To support internationalization, UBBThreads doesn't use strings in its PHP code. Instead, it maintains a message catalog file corresponding to each script. We only support English on our site, so the only message catalogs we need to concern ourselves with are in the subdirectory `/languages/english` — but if you're using another language or you do have i18n concerns, you must make sure that every string change that you make gets correctly translated and maintained in however many languages you support.

> **TIP:** By using the path `/languages/english` in every example that follows, we are not trying to enforce some kind of English-only trip on you. This particular site supports only English, so we happened to only work with the message cats in that subdirectory. Actually UBBThreads has good support for most European-origin languages plus Chinese.

A message catalog in the UBBThreads system looks something like this:

```php
<?php
$lang[STRING_ONE] = "This is a string.";
$lang[STRING_TWO] = "This is another string.";
$lang[STRING_WITH_VAR] = "This is a string with the variable
$_COOKIE['myname'] embedded in it.";
?>
```

As you can see, PHP constructs an associative array called $lang with all the strings necessary for that page as values. If you include this file from a PHP script, these array elements become immediately available to you as if they were in the script itself.

Open up the message catalog file /languages/english/ubbthreads.php. Add a line similar to this:

```php
$lang[TERMS_USE] = "Welcome to our developer forum. Please read the <A
HREF=\"/forums/forumstermsofuse.html\">Forums Terms of Use</A>.";
```

> **TIP:** You may be wondering why we use double quotes in the line of code that immediately precedes this sentence, although we didn't strictly need to and, in fact, the choice of double quotes forced us to escape the HREF. The reason is that we are going to be dropping this string into another string that is itself double-quoted — so we need to make sure that all the escaping of double-quotes is uniform across the larger string.

Now you want to add a box to the top of the main UBBThreads page that displays this message prominently. Open the script ubbthreads.php (not the message catalog — it would be less confusing if these files had different names) and add this section near the top. We slotted it in between the HTML header section and the checking groups section (approximately line 38), but you could do it anytime before HTML output begins again.

```php
// Customization: add a box with a link to the forum terms of use
  echo "<p>";
  $html -> open_table();
  echo "
<tr class=\"cleartable\">
<td class=\"cleartable\" align=\"center\">$lang[TERMS_USE]
  ";
  $html -> close_table();
  echo "<p>";
```

The result looks something like what you see in Figure 35-1.

Changing registration/login links

We are not using the login, logout, and newuserregistration functions that came with the forum. Instead, we want to use the main developer.knownow.com user log-in/register system.

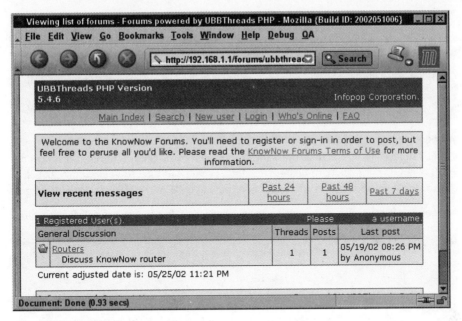

Figure 35-1: Link to terms of use page

We're also sticking to our pre-existing user-database schema and cookies, topics that we discuss in greater detail in the third bucket of forum integration tasks beginning in the "Alter schema" section below. For now, we just want to make sure that all links that point to login, logout, or registration pages are correct.

These links appear in two places. The first is the main forums page, which is either `ubbthreads.php` or `categories.php`. At the upper right of the forums or categories list box, unregistered users see a link that says `Please register a username`. The other location is the medium gray navbar at the top of each page, which displays registration and login/logout links depending on the status of the visitor (see Figure 35-1 for both links).

To change the `ubbthreads.php` `Please register a username` link, simply alter the `/languages/english/ubbthreads.php` message catalog entry so it points to the main site registration page:

```
$lang[WEL_PRIV_NO] = "Please <A HREF=\"/register.html\">register</A> a
username.";
```

The navbar links are in the file `ubbt.inc.php`, which contains an HTML display class and some other utilities. Look for the `send_header` function, which is part of the HTML class. You find two different menus, one for logged-in users and one for logged-out users, approximately 100 lines apart. Look for the comments `If they aren't logged in they get the standard menu`, and immediately below a bunch of `HREF`s that constitute the logged-out users' menu. You want to either delete the links pointing to `newuser.php`, `login.php`, and `logout.php`; or edit these lines to point to the registration and login scripts you want to use.

You should, however, definitely keep one of the links in the logged-in user's menu, as follows:

```
<a href = \"$phpurl/login.php?Cat=$Cat\">$lang[CONTROL_PANEL]</a>
$spacer
```

This line occurs at approximately line 297. Unfortunately, the file `login.php` has two functions: For logged-out users, it shows a login form; but for logged-in users, it displays the user control panel. Do not delete or change this line, or you can't get to your control panel. This is one of the few examples of confusing and unclear code in the UBBThreads package.

You also need to alter `login.php` so it no longer displays a log-in form. Look for this block:

```
if ($Username && $Password) {
  $html -> start_page($Username,$Password,$Cat);
  exit;
}
```

Delete everything after that. If you like, you can rename this script to something more logical, like `controlpanel.php`; remember to change the link in the logged-in user's menu.

At this point, your registration and log-in functions no longer work until you make some backend alterations, as we describe in the next bucket of integration changes beginning with the "Alter schema" section below.

Force registration/login on post attempt

The capability to force users to register before posting is very important to us. The default behavior of UBBThreads is to enable unregistered users to post, either with the username *Anonymous* or under a *nom de post* of their own choosing. Neither of these alternatives is at all acceptable to us, so we need to hack the posting scripts.

There are three posting scripts: `newpost.php`, `newreply.php`, and `addpost.php`. The first two show forms that submit to the third. The most efficient thing from an engineering point of view would be to add the login check to `addpost.php` because it's already the single point of entry. This is undesirable from a usability point of view, however, because users would only find out they needed to login after submitting the post — and they would almost certainly lose the text of their messages, which would irk them. Therefore, it's better to check for login before displaying the post or reply forms in the first place.

Simply add the following lines to both `newpost.php` and `newreply.php`. The proper place is in the section commented `Get the user info`, right after you set the variables `$Username` and `$Password` from the cookies or sessions. The following code will force a redirect to the main site login page if a user does not have the correct cookies.

```
if (!$Username || !$Password) {
```

```
  $origin = urlencode($REQUEST_URI);
  header("Location: /login.html?origin=$origin");
}
```

This will force redirect to your top-level login script if the user isn't logged in. If your login routines are properly designed, you will be able to return the user to the post/reply form after login by using the $origin variable in the URL.

Toggle subscribe/unsubscribe links

At the bottom of each forum display page (postlist.php) is a link that says Subscribe/Unsubscribe to Board for logged-in members. A cute, nice-to-have feature is to make these links toggle back and forth based on whether the particular user has actually subscribed to the board or not. In other words, instead of saying Subscribe/Unsubscribe in all cases, the link will say Subscribe if the user is not subscribed and Unsubscribe if the user is already subscribed. First we have to change the link text. Go into the generic message catalog file (/languages/english/generic.php) and alter the text of the link as shown:

```
$lang[FORUM_SUB] = "Subscribe to Board";
```

Also add another line there:

```
$lang[FORUM_UNSUB] = "Unsubscribe from Board";
```

Now you're ready to edit the code in postlist.php. Search for the variable $config[subscriptions], and change the case as shown in the code block below.

```
        if ($config[subscriptions]) {
          // Customization: this link to say "Subscribe" if unsubscribed,
          // "Unsubscribe" if already subscribed
          $Owner_q = addslashes($user['U_Username']);
          $query = "
                   SELECT  S_Username
                   FROM    w3t_Subscribe
                   WHERE   S_Username = '$Owner_q'
                   AND     S_Board    = '$Board_q'
                   ";
          $sth = $dbh -> do_query($query);
          if (!$dbh -> fetch_array($sth)) {
            echo " | <a
href=\"$config[phpurl]/togglesub.php?Cat=$Cat&Board=$Board&page=$page&vi
ew=$view&sb=$sb&o=$o\"><img border=0
src=\"$config[images]/subscribetoboard.gif\" align=top>
$lang[FORUM_SUB]</a>";
          } else {
            echo " | <a
href=\"$config[phpurl]/togglesub.php?Cat=$Cat&Board=$Board&page=$page&vi
ew=$view&sb=$sb&o=$o\"><img border=0
src=\"$config[images]/subscribetoboard.gif\" align=top>
$lang[FORUM_UNSUB]</a>";
```

```
      }
   }
```

Allowing users to control profile-display

UBBThreads establishes a user profile page for each new registered user. We happen to believe, however, that our visitors are more likely to feel comfortable sharing personal information with us if we enable them to control the display of that information. Our forum is about enterprise software, where potential developers tend to be extremely cagey about their identities and intentions; we, therefore, want to go beyond opt-out display and actually implement an opt-in user profile display preference. In cases where the creation of an online identity is more central to the mission of the site — as in a hobbyist community — this would be self-defeating.

First, you need to add a column to the w3t_Users table in your database schema. We called this column U_Public. It's easiest to just do this on the command line by typing the following line into the MySQL command-line client, but you may wish to put it in a script instead.

```
ALTER TABLE w3t_Users ADD COLUMN U_Public tinyint DEFAULT 0;
```

Also add this text string to the /languages/english/showprofile.php message catalog:

```
$lang[PRIVATE_PROFILE] = "This user has chosen not to display his or her
profile.<BR><BR>";
```

Now you can add the following code at the very top of the showprofile.php file, below the copyright notice:

```
/*************************************************
 * showprofile.php                              *
 * This page displays an opt-in user profile. *
 *************************************************/

// Require the library
  require ("main.inc.php");
  require ("languages/" .$lang['THIS_FILE']. "/showprofile.php");

// Customization: don't show the profile unless they opt in
  $User = rawurldecode($User);
  $Profile_user = addslashes($User);
  $query = "
    SELECT U_Public
    FROM   w3t_Users
    WHERE  U_Username = '$Profile_user'
  ";
```

```
    $sth = $dbh -> do_query($query);
    list($consent) = $dbh -> fetch_array($sth);
    $dbh -> finish_sth($sth);
    if ($consent != 1) {
        $html = new html;
        $html -> send_header("$lang[PROF_FOR]
$User",$Cat,0,$user['U_Username'],0,0,$user);
        $html -> table_header("$lang[PROF_FOR] $User");
        echo "<TABLE border=\"0\" width=\"$theme[tablewidth]\"
align=\"$theme[tablealign]\" class=\"lighttable\" cellspacing=\"0\">";
        echo "<tr><td>
            $lang[PRIVATE_PROFILE]
            </td></tr></table>";

    // ---------------
    // Send the footer
    $html -> send_footer();
    exit;
    }


// ----------------------
// Grab this user's info
[etc.]
```

When a new developer registers on the site, he or she is opted out of displaying the profile by default. Unless he or she goes to the user info management forms and changes this preference, his or her user profile will look like Figure 35-2.

You also need to give users a way of opting in to profile display. We deal with the management of this bit in the section "Alter user info management forms," a little later in this chapter.

Alter user pages to get rid of rejected features

Because we no longer have the private message or address book features, we need to expunge display references to them from user pages that contain them.

The main user page is the user control panel. For reasons that don't immediately make a lot of sense, the user control panel is the only display file that doesn't have a PHP script of its own. Instead it is (very confusingly) part of the HTML display class in ubbt.inc.php. You call it from another file like this:

```
$html -> start_page($Username, $Password, $Cat);
```

Ah, the joy of HTML display classes!

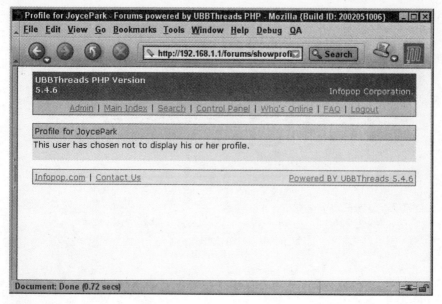

Figure 35-2: An opted-out user profile

First, we want to get rid of the PM flasher. This is a dynamic GIF on the top navbar that looks like a blinking envelope and is supposed to indicate to the user that he or she has a new private message. Look for a comment about the PM flasher on approximately Line 171 and comment out or delete that block.

Now we want to get rid of the private-messages and friends online boxes on the control panel. Luckily, they are in the same table row, which simplifies matters quite a bit. The sections are well commented; you merely need to delete or comment out the chunk of code from approximately Lines 866 to 977.

You also need to comment out a reference to the address book from the user profile page, `showprofile.php`. Again, the lovely style of UBBThreads code makes it simple: Look for a comment that says `Only show the address book link for logged in users`, and comment out that `if()` block (approximately Lines 191 – 196).

Figure 35-3 shows the user control panel with the offending features deleted:

Alter user info management forms

UBBThreads provides three forms that registered users can employ to change their information and preferences. We need to delete from these forms any reference to functions that we've removed. We must also add controls for new functionality, such as the opt-in user profile display.

Figure 35-3: User control panel

The three user management forms are: `editbasic.php`, `editdisplay.php`, and `editsubscribe.php`. We deal with them in turn. Remember that right now we are only going to deal with the UI; we change functionality in the next section.

Changes to `editbasic.php` depend to some extent on how you plan to handle user data. In particular, if you already have a means for your registered users to change their passwords and e-mail addresses, you may not want to let them do so from this form — thus you would want to remove the form fields associated with passwords and e-mail addresses from the HTML form on this page. The main change that we made to this form was to take out the `accept private messages` preference and add a `display private profile` pref in its place. This illustrates how to edit the form to suit your particular needs.

First, we want to change a line in the message catalog, `/languages/english/editbasic.php`:

```
$lang[PROF_DISPLAY] = "Display private profile?";
```

Next, we want to add the `U_Public` bit to the data we fetch. Do this by adding `U_Public` to the end of the long select statement near the top of the main `editbasic.php` file (in place of `U_AcceptPriv`) and also by adding `$Public` to the end of the list construct (in place of

$AcceptPriv). This has the effect of adding each user profile display preference to the bucket of data we fetch from the database and setting it to a variable called $Public.

Now we do the little trick to convert a bit into a two-radio–button display. Search for the block commented Set the default for accepting private messages, and alter it like so:

```
if ($Public == 1) {
  $publicyes = "checked";
} else {
  $publicno = "checked";
}
```

Finally we display the radio buttons. Look for this block at the end of the file, and alter it as shown:

```
//if ($config[private] == "1") {
  echo "
    $lang[PROV_PRIV]<br>
    <input type=radio name=Public value=1 $publicyes
class=\"formboxes\"> $lang[TEXT_YES]
    <input type=radio name=Public value=0 $publicno class=\"formboxes\">
$lang[TEXT_NO]
    <p>
    ";
//}
```

In other words, comment out the condition surrounding the block; change the name of the radio buttons to Public and their values to integers, and use the $publicyes and $publicno variables to display one of the two buttons pre-selected. We have basically replaced the private messages preference with a profile display preference, disturbing as little as possible along the way.

On the next form, editdisplay.php, we just want to take out a few form fields. We don't want to support multiple languages, skins, or user control of the main page — so we delete those three form fields and their associated message strings from the HTML form. If you want to be really neat, you could also delete the U_StyleSheet, U_Language, and U_FrontPage columns from the select statement, and the $StyleSheet, $chosenlanguage, and $FrontPage variables from the list construct.

On the third form, editmail.php, we just want to remove the radio button for private message notification. If you want to be really neat, you could also delete U_Notify from the select statement and $Notify from the list construct.

Inflection point: Bucket-two tasks complete

At this point, you should see the forum pretty much as you want to see it. All links should point to the correct locations. All display pages should be expunged of features you don't want, and all user management forms should show only the options you want to give your users.

Now we come to the biggest fork in the road: integrating forum user registration and login with sitewide user management. Basically, you need to make up your mind at this point whether you want to go for a full integration – where each piece of user data is unique, and lives in only one place in the database – or whether you want to do the quicker and dirtier thing, which is to repeat pieces of user information in the database and hope they stay synched up. The latter takes more effort from the programmer if you're using a lightweight database such as MySQL, which typically is not set up with transactional support.

The risk of your data coming unglued is not that high if you are just sticking a forum on your main site, end of story. This is especially true if your site never needs to scale to a level where database replication becomes a necessity. But if you eventually want to integrate lots of features – a forum, user diaries, photo albums, polls, trouble tickets, and so on — and have replication issues, you should seriously think about maintaining a clean, well-designed schema from the beginning. It's a principle of good design to never maintain a piece of data (especially an important one such as password) in multiple places, and if you violate this principle you're gambling that nothing bad is going to happen. It's your decision, but don't start whining if you lose the gamble.

Alter schema

In either the full or partial integration cases, you definitely want to do one thing: Change the forum users table so it no longer auto-increments user IDs. The main user ID is also going to be logged in the w3t_Users.U_Number field by your code, and you want to ensure that the database cannot cross you up by attempting to generate its own number for that field. The situation you want to avoid is registering a new user in the main user table, and then having something go wrong with the forum user registration — in which case the main user ID and forum user ID no longer match.

This is the SQL to remove auto-incrementing from the w3t_Users.U_number field (you also probably want to take this opportunity to get rid of the NULL default value, which works with the auto-incrementing):

```
ALTER TABLE w3t_Users alter column U_Number DROP DEFAULT;
ALTER TABLE w3t_Users DROP PRIMARY KEY;
ALTER TABLE w3t_Users MODIFY U_Number int(9) unsigned PRIMARY KEY;
```

Again, you can do this from the command line or put it in a script. If you've opted for partial integration, your job is now done. Kick back and pity the poor schmoes who must do a complete integration job.

For full integration, you must now remove all fields from `w3t_Users` that duplicate information found in your main user table. Furthermore, you must go through the entire UBBThreads codebase and alter all SQL statements so that they no longer refer to the removed fields, but instead reference the main user table fields.

The fields you will have to remove may include:

- ◆ U_Username
- ◆ U_Password
- ◆ U_Email
- ◆ U_Name
- ◆ U_Homepage
- ◆ U_Occupation
- ◆ U_Location
- ◆ U_Bio

Basically any data that already appears elsewhere on your main site must go. Obviously, the most important fields are username, password, e-mail, and name.

Now to the grind: altering all the SQL statements in UBBThreads to use the schema correctly. Comfort yourself with the thought that you're doing The Right Thing. Obviously, we can't show you every single line you need to fix, but here's an example from `showprofile.php`. Look for this chunk:

```
$Username = $w3t_myname;
$Password = $w3t_mypass;
$userob = new user;
$user = $userob -> authenticate("$Username", "$Password", "U_Username,
U_Password, U_PictureView, U_Number, U_TimeOffset");
```

Change it to the following:

```
$Username = $_COOKIE['w3t_myname'];
$Password = $_COOKIE['mainsite_pass'];
$userob = new user;
$user = $userob -> authenticate("$Username", "$Password",
"w3t_Users.U_Username, mainsite_Users.Password, w3t_Users.U_PictureView,
w3t_Users.U_Number, w3t_Users.U_TimeOffset");
```

Now just do that on every SQL query. The Unix utility `grep` is a big help in this type of work, as is a text editor that lets you make text searches.

Because you're going to be touching every file anyway (and think of the unmatched opportunity this gives you to learn the codebase!), you may also want to take this occasion to centralize the setting of the `$Username` and `$Password` variables. For some reason,

UBBThreads sets these variables to the cookie values at least once per script, which is not great design — especially if you're doing full integration and are using your main site password cookie. The easiest thing is to add the cookie values to main.inc.php:

```
$Username = $_COOKIE['w3t_myname'];
$Password = $_COOKIE['mainsite_pass'];
```

Then, in each other UBBThreads file, delete the setting of these variables (usually near the top of the file) and replace the lines with a comment like this:

```
// Moved these variables to main.inc.php
$Username = $w3t_myname; // Delete this line
$Password = $mainsite_pass; // Delete this line
```

Now if you need to change your cookie names again sometime in the future, it's a five-second change.

Import pre-existing user data

Now that your main site user and forum user schemas are all neatened up, you want to create forum users to match some or all your main site users. You want to write a script to do this. Probably if you only have a few users (less than 1000), you can use the Apache module version of PHP; but if you have many more users, you probably want to use the binary version.

This is the rare case where full integration takes less work than partial integration — which makes sense because the point of full integration is to move and copy as little data as possible. The full integration version is shown in Listing 35-2:

Listing 35-2: Script to move user data (importusers.php)

```php
<?php

/***********************************************
 * Script to copy user data to forums tables. *
 ***********************************************/

// Connect to the database
require_once('/usr/local/apache/protected/db_vars.inc');
$db = mysql_connect($mysql_host, $mysql_user, $mysql_pass);
mysql_select_db('ubbthreads');

//----------------------
// Get the main site user data
$query = "SELECT user_id, firstname, lastname
          FROM mainsite_Users
         ";
$result = mysql_query($query) or die(mysql_error());

// Cycle through the users
while ($olduser_arr = mysql_fetch_array($result)) {
```

```php
// Lay out the data nicely
$user_id = $olduser_arr['user_id'];
$firstname_q = addslashes($olduser_arr['firstname']);
$lastname_q = addslashes($olduser_arr['lastname']);
echo "Working on $firstname $lastname<BR>";


// ----------------------------
// Create a forum user
// Create username by concatenating firstname + lastname
// If not the first person with that combo, add an int
// to avoid having multiple people with the same username
$test_username = $firstname_q.$lastname_q;
$query = "SELECT U_Number
          FROM w3t_Users
          WHERE U_Username = '$test_username'";
$result = mysql_query($query);
$rl_rows = mysql_num_rows($result1);
if ($rl_rows > 0) {
  $Username_q = $firstname_q.$lastname_q.$rl_rows;
} else {
  $Username_q = $firstname_q.$lastname_q;
}

// Shove the data into the w3t_Users table
$query = "INSERT INTO w3t_Users (U_Username, U_Totalposts, U_Homepage,
U_Status, U_Sort, U_Display, U_View, U_PostsPer, U_Number, U_EReplies,
U_Post_Format, U_Registered, U_Groups, U_Title)
          VALUES ('$Username_q', 0, '$homepage_q', 'User', 5, 'flat',
'collapsed', 10, $user_id, 'Off', 'side', NOW(), '-3-', 'stranger')
          ";
  $result = mysql_query($query) or die(mysql_error());
}
echo "FINISHED TRANSFERRING OLD USERS";
?>
```

Listing 35-3 is the partial-integration version:

Listing 35-3: Script to copy user data (importusers_partial.php)

```php
<?php

/************************************************
 * Script to copy user data to forums tables. *
 ************************************************/

// Connect to the database
require_once('/usr/local/apache/protected/db_vars.inc');
$db = mysql_connect($mysql_host, $mysql_user, $mysql_pass);
mysql_select_db('ubbthreads');
```

```php
//------------------------
// Get the main site user data
$query = "SELECT user_id, firstname, lastname, email, password,
$homepage
          FROM mainsite_Users
        ";
$result = mysql_query($query) or die(mysql_error());

// Cycle through the users
while ($olduser_arr = mysql_fetch_array($result3)) {
  // Lay out the data nicely
  $user_id = $olduser_arr['user_id'];
  $firstname_q = addslashes($olduser_arr['firstname']);
  $lastname_q = addslashes($olduser_arr['lastname']);
  $email_q = addslashes($olduser_arr['email']);
  $password_q = addslashes($olduser_arr['password']);
  $homepage_q = addslashes($olduser_arr['homepage']);
  echo "Working on $firstname $lastname<BR>";

  // --------------------------------
  // Create a forum user
  // Create username by concatenating firstname + lastname
  // If not the first person with that combo, add an int
  // to avoid having multiple people with the same username
  $test_username = $firstname_q.$lastname_q;
  $query = "SELECT U_Number
            FROM w3t_Users
            WHERE U_Username = '$test_username'";
  $result = mysql_query($query);
  $r1_rows = mysql_num_rows($result);
  if ($r1_rows > 0) {
    $Username_q = $firstname_q.$lastname_q.$r1_rows;
  } else {
    $Username_q = $firstname_q.$lastname_q;
  }

  // Shove the data into the w3t_Users table
  $query1 = "INSERT INTO w3t_Users (U_Username, U_Password, U_Email,
U_Name, U_Totalposts, U_Homepage, U_Status, U_Sort, U_Display, U_View,
U_PostsPer, U_Number, U_EReplies, U_Post_Format, U_Registered,
U_RegEmail, U_Groups, U_Title)
            VALUES ('$Username_q', '$password_q', '$email_q',
'$firstname_q $lastname_q', 0, '$homepage_q', 'User', 5, 'flat',
'collapsed', 10, $user_id, 'Off', 'side', NOW(), '$email_q', '-3-',
'stranger')
          ";
  $result1 = mysql_query($query1) or die(mysql_error());
}
echo "FINISHED TRANSFERRING OLD USERS";
```

```
?>
```

This script will probably not exactly suit your needs (unless our taste in database design and variable naming is suspiciously similar), but just a little jiggering of variable names should make it useful to you. Be sure to save it to some filename like `importusers.php`.

After you import new users, you may need to reset your forum administrator permissions, and make sure that if you have a user who has the ID number 1, he or she doesn't have forum administrator permissions. The two database fields you need to look at are `w3t_Users.U_Status` and `w3t_User.U_Groups`. Administrators will have `Administrator` as the value of the former, and `-3-1-` (the order of the digits may be different) as the value of the latter. You may need to set these values by hand.

Import pre-existing posts

Recall that one of our project requirements was saving posts from an old message-posting system to a new forum. Now that we've transferred user data, we can turn to transferring data from the old message-posting system. This varies enormously with the design of your previous bulletin board; the following code (Listing 35-4) is only meant to be illustrative of how to fit one schema into another as neatly as possible. Again, you will be able to run the script in your browser if you have some fairly small number of posts (less than 1000); but the command line is probably a better idea if you have tons.

Listing 35-4: Script to move old posts (moveposts.php)

```php
<?php

/************************************************
 * Script to copy old posts to forums tables. *
 ************************************************/

// Connect to the database
require_once('/usr/local/apache/protected/db_vars.inc');
$db = mysql_connect($mysql_host, $mysql_user, $mysql_pass);
mysql_select_db('ubbthreads');

$query = "SELECT * FROM threads";
$result = mysql_query($query) or die(mysql_error());

// Cycle through the threads
while ($threads_arr = mysql_fetch_array($result)) {
  $id = $threads_arr[0];
  $cat_id = $threads_arr[1];
  if ($cat_id == 21) {
    $Board_q = 'router';
  } elseif ($cat_id == 24) {
    $Board_q = 'microservers';
  } elseif ($cat_id == 25) {
```

```php
  $Board_q = 'components';
} elseif ($cat_id == 31) {
  $Board_q = 'docu';
} elseif ($cat_id == 32) {
  $Board_q = 'sampleapps';
}
$user_id = $threads_arr[2];
$text = $threads_arr[3];
$code = $threads_arr[4];
$datetime = $threads_arr[5];
$disabled = $threads_arr[6];
if ($disabled == 1) {
  // disabled threads should not be moved
  continue;
}

$query = "SELECT U_Username, U_Totalposts
          FROM w3t_Users
          WHERE U_Number = $user_id
          ";
$result = mysql_query($query) or die(mysql_error());
$name_arr = mysql_fetch_array($result);
$username = $name_arr[0];
$totalposts = $name_arr[1];

echo "Working on Thread $id<BR>";
if ($text != "" && $code == "") {
  $Body = $text;
} elseif ($text != "" && $code != "") {
  $Body = $text.'\n\n'.$code;
} elseif ($text == "" && $code != "") {
  $Body = $code;
}
$Body_q = addslashes($Body);
$Subject = substr($Body_q, 0, 50);
$Subject_q = $Subject."...";
$Username_q = addslashes($username);
// -----------------------
// Up their totalposts by 1
$Totalposts = $totalposts + 1;

// -------------------------------------
// Update their profile
$query = "UPDATE w3t_Users
          SET    U_Totalposts = $Totalposts
          WHERE  U_Username   = '$Username_q'
          ";
$result = mysql_query($query) or die(mysql_error());
```

```
  // Add the post
  $query = "INSERT INTO w3t_Posts (B_Board, B_Number, B_Parent, B_Main,
B_Posted, B_Last_Post, B_Username, B_Subject, B_Body, B_Mail, B_Status,
B_Approved, B_Picture, B_Icon, B_Reged, B_UTitle, B_ParentUser,
B_Replies, B_UStatus, B_Topic, B_Convert)
          VALUES ('$Board_q', '$id', 0, '$id', NOW(), NOW(),
'$Username_q', '$Subject_q', '$Body_q', 0, 0, 'yes', 'http://',
'book.gif','y','stranger', NULL, 0, 'User', 1, 'both')
          ";
  $result = mysql_query($query) or die(mysql_error());

  // Update the board totals
  $query = "UPDATE w3t_Boards
          SET     Bo_Total   = Bo_Total + 1,
                  Bo_Last    = NOW(),
                  Bo_Poster  = '$Username_q',
                  Bo_Threads = Bo_Threads + 1
          WHERE   Bo_Keyword = '$Board_q'
          ";
  $result = mysql_query($query) or die(mysql_error());
}

echo "FINISHED TRANSFERRING OLD THREADS<BR><BR>";
?>
```

Add forum data to new-user registration

Whenever new users register on your main site, you also need to open a new forum user
account for them. If you forget to do this, they will not be able to use the forums correctly.

This is the full-integration version.

```
function devRegister($firstname, $lastname, $email, $user_id, $db,
$database_name) {
  mysql_select_db($database_name); //mysql_db_query has been
deprecated...

  // Create a forum user
  // Create username by concatenating firstname + lastname
  // If not the first person with that combo, add an int
  // to avoid having multiple people with the same username
  $firstname_q = addslashes($firstname);
  $lastname_q = addslashes($lastname);
  $query = "SELECT id
          FROM mainsite_Users
          WHERE firstname = '$firstname_q'
          AND lastname = '$lastname_q'
          ";
  $result = mysql_query($query);
  if (!$result) {
```

```
    return 1;
    exit;
  } else {
    $r_rows = mysql_num_rows($result);
  }
  if ($r_rows > 1) {
    $Username_q = $firstname_q.$lastname_q.$r_rows;
  } else {
    $Username_q = $firstname_q.$lastname_q;
  }
  $email_q = addslashes($email);
  $ip_q = $_SERVER['REMOTE_ADDR'];

  // Insert w3t_Users data
  // -----------------------------------------
  $query = "INSERT INTO w3t_Users (U_Username, U_Totalposts, U_Laston,
U_Status, U_Sort, U_Display, U_View, U_PostsPer, U_Number, U_EReplies,
U_Post_Format, U_Registered, U_RegEmail, U_RegIP, U_Groups, U_Title,
U_Color, U_Public)
            VALUES ('$Username_q', 0, NOW(), 'User', 5, 'flat',
'collapsed', '10', $user_id, 'Off', 'side', NOW(), '$email_q', '$ip_q',
'-3-', 'stranger', '', 0)
            ";
  $result = mysql_query($query);
  if (!$result || mysql_affected_rows($db) != 1) {
    return 1;
    exit;
  }
  return 0;
}
```

This is the partial integration version:

```
function devRegister($firstname, $lastname, $email, $user_id, $homepage,
$db, $database_name) {
  mysql_select_db($database_name); //mysql_db_query has been
deprecated...

  // Create a forum user
  // Create username by concatenating firstname + lastname
  // If not the first person with that combo, add an int
  // to avoid having multiple people with the same username
  $firstname_q = addslashes($firstname);
  $lastname_q = addslashes($lastname);
  $query = "SELECT id
            FROM mainsite_Users
            WHERE firstname = '$firstname_q'
            AND lastname = '$lastname_q'
            ";
```

```
$result = mysql_query($query);
if (!$result) {
    return 1;
    exit;
} else {
    $r_rows = mysql_num_rows($result);
}
if ($r_rows > 1) {
    $Username_q = $firstname_q.$lastname_q.$r_rows;
} else {
    $Username_q = $firstname_q.$lastname_q;
}
$email_q = addslashes($email);
$homepage_q = addslashes($homepage);
$ip_q = $_SERVER['REMOTE_ADDR'];


// Insert w3t_Users data
// -----------------------------------------
$query = "INSERT INTO w3t_Users (U_Username, U_Password, U_Email,
U_Name, U_Totalposts, U_Homepage, U_Status, U_Sort, U_Display, U_View,
U_PostsPer, U_Number, U_EReplies, U_Post_Format, U_Registered,
U_RegEmail, U_Groups, U_Title)
            VALUES ('$Username_q', '$password_q', '$email_q',
'$firstname_q $lastname_q', 0, '$homepage_q', 'User', 5, 'flat',
'collapsed', 10, $user_id, 'Off', 'side', NOW(), '$email_q', '-3-',
'stranger')
            ";
$result = mysql_query($query);
if (!$result || mysql_affected_rows($db) != 1) {
    return 1;
    exit;
}
return 0;
}
```

Whichever version of the function you choose, you must add it to your new-user registration scripts. We can't give you an example here for space reasons, but it should be possible with a little work to shoehorn this function into the `register.php` script from Chapter 38.

Set forum cookies on sitewide login

You need to add the setting of forums cookies to your sitewide login routines, so that whenever users log in anywhere on the site, they also receive the persistent data that they need to access the forums seamlessly.

It's very easy to do this if you have a well-designed user management system in the first place (see Chapter 38 for an example). The versions for full and partial integration differ only in the password cookie. For full integration we're assuming you are using your main site password cookie instead of $w3t_mypass.

The following code block ensures that your user cookies are set for use with the UBBThreads forum:

```
function devLogin($email, $password, $db, $database_name)
{
  mysql_select_db($database_name); //mysql_db_query has been
deprecated...

  // We'll be using the site password cookie rather than w3t_pass,
  // so we assume it's being checked and set in the sitewide login
function
  $trim_email = trim($email);
  $lc_email = strtolower($trim_email);
  $as_email = addslashes($lc_email);
  $trim_pass = trim($password);
  $as_pass = addslashes($trim_pass);
  $crypt_pass = crypt($as_pass);
  $query = "SELECT w3t_Users.U_Username
           FROM mainsite_Users, w3t_Users
           WHERE mainsite_Users.email='$as_email'
           AND mainsite_Users.password = '$crypt_pass'
           AND mainsite_Users.id = w3t_Users.U_Number
           ";
  $result = mysql_query($query);
  $num_username = mysql_num_rows($result);
  if ($num_username == 1) {
    $username_arr = mysql_fetch_array($result);
    $username = $username_arr[0];
    // Set the developer cookie(s)
    // ------------------------------
    setcookie("w3t_myname", $username, time()+3156000, "/forums");
    // Don't need to set w3t_mypass for full integration
    // Uncomment the following line for partial integration
    //setcookie("w3t_mypass", $crypt_pass, time()+31536000, "/forums");
  } else {
    // Failure for any reason
    return 1;
  }
}
```

Call this function at the same time you call your sitewide login functions; or just add the code to your sitewide login function. Remember that we want to use e-mail and password on login rather than username and password, and that email is unique and password is encrypted.

We will also need to unset these cookies on logout.

```
function devLogout()
{
  // Get rid of the developer cookie(s)
```

```
    setcookie("w3t_myname", "", time() - 3156000, "/forums");
    // Uncomment the following line for partial integration
    //setcookie("w3t_mypass", "", time() - 3156000, "/forums");
}
```

Alter user-management scripts

And finally, we need to update what happens if the user changes basic user information. The form `editbasic.php` is used to change things like e-mail address and sig; it submits data to `changebasic.php`, which does a big update. Basically what you need to do divide this update into two updates: one for the main user table data, and one for the forum user table data.

For full integration, change the section in `changebasic.php` after the `Formatting the query` words section, as shown:

```
// --------------------------
// Update the User's profile
  $query  = "UPDATE w3t_Users
          SET U_Fakeemail     = '$Fakeemail_q',
          U_Signature      = '$Signature_q',
          U_Occupation     = '$Occupation_q',
          U_Hobbies        = '$Hobbies_q',
          U_Location       = '$Location_q',
          U_Bio            = '$Bio_q',
          U_Extra1         = '$ICQ_q',
          U_Picture        = '$Picture_q',
          U_Visible        = '$Visible',
          U_Public     = $Public
          WHERE U_Username = '$Username_q'
          ";
  $dbh -> do_query($query);

  // Get the user id for the mainsite update
  $query = "SELECT U_Number
          FROM w3t_Users
          WHERE U_Username = '$Username_q'
          ";
  $dbh -> do_query($query);
  list($user_id) = $dbh -> fetch_array($sth);
  $dbh = finish_sth($sth);

  $query  = "UPDATE mainsite_Users
          SET password   = '$Password_q',
          email          = '$Email_q',
          WHERE user_id = '$user_id'
          ";
  $dbh -> do_query($query);
```

```
  // See if we need to reset the cookies
  if ($Password != $ChosenPassword) {
    setcookie("mainsite_pass", $ChosenPassword, time()+31536000, "/");
  }
  if ($_COOKIE['mainsite_email'] != $Email) {
    setcookie("mainsite_email", $Email, time()+31536000, "/");
  }

  return 0;
}
```

For partial integration, it's a little more work:

```
// --------------------------
// Update the User's profile
  $query  = "UPDATE w3t_Users
            SET U_Password    = '$Password_q',
                U_Email       = '$Email_q',
                U_Fakeemail   = '$Fakeemail_q',
                U_Signature   = '$Signature_q',
                U_Occupation  = '$Occupation_q',
                U_Hobbies     = '$Hobbies_q',
                U_Location    = '$Location_q',
                U_Bio         = '$Bio_q',
                U_Extra1      = '$ICQ_q',
                U_Picture     = '$Picture_q',
                U_Visible    = '$Visible',
                U_Public     = $Public
            WHERE U_Username = '$Username_q'
            ";
$dbh -> do_query($query);

  // Get the user id for the mainsite update
  $query = "SELECT U_Number
            FROM w3t_Users
            WHERE U_Username = '$Username_q'
            ";
$dbh -> do_query($query);
list($user_id) = $dbh -> fetch_array($sth);
$dbh = finish_sth($sth);

  $query  = "UPDATE mainsite_Users
            SET password  = '$Password_q',
                U_Email       = '$Email_q',
            WHERE user_id = $user_id
            ";
$dbh -> do_query($query);

  // See if we need to reset the cookies
```

```
if ($Password != $ChosenPassword) {
  setcookie("w3t_mypass", $ChosenPassword, time()+31536000,
"/forums");
}
if ($_COOKIE['mainsite_email'] != $Email) {
  setcookie("mainsite_email", $Email, time()+31536000, "/");
}

return 0;
}
```

Turn off register_globals

This optional change isn't so much difficult as it is super-tedious. You merely need to go through the entire UBBThreads codebase and change every GET, POST, cookie, or session variable to a correctly formed superglobal array member. You'd want, for example, to change all the $w3t_myname references to $_COOKIE['w3t_myname'], and so forth. Then you could turn off register_globals, which would make the site much, much safer.

You could write a PHP or Perl script to do some of it for you very quickly. In Perl, it would just be something like:

```
perl -pi -e "s/w3t_myname/_COOKIE\[\'w3t_myname\'\]/g" *.php
perl -pi -e "s/w3t_mypass/_COOKIE\[\'w3t_mypass\'\]/g" *.php
```

Unfortunately this won't work nicely in all cases, because of usages like this:

```
$Subject = str_replace("&", "&amp;", $Subject);
```

It's probably possible to do this type of string replacement:

```
$_POST['Subject'] = str_replace("&", "&amp;", $_POST['Subject']);
```

But not necessarily a good idea to manipulate your superglobal array variables by hand after the post.

If all this sounds significantly less fun than going to the dentist, you can take your chances and wait for Infopop to take care of it. UBBThreads 6.0 may deal with the issue in a better way.

Inflection point: Bucket-three tasks complete

Well, we did warn you it's a non-trivial amount of work to integrate other people's PHP. We hope you now have a very clear idea how it's done, especially the planning steps. The main message that we hope to convey is that dividing up integration and customization changes into manageable bite-sized tasks that can be tackled one at a time is crucial — otherwise, it's far too easy to get lost in someone else's codebase when you're in a hurry.

Deployment and maintenance

Deployment should be fairly straightforward if you've followed along so far. Make yourself a checklist, and test every step on it on several staging machines if you can.

1. Confirm that all necessary configuration changes have been made on the production servers. We once needed to roll back during a major feature push because the sysadmins had not set up DNS to enable e-mail to be sent from that server — not fun if you've already made schema changes.

2. `Tar` or `zip` up the entire UBBThreads directory tree and `scp` it to your production server(s).

3. Unzip and/or untar the directory in the desired location. Check all directory and file permissions.

4. Change domain names in `config.inc.php`.

5. Make a full dump copy of your database at this moment, structure and data — if you have to roll back the database, you will have lost at most a few minutes of data. Create the database by hand if you don't already have user data, set permissions. Create tables with `createtable.php`.

6. Run your schema-customization script(s). At this point, you probably lose some functionality for a few minutes.

7. Populate UBBThreads tables with imported data from main-user tables. Delete all database-editing scripts.

8. Set forum-administrator status, probably by hand if you already have users. Ensure that user ID 1 is not a forum administrator.

9. Test.

10. Enjoy a refreshing beverage — you deserve it!

> **TIP:** It can be very stressful to push out a large feature to production, especially if you have to make schema changes on-the-fly. Consider shutting down the entire site for an hour or so to give yourself room to move.

Maintenance will mostly involve deciding how frequently you want to sync up with UBBThreads development. Obviously if you've made extensive changes, you are not going to want to upgrade your UBBThreads software too frequently. We recommend thinking about upgrading once per major release cycle (for example, UBBThreads 5, UBBThreads 6, and so on). Wait until a few minor releases have gone by — in other words, upgrade on version 6.2.3, not 6.0 beta release candidate 1.

Remember that the better record-keeping you have done throughout the integration process, the easier your task will be in the future. It's amazing how easy it is to forget some incredibly simple change that took you hours and hours to figure out. You don't want to go through all this every time you upgrade your software package.

Summary

Integration is an increasingly important part of Web development. Because PHP has been explicitly designed from the ground up to play well with a multitude of other technologies, it has many advantages in knitting together several pieces of software into a seamless whole.

Common Web integration projects include PHP plus database packages such as forums, bug trackers, knowledgebases, and online photo albums. Integration can run the gamut from changing the colors of the text links to almost rewriting the entire codebase to tailor it more closely to your needs. We walk you through a realistic and complete integration project by using commercial PHP code, discussing the entire procedure from writing the spec to final deployment.

## Chapter 36

Security and Cryptography

In This Chapter

- ♦ Possible attacks
- ♦ Encryption
- ♦ Public-key encryption
- ♦ Single-key encryption
- ♦ Hashing
- ♦ Secure Server Layer

"Security is not a joking matter," proclaim signs at airports everywhere. The same sign should be posted near your PHP server. Anyone connecting a server to the Internet must take proper security measures or risk loss of data or even money to the keystrokes of malicious crackers.

The mantra of the security-conscious site designer is *"Don't trust the network."* If you're worried about the security of your site, chant this mantra as you code your pages. Any information transmitted to your server via the network — be it a URL, data from an HTML form, or data on some other network port — should be treated as potentially hazardous. This chapter suggests several techniques for "sanitizing" incoming information. You should apply these techniques and spend some time trying to discover other potential hazards and ways to prevent them.

The second rule of thumb for a secure site is *"Minimize the damage."* What if the program you just wrote, which you are *sure* is secure, is actually vulnerable? Just to be on the safe side, limit the damage an intruder can cause after he or she has taken advantage of the vulnerability.

When visitors come to your site, they trust that it contains valid information, that it is not harmful to them or to their computers, and that any information they provide to it is handled properly. Interacting with a site, whether an e-business, recreational, or informational site, involves certain security risks for a visitor. As a site designer, it is your responsibility to protect visitors from these risks. Besides being sure their information is safe on your server, this means you should take measures to safeguard their information while it is in transit from their computers to your server.

But all this should not scare you away from putting your e-business online. The first section of this chapter describes some possible attacks against your server and ways to avoid them. We then discuss cryptographic techniques for protecting your data. At the end of this chapter, we list some Web sites that contain up-to-the-minute information on the latest cracker techniques. By watching these sites, you may learn of possible security vulnerabilities before an attacker does and, thereby, avoid disaster.

Possible Attacks

Connecting your server to the Internet is like setting up a storefront on a busy street. You're likely to have quite a few visitors, but if you're not careful, some less than desirable visitors may take advantage of you.

Site defacement

Often more embarrassing than harmful, site defacements are fairly common because the cracker has an opportunity to publicize his or her exploitation. Site defacements are sometimes left as calling cards by a cracker who entered a system by more complicated means.

It is possible to deface a badly designed Web site using only a Web browser. Take, for instance, the following program:

```php
<?php if (IsSet($visitor)) {
  $fp = fopen("database", "a");
  fwrite($fp, "<li>$visitor\n");
  fclose($fp); } ?>
<HTML>
<HEAD></HEAD>
<BODY>
<H1>Visitors to this site:</H1>
<OL>
<?php $fp = fopen("database", "r");
  print(fread($fp, filesize("database")));
  fclose($fp) ?>
</OL>
<HR>
<FORM><INPUT TYPE="TEXT" NAME="visitor">
<INPUT TYPE="SUBMIT" NAME="submit" VALUE="Sign in!">
</FORM>
</BODY>
</HTML>
```

This program implements a very rudimentary guest book. In reading this code, however, you should feel a bit uneasy. *Don't trust the network.* This program accepts form data that we expect to contain the visitor's name (in the variable $visitor) and stores it in a text file for display to subsequent visitors. For the inputs we expect, there is no trouble.

Now put on your script-kiddie hat for a moment and imagine what would happen if the input contained HTML tags. This simple program would blindly insert those tags into the pages it generates, and other visitors' browsers would interpret them as usual. One particularly malicious tag is the <SCRIPT> tag. A cracker wishing to deface this Web page could duplicate the page's appearance on his or her own server (www.badsite.com) and then sign into the guestbook with the name:

```
<SCRIPT LANGUAGE="JavaScript">
window.location="http://www.badsite.com/"</SCRIPT>
```

When visitors load the guest book, their browsers receive this tag and immediately begin loading the hacked site. With a little ingenuity, the cracker could then take advantage of the visitors' trust of your site to extract personal information such as passwords or credit card numbers.

The solution to this problem is to sanitize the input data. In this case, we want any characters that have special meaning to a browser to be translated into something harmless. Luckily, PHP provides a way to perform just such a translation. The function htmlspecialchars() converts the characters <, >, ", and & to their representations as HTML entities (such as <). We change the first part of our program to use this new function as follows:

```
<?php if (IsSet($visitor)) {
  $fp = fopen("database", "a");
  $clean_visitor = htmlspecialchars($visitor);
  fwrite($fp, "<li>$clean_visitor\n");
  fclose($fp); } ?>
```

And we have patched a very significant security hole in our site.

Accessing source code

Even if your PHP source code isn't a trade secret, you should still protect it from exposure to the network. If an intruder can read your source code, then he or she need not experiment to find a weakness. Instead, the intruder can simply analyze the code, looking for common mistakes and other security holes. In general, the more helpful information you provide to potential intruders, the more likely an intrusion. By hiding such tidbits as source code, directory names, or usernames from the network, you can reduce the likelihood of an attack.

When PHP is used as a Web server module, there is little risk of source code being released by the Web server, as any file with the proper extension is parsed by the PHP module. If PHP is installed as a CGI program, however, things are not so simple.

If you cannot run PHP as a server module, the next most secure setup is to run it as an interpreter for CGI scripts, just as you would Perl or Python.

CRACKERS, SCRIPT-KIDDIES, AND OTHER FIENDS

The term "*hacker*" is commonly used to describe individuals more correctly labeled crackers. Within the computer community, "*crackers*" are those who, through luck or skill, break into computer systems and cause damage. "Hackers" are those who can "*hack*" — read and write efficient (and often obscure) code in many languages. To a programmer, being labeled a hacker is an honor, whereas being labeled a cracker probably means he or she should start reading the Help Wanted section.

As if "*cracker*" was not sufficiently derogatory, young crackers who use tools and scripts they find on the Web are called "*script-kiddies*." These budding lawbreakers often have little understanding of what they are actually doing. They are usually the culprits behind low-tech attacks such as site defacement. A fairly good indicator of the work of a script-kiddie is the excessive use of misspelling and capitalization, as in "W3 R KOOL DOODz."

Place all your PHP programs in the cgi-bin directory for your server or your account and arrange for the PHP interpreter to be invoked when they are executed. On Unix, this is done by adding a line similar to the following as the first line of every script:

```
#! /usr/local/bin/php
```

To use this setup, you must compile PHP with the --enable-discard-path configuration option. This setup has the disadvantage that the URLs for most of your pages contain /cgi-bin/.

The next most secure setup is a bit more complicated and is actually counter to the recommendations of CERT, a respected authority on computer security: We place the PHP interpreter itself in the cgi-bin directory. It is usually inadvisable to put an interpreter in the cgi-bin directory, because the rules for invoking CGI programs would allow any file on the server to be parsed as a program.

PHP is written to operate safely from the cgi-bin directory, however, if configured correctly. If you intend to use this setup, first carefully read the security and configuration sections of the PHP manual, as they may contain important information not available as this book went to press.

This setup relies upon the Web server to redirect URLs of the form:

```
http://your.server/program.php
```

to URLs of the form:

```
http://your.server/cgi-bin/php/program.php
```

The precise directives that will cause your Web server to do this vary. For Apache they are:

```
Action php-script /cgi-bin/php
AddType php-script .php
```

If you are using Apache, be sure to compile PHP with the `--enable-force-cgi-redirect` configuration option. This option utilizes a feature specific to Apache to prevent PHP from executing when invoked by URLs of the second form. Your setup is complete.

If you are using any other server software, you must compile PHP with the `--disable-force-cgi-redirect` configuration option. PHP cannot distinguish the two types of URLs and serves a document of either type. This allows a visitor to view files without regard for Web-server–based access restrictions. Assume, for example, that the URL `www.secrets.com/top/secret/hush.php` has access restrictions placed on it. A cracker could use the URL `www.secrets.com/cgi-bin/php/top/secret/hush.php` to read the file anyway.

In this case, the Web server is giving PHP the path name `/top/secret/hush.php`. PHP determines the location of the program file by prepending the configuration value `doc_root` to the given path name. By default, this value is the same as the Web server's document root (the directory corresponding to `www.secrets.com/`). Setting `doc_root` to another directory will limit PHP to programs in that directory and its subdirectories instead of the entire collection of Web-server documents. Any visitor may access any of the PHP programs by the method just described, however, without regard for Web-server–based access controls. *Be careful!*

Reading arbitrary files

A few common PHP programming mistakes can make it easy for a hacker to read almost any file on the server. Study the following page:

```
<HTML>
<HEAD></HEAD>
<BODY>
<?php if (IsSet($poem)) {
  $fp = fopen($poem, "r");
  print (fread($fp, filesize($poem)));
  fclose($fp);
  } ?>
<HR><FORM>Pick a poem:
<SELECT NAME="poem"><OPTION VALUE="jabb.html">Jabberwocky
<OPTION VALUE="graves.html">Cat-Goddesses</SELECT>
<INPUT TYPE="SUBMIT" VALUE="Show Me"></FORM>
</BODY>
</HTML>
```

This simple program displays a number of poems, selectable from a pop-up menu given in the form near the end. Invoke the security mantra: *Don't trust the network.* Clicking `Show Me` on this page results in URLs such as `...poetry.php?poem=graves.html`. A cracker may

substitute the file name of some more sensitive file, such as
`...poetry.php?poem=/etc/passwd`. The program, as given, would dutifully serve up
the Unix password file, possibly enabling the cracker to break into a visitor account and do
further damage.

The following is an appropriate solution to this problem:

```php
<?php if (IsSet($poem)) {
  switch ($poem) {
    case "jabb":
      $poem_file = "jabb.html";
      break;
    case "graves":
      $poem_file = "graves.html";
      break;
  }
  if (IsSet($poem_file)) {
    $fp = fopen($poem_file, "r");
    print (fread($fp, filesize($poem_file)));
    fclose($fp);
  }
} ?>
```

The advantage of this method is that it explicitly lists the acceptable inputs and gracefully
handles unacceptable inputs. If there were more poems to be processed, the `switch` statement
could be replaced with a database query, where failure of the query indicates invalid input.

This is not a good solution:

```php
<?php if (IsSet($poem)) {
  if (!strstr($poem, "/") && !strstr($poem, "\\")) {
    $fp = fopen($poem, "r");
    print (fread($fp, filesize($poem)));
    fclose($fp);
  }
} ?>
```

The second conditional in this code segment checks for pathname separators in the given file
name. This program explicitly describes a set of unacceptable inputs and considers anything
else acceptable. It depends on the programmer imagining and checking for every possible
undesired input. In this case, the programmer has missed something by making the implicit
assumption that no sensitive files are stored in the same directory as the script.

What if a file that should be private escapes your server anyway? There is a chance that some
misconfiguration (perhaps by someone else) or an unnoticed security hole will render some or
all of your server's files publicly accessible.

PHP allows you to explicitly specify the set of directories in which files can be opened with
the configuration value `open_basedir`. See Chapter 37 for more information on the PHP

configuration file. This configuration value can be useful to prevent access to entire directories and is a good way to *minimize the damage.*

Many sensitive files, however, must be opened from PHP programs as visitors access the site. A common example is a password file. Access to such a file cannot be blocked with open_basedir, but the sensitive information it contains can be encrypted to render it useless to anyone who may steal it.

A password-protected site must verify the password given by a visitor wishing to gain access. One way to do this would be to store a password for safekeeping in encrypted form and then decrypt it when we need to compare it to the user-supplied password. The problem is that if we can decrypt the password, others may be able to decrypt it too. Also, we would have to make sure that no one could see the password after we decrypted it for comparison. Instead, we can use an encryption function that only goes one way and is easy to use for encryption, but that can't be decrypted. Rather than decrypt a stored password and compare the decrypted versions, we *encrypt* the *given* password and compare the encrypted passwords. Unix uses this strategy with its own password file, /etc/passwd, and PHP allows programmers to use the same encryption function for their own password files.

The function crypt(password, salt) encrypts the given password. The salt adds an extra bit of chance and should be chosen randomly when the password is first recorded. (PHP chooses a random salt if this parameter is omitted.) The function returns the concatenation of the salt value and the encrypted version of the password. The following function will create a new password for a visitor:

```
function new_pw($given) {
  return crypt($given)
}
```

And this function will compare a password given by a visitor with a stored, encrypted password:

```
function verify_pw($given, $stored) {
  $salt = substr($stored, 0, CRYPT_SALT_LENGTH);
  $given_encrypted = crypt($given, $salt);
  return ($stored == $given_encrypted);
}
```

Running arbitrary programs

It's every system administrator's worst nightmare. The server's running more slowly than usual. A look at the running programs on the server reveals that a program entitled crack is burning 98 percent of the processor's time. Most likely, this program has been placed here by a cracker who is using it to decrypt (crack) passwords. The administrator logs in to kill the offending program but finds that his password is incorrect. His server has been "root compromised," and there is no telling how much damage has been done.

HUMAN ENGINEERING

Human engineering is an often overlooked part of cracking. Sometimes it's easier for crackers to extract information (particularly passwords) from human beings than from computers:

Cracker: Hi, John, This is Gary in the IT department. When was the last time you used your company account?

John: Well, I entered a few new purchase orders about an hour ago.

Cracker: Well, John, I'm afraid your account has been compromised. Some of the information in it may have been lost. This could cost the company millions if we don't catch the intruder quickly. We need to open your account and assess the damage immediately. Can you give me your password?

John: Sure, it's . . .

Worse yet, sometimes forgetful visitors note their passwords on scraps of paper in their desks! A determined cracker can easily find a job as a night janitor and look for such notes.

In a compromise such as this, an intruder gains interactive access to the server, usually via a Unix shell or MS-DOS command line. Clearly, this is the most difficult type of heist to pull off, but it also bears the greatest reward. Once "inside" a server, the cracker has virtually unlimited power to bring down the server, steal or modify information, or make use of the server's computational power for further wrongdoing. Worse yet, a truly skilled cracker can conceal his or her steps by editing log files and erasing any temporary files he or she has created.

PHP has several program execution functions: `system()`, `exec()`, `popen()`, `passthru()`, and the back-tick (`` ` ``) operator. As an example of the use of one of these functions, the following page returns the Unix `finger` information for a visitor specified through an HTML form:

```
<HTML>
<HEAD></HEAD>
<BODY>
<FORM>Get information on <INPUT TYPE="TEXT" NAME="username">,
<INPUT TYPE="SUBMIT" VALUE="Please"></FORM>
<?php if (IsSet($username)) { ?>
  <H1>Results for <?php echo $username; ?></H1>
  <pre><?php system("finger " . $username); ?></pre>
<?php } ?>
</BODY>
</HTML>
```

The program, as given, takes a user name from the HTML form and executes the Unix program `finger` to look up information about that user. You should hear *Don't trust the network* repeating loudly in your head. Unix commands are separated by a semicolon, so anything following a semicolon in the string passed to `system()` is treated as a new command. This new command is executed with all the permissions of the user under which the Web server is running.

Under Unix, the command `"rm -rf /"` will delete all files on the server. Imagine the damage if an ill-intentioned visitor typed `"; rm -rf /"` into the form and clicked `Please`.

The best solution to this problem is to filter out everything but valid user names before invoking `finger`. This requires specific knowledge about user name formats on your server, so we do not present an example here. PHP presents a solution that is almost as good. The function `escapeshellcmd()` will sanitize a string for use in a program execution command, rendering harmless any special characters such as the semicolon. We replace the line invoking `system()` in the preceding code snippet with:

```
<pre><?php
    system(escapeshellcmd("finger " . $username)); ?></pre>
```

Magically, no value the visitor may enter can result in arbitrary programs being executed. This does not, however, prevent the visitor from providing unexpected input to `finger`. Although `finger` does no harm if given incorrect input, other programs may not be so forgiving. If in doubt, err on the side of caution!

To *minimize the damage* of a compromise of this sort, most modern Web servers run as a dummy user (often called `nobody` on Unix systems). This user has only the permissions required to run the Web server (and any PHP scripts) and read and write the necessary files. But remember, any databases or files that your scripts can modify are modifiable by this user, and thus they are vulnerable if an attacker can run arbitrary programs.

Viruses and other e-critters

Visitors trust software coming from a trusted site. If your site allows visitors to download files uploaded by other visitors, you should warn your visitors to check files for viruses before running them, and you should consider periodically scanning the files on your server for viruses as well. This is a hard problem to solve, particularly with the possibility of embedding viruses in such seemingly harmless files as word processor documents. Indeed, Microsoft was caught in this very bind when they inadvertently released a CD-ROM with a Word document containing the Melissa virus.

> **CROSS-REFERENCE:** See the section "Site Defacement," at the beginning of this chapter, for other ways that your visitor may inadvertently receive malicious code.

SYSTEM ADMINISTRATORS

System administrators, also called *sysadmins*, are the folks who make sure the computers we all use keep on computing and that the Internet keeps on networking. Their jobs are shrouded in mystery: They hold the keys to the mysterious "machine room" where all the critical servers are stored. It's not unusual to see them hurrying into the office at midnight, surely to avert some crisis that could bring the company to its knees.

Sysadmins are also a very cautious lot. They tend to program their servers to report any unusual activity immediately (often to the large-screen alphanumeric pager they carry at all times) and to take swift, decisive action against anything they deem improper or unsafe.

A professor in a Computer Science department once asked his students, as homework, to break into his Linux desktop. To make things a little easier, he gave the encrypted text of his password (see the description of `crypt()` under "Reading Arbitrary Files"). In a testament to the security of the Unix `crypt()` function, none of the students cracked his desktop. Several of his students were denied access to their campus accounts, however, and questioned by university officials because they were running computationally expensive programs named `crack`!

If you aren't your own system administrator, but you are concerned about the security of your site, it is probably a good idea to befriend your local sysadmin. He or she can sometimes suggest ways to make your site more secure and can also be an enormous help in recovering from an incident.

E-mail safety

E-mail is the least secure of any of the Internet protocols. As it travels to its destination, it may be spooled on several intermediary servers. If security is weak on a server, it is not difficult for a cracker to read e-mail passing through that server. Send as little critical information as possible via e-mail. That is, *never* e-mail credit card numbers, and try to avoid sending passwords via e-mail unless absolutely necessary. It is interesting that most existing sites do not adhere to the latter point.

Whenever your site asks for your visitor's e-mail address, it should explain exactly how the address is to be used and to whom it is to be released. Whenever an e-mail address is presented on a Web page, it should be modified so as not to be easily identified by automated search engines picking up e-mail addresses to produce spam. The easiest and most elegant way to do this is to replace the @ symbol by the word at.

Unless absolutely necessary, avoid creating `mailto:` links. These links are excellent sources of spam addresses and are inconvenient for visitors who do not use their Web browser for sending e-mail.

Encryption

Encryption is the process of *encrypting* some message, referred to as *plaintext*, into unrecognizable *ciphertext*. Without certain information (a *key* of some sort), it is extremely hard to reconstruct the plaintext from the ciphertext. Someone equipped with the proper key, however, can easily *decrypt* the ciphertext, revealing the original plaintext — at least, if the chosen encryption function is not one-way.

We have already seen one use of encryption in this chapter: Passwords are stored in encrypted form. Password encryption, however, is usually one-way. There is no key to decrypt an encrypted password. Such a key is not needed, and the encryption can be made stronger if it doesn't need to be reversible. Encryption has many other uses in online business, both for storing data on the server and transmitting it across the network.

Public-key encryption

Meet Alice and Bob, professional cryptographic examples. They were chosen by the mathematical community, not for their acting talent, but because their names begin with A and B. Alice and Bob want to communicate securely, but their only method of communication is via Pony Express — not particularly secure. Each of them selects a public key and a secret key. We shall call Alice's keys P_{alice} and S_{alice} respectively and, likewise, Bob's keys P_{bob} and S_{bob}. They publish their public keys in the newspaper but hide their secret keys under their mattresses.

Alice has a sensitive message M for Bob. With her keys, Alice received a set of instructions for translating a message with a key. We write the translation like this: $P_{bob}(M)$. She translates her message with Bob's public key and hands the result to a shady-looking character on a pony.

Our friends' keys were not chosen arbitrarily. They have the special property that if they translate a message with one key, then translate the result with the other, they get the original message back. That is, $S_{alice}(P_{alice}(M)) = P_{alice}(S_{alice}(M)) = M$. There's no other way to resurrect the original message. In this case, Bob translates the message he receives, which he knows to be $P_{bob}(M)$ with his secret key. $S_{bob}(P_{bob}(M)) = M$, so he can read Alice's original message.

Bob knows that nobody else could have read that message, because nobody else has his secret key. But he does not know that it came from Alice: Anyone who reads the newspaper may have sent that message, signing the name `Alice` at the bottom.

Now Alice wants to send another message to Bob, and this time she wants no doubt that it was from her. First, she translates the message with her secret key and writes the result after her message as a *signature:* $M + S_{alice}(M)$. She sends this off to Bob, who reads Alice's message, which instructs him to translate the signature with her public key: $P_{alice}(S_{alice}(M)) = M$, and he sees her message again.

Because nobody else has Alice's secret key, she is the only one who could have created this signature, so this message must have come from her. But note that this time Alice sent her message *M* to Bob directly. Any rogue could have waylaid the Pony Express and read it. If she had so desired, she could have first signed the message, then encrypted the message and the signature using the first method, resulting in a signed, encrypted message.

There is a hitch in this scheme. Without meeting Alice, Bob can't be sure that the public key he found in the newspaper is really Alice's key. What if someone else had his or her key printed under her name? This could become a real problem if Bob communicates with lots of people — he simply doesn't have the time to check keys with each of them face-to-face.

Assume that there is at least one person everyone trusts; call him Tom. Tom picks a set of keys and offers to sign documents with his secret key, if the owner of the document shows proof of his or her identity. Alice has her public key signed by Tom, and then publishes the signed key, called a *certificate,* in the newspaper. Bob checks the signature on the key he sees in the newspaper, using Tom's public key. He knows that Tom signed that message, and Tom must have checked Alice's identification, so the key in the newspaper must really belong to Alice.

Single-key encryption

In single-key encryption, the same key can encrypt and decrypt a message. In general, it runs much more quickly than other forms of encryption, but it is more difficult to use for communication because the key must somehow be transmitted from one end to the other without any eavesdroppers picking it up. This is precisely where public-key encryption can lend a hand.

Returning briefly to our characterization, imagine Alice and Bob want to have a private conversation using single-key encryption. Alice asks Bob for his certificate, which contains his public key. She then picks a new single key and encrypts that key with Bob's public key, sending the result to Bob. Using his secret key, he decrypts the message to reveal Alice's single key and then uses it to begin a single-key encryption conversation.

The Unix version of PHP provides a set of functions that implement single-key encryption, using a publicly available library called `mcrypt`. To use these functions, you must download and install `mcrypt` (there is a link to the library's source available in the PHP manual) and recompile PHP with the `--enable-mcrypt` configuration option.

> **TIP:** As this book went to press, PHP was not compatible with the latest version of `mcrypt`. The latest compatible version was `libmcrypt-2.2.6`. Further, when compiling this version of `mcrypt`, you must specify the configuration option `--disable-posix-threads` during the `mcrypt` configuration. Missing this step causes Apache to crash.

`Mcrypt` offers a choice between a number of ciphers — different single-key algorithms. Each has its relative pros and cons in terms of speed and strength. In general, DES and Blowfish are fairly well-known algorithms with a good balance of speed and strength, but if you need extreme speed or great strength, you should research the algorithms available in your implementation (listed in mcrypt.h) and choose the one most suited to your needs.

Mcrypt also allows you to choose four cipher modes. These are summarized in Table 36-1.

Table 36-1: Cipher Modes Provided by mcrypt

Mode	Description	Initialization vector (IV)
ECB (electronic code book)	Just translate the block of data given. Suitable for small blocks of data that aren't very predictable, such as other keys. Do not use for text: The high frequency of letters and punctuation may be used to break the encryption.	no
CBC (cipher block chaining)	This stronger mode is far better suited for use with textual data.	opt
CFB (cipher feedback)	Like ECB, CFB is well suited for short blocks of data.	yes
OFB (output feedback)	OFB is very similar to CFB but designed to be better behaved when it encounters errors in its input.	yes

The last two modes require an initialization vector (abbreviated IV), which functions as a starting state for the encryption algorithm. The differences between these modes are relevant to interactive use, where individual keystrokes are encrypted one at a time. In that case, it is crucial that the algorithm not encrypt *a* the same way each time. The PHP interface to mcrypt only allows us to encrypt strings, however, so any of the modes except ECB are perfectly acceptable.

Depending on the cipher mode you want to use, call mcrypt_ecb(), mcrypt_cbc(), mcrypt_cfb(), or mcrypt_ofb() like this:

```
mcrypt_cbc(cipher, key, data, direction, [iv])
```

where *cipher* is MCRYPT_DES, MCRYPT_BLOWFISH, or whichever cipher you have chosen. (See the PHP documentation for an updated list of supported ciphers.) Pass your key and the data you wish to encrypt or decrypt in the key and data arguments, respectively. To encrypt, pass MCRYPT_ENCRYPT in the direction argument; to decrypt, pass MCRYPT_DECRYPT. Finally, for cipher modes that support initialization vectors, pass your own IV in the iv argument.

Your key must be of the correct size for your cipher. To find out what this size is, use:

```
mcrypt_get_key_size(cipher)
```

Again, *cipher* is the cipher you have chosen.

To generate a random IV or key, use:

```
mcrypt_create_iv(size, source)
```

Here, *size* is the size of the desired object and *source* is one of MCRYPT_RAND, MCRYPT_DEV_RANDOM, or MCRYPT_DEV_URANDOM, specifying the random number generator to use: rand(), /dev/random, or /dev/urandom, respectively. If you use rand(), be sure to call srand() to seed the random number generator first. (See Chapter 12 for more information on random numbers.) The proper sizes for IVs and keys are obtained by calling mcrypt_get_block_size(cipher) and mcrypt_get_key_size(cipher), respectively.

Note that all data handled by mcrypt is in the form of PHP strings of binary data. If you wish to display the data in some human-readable format or store it as a text string, you must apply some translation to it. PHP provides the functions base64_encode() and base64_decode() for just this purpose. Check the PHP manual for more information on these functions.

Encrypting cookies

Cookies your site sends to a visitor's browser contain information about that visitor. When the browser sends the cookie back, your site uses the information it contains to generate a new page. *Don't trust the network* — sound familiar? A cookie could be modified or forged by a malicious user, perhaps fooling your site somehow. This extremely simple program will serve as an example:

```
<?php
  $visits = $_COOKIE['visits'] + 1;
  setcookie("visits", $visits);
?>
<HTML><HEAD></HEAD>
<BODY>
<H1>You have been here <?php echo $visits ?> times</H1>
</BODY>
</HTML>
```

CROSS-REFERENCE: See Chapter 27 for more information on cookies.

Here a count of our visitors' visits to this site is kept in the cookie visits. A visitor could modify his or her cookie, however, to make the visit count 10,000. Our program would have no idea that this visitor has not been to the page 10,000 times and would blindly display, You have been here 10000 times.

But with some help from mcrypt and a few friends, we can make this impossible:

```
<?php
```

```
$key = base64_decode("NCiUmfiRByg=");
if (IsSet($_COOKIE['visits'])) {
  $encrypted = base64_decode($_COOKIE['visits']);
  $visits = mcrypt_cbc(MCRYPT_DES, $key, $encrypted,
                       MCRYPT_DECRYPT); }
$visits = $visits + 1;
$encrypted = mcrypt_cbc(MCRYPT_DES, $key, $visits,
                        MCRYPT_ENCRYPT);
setcookie("visits", base64_encode($encrypted));
?>
```

mcrypt deals with strings full of binary data, so we can't easily type them in or send them to browsers without modification. In this case, we have chosen to use the PHP base64 functions to turn them into well-behaved strings. Before writing this program, we invented a DES key with the following code:

```
<?php
  $key_size = mcrypt_get_key_size(MCRYPT_DES);
  $key = mcrypt_create_iv($key_size, MCRYPT_DEV_RANDOM);
  echo base64_encode($key);
?>
```

We copied and pasted the resulting key (in base 64 encoding) into our cookie program's first line. We store the number of visits in the cookie named visits, encrypted and in base 64 encoding. So if the visits variable is set, we first base64_decode it, then decrypt it. We then increment the counter, encrypt it, base64_encode it, and store it in a new cookie. The visitor sees cookie values such as IQ109yQCEgw%3D, which are not editable.

The program is not completely secure! The cookie value just given will *always* correspond to visit number 7. A cracker wishing to make your site believe he had only visited seven times could simply substitute this value for the visits cookie. If you know it would not benefit a visitor to return to a prior cookie (in this case, if the visitor wants a large visit count), however, this method is adequate: There is no way to easily invent a cookie for a state that has not been seen yet.

> **CROSS-REFERENCE:** To maintain a more useful visitor state, you should use sessions, which are described fully in Chapter 27.

This example should bring home the need to keep your source code private: If a cracker could view this program from his or her browser, he or she would have your site's encryption key and could decrypt your cookie values with ease.

Hashing

Signing a document with your private key produces a signature that is as large as the original document. This becomes a problem when we want to sign long documents such as files. For instance, most security software (including mcrypt) is digitally signed so that downloaders know that the latest version really was written by the author. Otherwise, sysadmins worry, an eager cracker could circulate a version of a security program into which he or she has installed a back door and then walk into the systems running that version with no difficulty.

What you need is a digital fingerprint for a large file. What if we treat the binary data of the file as a list of integers, add them all together, then chop off all but 128 bits of the sum? We call the final 128-bit number the *checksum*. The author of the file then encrypts the checksum with his or her secret key and attaches the result to the file as a signature.

Assume a cracker makes modifications to the file. He or she can then calculate the sum C of the changes and put the number $-C$ at the end of the file, creating a file that he or she knows to have the same checksum as the original. The cracker then appends the same encrypted checksum to the file as its signature.

When some unsuspecting user downloads the modified file, the user calculates the new checksum, decrypts the signature to find the original author's checksum, and sees that they match. The user proceeds to use the modified file, incorrectly assuming that it was written by the stated author.

Of course, the cryptographers are right on the spot with a solution. It should be very difficult to make changes to a file to produce a certain fingerprint. To ensure this, many *hashing* algorithms have been developed. Hashing algorithms are generally modifications of single-key encryption algorithms to make them create a ciphertext of a specific length, from which it is not possible to reconstruct the original message.

As you would expect, PHP provides a set of functions for hashing. These functions depend on the publicly available mhash library. You can find the latest version of the mhash library through a link in the PHP manual.

The function mhash(type, input) computes the hash value of input, using the method specified by type. Common values for this argument are MCRYPT_MD5 and MCRYPT_SHA1. For a complete list of possibilities, see the PHP manual.

Digitally signing files

Now let us present a PHP program to accept uploaded files only when they are correctly signed. We assume that our site is equipped with a list of usernames and Blowfish keys, where each user has a key known only to that user and our site. The function get_user_key(username) retrieves these keys for us. The uploader generates the signature for an upload by first hashing the upload file with the MD5 hash algorithm and then encrypting the resulting hash value with her Blowfish key.

```
<HTML><HEAD></HEAD>
<BODY>
<?php if (empty($file) || !IsSet($username) || empty($sig)) { ?>
<H1>Upload a file</H1>
<FORM ENCTYPE="multipart/form-data" METHOD="POST">
```

```
<INPUT TYPE="HIDDEN" NAME="MAX_FILE_SIZE" VALUE="2000000">
Upload the file: <INPUT NAME="file" TYPE="file"><br>
With this signature: <INPUT NAME="sig" TYPE="file"><br>
For user <INPUT NAME="username" TYPE="text"><br>
<INPUT TYPE="SUBMIT" VALUE="Go"></FORM>
<? } else {
  $fp = fopen($file, "r");
  $hash = mhash(MHASH_MD5, fread($file, $file_size));
  fclose($fp);
  $key = get_user_key($username);
  $encr_hash = mcrypt_cbc(MCRYPT_BLOWFISH, $key, $hash,
                          MCRYPT_ENCRYPT);
  $sfp = fopen($sig);
  $sig_data = fread($sig, $sig_size);
  fclose($sfp);
  if ($encr_hash != $sig_data)
    echo "<H1>Rejected -- signature did not match</H1>";
  else {
    echo "<H1>Accepted</H1>";
    // Continue handling the uploaded file
  }
} ?>
</BODY>
</HTML>
```

This program parallels the uploader's steps, first hashing the uploaded file and then encrypting the result with the user's key. If the results are the same, then the uploader must have used the same key, and we can assume they are genuine. If the results differ, then the upload is a forgery.

Secure Server Layer

The uses of cryptography presented so far protect the server's data. The single-key encryption example protects information the server stores on clients (cookies) from unwanted modification. The hashing example enables the server to detect forged files and refuse to accept them.

We now turn our attention to the security of your site's visitor. The visitor often transmits private information to your site. The visitor's password and credit card information must somehow travel from his or her machine to the server, across the untrustworthy network.

The *Secure Server Layer* (SSL) protocol provides a way to do this, making it impossible for an eavesdropper to listen in. It also provides a way for the site to prove its identity to the visitor and, optionally, for the visitor to prove its identity to the site. Although we won't delve into the cryptographic details, SSL does its work by using public-key encryption to prove the identity of the server and to exchange a new key to be used to encrypt the conversation. It then switches over to single-key encryption, which is much faster, using this new key.

Regardless of how you acquire and license the SSL software, you must purchase a certificate for your site from a well-known *certificate authority.* These authorities are the trusted third parties in the conversation between your server and a browser, but they do not give away their services for free.

It is beyond the scope of this book to make comparisons of competing SSL servers. In the tradition of open source, the authors believe that the free implementations are the best and most reliable; indeed, many of the commercial SSL servers are based on the open source implementations! If you buy a commercial implementation, however, you receive support from that company, and you satisfy management's desire to pay for something.

FYI: Security Web Sites

If you are losing sleep after reading this chapter, fear not. Every administrator and site designer around the world is grappling with the same issues, and there is a strong feeling of solidarity among computer security professionals. Many Web sites are devoted to computer security, and almost all of them contain full descriptions of recent security incidents and ways to protect your system from duplicate attacks. Some are designed for security professionals, whereas others have the cracker in mind. Either way, the information they provide is useful and often very interesting.

Begin your explorations by checking out these sites:

◆ **Computer Emergency Response Team (CERT)** (www.cert.org/): CERT is one of the most popular repositories of official descriptions of security incidents. It publishes advisories on all sorts of security issues, including very clear descriptions of the problem, vulnerable systems, and possible solutions.

◆ **Security-focus.com** (www.securityfocus.com/): Security-focus.com provides a great deal of information on all aspects of computer security, from the legal and political to the technical. It also hosts the well-known security mailing list, BugTraq (which can be found under Forums).

◆ **Rootshell** (http://rootshell.com/): Rootshell is a well-respected site that contains fairly technical descriptions of many, many security vulnerabilities, including detailed descriptions of how to exploit the vulnerability, as well as instructions on removing the vulnerability.

◆ **Insecure.Org** (http://insecure.org/): Insecure.Org is a fairly well-established site that is not afraid to make cracking tools available and to discuss the nitty-gritty details of many "exploits." This site can be extremely useful if you want to try to break into your own site.

♦ **L0pht Heavy Industries** (`http://www.l0pht.com/index.html`): L0pht is another on-the-edge site, run by people who crack into machines for a living. They are paid to do this in the hopes that they can find a vulnerability before someone with malicious intent does, and they report what they've done on this site and others. The site also contains lots of interesting opinions on its "soapbox."

Summary

For any significant Web site, security is a crucial part of the site's implementation. You should take extreme care to secure your server from attack and also be sure to protect your visitors' private information from prying eyes. In a time of enormous growth for online businesses, publication of a story about a major security breach can destroy visitors' confidence in your site, driving them to the competition and possibly leaving your site to evaporate as quickly as it appeared.

In this chapter, we've driven home three basic lessons:

Don't trust the network. Every byte of data that comes from the Internet should be treated as potentially hazardous. Be as restrictive as possible in defining the inputs you allow. Prefer the solution that lists the acceptable inputs to the one that lists the unacceptable inputs. Be sure that your Web server configuration does not allow clients to view your source code or to work around your access restrictions.

Minimize the damage. Where possible, make sure that the damage possible from a particular type of security breach is minimal. Encrypt sensitive data. If you run your own Web server, make sure it is running as a dummy user.

Finally, if you run your own server, spend some time breaking into it. If you're successful, then you've identified a vulnerability that you can patch before an intruder finds it. If you're unsuccessful, you've learned something about your server, and your security precautions have weathered a good test. If you don't run your server, find out who does, and see what he or she can tell you about your site's security.

## Chapter 37

Configuration and Tuning

In This Chapter

♦ Viewing environment variables

♦ Configuring Apache for PHP

♦ Configuring PHP

♦ Improving performance

In this chapter, we discuss the many configuration options available with PHP, particularly the Unix Apache module version, in some detail. The goal is for you to better understand the tradeoffs of each capability you may enable or disable, and how they may affect each other. We also touch on ways you can measure and improve the performance of your PHP scripts.

Viewing Environment Variables

To see any of the settings discussed in the following section, you have only to use the `phpinfo()` function in a valid PHP script. This function begins with a quick recap of the PHP version, your platform, date of build, and compile-time options; it then moves methodically through your PHP settings. You will also see some information about your Web server settings and environment variables.

Th output of the `phpinfo()` function is a potential bonanza for crackers, so you shouldn't leave it sitting around on a production server.

Understanding PHP Configuration

Like most of the best open source software packages, PHP is highly configurable. It's left up to you, the individual PHP user, to find your own balance among the competing virtues of power, flexibility, safety, and ease of use.

Configuration is difficult to describe fully because there are so many possible combinations of options — about 25 factorial combinations, as a matter of fact. In some cases, there is an obvious conflict between two configuration directives — you simply have to choose one or the other, end of story. In other cases, you can have both but may need to remember some workarounds. We try to point out as many of these implications as we can, but no one can honestly claim to have tested every possible combination.

Since the launch of PHP 4, the development group has made a truly Herculean effort to bring the Windows build up to the same level of functionality as Unix users have always enjoyed. The Windows version of PHP now ships with the most popular extensions (for example, MySQL) compiled in, and a startling number of shared libraries (.dlls) bundled with PHP itself. Many of these libraries have to be built from Unix source, so this effort represents a truly amazing amount of unremunerated, thankless work from the PHP build team.

In fact, the truth is that the PHP build for Windows (the so-called manual installation, not the installer version) now offers almost all the functionality of Unix builds with much less effort. Windows users only need to worry about the variables that can be set with the php.ini file — not all of which are applicable to Windows versions of PHP anyway. If you only use PHP on Windows, feel free to skip down to the "The php.ini file" section of this chapter, with a glance at the "Apache configuration" section if you run on Apache.

Unix users have a more specific palette of options. To take full advantage of this power, you need to clearly understand the various means by which you can analyze and control your PHP installation. The three most important on the Unix side are:

♦ Compile-time options

♦ Web-server configuration files

♦ The php.ini file

A few things can also be controlled with runtime options, system settings, or the presence/absence/configuration of other software packages.

Compile-time options

During the configure/make process, PHP allows you to specify a number of specific flags. This causes the appropriate extensions to be built into your custom version of the PHP module or binary. None of the information in this section is relevant if you are running a pre-compiled binary (for example, Windows, Mac OS X, or rpm build).

It's important to understand that most compile-time options are merely necessary preconditions for using a particular function set — but that this capability can still be turned on or off, or important configuration options set, in the php.ini file. The compilation step and the configuration file work together. Think of it this way: You must compile with the flag to use the functionality; but you needn't use the functionality just because you compiled with the flag.

> **TIP:** If you fail to employ the appropriate compile-time option, you get an undefined-function fatal error. This error is almost never seen outside of user-defined functions for any other reason, so it should be considered a red flashing light that you need to check your compilation options.

Most compile-time options are pretty self-explanatory. You merely install the required libraries, build PHP with the --with- [library] [=DIR] flag and, in some cases, set a configuration option in php.ini. In the following sections, we will only mention common cases that require special treatment of some kind.

> **TIP:** Remember that all third-party servers and libraries that you plan to use with PHP must be downloaded and installed *before* you attempt to build PHP. This means the Web server, a database server, mail and LDAP servers, XML, encryption, graphics, and bcmath libraries must all be in place before PHP.

--with-apache[=DIR]

This flag causes PHP to be built as a static Apache module. Even though the Apache module version is now, by far, the most popular build, the PHP developers have chosen to leave the CGI build as the default choice. If you forget this (or the --with-apxs) flag when trying to make a static Apache module, you will end up with the CGI version.

You almost certainly want to set the Apache base directory parameter because make may default to some unexpected location. Remember that Apache installs in different default directories in the source versus RPM builds — so if you've previously installed an httpd via RPM (perhaps as part of a Red Hat Linux installation), you should uninstall the package and leave a clean background for the source build you need now.

A static Apache build will have to be recompiled every time you change PHP versions. Apache server, at this point, changes rather slowly, whereas PHP adds new extensions and releases patches rather frequently, so this may be a significant factor in choosing the apxs build instead.

--with-apxs[=DIR]

This flag specifies that the PHP module be built as a dynamic Apache module. This saves disk space for Apache, and some people claim the build is easier. The main value of the apxs build is that you will be able to swap PHP modules (while upgrading, for instance) without recompiling Apache. If you upgrade frequently, or if you enjoy trying out experimental builds, this is the best option.

> **CAUTION:** Remember that you can build PHP with *either* the --with-apache or --with-apxs flags, not both.

--with-[database][=DIR]

All the databases supported by PHP use a similar compile-time flag. The directory need only be specified if it is not the default installation directory. For more information on choosing a database for use with PHP, see Chapter 16. The specific flags and default directories are listed in Table 37-1:

Table 37-1: Database Compile-Time Information

Database Name	Default Directory	Flag Syntax
Adabas D*	`/usr/local`	
DBase	`bundled`	`--enable-dbase`
Filepro	`bundled`	`--enable-filepro`
IBM DB2	`/home/db2inst1/sqllib`	`--with-ibm-db2[=DIR]`
Informix	`no default`	`--with-informix[=DIR]`
iODBC*	`/usr/local`	`--with-iodbc[=DIR]`
mSql	`/usr/local/Hughes`	`--with-msql[=DIR]`
MySQL	`bundled`	`--with-mysql[=DIR]`
Openlink*	`/usr/local`	`--with-openlink[=DIR]`
Oracle	`ORACLE_HOME`	`--with-oci8[=DIR]`
PostgreSQL	`/usr/local/pgsql`	`--with-pgsql[=DIR]`
SAP DB	`/usr/local`	`--with-sapdb[=DIR]`
Solid*	`/usr/local/solid`	`--with-solid[=DIR]`
Sybase	`/home/sybase`	`--with-sybase[=DIR]`
Sybase-CT	`/home/sybase`	`--with-sybase-ct[=DIR]`
Velocis*	`/usr/local/velocis`	`--with-velocis[=DIR]`

The databases marked with an asterisk use ODBC-based interfaces. These ODBC choices are mutually exclusive — you must limit yourself to a maximum of one.

Each database mandates slightly different configuration options in php.ini or other configuration files. Oracle, for example, has its own environment variables that obviate PHP settings. Sybase, Oracle, and some other databases escape single quotes with single quotes, which requires the magic_quotes_sybase option in php.ini. MySQL allows you to specify a default hostname, username, and password — not at all a good idea unless you understand the security implications! Most of these options are standard and self-explanatory, however, and they have little effect on other parts of PHP.

--with-mcrypt[=DIR]

This flag builds in the mcrypt library, which includes many of the most popular open cipher algorithms. mcrypt is available for download from Greece:

```
http://mcrypt.hellug.gr/
```

There is no documented default directory, although PHP can probably find the one mentioned in the libmcrypt documentation. libmcrypt must be compiled with the --disable-posix-threads option. See Chapter 36 for more information on using PHP's cryptography capabilities.

--with-java[=DIR]

This flag builds Java support into PHP. The DIR path should be set to the location of your JDK, and the Java settings in php.ini must all be set correctly. This extension cannot be used with a static Web server build (for example, --with-apache), and this flag will probably not work correctly with Solaris versions of PHP and Java. Please see the Java extension README in /php-4.x.x/ext/java for more information.

There is an alternate method of accessing Java from PHP, which is to integrate PHP into a Java Servlet environment using a SAPI module. You might want to do this if you use Java extensively, as it is the more efficient method. If you choose the servlet integration method, you do not need this extension.

--with-xml[=DIR]

This flag builds in the expat XML parser. expat is now bundled with all versions of PHP; if you do not specify a directory, PHP will use the bundled version. If for some reason you wish to use an external version of expat, you can download the package from:

```
www.jclark.com/xml/
```

In this case, you must also set the --with-expat-dir=DIR flag.

To use XML, you must disable short-open tags (such as <? ?>) with the --disable-short-tags compile-time flag or the short_open_tag directive in php.ini. The XML parser requires this style of tag for its own purposes, so PHP must not confuse the situation. As ever, the standard PHP tag (`<?php ?>`) is the best option, unless for some reason you can't use it.

> **CROSS-REFERENCE:** To learn more about XML and PHP, see Chapter 31.

--with-xmlrpc

This flag builds Dan Libby's XML-RPC and SOAP implementation into PHP. The XML-RPC package now comes bundled with PHP, so you do not need to specify a directory.

--with-dom[=DIR]

This flag builds with DOM XML support, using the GNOME xml library (a.k.a. `libxml`, `gnome-xml`). The `DIR` path should point to your `libxml` installation; if you don't set this value, it defaults to `/usr`. You can download and learn more about GNOME xml from:

```
www.xmlsoft.org/
```

--with-gd[=DIR]

This flag builds the graphics library, `gd`, into PHP. `gd` is available at:

```
www.boutell.com/gd/
```

`gd` has not supported gif format graphics since version 1.6 due to licensing issues. You will require separate external libraries to manipulate files in the jpeg, png, Xpm, FreeType, and Type 1 formats. These libraries must be installed before PHP is compiled, and an additional flag for each one (for example, `--with-jpeg-dir=DIR`) must be passed to PHP at compile time.

`gd` is one of the most problematic PHP extensions to configure — so much so that the PHP development team has recently announced plans to fork `gd` and take over distribution of the library in a form more usable to PHP. By press time, the `gd` situation may have stabilized for PHP users.

> **TIP:** Very common shared libraries, such as `libxml`, `gd`, and `libjpeg`, can cause fatal problems at PHP compile time even if you correctly set the directory paths in all the compile-time flags. Common issues include PHP looking for the files in the wrong place, incorrect versions of these libraries already being installed on your machine, or libraries having been built in a form inaccessible to PHP.
>
> The solution to most of these problems is to upgrade all such shared libraries to the latest version. However, if your client applications are old, this may break them. A possible workaround is to temporarily rename the installed versions of your shared libraries so they cannot be found by PHP; compile the new versions in different locations; compile PHP using these directory paths; and then re-name your old versions to their original names. Take good notes if you try this!

--enable-bcmath

This option builds support for arbitrary-precision mathematics from a bundled library. You can set the number of decimal places in `php.ini`.

--enable-calendar

This option builds support for calendar conversion functions (for example, Jewish to Julian) from a bundled library.

--with-config-file-path=DIR

This option allows you to specify the location of your `php.ini` file. You only need to use it if you've deliberately moved it away from the default location, `/usr/local/lib`.

--enable-url-includes

This option allows you to include or require *and execute* files from remote HTTP or FTP servers, like this: `include(http://remotehost/include.php.)`. This functionality should be carefully considered, as it has horrible security implications. If you merely want to read in HTML files from other servers, you do *not* need this flag.

--disable-url-fopen-wrapper

This flag turns off the default capability to open files on remote HTTP and FTP servers, like this: `fopen(http://remotehost/include.php.)`.

CGI compile-time options

All compile-time options just described are available for the CGI version, except for the module-specific flags (for example, `--with-apache`, `--with-apxs`).

Most users today who use PHP's CGI mode are interested in using it as a standalone binary, similar to Perl, rather than for Web development. If this is the case, safe mode is probably beside the point.

--enable-safe-mode

Safe mode was originally designed for and is still very strongly recommended for users of the CGI version of PHP. Module users generally do not use safe mode, although it's theoretically possible.

Safe mode basically does three things:

♦ It limits PHP parsing to files in a specified directory.

♦ Even within that directory, it prevents PHP from reading files that are owned by a user other than the one running the PHP process.

♦ It limits PHP to executing only external programs in a specified directory, such as `/usr/local/bin`.

Remember that *user* in this formulation means the PHP user rather than a systems user.

The increased security of safe mode comes at a cost — and that cost is inconvenience. Inconvenience is probably the number-one reason that people do insecure things in the first place — which leaves us right back where we started.

In general, if you lack root access on the server you can forget about using safe mode. The exception is if your ISP has set you up with a CGI version of PHP running under individual UIDs with suExec or functional equivalent. It's next to impossible to switch file ownership between a real Unix system user and Nobody without becoming the superuser once in awhile.

> **CAUTION:** Apache's suExec feature, which allows CGIs to be run under user IDs different than that of the `httpd`, is *not* compatible with PHP safe mode. You must choose one or the other, as your PHP binary will get dumped to the browser if you try to use both.

The safe mode restriction on executing programs is intended to limit access to system utilities. PHP can still connect to certain programs that are already running, regardless of their location or user — such as a database server or mail server — because it's talking to a port rather than running a program.

The main Apache configuration directive related to safe mode is `DocumentRoot`. Remember that under safe mode you can't `include` or `require` files from outside this directory, so set it at a high enough level. You can alternatively set the PHP document root in `php.ini` by means of the `doc_root` variable — you may choose to do it this way if, for instance, only part of your site is PHP-enabled. Configuration directives in `php.ini` related to safe mode include `safe_mode=on/off` and `safe_mode_exec_dir`. (You only need to set this if you want to change from `/usr/local/bin` to something else.) You can also use `include_path` to specify particular subdirectories *within your document root directory only* for your include files.

> **TIP:** Safe mode cannot be enabled or disabled in Apache's per-directory `.htaccess` files. Changes related to safe mode must be made in the main Apache configuration file, `httpd.conf`, or in php.ini as described above.

The function `set_time_limit()` cannot be used in safe mode. You must depend on the global configuration directive `max_execution_time` in `php.ini` instead.

--with-exec-dir[=DIR]

Another compile-time option relating to safe mode is `--with-exec-dir`. This option sets the default safe-mode execution directory to `/usr/local/bin`, but that can be changed with the `safe_mode_exec` directive in `php.ini`. Remember you can only run programs from this single directory under safe mode.

--enable-discard-path

If you'd like to place the CGI version of PHP outside the Web tree and call it as you would a Perl CGI script (such as with #!/usr/local/bin/php as the first line of each script), you need to specify this compile-time flag. You must also make all PHP CGI scripts executable.

--enable-force-cgi-redirect

This flag is a security must for the CGI module. It prevents browser users from calling CGI-bin files directly, thereby bypassing Apache security settings. This is an Apache-specific configuration directive; don't bother trying to enable it if you are running on a different Web server or as a standalone binary.

Apache configuration files

If PHP is used with Apache as a module or with CGI, much of PHP's basic file-serving capability is determined by Apache's configuration files. The main ones from recent versions of Apache Server are the httpd.conf file for global settings, and the .htaccess file for per-directory access settings. Older versions of Apache split up httpd.conf into three files (access.conf, httpd.conf, and srm.conf), and some users still prefer this arrangement.

In PHP 3, there were specific Apache configuration directives that could substitute for almost every php.ini setting. For example, instead of setting Engine = On in the first substantive line of php.ini, you could put php3_engine on in an .htaccess file for a similar effect. As the number of PHP configuration directives increased, however, people decided that too many flags were cluttering up Apache's namespace. The naming scheme was generalized, therefore, to encompass these four basic, configurable directives:

- **php_value name value:** Sets value of variable.
- **php_flag name on|off:** Sets Boolean.
- **php_admin_value name value:** Sets value of variable. Can only be used in main Apache configuration file(s) rather than .htaccess.
- **php_admin_flag name on|off:** Sets Boolean. Can only be used in main Apache configuration file(s) rather than .htaccess.

An example would be magic quotes for GET, POST, and COOKIE variables. In PHP 3, it could be set with this specific line in httpd.conf or .htaccess:

```
php3_magic_quotes_gpc Off
```

In PHP 4, you can use php_flag with the name of the variable, like this:

```
php_flag magic_quotes_gpc off
```

If this is all too confusing, don't worry: The new-style Apache configuration directive naming only applies to settings you can change in php.ini anyway.

Apache server has a very powerful, but slightly complex, configuration system of its own. Learn more about it at the Apache Web site:

```
www.apache.org/
```

The following headings describe settings in `httpd.conf` that affect PHP directly and cannot be set elsewhere.

Timeout

This value sets the default number of seconds before any HTTP request will time out. If you set PHP's `max_execution_time` to longer than this value, PHP will keep grinding away but the user may see a 404 error. In safe mode, this value will be ignored; you must use the `timeout` value in `php.ini` instead.

DocumentRoot

`DocumentRoot` designates the root directory for all HTTP processes on that server. It looks something like this on Unix:

```
DocumentRoot    "/usr/local/apache_1.3.6/htdocs"
```

It looks like this on Windows:

```
DocumentRoot    "C:/Program Files/Apache/htdocs/"
```

The document root can be almost any directory — it needn't be in the Apache installation directory. You can specify a subdirectory of this as the PHP document root, using the `doc_root` setting in `php.ini`. In this case, HTML files would be served out of the Apache document root and its subdirectories, but PHP would only be parsed in the specified PHP directory and its subdirectories.

AddType

The PHP MIME type needs to be set here for PHP files to be parsed.

Remember that you can associate any file extension with PHP; many administrators set the `.php3` and `.html` types for backward compatibility — but if you wanted to, you could have PHP parse files called `filename.asp` or `filename.jsp`. You can also add multiple types for different versions of PHP. The following are sample `AddType` lines; the first one is the most common for PHP 4, but you can add as many of the others as you wish.

```
AddType application/x-httpd-php .php .php4
AddType application/x-httpd-phps .phps
AddType application/x-httpd-php3 .php3 .phtml
AddType application/x-httpd-php .html
```

You can also set this on a per-directory basis with `.htaccess`, simply by adding type lines to `.htaccess` files. PHP files are then parsed only in one directory of your site, for instance in a forum folder. Alternatively, you can set up a directory with archived versions of files that may have old extensions — so just in that directory, Apache allow files with the `.phtml` extension to be parsed.

Action

You must set this line for the CGI version of PHP with Apache, generally used with Windows. You do *not* need to set this line for the module version of PHP.

```
Action application/x-httpd-php4 "/php/php.exe"
```

LoadModule

You must uncomment this line for the Windows or apxs module version of Apache.

```
LoadModule php4_module modules/php4apache.dll
```

AddModule

You must uncomment this line for the Windows or apxs module version of Apache.

```
AddModule mod_php4.c
```

The php.ini file

The PHP configuration file, `php.ini`, is the final and most immediate way to affect PHP's functionality. Important changes have been made in the structure of this file since the beta versions of PHP 4; so if you haven't bothered to really look at every line recently, now may be a good time.

The `php.ini` file is read each time PHP is initialized — in other words, whenever `httpd` is restarted for the module version or with each script execution for the CGI version. If your change isn't showing up, remember to stop and restart `httpd`. If it still isn't showing up, use `phpinfo()` to check the path to `php.ini` (near the top of the file); if necessary, recompile with the `--with-config-file-path` flag or just move `php.ini` to wherever PHP expects to find it.

> **CAUTION:** What happens if PHP can't find `php.ini`? Under Windows, right up until the formal release of PHP 4, you used to get an "unable to parse configuration file" fatal error. Under Unix and now under Windows as an ISAPI module, interestingly enough, you get no warnings or errors — PHP carries on with default settings, which are the same as if you had not changed any settings in `php.ini-dist`. You only need to install `php.ini` if you want to change the default settings.

The configuration file is well commented and thorough. Keys are case sensitive, keyword values are not; whitespace, and lines beginning with semicolons are ignored. Booleans can be represented by `1/0`, `Yes/No`, `On/Off`, or `True/False`. The default values in `php.ini-dist` will result in a reasonable PHP installation that can be tweaked later.

What follows are notes explaining the settings in `php.ini` that are not completely documented in the file or the PHP manual's `configuration.html` page.

short_open_tag = Off

Short open tags (called *short tags* in PHP 3) look like this: `<?  ?>`. This option *must* be set to Off if you want to use XML functions.

safe_mode = Off

If this is set to On, you probably compiled PHP with the `--enable-safe-mode` flag. Safe mode is most relevant to CGI use. See the explanation in the section "CGI compile-time options," earlier in this chapter.

safe_mode_exec_dir = [DIR]

This option is only relevant if safe mode is on; it can also be set with the `--with-exec-dir` flag during the Unix build process. PHP in safe mode only executes external binaries out of this directory. The default is `/usr/local/bin`. This has nothing to do with serving up a normal PHP/HTML Web page.

safe_mode_allowed_env_vars = [PHP_]

This option sets which environment variables users can change in safe mode. The default is only those variables prepended with "`PHP_`." If this directive is empty, most variables are alterable.

safe_mode_protected_env_vars = [LD_LIBRARY_PATH]

This option sets which environment variables users can't change in safe mode, even if `safe_mode_allowed_env_vars` is set permissively.

disable_functions = [function1, function2, function3...functionn]

A welcome addition to PHP 4 configuration is the ability to disable selected functions for security reasons. Previously, this necessitated hand-editing the C code from which PHP was made. Filesystem, system, and network functions should probably be the first to go because allowing the capability to write files and alter the system over HTTP is never such a safe idea.

max_execution_time = 30

The function `set_time_limit()` won't work in safe mode, so this is the main way to make a script time out in safe mode. In Windows, you have to abort based on maximum memory consumed rather than time. You can also use the Apache timeout setting to timeout if you use Apache, but that will apply to non-PHP files on the site too.

error_reporting = E_ALL & ~E_NOTICE

Until recently, this was a bitfield that added up to a maximum value of 15. Due to widespread misunderstanding, this directive seems to have been changed in PHP 4 to a string type. The default value is `E_ALL & ~E_NOTICE`, all errors except notices, which corresponds to the old value of 7. Development servers should be set to at least the default; only production servers should even consider a lesser value.

error_prepend_string = ["<font color=ff0000>"]

With its bookend, error_append_string, this setting allows you to make error messages a different color than other text, or what have you. We recommend setting the value to "<blink>" (and error_append_string to "</blink>", of course) for a special treat! The default values result in a red error message. Remember to uncomment these if you want to use them — they're commented out by default.

warn_plus_overloading = Off

This setting issues a warning if the + operator is used with strings, as in a form value.

variables_order = EGPCS

This configuration setting supersedes gpc_order. Both are now deprecated along with register_globals. It sets the order of the different variables: Environment, GET, POST, COOKIE, and SERVER (a.k.a. Built-in). You can change this order around. Variables will be overwritten successively in left-to-right order, with the rightmost one "winning" the hand every time. This means if you left the default setting and happened to use the same name for an environment variable, a POST variable, and a COOKIE variable, the COOKIE variable would own that name at the end of the process. In real life, this doesn't happen much.

register_globals = Off

Allows you to decide whether you wish to register EGPCS variables as global. This is now deprecated, and as of PHP 4.2, this flag is set to Off by default. Use superglobal arrays instead. All the code in this book uses superglobal arrays.

gpc_order = GPC

Deprecated.

magic_quotes_gpc = On

This setting escapes quotes in incoming GET/POST/COOKIE data. If you use a lot of forms which possibly submit to themselves or other forms and display form values, you may need to set this directive to On or prepare to use addslashes() on string-type data.

magic_quotes_runtime = Off

This setting escapes quotes in incoming database and text strings. Remember that SQL adds slashes to single quotes and apostrophes when storing strings and does not strip them off when returning them. If this setting is Off, you will need to use stripslashes() when outputting any type of string data from a SQL database. If magic_quotes_sybase is set to On, this must be Off.

magic_quotes_sybase = Off

This setting escapes single quotes in incoming database and text strings with Sybase-style single quotes rather than backslashes. If `magic_quotes_runtime` is set to On, this must be Off.

auto-prepend-file = [path/to/file]

If a path is specified here, PHP must automatically `include()` it at the beginning of every PHP file. `Include` path restrictions do apply.

auto-append-file = [path/to/file]

If a path is specified here, PHP must automatically `include()` it at the end of every PHP file — unless you escape by using the `exit()` function. `Include` path restrictions do apply.

include_path = [DIR]

If you set this value, you will only be allowed to include or require files from these directories. The `include` directory is generally under your document root; this is mandatory if you're running in safe mode. Set this to . in order to include files from the same directory your script is in. Multiple directories are separated by colons
`".:/usr/local/apache/htdocs:/usr/local/lib"`.

doc_root = [DIR]

If you're using Apache, you've already set a document root for this server or virtual host in `httpd.conf`. Set this value here if you're using safe mode or if you want to enable PHP only on a portion of your site (for example, only in one subdirectory of your Web root).

upload_tmp_dir = [DIR]

Do not uncomment this line unless you understand the implications of HTTP uploads!

session.save-handler = files

See Chapter 27.

ignore_user_abort = [On/Off]

This setting controls what happens if a site visitor clicks the browser's Stop button. The default is On, which means that the script continues to run to completion or timeout. If the setting is changed to Off, the script will abort. This setting only works in module mode, not CGI.

Improving PHP Performance

There are two basic schools of thought about Web performance. The first is that PHP script performance, theoretical Web server speed, chip clock speed, server RAM, and almost everything else is made irrelevant by throughput issues — so why sweat the small stuff? The other is that there's no thrill quite like that of shaving a few microseconds off your script execution time. This section is basically useless for proponents of the former view.

Before you can improve your performance, you have to measure it. The good people at Zend are working on a commercial tuning debugger, but at press time it was not available to the public. We default, therefore, to the time-honored programming performance metric: measuring microseconds. Whip up a little function like this:

```
function exec_time()
{
  $mtime = explode( " ", microtime());
  $msec = (double)$mtime[0];
  $sec = (double)$mtime[1];
  return $sec + $msec;
}
```

This function just reformats microtime output into a double for easier subtraction. Paste or include it at the top of the script you'd like to measure. Now divide the main body of your script into sections and scatter calls to exec_time() at strategic points, like so:

```
<?php
$start_db_call = exec_time();
$result = mysql_db_query("test", "SELECT * FROM user WHERE ID=1");
while ($testrow = mysql_fetch_array($result)) {
  echo $testrow[0];
}
$end_db_call = exec_time();
$runtime = $end_db_call - $start_db_call;
echo "Database call and echo took $runtime seconds";
?>
```

The next time you hit the Web page, voila! A self-timing PHP script, at your service.

> **CAUTION:** Using microtime() to measure PHP tells you only what happens between the time PHP begins working on the first measured line of code and the time it finishes working on the last measured line of code. It does not tell you how long your Web server is taking to spawn a child process or your CGI to start up, how much latency your server is suffering from, what traffic conditions at your Web farm are like, or a lot of other things that affect real-world performance at least as much if not more that actual PHP processing time. To find out that kind of thing, you need measuring tools far beyond PHP. A good start for Apache on Unix is the program called ab (a.k.a. Apache Benchmark tool) which ships with Apache.

Now that you know how long the various parts of your script are taking, you can take steps to improve performance. Actually, a little logic should tell you that functions that touch other files or call other daemons should take longer than those that are self-contained within a discrete file. So database calls, include and require statements, objects with inheritance, and XML parsing are just going to take longer than simple arithmetic or echoing a string. But because these advanced functionalities are the best part of PHP, obviously it would be pointless to get rid of them for the sake of squeezing out a few more microseconds.

What you can and should do instead is hunt and destroy gross programming errors that cause unnecessary latency. Infinite loops, you know, are never very stylish. If you can notice a script running slowly with the naked eye, especially on a localhost, it's cause for concern — whip out the microtime and find out where it's going wrong. Pay special attention to known bottlenecks such as: using regex instead of explode() in a tight loop; object-oriented programming where it's not needed; bad use of SQL; including multiple instances of the same files; and long loops.

Although it would be better to eliminate all errors in the code itself, you can also help matters by setting the Apache or PHP timeout and max-memory configuration variables as low as possible. Come on — no Web page should need a 300-second timeout and you know it. Another configuration setting that may have a good effect on extremely slow scripts is ignore_user_abort in php.ini.

Recent distributions of PHP have also offered an optimized php.ini that sets variables for maximum speed at the possible expense of other virtues. If you choose to use this file, please take the time to understand the effects of its changes — in other words, don't just slap on your server and then ask where your HTTP_*_VARS values went.

OPTIMIZERS AND CACHES

Until recently, speed-shavers had few options but homemade metrics like the microtime() function just described. But now, intriguing tools are beginning to become widely used to increase PHP performance.

One that is available without cost is the Zend Optimizer. This tool makes multiple passes over a PHP script and replaces slower constructs with faster ones that have the same effect. However, the Zend Optimizer is rumored to mostly help inexperienced coders – if you already write tight PHP, it may not be able to add much value.

Another Zend product which promises to affect performance positively is the Zend Accelerator. This product apparently compiles and stores a version of each page in memory, reducing disk reads and redundant compilation and thus speeding Web service. Reliable reports claim that the Accelerator can deliver 2 – 10X improvements in number of requests handled. Both the Zend Accelerator and the Zend Optimizer are availabe at the Zend Web site, www.zend.com.

There are also optimizing and caching products available without cost. Two popular choices are Nick Lindridge's PHP Accelerator (www.php-accelerator.co.uk) and APC (http://apc.communityconnect.com).

Summary

The good thing and the bad thing about PHP configuration are the same thing: There are a whole heck of a lot of options and more than one way to set many of them. The Unix Apache module is particularly rich in choices, but the development team has labored long and hard to make PHP as customizable as possible.

There are three main ways to configure PHP. The first is via build-time flags, which are only available to those who build from source. Many of these directives are only necessary preconditions, meaning they set default conditions that need to be confirmed or can be reversed elsewhere. The second is via Apache configuration files (`httpd.conf` and `.htaccess`), which are only available to users of Apache server. The third is via the `php.ini` file, which comes with every PHP distribution.

The `php.ini` file has experienced a few significant changes with PHP 4. One of the most important is the capability to disable functions on an individual basis. Certain features of PHP 3 and PHP 2 are beginning to be deprecated in this file, such as `register_globals`. And the `php.ini` is no longer an absolute necessity on Windows — versions of PHP 4 now recognize default values even without the file being present in the Windows path.

After you've run PHP for a while, you may wish to tune its performance. PHP 4 is considerably faster at the same tasks than PHP 3, and in general script execution time isn't the bottleneck to total performance — but you may want to maximize the efficiency of your PHP-enabled server anyway. The main tool available to measure performance is simply echoing `microtime()` at intervals throughout a script. With this simple method, you can try to narrow down and improve the parts of your scripts that are taking the most time. This does not measure anything outside PHP which may affect its performance; for that, you need external tools such as `ab` (Apache Benchmark).

Tools to help speed up PHP are becoming widely available. One of the most intriguing is Zend's Accelerator, which promises at a minimum to double pages served on the same hardware. There are also alternatives available without cost.

Chapter 38

Case Study: User Authentication

User data management is a core function of many Web sites. However, it's more difficult than it may seem to design a good, secure, extensible way to register, log in, and change user information. Even harder is architecting a toolkit for your administrators and editors. In this chapter, we walk you through a complete user registration and administrator authentication system, with notes on the fine points to keep in mind as you implement such a system for yourself.

Designing a User-Authentication System

By now, you're probably sick and tired of us telling you to think through your needs and write up some specs before you design any feature. Well, too bad, we're not going to let up on you now — because it's never more relevant advice than when you're dealing with user data.

There are quite a few common decisions that you should make before you write any code. Do you plan to use full names, or just usernames? If you're going to collect full names, always collect separate first and last names. If you've ever had to write a program to split a bunch of names (like the following) into first and last names, you'll know why keeping them separate is so important:

♦ Thomas St. John, Jr.

♦ Lee Min

♦ Michael de la Cruz

♦ Arantxa Sanchez Vicario

- ◆ David Ben Gurion
- ◆ M. Abu Ibrahim

As you can immediately see, there is no simple algorithm that can be immediately applied to names like these that will infallibly split them correctly.

Who will choose the passwords? Do you allow your users to set their own? Or do you generate passwords programmatically and e-mail them to your users? The former is easier for the user, but the latter allows you to more easily weed out users who give false e-mail addresses.

Is a user immediately logged in after registering? Or does he or she have to perform some other step, such as waiting for an e-mail with a password or a link to a confirmation form?

Is login based on e-mail and password or username and password? Must any or all these be unique?

Do you permit writes by anonymous users? If so, do they have one mass name (for example, Anonymous Coward) or do you allow them to choose ad-hoc temporary usernames?

How do you plan to deal with forgotten passwords and possibly usernames? Any number of schemes can be implemented to deal with these issues — programmatically generating a new password, sending the old password in plain text e-mail, permitting a temporary login just long enough to change the password, and so on — but they all have consequences. For instance, if you send the password via email, you probably will not be able to use a good encryption scheme.

Do you give users control over the display of their personal information? Do you have a clear user policy that requires this? Have you checked your proposed architecture against your user agreement?

How do you plan to handle permissions? Do your permissions come in buckets — all users get the same permissions — or do you need more fine-grained control?

What is your legal liability position in regard to user data? For instance, if you use a badly designed user validation scheme and someone manages to crack it enough to impersonate someone else — can enough harm be done that your organization could be sued? If your site is basically just a content or community resource, the stakes aren't usually very high — but if you handle money or goods in any form, you need a clear policy.

Do you plan to disable or delete bad users?

How will you maintain state (if at all)? Do you plan to use cookies or sessions or databases?

Do you need the ability to log in as a given user?

Is your site actually part of a suite of Web properties belonging to your organization? If so, do you need to make all the sites use the same user-management system?

If you can get clear answers to these questions, preferably written down in a spec, you are quite a way toward designing the precise user data-management architecture that you need.

Avoiding Common Security Issues

Some very common and easily avoidable security issues are far too often ignored by site designers. PHP is sometimes targeted with the accusation of being chintzy and insecure because individual programmers do not follow good software practices. Security practices are especially important in working with user data.

You can do a few basic things to greatly reduce the risk of your site being cracked. Remember that security is all about raising the difficulty level for crackers — it's one thing to be cracked by a professional crime ring, and another to have all your user's passwords stolen by a 15-year old kid who can't even program.

Every Web site should be taking these very basic steps to safeguard its users' personal data:

Turn off register_globals

Too many PHP developers still write code such as this:

```php
<?php
if (check_admin_priv()) {
  $admin = 1;
}

if ($admin == 1) {
  // Allow the user to see some privileged data
}
?>
```

This works fine for what you want it to do, which is set the $admin variable to 1 for legitimate administrators. But you also need to think about what your scripts can do that you *don't* want them to do. This particular usage also lets any user who cares to use a URL like badcode.php?admin=1 get administrator privileges if you have register_globals turned on. At the very least, you should be setting $admin to some other value if check_admin_priv() does not return true — but a better solution is to learn to live without register_globals.

PHP's register_globals feature, which makes all GET, POST, COOKIE, SESSION, ENV, and SERVER variables immediately available via their plain variable names, is very popular because it seems to make development so much easier. Crackers can exploit this feature, however, to spoof cookies, run external JavaScript functions, load unsafe data into a database, and many other security nightmares. In large and complicated sites, register_globals can also lead to strange bugs as variables overwrite each other — especially if your team has members who do not choose good variable names (and most teams do). Only you can prevent your global namespace from becoming polluted with unsafe or unnecessary values.

The truth is that register_globals merely saves you a few keystrokes in development, at the price of massive risk. PHP is slowly moving towards deprecating this feature for good, and as of 4.2.0 has turned off the register_globals flag by default. Instead, the team has implemented the new superglobal arrays, which force you to ask for COOKIE values in cookies, POST values from posts, and so on — the gain for you is true global scope.

You have time now to begin moving away from register_globals. Remember that you can easily write a shell, Perl, or PHP script to replace many of the global variables in your codebase — so this change doesn't necessarily entail enormous amounts of hand labor. Use of superglobal arrays also encourages good programming practice — because good code asks for data and evaluates conditions as specifically as possible.

Check for string length and safety

Many PHP user registration programs contain lines like this:

```
if ($username && $password && $email) {
  // Allow them to register
}
```

However, you should never assume that, just because you've provided some nice form fields named Username and Password, people are using those fields to enter usernames and passwords. The pseudo-code above just asks for the existence of a variable value without specifying anything about that value. You can and should be specifying precisely which types of data you accept into your database — the more precisely, the better.

There is no good reason, for example, that anyone should ever be choosing a username or password that is longer than, say, 25 characters. If someone wants to use a 100-character string as a username, that's a presumptive test that he or she may intend to do harm to your system. Why not just filter these people out before something bad happens, by testing for string length? It takes hardly any more development or runtime resources. This code snippet, for instance, will only allow users to register if all the variables contain fewer than 25 characters.

```
if (strlen($username) <= 25 && strlen($password) <= 25 && strlen($email)
<= 25) {
  // Allow them to register
}
```

Also, think about the type and content of these variables. If you have a form field for a user's age, there's no legitimate reason why anyone should be trying to stuff an array into it. You can use PHP functions like is_int, is_string, and is_bool to make sure your variable type is what it should be.

Be particularly careful of any string that has tags (especially HREF and SCRIPT tags), single-quotes, double-quotes, or semicolons in it. You should either reject these outright if there's no legitimate use for such characters — no username should have any of these characters in them, for example — or use escaping and encoding to turn them into strings which cannot evaluate in PHP or a browser.

> **TIP:** You're much safer, of course, if your database design fully supports the strategic goals of your code. So don't use expansive types such as `text` or `varchar` to represent an Boolean, integer, or date — make sure that the data type of each field is carefully matched to the actual data you intend to store in that field. Not only is your performance faster, but in the event someone manages to sneak unsafe code into your database, a restrictive type has a much better chance of choking on or truncating the bad data.

One-way encrypt passwords

A surprising number of "professional" Web sites store their user's passwords in plain text in their databases. In doing so they are running the risk that one break-in can result in the compromise of the entire user data system — which often means that financial or other systems can no longer be trusted. Password theft is also becoming a source of legal liability for companies who fail to prevent or try to cover up the theft of their users' personal data.

The most frequently heard excuses for this practice are that the site needs to e-mail passwords to users who have forgotten them; and that the site's employees need the capability to log in as a particular user to verify bugs reported by that user. Neither of these excuses washes. You have many other ways to deal with forgotten passwords and logging in as a particular user, some of which we will discuss in the "User Tools" and "Administrator Tools" sections below.

The easiest way to get out from under the technical and legal risks of password theft is to make it impossible for even you to know what your users' passwords are. The easiest way to accomplish this is to one-way encrypt user passwords on registration. You can do this either in PHP, or in the database itself. The MySQL way to store passwords, for example, is by wrapping them in a built-in encrypting function called `password()`:

```
INSERT INTO user_table (username, password) VALUES('$username',
password('$password'));
```

Now when a user tries to log in, you query for the password using the same function:

```
SELECT username, password FROM user_table WHERE username = '$username'
AND password = password('$password');
```

If you want to do the encryption on the PHP side, which has advantages, there's a code sample with explanations in the "Login" section below. Both methods use good one-way algorithms that, for most practical purposes, cannot be reversed as they require serious supercomputer time to decrypt. Whichever method you choose, the important point is to always encrypt your passwords before storing them.

> **CROSS-REFERENCE:** These are specifically user-data security issues. See Chapter 36 for general information on security and cryptography and Chapter 18 for more information about database-specific issues.

Registration

Now you can begin to implement all the design decisions and tips that we discuss in the "Designing a User Authentication" section at the beginning of this chapter. Obviously the first place to start is with new user registration. In the code in this section, which is based on some sample code written by Tim Perdue, we have chosen the following options:

- ◆ Check for a unique e-mail address on each registration.
- ◆ Have users choose their own usernames, which must be unique.
- ◆ Have the users choose their own passwords, which are then one-way encrypted.
- ◆ Confirm new registrations by click-through e-mail to cut down on spam and rogue users.

The particular method of one-way encryption used here is actually md5 hashing. This takes a string of any reasonable length, applies RSA's md5 algorithm to it, and returns a 32-character hexadecimal string that has a high chance of uniquely identifying that string later (unless you started out with an extremely large number of strings). It's kind of like getting a claim ticket for your shirt at the dry cleaner's — it has a number on it that increases your chances of later identifying the particular shirt you dropped off. By some definitions this is not strictly encryption — but for our purposes, it's one of the better one-way transformation algorithms. Unless you have unlimited supercomputers and time, you will not be able to figure out what the original password was.

> **TIP:** You may have seen md5 hashing used in another context, which is guaranteeing that software packages contain what they should contain. Open source projects often run their tarballs through md5 to generate a 128-bit key that is published separately. Any user should be able to run the same package through md5 and come up with the same number if the contents have not been altered. If a virus were introduced to the distribution somehow, the md5 hashes would not match, and he or she would know not to install the package.

The script in Listing 38-1 should be called `register_funcs.inc`. It contains all registration-related functions. You will call these functions from other PHP pages.

Listing 38-1: Registration functions (register_funcs.inc)

```php
<?php

// A file with the database host, user, password, and selected database
include_once('db_vars.inc');

// A string used for md5 encryption.  You could move it to a file//
outside the web tree for more security.
$supersecret_hash_padding = 'A string that is used to pad out short
strings for md5 encryption.';


function user_register() {
```

```php
  // This function will only work with superglobal arrays, because
  // I'm not passing in any values or declaring globals
  global $supersecret_hash_padding;

  // Are all vars present and passwords match?
  if (strlen($_POST['user_name']) <= 25 && strlen($_POST['password1'])
<= 25 && ($_POST['password1'] == $_POST['password2']) &&
strlen($_POST['email']) <= 50 && validate_email($_POST['email'])) {
    // Validate username and password
    if (account_namevalid($_POST['user_name']) ||
strlen($_POST['password1'] >= 6)) {

      $user_name = strtolower($_POST['user_name']);
      $user_name = trim($user_name);
      // Don't need to escape, because single quotes aren't allowed
      $email = $_POST['email'];
      // Don't allow duplicate usernames or emails
      $query = "SELECT user_id
                FROM user
                WHERE user_name = '$user_name'
                AND email = '$email'";
      $result = mysql_query($query);
      if ($result && mysql_num_rows($result) > 0) {
        $feedback = 'ERROR - Username or email address already exists';
        return $feedback;
      } else {
        $first_name = $_POST['first_name'];
        $last_name = $_POST['last_name'];
        $password = md5($_POST['password1']);
        $user_ip = $_SERVER['REMOTE_ADDR'];
        // Create a new hash to insert into the db and the confirmation
email
        $hash = md5($email.$supersecret_hash_padding);

        $query = "INSERT INTO user (user_name, first_name, last_name,
password, email, remote_addr, confirm_hash, is_confirmed, date_created)
                VALUES ('$user_name', '$first_name', '$last_name',
'$password', '$email', '$user_ip', '$hash', '0', NOW())";
        $result = mysql_query($query);
        if (!$result) {
          $feedback = 'ERROR - Database error';
          return $feedback;
        } else {
          // Send the confirmation email
          $encoded_email = urlencode($_POST['email']);
          $mail_body = <<< EOMAILBODY
Thank you for registering at Example.com.  Click this link to confirm
your registration:
```

```
http://localhost/confirm.php?hash=$hash&email=$encoded_email

Once you see a confirmation message, you will be logged into Example.com
EOMAILBODY;
        mail ($email, 'Example.com Registration Confirmation',
$mail_body, 'From: noreply@example.com');

   // Give a successful registration message
        $feedback = 'YOU HAVE SUCCESSFULLY REGISTERED. You will
receive a confirmation email soon';
        return $feedback;
      }
    }
   } else {
     $feedback =  'ERROR - Username or password is invalid';
     return $feedback;
   }
  } else {
    $feedback = 'ERROR - Please fill in all fields correctly';
    return $feedback;
  }
}
```

```
function account_namevalid() {

  // must have at least one character
  if
(strspn($_POST['user_name'],"abcdefghijklmnopqrstuvwxyzABCDEFGHIJKLMNOPQ
RSTUVWXYZ0123456789-") == 0) {
    return false;
  }

  // must contain all legal characters
  if
(strspn($_POST['user_name'],"abcdefghijklmnopqrstuvwxyzABCDEFGHIJKLMNOPQ
RSTUVWXYZ0123456789-_") != strlen($name)) {
    return false;
  }

  // min and max length
  if (strlen($_POST['user_name']) < 5) {
    return false;
  }
  if (strlen($_POST['user_name']) > 25) {
    return false;
  }

  // illegal names
```

```
   if
(eregi("^((root)|(bin)|(daemon)|(adm)|(lp)|(sync)|(shutdown)|(halt)|(mai
l)|(news)|(uucp)|(operator)|(games)|(mysql)|(httpd)|(nobody)|(dummy)|(ww
w)|(cvs)|(shell)|(ftp)|(irc)|(debian)|(ns)|(download))$",
$_POST['user_name'])) {
     return false;
   }
   if (eregi("^(anoncvs_)", $_POST['user_name'])) {
     return false;
   }

return true;
}


function validate_email () {
   return (ereg('^[-!#$%&\'*+\\./0-9=?A-Z^_`a-z{|}~]+'. '@'. '[-
!#$%&\'*+\\/0-9=?A-Z^_`a-z{|}~]+\.' . '[-!#$%&\'*+\\./0-9=?A-Z^_`a-
z{|}~]+$', $_POST['email']));
}


function user_confirm() {
   // This function will only work with superglobal arrays, because
   // I'm not passing in any values or declaring globals
   global $supersecret_hash_padding;

   // Verify that they didn't tamper with the email address
   $new_hash = md5($_GET['email'].$supersecret_hash_padding);
   if ($new_hash && ($new_hash == $_GET['hash'])) {
     $query = "SELECT user_name
               FROM user
               WHERE confirm_hash = '$new_hash'";
     $result = mysql_query($query);
     if (!$result || mysql_num_rows($result) < 1) {
       $feedback = 'ERROR - Hash not found';
       return $feedback;
     } else {
       // Confirm the email and set account to active
       $email = $_GET['email'];
       $hash = $_GET['hash'];
       $query = "UPDATE user SET email='$email', is_confirmed='1' WHERE
confirm_hash='$hash'";
       $result = mysql_query($query);
       return 1;
     }
   } else {
     $feedback = 'ERROR - Values do not match';
     return $feedback;
```

```
    }
}

?>
```

Notice that, during the registration process, we also one-way encrypted a variable consisting of the user's e-mail address plus a filler string. This will be used to confirm that e-mail is actually received at the e-mail address listed by the user.

Listing 38-2 should be called `register.php`. It shows a form and calls the `register()` function:

Listing 38-2: Registration form (register.php)

```php
<?php

/*********************************************************
 * New user registration page.  There are links to      *
 * this page from the header on every other page for     *
 * logged-out and logged-in users.  This may be a        *
 * design flaw however; it's entirely possible that      *
 * we may want to show this page only to logged-out      *
 * visitors.                                             *
 *********************************************************/

require_once('includes/register_funcs.inc');

if ($submit == 'Mail confirmation') {
  $feedback = user_register();

  // In every case, successful or not, there will be feedback
  $feedback_str = "<P class=\"errormess\">$feedback</P>";
} else {
  // Show form for the first time
  $feedback_str = '';
}



// ----------------
// DISPLAY THE FORM
// ----------------
include_once('includes/header_footer.php');
site_header('Registration');

// Superglobals don't work with heredoc
$php_self = $_SERVER['PHP_SELF'];

$reg_str = <<< EOREGSTR
<TABLE CELLPADDING=0 CELLSPACING=0 BORDER=0 ALIGN=CENTER WIDTH=621>
```

```
<TR>
  <TD ROWSPAN=10><IMG WIDTH=15 HEIGHT=1 SRC="../images/spacer.gif"></TD>
  <TD WIDTH=606></TD>
</TR>
<TR>
  <TD>

$feedback_str
<P CLASS="left"><B>REGISTER</B><BR>
Fill out this form and a confirmation email will be sent to you. Once
you click on the link in the email your account will be confirmed and
you can begin to contribute to the community.</P>
<FORM ACTION="$php_self" METHOD="POST">
<P CLASS="bold">First Name<BR>
<INPUT TYPE="TEXT" NAME="first_name" VALUE="$first_name" SIZE="20"
MAXLENGTH="25"></P>
<P CLASS="bold">Last Name<BR>
<INPUT TYPE="TEXT" NAME="last_name" VALUE="$last_name" SIZE="20"
MAXLENGTH="25"></P>
<P CLASS="bold">Username<BR>
<INPUT TYPE="TEXT" NAME="user_name" VALUE="$user_name" SIZE="10"
MAXLENGTH="25"></P>
<P CLASS="bold">Password<BR>
<INPUT TYPE="password" NAME="password1" VALUE="" SIZE="10"
MAXLENGTH="25"></P>
<P CLASS="left"><B>Password</B> (again)<BR>
<INPUT TYPE="password" NAME="password2" VALUE="" SIZE="10"
MAXLENGTH="25"></P>
<P CLASS="left"><B>Email</B> (required for confirmation)<BR>
<INPUT TYPE="TEXT" NAME="email" VALUE="$email" SIZE="30" MAXLENGTH="50">
</P>
<P><INPUT TYPE="SUBMIT" NAME="submit" VALUE="Mail confirmation"></P>
</FORM>

  </TD>
</TR>
</TABLE>
EOREGSTR;
echo $reg_str;

site_footer();

?>
```

The registration form looks similar to Figure 38-1.

Figure 38-1: User registration form

After the user registers, he or she gets a confirmation e-mail with a link to click. This link contains a confirmation hash and the e-mail address that the mail was sent to. The user can't log in to the site until he or she gets this e-mail and we check it against the hash that we set. Here we are trusting that our padding string remains secret. If someone learned it, he or she could spoof any e-mail address quite easily — but until we have reason to believe our system security has been broken, this can be considered "good-enough" proof that the hash was indeed set by us. None of this will necessarily stop a determined attack by a knowledgeable cracker, but it will greatly reduce the number of people who try to give patently false e-mail addresses in registration forms.

After the user clicks through the link, he or she will see the following page, `confirm.php` (Listing 38-3):

Listing 38-3: New-user confirmation page (confirm.php)

```php
<?php

/****************************************************
 * New user confirmation page.  Should only get here *
 * from an email link.                               *
 ****************************************************/


require_once('includes/register_funcs.inc');
include_once('includes/header_footer.php');

site_header('Account Confirmation');
```

```
if ($_GET['hash'] && $_GET['email']) {
  $worked = user_confirm();
} else {
  $feedback_str = "<P class=\"errormess\">ERROR - Bad link</P>";
}


if ($worked != 1) {
  $noconfirm = '<P class="errormess">Something went wrong.  Send email
to admin@example.com for help.  If you clicked through to this page
directly, please go to login.php instead.</P>';
} else {
    $confirm = '<P class="big">You are now confirmed. <A
HREF="login.php">Log in</A> to start browsing the site</P>';
}

$page = <<< EOPAGE

<TABLE CELLPADDING=0 CELLSPACING=0 BORDER=0 ALIGN=CENTER WIDTH=621>
<TR>
  <TD><IMG WIDTH=15 HEIGHT=1 SRC=../images/spacer.gif></TD>
  <TD WIDTH=606 CLASS=left>
  $feedback_str
  $noconfirm
  $confirm
  </TD>
</TR>
</TABLE>
EOPAGE;

echo $page;

site_footer();

?>
```

Login/Logout

If your registration process was well designed in the first place, it can help your login process be more effective. So, for example, if you strictly enforce e-mail and username uniqueness during registration, in theory, you do not need to check for those things during login. You may still want to as a belt-and-braces kind of thing, but it all depends on how much you trust your registration. In the case of the registration system in the preceding "Registration" section, our method of using a one-way hashing function to encrypt passwords and e-mails can also be adapted to enhance the reliability of cookies in an extremely scalable way.

Here's the problem we're trying to solve: After a user logs in, we want to set a cookie that uniquely identifies the user. Say we set a cookie that contains the user's username on our site, which is generally not a very private piece of information — in fact, it's a method of saving people from having to use their real names in public. A cookie, however, is just a text file — there's literally nothing stopping you from writing up a cookie file on your computer that claims you are someone else.

Sites deal with the cookie-verification problem in different ways, the most common of which is checking your cookie data against a database on every page load. This is not a very scalable solution, however, unless you have some kind of serious data-caching mechanism, because eventually the database becomes a bottleneck.

The solution that we use is a little bit different. When users log in, we look them up in the database by their usernames and passwords. If we find them in there, we set two cookies per user: one with the username and one with the hashed product of the username and a super-secret string known only to us. Now on every page load, we check for the existence of these cookies — but also we see if they match and if they were set by us, by hashing the value of the username cookie with the super secret string and then comparing it to the hash cookie. All this is done on the Web server at relatively little cost in time or cycles, rather than necessitating the opening of a connection to the database. Again, we must trust that the secret string is not compromised — but in the worst case scenario, we could change this string and merely cause everyone to be logged out suddenly.

After we confirm that the cookies do, in fact, match, we can optionally go even further by setting a global logged-in flag. This isn't the most secure method possible, but it's extremely fast. You may consider using a logged-in flag for reads and reserving every-page cookie-verification for tools such as adding content or changing passwords. You could do this by splitting the `user_isloggedin()` function in Listing 38-4 into two functions: one to detect the flag, and one to match up the cookies.

Listing 38-4 is called `login_funcs.inc`. It contains all login- and logout-related functions, which will be called from other PHP pages.

Listing 38-4: Login and logout functions (login_funcs.inc)

```php
<?php

// A file with the database host, user, password, and selected database
include_once('db_vars.inc');

// A string used for md5 encryption.  You could move it to a file
// outside the web tree for more security.
$supersecret_hash_padding = 'A string that is used to pad out short
strings for md5 encryption.';


$LOGGED_IN = false;
```

```php
unset($LOGGED_IN);


function user_isloggedin() {
  // This function will only work with superglobal arrays, because
  // I'm not passing in any values or declaring globals
  global $supersecret_hash_padding, $LOGGED_IN;

  // Have we already run the hash checks?
  // If so, return the pre-set var
  if (isSet($LOGGED_IN)) {
    return $LOGGED_IN;
  }
  if ($_COOKIE['user_name'] && $_COOKIE['id_hash']) {
    $hash = md5($_COOKIE['user_name'].$supersecret_hash_padding);
    if ($hash == $_COOKIE['id_hash']) {
      return true;
    } else {
      return false;
    }
  } else {
    return false;
  }
}


function user_login() {
  // This function will only work with superglobal arrays, because
  // I'm not passing in any values or declaring globals
  if (!$_POST['user_name'] || !$_POST['password']) {
    $feedback = 'ERROR - Missing username or password';
    return $feedback;
  } else {
    $user_name = strtolower($_POST['user_name']);
    // Don't need to trim because extra spaces should fail for this
    // Don't need to addslashes because single quotes aren't allowed
    $password = strtolower($_POST['password']);
    // Don't need to addslashes because we'll be hashing it
    $crypt_pwd = md5($password);
    $query = "SELECT user_name, is_confirmed
              FROM user
              WHERE user_name = '$user_name'
              AND password='$crypt_pwd'";
    $result = mysql_query($query);
    if (!$result || mysql_num_rows($result) < 1){
      $feedback = 'ERROR - User not found or password incorrect';
      return $feedback;
    } else {
      if (mysql_result($result, 0, 'is_confirmed') == '1') {
```

```
            user_set_tokens($user_name);
            return 1;
        } else {
            $feedback = 'ERROR - You may not have confirmed your account
yet';
            return $feedback;
        }
    }
  }
}


function user_logout() {
  setcookie('user_name', '', (time()+2592000), '/', '', 0);
  setcookie('id_hash', '', (time()+2592000), '/', '', 0);
}


function user_set_tokens($user_name_in) {
  global $supersecret_hash_padding;
  if (!$user_name_in) {
    $feedback =  'ERROR - No username';
    return false;
  }
  $user_name = strtolower($user_name_in);
  $id_hash = md5($user_name.$supersecret_hash_padding);

  setcookie('user_name', $user_name, (time()+2592000), '/', '', 0);
  setcookie('id_hash', $id_hash, (time()+2592000), '/', '', 0);
}

?>
```

Listing 38-5 is called `login.php`. It shows a form and calls the `login()` function. On success, it redirects to the home page.

Listing 38-5: Login form (login.php)

```
<?php

/**************************************************
 * Login page.  There are links to this page from *
 * the header on every other page for logged-out  *
 * users only.                                    *
 **************************************************/

require_once('includes/login_funcs.inc');

// If they're logged in, log them out
```

```php
// They shouldn't be able to see this page logged-in
// This allows the same page to be used as a logout script
if ($LOGGED_IN = user_isloggedin()) {
  user_logout();
  $_COOKIE['user_name'] = '';
  unset($LOGGED_IN);
}

if ($submit == 'Login') {
  if (strlen($_POST['username']) <= 25 && strlen($_POST['password'])
<=25) {
    $feedback = user_login();
  } else {
    $feedback = 'ERROR - Username and password are too long';
  }
  if ($feedback == 1) {
    // On successful login, redirect to homepage
    header("Location: index.php");
  } else {
    $feedback_str = "<P class=\"errormess\">$feedback</P>";
  }
} else {
  $feedback_str = '';
}


// ----------------
// DISPLAY THE FORM
// ----------------
include_once('includes/header_footer.php');
site_header('Login');

// Superglobals don't work with heredoc
$php_self = $_SERVER['PHP_SELF'];

$login_form = <<< EOLOGINFORM
<TABLE CELLPADDING=0 CELLSPACING=0 BORDER=0 ALIGN=CENTER WIDTH=621>
<TR>
  <TD ROWSPAN=2><IMG WIDTH=15 HEIGHT=1 SRC=../images/spacer.gif></TD>
  <TD WIDTH=606 HEIGHT=1><IMG WIDTH=606 HEIGHT=1
SRC=../images/spacer.gif></TD>
</TR>
<TR>
 <TD>

$feedback_str
<P CLASS="bold">LOGIN</P>
<FORM ACTION="$php_self" METHOD="POST">
<P CLASS="bold">Username<BR>
```

```
<INPUT TYPE="TEXT" NAME="user_name" VALUE="" SIZE="10"
MAXLENGTH="15"></P>
<P CLASS="bold">Password<BR>
<INPUT TYPE="password" NAME="password" VALUE="" SIZE="10"
MAXLENGTH="15"></P>
<P><INPUT TYPE="SUBMIT" NAME="submit" VALUE="Login"></P>
</FORM>

  </TD>
</TR>
</TABLE>
EOLOGINFORM;
echo $login_form;

site_footer();

?>
```

Figure 38-2 shows the login page in the midst of an error.

Figure 38-2: Login page

> **TIP:** Mozilla is far and away the best browser to develop on if you're working with the login functions of a site because it has the Cookie Manager feature (in the Tools menu). Mozilla enables you to see all your cookies in a nice alphabetized list and to delete or block cookies individually. The only thing to watch out for is that cookies may be classified under `example.com`, `servername.example.com`, or `www.example.com` depending on precisely how they were set.

Logging out is very simple — you just unset the cookies. Actually, if you are logged in and visit the `login.php` page , it happens automatically — so you can use `login.php` for both logging in and logging out.

User Tools

Registration and login are the core of your user management system, but you also need tools for various common situations, such as forgotten passwords, changing a password, or changing less sensitive user information.

Forgotten password

The most common way to deal with a forgotten password is to simply mail it to the e-mail address you have on file for a particular user. Many sites a lot larger than yours do this. Cases of stealing passwords this way may have been reported, but it's not a rampant problem — especially if people do the smart thing, which is to immediately change the password as soon as they can log on.

There are more elaborate ways to deal with forgotten passwords. One of us, for example, once worked on a system where an e-mail was sent containing a link that allowed the user to visit a special page which existed once and only once — which allowed the user to change his or her password without actually logging in. It was a somewhat neurotic solution to the problem, but it worked.

We believe the best compromise is simply to mail a new computer-generated random password. This will be fairly secure, and yet so difficult to remember that hopefully the user will be more motivated to immediately change his or her password to something more comfy.

You can also repurpose the password-generation part of this code if you plan to generate passwords during the registration process instead of letting the user choose the password as we do in the section "Registration," earlier in this chapter.

Listing 38-6 is called `forgot.php`. It shows a form, generates a random new password, and sends it to the user's recorded e-mail address.

Listing 38-6: Form to handle forgotten passwords (forgot.php)

```php
<?php

/********************************************
 * This file displays the forgot-password  *
 * form.  It submits to itself, mails a     *
 * temporary password, and then redirects   *
 * to login.                                *
 ********************************************/

// A file with the database host, user, password, and selected database
```

```php
require_once('db_vars.inc');

if ($HTTP_POST_VARS['command'] == 'forgot' && strlen($_POST['email'] <=
50)) {
  // Handle submission.  This is a one-time only form
  // so there will be no problems with handling errors.
  $as_email = addslashes($_POST['email']);
  $query = "select id from users where email = '$as_email'";
  $result = mysql_query($query);
  $is_user = mysql_num_rows($result);

  if ($is_user == 1) {
    // Generate a random password
    $alphanum =
array('a','b','c','d','e','f','g','h','i','j','k','m','n','o','p','q','r
','s','t','u','v','x','y','z','A','B','C','D','E','F','G','H','I','J','K
','M','N','P','Q','R','S','T','U','V','W','X','Y','Z','2','3','4','5','6
','7','8','9');
    $chars = sizeof($alphanum);
    $a = time();
    mt_srand($a);
    for ($i=0; $i < 6; $i++) {
      $randnum = intval(mt_rand(0,56));
      $password .= $alphanum[$randnum];
    }
    // One-way encrypt it
    $crypt_pass = md5($password);

    // Put the temp password in the db
    $query = "update univ_Users set password = '$crypt_pass' where email
= '$as_email'";
    $result = mysql_query($query) or die('Cannot complete update');

    // Send the email
    $to      = $_POST['email'];
    $from    = "forgot@example.com";
    $subject = "New password";
    $msg     = <<< EOMSG
You recently requested that we send you a new password for Example.com.
Your new password is:

        $password

Please log in at this URL:

        http://localhost/login.html

Then go to this address to change your password:
```

```
                    http://localhost/changepass.php
EOMSG;

    $mailsend = mail("$to","$subject","$msg","From: $from\r\nReply-
To:webmaster@example.com");

    // Redirect to login
    header("Location: login.html");
  } else {
    // The email address isn't good, they lose.
  }

}


// -----------------------
// Display the form nicely
// -----------------------

// Superglobal arrays don't work in heredoc
$php_self = $_SERVER['PHP_SELF'];

$form_str = <<< EOFORMSTR
<HTML>
<HEAD>
<STYLE TYPE="text/css">
<!--
BODY, P      {color: black; font-family: verdana; font-size: 10 pt}
H1           {color: black; font-family: arial; font-size: 12 pt}
-->
</STYLE>
</HEAD>

<BODY>
<TABLE BORDER=0 CELLPADDING=10 WIDTH=100%>
<TR>
<TD BGCOLOR="#F0F8FF" ALIGN=CENTER VALIGN=TOP WIDTH=150>
</TD>
<TD BGCOLOR="#FFFFFF" ALIGN=LEFT VALIGN=TOP WIDTH=83%>
<H1>Request new password</H1>
<p><b>Forgot your password?</b> Don't worry -- simply enter your email
address below, and we will email you a new password.<br><i>Please use
the email address you provided when you registered. If you've forgotten,
you can always <a href="/register.html">register again</a>.</i></p>

<form action="$php_self" method="post">
Email: <input type="text" name="email"><br />

<br /><br />
```

```
<input type="hidden" name="command" value="forgot">
<input type="submit" value="Send password">
</form>

</TD>
</TR>
</TABLE>

</BODY>
</HTML>
EOFORMSTR;

echo $form_str;

?>
```

Figure 38-3 shows the Forgot Password form in action.

Figure 38-3: Forgot password form

Changing sensitive user data

You probably want a little bit more security before you let users go changing their e-mail addresses and passwords — like, for instance, making extra sure they know the old password first. This is especially important if you use cookies with very long expiration times. It's easier to manage this extra verification if you have a separate form for e-mail and password changes, versus non-sensitive data, such as homepage or sig.

If you don't collect usernames on your site, and instead use email addresses as unique-identifying cookies, you will have to reset the cookies when you allow the user to change an e-mail address. Otherwise your whole user authentication scheme will no longer work properly.

Listing 38-7 is called `emailpass_funcs.inc`. It contains functions related to changing e-mail or password:

Listing 38-7: E-mail and password editing functions (emailpass_funcs.inc)

```
<?phpfunction user_change_password () {
  // Do new passwords match?
  if ($_POST['new_password1'] && ($_POST['new_password1'] ==
$_POST['new_password2'])) {
    // Is password long enough?
    if (strlen($_POST['new_password1']) >= 6) {
      // Is the old password correct?
      if (strlen($_POST['old_password']) > 1) {
        $change_user_name = strtolower($_COOKIE['user_name']);
        $old_password = strtolower($_POST['old_password']);
        $crypt_pass = md5($old_password);
        $new_password1 = strtolower($_POST['new_password1']);
        $query = "SELECT *
                  FROM user
                  WHERE user_name = '$change_user_name'
                  AND password = '$crypt_pass'";
        $result = mysql_query($query);
        if (!$result || mysql_num_rows($result) < 1) {
          $feedback = 'ERROR - User not found or bad password';
          return $feedback;
        } else {
          $crypt_newpass = md5($new_password1);
          $query = "UPDATE user
                    SET password = '$crypt_newpass'
                    WHERE user_name = '$change_user_name'
                    AND password = '$crypt_pass'";
          $result = mysql_query($query);
          if (!$result || mysql_affected_rows() < 1) {
            $feedback = 'ERROR - Problem updating password';
            return $feedback;
          } else {
            return 1;
          }
        }
      } else {
        $feedback = 'ERROR - Please enter old password';
        return $feedback;
      }
    } else {
      $feedback .= 'ERROR - New password not long enough';
```

```php
      return false;
    }
  } else {
    $feedback = 'ERROR - Your passwords do not match';
    return $feedback;
  }
}


function user_change_email () {
  global $supersecret_hash_padding;
  if (validate_email($_POST['new_email'])) {
    $hash = md5($_POST['new_email'].$supersecret_hash_padding);

    // Send out a new confirm email with a new hash
    $user_name = strtolower($_COOKIE['user_name']);
    $password1 = strtolower($_POST['password1']);
    $crypt_pass = md5($password1);
    $query = "UPDATE user
              SET confirm_hash = '$hash',
                  is_confirmed = 0
              WHERE user_name = '$user_name'
              AND password = '$crypt_pass'";
    $result = mysql_query($query);
    if (!$result || mysql_affected_rows() < 1) {
      $feedback = 'ERROR - Wrong password';
      return $feedback;
    } else {
      // Send the confirmation email
      $encoded_email = urlencode($_POST['new_email']);
      $mail_body = <<< EOMAILBODY
Thank you for registering at Example.com.  Click this link to confirm
your registration:

http://localhost/confirm.php?hash=$hash&email=$encoded_email

Once you see a confirmation message, you will be logged into Example.com
EOMAILBODY;
      mail($email, 'Example.com Registration Confirmation', $mail_body,
'From: noreply@example.com');
      // If you use email rather than password cookies,
      // uncomment the following line
      // user_set_tokens($user_name);
      return 1;
    }
  } else {
    $feedback = 'ERROR- New email address is invalid';
    return $feedback;
  }
```

```
}

?>
```

Listing 38-8 is called `changeemail.php`. It shows a form and calls the proper function. If you are not logged in, it redirects you to the homepage.

Listing 38-8: Form to change e-mail (changeemail.php)

```php
<?php

/****************************
 * Change email form page. *
 ****************************/

require_once('includes/emailpass_funcs.inc');
require_once('includes/login_funcs.inc');
if (!user_isloggedin()) {
  header("Location: index.php");
}


if ($_POST['submit'] == "Change my confirmation") {
  $worked = user_change_email();
  if ($worked == 1) {
    $feedback_str = "<P class=\"errormess\">A confirmation email has
been sent to you.</P>";
  } else {
    $feedback_str = "<P class=\"errormess\">$feedback</P>";
  }
}


// ------------
// DISPLAY FORM
// ------------

include_once('includes/header_footer.php');
site_header('Change Email');

// Superglobals don't work with heredoc
$php_self = $_SERVER['PHP_SELF'];

$form_str = <<< EOFORMSTR
<TABLE CELLPADDING=0 CELLSPACING=0 BORDER=0 ALIGN=CENTER WIDTH=621>
<TR>
  <TD ROWSPAN=2><IMG WIDTH=15 HEIGHT=1 SRC=../images/spacer.gif></TD>
  <TD WIDTH=606 HEIGHT=1><IMG WIDTH=606 HEIGHT=1
SRC=../images/spacer.gif></TD>
```

```
</TR>
<TR>
 <TD>
$feedback_str
<P CLASS=left><B>Change your email address</B><BR>
A confirmation email will be sent to you.<BR>
<FORM ACTION="$php_self" METHOD="POST">
<B>Password</B><BR>
<INPUT TYPE="password" NAME="password1" VALUE="" SIZE="10"
MAXLENGTH="15"><BR><BR>
<B>New email</B> (required for confirmation)<BR>
<INPUT TYPE="TEXT" NAME="new_email" VALUE="" SIZE="20"
MAXLENGTH="35"><BR><BR>
<INPUT TYPE="SUBMIT" NAME="submit" VALUE="Send my confirmation">
</FORM>
 </TD>
</TR>
</TABLE>
EOFORMSTR;

echo $form_str;

site_footer();

?>
```

The results of `changeemail.php` are show in Figure 38-4:

Figure 38-4: Form to change e-mail address

> **TIP:** It's not a bad idea to keep track of the original e-mail address that a user registered under. If someone has registered at your site with the intent to cause harm, such as harassing another user or otherwise making a pest of himself, he may attempt to cover his tracks by changing his e-mail address using your handy tools. In this case, at least you would have one e-mail address that was known to work at one time.

Listing 38-9 is called `changepass.php`. It shows a form and calls the proper function. If you are not logged in, it redirects you to the homepage.

Listing 38-9: Change password form (changepass.php)

```php
<?php

/*******************************
 * Change password form page. *
 *******************************/

require_once('includes/emailpass_funcs.inc');
require_once('includes/login_funcs.inc');
if (!user_isloggedin()) {
  header("Location: index.php");
}

if ($submit) {
  $worked = user_change_password();
  if ($worked == 1) {
    $feedback_str = "<P class=\"errormess\">Password changed</P>";
  } else {
    $feedback_str = "<P class=\"errormess\">$feedback</P>";
  }
}


// ------------
// DISPLAY FORM
// ------------

include_once('includes/header_footer.php');
site_header('Change Password');

// Superglobals don't work with heredoc
$php_self = $_SERVER['PHP_SELF'];

$form_str = <<< EOFORMSTR
<TABLE CELLPADDING=0 CELLSPACING=0 BORDER=0 ALIGN=CENTER WIDTH=621>
<TR>
  <TD ROWSPAN=2><IMG WIDTH=15 HEIGHT=1 SRC=../images/spacer.gif></TD>
  <TD WIDTH=606 HEIGHT=1><IMG WIDTH=606 HEIGHT=1
SRC=../images/spacer.gif></TD>
```

```
</TR>
<TR>
 <TD>
$feedback_str
<P CLASS=left><B>Change your password</B><BR>
<FORM ACTION="$php_self" METHOD="POST">
<B>Old password</B><BR>
<INPUT TYPE="password" NAME="old_password" VALUE="" SIZE="10"
MAXLENGTH="15"><BR><BR>
<B>New Password</B><BR>
<INPUT TYPE="password" NAME="new_password1" VALUE="" SIZE="10"
MAXLENGTH="15"><BR><BR>
<B>New password</B> (again)<BR>
<INPUT TYPE="password" NAME="new_password2" VALUE="" SIZE="10"
MAXLENGTH="15"><BR><BR>
<INPUT TYPE="SUBMIT" NAME="submit" VALUE="Change my password">
</FORM>
 </TD>
</TR>
</TABLE>
EOFORMSTR;

echo $form_str;

site_footer();

?>
```

The results of changepass.php are show in Figure 38-5:

Figure 38-5: Form to change password

Edit nonsensitive user data

We define non-sensitive user information as the kind of user data that you won't be sued for inadvertently revealing — things like favorite links, photos or avatars, and sex.

Non-sensitive user information is very straightforward to change. Just use a simple HTML form submit to a PHP form handler which will stash the data in the datastore. A sample form is included below; feel free to just grab it and change the variables to suit your own schema.

Figure 38-6: Changing incidental user information

The code for Figure 38-6 is contained in Listing 38-10, `edit_userinfo.php`:

Listing 38-10: Form to edit user data (edit_userinfo.php)

```php
<?php

/***********************************************
 * This file displays the change non-sensitive *
 * user data form.  It submits to itself, and   *
 * displays a message each time you submit.      *
 ***********************************************/

// A file with the database host, user, password, and selected database
require_once('includes/db_vars.inc');
include_once('includes/header_footer.php');
include_once('includes/login_funcs.inc');
```

```php
if (!user_isloggedin()) {
  echo '<P>You are not logged in, or this is not your user
profile.</P>';
} else {
  $user_name = $_COOKIE['user_name'];
  if ($_POST['submit'] == "Edit user data" && strlen($_POST['gender'])
== 1 && strlen($_POST['priv_profile']) == 1) {
    // Send data to db

    // I'm not bothering to check the stringlength of these
    // because I'm URL-encoding them
    $as_photo_url = addslashes($_POST['photo_url']);
    $ue_photo_url = urlencode($as_photo_url);
    $as_homepage_url = addslashes($_POST['homepage_url']);
    $ue_homepage_url = urlencode($as_homepage_url);
    $as_fav_link1 = addslashes($_POST['fav_link1']);
    $ue_fav_link1 = urlencode($as_fav_link1);
    $as_fav_link2 = addslashes($_POST['fav_link2']);
    $ue_fav_link2 = urlencode($as_fav_link2);
    $as_fav_link3 = addslashes($_POST['fav_link3']);
    $ue_fav_link3 = urlencode($as_fav_link3);
    $as_location = addslashes($location);

    $query = "UPDATE user
              SET photo = '$ue_photo_url',
                  homepage = '$ue_homepage_url',
                  link1 = '$ue_fav_link1',
                  link2 = '$ue_fav_link2',
                  link3 = '$ue_fav_link3',
                  location = '$as_location',
                  country = '$country',
                  gender = '$gender',
                  priv_profile = $priv_profile
              WHERE user_name = '$user_name'";
    $result = mysql_query($query);
    if (!$result) {
      $status_message = 'Problem with user data entry';
    } else {
      $status_message = 'Successfully edited user data';
    }
  } elseif (strlen($_POST['gender']) > 1 &&
strlen($_POST['priv_profile']) > 1) {
    // Bad user, smack on wrist
    $status_message = 'You\'re trying to do something very odd with this
form.  Stop it now.';
  }

  // Get previously-existing data
```

```
  $query = "SELECT photo, homepage, link1, link2, link3, location,
country, gender, priv_profile
            FROM user
            WHERE user_name = '$user_name'";

  $result = mysql_query($query);
  // Shall we have an error message if no data comes back?
  $user_array = mysql_fetch_array($result);

  $photo_url = urldecode($user_array['photo']);
  $photo_url = stripslashes($photo_url);
  $homepage_url = urldecode($user_array['homepage']);
  $homepage_url = stripslashes($homepage_url);
  $fav_link1 = urldecode($user_array['link1']);
  $fav_link1 = stripslashes($fav_link1);
  $fav_link2 = urldecode($user_array['link2']);
  $fav_link2 = stripslashes($fav_link2);
  $fav_link3 = urldecode($user_array['link3']);
  $fav_link3 = stripslashes($fav_link3);
  $location = stripslashes($user_array['location']);
  $country = $user_array['country'];
  $gender = $user_array['gender'];

  // Construct the multiple field types
  if ($gender == "M") {
    $gender_button_str = '<INPUT TYPE="RADIO" NAME="gender" VALUE="M"
CHECKED>M
<INPUT TYPE="RADIO" NAME="gender" VALUE="F">F';
  } elseif ($gender == "F") {
    $gender_button_str = '<INPUT TYPE="RADIO" NAME="gender" VALUE="M">M
<INPUT TYPE="RADIO" NAME="gender" VALUE="F" CHECKED>F';
  } else {
    $gender_button_str = '<INPUT TYPE="RADIO" NAME="gender" VALUE="M">M
<INPUT TYPE="RADIO" NAME="gender" VALUE="F">F';
  }
  $priv_profile = $user_array['priv_profile'];
  if ($priv_profile == 1) {
    $priv_profile_str = '<INPUT TYPE="RADIO" NAME="priv_profile"
VALUE="1" CHECKED>Yes
<INPUT TYPE="RADIO" NAME="priv_profile" VALUE="0">No';
  } elseif ($priv_profile == 0) {
    $priv_profile_str = '<INPUT TYPE="RADIO" NAME="priv_profile"
VALUE="1">Yes
<INPUT TYPE="RADIO" NAME="priv_profile" VALUE="0" CHECKED>No';
  } else {
    $priv_profile_str = '<INPUT TYPE="RADIO" NAME="priv_profile"
VALUE="1">Yes
<INPUT TYPE="RADIO" NAME="priv_profile" VALUE="0">No';
  }
```

```
   // --------------
   // Construct form
   // --------------


   site_header('User data edit page');


   $userform_str = <<< EOUSERFORMSTR
<TABLE ALIGN=CENTER WIDTH=621>
<TR>
   <TD ROWSPAN=10><IMG WIDTH=15 HEIGHT=1 SRC="../images/spacer.gif"></TD>
   <TD WIDTH=606></TD>
</TR>
<TR>
 <TD>
<P CLASS=bold>USER PROFILE<BR><BR><A HREF='/changeemail.php'>Change your
email address</A><BR><BR><A HREF='/changepass.php'>Change your
password</A>

<P><FONT COLOR="#ff0000">$status_message</FONT></P>

<FORM ACTION="$PHP_SELF" METHOD="POST">
<P CLASS=left>
<B>Photo URL</B> (i.e. http://www.my.com/foto.jpg)<BR>
<INPUT TYPE="TEXT" NAME="photo_url" VALUE="$photo_url" SIZE="40">
</P>
<P CLASS=left>
<B>Homepage URL </B>(e.g. http://www.my.com/page.html)<BR>
<INPUT TYPE="TEXT" NAME="homepage_url" VALUE="$homepage_url" SIZE="40">
</P>
<P CLASS=bold>
Favorite links<BR>
<INPUT TYPE="TEXT" NAME="fav_link1" VALUE="$fav_link1" SIZE="40">
</P>
<P>
<INPUT TYPE="TEXT" NAME="fav_link2" VALUE="$fav_link2" SIZE="40">
</P>
<P>
<INPUT TYPE="TEXT" NAME="fav_link3" VALUE="$fav_link3" SIZE="40">
</P>
<P CLASS=left>
<B>Location</B> (City, State)<BR>
<INPUT TYPE="TEXT" NAME="location" VALUE="$location" SIZE="35"
MAXLENGTH="50">
</P>

<P CLASS=left>
<B>Country<BR>
```

```
<INPUT TYPE="TEXT" NAME="country" VALUE="$country" SIZE="35"
MAXLENGTH="50">
</P>
<P CLASS=bold>
Gender<BR>
$gender_button_str
</P>
<P CLASS=bold>
Make user profile private?<BR>
$priv_profile_str
</P>
<P>
<INPUT TYPE="SUBMIT" NAME="submit" VALUE="Edit user data">
</FORM>
 </TD>
</TR>
</TABLE>
EOUSERFORMSTR;
  echo $userform_str;

  site_footer();
}

?>
```

Administrator Tools

Administrator tasks tend to be rather specific to particular sites, but there are a few general principles to keep in mind in designing administrator tools. The main one, obviously, is to protect these tools from being found and used by unauthorized users.

Authorization: Basic auth, cookie, database, IP

Although a full discussion of authentication is beyond the scope of this chapter, you need to understand permissions to design tools that act on user data.

First, we should clearly define the distinction between *authentication* and *authorization*. *Authentication* means we are trying to verify that you are who you say you are. Everything in this chapter so far has been about authentication, strictly speaking. Merely by being a particular user, certain abilities (such as the ability to change your own e-mail address) devolve upon you. *Authorization* is about determining whether you have permission to do what you want to do. Often an authorization step is built into authentication in a way that is transparent to the user, but they are fundamentally two separate tasks.

There are four main types of authorization: basic auth, cookie, database, and IP based.

Basic auth is a Web server specific method of authorization and authentication. You can tell the Web server to prompt for a password and check a list of authorized users before serving a page in a particular directory under your Web tree. Although, in a certain sense, the Web server is doing this on every page load, the browser can transparently handle multiple pages per session so that the user only has to enter a login and password once per browser session. A clear explanation of basic auth for Apache `http` server can be found here:

```
http://httpd.apache.org/docs/howto/auth.html
```

Cookie-based authorization, as the name implies, relies upon special cookies to identify browser sessions belonging to trusted users. Often the cookie must be set inside the firewall, so there is an element of IP authorization to this type of scheme also. The advantage of cookie-based designs is that they are easy to implement and can be used by several employees at once. The disadvantage is that, by themselves, cookies are easy to spoof and hard to track because they embody authorization without authentication. If you have six trusted users in your organization that are empowered to take a certain action, with cookies alone you won't know which of the six made a particular mistake.

Database authorization relies on a more formal concept of permissions, either individual or grouped into baskets. Individual permissions are stored in their own database tables, such as `permission` and `user_permission`. On each page load, the code checks to see whether this particular authenticated user has the particular permission necessary to use this particular tool. Baskets of permissions are often represented simply as a bit in the user table (`is_admin` or some such field). Database permissions are the most complicated to implement, but one of the safest designs. Furthermore, you can track individual actions with a database at a level of granularity not possible with the other schemes.

Finally, IP-based permissions attempt to restrict use of certain tools to only those behind a firewall or on a particular subnet. You may, for example, allow only one development server to connect to your live database on the other side of the firewall. IP-based plans should really be led by your IT staff or systems administrators because almost all the work and maintenance falls on them. If you, as the Web developer, do everything they tell you to do, but the network is cracked anyway, the responsibility should fall on them. Obviously IP-based authorization is non-authenticated — unless you work in a locked room, it's very difficult to prevent others from sneaking up to your computer while you're away and using the browser-based tool on your computer.

Remember that any or all these basic methods can be combined for stronger security. You could have a system where all tools lived in a particular password-protected directory on a particular server, for example, and would run only on that server, but permissions were stored on the live database in the field. This would combine basic auth, database, and IP-based authorization systems for a more secure result.

Login as user

Logging in as a particular user is not a tool per se. It may be something you must build it into the structure of your entire site, depending on how you implement it and the particulars of your site architecture. For instance, you may have a special cookie that means "I'm the administrator, but I want to see this user's user page as if I were the user."

If you used the registration and login code we laid out in the "Registration" and "Login" sections of this chapter, you could easily write a tool to basically give a particular user's cookies to the administrator of your site. Essentially, it would amount to using the login script without requiring a password — or rather without requiring the password of the user whose point of view you are taking. This would be an intrinsically insecure way to accomplish your task, and therefore should only be used in combination with one or more of the other security schemes discussed in the "Avoiding Common Security Problems" section of this chapter.

The `impersonate.php` form in Listing 38-11 looks exactly like the normal login form, `login.php`. Instead of entering his or her own username and password, however, the authorized user will enter the username of the user he or she wishes to impersonate, plus a special administrator password. If the administrator cookie is not detected, the form will automatically redirect to the front page of the site.

Listing 38-11: Administrator impersonation script (impersonate.php)

```php
<?php

/***************************************************
 * Script to set user cookie so admins can browse *
 * site from the viewpoint of a particular user.  *
 * Potentially VERY unsafe!!!  Protect it with     *
 * your life!                                       *
 ***************************************************/

// If this person isn't recognized as the admin, bounce them
if ($_COOKIE['user_name'] != 'Administrator') {
  header("Location: index.php");
}

require_once('includes/db_vars.inc');
require_once('includes/login_funcs.inc');

function user_impersonate() {
  // This function will only work with superglobal arrays, because
  // I'm not passing in any values or declaring globals
  if (!$_POST['user_name'] || !$_POST['password']) {
    $feedback = 'ERROR - Missing username or password';
    return $feedback;
  } else {
    $user_name = strtolower($_POST['user_name']);
    // Don't need to trim because extra spaces should fail for this
    // Don't need to addslashes because single quotes aren't allowed
    $password = strtolower($_POST['password']);
    // Don't need to addslashes because we'll be hashing it
```

```php
    $crypt_pwd = md5($password);
    $query = "SELECT user_name
            FROM user
            WHERE user_name = 'Administrator
            AND password='$crypt_pwd'";
    $result = mysql_query($query);
    if (!$result || mysql_num_rows($result) < 1){
      $feedback = 'ERROR - User not found or password incorrect';
      return $feedback;
    } else {
      if (mysql_result($result, 0, 0) == 'Administrator') {
        user_set_tokens($user_name);
        return 1;
      }
    }
  }
}

if ($submit == 'Login') {
  $feedback = user_impersonate();
  if ($feedback == 1) {
    // On successful login, redirect to homepage
    header("Location: index.php");
  } else {
    $feedback_str = "<P class=\"errormess\">$feedback</P>";
  }
} else {
  $feedback_str = '';
}


// ----------------
// DISPLAY THE FORM
// ----------------
include_once('includes/header_footer.php');
site_header('Login To OpenCortex');

// Superglobals don't work with heredoc
$php_self = $_SERVER['PHP_SELF'];

$login_form = <<< EOLOGINFORM
<TABLE CELLPADDING=0 CELLSPACING=0 BORDER=0 ALIGN=CENTER WIDTH=621>
<TR>
  <TD ROWSPAN=2><IMG WIDTH=15 HEIGHT=1 SRC=../images/spacer.gif></TD>
  <TD WIDTH=606 HEIGHT=1><IMG WIDTH=606 HEIGHT=1
SRC=../images/spacer.gif></TD>
</TR>
<TR>
 <TD>
```

```
$feedback_str
<P CLASS="bold">LOGIN</P>
<FORM ACTION="$php_self" METHOD="POST">
<P CLASS="bold">Username<BR>
<INPUT TYPE="TEXT" NAME="user_name" VALUE="" SIZE="10"
MAXLENGTH="15"></P>
<P CLASS="bold">Password<BR>
<INPUT TYPE="password" NAME="password" VALUE="" SIZE="10"
MAXLENGTH="15"></P>
<P><INPUT TYPE="SUBMIT" NAME="submit" VALUE="Login"></P>
</FORM>

  </TD>
</TR>
</TABLE>
EOLOGINFORM;
echo $login_form;

site_footer();

?>
```

Summary

User data management is a core function of many Websites. Unfortunately, often not enough thought is given to security, scalability, and modularity in these important subsystems. We demonstrate a complete user management package here, and walk you through the design principles you should keep in mind as you implement your own.

The main functions of a user management system include new user registration and confirmation, login and logout, forgotten password replacement, changing e-mail and passwords, changing other user data, and logging in as another user.

## Chapter 39

Case Study: A Trivia Game

In This Chapter

♦ A guessing game with approximate answers

♦ The object-oriented implementation of the game

♦ Database and session support

♦ Design considerations

In this chapter, we present a full working example of a small PHP application: a Web-based trivia game with a twist (the "Certainty Quiz"). The main virtue of the chapter is intended to be its completeness; Instead of using code fragments to illustrate talking points, as we do in most other chapters, we're showing everything, soup to nuts. As a result, this is one of the larger examples in the book, weighing in at more than 1300 lines of PHP code.

Concepts Used in This Chapter

The code in this chapter uses a wide variety of techniques, tricks, and technologies that we've presented elsewhere in the book. In particular:

♦ We make heavy use of the object-oriented features of PHP (Chapter 26).

♦ We rely on PHP's session mechanism to propagate game data from page to page (Chapter 27).

♦ We use a backend database (MySQL) to store questions and high scores (Chapter 18).

♦ We use the new superglobal variables whenever we process form input (Chapter 9).

♦ We do some behind-the-scenes mathematics, including approximating nth roots (Chapter 12).

♦ We use arrays for storing data and for manipulating data returned from the database (Chapter 11)

♦ We do a lot of string processing and concatenation to build our display pages, including the heredoc technique for templating pages (Chapter 10).

We highlight some of these topics in various sections later in the chapter as we delve into the code.

> **NEW FEATURE:** This entire chapter uses very modern (at this writing) features of PHP. It has been tested with PHP 4.1.2 and 4.2 but is very unlikely to work with versions that are any earlier than 4.1.

The Game

Several years ago, a friend asked one of us to try a quiz he'd seen somewhere on the Internet. After I agreed, he told me that he would ask me ten questions, each of which had a numerical answer (dates, weights, lengths, counts, and so on). The unusual part was that instead of giving my answer as a number, I was to give it as a lower bound and an upper bound on the answer. I could make the ranges as large as I wanted, and otherwise I had only one instruction: Make sure that you answer nine out of ten questions correctly.

I answered the questions confidently and was surprised at the end to find that my final score was six (or was it four?). At any rate, I did surprisingly badly, but my friend said that everyone else he had tried it on had done even worse. Now, how could anyone lose such an easily winnable game? After all, when asked when Shakespeare was born, I could have said "Sometime between 30,000 B.C. and 30,000 A.D." and been pretty sure that I would be right. What trips people up seems to be some combination of pride and overconfidence. The pride prevents you from giving a ridiculously large range (because then your questioner knows you don't have the foggiest idea when Shakespeare was born); the overconfidence makes you make you willing to narrow the range beyond your real range of certainty. In the end, the game isn't testing your knowledge — it's testing your knowledge of your own knowledge (or lack of knowledge).

Our version

In this chapter, we implement something like this quiz game, but with some changes to make it more Web-friendly. For one thing, rather than having the player type in numbers freely, we present a range of choices that the player narrows down further. For another, we don't rely on pride to make the ranges narrow (because people may end up playing this over the Web in the privacy of their own home). Instead we add incentives to the scoring system to make people guess narrowly rather than broadly. Finally, we add in some features familiar from online games, such as levels of difficulty and a list of top scorers.

The upshot is a game that, while it may or may not be fun, is certainly frustrating, which for many people is nearly as good.

Sample screens

Figure 39-1 shows the game screen as it may look to a new arrival. There is a welcome message to the right, and a question to the left, with radio buttons for choosing a range of answers.

Figure 39-1: Start screen

Figure 39-2 shows the screen immediately after the player has answered the first question. Another question is offered on the left, and now the state of the game score is highlighted on the right, showing the correct answers to date, the credit remaining, and the level attained. (See the next section for an explanation of what these things mean.)

Figure 39-2: Continuing play

Finally, Figure 39-3 shows "Game Over," complete with taunting message and a list of high scorers. (There's a corresponding "Game Won" screen in the unlikely event that the user survived all the questions the game could come up with.)

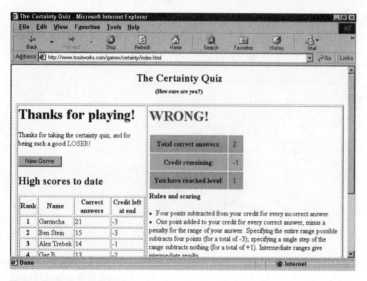

Figure 39-3: Game over

The rules

The basic play cycle is simple: The player is asked a question that requires a numerical answer, and the player responds by choosing a range of values that should include the answer. The goal is to answer as many questions correctly as possible, while surviving in the meantime. Survival depends on credit, which is accumulated by answering questions correctly with a narrow range and is spent by giving wrong answers, or answering questions too broadly.

The exact rewards and penalties are easily tweakable in the code, but in this chapter's version they are:

- ♦ **Correct answers:** One point added to credit, minus a penalty for the size of the range specified. The penalty ranges from zero for answers that use only one step of the possible range, up to four points for making the range as wide as possible.

- ♦ **Incorrect answers:** Four points deducted from credit.

Credit starts at five points, can only rise as high as fifteen points, and the game is over when credit goes below zero.

It is easy to pass by simply submitting your answer without making a choice, since the radio buttons are set to specify the widest possible answer range unless the player changes them.

The penalties are set up so that passing is costly (a total of 1 - 4 = -3 points), but not as costly as guessing wrong (-4 points). The player is better off narrowing the range as much as possible, while still being sure that the real answer is still included.

Playing the game yourself

We have a playable version of this game up at `www.troutworks.com/games/certainty/index.html`, containing many more questions than we include in the sample databases in this chapter. We may change some aspects of the publicly playable game between the time we are writing this and when the book comes out, so we can't guarantee that the public game matches this chapter's code in every respect. The code from this chapter, however, is available at the Web site for this book (`www.troutworks.com/phpbook`).

The Code

The code for this example is almost completely written in an object-oriented style (see Chapter 26 for an introduction to PHP's version of object-oriented programming). Among the classes we define are:

- ♦ **Question:** Each `Question` object includes the text of the question, the correct answer, the lower and upper bounds that are presented to the player, and enough information to display the range of choices that the player can choose from. In addition, `Question` instances track whether or not they are answered correctly.

- ♦ **Game:** There should be one and only one `Game` object in existence at a particular time. Game objects may include up to two question objects (the current question and the previous one), as well as a `GameParameter` instance.

- ♦ **GameParameters:** Contains all the numerical settings that affect how the game behaves and manages some globally available resources such as the database connection.

- ♦ **GameDisplay:** Contains a `Game` instance as a component and does all the work of actually displaying HTML and receiving input. Also contains an instance of `GameText`.

- ♦ **GameText:** A repository for boilerplate HTML that is not dependent on any knowledge of the state of the game. Only this class and `GameDisplay` actually have HTML code in them.

Code files

The code files include definitions for all the classes in the preceding section: `question_class.php`, `game_class.php`, `game_parameters_class.php`, `game_display_class.php`, and `game_text_class.php`. In addition, there are some code files that don't define classes:

- ◆ **index.php:** The first file loaded, that handles sessions and post arguments and creates the GameDisplay object.

- ◆ **certainty_utils.php:** A grab bag of initialization statements (seeding the random-number generator etc.) and math utility functions.

- ◆ **entry_form.php:** A form for adding new questions to the database.

- ◆ **dbvars.php:** The usual file with definitions for username, password, and host for the database connection.

We now take a tour of the code file listings. Rather than building from the ground up as we sometimes do, in this chapter we work from the top down; first the very first page that is actually loaded, then the code that page depends on, and so on until we bottom out in utility functions and database calls. Finally, at the end of the chapter, we show how to construct the database and populate it with questions.

index.php

Listing 39-1 shows index.php, which is the user's entry point. The primary job of this file is to determine where we are in the cycle of play, set up the appropriate PHP objects (either by creating them or by retrieving them from the user's session), and finally, to echo out the display code that the objects generate.

Where we are in the course of a game is determined by a combination of session and POST information; as users arrive for the first time, they find neither a current session nor any POST arguments. Successive pages, however, should have both an active session and useful information submitted from the previous page.

Listing 39-1: index.php

```php
<?php
// Include code files, start up session
include_once("certainty_utils.php");
include_once("game_display_class.php");
session_start();

// Determine state and handle post arguments

// CASE 1: Player is submitting name for high score list
if (get_session_value('game') &&
    get_post_value('HIGHSCORE')) {
  $game_display =
     new GameDisplay(get_session_value('game'));
  $game_display->handleHighScore();
}

// CASE 2: Player is in middle of game that we are tracking
elseif (get_session_value('game') &&
```

```
          !get_post_value('NEW')) {
  $lower = get_post_value('lower');
  $upper = get_post_value('upper');
  $game_display =
     new GameDisplay(get_session_value('game'));
  $game_display->updateWithAnswer($lower, $upper);
}

// CASE 3: Player has either just arrived or has
//    finished a game and asked for a new one.
elseif (!get_post_value('POSTCHECK') ||
        get_post_value('NEW')) {
  $game_display = new GameDisplay(new Game());
}

// CASE 4:  Something is wrong.
  // The page is the result of a POST operation,
  // yet we don't seem to have a live session, so
  // we are not successfully tracking a game.
  // The only thing to do is complain, and ask about
  // cookies.
else {
  $game_display =
    new GameDisplay(new Game());
  $game_display->setProblem(
   "We couldn't track your game.  You may need to ".
   "enable cookies in your browser to play");
}

// Construct string that will be displayed as page
$page_string = $game_display->display();
if (!($problem = $game_display->getProblem())) {
  // Everything is fine
  // Store game state in session so that next
  //    page can pick it up
  set_session_value('game',
                    $game_display->getGame());
}
else {
  // There is a problem somewhere.  Create
  //    an error page.
  $page_string =
    $game_display->makeErrorPage($problem);
  // hope to start fresh next time
  set_session_value('game', new Game());
}

// Actually echo page to browser
echo($page_string);
```

```
?>
```

The object types that `index.php` cares about are `GameDisplay` and `Game`. The `Game` object contains all the state information that needs to be preserved from page to page about where the user is in the game (score, questions asked already, and so on). The `GameDisplay` object contains a `Game` instance, and does everything necessary to produce an HTML page from it.

If the user is starting off for the first time, we create a new `Game` object, relying on the `Game` constructor to initialize it appropriately. For subsequent pages, though we rely on the automatic object serialization feature of PHP sessions to store the `Game` object for us. (The actual definitions of `get_session_value()` and `set_session_value()` are in `certainty_utils.php`, but all that is happening is that we stash the `Game` object in a session. PHP takes care of the serialization that is necessary to read the object into a session and back out again.)

> **CROSS-REFERENCE:** For more on what it means to serialize an object, see Chapter 26; for an explanation of sessions and their workings, see Chapter 27.

Regardless of whether we create a new `Game` object or retrieve the one from the last page, in both cases, we create a new `GameDisplay` object around it and then ask that object for a string that represents the entire HTML page. Our last act is to send that string off to the browser.

> **CAUTION:** PHP 4.1.2 was up to the challenge of automatically serializing our game object, but a test on PHP 4.0.3pl1 failed miserably. This is one of the reasons why we advertised the code in this chapter as only being appropriate for "modern" PHP installations.

game_display_class.php

Almost all of the look-and-feel action for this game is in `game_display_class.php`, as shown in Listing 39-2.

The code file depends on two other files: `game_class.php`, and `game_text_class.php` — the former contains most of the logic for the inner workings of the game, whereas the latter just contains some boilerplate text. The job of the `GameDisplay` class is to extract all the information from the game state necessary to produce actual HTML pages.

Although PHP class definitions cannot currently enforce public vs. private access, in this chapter we follow a convention that we mentioned in Chapter 26 — we separate the functions that are intended to be used publicly from the functions that are intended only for internal use.

The public functions (*interface*) to `GameDisplay` are:

♦ `GameDisplay()` (the constructor).

♦ Various accessor and setter functions for interacting with private member data.

♦ updateWithAnswer(), which is called with data from the user's submission of a guess.

♦ makeErrorPage(), which returns HTML to display if something has gone wrong.

♦ display(), which returns HTML to display when everything has gone right.

Listing 39-2: `game_display_class.php`

```php
<?php
include_once("game_class.php");
include_once("game_text_class.php");
class GameDisplay
{
  // PRIVATE VARIABLES

  //    presentation
  var $_pageTitle = "The Certainty Quiz";
  var $_blueColor = "#AAAAFF";
  var $_redColor = "#FFAAAA";

  //    contents
  var $_game = NULL;
  var $_gameText;
  var $_highScorePosted = FALSE;
  var $_problem = NULL;

  // CONSTRUCTOR

  function GameDisplay ($game) {
    $this->_game = $game;
    $this->_gameText = new GameText();
  }

  // PUBLIC FUNCTIONS
  //    accessors
  function getPageTitle() {
    return($this->_pageTitle);
  }
  function getBlueColor() {
    return($this->_blueColor);
  }
  function getRedColor() {
    return($this->_redColor);
  }
  function getGame() {
    return($this->_game);
  }
  function getHighScorePosted() {
    return($this->_highScorePosted);
```

```
  }
  function getProblem () {
    if ($this->_problem) {
      return($this->_problem);
    }
    if (!$this->_game) {
      return("No game object");
    }
    else return($this->_game->getProblem());
  }

  //   setters
  function setProblem($problem_string) {
    $this->_problem = $problem_string;
  }

  function updateWithAnswer ($lower, $upper) {
    $this->_game->updateWithAnswer($lower, $upper);
  }

  function makeErrorPage ($problem_string) {
    // constructs the HTML page to display when
    /// something has gone horribly wrong
    $top_matter_string =
        $this->_makeTopMatter($this->_pageTitle);
    $page_string = <<<EOT
$top_matter_string
</H2></CENTER>
<TABLE BORDER=2>
<TR>
<CENTER>
<H2>We're sorry, but the game is not available
right now.</H2><H4>($problem_string)</H4>
</CENTER>
</TR></TABLE>
</BODY></HTML>
EOT;
    return($page_string);
  }

  function display () {
    // returns entire page as string ---
    // backbone structure of page, plus
    // overridable methods to print components

    // sanity checks
    if (!$this->_game ||
        !is_object($this->_game)) {
      $this->_problem =
```

```
      "Cannot find valid game object";
  return("");
}
elseif (!$this->_game->getDbConnection()) {
  $this->_problem =
    "No database connection";
  return("");
}

// display of apparently valid page
else {
  $top_matter_string =
    $this->_makeTopMatter($this->_pageTitle);
  $current_question =
    $this->_currentQuestionString();
  $previous_question =
    $this->_previousQuestionString();
  $game_state =
    $this->_gameStateString();
  $introduction =
    $this->_gameText->introduction();
  $rules =
    $this->_gameText->rules();
  if ($this->_game->getGameLost()) {
    $left_side =
      $this->_gameText->gameLostText() .
      $this->_highScoreString();
  }
  elseif ($this->_game->getGameWon()) {
    $left_side =
      $this->_gameText->gameWonText() .
      $this->_highScoreString();
  }
  else {
    $left_side = $current_question;
  }
  if ($this->_game->getPreviousQuestion()) {
    $right_side =
      "<TABLE><TR><TD>
      $previous_question
      </TD></TR><TR><TD>
      $game_state
      </TD></TR><TR><TD>
      $rules
      </TD></TR></TABLE>";
  }
  else {
    $right_side =
      "<TABLE><TR><TD>
```

```
            $introduction
            </TD></TR>
            <TR><TD>
            $rules
            </TD></TR><TR><TD>
            $game_state
            </TD></TR>
            </TABLE>";
        }

    // actually construct page
$page_string = <<<EOT
$top_matter_string
</H2></CENTER>
<TABLE BORDER=2>
<TR>
<TD VALIGN=TOP WIDTH=40% >$left_side</TD>
<TD VALIGN=TOP WIDTH=60% >$right_side</TD>
</TR></TABLE>
</BODY></HTML>
EOT;
        return($page_string);
    }
  }

  function _makeTopMatter ($title) {
    // returns HTML fragment that heads both
    //  regular page and error page, containing
    //  HTML head and title
    $return_string = <<<EOT
<HTML><HEAD><TITLE>$title</TITLE></HEAD>
<BODY BGCOLOR=#FFFFFF><CENTER>
<H1>$title<BR>
<FONT SIZE=-1 COLOR=BLUE>
(How sure <B>are</B> you?)</FONT>
</H1></CENTER>
EOT;
    return($return_string);
  }

  function handleHighScore () {
    // Handles database update for case where player
    //  has earned high score, and has submitted
    //  a name for the record
    if (!$this->_highScorePosted) {
      $this->_highScorePosted = TRUE;
      if (get_post_value('NICKNAME') &&
          get_post_value('ANSWER_COUNT') &&
          get_post_value('CREDIT') &&
```

```
        get_post_value('CHECKSUM') &&
        $this->_checksumChecks(
          get_post_value('ANSWER_COUNT'),
          get_post_value('CREDIT'),
          get_post_value('CHECKSUM'))) {
      $name = get_post_value('NICKNAME');
      $answer_count = get_post_value('ANSWER_COUNT');
      $credit = get_post_value('CREDIT');
      $query = "insert into high_scores
                (name, answer_count, credit)
                values
                ('$name', $answer_count, $credit)";
      $connection =
       $this->_game->_gameParameters->getDbConnection();
      $result = mysql_query($query, $connection);
    }
    else {
      // do nothing -- failure to add high score
      // should not be a deal killer
    }
  }
}

// PRIVATE FUNCTIONS
function _currentQuestionString () {
  global $PHP_SELF;
  return("<H2>" .
         $this->_game->getCurrentQuestionText() .
         "</H2>" .
         "<FORM METHOD=POST ACTION=\"$PHP_SELF\">" .
         "<INPUT TYPE=HIDDEN NAME=POSTCHECK VALUE=1>" .
         $this->_distractorString(
             $this->_game->getCurrentQuestion()) .
         "</FORM>");
}

function _distractorString ($question) {
  // creates the actual HTML for presentation of
  //  radio-button alternatives for guesses.
  //  Assumes that the array representing the
  //    actual alternatives has been calculated in
  //    advance, retrievable from the question using
  //    getDistractorArray
  $distractor_array = $question->getDistractorArray();
  $distractor_string = "<TABLE><TR VALIGN=TOP><TD>";
  $distractor_string .=
    "<TABLE BORDER=1 BGCOLOR=\"AAAAFF\"><TR><TH>
     </TH><TH>At least</TH><TH>Not more than</TH>";
  $count = 1;  // 1-based labels are preferable,
```

```php
                    // so we can just use if ($label) ...
  $total = count($distractor_array);
  foreach ($distractor_array as $distractor) {
    $lower_selected = ($count == 1) ?
      "CHECKED" : "";
    $upper_selected = ($count == $total) ?
      "CHECKED" : "";
    $formatted_distractor =
      ($distractor >= 10000) ?
        number_format($distractor) : $distractor;
    $distractor_string .=
      "<TR><TD>$formatted_distractor</TD>
         <TD><INPUT TYPE=RADIO NAME=\"lower\"
             VALUE=$count
             $lower_selected ></TD>\n" .
      "<TD><INPUT TYPE=RADIO NAME=\"upper\"
         VALUE=$count
         $upper_selected ></TD></TR>\n";
    $count++;
  }
  $distractor_string .= "</TABLE>";
  $distractor_string .= "</TD><TD>";
  $distractor_string .=
    "<INPUT NAME=\"Submit guess\" VALUE=\"Submit guess\"
         TYPE=SUBMIT>";
  $distractor_string .= "</TD></TR></TABLE>";

  return($distractor_string);
}

function _previousQuestionString () {
  if (!$this->_game->getPreviousQuestion()) {
    $return_string = "";
  }
  else {
    $return_string =
      $this->_game->previousQuestionCorrect() ?
        $this->_rightString() :
        $this->_wrongString();
  }
  return($return_string);
}

function _rightString () {
  return("<H1><FONT COLOR=GREEN>RIGHT!</FONT></H1>");
}

function _wrongString () {
  return("<H1><FONT COLOR=RED>WRONG!</FONT></H1>");
```

```
}

function _highScoreEligible () {
  // takes a game-ending score, and queries the
  //  DB to see if the player is eligible for the
  //  high score list
  $query = "select name, answer_count, credit
            from high_scores
            order by answer_count desc, credit desc
            limit 10";
  $connection =
    $this->_game->getDbConnection();
  if ($connection && is_resource($connection)) {
    $result = mysql_query($query, $connection);
    $eligible = false;
    if (mysql_num_rows($result) > 9) {
      while ($row = mysql_fetch_assoc($result)) {
        $answer_count = $row['answer_count'];
        $credit = $row['credit'];
        if (($this->_game->getCorrectAnswers()
              > $answer_count) ||
            (($this->_game->getCorrectAnswers()
              == $answer_count) &&
            ($this->_game->_credit > $credit))) {
          $eligible = TRUE;
          break;
        }
      }
    }
    else {
      $eligible = TRUE;
    }
    return($eligible);
  }
  else {
    $this->_problem =
      "Game display has no database connection";
    return(FALSE);
  }
}

// Checksum is calculated when posting a score
//  (comprised of a number of correct answers plus
//  credit remaining) and the checksum is compared with
//  the submitted scores.  A first line of defense against
//  spoofing (unless, of course, the checksum scheme is
//  published in a book or something).
function _checksumChecks ($answer_count, $credit,
                          $checksum) {
```

```
      return($checksum ==
            $this->_makeCheckSum($answer_count, $credit));
}

function _makeChecksum ($answer_count, $credit) {
  return ((round($credit)) * 17) *
            ($answer_count * 31);
}

function _postHighScoreString () {
  // The greeting plus HTML form for actually submitting
  //  a name to the high scores list
  global $PHP_SELF;
  $answer_count = $this->_game->getCorrectAnswers();
  $credit = $this->_game->getCredit();
  $checksum = $this->_makeChecksum($answer_count, $credit);
  $result_string =
    "<H2>Congratulations! You have a high score</H2>".
    "Enter your name (or a nickname) for the high ".
    "scores list:".
    "<FORM METHOD=POST ACTION=\"$PHP_SELF\" >".
    "<INPUT NAME=NICKNAME TYPE=TEXT SIZE = 30>".
    "<INPUT NAME=ANSWER_COUNT TYPE=HIDDEN ".
      "VALUE=$answer_count>".
    "<INPUT NAME=CREDIT TYPE=HIDDEN ".
      "VALUE=$credit>".
    "<INPUT NAME=CHECKSUM TYPE=HIDDEN ".
      "VALUE=$checksum>".
    "<INPUT NAME=Submit TYPE=SUBMIT ".
      "VALUE=Submit >".
    "<INPUT TYPE=HIDDEN NAME=POSTCHECK VALUE=1>" .
    "<INPUT TYPE=HIDDEN NAME=HIGHSCORE VALUE=1>" .
    "<FORM>";
  return($result_string);
}

function _highScoreString () {
  // The table of high scores itself, including
  //  the database interaction necessary to retrieve it
  if ($this->_highScoreEligible() &&
      !$this->_highScorePosted) {
    $result_string = $this->_postHighScoreString();
  }
  else {
    $result_string = "";
  }
  $result_string .=
    "<H2>High scores to date</H2>".
    "<TABLE BORDER=1><TR><TH>Rank</TH>".
```

```
      "<TH>Name</TH><TH>Correct answers</TH>".
      "<TH>Credit left at end</TH></TR>";
    $query = "select name, answer_count, credit
              from high_scores
              order by answer_count desc, credit desc
              limit 10";
    $connection =
      $this->_game->_gameParameters->getDbConnection();
    if ($connection && is_resource($connection)) {
      $result = mysql_query($query, $connection);
      $rank = 1;
      while ($row = mysql_fetch_assoc($result)) {
        $name = $row['name'];
        $answer_count = $row['answer_count'];
        $credit = (int) ($row['credit']);
        $result_string .=
          "<TR><TH>$rank</TH><TD>$name</TD>".
          "<TD>$answer_count</TD><TD>$credit</TD></TR>";
        $rank++;
      }
      $result_string .= "</TABLE>";
      return($result_string);
    }
    else {
      $this->problem =
        "Game display has no database connection<BR>";
    }
  }

  function _gameStateString () {
    // The HTML table
    $correct_answers = $this->_game->getCorrectAnswers();
    $credit = round_to_digits($this->_game->_credit,2);
    $level = $this->_game->_level;
    return("<TABLE CELLPADDING=10>".
    "<TR BGCOLOR=$this->_blueColor><TH>Total correct answers:</TH>".
    "<TD>$correct_answers</TD></TR>".
    "<TR BGCOLOR=$this->_redColor><TH>Credit remaining:</TH>".
    "<TD>$credit</TD></TR>".
    "<TR BGCOLOR=$this->_blueColor><TH>You have reached level:</TH>".
    "<TD>$level</TD></TR></TABLE>");
  }
}
?>
```

Most of the class's internal functions involve querying the Game object for information that it
then wraps up in HTML strings. One of the more interesting functions of this type is
distractor_string(), which creates the actual display of alternatives for the answer
range. The general division of labor here is:

♦ The upper and lower bounds for the answer are specified in the database, as well as how many choices should be displayed and how they should be scaled.

♦ The Question object takes this information and creates all the intermediate steps of the answer range as it is constructed.

♦ The GameDisplay object queries the game for the current question and then queries that question to discover the upper and lower bounds and the intermediate steps. It then simply wraps those values in HTML to present radio-button alternatives, with the maximum answer range preselected.

game_text_class.php

Your humble authors try really hard to make this stuff interesting, but in this case, we must declare defeat. The GameText class just wraps up some boilerplate HTML into member functions so that the GameDisplay class can ask for it. Enough said?

The functions use our favorite technique for creating large chunks of boilerplate, which is the *heredoc* syntax. (See Chapter 10 for more on the uses of heredoc.) Listing 39-3 shows the game_text_class.php.

Listing 39-3: `game_text_class.php`

```php
<?php
class GameText
{

function GameText () {
  // no vars, nothing for constructor to do
}

function introduction () {
$intro = <<<EOT
<H2>Welcome to the Certainty Quiz!</H2>
The game that tests
<LI>how much you know about how much <B>and</B> <LI>how much you know
about
how much you know about how much!
<H4>The object</H4> The goal is to answer as many questions
correctly as possible.
Answer questions
(starting with the first one at the left), by choosing
values above and below where you think the right answer lies.
Answers are correct if they include the real answer in the range.
The narrower your guesses, the longer you'll survive.
There are ten levels;  if you think the questions are
too easy, keep going.
EOT;
  return($intro);
  }
```

```php
function rules () {
$rules = <<<EOT
<H4>Rules and scoring</H4>
<LI>Four points subtracted from your credit for every incorrect answer.
<LI>One point added to your credit for every correct answer,
minus a penalty for the range of your answer.  Specifying the
entire range possible subtracts four points (for a total of -3);
specifying a single step of the range subtracts nothing
 (for a total of +1).  Intermediate ranges give intermediate results.
<LI>Credit is capped at 15.
<LI>Whenever your credit falls below zero, the game is over.
EOT;
  return($rules);
}

function gameLostText () {
global $PHP_SELF;
$game_over = <<<EOT
<H1>Thanks for playing!</H1>
Thanks for taking the certainty quiz, and for being
such a good <FONT COLOR=RED>LOSER!</FONT><BR>
<FORM METHOD=POST ACTION="$PHP_SELF">
<INPUT TYPE=SUBMIT NAME=NEW VALUE="New Game">
<INPUT TYPE=HIDDEN NAME=POSTCHECK VALUE=1>
</FORM>
EOT;
return($game_over);
}

function gameWonText () {
global $PHP_SELF;
$game_over = <<<EOT
<H1>You won!</H1>
Thanks for taking the certainty quiz, and for
beating it.  We bow to your superior knowledge
of what you know, and what you don't know.
<FORM METHOD=POST ACTION="$PHP_SELF">
<INPUT TYPE=SUBMIT NAME=NEW VALUE="New Game">
<INPUT TYPE=HIDDEN NAME=POSTCHECK VALUE=1>
</FORM>
EOT;
return($game_over);
}

}
?>
```

game_class.php

In this section, we get to the basic logic of the game. The Game object contains everything worth remembering about the current state of the game, as well as methods for updating it.

Data members

It's worth listing the important pieces of data that the Game object tracks:

- The current question (an instance of class Question).
- The previous question, if any (an instance of class Question).
- The questions that have been asked at this level (an array of database IDs).
- The questions that could still be asked at this level (an array of database IDs).
- The game's numerical defaults (an instance of class GameParameters).
- Numerical variables that track the game's state (credit, questions answered, and so on).

Public functions

As with the GameDisplay class, let's list the functions that the Game class exposes to callers:

- The constructor function (Game()).
- Various accessor functions for member data.

updateWithAnswer() takes the player's upper and lower guesses and updates the game's state accordingly, including both update of scores and setting up the next question to be asked.

Database interaction

The actual questions and answers that the game displays are retrieved from a back-end MySQL database. There are two main types of interaction with that database:

- Whenever the player moves to a new level (including the first one), the Game object retrieves the IDs of all questions that may be asked at that level and scrambles their ordering. This randomized list is propagated along with the Game object from page to page within a particular level of the game.
- Whenever a new question is actually ready to be asked, the Game object pops its database ID off the list constructed and then queries the question database to retrieve all the rest of the question's information (the text of the question, the correct answer, the range of possible values to present, and so on).

Listing 39-4 shows the game_class.php.

Listing 39-4: game_class.php

```php
<?php
include_once("certainty_utils.php");
include_once("game_parameters_class.php");
include_once("question_class.php");
```

```
class Game
{
  // PRIVATE VARIABLES
  var $_gameParameters;
  var $_dbConnection = NULL;
  var $_currentQuestion = NULL;
  var $_previousQuestion = NULL;
  var $_credit = 0.0;
  var $_level;
  var $_questionIdsAtLevel;  // an array of ids
  var $_questionsAskedAtLevel = 0; // a count
  var $_totalQuestions = 0;
  var $_correctAnswers = 0;
  var $_problem = "";  // might be string indicating issue
  var $_gameLost = FALSE;
  var $_gameWon = FALSE;

  // CONSTRUCTOR
  function Game () {
    $this->_gameParameters = new GameParameters();
    $this->_dbConnection =
      $this->_gameParameters->getDbConnection();
    if (!$this->_dbConnection) {
      $this->_problem = "No database connection";
    }
    else {
      $this->_previousQuestion;
      $this->_currentQuestion;
      $this->_correctAnswers = 0;
      $this->_level =
        $this->_gameParameters->getStartingLevel();
      $this->_credit =
        $this->_gameParameters->getStartingCredit();
      // make a list of questions to be asked at the
      //   starting level
      $this->_setupQuestionIds();
      // actually retrieve the first question
      $this->_installQuestion();
    }
  }

  // PUBLIC FUNCTIONS
  // accessors
  function getGameParameters()
    {return($this->_gameParameters);}

  function getCurrentQuestion()
    {return($this->_currentQuestion);}
```

```php
function getPreviousQuestion()
  {return($this->_previousQuestion);}

function getCredit() {return($this->_credit);}

function getLevel() {return($this->_level);}

function getQuestionsAskedAtLevel()
  {return($this->_questionsAskedAtLevel);}

function getTotalQuestions()
  {return($this->_totalQuestions);}

function getCorrectAnswers()
  {return($this->_correctAnswers);}

function getProblem()
  {return($this->_problem);}

function getGameLost()
  {return($this->_gameLost);}

function getGameWon()
  {return($this->_gameWon);}

function getCurrentQuestionText() {
  if (!is_object($this->_currentQuestion)) {
    print("What is it?<BR>");
    print_r($this->_currentQuestion);
  }
  else {
    return($this->_currentQuestion->getQuestion());
  }
}

function previousQuestionCorrect() {
  return($this->_previousQuestion->getCorrect());
}

function getDbConnection () {
  if (!$this->_dbConnection) {
    $this->_dbConnection =
      $this->_gameParameters->getDbConnection();
  }
  return($this->_dbConnection);
}

function updateWithAnswer ($lower, $upper) {
```

```php
    // The main modifying function for a game object.
    // Takes a player's upper and lower guess, determines
    //  correctness, updates scores, determines if the
    //  player has graduated to the next level, and
    //  swaps in the next question.
    $this->_previousQuestion = $this->_currentQuestion;
    $this->_previousQuestion->updateWithAnswer($lower,
                                               $upper);

    $this->_updateScores();
    $this->_maybeChangeLevel();
    if (!($this->_gameLost || $this->_gameWon)) {
      $this->_installQuestion();
    }
  }
}

// PRIVATE FUNCTIONS
function _installQuestion () {
  // actually retrieve a question from the database
  //  and create a corresponding instance of Question
  if (count($this->_questionIdsAtLevel) > 0) {
    // pop a question off the randomized list
    $question_id =
      array_pop($this->_questionIdsAtLevel);
    $query =
      "select id, question, answer,
      upper_limit, lower_limit, scaling_type
      from question
      where id = $question_id";
    if (!$this->_dbConnection) {
      $this->_dbConnection =
        $this->_gameParameters->getDbConnection();
    }
    if ($this->_dbConnection &&
        is_resource($this->_dbConnection)) {
      $result = mysql_query($query,
                            $this->_dbConnection);
      if ($row = mysql_fetch_assoc($result)) {
        $this->_currentQuestion =
          new Question(
            $row['id'],
            $row['question'],
            $row['answer'],
            $row['lower_limit'],
            $row['upper_limit'],
            10,
            $row['scaling_type']);
        $this->_questionsAskedAtLevel++;
      }
      else {
```

```
          $this->_problem =
             "Problem retrieving question from database";
        }
      }
      else {
        $this->_problem =
           "Problem querying question database";
      }
    }
    else {
      $this->_problem =
         "Could not find any questions to ask";
    }
  }

  function _setupQuestionIds () {
    $this->_questionIdsAtLevel =
      $this->_getQuestionIdsAtLevel($this->_level);
  }

  function _getQuestionIdsAtLevel ($level) {
    // to be used at time of graduation to a new level -
    // retrieves the new ids (only) of all questions at
    // the level, and shuffles them into a random order.
    $return_array = array();
    $query = "select id from question
              where level = $level";
    $this->getDbConnection();
    if (!$this->_dbConnection) {
      $this->_problem = "No database connection";
    }
    else {
      $result = mysql_query($query,
                            $this->_dbConnection);
      while ($row = mysql_fetch_assoc($result)) {
        array_push($return_array, $row['id']);
      }
    }
    // randomize the order of the questions
    $return_array = create_randomized_array($return_array);
    return($return_array);
  }

  function _updateScores () {
    // Change the current score based both on
    //  whether the player got the answer right and on
    //  the spread between the player's upper and lower
    //  guess.  Calculations depend on settings from
    //  the GameParameters class.
```

```php
  if ($this->_previousQuestion->rightAnswer()) {
    $this->_correctAnswers++;
    $this->_credit +=
      $this->_gameParameters->getRightAnswerCredit() -
      ($this->_previousQuestion->getAnswerSpread() *
       $this->_gameParameters->getAnswerSpreadDebit());
  }
  else {
    $new_credit =
    $this->_credit =
      $this->_credit -
      $this->_gameParameters->getWrongAnswerDebit();
  }
  // enforce cap on credit
  $this->_credit =
    min($this->_credit,
        $this->_gameParameters->getMaximumCredit());
}

function _maybeChangeLevel () {
  if ($this->_credit < 0.0) {
    $this->_gameLost = TRUE;
  }
  else {
    $params = $this->_gameParameters;
    $current_level = $this->_level;
    if ($current_level >
        $params->getMaximumLevel()) {
      $this->_gameWon = TRUE;
    }
    else {
      // find out if questions remain to be
      //  asked at this level
      if (($this->_questionsAskedAtLevel >=
          $params->getQuestionsPerLevel($current_level)) ||
          (count($this->_questionIdsAtLevel) == 0)) {
            // either we have asked the limit of
            // questions per level, OR we have simply run out
            $this->_level++;
            $this->_questionsAskedAtLevel = 0;
            $this->_setupQuestionIds();
            // note recursive call --- it's possible
            //  that no questions were found, and we have
            //  to keep going
            $this->_maybeChangeLevel();
      }
    }
  }
}
```

```
function __sleep () {
  // make sure to serialize all fields except
  //  the database connection (has to be recreated)
  //  and the previous question (no point).
  return(array(
          '_gameParameters',
          '_currentQuestion',
          '_credit',
          '_level',
          '_questionIdsAtLevel',
          '_questionsAskedAtLevel',
          '_correctAnswers',
          '_totalQuestions',
          '_problem',
          '_gameLost',
          '_gameWon'));
  }
}
?>
```

Handling an answer

Here are the steps that a Game object goes through in dealing with a guess range submitted by a player (in the function updateWithAnswer):

1. Move the current question object to the previous question slot.

2. Update the (now previous) question with the upper and lower ranges of the guess (which are still in terms of step numbers from the form rather than actual values).

3. Query the previous question to discover the range of the guess and whether the question was correctly answered. Update all scores (credit, correct answers) appropriately.

4. Decide whether to promote the player to a new level now. If so, retrieve the database IDs of all questions that may be asked at that level. Randomize the order of the question list.

5. If the game has not yet ended, grab a new question ID from the randomized list and use it to ask the database for a new question. Turn that data into a Question object and make it the current question.

Serialization and sleep()

The sleep() function is called to do cleanup whenever an object is serialized and also returns a list of all the member variables that should be recorded in a serialization. The Game class makes use of only the latter capability — all member variables except the previous question and the database connection itself are retained as the object is stored in the session for the next page's use.

game_parameters.php

The single instance of the GameParameters class, shown in Listing 39-5, packages up all the default numbers that we may want to customize in making a new version of the game (the penalties and rewards, the number of levels, the starting and maximum credit, and so on). In addition, this object manages global access to the database connection.

Listing 39-5: `game_parameters.php`

```php
<?php
include_once("certainty_utils.php");
include_once("dbvars.php");  // should really be moved out of the web
tree

class GameParameters {

  // PRIVATE VARIABLES
  var $_dbConnection = NULL;
  var $_startingLevel = 1;
  var $_maximumLevel = 10;
  var $_startingCredit = 5.0;
  var $_maximumCredit = 15.0;
  var $_questionsPerLevel = 3;
  var $_rightAnswerCredit = 1.0;
  var $_wrongAnswerDebit = 4.0;
  var $_answerSpreadDebit = 4.0;

  // CONSTRUCTOR
  function GameParameters () {
    // all fields set by default values
  }

  // PUBLIC FUNCTIONS
  // accessors

  function getStartingLevel () {
    return($this->_startingLevel);
  }

  function getMaximumLevel () {
    return($this->_maximumLevel);
  }

  function getStartingCredit () {
    return($this->_startingCredit);
  }

  function getMaximumCredit () {
    return($this->_maximumCredit);
```

```
  }

  function getRightAnswerCredit () {
    return($this->_rightAnswerCredit);
  }

  function getWrongAnswerDebit () {
    return($this->_wrongAnswerDebit);
  }

  function getAnswerSpreadDebit () {
    return($this->_answerSpreadDebit);
  }

  function getQuestionsPerLevel () {
    return($this->_questionsPerLevel);
  }

  function getDbConnection () {
    global $host, $user, $pass, $db;  // included from dbvars.inc
    if ($this->_dbConnection &&
        is_resource($this->dbConnection)) {
      return($_dbConnection);
    }
    else {
      // suppress warnings about connection,
      // will handle at higher level if failed
      $connection =
        @mysql_connect($host, $user, $pass);
      if ($connection &&
          mysql_select_db($db, $connection)) {
        return($connection);
      }
      else {
        return(FALSE);
      }
    }
  }

  function __sleep () {
    return(array('_startingLevel',
                 '_startingCredit',
                 '_rightAnswerCredit',
                 '_wrongAnswerDebit',
                 '_answerSpreadDebit',
                 '_questionsPerLevel'));
  }
}
?>
```

certainty_utils.php

This code file, shown in Listing 39-6, is a grab-bag for capabilities and definitions that do not fit neatly into a particular class and that are used in more than one other code file.

Everything in `certainty_utils.php` fits into one of a few categories:

♦ Initial declarations (seeding the random number generator, setting the error-reporting level).

♦ Abstraction functions for session and post variables. (The treatment of these variables is changing as of PHP 4.1 and 4.2, and these functions attempt to paper over the dfferences.)

Utility functions for calculating intermediate answer values and for randomizing question lists.

Listing 39-6: `certainty_utils.php`

```php
<?php

// Definitions and utility functions for the
//   Certainty Quiz game
error_reporting(E_ALL);
// enumeration constants for the scaling of distractors
define("CERTAINTY_LINEAR", 1);
define("CERTAINTY_GEOMETRIC", 2);

// Seed the random number generator
srand((double) microtime() * 1000000);

// A hack to retrieve the value of POST values
//   without explicitly checking PHP versions.
function get_post_value ($var_name) {
  global $HTTP_POST_VARS;
  if (IsSet($_POST) &&
      IsSet($_POST[$var_name])) {
    return($_POST[$var_name]);
  }
  elseif (IsSet($HTTP_POST_VARS) &&
          IsSet($HTTP_POST_VARS[$var_name])) {
    return($HTTP_POST_VARS[$var_name]);
  }
  else {
    return(FALSE);
  }
}

function get_session_value ($var_name) {
  global $HTTP_SESSION_VARS;
  if (IsSet($_SESSION) &&
      IsSet($_SESSION[$var_name])) {
```

```php
      return($_SESSION[$var_name]);
  }
  elseif (IsSet($HTTP_SESSION_VARS) &&
          IsSet($HTTP_SESSION_VARS[$var_name])) {
    return($HTTP_SESSION_VARS[$var_name]);
  }
  else {
    return(FALSE);
  }
}

function set_session_value ($var_name, $value) {
  global $HTTP_SESSION_VARS;
  if (IsSet($_SESSION)) {
    $_SESSION[$var_name] = $value;
    $HTTP_SESSION_VARS[$var_name] = $value;
  }
  else {
    $HTTP_SESSION_VARS[$var_name] = $value;
  }
}

// Numerical functions

function round_to_digits ($number, $digits) {
  if ($number < 0) {
    return(- round_to_digits(- $number, $digits));
  }
  else if ($number == 0) {
    return($number);
  }
  else {
    $tens =
      floor(log10($number));
    $divisor = pow(10, ($tens - $digits));
    $significant = (1.0 * $number) /
      $divisor;
    $rounded = round($significant);
    return($rounded * $divisor);
  }
}

function nth_root_initial($product, $n)
{
  $estimate = sqrt($product);
  $roots = 2;
  while ($roots < $n) {
    $estimate = sqrt($estimate);
    $roots = $roots * 2;
```

```php
    }
    return($estimate);
}

function nth_root ($product, $n) {
  if (($product <= 1) ||
      ($n < 2)) {
    die("Arguments to nth_root should be ".
        "product (greater than 1) and " .
        "n (greater than 1)");
  }
  $initial_estimate =
    nth_root_initial($product, $n);
  return(nth_root_aux($product, $n,
          $initial_estimate,
          20000,
          0.0001));
}

function nth_root_aux ($product, $n,
                       $guess,
                       $iterations_left,
                       $desired_difference) {
  if ($iterations_left <= 0) {
    return($guess);
  }
  else {
    $guessed_product = pow($guess, $n);
    if (abs($guessed_product - $product)
        < $desired_difference) {
      return($guess);
    }
    else {
      $new_guess =
        $guess -
          ((pow($guess, $n) - $product) /
            ($n * pow($guess, $n-1)));
      return(nth_root_aux($product, $n,
                          $new_guess,
                          $iterations_left - 1,
                          $desired_difference));
    }
  }
}

function create_randomized_array ($in_array) {
   // Assumes input is simple list, with keys
   //  equal to 0,...,n
   // Returns similar list, with keys as in input
```

```
//  but values in randomized order
// Assumes prior call to srand()
$in_array_length = count($in_array);
$working_array = array();
for ($i = 0; $i < $in_array_length; $i++) {
   $rand_value = rand();
   $working_array[$i] = $rand_value;
}
asort($working_array);  // orders by random value
$return_array = array();
$working_keys = array_keys($working_array);
foreach ($working_keys as $int_key) {
   array_push($return_array,
       $in_array[$int_key]);
}
return($return_array);
}
?>
```

The functions in `certainty_utils.php` take care of figuring out all the intermediate guesses between the lowest value offered to the user and the highest value. In addition, there's a scaling option, which determines whether the intermediate values grow linearly or geometrically. (If you think that the number "between" 10 and 1000 is 100, then you are scaling geometrically; if you think the number between 10 and 1000 is 505, then you are scaling linearly.) The functions for finding nth roots are used in doing the geometric scaling.

The `create_randomized_array()` function is what we use to scramble the order of questions within a level. See Chapter 11 for our rant about this function and why we prefer it to `shuffle()`.

question_class.php

Finally, we get down to the actual questions that are pulled from our database of questions to ask. The definition of the `Question` class is shown in Listing 39-7. The public functions here are:

♦ The constructor (`Question()`), which is given the question, correct answer, the upper and lower bounds, the number of steps in the guesses, and the type of scaling (linear or geometric).

♦ Various accessor functions, such as `getAnswer()`, `getQuestion()`, `getScalingType()`

♦ `updateWithAnswer()`, which bottoms out here by actually translating the Web form's step numbers to values for the guesses, comparing those guesses to the real answer.

♦ `getAnswerSpread()`, which returns a measure of how narrow the guess was.

Listing 39-7: `question_class.php`

```php
<?php
include_once("certainty_utils.php");

class Question
{
  // PRIVATE VARIABLES
  var $_id; // ID in database
  var $_question; // text of question
  var $_answer; // correct numeric answer
  var $_lowerLimit; // smallest value in distractors
  var $_upperLimit; // largest value in distractors
  var $_distractorCount; // number of dist. presented
  var $_scalingType;  // representing linear vs. geometric
  var $_distractorArray; // contains all dist presented
  var $_lowerGuess = NULL; // player's lower bound
  var $_upperGuess = NULL; // player's upper bound
  var $_correct = NULL;  // TRUE or FALSE after guess

  // CONSTRUCTOR
  function Question($id, $question,
                    $answer,
                    $lower_limit,
                    $upper_limit,
                    $distractor_count,
                    $scaling_type) {
    $this->_id = $id;
    $this->_question = $question;
    $this->_answer = $answer;
    $this->_lowerLimit = $lower_limit;
    $this->_upperLimit = $upper_limit;
    $this->_distractorCount = $distractor_count;
    $this->_scalingType = $scaling_type;
    $this->_distractorArray =
        $this->_makeDistractors($lower_limit,
                  $upper_limit,
                  $distractor_count,
                  $scaling_type);
  }

  // PUBLIC FUNCTIONS

  // accessors

  function getId () {return($this->_id);}
  function getQuestion () {return($this->_question);}
  function getAnswer () {return($this->_answer);}
  function getCorrect() {return($this->_correct);}
```

```php
function rightAnswer() {return($this->_correct);}
function getDistractorCount() {return($this->_correct);}
function getScalingType() {return($this->_scalingType);}
function getDistractorArray() {return($this->_distractorArray);}
function getLowerGuess() {return($this->_lowerGuess);}
function getUpperGuess() {return($this->_upperGuess);}

function getAnswerSpread () {
  $answer_range = count($this->_distractorArray) - 1;
  if (IsSet($this->_lowerGuess) &&
      IsSet($this->_upperGuess)) {
    $lower = $this->_lowerGuess;
    $upper = $this->_upperGuess;
    if ($upper < $lower) {
      print("Range problem!");
    }
    else {
      $spread =
              (max($upper - $lower, 1) - 1)
              / ($answer_range - 1);
      return($spread);
    }
  }
  else {
    print("Answer vars not set!");
    return(1.0);
  }
}

function updateWithAnswer($lower, $upper) {
  // takes a lower and upper guess from player, and
  //  determines if the guesses bound the right answer
  $this->_lowerGuess = $lower;
  $this->_upperGuess = $upper;
  $upper_value = NULL;
  $lower_value = NULL;
  $count = 1;
  foreach ($this->_distractorArray as $distractor) {
    if ($count == $lower) {
      $lower_value = $distractor;
    }
    if ($count == $upper) {
      $upper_value = $distractor;
    }
    $count++;
  }
  if (IsSet($lower_value) && IsSet($upper_value)) {
    if (($lower_value <= $this->_answer) &&
        ($upper_value >= $this->_answer)) {
```

```
        $this->_correct = TRUE;
      }
    else {
      $this->_correct = FALSE;
      }
  }
  else {
    $this->_correct = NULL;
  }
}


// PRIVATE FUNCTIONS
function _makeDistractors ($lower, $upper,
                            $distractor_count,
                            $linear_or_geometric)
// Create the array of intermediate values between
//  the upper bound and the lower bound on guesses
//  that the player can choose from.  Depending on
//  a flag in each row of the question database,
//  the scaling of possible answers ("distractors")
//  can be linear (10, 20, 30 ...) or geometric
//  (10, 20, 40, 80 ...)
// Code for construction of geometric distractors can
//  blow up for some arguments, so arguments are
//  checked before calls to make_distractors_geometric
//  are allowed.  Failures default back to linear.
{
  if (($linear_or_geometric == CERTAINTY_GEOMETRIC) &&
      ($this->safeGeometricArguments($upper, $lower))) {
    return($this->_makeDistractorsGeometric(
      $lower, $upper, $distractor_count));
  }
  else {
    return($this->_makeDistractorsLinear(
      $lower, $upper, $distractor_count));
  }
}


function safeGeometricArguments ($upper, $lower) {
 // should probably really also include the number
 // of distractors as an argument.  Only tested for
 // # of distractors approx 10.
 return (($upper > 0) && ($lower > 0) &&
         ($upper > $lower) &&
         (($upper / $lower) < 10000000000));
}


function _makeDistractorsLinear
         ($lower, $upper, $distractor_count)
```

```
{
    $return_array = array();
    array_push($return_array, $lower);
    $current = $lower;
    $increment = (($upper - $lower) / $distractor_count);
    // add in all the intermediate values
    for ($x = 1; $x < $distractor_count; $x++) {
      array_push($return_array,
                 round_to_digits($lower +
                           ($x * $increment),
                                 3));
    }
    array_push($return_array, $upper);
    return($return_array);
}


function _makeDistractorsGeometric
        ($lower, $upper, $distractor_count)
{
  if (($lower >= $upper) ||
      ($distractor_count < 2)) {
    die("Args to _makeDistractorsGeometric should be " .
        "1) a lower limit, 2) an upper limit, " .
        "3) a count (>= 2) of divisions between them.<BR>" .
        "Args were 1) $lower, 2) $upper, 3) $distractor_count<BR>");
  }
  $return_array = array();
  array_push($return_array, $lower);
  $limit_ratio = $upper / $lower;
  $root = nth_root($limit_ratio, $distractor_count);
  $current = $lower;
  // add in the intermediate values
  for ($x = 1; $x < $distractor_count; $x++) {
    $distractor = round_to_digits(
                      $lower * pow($root, $x),
                      3);
    array_push($return_array,
               $distractor);
  }
  array_push($return_array, $upper);
  return($return_array);
  }
}
?>
```

dbvars.php

When we actually query the database, we need to have access information. The file shown in Listing 39-8 is loaded by GameParameters.php, and sets up the variables necessary for making a MySQL connection. Note that the current values are dummies and will *not work* on your system! You need to fill in the correct values for your own MySQL configuration. If your Web server is connected to the Internet, it's also a good idea to move this file somewhere outside the Web-server document tree, and change the reference in GameParameters.php to point to its new location.

Listing 39-8: `dbvars.php`

```php
<?php
$host = "YOUR_HOSTNAME";
$user = "YOUR_MYSQL_USERNAME";
$pass = "YOUR_MYSQL_PASSWORD";
$db = "certainty";
?>
```

Creating the database

The trivia game is fueled by a database of questions, and so far, we have said nothing about how to create such a database.

Table definitions

Listing 39-9 shows a MySQL dump file of all the table definitions used in the code, along with a few sample entries. Before loading it, you need to create a database called certainty; after that is done, you should be able to simply cat or pipe the contents of this file to the mysql command.

Note that the question table includes several fields that are not actually used in the current code. One of them is attribution, useful for recording the book or Web site that served as the authority for the answer. Another is include, which we intended for filtering out questions in development that were not ready to be displayed. A third is subjectID, which we use to tag questions according to subject area (Science, Geography, History, and so on.) although that association is not actually displayed anywhere. A final as-yet unused column is unitID, which could be used to record the unit (kilometers, years, furlongs, bushels) of the answer in case the unit affects how guesses should be displayed.

Listing 39-9: Table definitions

```
# MySQL dump 7.1
#
# Host: [host deleted]     Database: certainty
#-------------------------------------------------------------
# Server version   3.22.32

#
```

```
# Table structure for table 'high_scores'
#
CREATE TABLE high_scores (
  id int(11) DEFAULT '0' NOT NULL auto_increment,
  name varchar(30),
  answer_count int(11),
  credit double(16,4),
  PRIMARY KEY (id)
);


#
# Dumping data for table 'high_scores'
#

INSERT INTO high_scores VALUES (8,'Ben Stein',15,-3.0000);


#
# Table structure for table 'question'
#
CREATE TABLE question (
  ID int(11) DEFAULT '0' NOT NULL auto_increment,
  answer double(16,4),
  unitID int(11),
  level int(11),
  subjectID int(11),
  include tinyint(4),
  upper_limit double(16,4),
  lower_limit double(16,4),
  scaling_type tinyint(4),
  question varchar(255),
  attribution varchar(255),
  PRIMARY KEY (ID)
);


#
# Dumping data for table 'question'
#


INSERT INTO question VALUES
(1,5283755345.0000,1,1,1,1,200000000000.0000,1000000.0000,2,
'What was the human population of the world in the middle of 1990?',
'http://www.census.gov/ipc/www/worldpop.html');
INSERT INTO question VALUES (2,70.0000,1,1,1,1,95.0000,5.0000,1,
'What percentage of the Earth\'s surface is covered by water?',
'http:/www.sciencenet.org.uk/database/Geography/Original/g00057d.html');
INSERT INTO question VALUES
(4,1969.0000,NULL,1,2,NULL,2000.0000,1950.0000,1,
'In what year did human beings first walk on the moon?','');
```

```
#
# Table structure for table 'subject'
#
CREATE TABLE subject (
  id int(11) DEFAULT '0' NOT NULL auto_increment,
  subject varchar(255),
  PRIMARY KEY (id)
);

#
# Dumping data for table 'subject'
#

INSERT INTO subject VALUES (1,'Geography');
INSERT INTO subject VALUES (2,'History');
INSERT INTO subject VALUES (3,'Science');
INSERT INTO subject VALUES (4,'Mathematics');
INSERT INTO subject VALUES (5,'Miscellaneous');
```

The MySQL dump includes only three sample questions. You could always add more through a direct interaction with MySQL, but it's more convenient to do it via a Web form.

entry_form.php

Listing 39-10 shows a bare-bones Web form for entering more questions into the question database. This simply takes typed input (except for a pull-down association with the subject table), and trusts the results. Note that there is neither security nor error-checking here — this is intended for use only by the game creator, and if misuse is a concern you should probably add password protection or some other kind of authentication. (See Chapter 38 for more on creating authentication systems.)

Listing 39-10: `dbvars.php`

```php
<?php
include_once("certainty_utils.php");
include_once("game_parameters_class.php");
$params = new GameParameters();
$connection = $params->getDbConnection();

if (get_post_value('POSTCHECK')) {
  handleEntryForm();
}
displayEntryForm();

function handleEntryForm () {
  $question = get_post_value('QUESTION');
  $answer = get_post_value('ANSWER');
  $lower_limit = get_post_value('LOWER_LIMIT');
  $upper_limit = get_post_value('UPPER_LIMIT');
```

```
$level = get_post_value('LEVEL');
$subject = get_post_value('SUBJECT');
$scaling_type = get_post_value('SCALING_TYPE');
$attribution = get_post_value('ATTRIBUTION');
if ($upper_limit > $lower_limit) {
  $query =
    "insert into question
      (question, answer, lower_limit, upper_limit,
       level, subjectID, scaling_type,
       attribution)
      values
      ('$question', $answer, $lower_limit, $upper_limit,
       $level, $subject, $scaling_type,
       '$attribution')";
  $result = mysql_query($query);
  if ($result) {
    print("Entry was successful<BR>");
  }
  else {
    print("Entry was not successful<BR>");
  }
}
else {
  print("Upper limit must be > lower<BR>");
}
}

function displayEntryForm () {
global $PHP_SELF;
$linear = CERTAINTY_LINEAR;
$geometric = CERTAINTY_GEOMETRIC;
$subject_string = make_subject_string();
$form_string = <<<EOT
<FORM METHOD=POST TARGET="$PHP_SELF" >
Question:
<INPUT TYPE=TEXT NAME=QUESTION SIZE=60 ><BR>
Answer:
<INPUT TYPE=TEXT NAME=ANSWER><BR>
Lower:
<INPUT TYPE=TEXT NAME=LOWER_LIMIT><BR>
Upper:
<INPUT TYPE=TEXT NAME=UPPER_LIMIT><BR>
Level:
<INPUT TYPE=TEXT NAME=LEVEL><BR>
Subject:
$subject_string<BR>
Scaling type:
<SELECT NAME=SCALING_TYPE>
  <OPTION VALUE=$linear>Linear
```

```
    <OPTION VALUE=$geometric>Geometric
</SELECT><BR>
Attribution:
<INPUT TYPE=TEXT NAME=ATTRIBUTION><BR>
<INPUT TYPE=SUBMIT NAME=SUBMIT VALUE=SUBMIT>
<INPUT TYPE=HIDDEN NAME=POSTCHECK VALUE=1>
</FORM>
EOT;
echo $form_string;
}

function make_subject_string () {
  $result_string = "<SELECT NAME=SUBJECT>";
  $query = "select id, subject from subject order by id";
  $result = mysql_query($query);
  while ($row = mysql_fetch_row($result)) {
    $id = $row[0];
    $display = $row[1];
    $result_string .= "<OPTION VALUE=$id>$display";
  }
  $result_string .= "</SELECT>";
  return($result_string);
}
?>
```

General Design Considerations

What follows is a brief list of issues that we were forced to consider while writing the code in this chapter.

Separation of code and display

The question of separating code and display is a vexing one, especially in situations where you have different personnel assigned to maintaining logic and appearance. Our own view on this is that perfect separation of code and display is like a perfect vacuum — you can get asymptotically closer to the ideal as you expend infinite effort.

For large Web sites employing many people, some pretty good techniques exist for making a strong separation, including templating systems and database storage of graphics and display text. For this relatively small and informal example, we were satisfied by simply segregating all HTML into two display-oriented classes, leaving the remainder of the code focused on logic and data.

Persistence of data

There are several kinds of data in this game that survive longer than the execution time of a page. We chose to use PHP's session mechanism for all the data particular to a particular game invocation and a backend database for everything else (questions, answers, and high-score lists).

For reasons of efficiency, we didn't want to store too much data via the session mechanism. So we separated out the most important data (that could not be easily recreated) into the Game class, and stored only an instance of that class. Everything else (question text, boilerplate HTML text, high scores, and so on) were either embedded in code files or easily retrievable from the database.

Exception handling

Although we didn't touch on it much in the discussion of the code files, we do have some error-handling logic, which is mainly designed to make our pages look better whenever things go horribly wrong. Two categories of things that inevitably go wrong are database connectivity and session handling. Our database installation at our Webhost is not under our control, and neither is our user's decision whether to enable cookies. If, for whatever reason, we can't actually retrieve the information we need to display a good game page, we would rather display our own error message than random PHP error messages.

PHP lacks a thoroughgoing mechanism for exception handling, other than coding functions to watch for the error status returned by other functions. For this game we used a poor man's version of exception handling by using a problem field in each of the major classes (Game and GameDisplay) to store strings describing errors that arose during attempting to update and display the game. Just before actual display these slots are checked, and if any errors are present the game's real display is suppressed, and an error message is display. Although this does not make the game any more playable, it at least attempts to avoid informing our users of which code-file line numbers have errored out. (We hate that!)

Summary

The Certainty Quiz is a small, simple, self-contained PHP application which you should be able to install and enjoy in the privacy of your own home (after connecting it to your favorite Web server and a MySQL database, of course). Although small, the code relies on database interaction, OOP features, use of sessions, string processing, object serialization, and non-trivial arithmetic to achieve its effects. Although PHP has many capabilities that we didn't come close to touching on, this chapter uses a fair cross-section of its most popular features — if you understand everything in this example, you are well on your way to exploiting the power of PHP.

Part IV

Appendixes

Appendix A: PHP for C Programmers

Appendix B: PHP for Perl Hackers

Appendix C: PHP for HTML Coders

Appendix D: PHP Resources

Appendix A
PHP for C Programmers

In this appendix, we assume that you have more C (or C++) programming experience than PHP experience and are looking to get up to speed in PHP quickly. First we'll give a quick overview of PHP from a C perspective, then we'll break down the similarities and differences, and finally we'll point out which parts of the book you are likely to benefit from the most.

The simplest way to think of PHP is as interpreted C that you can embed in HTML documents. The language itself is a lot like C, except with untyped variables, a whole lot of Web-specific libraries built-in, and everything hooked up directly to your favorite Web server. The syntax of statements and function definitions should be familiar, except that variables are always preceded by $, and functions do not require separate prototypes.

Similarities

In this section, we offer some notes (by no means exhaustive) on ways in which PHP can be expected to be C-like.

Syntax

Broadly speaking, PHP syntax is the same as in C: Code is blank insensitive, statements are terminated with semicolons, function calls have the same structure (`my_function(expression1, expression2)`), and curly braces (`{` and `}`) make statements into blocks. PHP supports C and C++-style comments (`/* */` as well as `//`), and also Perl and shell-script style (`#`).

Operators

The assignment operators (`=`, `+=`, `*=`, and so on), the Boolean operators (`&&`, `||`, `!`), the comparison operators (`<`, `>`, `<=`, `>=`, `==`, `!=`), and the basic arithmetic operators (`+`, `-`, `*`, `/`, `%`) all behave as they do in C.

Control structures

The basic control structures (`if`, `switch`, `while`, `for`) behave as they do in C, including supporting `break` and `continue`. One notable difference is that switch in PHP can accept strings as case identifiers.

Many function names

As you peruse the documentation, you'll see many function names that seem identical to C functions. It's a safe bet that these functions perform the exact same task, although they may sometimes take a slightly different form in terms of arguments or the way results are returned. Most string-modifying functions, for example, return new strings as the value of the function rather than modifying a string passed as an argument. Note, however, that function names are not case sensitive in PHP.

Differences

Although PHP has quite a bit of C ancestry, it also has some other ancestors (Perl, shell scripts), as well as some unique features that are not at all C-like.

Those dollar signs

All variables are denoted with a leading $. Variables do not need to be declared in advance of assignment, and they have no intrinsic type — the only type a variable has is the type of the last value that was assigned to it. The PHP version of the C code:

```
double my_number;
my_number = 3.14159;
```

would simply be:

```
$my_number = 3.14159;
```

Types

There are only two numerical types in PHP: *integer* (corresponding to a long in C), and *double* (corresponding to a double in C).

Strings are of arbitrary length. There is no separate character type. (Functions that might take character arguments in their C analogues typically expect a one-character string in PHP (ord(), for example). Beginning with PHP 4, there is also a genuine Boolean type (TRUE or FALSE). (See following sections for arrays and objects.)

Type conversion

Types are not checked at compile time, and type errors do not typically occur at runtime either. Instead, variables and values are automatically converted across types as needed. This is somewhat analogous to the way arithmetic expressions in C will "promote" numerical arguments as needed, but it is extended to the other types as well. (See Chapter 6 for details of the conversion rules.)

Arrays

Arrays have a syntax superficially similar to C's array syntax, but they are implemented completely differently. They are actually associative arrays, and the "index" can be either a number or a string. They do not need to be declared or allocated in advance.

No structure type

There is no *struct* in PHP, which is partly because the array and object types together make it unnecessary. (The elements of a PHP array need not be of a consistent type.)

Objects

PHP has a very basic OOP syntax, which allows definition of classes with member data items and member functions. There are no destructors (see "Memory Management," which follows), no multiple inheritance, and no private variables or methods.

No pointers

There are no *pointers* per se in PHP, although the typeless variables play a similar role. PHP does support variable references. You can also emulate function pointers to some extent, in that function names can be stored in variables and called using the variable rather than a literal name.

No prototypes

Functions do not need to be declared before their implementation is defined. The only ordering rule in PHP3 is define-before-use (and putting a function call in another function's body does not count as use until the latter function is called itself). It suffices to define all functions before making any top-level calls to functions. In PHP 4, functions do not even need to precede their calls, as there is an automatic precompilation step before execution.

Memory management

The PHP engine is effectively a garbage-collected environment (reference-counted), and in small scripts there is no need to do any deallocation. You should freely allocate new structures — such as new strings and object instances — especially because they will reliably go away when your script terminates. If you need to free memory within a script's execution, call unset() on the variable that refers to it, which will release the memory for collection. External resources (such as database result sets) can also be explicitly freed within a script, but doing so is worth it only if the script would use an unacceptable amount of the resource before terminating.

Compilation and linking

There is no separate compilation step for PHP scripts — the development cycle is simply edit-reload. Errors and warnings show up in the browser output by default, although there is also an error-logging capability. Typically there is no dynamic loading of libraries (although such a capability exists) — you decide at PHP configuration time which function families to include in your module, and they are then available to any script.

Permissiveness

As a general matter, PHP is more forgiving than C (especially in its type system) and so will let you get away with new kinds of mistakes. Unexpected results are more common than errors. In particular, under the default error-reporting level PHP does not warn you if you use a variable that has not yet been assigned (although it does supply reasonable default values rather than garbage). If you would rather be warned, you can set the error-reporting level by evaluating error-reporting(E_ALL) early in your script, or set the error-reporting level to E_ALL permanently by editing the php.ini file.

Guide to the Book

In writing this book, we very intentionally did not assume that the reader had prior knowledge of C. Because PHP resembles C in many aspects, some of the chapters may cover familiar ground. This is especially true of Part I, which is essentially a language introduction.

In Table A-1, we label the chapters of Part I according to how familiar they are likely to be to C programmers. Parts III and IV are very PHP-specific and likely to be novel, but you may also find portions of Part II to be familiar if you have some experience with SQL databases.

Table A-1: Guide to Part I for C Programmers

Chapter	Chapter Title	Verdict?	Notes
1	Why PHP?	Novel	The chapter you need to justify PHP to your boss.
2	Server-side Web Scripting	Novel	Important if you have not seen Web-scripting languages before.
3	Getting Started with PHP	Novel	Installation, hosting, and so on.
4	Adding PHP to HTML	Novel but easy	"Hello world" for PHP.
5	Syntax, Variables, and Printing	Mostly familiar	Skimmable until the section on variables (which really are different in PHP).
6	Types in PHP	Somewhat familiar	PHP performs automatic type conversions. Also see the late material on arrays and objects.

7	Control	Familiar	All the PHP control structures (`if`, `while`, `switch`, `for`) work the same way as in C.
8	Using and Defining Functions	Mostly familiar	Skimmable — differences include scoping rules, treatment of number of arguments, and the final section on variable function names.
9	Passing Information between Pages	Novel	Specific to Web-scripting.
10	Strings and String Functions	Mostly familiar	Some identically named string functions (`sprintf`) return new strings rather than operate on a passed string. Doubly quoted strings do automatic interpolation of variable values. Material late in the chapter on built-in functions for regular expressions, URLs.
11	Arrays and Array Functions	Novel	Deceptively familiar — PHP arrays are syntactically like C arrays but behave totally differently.
12	Math	Familiar	Similarly named functions behave the same way. Novel section on arbitrary-precision arithmetic ("bc" functions).
13	Filesystem and System Functions	Mostly familiar	Some novel touches, including reading a remote Web page (via HTTP) exactly like a file.
14	PHP Style	Mostly familiar	The same stylistic mandates as with C code — only the final sections are specific to Web site design.
15	Basic PHP Gotchas	Novel	Error messages and stumbling blocks do not have much overlap with C.

A Bonus: Just Look at the Code!

As a final bonus, C programmers are uniquely qualified to benefit from the open-source nature of PHP. Although the combination of this book and the online manual should answer almost all your questions, if you have the PHP source available you may be able to gain some extra insight by poking around in it and seeing how things are implemented. Although you would need to be familiar with lexing/parsing technology to get much out of the parser code itself, many PHP functions are simple wrappers around their C counterparts, and some others that have no C counterparts are at least written in clear and simple C.

It's also very easy for C programmers to add new capabilities to the language, whether for their own use or eventual use by the PHP community. Most PHP programming tasks are addressed by writing PHP (often by defining functions in PHP), but you can also pop the hood and add functionality to the underlying language by adding a new module, written (of course) in C.

Appendix B

PHP for Perl Hackers

In this appendix, we assume that you know Perl, but not PHP, and are looking to quickly get up to speed in PHP. The good news is that the two languages are very similar indeed.

This is by no means a comprehensive guide to how Perl and PHP compare. Although similar, and sharing some ancestry, they really are distinct languages with distinct syntaxes and feature sets, and there is no replacement for getting to know them individually. Our main goal for this appendix is to save you some time up front — to warn you, for example, that `elsif` means nothing in PHP, rather than letting you debug your way to that realization.

Similarities

In this section, we discuss some ways in which PHP and Perl are similar.

Compiled scripting languages

First, the obvious: Both Perl and PHP are "scripting" languages. This means that (unlike compiled languages like C) they are not used to produce native standalone executables in advance of execution, which can then be run without reference to what language they were written in. Instead, Perl or PHP source files are both fed to an appropriate engine at execution time. This does not mean, however, that Perl/PHP code is interpreted line by line at execution time; in the case of both Perl and PHP 4, scripts are quickly and automatically compiled at execution time, and then executed. But it does mean that the development cycle for PHP/Perl programmers is edit-execute, rather than edit-compile-execute, as in C.

Syntax

PHP's basic syntax is very close to Perl's, and both share a lot of syntactic features with C. Code is blank insensitive, statements are terminated by semicolons, and curly braces organize multiple statements into a single block. Function calls start with the name of the function, followed by the actual arguments enclosed in parentheses and separated by commas.

Dollar-sign variables

All variables in PHP look like scalar variables in Perl; a name with a dollar sign ($) in front of it. (See the Differences section for what happened to @ and %.)

No declaration of variables

As in Perl, you don't need to declare the type of a PHP variable before using it. The following line is valid in both languages, with no prior mention of the variable:

```
$the_answer = 42;
```

Loose typing of variables

As in Perl, variables in PHP have no intrinsic type other than the value they currently hold. The following sequence of two lines is legal in both languages:

```
$the_answer = 42;
$the_answer = "the answer";
```

The variable $the_answer is assigned sequentially to an integer and a string. This would not be legal in more strongly-typed languages like C, Pascal, or Java.

Strings and variable interpolation

Both PHP and Perl do more interpretation of doubly-quoted strings ("string") than of singly-quoted strings ('string'). In particular the value of $ variables is spliced into doubly-quoted strings at the time the strings are read.

The following code fragment is both legal Perl and legal PHP, and it has the same behavior in both languages.

```
$the_answer = 42;
$the_statement = "the answer is $the_answer";
```

At the end of the second line, the variable $the_statement contains the string:

```
'the answer is 42'
```

Differences

This section warns you (again, not exhaustively) about some ways that Perl and PHP diverge from each other.

PHP is HTML-embedded

Although it is possible to use PHP for arbitrary tasks by running it from the command line, it is more typically connected to a Web server and used for producing Web pages. The code for these pages can consist partially (or even completely!) of straight HTML, with fragments of PHP embedded in them to produce the dynamically generated portions.

If you are used to writing CGI scripts in Perl, the main difference in PHP is that you no longer need to explicitly print out large blocks of static HTML using print statements, and instead can simply write the HTML itself. Also, for typical pages, there is no need to explicitly send HTTP headers from PHP code.

No @ or % variables

PHP only has one kind of variable, which starts with a dollar sign ($). Any of the datatypes in the language can be stored in such variables, whether scalar or compound. For example, The expression `$my_array[0]` refers to the first element in an array, while `$my_array` refers to the array itself.

Arrays vs. hashes

PHP has a single datatype called an *array* that plays the role of both hashes and arrays/lists in Perl. For all the details, see Chapter 11; the short version is that a PHP array acts like a Perl hash when you supply keys and like a Perl (non-associative) array when keys are omitted. Values can be extracted by key (as in Perl hashes) or by iteration through the array (as with Perl arrays).

Specifying arguments to functions

Function calls in PHP look pretty much like subroutine calls in Perl. Function definitions in PHP, on the other hand, typically require some kind of list of formal arguments as in C or Java. For example, although the typical syntax for a two-argument subroutine in Perl might look like:

```
sub two_arg_sub () {
    my ($first_arg, $second_arg) = @_;
    ...
}
```

The corresponding PHP function definition would be:

```
function two_arg_function ($first_arg, $second_arg) {
    ...
}
```

Although your humble authors try hard not to be partisan, we feel strongly that subroutine arguments in Perl are a bug, and function arguments in PHP are a feature. Two kinds of silliness common in Perl that don't usually arise in PHP are: 1) popping the argument stack at various points in a subroutine (so that it is hard for a reader of the code to figure out what the formal arguments are supposed to be), and 2) compound arguments bleeding into one another because arguments are passed as a list of scalars. PHP arguments arrive intact and without confusion regardless of number and type.

Variable scoping in functions

In Perl, the default scope for variables is global. This means that top-level variables are visible inside subroutines, and often this leads to promiscuous use of globals across functions.

In PHP, the scope of variables within function definitions is local by default. This means that (with some exceptions) the only variables that are visible within functions are the formal parameters and variables assigned locally within the function. If you want to refer to a variable from the global context within a function, you must declare it by name in the function definition itself, using the `global` keyword.

No module system as such

In PHP there is no real distinction between normal code files and code files used as imported libraries. To import a PHP code file full of function or class definitions, you simply use `include()` or `require()`, which have much the same effect as splicing the definitions in at the point of the `include` statement.

Break and continue rather than next and last

Perl has some idiosyncratic language keywords, which are not the same as the corresponding C constructs. In general, if Perl and C disagree about such a name, you will find that PHP follows C rather than Perl. In particular, if you want to skip to the end of a `for` or `while` iteration, use `continue` (not `next`); if you want to break out of the loop altogether, use `break` (not `last`).

No elsif

A minor spelling difference: Perl's `elsif` is PHP's `elseif`. Also, its use is not mandatory. In PHP, the following is legal:

```
if ($boolean_var) {
    # case 1
}
else if ($other_boolean) {
   # case 2
}
```

In Perl, on the other hand, if you for some reason decline to use `elsif`, then your other alternative is the more awkward form:

```
if ($boolean_var) {
    # case 1
}
else {
  if ($other_boolean) {
       # case 2
  }
}
```

More kinds of comments

Perl people like the phrase "There's More Than One Way To Do It," and yet they suffer with a really impoverished set of options for comments. In addition to Perl-style (#) single-line comments, PHP offers C-style multiline comments (`/* comment */`), and Java-style single-line comments (`// comment`).

Regular expressions

PHP does not have a built-in syntax that is specific to regular expressions, but has most of the same functionality in its "Perl-compatible" regular expression functions. See Chapter 30 for the details.

Miscellaneous Tips

Following are answers to a couple of questions that that Perl programmers might have on their minds.

What about use strict "vars"?

Like Perl, PHP allows you to use variables without declaring them or initializing them, and (as in Perl) this capability is a frequent source of bugs. If you would like a declaration like Perl's `use strict "vars"`, try `error_reporting(E_ALL);`, which will at least warn you about the use of any unassigned variables.

Where's CPAN?

PHP doesn't yet have a code repository as comprehensive as the Comprehensive Perl Archive Network (CPAN), but a good effort is underway in the PEAR project (`http://pear.php.net`).

Guide to the Book

As in Appendix A (PHP for C programmers), in this section we offer Perl hackers a quick guide to Part I of the book to give a sense of which chapters are likely to already be familiar.

Table B-1: Guide to Part I for Perl Programmers

Chapter	Chapter Title	Verdict?	Notes
1	Why PHP?	Novel	The chapter you need to justify PHP to your boss
2	Server-Side Web Scripting	Possibly novel	Familiar to Perl CGI and mod_perl programmers; important if you have not seen Web scripting before

3	Getting Started with PHP	Novel	Installation, hosting, and so on
4	Adding PHP to your HTML	Novel but easy	"Hello world" for PHP
5	Syntax, Variables, and Output	Mostly familiar	Basic syntax is very familiar; variables are different
6	Types in PHP	Somewhat familiar	The scalar types are very similar; compound types are very different
7	Control	Mostly familiar	Basic constructs are similar, with syntactic differences
8	Using and Defining Functions	Somewhat familiar	Argument-passing and variable scoping very different
9	Passing Information between Pages	Novel	Specific to Web scripting
10	Strings and String Functions	Mostly familiar	Treatment of singly-quoted and doubly-quoted strings essentially the same, functions are mostly novel.
11	Arrays and Array Functions	Novel	No exactly corresponding datatype in Perl.
12	Math	Mostly familiar	Novel section on arbitrary-precision (BC) math functions.
13	File System and System Functions	Mostly familiar	Largely familiar (for example there is a `stat()` function).
14	PHP Style	Mostly familiar	Same stylistic issues as in Perl, with the addition of issues around when to print explicitly versus HTML-embedding.
15	Basic PHP Gotchas	Mostly familiar.	Same gotchas around unintentionally unassigned variables; other gotchas specific to PHP parsing.

Appendix C
PHP for HTML Coders

This appendix contains specific advice for HTML-only jocks looking to trade up to something a little more powerful on the server side. If you already know ASP, JavaScript, or almost any real programming language, this appendix is not going to help you much.

The Good News

If you're already proficient at HTML, starting to use PHP is not a huge step. Because PHP is usually embedded in HTML, extending the functionality of static Web pages with a programming language can be a very natural progression. So there are plenty of reasons to believe that you can learn PHP fairly quickly, such as the following factors.

You already know HTML

Because PHP is usually embedded in HTML, and because PHP uses HTML for all its display functions, you won't be able to see anything that your scripts are doing unless you output HTML. In fact, you can think of PHP as simply adding functionality to Web pages —it can do other things, but lots of people use it mostly for form handling and dynamic page generation.

You presumably have a lot of practice debugging HTML, which is all to the good. Many errors occur within the HTML parts of scripts or during the transitions between modes, so the ability to read and write HTML with great facility is crucial.

If you're strong on the design side, as are many HTML coders, you have the ability to produce a good-looking and well-laid-out product. This skill is important for the community because a lot of early PHP developers were not exactly known for their UI skills (including ourselves, we hasten to admit). So go out there and show the world that PHP sites don't need to be ugly, clunky, or at best really plain — you can make us all proud.

PHP is an easy first programming language to learn

Unlike many major programming languages, PHP enables you to do useful stuff from the very beginning instead of making you play endless games of tic-tac-toe or code up abstruse math problems. The Web browser and markup languages, however primitive and clunky they are now, point the way to the universal I/O, windowing, and multimedia solution that the world has been waiting for. PHP takes full advantage of the Web's power; plus it has very little overhead and takes a loose, inclusive approach to issues such as types, variables, and syntax.

All the nitpicky angst that programmers used to put into these areas you can now apply more directly to functionality.

And frankly, PHP enables you to learn just those parts that are useful to you and ignore the rest. Unlike some programming languages, which pretty much require a firm grasp of all the basic principles before you can do anything useful — try telling a C programmer that you just haven't seen a need for structs yet if you want a laugh — no one is going to give you a quiz on all the hundreds of PHP functions before entrusting you with a text editor. So if you don't need to write some huge math function right off the bat, go ahead and skip that chapter — we promise not to tell. If and when you ever need them, the math capabilities will still be there.

Web development is increasingly prefab anyway

Finally, the Web is increasingly making development a matter of altering prefab open-source code rather than hacking it all up yourself. Much of this work is about changing how the page looks rather than how it functions. Learn to be a smart script shopper and you're more than halfway there.

The Bad News

Before we get too carried away, honesty compels us to admit you may face a few hurdles before you become a power PHP user.

If programming were that easy, you'd already know how

PHP is a real programming language, similar to C (albeit generally Web-server dwelling), rather than a tag-based markup concept such as HTML or ColdFusion. This point introduces whole new levels of complexity. It simply takes time and practice to develop a bag of tricks, work out routines for solving problems, and just get better at development — and there are no shortcuts for these skills.

So here's the bottom line: Most of PHP is probably completely new to you. Unlike new PHP developers who are already proficient with ASP, JavaScript, or C, you can't expect to pick up any specific points here that are highly similar to things you already know how to do. Uh, sorry.

However, if you already know some JavaScript or have taken an "Intro to C" class in school — even if you wouldn't describe yourself as a JavaScript or C guru — you're ahead of the curve. Some of the logic is sure to come back to you as you begin to work with PHP.

Also, PHP training courses are beginning to pop up for those who are comfortable learning in the classroom. Check out the following Web sites:

```
http://www.phpbootcamp.com (USA)
http://www.rmit.edu.au (Australia)
http://www.thinkphp.de (Europe)
```

Backend servers can add complexity

PHP is mostly useful in conjunction with backend servers, such as database and mail servers, which have their own syntax and implementation issues that you need to learn about. Because open source software such as PHP is commonly used in noncorporate settings, most PHP developers probably don't have the luxury of a team of database, network, and design experts doing their various things while they just worry about the middle tier.

If possible, don't try to learn everything at once. The most important task is to become comfortable with the Web server itself; Apache, in particular, is an extremely powerful but involved piece of software that rewards study. (This advice may not be relevant if you have IT staff to install and maintain the Web server for you.) After that, you will almost certainly want to learn SQL if you don't know it already; and mail service is also a very rewarding subject. After you master those three, other new servers should be easier to learn.

Concentrate On . . .

One of your humble authors was an experienced programmer before learning PHP, but the other had basically done only HTML before — so we can dare to offer a few words of advice from our own learning experience. The steps to learning programming that we describe in the following sections may make the task a bit easier.

Reading other people's code

Learning to read other people's code can be harder than it sounds. One of the best things about PHP is its loose syntax and inclusive "don't worry, be happy" design — but that can also mean that different scripts can look very different, even if they return similar results. Beginners can be boggled by stylistic issues, and may find it difficult to sort out which parts of a script are functionally irreducible and which are the product of one individual's programming quirks. But regardless of difficulty, the sooner you can parse other people's PHP and the more code you can look at, the better off you'll be.

One potentially helpful exercise is to visit the mailing-list archive or a code exchange (see Appendix D) and print out multiple examples of code that solve the same issue (preferably one you're interested in). Then lay the sheets side by side, take a big ol' red pen, and go through it all, circling the common parts. Give extra brownie points to any scripters who comment their code well (which doesn't necessarily mean the most voluminous comments but rather the most useful) and look for more code from those people. Also look for code that is generally well laid out and logically organized, even if it isn't extensively commented.

Work on what interests you

We firmly believe that learning is motivation. If you find tasks that you want to accomplish, you will automatically be motivated to learn what you need to know to accomplish them. Don't let anyone tell you that "the right way" to learn programming is through some highly structured program of math problems, games, and stock-market simulations. Wanting to put pictures of your dog on the Internet is much more important than making sure that you know what's in every byte of memory your program is using.

Thinking about programming

As we said 10 paragraphs ago, learning PHP is inevitably going to take time, practice, and lots of example code. There is just no way around it, and really there is not a whole lot more to say on the subject.

One thing that may prove helpful to new developers, particularly those of a narrative rather than mathematical bent, is the judicious use of pseudocode. For example, you might start out with mostly pseudocode and gradually add more real PHP as we do in the steps below.

1. Write down the tasks that you want this page to accomplish. Being complete is more important at this stage than being cogent. Following is an example of a script mission statement:

   ```
   This page should display a form with any old answers already filled in.
   Then you can submit the form to update some of the values if you want
   to. And I want the form to be password-protected, so it needs to handle
   a User ID passed in from the login screen.
   ```

2. Break the mission statement down into steps and substeps, as in a recipe. Rearrange these if necessary. Following is an example of this step:

   ```
   1. Get the User ID that is passed from the login screen; if none, don't
   display anything.
   2. Display the HTML form.
   3. Make any old values from the database appear in the form.
      a. Connect to the database server.
      b. Download data about this item.
      c. Put the data into the HTML form's "value=X" variables.
   4. Change the values and put them into the database too.
   5. Pass the User ID to the next page.
   ```

3. Pick one of the steps and turn it into actual PHP code. Starting with a core PHP task — such as sending e-mail or returning something to the screen — is generally easier than beginning with peripheral tasks, such as connecting to a database. Any time that you might want to connect to a database, use a commented variable, array, or include file for the moment. The following example illustrates this step:

   ```
   1. Get the User ID that is passed from the login screen; if none, don't
   display anything.

   <?php
   // Dummy UserID pretending to be passed from login.
   ```

```
// Will be superseded later.
$UserID = 1;
?>
2. Display the HTML form.

<HTML><HEAD></HEAD>
<BODY>
<FORM>
First name: <input type="text" size=30 name="FirstName"><BR>
Last name: <input type="text" size=30 name="LastName"><BR>
E-mail: <input type="text" size=30 name="Email">

3. Make any old values from the database appear in the form.

<?php
// I'm using these variables now, but later I'll get
// them from the database instead.

$FirstName = "Joyce";
$LastName = "Park";
$Email = "root@localhost"
?>
Oh, I think I need to put them in before the form is rendered.

4. Change the values and put them into the database, too.
5. Pass the User ID to the next page.
```

4. Gradually fill in more and more of the code, fixing any new issues that arise. You may want to keep some of the pseudocode, suitably edited, as comments, as shown in the following example:

```
/* Pass the User ID to the next page. The best way is to have it show
up as a hidden input type and PHP variable in the form; then HTML can
pass it with the rest of the POST values. */
```

Learning SQL and other protocols

Spending some time interacting with backend servers directly, via whatever interface the server provides, is generally a good idea before you add the complexity of PHP between you and the server.

You can kill two birds with one stone by using the backend server's own interface to construct the database (or whatever), even though there may be nice PHP tools for some of these tasks. For instance, even though Tobias Ratschiller's phpMyAdmin tool is a very slick and handy way to deal with the MySQL database, the newbie database administrator can learn a heck of a lot more by using MySQL's deliberately primitive command-line interface.

Making cosmetic changes to prefab PHP applications

Jumping right into customizing a prefab application, such as Phorum or IMP, may help motivate you client-side types. Following are a few hints:

♦ First try just changing the colors — that's generally pretty safe. If that goes well, try customizing the buttons. The next safest thing is spacing — table widths, columns, and so on. You can also add graphics, add links, or play around with style sheets pretty much without worries.

♦ If the application has include files (especially `header.inc`), the cosmetic part is often in there. Look first in headers and footers for colors, the basis of page layouts, and so on. Remember to match header changes with corresponding footer changes and vice versa.

♦ Never, *ever* erase a line beginning with a conjunction (such as `if`, `while`, or `for`). If you are not 100% sure what you are doing, comment out code blocks rather than deleting them.

Debugging is programming

Few people truly enjoy debugging; as one of our colleagues once observed, "I'd rather implement new features than eat someone else's leftovers." Debugging can turn out to be a useful learning experience, however, because you can fix things at the edges of a big project instead of jumping into writing the whole thing from scratch.

One of the most efficient ways to debug is in pairs. Particularly if you're tired or have seen a piece of code too many times, focusing on every detail can prove difficult. At this point, talking through your logic becomes very helpful — one of you briefly stating why you're doing what you're doing and the other checking each step off very deliberately. A fresh set of eyes can often find cheap mistakes such as misspelled variable names or missing brackets, more quickly, too. If you get an opportunity to debug with a more experienced programmer, take it.

Avoid at First

A few things in PHP are extremely unfamiliar to HTML coders and generally are not extremely necessary to writing functional PHP. Try to avoid the elements that we describe in the following sections if you can, at least at first.

Objects

Objects can prove confusing even for experienced nonobject-oriented programmers, so do yourself a favor and avoid them if at all possible. Because PHP is not even a truly object-oriented language, the "object notation" can also cause problems later.

Maximal PHP style

See Chapter 14 on PHP style. The maximal style is deprecated by Rasmus Lerdorf himself, and only hardcore C programmers have the slightest excuse to use it, except in very specific, brief instances. It includes just too many single quotes, double quotes, forward slashes, backslashes, ASCII line breaks, and HTML line breaks for most coders. Beginners are better off if they don't waste their time worrying about stray punctuation when they could be spending the time and effort grasping larger concepts instead.

Programming large applications from scratch

Why reinvent the wheel? In Open-sourceland, you don't need to. Becoming a good customizer and recycler of other people's code is often more efficient than trying to become the world's greatest programmer from scratch. Learn to shop for what you need.

Consider This . . .

The ideas in the following sections are completely optional but may prove helpful. You may not agree with them all, but we offer them for what they're worth.

Reading a book on C programming

Unfortunately, we can't write a complete programming tutorial. Part I of this book explains these topics but necessarily very briefly. We've tried to comment our code samples extensively, but we can only do so much to explain these techniques in passing.

Mailing-list regulars frequently counsel new PHP developers to buy a book on C programming — but in a snotty, RTFM way that too often elicits a naturally passive-aggressive response. Nevertheless, if you separate it from the unspoken message that you must be a clueless idiot, it's good advice and something to seriously consider if you're having trouble with the programming aspect of PHP.

A clearly written, brief tutorial book is Patrick Henry Winston's *On to C* (Addison-Wesley, 1994). It's fewer than 300 pages long, and a lot of the PHP-relevant material is right at the beginning. The standard reference is *The C Programming Language*, by Brian W. Kernighan and Dennis M. Ritchie (Prentice Hall, 1988), which is quite definitive but more reference-oriented and, therefore, perhaps less appropriate for HTML-only coders. A friendlier introduction might be Dan Gookin's two-volume *C for Dummies* (Hungry Minds, 1997), which has cartoons and dry humor.

Minimal PHP style

Of the range of PHP styles, the easiest for the HTML coder to work with at first is the most minimal. In other words, we suggest that you separate the HTML and PHP sections completely. Not only does this technique avoid many stylistic difficulties, but by using this method, you avoid mixing PHP and HTML glitches on the same page, which makes diagnosing problems more than twice as hard. We discuss this topic more completely in Chapter 14.

Perhaps the easiest way to use the minimal style is to finish the HTML pages first, using whatever tool you're most enamored of. Take the time to debug your HTML completely and perhaps run it through a tidying utility. Then, and only then, tackle the PHP parts, secure and comfy in the knowledge that any difficulties you encounter are certainly on the PHP side rather than the HTML side.

One downside of this style is that you can't have pages pass their variables back to themselves. This is particularly relevant with forms; so if your site has a lot of forms, you may want to change your style a bit as your PHP skills improve.

Use the right tools for the job

Finally, you want to strongly consider using a PHP-enabled text editor for the PHP parts of your scripts. (See Chapter 4 for a discussion of text editors versus WYSIWYG tools.) Some people can do wonders with just Notepad or `emacs`, but a lot of frustrated beginners are certainly using those tools just because someone told them that's what the cool programmers do. As Zsa Zsa Gabor said (in a slightly different context), macho does not mean mucho. If you work more effectively with `vim` or Visual SlickEdit, by all means use those tools.

Syntax highlighting (printing different parts of the code in different colors) can help you a lot, as it will usually make clearer when you have failed to close off a parentheses or double-quote. Some programmer's text editors will automatically line up your curly braces for you, which helps you verify that you've closed off all of a set of nested cases. We would not even consider using a text editor without line numbering, since PHP's built-in error messages always refer to lines in your code. And last but not least, do not forget the power of "View Source" in the browser — this will help you verify that the output you are producing is in fact what you intended.

CAUTION: This advice does *not* apply to WYSIWYG editors, the use of which we deprecate. Sooner or later, you need to fix up the HTML into a human-readable form, which no WYSIWYG editor can yet produce. If it's your choice to use one, fine — but you should in no way think of this tool as a substitute for understanding and writing clean HTML by hand.

Appendix D
PHP Resources

This appendix lays out some basic resources that will help you learn more about the language. We have also tried to mention specific resources and products throughout the text.

The PHP Web Site

The URL for the PHP Web site (engrave it on your heart) is as follows:

```
www.php.net
```

Here you'll find the latest official news, the freshest downloads, the PHP bugtracker, a growing list of PHP users' groups, and links to PHP-friendly ISPs.

Most important, you'll find the PHP manual in the Documentation section of the PHP Web site. It's available in several versions for your universal reference pleasure, including the following:

♦ Numerous translations — many European languages, Japanese, Korean, and so on.

♦ Several PDF, Windows Help, and HTML download versions (useful when you're traveling; HTML versions are included with the PHP download).

♦ Two PalmPilot versions.

♦ A plain HTML online version.

♦ Links to the PHP-GTK (client-side PHP) and PEAR (PHP codebase) manuals.

> **CAUTION:** The PEAR manual, which used to be a chapter of the general PHP manual, has now been moved to its own server. You can find it at `http://pear.php.net/manual/`.

But when people talk about "*the* PHP manual," they mean the big annotated online version for which PHP is famous. Users from around the world have added notes and comments to each page. These additions are often clarifications of points made in the main text, additional insights, and reports of PHP's behavior on various platforms.

However, you may want to keep a couple of points in mind when using this manual:

♦ The canonical manual text is written in a super-terse programmer's style; and it is organized in a not-particularly discursive, notebook-like format.

> **CAUTION:** The online manual is *not* the place to ask questions! It's intended for meaningful comments and observations only. Send e-mail to one of the previous commentators who provide their addresses — many of them will be happy to help you. Or subscribe to the mailing list or post to a PHP forum, which is faster anyway. Remember, a stupid question posted to the manual errata *will* go down on your (semi)permanent record.

♦ The comments are edited, weeded, and verified only on an episodic (not to say extremely infrequent) basis. Proceed with extreme caution — there have been numerous instances of problems actually getting worse because a user uncritically followed the advice in the manual notes. You can write to the person to make sure that the advice is appropriate for you or even to determine whether the person really knows what he or she is talking about.

♦ The manual may lag behind development by a considerable time period.

> **CAUTION:** Our experience suggests that something about the organization of the manual makes it difficult or discouraging for many users to quickly find what they're looking for. To locate information about a function or construction, you sort of need to know that it's there and what kind of thing it is (not always clear from the headings — for example, date functions versus calendar functions), and often it helps to have an idea of what the PHP team might have named it If you can't accurately guess these three things, you're likely to spend a lot of time wandering around looking at not-quite-right function pages. We have nothing comforting to tell frustrated users, except that PHP has so many functions and configuration options and styles that writing about and organizing them all in a way that makes sense to an outsider is very difficult. Our hope is that books such as this one can help introduce you to the main categories (for example, array functions) and the most commonly used functions — and then you'll be more prepared to use the riches of the online PHP manual.
>
> One extremely helpful thing we recommend is reading the introductory page for each section of the online PHP manual. The manual is broken up into sections or chapters, such as "Arrays" and "Regexps"; each section has a "front page" which can be accessed via the "Function Reference" part of the online manual's table of contents. Usually (although not always) this page will have a lightning-quick introduction to the subject of the manual chapter, helpful hints, and a list of the functions in that section. By reading through these introductions, you will have a much better idea of the various things that PHP can do, and greatly increase your chances of being able to put your finger on just the function you need at any given moment.

> **TIP:** The English-language version of the online PHP manual has a cool feature that can save a lot of time for certain users, particularly those experienced in another programming language. If you type the name of a function as a top-level URI, the PHP site automatically forwards you to either the page devoted to that function (if it exists) or a search page with a completed search for that term (if it doesn't exist or doesn't have a discrete page). So, for instance, if you type **http://www.php.net/popen**, you'll be redirected to `www.php.net/manual/en/function.popen.php`. If you're looking for a PHP function that is similar to one in C or Perl, this trick can prove a great timesaver over navigating the manual by hand. It's also useful in cases where you know the name of the function but just want to check on the type of variable returned or the order of arguments to pass in.

The PHP Mailing Lists

The "official" PHP community meets and greets on the PHP mailing lists. With the advent of PHP4, a decision was made to split up the lists into more specific topics — so if you're surprised that volume on the main list seems to have dropped off of late, that's why.

Signing up

To subscribe to any of the PHP mailing lists, go to the following URL:

```
www.php.net/mailing-lists.php
```

You should see a large form listing the various mailing lists and options for viewing them. Just choose the list that you want, specify normal or digest versions, enter your e-mail address, and click the Subscribe button. You can also unsubscribe from a list here.

The PHP mailing list manager almost instantaneously sends you an e-mail message asking you to confirm your subscription. You aren't subscribed until you reply to this e-mail.

> **TIP:** You also find links to local (non-English) mailing lists and newsgroups at the bottom of this page. If you want to discuss PHP in Turkish or Japanese, this page is the place to start!

Users' lists and developers' lists

Many of the user-oriented lists are new with PHP4 or later. The following are the most popular PHP users' mailing lists:

php-general	The main mailing list — very heavy traffic, 80+ e-mail messages per day
php-windows	Specific mailing list for Windows users
php-install	An installation-related mailing list, mostly for new users
php-db	The database-related issues mailing list
php-i18n	Internationalization and localization mailing list
pear-general	The PEAR users' list
php-gtk-general	The PHP-GTK users' list
phplib	The PHPLIB users' list
smarty-general	The Smarty templates users' list
php-announce	Announces new releases — very occasional

Lists also are available for popular PHP-based projects such as Midgard and phpNuke; you subscribe to those lists through the products' own Web sites. We list the URLs of some of these sites in the "Major PHP Projects" section of this chapter below.

The following three lists are mostly intended for active developers and very early adopters — people who are going to get down in the C code and battle bugs to the death:

php-dev	The main PHP developers' list
php-gtk-dev	The PHP-GTK developers' list
pear-dev	The PEAR developers' list

These lists are low-to-medium volume, meaning approximately 100 to 1,000 messages a month. They are highly technical and mostly not enlightening unless you're an active team member. Various CVS lists for developers are also available, which mail out all CVS commits on a particular branch to all subscribers; and special lists for documentation writers and QA team members also exist.

If you're comfortable with Internet newsgroups (which many newer users are not), you can access the PHP mailing lists at the news gateway at the following location:

```
news.php.net
```

This option has one great advantage: You can send messages to the mailing lists without subscribing to them. Many new users, however, should think in terms of searching the archives for answers to old questions before (or rather than) asking new questions anyway.

Most of these mailing lists are archived and searchable at the following site:

```
http://marc.theaimsgroup.com
```

This archive dates all the way back to at least 1998, although the older posts are usually less complete.

> **TIP:** Trying a quick keyword search on the PHP site, mail archives, and perhaps some of the other major PHP Web sites before contacting the mailing lists is the polite thing to do. It's actually faster for you; plus the less time the developers must spend answering the same questions over and over, the more time they have to implement new features in the language. Actually, searching the archives is no longer just polite — it's a necessity. With so many new users, so-called "RTFM" (read the effing manual) questions are not (politely) answered on the PHP lists anymore. Also, try to ask your question on a specific list if it exists — especially installation-related questions.

Regular and digest

The main PHP user list is so high-volume that it has a twice-daily digest version. The new specialized mailing lists also typically have digest versions. The raw and digested versions each have advantages and disadvantages.

If you've never had 100+ e-mail messages a day pouring into your mailbox, you have no idea how distracting and time-consuming this experience can be. Just reading-and-deleting can take up a couple hours, whereas actually answering them can easily become a full-time job. Under no circumstance should you request the full user list if your primary mailbox is a Web-based free e-mail service such as Yahoo! mail or Hotmail.

> **TIP:** Setting up a separate mailbox for PHP mail is almost mandatory if you're subscribing to the full user mailing list, unless you've set up good mail filters. Otherwise, you quickly start to lose mail from other sources in the flood of similarly named threads.

On the other hand, the digest version makes getting into the flow more difficult. The few brave community members who get the full user list seem to answer all the questions on the half-volley before you even get the digest, making participation difficult for the time-stressed community member.

For beginners, we recommend the digest version. You can always trade up later, whenever you're ready to stop lurking and participate actively.

Everyone should also consider using one of the PHP forums (see the section on "Other PHP Web Sites" below) instead of or in addition to the user mailing list. These forums are great for those who dislike mailing lists. The downside is that PHP developers generally don't hang out here, so extremely abstruse infrastructure questions usually go unanswered. The upside is that they tend to be friendlier, especially to repetitive newbie questions, because the answerers can control the amount of contact they prefer and go away if they start to become annoyed.

Mailing list etiquette

Open-source mailing lists can be intimidating places, and the PHP general-users list is particularly active and fast-paced. The denizens of the mailing lists are people, and learning about their different personalities and plans over time can be fun — but they can get annoyed and fed up, too. A little netiquette can take the user a long way. The following sections offer a few tips to follow.

Remember, the community does all this work for free!

Before you turn on the flamethrower, remind yourself of your last experience with commercial-software tech support. Did it solve your problem the same day? Did it cost money? How long did it take? At what point did you get to talk to the developers of the program?

People might be sick of your question

Perhaps you're trying to install PHP for the first time and can't get it working as an Apache module — but we can assure you that tens of thousands of iterations of that question have appeared on the mailing lists over the years. People on the mailing lists are experiencing fatigue at answering questions that they and others have answered in a lot of other information sources — the FAQs, the online manual, the mailing-list archives, and any number of other Web sites. If you ask one of these basic questions on the general mailing list, it proves that you didn't take seriously the numerous polite requests on the PHP site to search for an answer to your question before posting. You may get an irritated e-mail informing you of all the above — or you may get no responses at all. Neither response means that the PHP community is cold-hearted and unhelpful. Try to see things from the point of view of community members of longer standing, and avoid these problems by searching for the answer to your question before you post.

Give detailed descriptions

Say as much as you can about your platform, the problem, and any steps you've already tried. Don't worry about being concise; you're far better off maundering on a little than making everyone go back and forth an extra time.

Code fragments are the very most efficient way to state your problem for debugging by the community. Many people edit their raw code to make it more anonymous and/or abstract. Remember to take out any passwords!

> **TIP:** Copy and paste your code fragments; don't retype them. List participants often post perfect code, only to be frustrated that nobody can find anything wrong with it — because they corrected their errors while retyping!

Make sure that you use a specific subject line — the more specific the better. "Subject: PHP Help" gets you ignored by most of the mailing-list regulars. You want to say something more descriptive such as, "Subject: mysql_connect arguments not being passed in 4.0.0".

PHP is international

PHP is developed and used by people literally all over the world. In fact, the active development team has only a smallish minority of native English speakers on it at any given time.

Native English speakers should feel supremely lucky that theirs is the *lingua franca* of the Internet in general and the PHP world specifically. They should feel awed by the linguistic dexterity of all the citizens of other nations and perhaps slightly abashed that they can't return the favor in Finnish or Urdu. In other words, cut people some slack already! Don't assume that someone is an idiot because his or her messages aren't couched in perfectly grammatical and smooth English. Instead, you might spend the time learning how to write "Thank you" in all the languages of the various PHP community members — it makes a nice `sig` file for your mailing list posts.

> **TIP:** If you don't know English well, you may want to write your question twice — once in English, once in your native language. This will increase the odds that someone will be able to decipher your meaning.

There are limits

The mailing list and other resources are meant to help you, but you must prepare to make a good-faith and even strenuous effort of your own. Help does not mean that someone comes to your office and writes your code — this is not a remake of the Disney version of Cinderella, with dancing, sewing, chore-doing mice! Please don't ask community members to go into your server and debug your scripts for you.

Every once in a while, someone gets on the mailing list and whines about how PHP doesn't have precisely the feature that he or she is looking for — to which the developers very sensibly reply, "Why don't you implement it yourself?" Or, if you're not a good C programmer yourself, you could always pay someone else to develop your feature and contribute it to the PHP community. At the very least, you can avoid doing things that may alienate others or cause developers to burn out on the whole idea of developing open-source software!

Do it yourself

Open-source software may be free to use, but you should not consider it free of all responsibilities. You are technically a "free rider" until you give back — or pay forward — to the community at large. It's your task to figure out where and how to best deploy your talents, and then to do that thing as you can. We don't mean that every casual PHP user must become a C developer, but you can contribute in many other ways. Answering questions on the PHP mailing lists or Web sites is always a good thing, because it lightens the load on the core developers. If you figure something out that seemed obscure in the online PHP manual, be sure to post your findings to the User-contributed notes section of the manual. Use the PHP bug-tracker according to the instructions. Simple steps like these, in aggregate, contribute to the healthy community that has made PHP so successful.

It's probably you

If you experience a failure to communicate, you need to ask yourself whether the problem could possibly lie with you. If you do find yourself in the middle of a flame war, which happens occasionally on any mailing list, people enjoy nothing more than a little public acknowledgment of what a jerk you've (unknowingly) been.

There are now commercial alternatives

If the whole ethos of the PHP mailing lists is driving you crazy, remember that you can now pay to play instead. Many companies are now staffed by well-known PHP developers who are willing to do everything from answering single questions to building a custom PHP extension for you. ThinkPHP (`www.thinkphp.de`), for example, is a German consultancy, associated with PHP team member Thies Arntzen, that offers support, training, and performance evaluations. In America, the supremely helpful Richard Lynch of PHP-mailing-list fame takes requests at `www.l-i-e.com`.

Other PHP Web Sites

Besides the "official" PHP resources that we mention in the preceding sections, some well-known community members have put up some extraordinarily helpful Web sites. Some of these enjoy a special relationship with PHP, and are "quasi-official." The following sections describe some of these sites.

Core scripting engine and tools

The core of PHP is the Zend scripting engine. It is produced by an Israeli company called Zend, and besides being a free part of PHP, it can also be embedded in other applications. Zend also produces various PHP tools and add-ons, such as a graphical debugger and a precompiler. You can find information on Zend products at the following URL:

`www.zend.com`

Zend.com is the home of the core PHP4 scripting engine, as well as a center of PHP commercialization. Although the company sells support and custom development services to larger companies, the vast majority of PHP developers are most interested in the add-on products being developer by core developers Zeev Suraski and Andi Gutmans and their team.

For most PHP users, the most useful product is the Zend Studio IDE, now in 2.0 release. (See Chapter 3 for more information and a screenshot.) This program is the first PHP-specific development tool available, with many well-designed features for the PHP professional. Because of Zend's unique relationship to PHP development, the company understands the language completely and can design an editing tool that is customized to the needs of hardcore PHP users.

Two other Zend products are primarily of value to companies. PHP consulting firms should find the Zend Encoder useful, as it enables them to ship their code in a platform-independent, optimized intermediate representation. Large PHP sites can get a quick return on investment by using the Zend Accelerator, which boosts performance by optimizing and caching, thereby requiring less capital investment in hardware.

The Zend site also offers unique content on a regular basis, including biographies of major figures in the PHP world, a handy weekly newsletter summarizing current issues in the development of our beloved programming language, and great articles on advanced topics in PHP development. Zend.com is one of the few Web sites that consistently offers articles of interest to corporate PHP developers and architects, often showcasing the finer points of PHP functionality, such as reference counting, output buffering, and changes to the `include` functions. Topics such as these may seem abstruse at first, but advanced users usually enjoy learning about the underlying structure and logic of the programming language so that they can write the tightest, cleanest, most secure, best-architected, and most well-thought-out PHP code possible. C programmers who want to contribute to PHP can also find inspiration and information in these articles — because Zeev and Andi are driving the course of PHP core development, getting a feeling for their aesthetic and decision-making is important if you want to delve into the heart of PHP.

PHP knowledgebase

PHP has a great knowledgebase, something like a FAQ-o-matic but more full-featured, called PHP Faqts (previously known as E-gineer). It is available at the following URL:

```
http://php.faqts.com
```

PHP Faqts is an interesting and nicely executed concept: an archived knowledgebase of answered and unanswered questions from real PHP users with a decent search function. For common questions, this site is much easier to use than the mailing lists or even many forums — and for that reason, we recommend it to new PHP users.

The way that Faqts (brainchild of Australian PHP whiz Nathan Wallace) works is that community members ask questions in one of several "buckets," such as Installation and Setup, Common Problems, Database Backed Sites, and the extremely cool Not Quite PHP. Other community members come along and add multiple answers to these questions. They can also associate other questions (basically other ways of stating the same thing) with that question/answer pair. Everyone can vote anonymously on whether the question/answer was useful or not. Thus, you get an accretion of knowledge over time and some way to discern whether a particular answer is good at a glance.

Going to this site, however, is not the fastest way to get your question answered, and it remains to be seen whether Faqts can scale indefinitely — but it's a cool idea and definitely a resource to try.

Articles and tutorials

Articles and tutorials take a "teach a man to fish . . ." approach. Often they can't really walk you through all the steps involved in building your Web site; instead, they attempt to guide you in thinking about what to do. Following are two sites that we recommend for such information.

PHPBuilder

```
www.phpbuilder.com/
```

Founded by Tim Perdue, the top PHP app developer responsible for Sourceforge.net and Geocrawler.com, this site has long been one of the most comprehensive and well-run PHP sites. The specialty of the site is a deep backlog of articles that focus on the correct architecture of PHP sites, with subjects such as user authentication, cross-platform development, database abstraction, and documentation and style. PHPBuilder also boasts one of the most active PHP-related Web forums, with excellent response times to most questions.

One downside to the site is that articles are not dated, so determining whether the advice is still relevant to current versions of the programming language can prove difficult. Despite this drawback, PHPBuilder is a must-visit for the more conceptual PHP programmer who wants to read well-argued position papers on the right way to code PHP.

Devshed

`www.devshed.com/Server_Side/PHP/`

A big commercial site with good tutorials and a forum, Devshed covers all the scripting languages (ASP, JavaScript, Python, and so on), making it the best one-stop for those still in the shopping phase.

PHP codebases

Codebases take a "give a man a fish . . ." approach, simply offering their donated wares to all takers. The code quality can vary widely, from first scripts to elegant classes contributed by experts in a particular area. The following sections describe a few such sites that you can visit.

> **CAUTION:** Although codebases can seem attractive to new developers and do embody the power of open source, there are reasons to be wary. For one thing, no one is guaranteeing the quality or safety of this code. If you're more comfortable cutting and pasting than writing it yourself, you may not have sufficient skill at reading other people's PHP to use contributed code in an intelligent way. Proceed with caution!

PHP Classes Repository

`www.phpclasses.org`

Originally a collection of classes by Manuel Lemos, this site is now a hotbed of OOP PHP. We would probably not recommend this site to beginners, both because of the heavy use of object-oriented programming and the strong leaning toward code in the "Sure you can, but is it a good idea?" category. If you're good at intelligently reading other people's code and adapting it to your own needs, however, this site can prove instructive.

PX: PHP Code Exchange

`http://px.sklar.com/`

A super-plain and uninformative site design nonetheless leads to a large variety of scripts — mostly smaller ones. Look here for a standalone snippet or function in a specialized area, such as graphics or math.

EvilWalrus

`www.evilwalrus.com`

This site is very attractive and well laid out with a bit of a Windows orientation and a fresh, growing code base. It also offers chatty news write-ups of interest to PHP developers.

> **TIP:** A quick rule of thumb in judging contributed code: If you can't follow along pretty well just by reading the comments, take a pass and look for another code sample. It's pretty rare for a good commenter to be a bad or malicious programmer.

Major PHP projects

These are the more ambitious standalone projects based on PHP which are becoming well-known in their own right. Even organizations that are not necessarily in love with PHP are beginning to consider these projects as the best-of-breed and/or most cost-effective option in their various categories.

PHPMyAdmin

http://www.phpmyadmin.net

Originated by Tobias Ratschiller, this program is a graphical front-end to MySQL that has brought database administration to the ranks of the command-line phobic. See Chapter 18 for more detailed information on how to use it.

PHP-Nuke

http://phpnuke.org

This site offers a newslog-style content management system that enables multiple users on an intranet or the Web to post stories and comments on an on-going basis. You can find lots of add-on packages written by enthusiastic users as well.

PHPSlash

http://phpslash.sourceforge.net

This site also offers a newslog-style content management system. It was originally a rewrite of Slashcode (the Perl codebase behind Slashdot) in PHP, although PHPSlash development has now diverged somewhat.

Midgard

www.midgard-project.org

This site offers a highly customizable content management system, similar to Vignette Story Server. Midgard doesn't simply enable users or editors to post short pieces in a constant format on a Web page; you can also use the program to manage workflow on all kinds of content-rich sites.

phpBB

www.phpbb.com

This is an object-oriented, template-based bulletin-board system offering threaded or flat view, skins, avatars, and other attractive display features.

Phorum

www.phorum.org

Phorum is a lighter-weight bulletin-board system with no graphics. Unlike most other PHP bulletin boards, Phorum displays an outline of the thread, plus the current message, plus a form to reply to that message on a single page.

SquirrelMail
`www.squirrelmail.org`

IMAP webmail client

PHPGroupware
`www.phpgroupware.org`

This large integrated suite of PHP programs offers you Web-based group-scheduling and interaction tools, including Web mail, a calendar, to-do lists, chat, forums, and more.

Sourceforge.net
`http://sourceforge.net/projects/alexandria-dev`

This is a Web-based engineering management toolkit that includes a task tracker, a bug tracker, a CVS front-end, forums, a documentation manager, and news releases. The codebase went closed-source in 2001. Version 2.7 is promised in August, but the 3.0 branch is commercial-only.

Our Web Site

We've set up a Web site for this book at the following URL:

`www.troutworks.com/phpbook/`

There you can find most of the larger chunks of code from this book in a convenient source format, which saves you from retyping them.

You can also find corrections for the few paltry errors that slipped through the eagle eyes and sharp electronic red pencils of our editors. We will also try to put up information about new features and new code samples as they become available.

> **TIP:** Unfortunately, we are pretty much monolingual in English — although we're extremely impressed with all the e-mail we've received from PHP users around the world who are nonnative English speakers. All the text on our Web site is in English. If you write to us in a language other than English, we will attempt to put your e-mail through a Web translator. If we can understand the question after that, we will write an answer and put it through the translator; otherwise, we'll just write back and tell you that we can't parse your e-mail. So if you get an e-mail from us in terrible, mechanical French or Italian, now you know why. If you write to us in an encoding that we can't read, such as Mandarin or Arabic, we can't reply at all — apologies in advance.

Last but not least, you can also contact us on the site and flame away! (Or maybe just ask us a few questions.) We love to hear from readers, so please visit and drop us a line.

Glossary

Active Server Pages (ASP, ASP.NET)

Microsoft proprietary server-side execution environment. The ASP engine is built into Microsoft's proprietary Web server, Internet Information Server (IIS). The latest version, ASP.NET, is built on top of Microsoft's Web-services development platform. PHP predates ASP, and should not be considered an "open-source copy" of the proprietary product.

Actual parameters

The arguments (or inputs) that are given to a function as it is called. (The corresponding arguments that appear in the function definition are called the *formal parameters*.)

Apache HTTP server

The most popular open-source Web server. Also called *Apache server*, *Apache httpd*, and simply *Apache*.

Apache Software Foundation

Nonprofit foundation which oversees several open source software projects, notably Apache HTTP server.

API

See *Application Program Interface*.

Applet

A Java program that can be quickly downloaded from a Web page and that executes within the environment of the user's browser.

Application Program Interface (API)

A standard specifying how a program should be coded to interact with a particular operating system or service. Usually, this is in the form of a small set of specified functions that can be called from the application's code.

Argument

An input to a function or operator.

Array

In PHP, a basic datatype that holds values in association with indices.

ASP

In the context of this book, see *Active Server Pages*, although, in other contexts, may also mean *A*pplication *S*ervice *P*rovider.

Assignment

A process or statement that stores a value in a variable.

Back end

Loose term for the part of a computer program or service that is far away in the process from what the user actually sees. In Web programming, database servers often occupy the back end, and browsers and HTML-producing programs are the front-end.

Binary

Several senses are relevant to this book: 1) adjective for base two, as in *binary arithmetic*; 2) description of the on-off encoding used in computer memory; 3) a computer file which uses the full range of possible byte values, not just the values that correspond to human-readable text. Files that are directly executable computer programs are often called *binaries*, for example, to distinguish them from human-readable source code. (See also *Compilation*, *Interpretation*, *Source*.)

Bitmapped graphics

Term for modern computer display technology where color values of pixels are maintained in computer memory. Also refers to a style of graphics programming where primitive operations change the color values of real or virtual pixels. (Compare entry for *Vector graphics*.)

Boolean

An adjective referring to true-or-false logic. In PHP, the datatype that has only two possible values: TRUE or FALSE.

Browser

See *Web browser*.

C

A major popular programming language used for operating-system and programming-language code as well as for general-purpose programming. Closely associated with the Unix family of operating systems. Most of PHP is written in C, but knowledge of C is unnecessary to use PHP.

C++

A successor to C that includes object-oriented constructs.

Cascading Style Sheets (CSS)

A standard for specifying the cosmetic attributes of a Web site in a centralized and general way, which individual browsers can then interpret and render appropriately.

Case sensitive

Describes programs, names, or documents where capitalization of letters makes a difference. The opposite is case insensitive.

CGI

See *Common Gateway Interface*.

Class

Object-oriented programming term for the programmer-defined blueprint for object instances of a certain type.

Client-side

General term for computation that happens on the client machine in a client-server relationship. In a Web programming context, it refers to computation that happens on the machine the user is browsing from, rather than on the machine the Web site is being served from. (See *Server-side*.)

ColdFusion

Proprietary Macromedia tag-based Web-scripting product.

Co-location

Special type of Web hosting where the customer provides the machine that the Web server runs on and takes care of its administration remotely, while the service provider offers the location, the electric power, the Internet hookup, and possibly other services such as data backups. (See *Hosting*.)

Column

In a database context, this refers to the fields that are prescribed by the definition of a database table. Each row entry in the table contains values for all the columns.

COM

See *Component Object Model*.

Common Gateway Interface (CGI)

A particular protocol for the communication between Web servers and programs that produce HTML pages on demand. Now replaced to some extent by more direct integration of Web servers and Web-scripting languages.

Common Object Request Broker Architecture (CORBA)

A standard for distributed object-oriented programming, sponsored by the Object Management Group, a computer-industry consortium. CORBA allows communication between different pieces of software running on different machines.

Constructor

In object-oriented programming, a constructor is the function that is automatically run at object creation time to do appropriate initialization. Programmers typically define constructor functions as they write object class definitions. See also *destructor*.

Cookie

A small piece of information stored by a Web server in a user's browser or on the hard disk of the user's machine.

Compilation

The automated process of translating a text-file program (as written by a programmer) into an executable program that runs on a computer. Compilation typically happens all at once so that the translation is finished before any part of the executable program is run. (See *Interpretation.*)

Component Object Model (COM)

A Microsoft-sponsored standard for distributed object-oriented programs, which allows communication between different programs running on the same machine. (See *DCOM, CORBA.*)

CORBA

See *Common Object Request Broker Architecture.*

Datatype

A blueprint for a kind of value in a computer program. A datatype determines both a range of legitimate values and also the way that such values are represented in computer memory. The basic datatypes in PHP are *integer, double, Boolean, string, array, NULL, resource,* and *object.*

DCOM

See *Distributed Component Object Model.*

Debugger

A piece of software that helps programmers find bugs in their code.

Destructor

In object-oriented programming, a destructor function is one that is automatically called just before an object instance is deleted or destroyed. This function has the responsibility of freeing any memory or resources associated with the instance. PHP does not have destructor functions per se, although future PHP versions based on Zend Engine 2 may support them.

Document Type Definition (DTD)

A document that specifies the structure of a class of XML documents in such a way that the documents can be automatically checked (or validated) to see if they conform to it.

Document Object Model (DOM)

A standardized interface (or API) for programs that interact with XML parsers. Under the DOM, XML parsers read in an entire XML document and construct a parse tree. The application program may then query or manipulate the tree. (See *SAX, API.*)

DNS

See *Domain Name Service.*

DOM

See *Document Object Model.*

Domain name

The name of a machine or service on the Internet, such as www.troutworks.com. A second-level domain name is a more general grouping, such as ibm.com, which may include many domain names.

Domain Name Service

A type of Internet server program that translates domain names (for example, www.ibm.com) into their underlying Internet Protocol (IP) addresses. (See *IP address, Domain name.*)

Double

A basic PHP datatype that represents floating-point numbers. (See *Floating-point, Integer.*)

DTD

See *Document Type Definition.*

Dynamic

Adjective used loosely to describe Web pages using HTML, plus more sophisticated technologies. On the server side, denotes pages assembled on-the-fly.

Dynamic HTML (DHTML)

Loose term for a set of HTML extensions and browser-side programming techniques for control of the graphic aspects of Web-site presentation.

ECMAScript

The new official name for JavaScript now that the standard is controlled by ECMA.

Editor

Software for editing text files, especially the text of program code.

Event

General term for a kind of signal from one program to another or from one program subsystem to another, which the receiving program is expected to notice and respond to.

Expression

In PHP, a combination of basic values, language constructs, operators, and function calls that itself has a value. (See *Statement.*)

fhttpd

A small, fast, open-source Web server written by Alex Belits.

File pointer

The value in a computer program that marks the current position of an ongoing read from a disk file.

File Transfer Protocol (FTP)

Standard method for transferring files from one machine to another over the Internet.

Filesystem

The combination of a computer's files and directories with the low-level operating system programs that manipulate them. Application programs typically interact with filesystem, rather than directly controlling the disk-drive hardware.

Flat-file database

A database system that holds a database in a single unified table rather than splitting it up into a multiple-table relational database. (See *Relational database.*)

Floating point

Term for numbers that have a fractional portion represented as numbers to the right of the decimal point. Also refers to arithmetic on such numbers. In PHP, identical to the *double* type.

Form-processing agent

A program that handles data passed by an HTML form. PHP can be used as a form-processing agent.

Formal parameters

The variable names that are associated with incoming arguments in a function definition. (The arguments given to a function as it is actually called are the *actual parameters*.)

FreeBSD

A free, open-source version of the Unix operating system.

Front end

Loose term for the parts of a program or service that are closest to the user. A pull-down menu in the browser display of a Web site is part of the front end, while the database on the server machine that records the corresponding transaction is part of the back end.

FTP

See *File Transfer Protocol*.

Function

A basic programming language construct that allows you to name a block of code and use it in different situations with different inputs.

gd

A graphics library often used in conjunction with PHP to produce or manipulate graphic images.

General Public License (GPL)

A type of software license championed by the Free Software Foundation, which encourages free source distribution and which permits distribution of modifications to GPL'ed software as long as the modified versions are themselves made freely available under the GPL.

GET

A basic HTTP method for submitting information in a request for a Web page. GET methods are often what a user invokes in following a link. (See *Post.*)

Global

Adjective describing information or values that are available throughout the code of a particular computer program. Opposite of *Local.* (See also *Scope.*)

GPL

See *General Public License.*

Hardcode

Including a literal value directly in program code, when it may be better as a variable or function argument.

Hosting

Providing the parts and labor necessary to serve up a Web site that someone else may have coded and designed. Hosting services usually include the necessary hardware, the Internet connection, and the administration needed to keep the site live.

HTML

*H*yper*T*ext *M*arkup *L*anguage, a subset of SGML that is the standard method to mark up Web pages.

HTTP

*H*yper*T*ext *T*ransfer *P*rotocol. The basic protocol by which Web browsers and Web servers communicate over the Internet.

http daemon

Program that runs constantly on Web-server machines, looking out for requests for Web pages

IDE

See *Integrated Development Environment.*

IE

See *Internet Explorer*.

IMAP

*I*nternet *M*essage *A*ccess *P*rotocol. A mail-retrieval protocol meant to supplement or supplant POP.

Inheritance

The relationship between an object-oriented class and a more general class that it is based on.

Instance

In object-oriented programming, a single data structure that is created according to the definition given by the object class. Also called *object*, or *object instance*. See also *instantiation, class*.

Instantiation

The process of making a particular instance of a general schema or pattern. In an object-oriented context, instantiating a class means creating an object that is an instance of the class.

Integer

In mathematics, a whole number with no fractional part, which may be positive or negative. In PHP, a basic datatype that represents such whole numbers.

Integrated Development Environment (IDE)

An IDE combines several different pieces of software that help software developers write code. At a minimum, an IDE typically includes a source-code editor, a debugger, and some kind of system for managing code revisions.

Internet Explorer (IE)

The Microsoft Web browser.

Internet Information Server (IIS)

Microsoft proprietary Web server.

Interpretation

In the context of computer languages, the process of running a computer program by successively translating and executing individual statements from a source file. Usually opposed to compilation, which performs all the translation before any execution.

IP address

Internet Protocol Address. A number by which each networked resource (server, desktop, printer) on the Internet or an Intranet is uniquely identified. An IP address currently takes the IPv4 form *x.x.x.x* where *x* is an integer between 0 and 255; plans are underway to expand the address space to 6 integers.

ISP

Internet Service Provider. A provider of Internet services, such as Internet access or Web hosting.

Java

An object-oriented programming language designed and promoted by Sun Microsystems, with an unusual method of compilation that makes it highly portable. In particular, it is possible to write applets in Java that are executable within several different browser environments.

Java Database Connectivity (JDBC)

Database connectivity standard promoted by Sun Microsystems, which allows Java programs to connect to disparate database systems.

Java Server Pages (JSP)

Server-side Web-scripting standard, promoted by Sun Microsystems, in which fragments of Java code can be embedded in HTML. PHP predates JSP by a considerable head-start.

JavaScript

A client-side Web-scripting language that extends the user-interface capabilities of browsers. No real relationship to Java. (See *Client-side, ECMAScript.*)

Java Virtual Machine (JVM)

Program that executes arbitrary Java code. JVM's embedded in Web browsers allow them to run downloaded applets. (See *Java, Applet, Web Browser.*)

JDBC

See *Java Database Connectivity*.

JScript

Microsoft's proprietary and non-standards-compliant implementation of JavaScript.

JSP

See *Java Server Pages*.

JVM

See *Java Virtual Machine*.

Linux

A free, open-source version of the Unix operating system.

Local

Adjective describing variables or values in a computer program that are only accessible from a restricted part of the code, or during a limited portion of the program's execution. Opposite of *global*. (See also *Scope*.)

Localhost

Networking designation for the very same machine a program is running on.

Lossy compression

Type of compression where the original data may not be exactly preserved by the compression-decompression cycle. Opposite of lossless compression. Often encountered in the context of compressing graphic images, notably in the JPEG standard. Note that lossy is not necessarily a derogatory term because savings in time or memory consumption may make up for small losses in fidelity.

Mailing list

Named set of e-mail addresses of people with a special interest. Mail sent to the list's address is remailed to everyone on the list.

Member function

In object-oriented programming, a function definition that is local to a class definition. Nearly synonymous with *method*, although for languages that support polymorphism, some would use member function to refer to a collection of methods with the same name that have different argument lists. (This distinction is not applicable to PHP, however, since each class can have only one method with a given name.)

Member variable

In object-oriented programming, a variable that is local to a class definition. Each instance of a class typically has its own copy of such variables, unless the variable is declared to be a class or static variable.

Metadata

Data about data. In a Web context, this usually means tags in a document that describe that document.

Method

In object-oriented programming, a function definition that is local to a class definition. See the discussion in the entry for *member function*.

MySQL

A free, open-source relational database system, often teamed up with Linux, PHP, and Apache for a complete Web-server package.

Navbar

Shorthand for *navigation bar*, meaning a visually prominent collection of links that is largely consistent across the different pages of a Web site.

Netscape Navigator

Web browser produced by Netscape (now part of AOL). (See *Web browser*.)

Open Database Connectivity (ODBC)

Standard promoted by Microsoft that facilitates communication between applications and disparate databases.

Object

Program construct that encapsulates both data and procedural information. Often used to refer to an instance of a class (see *instance*).

Object-Oriented Programming (OOP)

Programming using a style and/or language that bundles data and functions together into objects, which often model objects or entities in the real world. Optionally includes special programming language support for programming with objects, including *inheritance* and *polymorphism*.

ODBC

See *Open Database Connectivity*.

Open-Source Software (OSS)

Software that is distributed as (or includes) source code, with permission to modify that code. The term is used in contrast to *closed-source software*, where the distribution is of the executable or binary, which cannot in practice be modified or customized.

Operating System (OS)

The main program that runs a computer and, in turn, enables application programs to run and communicate with the hardware. Examples of operating systems include various flavors of Unix (Linux, FreeBSD, Solaris), Windows (Windows NT, Windows 2000, Windows 98, Windows XP), and the Macintosh OS.

Operator

A programming language construct with up to two inputs, found to the immediate left and/or immediate right of the operator in an expression.

Operator precedence

The set of priority rules that determines which operator has first claim when there are operators on both left and right sides of an argument or input.

OS

See *Operating system*.

Pathname

A string of characters denoting the location of a file in a filesystem, including any necessary directory or folder names.

Perl

An open-source scripting language, especially loved by Unix sysadmins and other Unix programmers.

PHP

PHP:Hypertext Preprocessor, an open-source HTML-embedded, server-side scripting language and engine.

Personal Web Server (PWS)

Microsoft proprietary intranet server.

Personalization

In a Web programming context, the process of producing dynamic Web pages with content that varies depending on who is browsing.

Polymorphism

For functions and methods, the property of having different behavior depending on the number and types of arguments.

POST

A basic HTTP method for submitting information in a request for a Web page. POST methods are often what a user invokes when submitting a form. (See *GET*.)

POP

In the context of this book, usually the *Post Office Protocol* for retrieving e-mail from a mail server. In other contexts, can also mean a *Point-of-Presence* on the Internet, such as an IP address.

Precedence

See *Operator precedence*.

Procedural abstraction

The process of wrapping lines of code up into named procedures or functions.

Programming language

A standard that defines a particular set of constructs in which computer code can be written. When there is a difference between a language's specification and an implementation of a compiler or interpreter for the specification, "*programming language*" refers to the specification. Examples of programming languages include C, C++, Common Lisp, Scheme, Basic, Pascal, Fortran, Perl, PHP. (Scripting languages are also programming languages.) (See *Scripting language, Compilation, Interpretation.*)

Relational database

A database system with the capability of splitting data into multiple tables, which are, in turn, associated by relationships between the column data of the different tables.

REST

*Re*presentational *S*tate *T*ransfer. A Web services protocol that uses URI namespace addressing, and returns plain XML.

Row

In a relational-database context, an entry in a database table, which includes values for the columns that are implied by the table definition.

RPM

*R*ed Hat *P*ackage *M*anager. A system of precompiled binaries for the Red Hat distribution of Linux and its derivatives.

Runtime

The time of program execution. Usually opposed to the time of program compilation. (See *Compilation.*)

SAX

See *Simple API for XML.*

Scope

The set of rules in a programming language that determines whether multiple occurrences of the same name refer to the same thing.

SCP

Secure copy utility. Encrypted replacement for cp and ftp.

Scripting language

A programming language that does not require an explicit compilation step by the programmer. Early versions of scripting languages are usually interpreted rather than compiled and are usually less powerful or more limited in usage than corresponding general-purpose languages. Usually this changes as they evolve, however, and many scripting languages (Perl, PHP 4) are now compiled (although without a separate step for the programmer) and quite powerful, providing flexibility and rapid development. (See *Interpretation, Compilation*.)

Server-side

General term for computation that happens on the server machine in a client-server relationship. In a Web-programming context, it refers to computation that happens on the Web-server machine rather than the machine the user is browsing from. (See *Client-side*.)

SGML

See *Standard Generalized Markup Language*.

SOAP

A Web-services standard for making remote procedure calls over HTTP. The acronym is usually thought to stand for *S*imple *O*bject *A*ccess *P*rotocol, although some members of the standards committee dispute this.

SSH

*S*ecure *Sh*ell, an encrypted replacement for Telnet. Usually distributed with scp, a secure file-copying utility.

Side effect

Any effect of an expression in a programming language other than the main value returned by the expression.

Simple API for XML (SAX)

A standardized interface (or API) for programs that interact with XML parsers. Under SAX, the parser reads in an XML document and notifies the application program of events corresponding to tags or contents as the parse progresses. (See *DOM, API.*)

Solaris

A proprietary version of the Unix operating system sold by Sun Microsystems.

Source

See *Source code.*

Source code

The actual text of code written by the programmer, as opposed to the executable program that is produced from it. (See *Compilation, Binary.*)

Standard Generalized Markup Language (SGML)

A standard for defining markup languages, which, in turn, are languages that structure documents so that they can be both displayed to people and manipulated by programs. HTML is a kind of markup language, although it's not technically an SGML language because it breaks many of SGML's rules.

Statement

In PHP, an expression terminated by a semicolon.

Static

This has several different meanings depending on context. In a programming language, a static variable in a function definition is one that retains its value between invocations of the function. Also, an adjective used to describe HTML pages that do not change rapidly or feature any visible client-side functionality.

Superglobal arrays

Replacement for EGPCS arrays, with true global scope everywhere. Strongly recommended by PHP group since PHP 4.2.1, allowing developers to turn off `register_globals`.

Typecast

Programming language expression that explicitly requests the conversion of a value from one datatype to another. Rarely needed in PHP.

Type conversion

Translation of a value from one datatype to another. May or may not be the result of an explicit typecast; can also be done by PHP itself.

Universal Resource Indicator (URI)

An Internet address. This term is an extension of Universal Resource Locator (URL).

Unix

A family of related operating systems that runs much of the Internet, except for the bit on the desks of users. Unix implementations include Linux, FreeBSD, and Solaris.

Valid

In an XML context, a valid document is one that not only is well-formed, but also follows the prescriptions of its Document Type Definition. (See *Valid, Document Type Definition.*)

Validating parser

In an XML context, a validating parser is an XML parser that checks parsed documents to make sure they conform to their Document Type Definitions. Not all XML parsers validate, although they all check if a document is well formed.

VBScript

Proprietary Microsoft scripting language based on Visual Basic.

Vector graphics

Style of graphics programming where lines and shapes are drawn by specifying the motions in a coordinate plane of a virtual pen. See *Bitmapped graphics.*

Web browser

The application program commonly used to browse Web pages. Examples include Netscape Navigator, Microsoft Internet Explorer, and Opera.

Web server

Program responsible for replying to requests for Web pages. Examples include Apache, Microsoft IIS, and iPlanet.

Web service

Program on the Internet with methods accessible via XML over HTTP.

Weblog

A personal diary, topical journal, or frequently updated news-link collection published on the Web

Web mail

A Web-based program for reading and sending electronic mail.

Well-formed

In an XML context, a well-formed document is one that conforms to the minimal syntactical requirements of XML, with tags properly closed off and so on. (See *Valid*.)

White space

Characters in a text file or computer program which display as blanks. White space includes spaces, tabs, linefeeds, and end-of-line characters.

World Wide Web Consortium (W3C)

International consortium that promulgates major Web protocols, such as HTTP, HTML, CSS, and XML.

WYSIWYG

Shorthand for "*W*hat *Y*ou *S*ee *I*s *W*hat *Y*ou *G*et," which describes programming, word processing, and design tools with visual interfaces that closely approximate the look of the thing you are designing.

XML

Short for e*X*tensible *M*arkup *L*anguage. A descendant of SGML and a more structured proposed successor to HTML, designed both for display in browsers and as a data-interchange format.

XML-RPC

*R*emote *p*rocedure *c*all over XML. Using XML to trigger a program action on a remote server.

XSL

e*X*tensible *S*tyle-sheet *L*anguage. A companion standard to XML, which specifies the transformation and display of XML documents.

Zend

Name for the parsing and execution engine at the core of PHP 4. Also the name of a company started by the designers of that engine (*Z*ee*v* Suraski and A*nd*i Gutmans) which markets commercial consulting services, add-ons, and tools for PHP.

Index